Anti-Money Laundering: International Law and Practice

Other Wiley Editorial Offices

John Wiley & Sons Inc., 111 River Street, Hoboken, NJ 07030, USA

Jossey-Bass, 989 Market Street, San Francisco, CA 94103-1741, USA

Wiley-VCH Verlag GmbH, Boschstr. 12, D-69469 Weinheim, Germany

John Wiley & Sons Australia Ltd, 42 McDougall Street, Milton, Queensland 4064, Australia

John Wiley & Sons (Asia) Pte Ltd, 2 Clementi Loop #02-01, Jin Xing Distripark, Singapore 129809

John Wiley & Sons Canada Ltd, 6045 Freemont Blvd, Mississauga, Ontario, L5R 4J3, Canada

Wiley also publishes its books in a variety of electronic formats. Some content that appears
in print may not be available in electronic books.

Library of Congress Cataloging-in-Publication Data

Anti-money-laundering : international law and practice / edited by Wouter H.
Muller, Christian H. Kälin, John G. Goldsworth.
        P. cm.
Includes bibliographical references and index.
ISBN 978-0-470-03319-7 (cloth : alk. paper)
1.   Money laundering–Prevention. 2.   Money–Law and legislation Criminal
provisions. 3.   Criminal law–International unification.   I. Muller, Wouter H. II.
Kälin, Christian. III. Goldsmith, John G.
K1089.A958 2007
345′.0268–dc22

                                                          2007004228

British Library Cataloguing in Publication Data

A catalogue record for this book is available from the British Library

ISBN: 978-0-470-03319-7 (HB)

Typeset in 10/12pt Times New Roman by Laserwords Private Limited, Chennai, India
Printed and bound in Great Britain by Antony Rowe Ltd, Chippenham, Wiltshire
This book is printed on acid-free paper responsibly manufactured from sustainable forestry
in which at least two trees are planted for each one used for paper production.

Edited by
Wouter H. Muller
Christian H. Kälin
John G. Goldsworth

Anti-Money Laundering: International Law and Practice

BICENTENNIAL
1807
WILEY
2007
BICENTENNIAL

John Wiley & Sons, Ltd

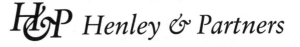

Henley & Partners

Anti-Money Laundering: International Law and Practice

Editors

Wouter H. Muller
Henley & Partners

Christian H. Kälin
Henley & Partners

John G. Goldsworth
Trusts & Trustees

Foreword by

Professor Kader Asmal
President FATF 2005–2006

Authors of the General Chapters

*Compliance and AML – Standards,
education and training*
William B. Howarth
International Compliance Association
Birmingham

*Anti-Money Laundering Regulation
and Trusts*
Martyn Frost, TEP
Society of Trust and Estate
Practitioners, London

*The United Nations Security Council and the
effort to combat money laundering
and the financing of terrorism*
Joel Sollier
UNSC Counter-Terrorism Committee, New York

*UN Anti-Money Laundering
Initiatives*
Rick McDonell
United Nations Office on Drugs and Crime, Vienna

Initiatives of the European Commission
Franco Frattini
EU Commission, Brussels

The Financial Action Task Force
Alain Damais
FATF – GAFI, Paris

The Egmont Group
Wouter H. Muller, TEP
Henley & Partners, Zurich

The Wolfsberg Process
Mark Pieth
University of Basel, Faculty of Law, Basel

Authors of Country Chapters

USA
John W. Moscow
Rosner Moscow & Napierala, LLP, New York

Canada
Nancy Carroll / Barbara McIsaac
McCarthy Tétrault LLP, Toronto

Panama
Ricardo M. Alba / Eloy Alfaro de Alba
Tapia, Linares & Alfaro, Panama City

Argentina
Sebastián A. Soler
Marval, O'Farrell & Mairal, Buenos Aires

Brazil
Eliana M. Filipozzi / Robert E. Williams Noronha
Advogados, London / São Paulo

Uruguay
Fabian Rivero / Ady Beitler
Estudio Bergstein, Montevideo

Chile
Cristóbal Eyzaguirre B. / Felipe Dalgalarrando /
Patricio Middleton
Claro Y Cia, Santiago de Chile

Bermuda and British Virgin Islands
Craig W. MacIntyre, TEP
Conyers Dill & Pearman, Hamilton

Bahamas
Cheryl E. Bazard / Tanya C. McCartney
Bahamas Association of Compliance
Officers, Nassau

Cayman Islands
Martin Livingston
Maples & Calder, Georgetown

Barbados
Carolyn Hanson
International Compliance Association
Christ Church

Netherlands Antilles and Aruba
Aede Gerbranda
Smeets Thesseling van Bokhorst, Amsterdam

St. Kitts and Nevis
Shawna Lake / Idris Clarke
Government of St. Kitts & Nevis, Basseterre

Switzerland
Judith Schmidt
Money Laundering Control Authority, Bern

Liechtenstein
Johannes Gasser / Markus Schwingshackl
Advokaturbüro Dr. Dr. Batliner
& Dr. Gasser, Vaduz

Austria
Thomas Shirmer / Markus Uitz
Binder Grösswang, Rechtsanwälte, Wien

United Kingdom
Peter Burrell / Kate Meakin
Herbert Smith LLP, London

Jersey
Andrew le Brun
Jersey Financial Services Commission, St. Helier

Guernsey
Mark G. Ferbrache, TEP
Ferbrache Richardson, Advocates, St. Saviours

Cyprus
David Stokes
Andreas Neocleous & Co., Limassol

Isle of Man
Nick Verardi / Marc Conway
Dickinson Cruickshank, Douglas

Ireland
John Handoll
William Fry Solicitors, Dublin

Germany
Olaf Otting
Gleiss Lutz, Frankfurt am Main

France
Philippe Blaquier-Cirelli / Pierre-Yves Couturier
Avocats à la Cour Jeantet Associés, Paris

Monaco
Donald Manasse, TEP / Sophie Marquet
Donald Manasse Law Offices, Monte Carlo

Spain
Javier García Sanz / Guillermo San Pedro
Uría Menéndez, Madrid

Italy
Alberto Giampieri / Paolo Iemma
Gianni, Origoni, Grippo & Partners, Rome

Greece
D. Karamagiolis
Tsibanoulis & Partners, Athens

Belgium
Françoise Lefèvre / Olivier Praet
Linklaters, Brussels

Netherlands
Enide Perez / Max Vermeij
Stibbe N.V., Amsterdam

Luxembourg
Pit Reckinger
Elvinger, Hoss & Prussen, Luxembourg

Russian Federation
Valery Tutykhin
John Tiner & Partners, Moscow

Ukraine
Dmytro Korbut
Andreas Neocleous & Co., Kiev

United Arab Emirates
Graham Lovett / Charles Barwick
Clifford Chance LLP, Dubai

Singapore
Chee Fang Theng, TEP
Khattar Wong, Singapore

Japan
Takashi Nakazaki
Anderson, Mori, Tomotsune, Tokyo

China
Donna Li
AllBright Law Offices /
Xiao Rong Gu
Institute of Law of Shanghai
Shanghai

Hong Kong
Steven Sieker, TEP / L. Travis Benjamin, TEP
Baker & McKenzie, Hong Kong

Australia
Andrew White
University of Melbourne, Melbourne

New Zealand
David Craig / Simon David
Bell Gully, Barristers and Solicitors, Wellington

South Africa
Pieter K. Smit
Financial Intelligence Centre, Pretoria

CONTENTS

Acknowledgements

This publication arose from the idea and need for a really first-rate, up-to-date and useful handbook on Anti-Money Laundering Laws and Regulations, simply because nothing of this kind had been attempted before. The publishers, *John Wiley & Sons*, concurred with this idea. They and the editors are now pleased to present the result to interested readers.

A great deal of specialist knowledge, work and effort has gone into this project, and it has certainly proved worthwhile. As an expression of its overall concept, this volume can unquestionably be seen as a pioneering achievement. The authors, editors and publishers hope that the users of this handbook share this viewpoint as well as their enthusiasm for the project.

At this point we would like to express our sincere thanks to all those who have contributed to and supported this book. Special thanks are due to our colleagues at *Henley & Partners*, in particular to *Rebecca van der Burg*. Furthermore, we also thank all the authors, the publishers as well as the *Society of Trust and Estate Practitioners*, the *International Compliance Association* and *Henley & Partners*. Thanks to their valuable support, they have also contributed to the successful publication of this handbook.

Zurich and London, October 2006

Wouter H. Muller
Christian H. Kälin
John G. Goldsworth

Alliance Partners

H&P Henley & Partners

Henley & Partners

Henley & Partners are specialized advisors to private clients and businesses. Internationally recognized for its unique expertise in private residence planning, the firm has also acquired a reputation in multi-jurisdictional real-estate advisory, tax-planning and fiduciary services.

In this context, Henley & Partners has also developed considerable expertise with regard to compliance and regulatory issues, including and in particular with regard to Anti-Money Laundering regulations and procedures in many jurisdictions. Several of the firm's principals are involved with regulatory matters affecting lawyers, tax consultants and fiduciaries, as well as advising governments on such regulatory matters.

Like its clients, Henley & Partners place particular emphasis on reliable, efficient service and impeccable quality. By implementing practical and creative solutions on the basis of solidly grounded expertise and extensive experience, the firm attract clients who are accustomed to expect success.

www.henleyglobal.com

International Compliance Association

The International Compliance Association

The International Compliance Association (ICA) is a professional organisation dedicated to supporting the best compliance and anti-money laundering practice in the financial services and allied sectors. The ICA transcends national boundaries by educating and supporting compliance and financial crime professionals throughout the world, through the provision of internationally recognised training and qualifications, member information exchange and continuing professional development.

The ICA focuses on education, training and research in the AML and compliance areas. It provides a range of courses and qualifications leading to professional and fellowship level qualifications in order for those working in the sector to demonstrate competence.

All ICA courses and qualifications are awarded in association with the University of Manchester Business School under a quality assured educational partnership that enables delegates across the world to be taught by an integrated education package consisting of

- detailed course manuals
- e-support systems
- workshops (in over 20 centres globally).

The courses and qualifications offered by the ICA include:

- International Diploma in Anti-Money Laundering – Int Dip (AML)
- International Diploma in Compliance – Int Dip (Comp)
- International Diploma in Financial Crime – Int Dip (Fin Crime)
- Certificate in Compliance
- Certificated Anti-Money Laundering awareness training for all staff.

www.int-comp.org

STEP
Society of Trust and Estate Practitioners

The Society of Trust and Estate Practitioners

The Society of Trust and Estate Practitioners (STEP) is the leading professional body for the trust and estate profession worldwide.

STEP members come from the legal, accountancy, trust and corporate administration, banking, financial planning, insurance and related professions and are involved at a senior level in the planning, creation, management of and accounting for trusts and estates, executorship administration, and related taxes.

Members of STEP include the most experienced and senior practitioners in the fields of trusts and estates.

STEP was founded in 1991 with the aim of bringing together all the senior practitioners in the various fields and cutting across professional boundaries. Through meetings, seminars, lectures and the exchange of technical papers and reports, members share information knowledge and experience, and benefit from the network of contacts that membership provides.

www.step.org

About this book

This book presents thorough yet practical information on the most important issues concerning international anti-money laundering laws and regulations. It is designed as a guide for **lawyers, bankers, regulators, business advisors, private-client advisors**, **family offices** and others who have to deal with the ever-increasing anti-money laundering maze. The use of concise and precise language reflects its character as a handbook and reference source. In particular, the authors have endeavored to express the terms and concepts involved as straightforwardly as possible in order to make them easily accessible, especially to those without a legal background. Footnotes are mostly avoided for the sake of clarity.

The book is divided up into many different **chapters**. The general chapters at the beginning cover broader issues readers should know about, whereas the various country chapters cover the most important areas that are relevant in practice for each jurisdiction. The individual chapters aim to explain the details without however being too technical.

The individual chapters of this book have been written by different co-authors. **Each of the authors is responsible for the contents of his/her chapter only** and it does not imply that a co-author or the organization he or she is affiliated with agrees with the contents of chapters contributed by other co-authors or their organizations.

This book can in no way substitute legal or other advice. The editors, publishers and authors therefore unreservedly exclude any liability for any losses or damages of any kind – be these direct, indirect or consequential – which may result from the use of this book or the information it contains. Although all the authors have undertaken their researches with great care, they obviously cannot guarantee their completeness and correctness any more than the editors or publishers.

Any **comments and suggestions, praise or criticism** will be gratefully received. If you as the reader feel that a particular topic or address should be removed from or added to this volume, please let us know.

By all means write to the editors via e-mail at zuerich@henleyglobal.com or by conventional mail at the following address: Wouter H. Muller, *Henley & Partners*, Kirchgasse 22, 8024 Zurich, Switzerland. The publishers will be happy to recompense useful information with a product from their current program.

About the editors

Wouter H. Muller, Senior Consultant at Henley & Partners in Zurich, Switzerland, is a lawyer and trust specialist with more than 30 years of experience in international trust management and private banking. He is also a Member of the Board of Verica Trust & Capital Management AG, an investment advisory firm, a member of the Society of Trust and Estate Practitioners (STEP) as well as of numerous other professional organizations.

He obtained a doctorate in civil law at the Law School of the University of Groningen in 1971 and then worked for 10 years as a solicitor in the Netherlands, specializing in family, real estate, corporate and tax law. In 1981 he joined Pierson, Heldring & Pierson N.V., a Dutch merchant bank in Amsterdam. For PHP he worked first in Luxembourg at their joint venture with Sal. Oppenheim & Cie. as director of their Luxembourg trust company. In 1987 he was appointed managing director of the PHP trust company in Curaçao (Netherlands Antilles) and in 1991 as director of the private bank in Luxembourg, being responsible a.o. the trust operations. In 1996, after the merger of PHP with Bank Mees & Hope into MeesPierson, Mr Muller went to Switzerland as director of the private bank, responsible for the Zurich office and for sales and marketing. Later he was also appointed as managing director of the trust office in Zug.

In 2003 he joined Henley & Partners as a senior consultant, where he deals specifically with government advisory, regulatory and compliance matters in the context of international legal and financial services.

Christian H. Kälin is an international real estate, tax and estate-planning specialist and a Partner at Henley & Partners, Zurich, as well as one of the founding partners of Verica Trust & Capital Management AG, Zug, an investment advisory firm. He is also a member of the Board of the International Financial and Legal Network (IFLN), a member of the Society of Trust and Estate Practitioners (STEP) as well as of numerous other professional organizations.

After completing Zurich Business School and his training at a Swiss private bank, he lived and studied for many years in France, the USA, New Zealand and Switzerland. A holder of a cum laude Masters degree in law from the University of Zurich, he is a frequent writer and speaker on international tax-planning issues, in particular on cross-border business relocation and private residence planning and is regularly quoted in international and Swiss media. He is the editor and one of the co-authors of the Switzerland Business & Investment Handbook. This is the key publication on the subject, supported by the Swiss Government, Credit Suisse and many other important companies and institutions, and with contributions by more than 40 leading authors covering all aspects of doing business, investing and living in Switzerland.

He also specializes in real-estate structuring and real-estate investments and is a member of the panel of judges for the Bentley International Property Awards. He is the editor and one of the co-authors of the International Real Estate Handbook, a standard work in the field.

John G. Goldsworth is a Barrister at Gray's Inn in London as well as the Editor of Trusts & Trustees, the leading independent professional journal in this field. An expert in international trust law and practice, he holds the degrees of LLB (Hons) from the University of London, and LLM in International Business Law from the University of Exeter and was called to the Bar at the Middle Temple in 1965.

Mr Goldsworth acts as 'of counsel' to a US law practice where international structures are recommended to international investors, and he is in Chambers at 8 Gray's Inn Square, London where, as a founder member of the Offshore Development Group within these Chambers, he advises governments, institutions and companies on the proper use and development of offshore financial activities and the development of legislation for inward and outward investment including company law, trusts, tax law, and financial law. This activity has included advising the governments of Iceland, Mauritius, Anguilla, the Seychelles and others. In his capacity as advisor to the Seychelles Ministry of Finance, his activities included attending the Commonwealth Finance Ministers Conference, sessions of the OECD and negotiating with international bodies such as the FATF and the UN. In addition many less formal contacts have existed with other countries on international law matters.

Mr Goldsworth is a member of several professional organizations and was chairman of a sub-committee of the International Bar Association on Transnational Litigation, 1985–1987. He is frequently a chairman and lecturer at professional conferences, currently including the most important annual conference on Trust Law, the International Trusts Congress in London. He is also a lecturer for the Certificate and Diploma Course of the Society of Trusts and Estate Practitioners (Guernsey, Monaco and Singapore).

Foreword

I was very pleased when I was approached to contribute to a work of a truly multinational character such as this handbook. Knowledge about technical matters and techniques to deal with money laundering is very important. However, I believe that among all the technical discussions about money laundering we often lose sight of the fact that combating money laundering is about combating large-scale criminality, protecting the integrity of financial systems and, most importantly, promoting transparency and good governance.

A handbook such as this, drawing together the combined wisdom and knowledge of contributors from a diverse range of jurisdictions and backgrounds, is therefore a major step to the promotion of awareness of the fundamental purpose of the fight against money laundering.

I believe that a work of this nature will be invaluable to practitioners and policy makers alike in all parts of the world.

It is common knowledge that one of the primary reasons for people to engage in criminal activity, especially at an organized level, is to make money. However, criminals are not only interested in making money but also in enjoying their criminal proceeds and reinvesting them in future criminal activity. They need to do this without drawing attention to the illegal sources of their wealth. Criminals must therefore have access to financial resources in order to survive and grow. In this way the scourge of money laundering works to perpetuate all manner of criminal activities of the most serious nature – activities such as drug distribution, terrorism, corruption and trafficking in women and children. It is with this in mind that we should consider the impact of money laundering on our societies.

The motivation for criminals to engage the financial sector is not the same as that of legitimate business and they do not share the same objectives. As a result illicit proceeds do not necessarily behave in accordance with normal market principles when they are laundered. Illicit proceeds contribute minimally to economic growth. The consequences of money laundering include greater risks to the soundness of financial institutions and contamination of legal financial transactions, while legitimate business gets displaced to more secure jurisdictions.

Continued laundering of criminal proceeds gives criminals financial power which they can use to further social disintegration, to undermine government structures and to violate community cohesion. It is painful to realize the degree of devastation of lives and communities that criminals cause when they wield this sort of power.

The reaction of the international community was slow but certain. Countries first developed measures to combat money laundering in the 1980s, which led to the formation of the Financial Action Task Force in 1989 – the most coherent response by the international community to the challenge of money laundering. The FATF is generally regarded as being at the forefront in giving shape and direction to the policies and measures aimed at regulating and controlling money laundering. Today, more than 150 countries have committed themselves to implementing the measures to combat money laundering recommended by the FATF.

Measures such as those recommended by the FATF are necessary to protect the integrity of a country's financial sector, to ensure that proceeds of criminal behaviour are detected and confiscated, and that criminals are prosecuted and convicted. If we do this, measures to combat money laundering help reinforce the rule of law, and are important for an effective legal system, a business friendly environment and long-term economic and financial development. These measures when fully and effectively implemented, are an integral part of good governance, sound financial management and an important part of the fight against all forms of criminal activity that threaten our communities: local, national and international.

Practitioners in this area now have a practical handbook from different jurisdictions at hand. We should therefore be grateful to the editors for this initiative, which I heartily support.

Professor Kader Asmal, M.P.
President, Financial Action Task Force, 2005–2006

Anti-Money Laundering – A short history

A personal view from one of the editors

Wouter H. Muller

Senior Consultant

Henley & Partners AG
Kirchgasse 22
CH-8001 Zürich
Switzerland

Tel +41 44 266 22 22
Fax +41 44 266 22 23
wouter.muller@henleyglobal.com
www.henleyglobal.com

Anti-Money Laundering: International Law and Practice.
Edited by W.H. Muller, C.H. Kälin and J.G. Goldsworth
© 2007 John Wiley & Sons, Ltd

Contents – Anti-money Laundering – A short history

1   Introduction

Money laundering is probably as old as money itself. In the past, however, nobody looked at it as a crime as such. It was more the underlying crime that was looked at than what was done with the proceeds of that crime.

It is undeniable that during the **Prohibition** period in the USA (1920–1933) enormous amounts of money must have been laundered. It is interesting to note that when Al Capone, the most notorious gangster in the *USA* in that time, was indicted for the first time in 1931, it was neither on charges of violating the *Volstead Act* that created the Prohibition (banning a.o. the transportation and sale of beverages with more than 0.5% alcohol) nor on charges of the numerous murders committed by him and his gang. It was on charges of evading Federal Taxes during the tax years 1925–1929.[1] At the time this was the closest a US Attorney came to indict someone for money laundering. It is also interesting to note here that, where police forces with guns endlessly chased these gangs without success, it was the people behind desks without guns who were eventually successful in getting these gangsters indicted and charged.

After Al Capone was sent away for 11 years it was clear to the mob that other ways had to be found to remain successful in their 'business'. Since **tax evasion** had proved to be a successful way to arrest and convict these 'business men' a way had to be found to mislead the tax authorities. 'Money that could not be found could not be taxed', so ways had to be found to safely put that money out of sight.

2   Bank secrecy

It is a coincidence that *Switzerland*, by strengthening its **bank secrecy** laws in the early 1930s, more with the aim of helping people hide away money in fear of the Nazi regime than for other reasons, came into the view of people who wanted to hide money for all kinds of legitimate and less legitimate reasons at that time. Not that *Switzerland* was alone in having bank secrecy rules, but it already had for a long time a well-established name for being discreet. Tax evasion not being a crime in Switzerland at the time, money could be safely put away without too many questions being asked. Only two directors of the bank in question had to know the identity of the client. For all others it was a numbered account or an account with a certain agreed code. Putting away money, however, was one thing, but using this money in a way that it could help to make 'business' grow was another.

3   Offshore

It was already in the late 19th century that the 'offshore' world was created. New Jersey was the first to offer companies, established in that state and doing business in another state, to pay the lower New Jersey tax rate. The state of Delaware was quick to follow and is to date still one of the most important offshore centers in the world and certainly the most important within the USA.

The Bahamas, next door to the USA, became an important offshore center when it was detected by the 'gambling industry' and international trading companies. Goods were traded from one

---

[1] Later that same year he and his gang were indicted on over 5000 violations of the Volstead Act.

country to another and 'on paper' via a Bahamian company who had to pay little or no taxes at all. When this trading business started to grow the need for offshore banks was evident. Well-known and reputable banks settled on the Bahamas to facilitate this business. Also, wealthy individuals were in a position to establish offshore trusts to safeguard their wealth for others than their designated beneficiaries.

World War II, however, was the factor that initiated the big growth for the 'financial offshore industry'. International companies like Shell and Philips moved their corporate seats to Curaçao in *the Netherlands Antilles* to be safe from the invading Third Reich in Europe. Based on this occurrence *the Netherlands Antilles* adopted the Law Seat Transfer in order to accommodate companies to transfer their seats in case of threat of war. Certainly during the period of the Cold War lots of companies included these kinds of safety measures into their company articles.

4   Euro dollars and offshore lending

The 'big boom' for the financial offshore industry in the Netherlands Antilles started in the late 1960s a.o. with the creation of the so-called 'Euro dollars'.

4.1   Euro dollars

Euro dollars already existed for a long time. With the implementation of the **Marshall Plan** after WW-II **US dollars** started to flow into *Europe*. As the USA became the biggest export market for Europe after the rebuilding of its industry, even more dollars flowed into Europe and so enormous amounts of US dollars were held in custody by non-US banks in *Europe*. The *Soviet Union* at that time also held US dollars, however in US banks, secured by Certificates of Deposit. After the invasion of *Hungary* in 1956, when the Cold War started to become really grim, the *Soviet Union* feared that the USA might freeze their US dollar deposits held in US banks. It was then that a British bank came up with the solution. The Soviets could place their US dollar deposits with the British bank and the British bank would then deposit its US dollars with a US bank. The USA could never freeze these dollars now that they no longer belonged to the Soviets but to the British bank. It is said that this transaction was the first to create the so-called 'Euro dollars'.

4.2   Euro dollar bond loans

Later, also because of the historically lower US interest rate, it became attractive for companies in Europe, used to much higher interest rates and in need of extra capital, to borrow on the US Capital Market. Making use of the immense treaty network of *the Netherlands*, Dutch Finance Companies, owned by non-US international corporations, issued US dollar bond loans through a Netherlands Antilles' subsidiary on the US market. Under the applicable treaties interest could be paid free from the usual 30% withholding tax. For the institutional investors this was a lucrative investment tool, for the internationally operating companies an interesting tool to get access to the vast US dollar Capital Market. In the heydays of this money-lending scheme, billions of US dollars, or better Euro dollars, floated through this money-lending circuit.

5   Closing the loophole

However, as it mostly goes with these inventive financial products, this mechanism of money lending was misused by others than for which the mechanism was initially developed. Less honorable institutions more and more started to use – or rather misuse – this finance vehicle and the whole scheme ended when in 1987 the *USA* abolished the treaty with the Netherlands Antilles.[2] Together with *FIRPTA*[3] in the early 80s these were the kind of measures taken by the US Government to make the investment of undeclared and illegally obtained money more difficult.

6 Tax avoidance and tax evasion

Still, these measures were aimed more at making tax evasion less attractive if not impossible. Whereas tax avoidance was still acceptable, tax evasion was considered by many states as an illegal act and therefore punishable under a Penal or Criminal Code. However, the difference between tax avoidance and tax evasion was – and still is – a thin line. 'The difference between tax avoidance and tax evasion is the thickness of a prison wall.' It is not clear from whom this saying originates and the meaning is also not very clear. Most probably it indicates that evasion is illegal and avoidance is not, but there is no moral difference.

The IFA,[4] on the occasion of its Annual Meeting in Venice in 1983, dedicated one of its seminars to the difference between tax avoidance and tax evasion. As was to be expected, no general conclusion was reached. I remember well that in the discussion of this seminar a South American delegate ventured the – by all delegated already long expected – statement that the difference between avoidance and evasion could not be generally defined because it could very well be possible that what was considered to be evasion in Europe or the USA was to be considered avoidance in South America!

7 Public scandals around the misuse of the financial (offshore) system

It was the scandals around Bernie Cornfield's *IOS*, having its headquarters in Geneva before the Swiss authorities withdrew his license and forced him to go completely offshore, and at one time having more than 15 000 salesmen working over the world in more than 100 countries, that made the general public aware of the existence of the financial offshore world and the possible misuse.

Later the collapses of **Banco Abrosiano** in Italy in 1982 and the *BCCI*,[5] worldwide represented but investigated and eventually closed by a joint action of the British and Luxembourg regulators and in the USA by the Manhattan District Attorney Robert Morgenthau in 1991, made it clear that even fully licensed **banks**, supervised by well-respected national institutions, were used for other ends than the normal day-to-day banking transactions.

In the USA the scandal of the collapse of **S&L's**,[6] that after deregulation in 1982 left the US taxpayer with an unpaid savings and loan repair bill of over US$200 billion by the end of 1988, as well as the bankruptcy on 13 February 1990 of Drexel Burnham, demonstrated that, in spite of Federal supervision, banks could easily be used for other non-reputable ends. The fact that these institutions were largely used by the men in the street disguised the real aim of these institutions. The worldwide network, however, made it difficult if not almost impossible for the supervisor to

---

[2] A grandfathering clause was however agreed to for bond loans that had not yet matured.
[3] Foreign Investment in Real Estate Property Act.
[4] International Fiscal Association.
[5] Bank of Credit and Commerce International.
[6] Savings and Loans Banks.

detect the misuse and the criminal background. All these institutions eventually turned out to be the means to an end: money laundering.

IOS was used by Meyer Lanski for laundering his 'silver dollars' from the gambling tables before he purchased his own bank, Miami National. Banco Ambrisiano maintained a scheme of offshore companies to launder money for the Mafia and the P2 Lodge and *BCCI* was used by big-time arms traders, the one time Panamanian dictator Manuel Noriega and the **Medellín cartel**.

8   The international fight against money laundering

The ever-increasing production, trade and subsequent use of narcotics have led to an ever-increasing stream of drugs money. The paradox here is that the constantly improving automation of international money transfers makes it easier for criminals to transfer money on all sides of the world from one account to another in a split second, but at the same time makes it easier for the regulators to check and monitor international money movements and detect unusual patterns of money movements.

8.1   The FATF

8.1.1   Forty recommendations

Recognizing the immense thread of these developments the G7 at its summit in 1987 decided that international action was needed to combat the increasing misuse of the worldwide financial system by criminals laundering drugs money. It was then that it was decided to establish an intergovernmental body to set worldwide standards to fight money laundering, the 'Financial Action Task Force' (*FATF*). The FATF was quick in setting global **AML Standards** by issuing its **Forty Recommendations** in 1990.

8.1.2   NCCT

It proved to be a powerful tool to convince countries to change their legislation in such a way that it adhered to these Recommendations. Countries that refused to adopt these Recommendations were put on a list, sometimes referred to as the 'Black List',[7] of 'Non Cooperative Countries and Territories' (*NCCT*). To be on this list turned out to be negative for the particular country and in October 2006 Myanmar (Burma) was the last country to be removed from the list.

8.1.3   Nine special recommendations

After the tragic events of **11 September 2001** it was evident that the world was no longer the same. A new phenomenon, **terrorism**, although already existing for a long time,[8] became the new focus and the Axes of Evil were a fact. Nobody new where a new deed of terror was going to take place and the attacks in *Madrid* and *London* proved that it could be anywhere and anytime.

---

[7] The OECD Tax Competition Group also uses a blacklist which is, however, more related to tax matters than to AML/CFT.
[8] For example, the RAF in Germany in the late 1960s and 1970s, the IRA in Northern Ireland and England and the ETA in Spanish Basque territory.

The *FATF* was very fast in responding to the events of 9/11 and already in October 2001 its mandate was extended to deal with all issues related to terrorist financing (*CFT*). In that same month the *FATF* adopted eight **Special Recommendations** on terrorist financing, complementary to the already existing 40 Recommendations and a ninth Special Recommendation was added in October 2004. In the meantime, as a result of changed and more sophisticated money laundering techniques, the 40 Recommendations were amended twice, in 1996 and 2003, to become more effective by reflecting those changes.

8.2   Response of the world

As a result the whole financial world has changed in general and the financial offshore world in particular. Whereas the 1980s were often referred to as the decennium of 'Total Greed' and the 1990s as the decennium of 'Cleaning Up',[9] the new millennium has become the time to really clean up the financial world.

Even the US banking world, after it first vehemently opposed **due diligence** and *KYC* rules, which were already common practice in the European banking world, now had to implement these very strict rules after the adoption of the *USA Patriot Act*.[10]

The rest of the world were now confronted with the *QI system*,[11] by which every account holder had to be identified when investing in US securities in order to establish whether or not the (ultimate) beneficial owner of that account, when claiming the benefits under a double tax treaty, was entitled to those benefits and not misusing the applicable treaty.

8.3   FIUs

Countries are more and more encouraged to join the FATF, which now consists of 31 countries and governments, and to become compliant with the 40 + 9 Recommendations. It became apparent that financial institutions are the source of information with regard to unusual or suspicious financial transactions. Obligations under national law, based on the FATF Recommendations, forces financial institutions to report these transactions to their Money Laundering Reporting Offices. These offices are mostly referred to as **Financial Intelligence Units** (*FIUs*) or sometimes Financial Investigation Units. Exchange of information between member countries of these confidential – financial – data became an important tool to effectively combat money laundering and terrorist financing. In order to be able to make effective use of this information, but, on the other hand, to protect its confidentiality, it became apparent that the exchange of this information had to be institutionalized.

8.4   The Egmont Group

In the early 1990s an informal global network of *FIUs* came into being. In June 1995, during a meeting of representatives of these *FIUs* in the Egmont–Arenberg Palace in Brussels, the **Egmont**

---

[9] It was in those years that people like Ivan Boesky, Dennis Levine and Michael Milken were convicted. The plea bargains of Boesky and Milken eventually led to the demise of Drexel Burnham.

[10] The Uniting and Strengthening America by Providing Appropriate Tools Required to Intercept and Obstruct Terrorism Act of 2001, Public Law 107-56, signed by President George Bush on 26 October 2001.

[11] Under the QI system every Qualified (financial) Intermediary has the obligation to identify the owner of an account through which investments in US securities are made. When the (beneficial) owner of that account is a US citizen or holder of a US Green Card, the QI has to withhold 30% Dividend c.q. Interest Withholding Tax on dividends c.q. interest paid out on US securities. Under the QI Agreement the QI is obliged to inform the US IRS about the identity of the account holder when requested.

Group was born, an informal group of government agencies that all had sensitive confidential information at their disposal. The Egmont Group defined as its common goal 'To provide a forum to enhance mutual cooperation and to share information that has utility in detecting and combating money laundering and terrorist financing'. The Legal Working Group of the Egmont Group, on the basis of the evaluation of answers on questionnaires distributed among members of the group, devised a definition of a *FIU*, which was approved by the members in 1996 and later amended in 2004 to reflect the growing emphasis on terrorist financing. At the moment of writing this chapter 101 *FIUs* around the world now meet the Egmont definition!

8.5   FATF Mutual Evaluation Reports

In the meantime the FATF conducted mutual evaluations of member countries in order to monitor the implementation of the 40 Recommendations and to assess the effectiveness of the AML systems in its member countries.

In January 2005 the FATF started a third round of mutual evaluations. This round, however, focused more than in the past on CFT now that the nine Special Recommendations and the AML/CFT Methodology 2004 were implemented. Evaluations are conducted by a team of specialists from the financial, legal and law enforcement areas from a member country and the FATF Secretariat. The eventual findings of the assessment team are compiled in a **Mutual Evaluation Report** to be presented to and discussed during the Plenary Meeting of the FATF. Members have agreed that the full evaluation reports will be made public and a summary be published on the FATF's website.[12]

The fact that these reports are shared with FATF-style Regional Bodies (*FSRBs*), the Offshore Group of Banking Supervisors (*OGBS*), the *IMF* and the **World Bank** make it a very strong tool to encourage countries not only to implement the Recommendations in their legislation, but also to make sure that the necessary actions are taken to really combat money laundering and terrorist financing effectively.

9   Private initiatives

It is evident that a lot of effort is given on a supranational level, international and national level to fight money laundering and terrorist financing. It is also evident that, on the basis of these initiatives, private initiatives became more and more important in order to keep their profession clean. The **Basel Committee on Banking Supervision** (*BCBS*), for instance, is a good example of such initiatives.

In October 2001 it set the Standards for Customer Due Diligence for Banks. In February 2003 it adopted and published, as an attachment to these Standards, General Guidelines to Account Opening and Customer Identification. Banks, established in member countries, generally adopted these standards and guidelines. In June 2003 the BCBS, in a joint exercise with the International Association of Insurance Supervisors (*IAIS*) and the International Organisation of Securities

---

[12] www.fatf-gafi.org: In 2005 and 2006 the following countries were evaluated: Australia, Belgium, Denmark, Ireland, Italy, Norway, Spain, Sweden, Switzerland and the USA.

Commissions (*IOSCO*), published a joint note providing an overview of the common AML/CFT standards that apply to each of these sectors. It assessed whether there were gaps or inconsistencies in approaches and recommendations. It also assessed, for each sector, the relationship between the institutions and their customers and the products that were particularly vulnerable to money laundering, offered by each sector to their customers and how each sector has dealt with these vulnerabilities. In an update, published in January 2005, the three sectors described the progress and developments since the first publication in 2003.

10   Conclusion

It is because of these international, national and private initiatives that money laundering and terrorist financing is and can be effectively fought. The Swiss Money Laundering Reporting Office (*MROS*), in its Annual Report of 2005, reported for the second consecutive year a significant decrease (11.2%) of reports on suspicious transactions. Statistical findings of FIUs in general confirm this trend. However, a study report, issued by the **Swiss Banking Institute** of the University of *Zurich* on 4 August 2006, on the impact of the Swiss and foreign *AML* regulations on the competitive position of the banking sector,[13] gives the following summary conclusion:

> ... the goal of *AML* efforts, namely the prevention of drug trafficking and organized crime, has not been achieved, although significant effort has been contributed by the financial sector. So, the *AML* activities of the Banks have become a sole requirement to conduct successful business locally and abroad. They generate however considerable expenditures.

This gives the impression that implementation of *AML*/CFT regulations has become a marketing tool rather than an effective mechanism to combat money laundering and terrorist financing.

This seems in contradiction with the report of the *MROS*. It may, however, be true for 'sophisticated' financial centers. But, what about less sophisticated centers? As long as bribery and corruption are still commonplace in certain countries it is difficult to assess the real impact of these regulations, although they are adopted in the law. Mutual Evaluation Reports will certainly help to improve that situation and the results are certainly impressive. But powerful criminal organizations have certain ways to seriously disrupt the process. It is frightening that on 14 September 2006 it was reported that the Vice President of the Russian Central Bank, Mr Andrey Kozlov, responsible for the supervision of banks, was murdered.

The title of this chapter is: 'Anti-Money Laundering – A short history'. That the history of AML is much more complex is evident. It is written from a personal perspective and largely as I have experienced it in my practice from 1971 till today.

This book is meant to help improve the fight against money laundering and terrorist financing. Money laundering and terrorist financing destabilize our economies and are an immediate threat for world peace. If we don't persevere in effectively combating money laundering and terrorist

---

[13] The results of the study were presented at the general assembly of the Association of Swiss Commercial and Investment Banks on 6 April 2006 by Professor Hans Geiger and Oliver Wünsch. The full study is available in German at: www.isb.unizh.ch/publikationen/amls/amls.php.

financing we run the risk that too many economies are run by criminals and corrupt governments. And that is a scenario no one is really looking for.

Bibliography

Beaty, J./Gwynne, S.C.: The Outlaw Bank – A wild ride into the secret heart of BCCI, Random House, New York, 1993.

Bennet, T.: International Initiatives Affecting Financial Tax Havens, Butterworths Tolley, London, 2001.

Biggs, S., Farrell, S./Padfield, N.: The Proceeds of Crime Act 2002, Butterworths LexisNexis, 2002.

Bruck, C.: The Predator's Ball – The Inside Story of Drexel Burnham and the Rise of the Junk Bond Raiders, Penguin Books USA Inc., New York, 1988–1989.

Clark, A./Burrell, P.: A Practitioners Guide to International Money Laundering Law and Regulation, City & Financial Publishing, Old Woking, 2003.

Evans, C.: The Euromoney Compliance Officer's Handbook 2004, Euromoney Institutional Investors PLC, Colchester, 2004.

Graham, T.: Butterworths International Guide to Money Laundering and Practice, Butterworths LexisNexis, 2003.

Gurwin, L.: The Calvi Affair, Macmillan, London, 1983.

Lascelles, D.: Behind Closed Doors – BCCI: The biggest bank fraud in history, Financial Times, London, 9–16 November 1991.

Manual on Countering Money Laundering and the Financing of Terrorism, The Asian Development Bank, Manila, 2003.

Moscow, J.: Money Laundering: A View from North America, London School of Economics Financial Markets Group, June 2002.

Müller, L.: Tatort Zürich, Econ-Ullstein Buchverlage GmbH, Berlin, 2006.

Pizzo, S./Fricker, M./Muolo, P.: Inside Job – The Looting of America's Savings and Loans, McGraw-Hill Publishing Company, New York, 1989.

Robinson, J.: The Laundrymen, Simon & Schuster UK Ltd, London, 1998.

Robinson, J.: The Sink, Constable & Robinson Ltd, London, 2003.

Schott, P.: Reference Guide to Anti-Money Laundering and Combating the Financing of Terrorism, 2nd edn, World Bank, 2006.

Stessens, G.: Money Laundering, A New International Law Enforcement Model, Cambridge University Press, Cambridge, 2000.

Stone, D.G.: April Fools – the Rise and Collapse of Drexel Burnham, Donald I. Fine Inc., New York, 1990.

Trepp, G.: Swiss Connection, Unionsverlag, Zürich, 1996.

Van den Heuvel, J.: Sneeuw over Curaçao, Uitgeverij BZZTôH, 's-Gravenhage 2002.

Walter, I.: The Secret Money Market, Harper & Row, New York, 1990.

Ziegler, J.: La Suisse lave plus blanc, Editions du Seuil, Paris, 1990.

INTERNATIONAL ISSUES

William B. Howarth is the Chief Executive of the International Compliance Association (ICA). In recent years, as a director of Central Law Training, Europe's largest provider of post-qualification legal training, he has developed, designed and delivered the STEP Global education system. He is currently responsible for global compliance and anti-money laundering initiatives and is still closely involved in the delivery of the Manchester Business School MBA for Wealth Managers. Former positions include Principal and Managing Director of a distance learning college; several university posts, including academic and directorial positions. Bill has written extensively in the field of trusts, estates and international law and has lectured around the world. Through his experience as a senior examiner and assessor for universities and professional bodies globally over an extensive period, he has initiated the ICA Quality Assurance systems to comply with the highest international standards. Bill is the general editor of the ICA course manuals and materials.

Compliance and AML

Standards, education and training

William B. Howarth

Chief Executive

The International Compliance Association
Wrens Court
52–54 Victoria Road
Sutton Coldfield B72 1SX
United Kingdom

Tel +44 121 362 7501
Fax +44 121 240 3002
bhowarth@int-comp.org
www.int-comp.org

Anti-Money Laundering: International Law and Practice.
Edited by W.H. Muller, C.H. Kälin and J.G. Goldsworth
© 2007 John Wiley & Sons, Ltd

Contents – Compliance and AML

1   The International Compliance Association

The *International Compliance Association (ICA)* is a global organisation dedicated to supporting the best compliance and anti-money laundering practice in the financial services and allied sectors. The *ICA* transcends national boundaries by educating and supporting compliance and financial crime professionals throughout the world, through the provision of internationally recognised training and qualifications, member information exchange and continuing professional development.

With a presence in 25 jurisdictions on four continents the *ICA* operates as a federal organisation and has reciprocal links with compliance officers associations and AML forum groups across the world. The *ICA* qualifications are recognised and supported by regulators, governments and industry globally as focussed, relevant education for the individuals who carry out AML and compliance functions for staff.

1.1   Course delivery

All *ICA* certificated education programmes are offered in association with the *University of Manchester Business School* under a quality assured educational agreement and programmes are delivered globally through a number of educational and collaborative arrangements with professional bodies, agencies, business schools and banking associations.

The *ICA* in association with the *University of Manchester Business School* offer a number of one-year professional/graduate diplomas through an integrated part-time study mode:

- Diploma in AML (UK and international version).
- Diploma in Compliance (UK and international version).
- Diploma in Financial Crime (UK).
- Certificate in Compliance (UK and international).
- AML awareness certificate (UK and international).

The programmes are delivered in an integrated educational format, including:

- Detailed course manuals.
- Face-to-face workshops (multiple jurisdictions).
- E-support (on-line library, discussion forums, tutor and news service).

The *ICA* has a team of international tutors who travel the world delivering the workshops in centres such as *The Bahamas, Bermuda, Cayman, Hong Kong, Singapore, Miami, New York, Channel Islands, Switzerland, Portugal, etc.*

1.2   The qualifications

The *ICA*'s diploma courses carry graduate status (120 credits at HE3 level) and are recognised by many universities globally for entry or an exemption from appropriate modules on Master's level qualifications. For example, the MSc in Financial Crime and Compliance of the City of London

University (Cass Business School) will give diploma holders exemptions so that the MSc can be completed within one year of part-time study (www.cass.city.ac.uk).

1.3   The students

In the last 5 years over 3000 students have been trained in AML and compliance, many of whom have gone on to acquire responsible positions as compliance officers and MLROs.

In all of the *ICA* programmes the work of global bodies such as *FATF, OECD, World Bank* and *EU* are central to the studies of the students.

2   Occupational standards of competency for compliance and money laundering prevention

The compliance and money laundering prevention functions have emerged as important corporate issues in recent times. Whether it is protecting systems against criminal misuse or ensuring that sales teams work to the highest ethical standards, the price of failure, in systems or controls, is high.

Safeguarding the integrity of a business is good business. That is why the *UK Financial Services Skills Council (FSSC)*,[1] in association with the *ICA* have developed occupational standards[2] and qualifications for all of those working in the compliance/AML field.

2.1   Market-led to meet business needs

The Standards will help meet regulatory requirements but regulation is not the main motivation for this project. The business need is to avoid the costs of damaged reputations, and loss of confidence that can result from the fraudulent misuse of systems. The project is a response to market demand for high-quality competence-driven education and training in compliance and money laundering prevention. Standards will provide the benchmark to guide that education and training, both nationally and internationally.

2.2   How the standards have been developed

A specialist research team and a series of practitioner groups analysed information about jobs and roles to produce a functional map of each area. The maps proceeded logically from an overarching statement of the purpose of the activity to descriptions of functions that can be assigned to individuals as their job responsibilities. Each function was then analysed to define the performance standard(s) to be achieved if the function is to be performed competently.

2.3   Using the occupational standards within the firm

Good standards have many practical uses. They can:

• Help employers to set competence requirements for recruitment and promotion.

---

[1] FSSC is recognised by the UK Government as the authoritative voice in occupational standards in the financial services sector. It represents employers' interests and directly influences the planning and funding of education and training across the UK with relevant government, national and international organisations.
[2] The standards can be viewed at www.fssc.org.uk.

- Provide a basis for job specification and job evaluation.
- Offer a benchmark for use when appraising performance.
- Allow training needs to be identified.
- Enable businesses to demonstrate that regulatory requirements have been met.
- Provide a basis for high-quality qualifications.

2.4 Defining competence and effective performance

The performance standards are intended to add to, not replace or compete with, an organisation's approach to defining competence. They provide a further dimension to effective performance – achievement against national and international competence benchmarks. They can be used as a framework for those organisations that have not yet developed their own competence systems or have not yet formally codified their own practice standards.

A number of businesses in the industry have already selected relevant Performance Standards, and used them as a basis for clarifying company standards, policies and procedures. Employers will be able to use the FSSC Standards menu to select and profile the competence requirements of different jobs within their firm.

The Standards therefore define competent performance. A test of the Standards is whether they apply to the range of senior and junior roles in compliance and anti-money laundering.

2.5 What is a standard?

Standards describe both performance and knowledge requirements and have the following features:

- Each standard is a single specification of competent performance.
- Each standard sets out separately performance criteria in terms of critical outcomes and critical behaviours.

Knowledge and understanding are crucial to effective performance and as such the Standards describe the types of knowledge that underpin performance to each standard.

2.6 How are the standards structured?

The activities that make up the compliance and AML functions have been developed and grouped into key areas of related functions. Each area specifies what is needed in terms of:

- Performance outcomes – what individuals contribute to the business.
- Knowledge – of law, regulations, procedures, etc. that must be mastered.
- Understanding – of risks, threats, public policies and why procedures work the way they do.
- Critical behaviours – how people apply knowledge and understanding.

Together, these make up the competence that staff need to do their jobs effectively and are the basis of the Standards.

2.7   Standards and qualifications

FSSC have designed a framework of qualifications based on the Standards of Competence. Within this framework awarding bodies will design and put forward for mapping against the Standards a coherent series of qualifications, reflecting the different roles and levels of responsibility within the compliance and AML functions.

Qualifications are proposed for compliance and AML at two distinct levels:

Level 4   Professional – targeted primarily at AML and compliance managers and senior professionals.

Level 3   Support professionals – targeted at managers/team leaders and some specialists.

The qualifications are organised around a set of core units (which all candidates must achieve) and option groups, which allow candidates to select units most appropriate to the responsibility of their particular jobs.

3   The future

The Standards were formally adopted as National Occupational Standards of Competence by Government Education Bodies in November 2006. Qualification mapping has commenced and the qualification framework and validation should be in place by early 2007.

The Standards have been designed with a global perspective so that they are readily usable by international organisations, regulators and governments as a guide in structuring the drive for competency and fitness and properness within the industry.

FSSC and *ICA* will be liaising with jurisdictions on a cooperative basis in an attempt to have a set of global Standards of Competency for compliance and AML put in place in 2007.

In an ideal world all jurisdictions should insist that the AML and compliance functions within an organisation are staffed by competent professionals who are fit and proper to carry out the role effectively. Education and training is an integral part of the continuous battle against AML, terrorist financing and fraud. Too often we are approached at the *ICA* by individuals who state that they have just been appointed as the MLRO/compliance officer of the organisation and could we tell them what their job is and how they should carry it out.

Martyn Frost, FCIB TEP is a consultant with Lane–Smith & Shindler LLP in Manchester having previously worked for over 30 years with a major UK trust company. As well as being an editor of Trust Quarterly Review, Martyn is also an editor of the Wills and Trusts Law Reports. Martyn has been a member of STEP Council for a number of years and has served on a variety of committees. He was a Deputy Chair and is heavily involved in STEP representation regarding money laundering and regulation. Martyn is the author of several books on trust and estate issues and lectures frequently on these issues both in the UK and internationally.

Anti-Money Laundering Regulation and Trusts

Martyn Frost
Deputy Chairman

The Society of Trust and Estate Practitioners

26 Grosvenor Gardens
London
SWIW OGT
United Kingdom

Tel +44 145 787 28 99 (direct)
Mobile +44 79 742 54 637
martyn.frost@gmail.com
www.step.org

Anti-Money Laundering: International Law and Practice.
Edited by W.H. Muller, C.H. Kälin and J.G. Goldsworth
© 2007 John Wiley & Sons, Ltd

Contents – Anti-money Laundering Regulation and Trusts

1   Introduction

Trusts pose a particular problem for anti-money laundering ('AML') regulation in that they are a unique legal concept that is often not understood at all well by either legislators or law enforcement agencies. Because the trust is particularly a creation of equity, and not statute, and mainly found in common law jurisdictions, there can be a very substantial lack of understanding, within civil law jurisdictions, of its features, value and legitimate uses. Although it must not be overlooked that the usefulness and adaptability of trusts does make them of increasing interest to some civil law jurisdictions who have legislated to introduce the concept into their legal structure. However, they are also not necessarily properly understood by legislators in common law jurisdictions.

Any lack of understanding can, in turn, create an atmosphere of suspicion when a trust is encountered even though there may be a lack of evidence to support any suspicion. Hence an earlier edition (now withdrawn) of the UK Joint Money Laundering Steering Group's Guidance Notes for Financial Institutions had described trusts as being popular vehicles for money launderers although it is very doubtful if sufficient statistical, or other, evidence existed to justify this statement in either a UK or global context. Quite clearly, the discussion of AML and trusts going forward needs to be informed with statistics as to the extent to which trusts are known to have been used to launder money. This so far appears to be lacking in the AML debate over trusts and had such information been collated already then the current approach to AML and trusts and trust service providers might be quite different. I think that in this context it is very important to make a distinction between:

(a) trusts being used as an integral part of the actual process of laundering criminal, or terrorist, funds and

(b) trusts being simply an end-use investment vehicle for funds that have already been laundered by other means.

In the latter case the fact of the investment being a trust, a painting or an apartment is not particularly relevant to the debate.

The trust does not offer any advantage to the money launderer in the placement step of money laundering.[1] It is not a vehicle that has any obvious features that will assist with this vital first step. However, like any other method or ownership (e.g. a company) or an investment medium (e.g. an investment account or antique) the trust can, and clearly does, play a part in the subsequent layering and integration process. However, this does not make the trust *per se* of any greater AML risk than any other asset or form of ownership in use.

2   What is a trust?

The act of a settlor placing assets into a trust is a gift by him to the trustees[2] for the trustee to hold, subject to the terms of the trust deed, for the beneficiaries of the trust and the settlor no longer has any ownership of the assets. The trustee has then become the legal owner of the assets. This latter point is one which can be difficult to grasp, or accept.

---

[1] Using the three-stage analysis of placement, layering and integration.
[2] And from an AML perspective this is a crucial point for checks and monitoring.

A trust is a number of obligations:

- that are accepted by, and are legally binding on, the trustee;
- to manage and control the property that the settlor has placed under the trustee's control for the benefit of the beneficiaries of trust;
- that are enforceable by the beneficiaries through a court of law;
- which include distributing the income and capital of the trust at a time and in a manner defined by the terms of the trust.

The property held by the trustee, whilst legally owned by him, will not form part of his personal estate.

It should also be noted that the trust is not a modern invention. It has its origins in medieval England and has been a prominent feature of common law property ownership and succession ever since.[3]

3 Duties of a trustee

The trustee, in accepting a trust, has placed on him certain duties which can be summarised as follows:

- To act exclusively in the interests of the beneficiaries, and not his own, in his dealings with, and management of, the trust.
- To account to the beneficiaries for the management of the trusts.
- To act lawfully in the management of the trust and, as the legal owner of the funds, to account for taxes, charges and similar liabilities imposed on the trust either by law or by any contract entered into by the trustee.
- Not to breach the terms of the trust, or if he does, to be personally accountable for the losses incurred.

4 Beneficiaries

These are usually individuals, but may also be charities (and sometimes companies), who will receive some part of the trust assets either immediately or at a future date. The extent of their benefit (which can be in capital, income or both) will be defined in the trust deed. Sometimes the settlor may give the trustee a discretion as to which beneficiaries receive what amount and at what time. The beneficiaries, both collectively and individually, have the right to enforce the terms of the trust against a defaulting trustee and to compel the trustee to act in their interests. They also have very wide rights to information, including the inspection of trust accounts and trust papers.

---

[3] Albeit that there have during this time been occasional legislative curbs on some features, but more often with legislative measures to make the trust more effective (a recognition of its fundamental importance to the common law property system). Common law jurisdictions have each developed different features of trusts to meet the needs of individual jurisdictions. The same can be said of those civil law jurisdictions that have introduced the trust into their codes.

5   Trustees

There is <u>no</u> requirement that the trustee:

- should not be a beneficiary (although where he is there are issues of conflict of interest to be considered if a beneficiary is to be appointed a trustee as well);

- be a professional trustee, although in practice for many trusts, where a non-professional trustee is appointed, the non-professional trustee will require considerable professional advice in order to understand his duties and discharge his obligations in the correct management of the trust;

- undertakes all the work personally (unless the deed requires it) and most jurisdictions permit the delegation of certain areas of management (such as asset management) to professionals selected by the trustee.

In common law jurisdictions, where trusts are ubiquitous, trustees are much more frequently private individuals[4] than they would be in off-shore centres. This is understandable as, quite reasonably, there is no legal compulsion to use professional trustees. However, this poses a further challenge to AML regulation – if the burden of regulation on the professional trustee becomes disproportionately onerous or expensive there will be a greater tendency towards the use of private trustees and that cannot be a help for AML.

The trustee, being the legal owner of the trust property, has placed on him the full burden of compliance with the AML requirements of the jurisdiction in which the trust is located, the jurisdiction in which he is resident (if this is different), the jurisdiction(s) in which trust assets are invested or located, and on distribution of all or part of the trust fund the AML requirements of where the trust is located, the jurisdiction in which he is resident and the countries in which payments to the beneficiaries are made. These requirements may be of differing complexity but nonetheless the trustee needs to be aware of what is required in all of the countries in which his trust carries out transactions.

Where the trustee concerned is a corporate trustee, AML authorities will have good reason for fit and proper testing of those who control or operate the trust company. There are still differences of opinion between jurisdictions as to the extent that this process is a simple test for an absence of negatives (e.g. no criminal convictions) or whether it should be a deeper process involving (1) the extent to which those in control encourage and establish a compliant AML culture and (2) the qualifications and professional experience of those who control and manage. There is a strong case that the more thorough process, apart from its costs, could jeopardise smaller participants particularly within a domestic market.

6   Protectors

Increasingly in off-shore jurisdictions settlors are appointing what are generally known as protectors. Whilst not unknown in 'on-shore' jurisdictions protectors are, by comparison, much less frequently used on-shore.

The role of a protector is not standard and will vary from trust deed to trust deed. The protector is not a trustee and he will not have any of the trust property vested in him. His general function is

---

[4] This will usually be for trusts on death (wills and intestacies), trusts of lifetime settlements, trusts associated with life products, charitable trusts, pension schemes and trusts of joint property.

usually to supervise the work of the trustee (he will frequently have powers to require accounts, approve investment managers or appoint trustees) and will also often act to ensure that the settlor's wishes are complied with when the trustee exercises discretions in the trust deed.

7   Language

Language is a factor in the approach to trusts by commercial enterprises. The vast majority of trust deeds are in English and this places an immediate obstacle in the way of understanding for jurisdictions where English is not the national language. Even where good English skills exist, trust deeds are problematic as they are technical documents, written in a technical language with many phrases and expressions that are obscure to those with no trust training. It is not surprising that there is some anecdotal evidence of at least one non-English speaking jurisdiction where banks currently turn away trust accounts.

Even within England the language and technical nature of trust deeds is a major obstacle to customer-facing staff of banks, estate agents, investment managers, etc. comprehending what the terms of a trust are. Expecting someone who does not have the relevant legal training to understand the risk involved in a deed that they do not understand (or to comprehend '*the ownership and control structure of the customer*'[5]) is not particularly realistic. From an AML point of view, more effective control is far more likely to be obtained by looking towards the trustee for compliance, i.e. that the burden of the control would not then fall on those who do understand the trust.

This issue of language can be taken one step further by posing the question as to whether or not AML rules that are workable and appropriate to trustees will be likely in non-common law jurisdictions, where usually trusts will not be catered for in the existing legal code, and where English is not the first language?

8   The uses of trusts

In order to get an understanding of the AML risks of trusts, it is essential to understand the multiplicity of uses for trusts in both common law jurisdictions and also those civil law jurisdictions that enacted specific provision for trusts. It is also important to appreciate that the use of trusts and the features of the professions involved with them vary between jurisdictions. An 'off-shore' centre, for example, typically has high-value, low-volume trusts, mainly, but not exclusively, for private clients, with professional trustees. This would provide a radical contrast to an 'on-shore' common law jurisdiction which will have many more lower value trusts as well as much wider diversification of trust type.

Taking England & Wales as an example (perhaps aptly as the trust originated here) trusts continue to provide a cornerstone of English property ownership and wealth management. It is my view that the vast majority of English citizens will, throughout their life, encounter trusts on more than one occasion. Trusts:

1. Provide the legal mechanism for the ownership of all jointly owned property.

2. Are found in all wills.

---

[5] As required by *Article 8 (1)(b) Third Money Laundering Directive* and recommended in *FATF Recommendation 5*.

3. Are imposed by law on the estates of those who die without a will.

4. Are the basis of many charities (acknowledging that this will provide a vast array of social, community and educational purposes).

5. Are used to safeguard the members' interests in pension funds.[6]

6. Are routinely involved in a wide variety of retail savings products provided by mutual funds and life assurance companies.

7. Are used by settlors, and are found within wills, to make safe financial provision for the disabled, financially vulnerable or spendthrift.

8. Are used by settlors, and testators, to create orderly and tax-efficient succession to family wealth through several generations.

9. Underlie employee share benefit schemes to promote wider share ownership by employees of all types of business.

10. Underlie many corporate ventures, as well as being core to the issue of most international corporate debt and domestic corporate debt.

11. Used to safeguard customers' monies that have been pre-paid for goods and services until the purchase has been delivered.

In other jurisdictions, particularly common law jurisdictions, the trust is routinely used for many of the same purposes as well as other purposes such an alternative to probate formalities (e.g. Canada and USA), trusts for diversified real estate ownership (USA), trusts of land and mineral rights for aboriginal populations (e.g. Canada and USA). Within civil law jurisdictions that have adopted the trust there is generally a more limited range of uses (often for personal trusts only).

In the 'off-shore' centres trusts can be used, and are used, for the same reasons, but can offer particular scope for use where the tax planning and succession issues have an international aspect, such as:

1. The avoidance of forced heirship provisions or community of property regimes (which may in themselves fail to recognise the reality of the modern family unit and quasi-family arrangements).

2. Substituting for prenuptial agreements (particularly where other jurisdictions may be uncertain in the effectiveness of such agreements).

3. Asset protection from creditors, within certain limits and with an effectiveness that varies greatly between jurisdictions.

The latter is not really effective in some larger jurisdictions that have specific legislation to prevent trusts being used as vehicles to defraud creditors (e.g. England & Wales and USA).

Assessment of AML risk is not a practical proposition without an understanding of the use and purpose of the individual trust, but once having established this, then a risk-based approach to AML becomes possible. Any regulatory body or financial institution ought to be able to assess tables of factors that will lead to varying levels of appropriate monitoring. A one-size-fits-all approach treating all trusts the same will waste resources. The factors involved in any

---

[6] And in this context also provide the legal basis for recovery of missing funds, for example, after the death of Robert Maxwell in early 1991.

risk assessment must be based on the experience of the individual jurisdiction, but will range across:

- the identity of the trustee,
- the value of the trust,
- the origin of the settled funds (and any later added funds) including the jurisdiction that they originate from,
- the nature of the property being settled,
- the transparency of the trust objects,
- the identity of the settlor (including issues of politically exposed persons),
- the purpose of the trust, and
- the nature of individual transactions being undertaken (particularly the extent to which they fit in with the known circumstances of the trust).

This is not to say that any single factor is an indication of a problem, it is merely one factor among others in assessing the overall risk.

9　Shams

In looking at the legitimate uses of trusts, it is important to understand the concept of 'sham trusts'; that is to say trusts which apparently exist on the face of the trust documents but where the trust documents are merely intended to deceive everyone but the trustee and settlor. Such 'trusts' are not in fact trusts and are no different to sham transactions or sham documentation in any other area of business. In England (and also Jersey) for a trust to be a sham trust there must be a prior agreement between the trustee and settlor that the trust property will be dealt with in a way different to that set out in the deed and the deed will in fact only be used to deceive the rest of the world.[7]

A finding of sham by a court is a finding that the trust does not, and never has, existed. A trustee who has colluded with a settlor to create a sham exposes himself to significant financial and regulatory risk, because of the inherent element of deception involved in creating a sham. But, where a sham is discovered, any regulatory reaction should be carefully drawn as a measure against false description or fraudulent action and not as a measure affecting valid trusts, as the sham was not a trust but the mere pretence of one.

A sham is not the same as where there is a valid trust, but the trustee for whatever reason defaults on his duties and fails to administer the trust according to the trust deed or his other legal duties – that is a breach of trust for which the trustee is personally liable to the beneficiaries of trust for the losses he has caused.

---

[7] *Shalson v Russo* [2003] EWHC 1637; *Abacus (CI) Ltd, trustee of the Esteem Settlement v Grupo Torras* [2003] JRC 092.

10   The domestic environment in which trusts are regulated

Attention has turned towards the effectiveness of AML regulation in individual, and often markedly different, jurisdictions and there is recognition that the quality and degree of regulation is a factor in assessing a jurisdiction's performance in AML terms. But it must also be worth acknowledging that other legal controls in a jurisdiction affecting trusts play a significant role in deterring the use of trusts for illegitimate purposes. For example, in England & Wales, trusts are subject to Inland Revenue control of their taxation (with substantial powers to assess and obtain payment of taxes for trustees), and statutory provisions to prevent trusts being used to defraud creditors,[8] avoid provision on divorce,[9] avoid pension provision on insolvency,[10] avoid nursing home costs[11] or defeat claims from family members on death.[12] In addition there are also significant powers of tracing and recovery that can be used to obtain restitution of funds to which the settlor may have had no valid title.[13] The English courts have a long and well established jurisdiction over trusts. This has led to a detailed understanding of trusts and their close judicial supervision.

Trustees, as the legal owner of the trust property, are fully subject to the whole range of legal and regulatory controls on property use and ownership that apply to the rest of the population in the jurisdiction and this, of course, includes money laundering regulations.

11   Trusts and companies

An understanding of trusts is not helped by the general approach of viewing them as a species of company and putting consideration of them in with consideration of corporate vehicles for AML purposes. It is true that trusts are often to be found in personal wealth structures alongside companies, but that of itself does not make them the same thing. Considering them together tends to channel consideration into a corporate vehicle regulatory project and then trying to adapt the terminology and recommendations to fit the trust as well. A prime example of this is the focus that has been placed on identifying the 'beneficial owner' of a trust for AML purposes. Trust practitioners do not use this expression, as it does not accurately reflect a beneficiary's relationship with the trustee or the trust property. Trusts are not a form of nomineeship, nor does a beneficiary of a trust have ownership, legal or equitable, of any of the underlying individual trust assets.[14]

To focus too much attention on the 'beneficial owner' can further divert AML resources from regulating the key event – the placing of assets in the trust. The *Third Money Laundering*

---

[8] *ss.339* and *423 Insolvency Act* 1986; *CIR v Hashmi* [2002] WTLR 1027.

[9] *ss.24* and *37 Matrimonial Causes Act 1973*.

[10] *s.342 Insolvency Act 1986*.

[11] *ss.21–22 National Assistance Act 1948*.

[12] *s.10 Inheritance (Provision for Family and Dependents) Act 1975*.

[13] It may intrigue those cynical about the valid uses of trusts that one of the principles involved uses a trust doctrine (that of constructive trusts) to aid in this recovery.

[14] This rather sweeping statement does ignore the far less common issues of bare trusts, constructive and resulting trusts. I would not argue against a nominee-style approach being more fitting to a bare trust, but constructive and resulting trusts are not generally deliberately used for property and wealth management and are best ignored for the purposes of establishing general principles in the AML context.

Directive[15] (*'3MLD'*), for example, treats a beneficial owner as being someone who will, at some future time, receive 25% of the capital of a trust. Such a person will be subject to AML checks during the lifetime of the trust[16] although they have no ownership of the trust property and will not usually have been the source of the trust property.[17] The trustee on the other hand will have legal ownership of the property, and legal full accountability for all his dealings with it (including, of course, when he is a professional trustee, the accountability for AML checks when receiving managing and disbursing trust monies).

The concentration on 'beneficial owner' is misleading in that it betrays an approach that has failed to appreciate the function of the trustee. The AML check on the assets being placed in trust and adequate controls on the trustee are instead the key.

There have also been suggestions in different international forums that national registers of beneficial interests, particularly those in trusts, would advance the AML cause. It is difficult to see such a huge bureaucratic exercise as doing anything of any significance for AML. Firstly, it would catch unimaginable amounts of useless data, unless the types of beneficial interests are very carefully defined. Secondly, it would not show any significant data where beneficiaries were part of a wide discretionary class. Thirdly, what use would be made of such a register or who would be able to access it and for what reason? There are some very significant issues of privacy involved with this question. Allied to the question of registers of beneficial interests are proposals that have been floated for trust registers. Similar issues arise in respect of them.

12   The implications for anti-money laundering of the variety of uses of trusts

Given the wide variety of functions of the trust, any AML regulation that approaches trusts with a single regime for all types of trust is in grave danger of wasting enforcement resources through monitoring and regulating transactions of no significant risk. The converse of the unnecessary diversion of resources is that the correct level of resource may well not be applied to the trusts of potentially greater risk.

An example of this is the English trust, applied by statute, to the co-ownership of all jointly owned land and buildings. It is accepted that UK real property is a common vehicle for the investment of proceeds of crime (and it has been described as the most popular[18]). However, I would submit that this popularity, or otherwise, has nothing to do with the trust that is applied where the property is to be jointly owned, as such an administrative trust neither facilitates nor hinders the transaction and has no more relevance to money laundering than the mechanics of joint ownership employed in civil law jurisdictions. However, as currently drawn the *3MLD* draws no distinction between

---

[15] Directive 2005/60/EC of the European Parliament and Council dated 26/10/05, which requires compliant money laundering regimes throughout the Member States by 15/12/07.

[16] *3MLD* currently requires any party subject to the Directive to ID&V beneficial owners whenever they enter into a business relationship with a trustee (wherever that trust is based).

[17] But where a beneficiary is also the settlor the key event for AML purposes should be the placing of the funds into the trust. If that is a clean transaction for AML, what changes the nature of the funds to the extent that further checks are required on the 'beneficial owner'? If the transaction had been a gift and not a trust neither donor nor donee would be subject to a continuing AML regime.

[18] NCIS report '*UK Threat Assessment of Serious and Organised Crime 2003*' Chapter 6 '*Money Laundering*'.

these trusts and any others.[19] Similar comments can be made about other trusts, such as savings products, that are trust-based or pension funds.

The use of trusts within wills and intestacies[20] under the common law system is another area where a one-size-fits all approach to AML and trusts is likely to create a lot of wasted effort. Whilst estates are already subject to AML checks for the suspicious assets that may need to be reported for anti-crime purposes, classifying will trusts and trusts for additional regulation of trust service providers appears to add nothing but expense. As a significant number of estates are dealt with by private individuals acting as personal representatives without, or with minimal, legal assistance imposing an AML trust regime solely on professional trust service providers appears to suggest that those with money to launder would be better off using private executors – something that I am sure wasn't intended but does indicate a less than incisive understanding of the role of trusts.

In only one area has *3MLD* recognised trusts of a markedly different character and these are trusts which are commercial in wholesale markets that are 'comprehensively supervised' and exempted them from the necessity of identifying the beneficial owner.[21]

13   Conclusion and recommendations

(1) In order for AML regulation to target effectively the risk areas of trusts, it seems to me to be essential for those proposing the methods of regulation, national legislators and regulatory bodies to have an understanding of:

- trusts generally,

- the diversity of types of trusts and their uses,

- the diversity of jurisdictions that use trusts,

- the position of trustees and the degree to which any jurisdiction makes them properly accountable for their actions.

In order to construct a risk-appropriate, economical and effective AML regime.

(2) Any regulatory regime that does not target properly the areas of concern is likely to lead to significant wasted effort and useless checks. Such work detracts from the value of AML in particular and generates a mechanical or unthinking approach to checks.

(3) Statistical information on money laundering and trusts is needed[22] in order to establish the extent of the problem and this should help with point (1) above. This should embrace

---

[19] STEP unsuccessfully attempted to obtain changes to exclude trusts of no significant risk from *3MLD* through lobbying in Brussels. Members of the European Parliament tabled a considerable number of amendments with the same aim, but these were all lost in the passage of the Directive through Parliament. All of this process revealed an unwillingness to consider the actual uses of trusts and the diversity of the AML issues involving trusts.

[20] An intestacy is the death of someone without a valid will.

[21] See paragraph 13 of the preamble to *3MLD*; an example of this type of trust is that used as the basis of much international corporate debt in which the City of London is a world leader.

[22] Obviously as money laundering is an illicit activity no accurate statistics for the entire 'business' will exist, but statistical analysis of what is known would benefit this debate.

a thorough and analytical approach to determine if trusts are indeed vehicles for money laundering. Too much that is put forward in this context at present is anecdotal, generalised and often out of date.

(4) An AML regime for trusts will not work effectively, or at reasonable economic cost, if regulation requires financial institutions and individuals to have an understanding of trusts that is beyond what they need for their profession or job (and is in my opinion beyond the level of understanding that currently those legislating for AML have).

For the above to be achieved, some constructive dialogue with trust practitioners and legal experts is essential.

INTERNATIONAL ORGANIZATIONS AND INITIATIVES

Joel Sollier is a French judge who has occupied a number of posts in national courts, in the Ministry of Justice and abroad. He is currently an adviser to the United Nations Security Council Counter-Terrorism Committee. As a member of the Committee's Executive Directorate, he handles legal and financial matters and represents the Committee in its dealings with various international bodies responsible for combating financial crimes. He has been involved in negotiations leading to the adoption of several United Nations counter-terrorism conventions and helped draft the Convention for the Suppression of the Financing of Terrorism.

Address

United Nations
Security Council
Counter-Terrorism Committee
Executive Directorate
42nd Street and 1st Avenue
New York, NY 10017, USA

Organization's profile

The **Counter-Terrorism Committee** derives its mandate from Security Council resolution 1373 (2001), adopted unanimously on 28 September 2001 following the 11 September terrorist attacks in the United States. Through this resolution, the Council imposed certain obligations on Member States in the field of counter-terrorism, including the criminalization of terrorism financing and related activities. Composed of the 15 Council delegations, the Committee monitors implementation of the resolution and, where necessary, facilitates the provision of relevant technical assistance to Member States.

The United Nations Security Council

And the effort to combat money laundering and the financing of terrorism[1]

Joel Sollier

Magistrate and Adviser to the Security Council Counter-Terrorism Committee[2]

United Nations

The Chrysler Building

405 Lexington Avenue, Rm 5127

New York, NY 10174

USA

Tel +1 212 457 18 56

Fax +1 212 457 4041

sollier@un.org

[1] Translated by M. Victoria Guerin.
[2] The ideas expressed by the author are his own and do not represent those of the United Nations.

Anti-Money Laundering: International Law and Practice.
Edited by W.H. Muller, C.H. Kälin and J.G. Goldsworth
© 2007 John Wiley & Sons, Ltd

Contents – The United Nations Security Council

1   Introduction

The delegates who adopted the *Charter of the United Nations* in San Francisco, in 1945, would doubtless have been astonished to learn that the Organization, established in order to '*maintain international peace and security*' and '*to develop friendly relations among nations*,'[3] would one day be called upon to deal with technical matters such as money laundering and the financing of terrorism.

In fact, however, the *United Nations* has taken action on such matters on a number of occasions, not only through its political and legal bodies in New York *(the General Assembly and the Security Council)*, but also through its standard-setting institutions and specialized agencies which are located throughout the world and work to ensure the practical implementation of counter-terrorism measures and the provision of technical assistance to States. The Organization's influence in this area is further expanded through the work of the *International Monetary Fund (IMF)* and the *World Bank*, which constitute the core of the global financial system.

The Security Council has attracted the most attention in recent years because of its counter-terrorism resolutions, especially those with an impact on the financial system. This development in the Council's work is not accidental; it arose from a specific context which has given rise to new modalities for action that it is now possible to evaluate.

2   The context of the council's action

2.1   The political context: the international community's response to the events of 11 September 2001

Once the initial shock of the **11 September 2001** attacks on New York and Washington had passed, these horrific events led to the realization that **the nature of terrorism had changed** and that its new manifestations called for solidarity among States and immediate action aimed at breaking the vicious circle of this violence.

The solution was not a one-time, coercive reaction to a specific event; a better course of action was to develop a long-term strategy that would strengthen international cooperation by establishing obligations common to all. This policy should also be compatible with the broader purposes of the *United Nations* and should therefore take **a legal approach to the counter-terrorism effort** by giving priority to the adoption of legislation.

However, the international community has not reached consensus on the subject of terrorism; on the contrary, the issue is a major source of conflict. The trauma of 11 September 2001 and the fact that the attack took place in the city in which United Nations Headquarters is located were doubtless among the primary causes of **the *Security Council's* unanimous adoption of important resolutions** in the days following the attacks.

2.2   The legal context: an impressive but little-used arsenal of counter-terrorism mechanisms

The persistence of terrorism throughout history and its spectacular growth during the 1960s prompted international institutions to make several attempts to codify international law in

---

[3] **Charter of the United Nations** Chapter I, article 1 (1) and (2).

this area. In the 1930s, the *League of Nations* had prepared an initial draft of an international counter-terrorism convention that was never adopted, but it was the *United Nations* which was responsible for standard-setting in this area by encouraging the preparation, under its auspices, of a group of conventions that are the basis of international counter-terrorism law as it exists today. These instruments, sectoral in nature, cover the principal terrorist acts: hijacking of ships and aircraft, hostage-taking, bombings and the financing of terrorism.[4]

In parallel to the preparation and adoption of these conventions, the *General Assembly* and the *Security Council* have adopted extremely clear resolutions in which they require States to prevent terrorism and call on them to adopt counter-terrorism measures. The first of these initiatives is *resolution 2625 (XXV) of 24 October 1970*, which establishes the principle that:

> *Every State has the duty to refrain from organizing, instigating, assisting or participating in acts of civil strife or terrorist acts in another State or acquiescing in organized activities within its territory directed towards the commission of such acts, when the acts referred to in the present paragraph involve a threat or use of force.*

This resolution, essentially political in nature, will later be supplemented by the *Declaration on Measures to Eliminate International Terrorism*, contained in *General Assembly resolution 49/60 of 9 December 1994*, which may be viewed as the basis for United Nations counter-terrorism policy:

> *States must also fulfil their obligations under the Charter of the United Nations and other provisions of international law with respect to combating international terrorism and are urged to take effective and resolute measures in accordance with the relevant provisions of international law and international standards of human rights for the speedy and final elimination of international terrorism, in particular:*
>
> *(a) To refrain from organizing, instigating, facilitating, financing, encouraging or tolerating terrorist activities and to take appropriate practical measures to ensure that their respective territories are not used for terrorist installations or training camps, or for the preparation or organization of terrorist acts intended to be committed against other States or their citizens;*
>
> *(b) To ensure the apprehension and prosecution or extradition of perpetrators of terrorist acts, in accordance with the relevant provisions of their national law;*
>
> *(c) To endeavour to conclude special agreements to that effect on a bilateral, regional and multilateral basis, and to prepare, to that effect, model agreements on cooperation;*
>
> *(d) To cooperate with one another in exchanging relevant information concerning the prevention and combating of terrorism;*
>
> *(e) To take promptly all steps necessary to implement the existing international conventions on this subject to which they are parties, including the harmonization of their domestic legislation with those conventions; [and]*
>
> *(f) To take appropriate measures, before granting asylum, for the purpose of ensuring that the asylum seeker has not engaged in terrorist activities and, after granting asylum, for the purpose of ensuring that the refugee status is not used in a manner contrary to the provisions set out in subparagraph (a) above.*

---

[4] A full list of the international counter-terrorism instruments may be found on the internet: (http://untreaty.un.org/English/Terrorism.asp).

This resolution, which is fundamental to international counter-terrorism law, was complemented by *General Assembly resolution 51/210 of 17 December 1996*, particularly noteworthy for the details of its provision on combating the financing of terrorism; it calls upon all States:

> (f) To take steps to prevent and counteract, through appropriate domestic measures, the financing of terrorists and terrorist organizations, whether such financing is direct or indirect through organizations which also have or claim to have charitable, social or cultural goals or which are also engaged in unlawful activities such as illicit arms trafficking, drug dealing and racketeering, including the exploitation of persons for purposes of funding terrorist activities, and in particular to consider, where appropriate, adopting regulatory measures to prevent and counteract movements of funds suspected to be intended for terrorist purposes without impeding in any way the freedom of legitimate capital movements and to intensify the exchange of information concerning international movements of such funds.

Despite this broad, consistent framework, however, there would be little effort to apply these standards; while the conventions on air piracy would be duly ratified as a condition for international certification of airports and airlines, this would not be true of the more recent conventions with broader scope, such as the *International Convention for the Suppression of Terrorist Bombings* (which covers 80% of all terrorist attacks committed worldwide) and the *International Convention for the Suppression of the Financing of Terrorism* which, at the time of the attacks of 11 September 2001, had been ratified by only three States). The situation was hardly better with respect to the sanctions mechanism; the staggering discrepancy between the relevance of resolutions concerning *Al-Qaida and the Taliban*[5] and the lack of any practical results of these resolutions would ultimately lead to the events of 11 September 2001 and, in part, to other acts committed by *Al-Qaida*. Generally speaking, by the late 1990s, despite this years-long cumulative standard-setting effort, counter-terrorism was at a standstill from the point of view of both international law (owing to the failure to reach consensus on a general definition of terrorism) and multilateral cooperation between States.

2.3   Criminal law policy-making in an international context: the financial approach

In recent years, the growth of organized crime has led to dissemination at the international level of methods that have proved successful in countries faced with sophisticated organized crime, such as the *United States* and *Italy*. **One such method involves a financial approach aimed at denying criminals access to the proceeds of their trafficking and weakening their logistical resources in order to make it more difficult for them to operate, and thus to cause harm to others.** A series of conventions, developed in the 1960s in an effort to combat international drug trafficking, marked the beginning of this movement. But it was the *United Nations Convention Against Illicit Traffic in Narcotic Drugs and Psychotropic Substances, adopted on 19 December 1988*, that laid the legal foundation for the international effort to combat crime from a financial perspective by establishing new offences (i.e. money-laundering) and new means of detecting them and seizing their proceeds, and by developing new procedures for international cooperation. This movement was subsequently expanded through the adoption of regional conventions and the creation of international standard-setting bodies such as the *Financial Action Task Force (FATF)* and other, more operational bodies.

---

[5]. About a dozen sanctions resolutions targeting Al-Qaida and the Taliban have been adopted; chief among these are resolutions 1267 (1999), 1390 (2002) and 1455 (2003).

During this period (1990–2000), with the end of the Cold War that had frustrated all attempts at coercive measures by the *Security Council*, it finally became possible to develop *an active policy of economic and financial sanctions* against States, entities and even individuals. The 15 sanctions regimes established by Council resolutions during this period include economic sanctions such as embargos on oil (against Iraq and the União Nacional pela Independência Total de Angola (UNITA)) and diamonds (*against UNITA, Sierra Leone and Liberia*) and targeted financial sanctions (*against UNITA and against Al-Qaida and associated individuals and entities*). The most successful of these is *resolution 1267 (1999)* adopted on 15 October 1999, which obliges States to freeze the assets of persons and entities on lists that are issued and periodically updated by the Security Council; to date, 34 States have seized 93 million dollars belonging to Al-Qaida and the Taliban.

Although international instruments carefully maintain the conceptual distinction between '*terrorism*', which is generally of a political or ideological nature, and '*organized crime*', the objectives of which are solely lucrative, the methods of combating them proposed by the international conventions are the same. The appeal for strengthened international cooperation in combating transnational problems applies particularly to terrorist groups, which often have their bases outside the borders of the countries in which their attacks take place.

3 Modalities for security council action

3.1 Imposition of binding obligations

The Security Council put its counter-terrorism policy into practice through a series of complementary, inter-related measures that were adopted over time.

The first important measure, *resolution 1368 (2001) adopted on 12 September 2001*, was of symbolic value; in paragraph 1, the Council asserts forcefully that it '*regards... any act of international terrorism... as a threat to international peace and security*'. This declaration of principle gave the Council a legal justification for taking all necessary measures, including coercive, under *Chapter VII of the Charter* in order to put an end to terrorist acts. However, this extension of the concept of a '*threat to international peace and security*' has not been universally acclaimed; some Member States consider that the Council has gone too far by expanding its powers in this manner in the absence of consensus on a legal definition of terrorism.

Nevertheless, this initial resolution would be followed, days later, by another fundamental decision: Security Council *resolution 1373 (2001), adopted on 28 September 2001*, sets forth the measures that the Council wished to promote in the context of a targeted, universal counter-terrorism effort. This resolution covers all aspects of counter-terrorism but focuses particularly on the financial element by imposing on States two specific obligations:

- **Criminalize the financing of terrorism**

Having established this principle in paragraph 1 (a) of the resolution, the Council goes on to explain, in paragraphs 1 (b) and 2 (e), the manner in which this is to be done, borrowing language from the *Convention for the Suppression of the Financing of Terrorism of 9 December 1999*:

> *The Security Council,*
>
> *Acting under Chapter VII of the Charter of the United Nations,*

1. Decides that all States shall:

(a) Prevent and suppress the financing of terrorist acts;

(b) Criminalize the willful provision or collection, by any means, directly or indirectly, of funds by their nationals or in their territories with the intention that the funds should be used, or in the knowledge that they are to be used, in order to carry out terrorist acts; [and]

. . ./. . .

2. Decides also that all States shall:

(e) Ensure that any person who participates in the financing, planning, preparation or perpetration of terrorist acts or in supporting terrorist acts is brought to justice and ensure that, in addition to any other measures against them, such terrorist acts are established as serious criminal offences in domestic laws and regulations and that the punishment duly reflects the seriousness of such terrorist acts. . .

- **Freeze the proceeds of crime**

This obligation is established in paragraph 1 (c) of the resolution, in which the Council decides that all States shall

(c) Freeze without delay funds and other financial assets or economic resources of persons who commit, or attempt to commit, terrorist acts or participate in or facilitate the commission of terrorist acts; of entities owned or controlled directly or indirectly by such persons; and of persons and entities acting on behalf of, or at the direction of such persons and entities, including funds derived or generated from property owned or controlled directly or indirectly by such persons and associated persons and entities. . ..

This obligation to freeze funds that may be used for the commission of terrorist acts is designed to ensure that States have rapid freezing and confiscation mechanisms at their disposal. These mechanisms need not be of an administrative nature; the resolution simply requires that a State's authorities be capable of freezing funds *'without delay'* pursuant to a request for legal assistance from another State or in implementation of sanctions imposed under *Chapter VII of the Charter.*

Resolution 1373 (2001) is highly significant from the political and legal points of view because it represents a synthesis of many normative provisions and provides a new, unified and current expression of a body of rules which had been laid down in the past but whose implementation had been wholly unsatisfactory. The resolution also gave these provisions a special status since, under *articles 25 and 48 of the Charter*, Security Council resolutions adopted under *Chapter VII* are binding on all United Nations Member States.

3.2   Cooperation with financial bodies

The Security Council's counter-terrorism policy also involves cooperation with numerous international organizations and entities in a position to support its action. The Council has called indirectly for *the establishment of new standards* for combating the financing of terrorism; at a meeting of *FATF* held in Washington in October 2001, the Task Force's mandate, initially limited to money laundering, was expanded to include terrorist financing at the request of its most influential members (which are also permanent members of the Council) because they considered it important to establish minimum international standards in an area where further action was needed. In the following years, *FATF* developed a series of special recommendations on terrorist financing, accompanied by technical notes on their implementation and best practices for the guidance of States.[6]

Through its specialized body, the *Counter-Terrorism Committee*, the *Security Council* has subsequently *promoted these standards* in its dialogue with Member States; in the absence of any other such norms, they quickly became the only international standards for the prevention of terrorist financing. In paragraph 7 of its *resolution 1617 (2005) adopted on 29 July 2005*, the Security Council:

> *Strongly urges all Member States to implement the comprehensive, international standards embodied in the Financial Action Task Force's (FATF) Forty Recommendations on Money Laundering and the FATF Nine Special Recommendations on Terrorist Financing...*

Thereby conveying the importance that it attaches to these non-binding recommendations, lending its political support to the technical work of FATF and institutionalizing cooperation between the two bodies.

This cooperation also has a role to play in the area of technical assistance; the Committee works with the *International Monetary Fund (IMF)*, the *World Bank* and some of the *FATF-style regional bodies* in providing States, at their request, with assistance in preparing draft legislation, creating monitoring bodies and training the officials involved in this work. These bodies also consider each other's reports on country visits and evaluations of States' implementation of their respective instruments and standards; where permitted, this exchange of information both avoids duplication and greatly enriches each body's work by giving it access to additional information and allowing it to take different approaches into account.

3.3   An international approach to financial crime

The *Security Council* does not dissociate the *nine special recommendations on terrorist financing from the FATF's 40 recommendations on money laundering* and; thus, the entire prudential system that has been developed since the creation of FATF in 1989 is endorsed as an effective means of combating illicit financial transactions. This is especially true in the case of the *Counter-Terrorism Committee*, where anti-money laundering legislation is considered an essential means of protecting States' financial systems from such transactions, particularly those intended to finance terrorist acts or to support the logistical activities of terrorist groups. In monitoring States' counter-terrorism mechanisms, the Committee verifies that they have appropriate legislation in place and that the monitoring bodies necessary to its implementation have been established.

The complaint that Security Council resolutions take a selective approach to financial crime by focusing only on the financing of terrorism without requiring prudential identification and detection mechanisms appears to have no basis in fact. Although terrorist financing and money laundering differ in both purpose and practice, the development of mechanisms to protect all financial systems will prevent or intercept suspicious transactions, regardless of their ultimate goal. The Committee is well aware of the interaction between money laundering and the financing

---

[6] All the FATF recommendations and related material are available on the internet: www.fatf-gafi.org.

of terrorism and of the need for a single approach to combating them. With that in mind, it has chosen to interpret *resolution 1373 (2001)* broadly by viewing anti-money laundering mechanisms as one of the modalities for combating the financing of terrorism.

4   The effectiveness of the system

4.1   Direct effectiveness

The effectiveness of the Security Council's effort to combat money laundering and the financing of terrorism can be measured in various ways; one of these is **the exponential increase in the ratification of counter-terrorism conventions,** and especially of the *International Convention for the Suppression of the Financing of Terrorism*, since 2001. It will be borne in mind that one of the Council's goals was to strengthen the network of international cooperation between States and, to that end, to harmonize States' national legislation through the expansion of treaty law. To date, there are 154 States parties to the Convention; this means that 75% of the world's States are linked by a general definition of terrorism *(art. 2.1 (b))*, a shared concept of the financing of terrorist acts and a common obligation to adopt certain prudential measures *(art. 18)*. By requiring States to take steps to combat the financing of terrorism and calling for ratification of the Convention, the Security Council has helped to lay the essential legal foundation for all cooperation; this is, indisputably, a significant achievement.

In practice, the process put in motion by the Council has promoted greater international cooperation in an area where prudence is called for. Banking secrecy is not a valid justification for refusing requests for mutual assistance between States parties to the Convention *(art. 12.2);* moreover, in practice, States and their financial institutions have become more flexible in their modalities for international cooperation. No banking institution wants to lay itself open to prosecution for complicity in the financing of terrorism or even, in good faith, to allow terrorist organizations or individuals to maintain accounts. Similarly, States which, five years after the adoption of binding Security Council resolutions, have failed to adopt prudential legislation or to criminalize the financing of terrorism find themselves in a tenuous diplomatic position and subject to international pressure that may be quite strong, particularly after a country visit by the *Counter-Terrorism Committee*[7] or an international financial institution such as FATF, IMF or the World Bank. Some 40 countries are currently in this position; most, but not all, of them are small States.

4.2   Indirect effectiveness

The political impetus provided by the *Security Council* has had an impact on other international bodies, which have developed their own programmes with the same goals as those of the *United Nations*. Of particular note is the adoption by regional political organizations of plans of action and technical measures that systematically incorporate a financial component. These organizations generally make direct reference to the work of the *United Nations*, and especially the *Security Council*, in order to give their programmes a solid legal basis and, more importantly, political legitimacy.

Similarly, the discussion of highly technical subjects at the highest levels of diplomacy has brought money laundering and terrorist financing into the public eye as never before; they

---

[7] The Security Council agreed in principle to the Committee's country visits in its resolution 1535 (2004).

are discussed at summits of heads of State, ministerial meetings and international events. Thus, the financing of criminal activity has become a political as well as a technical issue. This new focus of activity has had consequences at the national level, where the authorities are called upon to work with financial experts and to increase surveillance of all areas of the economy that may be vulnerable to exploitation by criminals.

Now that national authorities have become more aware of the risk of money laundering and, more recently, terrorist financing, it has been deemed necessary to regulate certain high-risk activities and sectors, including by monitoring non-profit organizations which handle large sums of money and verifying the charitable or religious nature of some activities. This increased supervision of private-sector activities with financial ramifications sometimes meets with resistance on the part of the general public; the line between national security and public freedom is not clearly drawn and it is important to find a balance between the two.

4.3   The limits of the system

The majority of the difficulties encountered are of a technical nature; while we know a good deal about money laundering networks and methods, the financing of terrorism is a new issue that is extremely difficult to understand. The anti-money laundering mechanisms developed progressively over more than 20 years are not always appropriate in combating terrorist financing, particularly when funds are transferred outside the traditional banking system. In the developing countries, for example, cash transfers are the norm and are almost impossible to trace. Thus, in the case of terrorist financing, a shortage of methodological tools and flexible technical solutions that can be adapted to economies with varying degrees of sophistication makes it difficult for States to fulfil the obligations imposed on them by the Security Council.

At the political level, too, there are many obstacles. Some States implicitly refuse the Council's authority, viewing it as an 'old boys' club' and challenging its right to adopt quasi-legislative measures under *Chapter VII of the Charter*, traditionally reserved for crisis settlement, in violation of the rights of the *General Assembly*. International standards for combating the financing of criminal activities also give rise to sometimes angry discussion; some developing countries consider that the rules designed to protect the financial system unfairly benefit rich countries since they were dictated by the international financial institutions, in which wealthy States have the greatest influence. Hence, the imposition of prudential measures and monitoring of their application is viewed as interference in their internal affairs and a genuine infringement on their sovereignty. Other States severely criticize financial sanctions such as those imposed pursuant to *Security Council resolution 1267 (1999) concerning Al-Qaida and the Taliban* and associated persons and entities on the grounds that the lack of precision in the listing process and permanent freezing of assets give rise to human rights violations.

Still other problems are linked to international financial structures that conflict with all policies in the area of criminal law, including those of the Security Council. In order to be effective, any effort to deprive organized crime of its sources of funding requires an in-depth reform of the international financial system and an end to tolerance of certain illicit activities and of the illegal practices of certain territories. However, economic imperatives, national interests and diplomatic alliances make it impossible to achieve consensus on radical reform. The proposed solutions therefore consist of more limited measures that seek to block the illicit movement of funds and to penalize the most serious transgressions. This policy may hinder criminal activity, but it cannot wholly eradicate it.

Recent Security Council resolutions which require States to combat terrorism by adopting economic and financial measures mark an important turning point in the international effort to prevent and punish the most serious crimes. It is now an international obligation for all States to combat money laundering and the financing of terrorism and to submit to the Council's monitoring. This action is giving new impetus to the 20-year effort to protect financial systems from transnational crime, but its success is largely dependent on the good will of States and on their awareness of the serious threat that terrorism and organized crime pose to their societies.

Bibliography

Bannelier, K./Christakis, Th./Corten, O./Delcourt, B.: 'Le droit international face au terrorisme', Pedone, Paris, 2002.

Bassiouni, M.C.: International Terrorism: Multilateral Conventions (1937–2001), Ardsley, New York, 2001/A compilation of UN Documents (1972–2001), 2 volumes, Ardsley, New York, 2002.

Halberstam, M: 'The Evolution of the United Nations Position on Terrorism: From Exempting National Liberation Movements to Criminalizing Wherever and by Whomever Committed', Columbia Journal of Transnational Law, vol. 41, p. 573, 2003.

International Monetary Fund: Suppressing the Financing of Terrorism: a handbook for legislative drafting, *Legal Department, Washington DC, 2003.*

Reisman, W.M.: 'International Legal Responses to Terrorism', Houston Journal of International Law, vol. 22, 1999, p. 3.

Rosand, E.: 'Security Council Resolution 1373, the Counter-Terrorism Committee, and the Fight Against Terrorism', American Journal of International Law, April 2003.

Rick McDonell was appointed to the post of Chief, UN Global Programme against Money Laundering in April 2006. He is a lawyer with extensive experience nationally and internationally in organised crime investigations, prosecutions and anti-money laundering policy and practice. In 1995, he was appointed under the auspices of the Financial Action Task Force (FATF) to begin work in the Asia Pacific region towards implementing the international AML/CFT standards. In that capacity, he was instrumental in establishing the Asia Pacific Group on Money Laundering (APG) and became the Executive Secretary of that body at its foundation in 1998 and remained so until this year. Rick guided the growth and cohesiveness of the APG and it is now recognised as one of the most successful FATF-style regional bodies.

Organisation's profile

Description of UNODC – taken from UNODC's brochure 'Making the world safer from crime, drugs, and terrorism'. The **United Nations Office on Drugs and Crime** (UNODC) is a global leader in the fight against illicit drugs and international crime, and the United Nations lead programme on terrorism. Established in 1997, UNODC has approximately 500 staff members worldwide. Its headquarters are in Vienna and it operates 21 field offices as well as a liaison office in New York and a permanent presence in Brussels.

UN Anti-Money Laundering Initiatives

Rick McDonell

Chief UN Global Programme against Money Laundering

UNODC

Anti-Money Laundering Unit (AMLU)

P.O. Box 500

1400 Vienna

Austria

Tel +43 1 260 60 42 22 (gen.)

    +43 1 260 60 45 08 (direct)

Fax +43 1 260 60 68 78

rick.mcdonell@unodc.org

www.unodc.org

Anti-Money Laundering: International Law and Practice.
Edited by W.H. Muller, C.H. Kälin and J.G. Goldsworth
© 2007 John Wiley & Sons, Ltd

Contents – UN Anti-Money Laundering Initiatives

1 UN Global Programme against Money Laundering (GPML)

The Anti-Money Laundering Unit (AMLU) of the United Nations Office on Drugs and Crime (UNODC) is responsible for carrying out the Global Programme against Money Laundering (GPML), which was established in 1997 in response to the mandate given by the 1988 UN Convention against Illicit Traffic in Narcotic Drugs and Psychotropic Substances.

The UN Convention against Transnational Organised Crime, which entered into force on 29 September 2003, widens the definition of money laundering to include the proceeds of all serious crime, and gives legal force to a number of issues addressed in the 1998 United Nations General Assembly Special Session's (UNGASS) Political Declaration.

The UN Convention against Corruption, which was entered into force on 14 December 2005, creates as an offence the concealment and laundering of the proceeds of acts of corruption and includes further extensive measures to combat money laundering.

The International Convention for the Suppression of the Financing of Terrorism which entered into force on 10 April 2002, requires Member States to take measures to protect their financial systems from abuse by persons planning or engaged in terrorist activity.

In keeping with the requirements of the UN Conventions and other internationally accepted standards such as the Recommendations of the Financial Action Task Force, the broad objective of the Global Programme against Money Laundering is to strengthen the ability of Member States to implement those standards.

More specifically, GPML's objectives are:

- To assist in the achievement of the objective set up by the UN General Assembly Special Session (UNGASS) for all States to have in place legislation on money laundering.

- To equip States with the necessary knowledge, means and expertise to implement national legislation and the UN Plan of Action against Money Laundering.

- To increase the capacity of States successfully to undertake financial investigations and prosecutions.

- To equip States with the necessary legal, institutional and operational framework to comply with international standards on countering the financing of terrorism including the relevant UN Security Council Resolutions.

- To assist States in detecting, seizing and confiscating illicit proceeds.

The Programme also encourages money laundering policy development, raises public awareness about money laundering and the financing of terrorism, and acts as a coordinator of anti-money laundering initiatives between the United Nations and other organisations.

2 Technical assistance

The technical assistance component of GPML is aimed at meeting the needs of UN Member States at the national and/or regional level in the implementation of their AML/CFT policies. Its wide range of activities include:

- reviewing legal and institutional AML/CFT frameworks;

- assisting in the drafting or upgrading of legislation and related regulations;

- ensuring that the necessary AML/CFT mechanisms are put in place and are efficiently implemented;

- fostering the awareness, understanding and implementation of best practices in the regulation of financial services; and

- conducting training workshops and seminars for law enforcement agencies, regulatory bodies, central banks, the banking and finance sector and the judiciary.

GPML continues to focus on capacity building in its work with Member States. Hands-on advice and assistance are being provided to AML/CFT practitioners, law enforcement, prosecutors, judges, financial regulators and FIU personnel. In keeping with the 'power of partnership' theme set by the Executive Director of UNODC, GPML has joined forces with several international bodies and governments to provide assistance.

3   Model legislation

GPML has developed, in collaboration with the UNODC Legal Advisory Section, the Common-wealth Secretariat and the International Monetary Fund (IMF), model laws for both common law and civil law legal systems to assist countries in drafting AML/CFT legislation in order to be in full compliance with the applicable UN Conventions and the FATF Recommendations.

The model laws serve as working tools for Member States and are continually being upgraded in order to encompass any new international standards. The model laws are intended to be adjusted to the particularities of national legal and administrative systems.

4   Expert mentors in the field

In 1999, GPML launched a 'mentoring programme' in order to provide in-depth and long-term assistance to States in the fight against money laundering and the financing of terrorism. GPML continues to expand the deployment of professional expertise in the field to train people and build institutions, deliver direct technical assistance and to improve AML/CFT capacity. Currently expert mentors are deployed in the Middle East and North Africa, Central Asia, West and Central Africa, South East Asia, the Pacific Islands, Eastern and Southern Africa, and Central America. Expert mentors can be deployed in the field for periods of one to four years depending on the needs of the countries requesting assistance.

5   Strengthening Financial Intelligence Units (FIUs)

Assistance in establishing FIUs has become a priority in GPML technical assistance activities. An FIU is responsible for receiving, analysing and disseminating to the competent authorities disclosures of financial information concerning suspected proceeds of crime in order to counter money laundering or financing of terrorism. A national FIU needs to provide a facility for the collection, analysis and rapid dissemination of financial information both nationally and internationally, while ensuring confidentiality of the data collected. An effective FIU is now a requirement of the FATF standards.

The Egmont Group, established in 1995, in which the (currently) 101 members pursues best practice among FIUs and promotes international cooperation in the fight against money laundering and financing of terrorism. This cooperation also includes the exchange of financial intelligence on a secure computer network (the Egmont Secure Web-site). GPML participates in Egmont Group meetings and conducts workshops in cooperation with the Egmont Group. GPML assist developing countries to meet best FIU practice and to be admitted as Egmont members.

6 Computer-based training

GPML in collaboration with the UNODC Regional Field Office in Bangkok launched its first set of AML Computer-Based Training (CBT) modules in 2003. This training CD-ROM – an introductory course on money laundering – was designed to help develop financial investigation expertise in law enforcement agencies.

Since then, GPML has developed 13 anti-money laundering modules that are being delivered through global CBT centres.

The training programme has flexibility in language, level of expertise, target audience and theme. The current prototype is an awareness-raising introduction for officials with a fairly basic skills level. Future courses will also be targeted at specialists, to cover such topics as FIU systems, asset forfeiture, know your customer requirements, specialised investigative techniques, mutual legal assistance, counter-financing of terrorism and investigating alternative remittance systems.

Computer-based training is particularly applicable in countries and regions where resources are few, and law enforcement skills and knowledge are low. GPML is working daily with many governments faced with this shortfall in front-line law enforcement expertise. As an approach, CBT lends itself well to GPML's global technical assistance operations.

The training includes high-quality voice, pictures, graphics, interactive video and animation, simulation and student tests.

GPML has delivered computer-based training in Africa, Asia, Latin America and the Pacific.

7 Website, database and research

7.1 International Money Laundering Information Network (IMoLIN)

IMoLIN, a one-stop AML/CFT research resource, was established in 1998 by the United Nations on behalf of a partnership of international organisations involved in anti-money laundering. AMLU now administers and maintains IMoLIN on behalf of the following 10 partner organisations: the Asia Pacific Group on Money Laundering (APG), the Caribbean Financial Action Task Force (CFATF), Commonwealth Secretariat, the Council of Europe–MONEYVAL, the Eastern and Southern Africa Anti-Money Laundering Group (ESAAMLG), the EuroAsian Group (EAG), the Financial Action Task Force (FATF), Financial Action Task Force on Money Laundering in South America (GAFISUD), Interpol, and the Organization of American States (OAS/CICAD). In the first half of 2004, AMLU relaunched IMoLIN, after completing an extensive renovation of the site's 'look and feel' and its content, in collaboration with UNODC's IT Section (www.imolin.org).

7.2   Anti-Money Laundering International Database (AMLID)

Within IMoLIN is AMLID, a unique password-protected service cataloguing world AML/CFT laws in an easily searchable format. In it, GPML maintains the largest available online legal library of AML/CFT national legislation. The database now contains legislation from some 163 jurisdictions and, since January 2005, more than 300 new and amended AML/CFT laws and regulations were included in the database.

In addition, AMLID also reflects the legal analysis of UN Member States' AML/CFT regimes. On 27 February 2006, GPML launched the AMLID 2nd Round of Legal Analysis and the database currently reflects the legal analysis of 32 countries and/or jurisdictions. The AMLID questionnaire was updated to reflect new money laundering trends and standards, and takes into account provisions related to terrorist financing and other current standards, such as the revised FATF 40 + 9 Recommendations. In addition, the revised AMLID questionnaire now includes a Conventions Framework section. This new section gives an overview of the status of a country or territory to the international conventions applicable to AML/CFT as well as the status of a country or territory to bi-lateral/multi-lateral treaties or agreements on mutual legal assistance in criminal matters and extradition. The old 72-subject questionnaire was expanded to 100 subjects reflecting the above-mentioned.

8   AMLU global press review

The AMLU Global Press Review is a periodic service designed to allow the Programme to share with colleagues some of the information about money laundering and related matters that the United Nations collects on a global basis. The Global Press Review collates recent news stories from print and audiovisual media. It is circulated to some 650 subscribers working in the UN system, international organisations and governments, all of whom have a particular interest or are involved in the AML/CFT field.

9   Collaboration

GPML continues to work in cooperation with other international organisations active in the fight against money laundering and terrorist financing, such as the Commonwealth Secretariat, the Organisation for Security and Cooperation in Europe (OSCE), the IMF, World Bank, the Egmont Group, the European Union, UNCITRAL, as well as the US Department of Justice (OPDAT). GPML has reached observer status within the FATF and the Financial Action Task Force-Style Regional Bodies (FSRBs); the Asia/Pacific Group on Money Laundering (APG), the Caribbean Financial Action Task Force (CFATF), the Council of Europe – MONEYVAL, the Eastern and Southern Africa Anti-Money Laundering Group (ESAAMLG), the EuroAsian Group (EAG), the Middle East and North Africa Financial Action Task Force (MENAFATF), and the Intergovernmental Group for the Fight against Money Laundering in West Africa (GIABA).

Abbreviations

AML	Anti-Money Laundering
AMLID	Anti-Money Laundering International Database
AMLU	Anti-Money Laundering Unit
APG	Asia Pacific Group on Money Laundering
CBT	Computer-Based Training
CFATF	Caribbean Financial Action Task Force
CFT	Combatting the Financing of Terrorism
EAG	EuroAsian Group
ESAAMLG	Eastern and Southern Africa Anti-Money Laundering Group
FATF	Financial Action Task Force
FIU	Financial Intelligence Unit according to the Egmont definition
FSRBs	Financial Action Task Force-Style Regional Bodies
GAFISUD	Financial Action Task Force on Money Laundering in South America
GIABA	Intergovernmental Group for the Fight against Money Laundering in West Africa
GPML	Global Programme against Money Laundering
IMF	International Monetary Fund
IMoLIN	International Money Laundering Information Network
MENAFATF	Middle East and North Africa Financial Action Task Force
MONEYVAL	Council of Europe Select Committee of Experts on the Evaluation of Anti-Money Laundering Measures
OAS/CICAD	Organization of American States
OPDAT	US Department of Justice
OSCE	Organisation for Security and Cooperation in Europe
UNCITRAL	United Nations Commission on International Trade Law
UNGASS	United Nations General Assembly Special Session's
UNODC	United Nations Office on Drugs and Crime

Franco Frattini (born in Rome on 14 March 1957) is an Italian politician, currently serving as European Commissioner for Justice, Freedom and Security. He is also one of five vice-presidents of the 25-member Barroso Commission. Mr Frattini studied law and graduated in 1979. Before entering into politics Mr Frattini was a State Attorney until he was appointed 'Council of State' Judge in January 1986. After having served in several public functions, Mr Frattini was appointed Minister for the Civil Service and Regional Affairs from 1995 to 1996. In April 1996 Mr Frattini was elected Member of Parliament. He was secretary of the Parliamentary Committee for Intelligence and Security Services and State Secrets from 1996 to 2004. In June 2001 Mr Frattini became a member of Silvio Berlusconi's government as Minister for Civil Service and for Coordination of Intelligence and Security Services. In November 2002 he was appointed Minister of Foreign Affairs until on 4 November 2004 he was nominated to take up the Justice portfolio in the European Commission.

Initiatives of the European Commission

Franco Frattini

Vice-President and EU Commissioner responsible for Justice, Freedom and Security

European Commission
B-1049 Brussels
Belgium

Tel +32 2 298 75 00
Fax +32 2 298 85 95
franco.frattini@cec.eu.int
europa.eu.int/comm/commission_barroso/frattini/index_en.htm

Anti-Money Laundering: International Law and Practice.
Edited by W.H. Muller, C.H. Kälin and J.G. Goldsworth
© 2007 John Wiley & Sons, Ltd

Contents – Initiatives of the European Commission

1   Introduction

We live at a time in history when new challenges have to be tackled at an unprecedented pace. Against these challenges there can be only collective responses, essential to our freedom and security. Ranking high on the list of challenges is fighting against new types of crime, such as money laundering or terrorist financing. Yet the response must consider the times we live in: the union of the international community, the respect for the rule of law and the assertion of collective responsibility. In this context, the European Commission has striven to develop over the years measures to tackle money laundering, organised crime and terrorist groups. This is a continuous process where new threats alert us of the need to carefully assess the nature of measures in place at the level of the European Union.

Organised crime groups tend to behave like any other organisation. Having worked hard to accumulate wealth through deception and violence, their members and relatives seek to enjoy their ill-gotten gains in peace. This entails protection from intrusive forms of scrutiny and maintaining the appearance of your typical law-abiding citizen. It is therefore important for them to conceal the dubious origin of their wealth. Criminals organise themselves into structured organisations; they get large amounts of banknotes, with the practical issues associated with their physical handling and eventual transformation into clean money. This illustrates how over the years money laundering has become a lucrative business. While petty criminals may tend to focus on the concealment aspect – where monies are intended for deferred personal consumption – larger criminal organisations are more interested in securing and enhancing value over time. Far from wishing to destabilise financial markets, criminals are looking for stable, prosperous and, above all, deep markets. The deeper and the stronger they are, all the easier to conceal the profits.

Thus the stage is set for an unlikely alliance between criminals and outwardly respectable professions, whose skills aid organised crime in concealing its profits. This is without doubt a Faustian pact. There is no easy way out for the banker, the lawyer or the accountant who becomes involved in such an association. Associations of this kind are a matter of great concern for decision-makers everywhere, perverting the functioning of our democratic societies and the rule of law. From such associations, criminals can access relays in society that could thwart efforts to fight organised crime. Take, for example, a situation where the proceeds of crime, when channelled into a small domestic economy, result in the aligning of the interests of the State with those of organised crime as the major investor in the domestic economy.

This leads us to the wider ramifications of money laundering as impacting on both economic and financial levels. This requires money laundering to be prosecuted as an offence in its own right. At the same time consideration should be given that the causal link with the **predicate offence** (the offence that generated crime) is preserved in one way or another, given that in most jurisdictions there is the need to prove that funds originated from illegal activities. In this context money laundering cannot simply be construed as a 'technical' offence like insider trading or market manipulation. It is more closely linked to the law enforcement chapter, with the attendant consequences in terms of shared responsibility between law enforcement authorities and other administrative bodies responsible for preventive measures. Essential to the prosecution of heads of organised crime groups for money laundering activities is **tracing** funds back to their ultimate owner. In this way making connections with predicate offences strikes at the heart of organisations busy washing and drying the proceeds of crime. In this respect the fight against money laundering is inseparable from the wider fight against organised crime. Accordingly, a key component in the fight against money laundering is ensuring coordination across all relevant parties, whether public or private, with regulatory or supervisory powers, of an administrative, police or judicial nature. In the following section I will demonstrate how the European Commission has endeavoured over the years to pursue an integrated approach of linking preventive measures to law enforcement matters.

2 The action of the European Commission in the fight against money laundering: preventive measures

It is to the European Commission's credit that it became aware early on of the need to effectively respond to the threat of money laundering. A Community regulation was first laid down in 1991, through *Directive 91/308/EEC* **on the prevention of the use of the financial system for the purpose of money laundering.**[1] The need for Community intervention countering the criminal use of the system was deeply felt, especially given the then recently introduced freedom of capital movements and the principle of the freedom to supply financial services. The Commission was eager to demonstrate that the benefits of moving capital across borders did not accrue to organised crime. Law and order considerations had been put forward to justify former capital movement restrictions and it was important to prove that freedom of capital movements did not provide criminals with increased opportunities to move funds around, especially within an increasingly globalised economy.

Directive 91/308/EEC's definition of 'money laundering' specifies categories of financial intermediaries and their obligations and requirements, defines these obligations and requirements, and indicates the public authorities responsible for the control functions. This general framework was devised as consistent with the 40 recommendations of the **Financial Action Task Force** on money laundering (*FATF*), the global standard-setter created shortly before.

Key to this directive was distinguishing between 'competent authorities' and 'authorities responsible for combating money laundering'. This recognised that the authorities responsible for combating money laundering were mainly those who received and carried out analyses of suspicious transactions. When reporting entities or supervisory authorities become aware of such transactions, they are required to forward these on for subsequent analysis to the national authority responsible for combating money laundering. This distinction is fundamental to the anti-money laundering framework developed according to *FATF* recommendations. It provides for a clustering of public sector expertise to analyse what could be very complex schemes. The dual nature of this system also recognises the early warning role of the private sector in the prevention of money laundering. Leads provided from this source are purely indicative and are subject to a series of filters established by the authority responsible for combating money laundering. After filtering, selected material can then be used by 'competent authorities', i.e. traditional law enforcement authorities, who are thus better able to focus their investigative and judicial powers on relevant facts.

Directive 91/308/EEC was also a landmark text in the sense that most of the key preventive measures that subsequently proved useful were first introduced here. These consisted of the need

---

[1] Official Journal L166 of 28.06.1991, p. 77.

for customer identification, record-keeping and reporting requirements associated with suspicious transactions. For a suspicious transaction to lead to investigation, reporting entities were required to maintain sufficient customer details and the relevant documentation admissible as evidence to an investigation into money laundering. Consistent with such an integrated approach, all reporting entities were required to implement appropriate internal control and communication procedures. In addition they had to properly train their employees to be aware of possible laundering patterns.

The Commission closely monitored Member States' transposition of this directive into domestic legislation and produced two insightful evaluation reports. The dialogue conducted under the **contact committee**, created in the Directive, was especially useful allowing the Commission to collect feedback from national authorities involved in the fight against money laundering. The European Parliament, while generally positive to such Commission reports, noted that further progress was required to enhance the effectiveness of EU and national anti-money laundering frameworks. In addition, typological studies undertaken by *FATF* and other bodies involved in the fight against money laundering provided useful examples on how launderers were reacting to the introduction of new legislation. Out of this wealth of information, it was possible to move forward.

14 July 1999 saw the Commission present a proposal for an amended Directive that became known as the *second money laundering directive*.[2] Its aim was to refine existing provisions and to plug perceived gaps arising out of the successful implementation of the first directive. Of particular note was extending the scope of **predicate offences** to all forms of large-scale criminal activity with links to organised crime, and thus liable to generate significant 'launderable' revenues. Similarly it was decided that crimes defined in article 3(1a) of the Vienna Convention, included in *Directive 91/308/EEC*, would be supplemented by that of the offence of serious fraud to EC financial interests, corruption and participation in the activities of criminal organisations. The latter directive, linked to the definition of *Joint Action of Council 98/733/JHA* of 21 December 1998, demonstrates the cross-fertilisation between pillars as an example of the interoperability of legislative acts adopted under different EU procedures.

Other elements introduced in the second directive included extending the scope of reporting entities. The European Parliament and some typological work drew the Commission's attention to launderers passing numerous low-value wire transfers through bureaux de change and money remittance outlets in reaction to a heightened culture of surveillance in the banking sector. Naturally, as larger institutions tightened their controls, organised crime turned to financial intermediaries operating under less stringent scrutiny. A result of this was to broaden the scope of financial institutions covered in the directive to include both mutual funds and independent legal professionals. The latter's inclusion gave rise to animated exchanges between Council and Parliament, with MEPs asserting that this represented a violation of lawyer–client confidentiality. Under the proposed scheme, lawyers would have to report suspicions related to their clients to authorities responsible for combating money laundering. While the inclusion of other non-financial professions, such as real estate agents and accountants, was not seriously challenged, Parliament stressed that at issue were certain fundamental rights related to the integrity of court proceedings. As this was never the Commission's intention a compromise was reached, limiting the reporting role of lawyers to their participation in financial or corporate transactions, including providing tax advice. Information received in their role of defending or representing a client was

---

[2] Official Journal L344 of 28.12.2001, p. 76.

exempted from the reporting obligation. Self-regulatory bodies were recognised as the first filter in the detection of suspicious transactions, if member States allow them to do so.

This was deemed a reasonable compromise from the Commission's point of view. That it remains unaltered in the *third directive* is a sign that the Commission considers it too early to draw conclusions given the brief implementation period of such a provision. The susceptibility of legal professions to involvement in money laundering operations does exist and the Commission has taken steps to deter conduct of this kind.

The above episode should not detract from the fact that the majority of discussions on anti-money laundering legislation proposed by the Commission have taken place in a consensual atmosphere. In particular the lack of criticism of the Commission's general approach gives a clear indication as to the quality of the tabled legislation. The Commission has always been careful to implement its policies in a fair and transparent manner and endeavoured to reach early agreement through proper consultation with all interested parties. In this regard it goes without saying that the support of affected industries and the general public are essential to effectively combat money laundering.

This consensual spirit was also present when the Commission tabled a proposal for a *third money laundering directive*, and is noteworthy given the potential irritation of it following so soon after the *second directive*. In particular, some Member States had not even completed transposition of the *second directive* when the draft of the *third directive* was released. Another explanation for the swift adoption of the third money laundering directive lay in the very changed circumstances emerging in the wake of the 11 September and Madrid bombings. It was also facilitated by building on existing measures. Put simply, the third release extended the scope to the financing of terrorism, defining the **predicate offence** as a serious crime whose definition lies in the *Framework Decision 2001/500/JHA* (another example of cross-fertilisation between pillars), and constitutes the most elaborate attempt yet to specify **customer due diligence** rules. Within this framework the identification of **beneficial ownership** is crucial. Financial intermediates can no longer stop at knowing the identity of managers of a legal arrangement, such as a company or a trust. They are required to go beyond the middleman in order to determine who exactly the beneficiaries of deposited funds are. The directive adopts a risk-based approach in consideration of the daunting overhead such extensive cross-checking entails. As such, financial intermediaries have to set up adequate internal procedures to pinpoint areas of high, medium and low risk and adjust their level of scrutiny accordingly. While such a sophisticated approach presents a number of difficulties, the Commission believes that it strikes the right balance between comprehensiveness and accuracy. Provisions in the directive call for specific procedures according to certain high-risk or low-risk situations. The definition of the circumstances triggering such special procedures is adopted through comitology procedures for added flexibility in the implementation of the directive. In particular, in the wake of the Abacha case in the United Kingdom, politically exposed persons will always be considered high risk under the terms of the directive. After an uneventful first reading, the third money laundering directive was adopted and published in November 2005. From that point on Member States have 24 months to implement this challenging text.

In the following section I will focus on the other side of the legislative coin, namely the law enforcement aspects of the fight against money laundering.

3 The action of the European Commission in the fight against money laundering: law enforcement measures

The European Union, through a series of reforms outlined in the ***Amsterdam Treaty***, has undertaken to construct an area of Justice, Freedom and Security. These three democratic ideals have been at the top of the Union's agenda for the last five years. However, this rapid expansion has not only resulted from an expansion of the competencies of the Union per se, but more so due to contingent events that have demonstrated the need for common policies in a number of key areas close to the daily life of every citizen. An area without internal frontiers must be an area of justice in order to serve its citizens, one where criminals can find no safe havens, and where citizens and business are not discouraged by cross-border obstacles in the exercising of their rights.

This objective was unambiguously reaffirmed in the ***Tampere declaration*** following the European Council of October 1999. An entire paragraph was dedicated to actions necessary to counter money laundering. In particular, the European Council affirmed that:

> *Money laundering is at the very heart of organised crime. It should be rooted out wherever it occurs. The European Council is determined to ensure that concrete steps are taken to trace, freeze, seize and confiscate the proceeds of crime.*

No matter how effective preventive measures may be, crucial to the success and credibility of the anti-money laundering scheme is that further action is taken 'down the pipeline'. This requires that suspicions of money laundering are effectively dealt with by the judiciary and lead to the swift implementation of appropriate sanctions. Indeed, nothing depresses the public more than a criminal at large as a result of the undue leniency of sentence whether it be wholly, partially or not even applied at all.

An obvious starting point for action in this field was ***Convention n° 141 of 1990 from the Council of Europe***.[3] This laid down a comprehensive system of rules aimed at covering all procedural aspects connected with money laundering – from the initial investigations to the adoption and execution of the confiscation sentence. It provided for special mechanisms promoting the widest possible cooperation required to deny criminal organisations access to money laundering instruments and to the proceeds of crime. More than a deepening of existing mutual legal assistance instruments, it laid out detailed – and thus more effective – rules on the form international cooperation should take in the specific context of the fight against money laundering. International cooperation is indeed critical in many laundering cases, where the proceeds of crime are often laundered in another country. The fact that all EU Member States have signed and ratified Convention n°141, an infrequent occurrence for *Council of Europe* instruments, illustrates the value placed upon this instrument.

Capitalising on existing instruments, the *Council of the Ministers of Justice and Home Affairs* of 3–4 December 1998 adopted a Joint Action[4] wherein member states committed to ensuring that no reservations were made or upheld in respect of *articles 2 and 6 of the Convention of 1990 of the Council of Europe*. Thus the possibility allowed by the Convention to make reservations was eliminated with respect to Member States. Confiscation would be possible for all offences punishable by a detention order in excess of one year, this scope of predicate offences for money

---

[3] Available at www.coe.int.
[4] Joint Action 98/699/JHA, Official Journal L333 of 9.12.1998, p. 1.

laundering cannot be narrowed above that same threshold. In addition to this obligation, the 1998 instrument lays down further provisions aimed at facilitating both the freezing of assets of persons under investigation and cooperation between the associated authorities.

This instrument was converted and updated in 2001 through the adoption of a Framework Decision,[5] i.e. the third pillar equivalent of a directive (though without direct effectiveness). While retaining the dispositions applicable to *Convention n° 141*, it introduced a first attempt, admittedly modest, to harmonise penal sanctions related to money laundering. Under such provisions, each Member State shall take the necessary steps to ensure that money laundering as defined in *Convention n° 141* is punishable by deprivation of liberty for a maximum of not less than 4 years. Rules related to value confiscation are also provided for: in cases where proceeds cannot be seized, it shall be possible to confiscate property to a value corresponding to such proceeds. To date the Commission has undertaken two evaluations in 2004 and 2006 on Member States' implementation of this framework decision. Implementation has on the whole been satisfactory, including in the new Member States, yet it also reflects the relatively cautious approach taken in the Framework Decision. For example, there are still wide variations in the maximum penalty applicable to money laundering: it ranges from four years of detention in the Netherlands to 14 years in the United Kingdom and Ireland. With the adoption in May 2005 of a revamped Council of Europe instrument (*Council of Europe Convention n° 198 on Laundering, Search, Seizure and Confiscation of the Proceeds from Crime and on the Financing of Terrorism*[6]) and the publication in November 2005 of the **third money laundering directive**, the Commission, true to its role, will reflect on these new developments as related directly or indirectly to penal law.

Fostering international cooperation is of course key to a successful enforcement strategy. On regulatory aspects, the European Commission attaches great importance to its participation in international fora such as *FATF*, and watches with interest the recent emergence and development of regional anti-money laundering groups modelled on *FATF*, including Moneyval for Eastern Europe or MENAFATF for Maghreb and Middle East countries. Central to the exchange of operational information are *financial intelligence units (FIUs)*. The fact that their legal standing has been by now recognised in many international and European instruments highlights their important role in a globalised age. This reflects the need to go beyond bilateral memoranda of understanding on the exchange of information in order to forge a common approach irrespective of their status, often varying from one country to another. Hence *Council Decision of 17 October 2000 (2000/642/JHA)* laid down minimum standards of cooperation in the exchange of information between *FIUs* in EU Member States.[7]

Fighting money laundering cannot be carried out in isolation, using only specific instruments. To this end the fight against money laundering has been enhanced by a general improvement in the quality of police cooperation and judicial mutual legal assistance within the European Union. It is not an overstatement to say that the European Union has, in the last few years, made tremendous progress in this regard, fostering day-to-day cooperation through the creation of structures such as *Europol* and *Eurojust*, and through the adoption of legal instruments that deepen **police and judicial cooperation**. Such instruments include the second protocol to the Convention on the protection of the financial interest of the Community, which criminalises

---

[5] Official Journal L182, 05.07.2001, p. 1.
[6] Available at www.coe.int.
[7] Official Journal L271 of 24.10.2000, p. 4.

money laundering and provides for the confiscation of the proceeds from Community frauds. Important progress has also been made in the ***Convention on mutual assistance in criminal matters of 29 May 2000***[8] and its protocol of 16 October 2001.[9] In the latter, a special section is devoted to the promotion of the exchange of bank account information, crucial to reconstituting trails between entities or persons during money laundering investigations. Finally, the European Union is also making headway on sectoral instruments including the Council decision on joint investigation teams (2002/465/JHA),[10] the ***Framework decision on the freezing of property (2003/577/JHA)***,[11] which allows for the mutual recognition of freezing decisions delivered by a judicial authority, and the ***Framework decision on confiscation of crime-related proceeds, instrumentalities and property (2005/212/JHA)***,[12] setting out extended measures of confiscation. All of these background elements aid law enforcement agencies throughout Europe in taking better-informed and faster decisions in complex cross-border cases.

It could even be said that the best contribution the European Commission can make to the fight against money laundering is to continue building a space of Justice, Freedom and Security for all European citizens.

4   Terrorist financing: taking up the gauntlet

Terrorist financing covers two distinct areas – first, the financing of terrorist attacks and second, the financing of terrorist networks, including recruitment and the promotion of terrorist causes. What have to be targeted here are the financial supports of terrorism.

Money laundering and terrorist financing share many similar traits by combining a financial, non-violent part with a criminal action. The similarity between terrorist financing and money laundering is visible in the techniques used to launder money and to conceal the sources and the use of terrorist financing. However, there are a number of differences between the two. Indicative evidence points to generally low-value monetary transactions used to finance terrorist networks and attacks. Such small sums in themselves are unlikely to generate suspicion as they move through the financial system, thereby complicating their detection. In this light anti-money laundering legislative measures are less effective where funds involved in terrorist financing originate from legitimate sources. The essential difference being that, unlike money laundering, the criminal action takes place after the collection of funds and not before. Therefore additional measures have to be developed to tackle terrorist financing.

This problem is further complicated by the global character of terrorism. Traditional and domestic forms of terrorism previously employed direct financing methods, since those who financed it were generally situated in the same territory where attacks took place. Little use was made of the financial system and traditional police action was considered sufficient to counter it. Nowadays, terrorist groups operate across the globe and financing is carried out at various entry points in the financial system where low-value sums arouse little suspicion. This aspect requires coordinated action with various bodies operating in the fields of security and intelligence. In addition to this, empirical evidence has identified three mechanisms co-opted to the financing of

---

[8] Official Journal L197 of 12.7.2000, p. 1.
[9] Official Journal L196 of 21.11.2001, p. 1.
[10] Official Journal L162 of 20.6.2002, p. 1.
[11] Official Journal L196 of 2.8.2003, p. 45.
[12] Official Journal L68 of 15.3.2005, p. 49.

terrorist activities: use of **non-profit organisations**; **alternative fund remittance systems**; and **cross-border transportation of currency**.

In October 2001, FATF adopted the *Special Recommendations on Terrorist Financing* addressing legislative and regulatory steps required to combat terrorist financing. The *European Commission* has been responsive to these new threats and has engaged a multi-pronged action. The *Commission* proposed a regulation on cash controls at the external borders of the EU in order to establish an appropriate instrument to address the use of cash couriers. This regulation was published in November 2005.[13] The Commission has adopted a draft *Regulation on payer's information accompanying fund transfers,*[14] the content of which is under discussion at *Council* and *Parliament*. Lastly, a proposal of a draft directive on a new legal framework for payments in the internal market is on the table since December 2005.[15] This is intended, in conjunction with enhanced supervision provided for in the *third money laundering directive*, to aid the control of transactions outside the formal financial system.

As regards the freezing of terrorist assets, *United Nations Security Council Resolutions 1373 and 1267* have been implemented at EU level. The remaining key issues concern how to handle effective listing and delisting procedures and the need to ensure that EU level instruments are complemented by national measures that facilitate robust preventive freezing mechanisms. In this vein a joint initiative of the *European Commission* and European banks has established the *electronic-Consolidated Targeted Financial Sanctions List (e-CTFSL)* database,[16] one containing information related to all persons and entities subject to EU financial sanctions.

Finally, the *Commission* has begun work on possible measures to be adopted by the **non-profit sector** in order to increase its resilience to infiltration by terrorist groups. The *Commission* released in 2005 a communication proposing several steps towards increased transparency and accountability of non-profit organisations, including a proposal for a framework code of conduct.[17] Given the diversity of this sector throughout the *European Union*, it is expected that such a process will take time. Nevertheless, considerate of international standards, the *Commission* will continue to consult and inform parties in a timely manner so that our common reflection can bear fruit.

5   Conclusion: a look at upcoming challenges

The *European Commission* cannot allow any measure of complacency concerning the Union's current anti-money laundering architecture. We must remain open to criticism and be pragmatic where our assumptions do not stand up in practice. Thus, in the coming years, we must remain open to adapting our schema as contingencies and reality dictate. However, our counterparts in Member States and in the private sector can still expect us to ground our proposals on solid empirical experience derived from more than a decade of experience in this area. The *third money laundering directive* will be the first serious test for this new comprehensive system. As to whether our assumptions in this text will stand the test of time, it is too early to say.

Apart from the implementation of the *third money laundering directive*, I would like to pose a few questions to stimulate what are, from a *Commission* perspective, important discussions that may take place in the coming years.

---

[13] Regulation (EC) No. 1889/2005, Official Journal L309, p. 9.
[14] COM(2005)343 of 26.7.2005.
[15] COM(2005)603 of 1.12.2005.
[16] Accessible at http://europa.eu.int/comm/external_relations/cfsp/sanctions/list/consol-list.htm.
[17] COM(2005)620 of 29.11.2005.

- Are non-financial professions sufficiently equipped to implement a framework specifically designed for financial institutions? Some might answer that the level of compliance for these professions is dangerously low while others point out that Member States have not conducted outreach activities informing these professions of their new responsibilities. In both cases, a more open dialogue with these professions and their respective supervisory authorities is needed.

- Is customer due diligence evenly and effectively implemented within the European Union? It is crucial that the detailed provisions, due to enter into force once the ***third money laundering directive*** is transposed, are properly applied by entities covered under the directive. For this to be effective coordination between supervisors is warranted, not only for the sake of efficiency – preventing regulatory arbitrage – but also to ensure fair competition between similar entities within the single market in financial services. Especially in consideration of the verification and cross-checking overheads that would put law-abiding banks at a disadvantage where non-compliance is not properly addressed amongst less scrupulous competitors.

- Are corporate vehicles properly regulated? Highly publicised cases, such as Enron in the United States of America and Parmalat in Europe, have demonstrated the toxic combination of specific legal arrangements with offshore financial locations. The whole anti-money laundering scheme could be rendered less effective were particular loopholes left untouched. *FATF*, through its new recommendations 33 and 34 put forward in 2003, has raised awareness of the threat. Now is the time to think about what needs to be done at the European level to properly address the issue of the transparency of corporate vehicles.

- Are sanctions for breach of anti-money laundering provisions properly designed? As the EU preventive mechanism has been devised at the Community level to avoid the possibility of regulatory arbitrage, one could assert that the same reasoning could apply to sanctions, i.e. criminals could hide their money where law enforcement agencies are perceived to be soft or sanctions are deemed to be ineffective or seldom enforced. Member States may argue on the feasibility of harmonising sectoral provisions without jeopardising the consistency of national legal systems. Whatever the upshot, expect a lively debate on this issue.

Overall, the *European Commission* has a duty to remain alert to any new threat. I believe we should not balk at interrogating areas of legislation or supervision that are not living up to expectations. Only by adopting such open-mindedness can we convey our message efficiently. Rest assured though, that in an increasingly dangerous world, our resolve to fight money laundering and terrorist financing is stronger than ever.

Address

European Commission
B-1049 Brussels
Belgium
Tel +32 2 299 11 11
Fax +32 2 296 74 81
http://europa.eu.int/comm/
Contact person: Jonathan Faull
jonathan.faull@cec.eu.int

Alain Damais is Executive Secretary of the Financial Action Task Force (FATF) since January 2005. Prior to this appointment, he worked with the French Treasury between 1997 and 2002, in particular on anti-money laundering and anti-corruption issues from 1997 until 2001: at that time, he held the position as Deputy Head of the French delegation to the FATF, as well as Head of the French delegation to the OECD working group on bribery. He also worked on securities market issues between 2001 and 2002. More recently, from May 2002 to the end of 2004, he was Senior Financial Sector Specialist at the Financial Market Integrity Unit (FSEFI) of the World Bank, in charge of coordinating the anti-money laundering and combating terrorist financing assessment program of the World Bank.

The Financial Action Task Force

Alain Damais

Executive Secretary

Financial Action Task Force (FATF)
Paris
France

Anti-Money Laundering: International Law and Practice.
Edited by W.H. Muller, C.H. Kälin and J.G. Goldsworth
© 2007 John Wiley & Sons, Ltd

Contents – The Financial Action Task Force

1   Introduction

The Financial Action Task Force (FATF) was established by the G-7 Summit held in Paris in July 1989, in response to mounting concerns of the international community over the risks of money laundering. Recognizing the threat posed to the banking system and to financial institutions by the laundering of proceeds of crime, the G-7 Heads of State or Government and the President of the European Commission convened a Task Force from the G-7 member States, the European Commission, and eight other countries.

The Task Force was given responsibility for examining money laundering techniques and trends, reviewing the action which had already been taken at a national or international level, and setting out the measures that still needed to be taken to combat money laundering. In July 1990, one year after its creation, the FATF issued a report containing a set of Forty Recommendations providing a comprehensive plan of action needed to fight against money laundering. Since then the FATF has become the recognized world standard setter in the fight against money laundering. It has updated the Forty Recommendations twice (in 1996 and 2003) to reflect the changes which have occurred in money laundering operations, and has sought to encourage all countries around the world to adopt measures based on these recommendations.

After the terrorist attacks of September 11, 2001, the development of international standards in the fight against terrorist financing was added to the mission of the FATF. It issued the Eight Special Recommendations on Terrorist Financing in October 2001 and added a Ninth Special Recommendation in October 2004.

Today, the 40+9 Recommendations together with their interpretative notes, guidance and best practices, form the international standard against money laundering and terrorist financing. This was recently endorsed by the United Nations Security Council, which in its Resolution 1617 of 29 July 2005 *'strongly urges all Member States to implement the comprehensive, international standards embodied in the Financial Action Task Force's (FATF) Forty Recommendations on Money Laundering and the FATF Nine Special Recommendations on Terrorist Financing'*.

2   A Task Force of 33 members committed to fight money laundering and terrorist financing

2.1   A broad mandate

The FATF is an inter-governmental body whose purpose is the development and promotion of policies, both at national and international levels, to combat money laundering (ML) and terrorist financing (TF). It is therefore a 'policy-making body' which works to generate the necessary political will to bring about national legislative and regulatory reforms in these areas.

Following the expansion of its mandate in 2001 to include the fight against terrorist financing and the introduction of the Eight Special Recommendations, the FATF opened up an entirely new area of work. Although much has already been done, there is an obvious need for continuing mobilization at the international level to deepen and broaden both anti-money laundering action and the fight against terrorist financing.

Over the years, the FATF's role as an international standard setter has become increasingly important. The current FATF mandate, adopted in May 2004 at the FATF ministerial meeting, calls on the Task Force to:

- Establish international standards for combating money laundering and terrorist financing.

- Ensure global action to combat money laundering and terrorist financing.

- Ensure that FATF members have implemented the revised Forty and the [Nine] Recommendations in their entirety and in an effective manner (through a peer or mutual evaluation process).

- Ensure the enlargement of the international network against money laundering and financing terrorism and promoting worldwide application of the FATF standards.

- Enhance the relationship between FATF and International organizations, regional bodies and non-member countries.

- Further develop the typologies exercises (examining money laundering and terrorist financing techniques and trends).

- Reach out to all the parties affected by the FATF's standards (e.g. private financial institutions and certain non-financial businesses and professions).[1]

The FATF does not have a tightly defined constitution or an unlimited life span. It reviews its mission every four or five years. The FATF will only continue to exist and to perform its function if its member governments agree that this is necessary. The FATF has been in existence since 1989, and the Members have agreed that the current mandate will extend through the end of 2012.

2.2   A light, simple and efficient organizational structure which aids decision making

The FATF is composed of three main components:

- The Plenary gathers the 33 Members[2] and takes all decisions of the FATF, by consensus of the Members. Matters for decision by the Plenary are prepared by experts in the framework of dedicated working groups.

- The Presidency: each year, the FATF members select one of their Member jurisdictions to hold the Presidency for 12 months. The position of President is usually held by high-level government officials from member jurisdictions.

- The Secretariat, which prepares and implements the work/decisions of the Plenary and supports the President. It has to be noted that although the FATF Secretariat is housed at the OECD Headquarters in Paris, France, the FATF is fully independent from the OECD.

---

[1] Mandate for the future of the FATF (September 2004–December 2012), available at: www.fatf-gafi.org/.
[2] The 31 member countries and governments of the FATF are: Argentina (2000); Australia (1990); Austria (1990); Belgium (1990); Brazil (2000); Canada (1990); Denmark (1991); Finland (1991); France (1990); Germany (1990); Greece (1991); Hong Kong – China (1991); Iceland (1992); Ireland (1991); Italy (1990); Japan (1990); Luxembourg (1990); Mexico (2000); the Kingdom of the Netherlands (1990); New Zealand (1991); Norway (1991); Portugal (1991); the Russian Federation (2003); Singapore (1992); South Africa (2003); Spain (1990); Sweden (1990); Switzerland (1990); Turkey (1991); the United Kingdom (1990); and the United States (1990). Two international organizations are also members: the European Commission (1990) and the Gulf Cooperation Council (1991).

All of these components interact in a flexible manner to allow issues to be discussed and decisions to be taken in a rapid manner when necessary. For instance, in the aftermath of the September 11 attacks, the FATF received mandate from the G-7 Finance Ministers to elaborate measures to prevent, detect and prosecute terrorist financing operations. In a special Plenary meeting held in Washington, DC, on 29–30 October 2001, the FATF Plenary adopted the Eight Special Recommendations on Terrorist Financing. An entirely new standard had been framed in less than 7 weeks. Following from these decisions, a dedicated working group was put together to elaborate detailed measures and guidance to implement the Eight Special Recommendations, and the working group produced Interpretative Notes, Best Practices Papers, and other studies to help governments around the world to take the necessary actions against terrorist financing. This example illustrates how the FATF reacts in situations where emerging threats are identified or urgent action is needed.

2.3   An expanding membership and delegates with a range of expertise

The FATF has expanded its membership in three different phases:

- In 1991 and 1992, the FATF expanded its membership from the original 16 Members to 28, comprising all jurisdictions that were members of the OECD at that time.

- In June 2000, 3 other Member countries from South America (Argentina, Brazil and Mexico) joined the FATF.

- Lastly, in June 2003, the Republic of South Africa and the Russian Federation also became full Members of the FATF.

The FATF is therefore currently composed of 33 Members from six continents. These jurisdictions represent almost all major financial centers in the world.

Additionally, the People's Republic of China became an observer on 21 January 2005, with a view to becoming a full Member of the organization: at this stage, the membership process for China is continuing at a steady pace. Also, more recently, the Republic of Korea became an observer (July 2006) and India also (December 2006) with a view for India and Korea to become full Members in the future.

Members are represented in FATF by delegations which include experts from a wide range of agencies. They primarily include officials from the Ministries of Finance, Justice, Internal and External Affairs, as well as experts from financial regulatory authorities (whether banking, securities, insurance and others) and law enforcement agencies (FIU, police, prosecutors, etc.). The variety of expertise of its delegates is particularly important for the FATF, as the fight against money laundering and terrorist financing is multifaceted and requires multidisciplinary perspectives. The composition of its delegations allows the FATF to obtain and process information from a very large spectrum and make fully informed decisions.

3   A standard for the world: the FATF 40+9 recommendations

The FATF's Forty Recommendations on Money Laundering, combined with its Nine Special Recommendations on Terrorist Financing, set out the basic framework for detecting, preventing and suppressing ML and TF. The FATF Recommendations have been endorsed by more than 170 countries, are widely accepted as the international anti-money laundering and counter-terrorist financing standard, and have been, or are being, successfully implemented.

3.1   A standard updated in June 2003. . .

The FATF Recommendations were first adopted in 1990, and then revised a first time in 1996. In June 2003, the FATF completed another revision of its Recommendations, in light of the most recent changes in money laundering methods and techniques, and in response to requests to develop efficient counter-measures to meet the new trends.

A couple of factors were at the root of this comprehensive revision. First, at the end of the 1990s, the FATF had noted through its Typologies exercise an increasingly sophisticated combination of techniques being used by money launderers, involving a broad scope of professionals, including some outside of the financial sectors. Also, there had been developments at the international level, such as adoption of the UN Convention on Transnational Organized Crime, adoption of the second European Union Directive 2001/97/EC on fighting money laundering, and the adoption of the Eight Special Recommendations on Terrorist Financing by the FATF in 2001. All these factors, combined with the experience gained through the FATF's NCCT process, led the FATF to review and revise the Forty Recommendations into a new more comprehensive framework. The review process was open to Members and non-Members of the FATF, observers, representatives of the financial sectors and other interested parties.

3.2   . . . to enhance the effectiveness of AML/CFT regimes throughout the world and offer concrete measures against emerging threats

The revision of the FATF standards primarily (i) enlarged and harmonized the definition of the money laundering offence to include a wide range of predicate offences generating high volume of proceeds (Recommendations 1 and 2), (ii) provided for more detailed Customer Due Diligence measures by financial institutions (Recommendation 5), (iii) called for the creation of Financial Intelligence Units in all countries (Recommendation 26) and (iv) called for improved efficiency, comprehensiveness and speed of international cooperation (Recommendations 35 to 40).

It also included a wide range of concrete measures to protect the international financial system against identified threats that were emerging from the international financial globalization, in particular:

- The risks posed by foreign Politically Exposed Persons (PEPs), and the need to call for increased due diligence in such (and other) high-risk situations (Recommendation 6).

- The vulnerability of cross-border correspondent banking operations (Recommendation 7).

- The threats that may arise from new technologies, in particular the risk associated with non-face-to-face transactions (Recommendation 8).

- The use of shell banks by money laundering networks (Recommendation 18).

- The use of professionals outside of the financial sectors in the design or performance of money laundering operations, in particular legal professionals and accountants (Recommendations 12 and 16).

- The renewed vulnerability of the real estate sector to money laundering operations (Recommendations 12 and 16).

- The interest of money launderers in precious metal and stones to hide/invest their criminal assets (Recommendations 12 and 16).

- The growing threats posed by casinos in money laundering operations (Recommendations 12 and 24).

- The misuse of corporate vehicles and/or legal arrangements, such as trusts, by money launderers (Recommendations 33 and 34).

The FATF is still reviewing some of these threats through its Typologies exercise (i.e. consideration of risks associated with new payment technologies).

3.3   A standard against terrorist financing as well as against money laundering

As mentioned above, following the attacks against New York and Washington on September 11, 2001, the FATF expanded its mandate to address the financing of terrorism. On 30 October 2001 – just seven weeks after the 9/11 attacks – the FATF issued Eight Special Recommendations that were specifically designed to confront terrorist financing. These recommendations reinforced certain of the measures called for by the United Nations Convention for the suppression of the financing of terrorism – criminalization of terrorist financing, freezing of terrorist assets, for example – however, they also focused on three major channels used by terrorist organizations for moving their funds:

1. alternative remittance systems,

2. electronic wire transfers, and

3. non-profit organizations.

These three methods were addressed directly through FATF Special Recommendations VI, VII and VIII, respectively.

Further investigation since 9/11 clearly indicated yet another major channel for the movement of terrorist funding, that is, the physical carrying of funds in cash across borders or 'cash couriers'. Reacting to this new trend and closing a gap in international measures regarding the physical transportation of funds related to terrorist financing or money laundering, the FATF issued in October 2004 a new Special Recommendation, the ninth, to address this specific issue.

4   A monitoring process to ensure compliance with the standards: the mutual evaluations

Since the beginning of its work, the FATF has conducted mutual evaluations of its member countries to check their compliance with the FATF Recommendations. The mutual evaluation process is key in ensuring the credibility of the Recommendations and their successful implementation, and represents a central pillar of the work of the FATF over the last 10 years.

Through this peer review process, the FATF is assessing the implementation of the FATF Recommendations and the effectiveness of anti-money laundering systems in all its Member jurisdictions. Each Member country is examined in turn by the FATF on the basis of an on-site visit conducted by a team of three to six selected experts in the legal, financial and law enforcement fields from other Member governments. The team draws up a report assessing the extent to which the evaluated country has implemented an effective system to counter money laundering. The report highlights areas in which further progress may still be required and includes a table summarizing the compliance ratings with each of the 40+9 Recommendations.

The FATF follows up on assessments when deficiencies are identified. The FATF's policy for dealing with Members which are not in compliance with the Forty Recommendations represents a graduated approach aimed at reinforcing peer pressure on Member governments to take action to tighten their anti-money laundering systems. The policy starts by requiring the country to deliver a progress report at Plenary meetings. Further steps include a letter from the FATF President or sending a high-level mission to the non-complying Member country. The FATF can also apply Recommendation 21, which results in issuing a statement calling on financial institutions to give special attention to business relations and transactions with persons, companies and financial institutions domiciled in the non-complying country. Also, as a final measure, the FATF membership of the country in question can be suspended.

4.1   Assessments are done throughout the world using the same methodology

To ensure global consistency of assessments, the FATF and all the bodies and organizations that produce assessment reports based on the FATF Recommendations have adopted a common methodology as well as common documents and procedures.

The methodology was most recently updated in early 2004 to reflect the revised Forty Recommendations that were adopted in June 2003 as well as a number of interpretative notes that were issued by the FATF on the Nine Special Recommendations. The revised methodology, which was endorsed by the FATF Plenary on February 2004, is fully in line with the FATF Recommendations.

4.2   The third round of mutual evaluations

The FATF started a third round of mutual evaluations for its Members in 2005, with the discussion and adoption of the mutual evaluation reports on Belgium and Norway in June 2005. Since then, eight other Member countries have been assessed: Australia, Italy and Switzerland in October 2005; Ireland and Sweden in February 2006; Denmark, Spain and the United States in June 2006.

The FATF is promoting increased transparency in the assessment process through the publication of mutual evaluation reports: since the beginning of the third round, all reports adopted have been published and are available on the FATF website (www.fatf-gafi.org).

5   The FATF objective: the worldwide implementation of its anti-money laundering and counter-terrorist financing measures to achieve concrete results

The FATF since its formation in 1989 has emphasized the importance of building a worldwide network of countries against money laundering. The globalization of financial markets throughout the 1990s has created new opportunities for both legitimate and non-legitimate operators and users of the international banking system. The open financial system of today's global village is characterized by high and rapid mobility of funds, as well as the ever-lasting modernization of new payment technologies. While these developments have created new opportunities to do business all over the world, to move assets and secure personal wealth without barrier, they have also offered new tools and techniques for criminals to launder the proceeds of their crimes or hide their illegal assets.

At this time of ever-increasing globalization, the actual effectiveness of the overall system against money laundering equals the effectiveness of the weakest link in the global chain. Therefore, since its inception, the FATF has considered as one of its key priorities to convince countries around the globe, outside its limited membership, to follow the FATF standards and implement actions and measures to combat money laundering and, since 2001, terrorist financing.

In order to reach out far beyond its membership, the FATF has over time forged dozens of partnerships with a very broad range of international and regional organizations, which are observers in the FATF.[3]. Also, the FATF has not been shy in using the necessary tools to put pressure on countries or territories which refuse to cooperate in the fight against money laundering and terrorist financing.

5.1   Coordinated action with FATF-Style Regional Bodies (FSRBs)

The FATF has, since the mid-1990s, encouraged the development of regional groups based on its model and following its recommendations and principles. These groups work to ensure concrete implementation of the FATF standards at the regional level, through awareness raising, technical assistance and peer pressure at regional level on AML/CFT issues.

Today, nine regional groups have been created and recognized by the FATF.[4] All of these regional groups have similar form, functions and procedures to those of the FATF, and all of these groups conduct mutual evaluations of their members to check their compliance with the FATF 40+9 Recommendations. These groups are the key elements of the international network against money laundering and terrorist financing that the FATF is leading. The members of these groups have all committed to implement the FATF 40+9 Recommendations. Together, with the members of the regional groups, there are 172 jurisdictions around the globe that have committed to implement the FATF standards.

---

[3] 29 international and regional organizations are observers in the FATF. They include among others: the African Development Bank, the Asian Development Bank (ADB), the Commonwealth Secretariat, the Egmont Group of Financial Intelligence Units, the European Bank for Reconstruction and Development (EBRD), the European Central Bank (ECB), Europol, the Inter-American Development Bank (IDB), the International Association of Insurance Supervisors (IAIS), the International Monetary Fund (IMF), the International Organisation of Securities Commission (IOSCO), Interpol, the Organisation of American States/Inter-American Drug Abuses Control Commission (OAS/CICAD), the Organisation for Economic Cooperation and Development (OECD), the United Nations Office on Drugs and Crime (UNODC), the United Nations Counter-Terrorism Committee of the Security Council, the World Bank, and the World Customs Organisation (WCO).

[4] FATF-style regional bodies are: the Asia/Pacific Group on money laundering (APG), the Caribbean Financial Action Task Force (CFATF), the Eastern and Southern Africa Anti-Money Laundering Group (ESAAMLG), the Eurasian Group (EAG), the Financial Action Task Force on Money Laundering in South America (GAFISUD), the Intergovernmental Action Group Against Money Laundering in Africa (GIABA), the Middle East and North Africa Financial Action Task Force (MENAFATF), MONEYVAL (Council of Europe Select Committee of Experts on the Evaluation of Anti-Money Laundering Measures), and the Offshore Group of Banking Supervisors (OGBS).

5.2   Cooperation with several international organizations

Further to its close partnership with regional groups specialized in anti-money laundering issues; the FATF is cooperating with large multidisciplinary organizations, at both regional and international level.

The cooperation with the International Monetary Fund (IMF) and the World Bank is particularly exemplary in this respect. The FATF Members have successfully encouraged the IMF and the World Bank to create and develop programs designed to help their Member countries to build their AML/CFT systems through the provision of technical assistance. In 2002, the Executive Boards of the IMF and the World Bank recognized the FATF Recommendations as the international standards against money laundering and terrorist financing, and since then these organizations have provided assistance and training to help their members to increase compliance with the FATF 40+9 Recommendations. Also, the IMF and the World Bank participate in the global assessment program led by the FATF and the FSRBs, and conduct assessment of compliance of their member countries with the FATF Recommendations, using the FATF assessment methodology.

The FATF also focuses on cooperation with other organizations, such as the United Nations and various donor organizations. The FATF is closely cooperating in a number of areas with the United Nations agencies, primarily the Global Program against Money Laundering (GPML) and the Counter-Terrorism Executive Directorate (CTED), which is working under the Counter-Terrorism Committee (CTC) of the United Nations Security Council. This cooperation with the United Nations will further increase following the recognition by the UN Security Council in its Resolution 1617 of the FATF Recommendations as the international standards to combat money laundering and terrorist financing.

5.3   Targeting non-cooperative countries and territories

The FATF has complemented its diplomatic efforts by an initiative designed to name and shame countries or territories that refuse to cooperate in the fight against money laundering or have severe deficiencies in their national AML regimes. The Non Cooperative Countries and Territories (NCCT) initiative, famously termed the 'FATF blacklist', has produced excellent results: it has raised the global awareness on these issues, increased the political profile of the fight against financial crime and provided very strong and powerful incentives to many jurisdictions to improve their laws and practices regarding the fight against money laundering, and eventually join the international community in this global fight.

In June 2000, the FATF published its first NCCT list, with 15 countries and territories on it. Overall, a total of 47 countries or territories were examined in two rounds of reviews (in 2000 and 2001), and 23 countries or territories were listed either in June 2000 or June 2001. Out of these, 22 have now been de-listed after (i) modifying their legislation, (ii) creating the necessary authorities to supervise financial institutions, analyze suspicious transaction reports and/or enforce the criminal laws and prosecute criminals, and (iii) demonstrating that they were concretely implementing their legislation and would not block international cooperation. The only country remaining on the NCCT list, Myanmar, has also made progress, but not enough to yet be de-listed.

This initiative has had long-lasting effects on a much broader range of countries than the 23 listed, as it has created a global incentive for countries to either create or improve their AML/CFT regimes, and better cooperate at the international level. In addition, this initiative encouraged many other countries and territories to adopt and implement measures for the prevention, detection and punishment of money laundering and terrorist financing, to prevent any listing by FATF.

Overall, the NCCT initiative fulfilled its main objective well, i.e. it reduced the vulnerability of the worldwide financial system to money laundering by ensuring that all major financial centers adopt and implement AML/CFT measures.

5.4   Concrete results are obtained against criminals

The effective implementation of the FATF standards has already produced important results in the fight against organized crime. These concrete results are measured on a regular basis, through the mutual evaluation process, and all mutual evaluation reports include figures and statistics, as well as an overall comment on how the AML/CFT system is working concretely. As a matter of course, these figures only refer so far to the 10 countries which have been assessed since early 2005 (see above), and will be completed throughout the third round of mutual evaluations. Nevertheless, as a matter of example, the number of convictions for money laundering or terrorist financing, and the amount of criminal assets forfeited, which are two interesting indicators of success, are very significant and disclosing in this regard.

Convictions: assessments are showing that there is an effective enforcement of the money laundering offence in all the FATF Member states and that continued progress is being made. For instance, it has increased from 2 in 1991 to 50 in 1995 and to 117 in 2003 in Switzerland. In Belgium, the total number of convictions for money laundering has been multiplied by two between 2000 and 2003 from 263 convictions in 2000 to 513 in 2003. Between 2000 and 2004, 2903 cases led to a conviction (an average of 580 per year) in Italy. The number of convictions for money laundering in the United States reached 1075 in 2005, and the United States is now on an average trend of more than 1000 convictions a year. These results show that money launderers are being caught and convicted, and are evidence of the effective implementation of the FATF standards.

Confiscation: the same conclusion can be reached regarding the amount of criminal assets forfeited. In 2003, for instance, almost USD 8 million were confiscated in Australia, nearly EUR 56 million in Belgium, approximately EUR 112 million in Italy, and USD 564.5 million in the United States. All available statistics show that the amounts of criminal proceeds that have been confiscated in recent years are continuously increasing, demonstrating that the Member States of the FATF are achieving continuous progress and increasing results in the fight against financial crime.

These concrete results against criminals and their assets also show the benefits of the preventive measures applicable to private businesses (such as banks, financial institutions and other professionals which are subject to FATF measures). The role of these professionals in preventing and detecting money laundering/terrorist financing operations is more than ever a key to the overall success of any AML/CFT system.

6   Current challenges: reaching out further to the private sector and the effect of corruption on AML/CFT systems

The FATF regards engagement with the private sector as critical to effective implementation of the FATF Recommendations. The FATF Secretariat is in regular contact with the various representatives of the banking sector, such as the Wolfsberg Group (an association of several global banks) and more recently the International Banking Federation (IBFed is the representative body for the Australian, Canadian, European, Japanese and US banking associations).

The FATF has already taken three steps to improve dialogue with the private sector. First, the FATF decided on publishing, as a general rule, all future mutual evaluation reports. These reports will assist the private sector by providing detailed information on the quality of the AML/CFT systems of FATF Members. Second, the FATF Typologies work has been redesigned to emphasize more in-depth analysis of money laundering/terrorist financing methods. The published Typologies reports thus may serve as a reference for the private sector on typologies and trends in this area. Third, the FATF has decided to improve its dialogue with the private sector by developing new contacts and maintaining a principle of consultation with the private sector on a systematic basis when creating new standards.

Private sector outreach events have also been designed to further improve consistency in the application of the FATF standards throughout the world. A December 2005 private sector outreach seminar included both the banking and securities sectors, which face similar issues in the implementation of certain standards. It helped to identify problems and issues that need clarification, transfer knowledge and increase consistency.

Another challenge for the future will be to assess damaging effects of corruption on the effectiveness of AML/CFT systems. Following the efforts led by the former President of FATF, Professor Kader Asmal (South Africa), these issues are now taken into account in AML/CFT assessments. But there is still a need for a comprehensive study, in particular with respect to its impact on developing countries and economies. The challenge posed by money laundering and corruption to nations in the developing world is enormous. It impacts on a government's ability to deliver on development objectives and to meet worthy socio-economic causes such as education, healthcare and housing. The overall social costs of money laundering and corruption are particularly high for developing economies. Corruption raises serious questions about the integrity of law enforcement systems as well as that of financial markets. Corruption associated with money laundering, whether private or public, corrodes society's moral values and poses challenges to good governance practices and the legitimacy of nationhood. The FATF will continue to raise awareness on these issues, so that the devastating effects of corruption and money laundering on development can no longer be ignored.

Abbreviations

ADB	African Development Bank, the Asian Development Bank
AML/CFT	Anti-Money Laundering and Counter Financing of Terrorism
APG	Asia/Pacific Group on money laundering
CFATF	Caribbean Financial Action Task Force
CTC	United Nations Counter-Terrorism Committee
CTED	United Nations Counter-Terrorism Executive Directorate
EAG	Eurasian Group
EBRD	European Bank for Reconstruction and Development
ECB	European Central Bank
ESAAMLG	Eastern and Southern Africa Anti-Money Laundering Group
EU	European Union

FATF	Financial Action Task Force on Money Laundering
FIU	Financial Intelligence Unit
FSRBs	FATF-Style Regional Bodies
GAFISUD	Financial Action Task Force on Money Laundering in South America
GCC	Gulf Cooperation Council
GIABA	Intergovernmental Action Group Against Money Laundering in Africa
GPML	United Nations Global Program against Money Laundering
IAIS	International Association of Insurance Supervisors
IDB	Inter-American Development Bank
IMF	International Monetary Fund
IOSCO	International Organisation of Securities Commission
MENAFATF	Middle East and North Africa Financial Action task force
ML	Money Laundering
NCCT	Non Cooperative Countries and Territories
OAS	Organization of American States
OECD	Organization for Economic Co-operation and Development
OGBS	Offshore Group of Banking Supervisors
PEP	Politically Exposed Person
TF	Terrorist Financing
UN	United Nations
UNODC	United Nations Office on Drugs and Crime
WCO	World Customs Organisation

The Egmont Group

The Egmont definition of a Financial Intelligence Unit[1]

Wouter H. Muller

Senior Consultant

Henley & Partners AG
Kirchgasse 22
CH- 8001 Zürich
Switzerland

Tel +41 44 266 22 22
Fax +41 44 266 22 23
wouter.muller@henleyglobal.com
www.henleyglobal.com

[1] This chapter is, on the advice of the Egmont Committee, edited from official documents published by the Egmont Group.

Anti-Money Laundering: International Law and Practice.
Edited by W.H. Muller, C.H. Kälin and J.G. Goldsworth
© 2007 John Wiley & Sons, Ltd

Contents – The Egmont Group

1 Background

The fight against money laundering is an essential part of the overall struggle to combat and prevent **financial crimes** ranging from illegal narcotics trafficking to the funding of terrorist activity. Governments around the world recognize the corrosive dangers that unchecked financial crimes pose to their economic and political systems. The key issue involved in the anti-money laundering effort is ensuring that the critical piece or pieces of information reach the investigators and prosecutors charged with **putting criminals behind bars** and **taking their illegally obtained wealth away.**

The information needed to support anti-money laundering investigations and combat and prevent the financing of terrorism often involves a wide range of human activity beyond that based purely on criminal motivation. Countering money laundering and other financial crimes effectively requires not only knowledge of laws and regulations, investigations and analysis, but also of banking, finance, accounting and other related economic activities. Financial crimes of all types are after all an economic phenomenon; launderers rely to a certain extent on already existing financial and business practices as a way of hiding illegally obtained funds or using legally obtained funds for terrorist acts and related criminal activity.

Financial crime investigations conceivably touch a number of law enforcement agencies within a particular jurisdiction. This means that a completely effective, multi-disciplined approach for combating and preventing financial crime is often beyond the reach of any single law enforcement or prosecutorial authority. Since money may transfer hands in a matter of seconds or be relocated to the other side of the world at the speed of an electronic wire transfer, law enforcement and prosecutorial agencies that investigate financial crimes must be able to count on a virtually immediate exchange of information. This information exchange must also be at an early point after possible detection of a crime – the so-called 'pre-investigative' or intelligence stage. At the same time, the information on innocent individuals and businesses must at all times be protected.

2 The creation of FIUs

Over the past years, specialized governmental agencies have been created as countries develop systems to deal with the problem of money laundering and other financial crimes. These entities are commonly referred to as '**financial intelligence units**' or '**FIUs**'. They offer law enforcement agencies around the world an important avenue for **information exchange**.

An FIU, quite simply, is a central office that obtains financial reports information, processes it in some way and then discloses it to an appropriate government authority in support of a national anti-money laundering effort. FIUs have attracted increasing attention with their ever more important role in anti-money laundering programs. They are able to provide a rapid exchange of information (between financial institutions and law enforcement/prosecutorial authorities, as well as between jurisdictions), while protecting the interests of the innocent individuals contained in their data.

Two major influences shape the creation of the FIUs: implementing anti-money laundering measures alongside already existing law enforcement systems (the Judicial, Law Enforcement and Hybrid models) or providing a single office for centralizing the receipt and assessment of financial information and sending the resulting disclosures to competent authorities (the Administrative and Hybrid models).

2.1   The judicial model

The Judicial Model is established within the judicial branch of government wherein 'disclosures' of suspicious financial activity are received by the investigative agencies of a country from its financial sector such that the judiciary powers can be brought into play, e.g. seizing funds, freezing accounts, conducting interrogations, detaining people, conducting searches, etc.

2.2   The law enforcement model

The Law Enforcement Model implements anti-money laundering measures alongside already existing law enforcement systems, supporting the efforts of multiple law enforcement or judicial authorities with concurrent or sometimes competing jurisdictional authority to investigate money laundering.

2.3   The administrative model

The Administrative Model is a centralized, independent, administrative authority, which receives and processes information from the financial sector and transmits disclosures to judicial or law enforcement authorities for prosecution. It functions as a 'buffer' between the financial and the law enforcement communities.

2.4   The hybrid model

The Hybrid Model serves as a disclosure intermediary and a link to both judicial and law enforcement authorities. It combines elements of at least two of the FIU models.

3   Beginning of the Egmont Group

Despite the fact that FIUs were created in several jurisdictions throughout the world during the first years of the 1990s, their creation was still seen as isolated phenomena related to the specific needs of those jurisdictions establishing them. In June 1995, government agencies and international organizations gathered at the Egmont–Arenberg Palace in Brussels to discuss money laundering and ways to confront this global problem. Out of this first meeting was born the Egmont Group ('Egmont'), an informal body of government disclosure receiving agencies that share a common goal – **to provide a forum to enhance mutual cooperation and to share information that has utility in detecting and combating money laundering and, more recently, terrorism financing.** Over time, working groups have developed to carry out the tasks of Egmont. Today, Egmont has five working groups: Legal, Training and Communication, Outreach, Operational and IT (see later).

Early on, the participants in Egmont recognized the need for developing effective and practical means of cooperating, especially concerning information exchange and the sharing of expertise. To meet those challenges, the Legal Working Group examined obstacles related to information exchange among government agencies that specifically combat money laundering through the processing of financial information. To identify financial disclosure receiving agencies around the world and to better understand how such government agencies function, jurisdictions completed questionnaires and submitted them for review by the Legal Working Group. On the basis of the answers provided from the questionnaires, the Legal Working Group devised a functional definition of an FIU.

Although initially the focus of the Egmont FIU was essentially on money laundering, FIUs are also playing an important role in the international effort to combat the financing of terrorism. The financial disclosures that FIUs currently receive, analyze and disseminate have proven to be invaluable sources of information for those national agencies that investigate terrorism financing. In order to meet international mandatory standards, countries have or are in the process of amending their domestic legislation to bring terrorism financing within the remit of their FIU as an autonomous offence, beside as a predicate offense for money laundering, thus expanding the scope of the FIU's overall functions.

4   Egmont definition of an FIU

Based upon the work of the Legal Working Group, Egmont approved the following definition of an FIU in 1996, consequently amended in 2004 to reflect the FIU's role in combating terrorism financing:

> **A central, national agency responsible for receiving (and as permitted, requesting), analyzing and disseminating to the competent authorities, disclosures of financial information:**
>
> **(i) concerning suspected proceeds of crime and potential financing of terrorism, or**
>
> **(ii) required by national legislation or regulation, in order to combat money laundering and terrorism financing.**

The definition of an FIU can best be understood through a brief explanation of each of its component parts.

4.1   A central, national agency

A central, national agency. Egmont's focus on international cooperation requires that **only one government agency per territory or self-autonomous jurisdiction, recognized by international boundaries, serve as the contact point for international exchanges.** It must operate in a jurisdiction that is governed by the laws of that territory. To be clear, use of the phrase '**central, national agency**' carries with it no political designation or recognition of any kind.

An anti-money laundering/terrorism financing government agency operating in a jurisdiction that in political terms constitutes a dependency of another nation, may be considered an FIU as long as it is the only government agency that carries out these efforts in that internationally recognized boundary. Recognition that such government agency meets the Egmont definition of an FIU does not necessarily equate to sovereignty.

In federal systems, the phrase 'central, national agency' implies that only one government agency may be considered an FIU under Egmont. Even though federal systems have multiple subdivisions, only one centralized agency serves as contact point for information exchange for Egmont.

4.2 Responsible for

Responsible for. This word denotes that the legal framework, which establishes the FIU, authorizes, at a minimum, the functions outlined in the Egmont definition.

4.3 Receiving, analyzing and disseminating

Receiving (and as permitted, requesting), analyzing and disseminating. This phrase designates the three principal activities of all Egmont FIUs, and the functions that make them unique.

4.3.1 Receiving

Receiving. FIUs serve as the central reception point for receiving financial disclosures. This takes into account FIUs that have more than one office and FIUs that receive disclosures from different domestic agencies. This concept also distinguishes FIUs from law enforcement agencies with a general (overall) law enforcement mission.

4.3.2 And as permitted, requesting

(And as permitted, requesting). Some but not all FIUs have the ability to query specific financial information from certain financial institutions and other non-financial entities beyond the financial disclosures that FIUs normally receive from reporting entities. For this reason, the language is in parentheses and is limited in scope.

4.3.3 Analyzing

Analyzing. Analysis involves an initial evaluation of the utility or relevance of disclosures received from reporting entities at the pre-investigation stage. Analysis of information reported to FIUs may occur at different stages and take different forms. Some FIUs analyze every financial disclosure when it arrives at the FIU. For other FIUs, such a system is impossible due to the sheer volume of financial disclosures that they receive. Those FIUs make the financial disclosures immediately available to appropriate investigative authorities and the FIUs analyze financial disclosures in response to requests for information or on their own accord but not in response to each and every financial disclosure reported to it. In an increasing manner, many FIUs have incorporated analytical software that assists in determining money laundering trends and patterns for use by law enforcement, to provide feedback to the reporting institutions and in some cases for purposes of proactive targeting. In all cases, some *de minimis* level of analysis must occur in order to categorize a given piece of information and determine which agency, or group of agencies, should be entitled to receive it.

4.3.4 Disseminating

Disseminating. FIUs at a minimum must be able to share information from financial disclosures and the results of their analysis regarding money laundering and related crimes, as determined by domestic legislation, and terrorism financing, firstly with domestic competent authorities and, secondly, with other FIUs. A critical element in assessing dissemination capability involves assessing the extent to which a candidate FIU's law permits the cooperation with other FIUs through the exchange of information.

4.4 Disclosure of financial information

Disclosures of financial information. These are the materials that FIUs use and share with each other to detect and combat money laundering and terrorism financing. In this regard, FIUs may share publicly available as well as sensitive information (whether financial disclosures or law enforcement information) with competent authorities under terms that protect the information against misuse.

4.5 Suspected proceeds of crime and potential financing of terrorism

Concerning suspected proceeds of crime and potential financing of terrorism. The first type of disclosure of financial information concerns the reporting of suspicious or unusual transactions or activities regarding funds that are suspected of having originated from criminal activity or of being intended to support terrorist activity.

[Disclosures otherwise] required by national legislation, or regulation. This requirement encompasses all other mandated types of reporting requirements required by law, whether involving currency, checks, wires or other transactions.

4.6 To combat money laundering and terrorism financing

In order to combat money laundering and terrorism financing. This phrase re-emphasizes the common purpose of every FIU.

5 Organizational structure of the Egmont Group

The goal of the Egmont Group is to provide a forum for FIUs **to improve support to their respective national anti-money laundering programs.** This support includes expanding and systematizing the exchange of financial intelligence information, improving expertise and capabilities of personnel of such organizations, and fostering better communication among FIUs through application of technology. In order to accomplish its mission of development, cooperation and sharing of expertise, the Group has developed five working groups and an Egmont Committee. The working groups and their functions are listed below:

- **The Legal Working Group** (LWG) reviews the candidacy of potential members and handles all legal aspects and matters of principle within Egmont, including cooperation between FIUs.

- **The Outreach Working Group** (OWG) works to create a global network of FIUs by identifying candidates for membership and working with those countries to ensure that they meet international standards.

- **The Training Working Group** (TWG) identifies training needs and opportunities for FIU personnel, and conducts training seminars for Egmont members as well as for non-Egmont jurisdictions.

- **The Operational Working Group** (OpWG) seeks to bring FIUs together on typologies development and long-term strategic analytical projects.

- **The IT Working Group** (ITWG) provides advice and technical assistance to new and existing FIUs to develop, enhance, or redesign their IT systems, and examines new software applications that might facilitate analytical work.

- **The Egmont Committee serves as the consultation and coordination mechanism** for the Heads of FIUs and the five Working Groups. Among its primary functions are to assist the Egmont Group in a range of activities from internal coordination and administrative consultation to representation at other international fora. The Committee is composed of a Chair, two co-vice Chairs, the Chairs of the above-mentioned five Working Groups, and regional representation from Africa, Asia, Europe, the Americas, and Oceania. The regional representation reflects the strength of Egmont membership in each part of the world. The Committee and the Working Groups meet three times a year, including the annual plenary during which the Egmont Group meets as a whole. Since the Egmont Group is not a formal organization, there is no permanent secretariat at present. Administrative functions are therefore shared on a rotating basis. However, as from 2007 a permanent secretariat will be set up in Canada. Aside from the Egmont Support position, the above-listed Working Groups and Egmont Committee are used to conduct common business.

The **Statement of Purpose**[2] adopted at the 5th Egmont Group Plenary held in Madrid on 24 June 1997 and amended at The Hague on 13 June 2001, in Sydney on 23 July 2003 and in Guernsey on 23 June 2004, called for a formal articulation of the process by which a financial intelligence unit is recognized as meeting the Egmont FIU definition in order to become an Egmont Group member. This process is now delineated in the document **Procedure for Being Recognised as an FIU by the Egmont Group.**[3]

6 Information exchange

It is the exchange of information that is central to the Egmont Group. The two documents **Principles for Information Exchange** (June 2001)[4] and **Best Practices for the Exchange of Information**[5] have been adopted in order to enhance information exchange and to provide **guidelines in terms of best practices for the exchange of information** between FIUs.

The **Principles** provide in part that FIUs should be able to exchange information freely with other FIUs on the basis of reciprocity or mutual agreement and consistent with procedures understood by the requested and requesting party. Furthermore, the Egmont members have agreed that information exchanged between FIUs may be used only for the specific purpose for which the information was sought or provided. The requesting FIU may not transfer information shared by a disclosing FIU to a third party, nor make use of the information in an administrative, investigative, prosecutorial, or judicial purpose without the prior consent of the FIU that disclosed the information. Along these lines, the Egmont Group members have agreed that all information

---

[2] www.egmontgroup.org/statement_of_purpose.pdf.
[3] www.egmontgroup.org/procedure_for_being_recognised.pdf.
[4] www.egmontgroup.org/princ_info_exchange.pdf.
[5] www.egmontgroup.org/bestpractices.pdf.

exchanged by FIUs must be subjected to strict controls and safeguards to ensure that it is used only in an authorized manner, consistent with national provisions on privacy and data protection.

7   Conclusion

Money laundering and terrorist financing are international issues that can only be effectively addressed through international cooperation and coordination, to which the Egmont Group is firmly committed.

Mark Pieth is Professor of Criminal Law at Basel University, Chairman of the OECD Working Group on Bribery in International Business Transactions, and Member of Swiss Federal Gaming Commission, Chairman of the Board of the Basel Institute on Governance. Formerly a Member of the Independent Inquiry Committee into the Iraq Oil-for-Food Programme, the Financial Action Task Force on Money Laundering (FATF) and Head of Section of Economic and Organised Crime at the Swiss Ministry of Justice & Police, member of Chemical Action Task Force on Precursor Chemicals, Chairman, UN Intergovernmental Expert Group Commission to determine the extent of illicit trafficking in drugs. Mark Pieth has published extensively in the fields of economic and organised crime, money laundering, corruption, sentencing and criminal procedure.

The Wolfsberg Process

Mark Pieth

Professor of Criminal Law at the University of Basel
Chairman of the OECD Working Group on Bribery
Chairman of the Board of the Basel Institute on Governance

University of Basel
Faculty of Law
Peter Merian-Weg 8
Postfach
4002 Basel
Switzerland

Tel +41 61 267 25 38
Fax +41 61 267 25 49
mark.pieth@unibas.ch
www.pieth.ch
www.baselgovernance.org
www.ius.unibas.ch

Anti-Money Laundering: International Law and Practice.
Edited by W.H. Muller, C.H. Kälin and J.G. Goldsworth
© 2007 John Wiley & Sons, Ltd

Contents – The Wolfsberg Process

1 Introduction

'Wolfsberg' is the name of a UBS training centre overlooking Lake Constance in Switzerland. However, since the Wolfsberg 'Global Anti-Money-Laundering Guidelines for Private Banking' were published in October 2000,[1] 'Wolfsberg' has become a household name in the banking industry. This chapter examines the process that brought together the major 12 private banking institutions and led them to draft their common customer due diligence (CDD) standards. It also investigates how it was possible that this self-regulatory instrument could gain such prominence within only a few years: it is now regularly cited together with other key international public sector texts on CDD and anti-money laundering (AML), such as the Basel Committee on Banking Supervision (BCBS) CDD paper[2] and the Forty Recommendations of the Financial Action Task Force on Money-Laundering (FATF).[3] Increasingly, the Wolfsberg publications are regarded as the 'gold standard' by the industry worldwide, and the Wolfsberg Group has become a preferred interlocutor with regulators. Obviously, this invites a critical discussion of the various contents of the Wolfsberg documents and the role of this exclusive club of key players in the industry. Before going into this analysis, the next section will briefly sketch the background of the developments.

2 The 'Wolfsberg history'

2.1 Background

Rules on customer identification in banking began to emerge as early as the 1970s and 1980s.[4] Similarly, AML is not a new topic: the first national criminal law provisions against money laundering date back to 1986,[5] the first international standard to 1988.[6] However, the issue suddenly began to gain momentum when the G7 created the FATF in 1989. Even though it was merely based on 'soft law' and 'peer pressure', this task force managed to merge the criminalization agenda (money laundering defined as obscuring the proceeds of illicit drug trade as well as the forfeiture of ill-gotten gains) with upcoming regulatory rules (on identification and customer due diligence).

The financial services industry was caught off-guard by regulators and law enforcement agencies, when the new rules were rapidly extended in three ways: first, beyond banks to non-banking financial institutions and even to some non-financial institutions (especially so-called 'gate keepers', e.g. lawyers);[7] second, to further predicate offences;[8] and third, to new geographic

---

[1] Wolfsberg, 'Global Anti-Money-Laundering Guidelines for Private Banking', 30 October 2000, revised in 2002.

[2] BCBS CDD 2001, Bank for International Settlements, Basel Committee on Banking Supervision, 'Customer due diligence for banks', October 2001.

[3] FATF 40/2003, 'The Forty Recommendations of the Financial Action Task Force on Money Laundering 1990', revised 20 June 2003.

[4] For example, 'Swiss Bankers Code of Conduct (CDB)', 9 December 1977; 'Basel Statement of Principles' (BSP), 12 December 1988.

[5] UK: Drug Trafficking Offences Act 1986; Money Laundering Control Act 1986 (Pub. L. No. 99–570, 100 Stat. 3207-18, Title 18, Part I, Chapter 95, §1956).

[6] 'United Nations Convention Against Illicit Traffic in Narcotic Drugs and Psychotropic Substances', adopted on 19 December 1988.

[7] FATF 40/1996; FATF 40/2003, Recs. 8 and 9; cf. also EU 2005, 'Third Directive on Prevention of the Use of the Financial System for the Purpose of Money Laundering or Terrorist Financing (Ref. IP/05/682)', 26 May 2005.

[8] FATF 40/2003, Rec. 1 and Glossary (cf. note 7).

horizons beyond the area covered by OECD Member states.[9] Especially multinational corporations were confronted with continuously growing expectations by multiple regulators, and the emphasis differed from country to country, despite increasing efforts in the area of law harmonization. Whereas the USA was primarily interested in systematically generating data on cash transactions and wire transfers, the UK took pride in inventing and promoting the system of suspicious transaction reporting (STR) to financial intelligence units (FIUs). The Swiss regulators, finally, placed their emphasis more on customer identification and aimed at exporting their own system in order to reduce regulatory arbitrage.[10]

2.2   The emergence of the group

Such was the situation when civil society facilitators suggested the formation of a self-regulatory group to two banking institutions.[11] The time was apparently ripe for a variety of reasons. The immediate reason may have been a sequence of concrete scandals (e.g. Salinas and Abacha) tarnishing the reputation even of well-established corporations on both sides of the Atlantic. Credibility had become a serious business issue. However, the deeper logic that led to the formation of the group was most certainly the desire to create a level playing field for key competitors. Especially the need to bridge the 'transatlantic gap' with private means became apparent when the US Congress, dominated by the Republicans, rebuffed a proposal by the Clinton Administration to raise the regulatory CDD standards, especially for the 'know-your-customer' (KYC) rules. Another motivation was, however, the banks' interest in managing expectations and in keeping the costs of compliance on a reasonable and comparable[12] level.

From the outset, the Wolfsberg Group was planned as a 'multistakeholder initiative', even if three very different partners were involved. On the one hand, there were the 12 banks, represented by their chief compliance officers or heads of corporate AML units. On the other hand, two civil society entities, the anti-corruption watchdog Transparency International (TI),[13] including a former head of FinCEN[14] as a resource person and the university research facility 'Basel Institute on Governance',[15] represented by the Chairman of the OECD Working Group on Bribery. The challenge of this multistakeholder approach was to prevent the Wolfsberg Group from becoming a mere elitist lobbying group. While the banks are in possession of the detailed know-how, the role of the non-banks is to raise new issues (like the money management of corruption) or to act as mediators between regulators and banks by asking critical questions about touchy issues (like the financing of terrorism) in an otherwise industry-driven process.

In 2000, the group presented a first standard, focusing on private banking and continuously refining the existing regulatory standards for KYC, CDD, increased diligence, monitoring, documentation and training.[16] A series of further documents followed, which are either of a more policy-orientated nature (on financing of terrorism, on the laundering of corruption money and on the risk-based approach), or they add operational detail to the fundamental principles, for the benefit of their constituency and for competitors. The mechanism developed to reduce cost

---

[9] Pieth/Aiolfi 2004, 19 et seq.

[10] Ibid., 7 et seq.

[11] City Group and UBS.

[12] Pieth/Aiolfi 2003, 273 et seq.

[13] Transparency International, a Berlin-based anti-corruption NGO.

[14] Stanley E. Morris, former head of FinCEN and Head of Staff of Interpol.

[15] Mark Pieth, Chairman of the Basel Institute on Governance and the Working Group on Bribery (WGB) of the OECD.

[16] Cf. note 1.

in vetting correspondent banks (certification of correspondence and creation of an international registry) goes a step further towards a joint business venture (see below also).

The Wolfsberg Group has gone beyond standard setting: in order to involve both regulators and a larger group of major competitors, it has opened its doors to a wider circle for the past three years on the occasion of an annual event called the 'Wolfsberg Forum'. Wolfsberg has also held training seminars, both for member institutions and for outside guests (most recently in Russia and in China).

2.3   Primary goal: to negotiate a risk-based approach

Even if it is rarely explicitly said, the fundamental thrust of the Wolfsberg texts is to convince national and international regulatory agencies to adopt a **risk-based approach** to AML. This idea was already inherent in the first text of 2000 and becomes more and more visible, particularly in the 2006 paper on 'A Risk-Based Approach for Money Laundering Risks'.[17] Interestingly, the Working Group preparing this document invited several non-Wolfsberg banks who had participated in the Wolfsberg Forum to help write the document.

Whereas the traditional rule-based approach was rather ineffective, because it asked banks to take specific measures depending upon set thresholds or predefined criteria, the risk-based approach is more flexible, it identifies risk variables (e.g. country risk, customer risk or services risk), but leaves it up to the institution to set its own priorities for each criterion.

According to the risk-based approach, each institution is expected to develop its own compliance system, based on risk variables and addressing the particular situation as well as the business and client segment of the institution. The idea is that the bank knows its own risks best, and regulatory as well as criminal responsibility is attached to the potential malfunctioning of the system rather than an individual case that may be a mere 'accident'.

This approach is demanding, but it allows for a greater margin of flexibility. On the one hand, the bank is able to reduce costs when dealing with already heavily supervised customers (financial institutions in an FATF area or companies listed at the stock exchange). No additional diligence is required vis-à-vis central banks or MDBs. On the other hand, increased scrutiny is applied to 'higher risk situations'.[18] The Wolfsberg 'Risk-Based Approach' paper of 2006 lists examples of risk situations and measures to be taken against increased country, customer and services risks.[19] The risk-based approach basically allows the allocation of scarce resources to where they are most needed. It does, however, depend on the availability of information about risky clients, transactions and money laundering patterns. Several more detailed indicators are to be found in other papers, e.g. the FAQs on private bank intermediaries or on politically exposed persons (PEPS).[20]

It appears that the Wolfsberg strategy has been successful. Regulators began to participate in the Wolfsberg Forum in 2003, the FATF was responsive in its 2003 version of the Forty Recommendations and, more recently, with the help of its 'Electronic Advisory Group on the Risk-Based Approach': the FATF Secretariat has invited financial institutions to report on their

---

[17] Wolfsberg Statement, 'Guidance on a Risk-Based Approach for Managing Money Laundering Risks', March 2006.
[18] Cf. note 1, Art. 2.4 and 'The Wolfsberg AML Principles – Questions & Answers on "High-Risk Activities"', 7 May 2002.
[19] Cf. note 17.
[20] Cf. note 18.

application of the risk-based approach to combating money laundering (AML) and financing of terrorism (CFT). If the banks, in principle, seek to extend these methods developed in the credit industry to legal risks, they are aware of their own limits, especially regarding access to intelligence. They, therefore, depend on the feedback of financial intelligence units (FIUs).

3 Standards for anti-money laundering and combating the financing of terrorism

3.1 AML principles for private banking

When the **Wolfsberg Group** first published its **CDD** standards for private banking,[21] regulators and other commentators alike remained unimpressed. They asked what was new about the standards. It is true that the paper published in 2000 goes over the same terrain as many national guidelines and regulations as well as the FATF standards. Therefore, the BCBS CDD document merely mentions Wolfsberg in a footnote in its 2001 version.[22] Nevertheless, the Wolfsberg text is significant in that it gives a concise and clear overview of the rules for client acceptance and ongoing monitoring. With regard to client acceptance, it goes into some detail about **KYC** and CDD, including delicate issues like the treatment of intermediaries. Here, the 'Questions and Answers' paper to the Principles[23] is probably the more relevant document: it distinguishes between identification and due diligence rules for 'introducing intermediaries', 'managing intermediaries' and 'agent intermediaries'. Furthermore, it was one of the first texts to elaborate in detail what 'due diligence' requires and, especially, what determining the source of wealth and the source of funds entails in practice. The text also indicates what heightened scrutiny of high-risk and best-practice on **politically exposed persons (PEPs)** could mean.

In 2002 Wolfsberg reacted to the 2001 BCBS CDD paper with a revised version of its standards, and thus started an ongoing game of 'ping-pong' between the public and the private sector.[24] The key achievement of the Wolfsberg Principles remains the extension of a unified approach to roughly 60% of the industry, including an estimated 50% of the market share in each key off-shore destination.[25]

3.2 Combating the financing of terrorism

Wolfsberg reacted to 9/11 almost immediately with a declaration of support.[26] Its statement of 2002 entitled 'The Suppression of the **Financing of Terrorism**',[27] however, serves mixed purposes. It indicates the industry's readiness to cooperate with the authorities and stresses that established KYC procedures are useful, especially in conjunction with search lists provided by law enforcement agencies. As far as due diligence and heightened scrutiny are concerned, the paper tries to impress on governments that fighting terrorism is not really a subject to which the risk-based approach can be applied, because banks typically lack the type of information

---

[21] Cf. note 1.
[22] Cf. above, note 2 (note 4 in the text).
[23] Cf. note 18.
[24] Pieth/Aiolfi 2004, 33.
[25] Pieth/Aiolfi 2003, 273.
[26] 'Wolfsberg Group Pledges Anti-Terrorism Support', Press Statement, 5 October 2001.
[27] 'The Suppression of the Financing of Terrorism, Wolfsberg Statement', 11 January 2002.

primarily available to secret services and police forces. Here, an entire paragraph lists 'Areas for Discussion with Government Agencies' regarding the public–private cooperation. Wolfsberg obviously seeks a fair repartition of the responsibilities between the public and the private sectors.

3.3   Correspondent banking

In 2002, following basically the new rules of the US Patriot Act[28] for **correspondent banking** which were later also picked up by the new Forty Recommendations of the FATF, Wolfsberg developed a detailed set of rules for correspondent banking. The Principles of 2002[29] define what a risk-based approach in correspondent banking could entail and essentially distinguish between 'standard' due diligence for correspondent banks and 'enhanced' diligence for institutions dealing with higher risk indicators. Detailed 'frequently asked questions' ('FAQs') serve as an operational manual.[30] Wolfsberg has recently taken yet another step by encouraging private businesses to act as central certification agencies and create an international registry of due diligence data gathered by correspondent banks. This step allows banks to operate much more economically than within the traditional system, in which every bank had to apply its own due diligence to every potential correspondent. The system is intended to be open and it is envisaged that, ideally, as many banks as possible use these services, thus keeping the costs low. The Wolfsberg banks themselves merely acted as 'first movers'.

3.4   Further technical standards

Over the last years the Wolfsberg Group has published a series of further, more technical, papers, which indicate a move beyond private banking to other areas of the industry: e.g. the 'Anti-Money Laundering Guidance for Mutual Funds and other Pooled Investment Vehicles',[31] the 'FAQs on Selected Anti-Money Laundering Issues in the Context of Investment and **Commercial Banking**',[32] as well as the more recent deliberations of working parties with regard to 'Card-Based Banking'[33] and on 'Cross-Border Wire Transfers'.[34]

Yet another statement, enacted in 2003, deals with issues of 'Real Time Screening', 'Retroactive Searches' and 'Transaction Monitoring' – techniques applied to all areas of AML and CFT – in a cross-cutting way.

3.5   The money management of corruption

The discussions regarding **corruption** and money laundering, which have taken place within the Wolfsberg context for over three years, are on a different level. In fact, the connection

---

[28] US Patriot Act 2001, 'United States Uniting and Strengthening America by Providing Appropriate Tools Required to Intercept and Obstruct Terrorism', 24 October 2001, sections 312 et seq.

[29] 'The Wolfsberg Anti-Money Laundering Principles for Correspondent Banking', 21 October 2002.

[30] 'Wolfsberg Frequently Asked Questions ("FAQs") on Correspondent Banking', 2006.

[31] 'Wolfsberg Statement – Anti-Money Laundering Guidance for Mutual Funds and other Pooled Investment Vehicles', March 2006.

[32] 'Wolfsberg Frequently Asked Questions ("FAQs") on Selected Anti-Money Laundering Issues in the Context of Investment and Commercial Banking', 2006.

[33] 'Card-based Banking, Principles and Typologies', Working Session I-C, Wolfsberg Working Group Paper, 1 June 2006.

[34] 'Cross-Border Wire Transfers, Issues and Best Practices', Working Group Session I-B, Wolfsberg Working Group Paper, 1 June 2006.

between corruption and money laundering was one of the reasons – especially for the members of civil society – to set up the group in the first place. Therefore Wolfsberg decided to publish a further statement focusing, in particular, on risks related to graft and corruption. Even though several aspects of the problem have already been covered by earlier papers (money laundering and PEPs), others pose additional challenges. It is, under ordinary circumstances, extremely difficult to detect whether an, in principle, bona fide company obtains contracts by means of bribery; and it would pose an even bigger problem to determine whether funds are prepared for corrupt uses (so-called 'slush funds'). Understandably, banks are very shy to make promises they cannot fulfill: a pro-active client-screening for bribery is beyond their means. What they can do, however, is to keep their own house in check and, as far as their clients are concerned, apply their established risk-based approach. Unusual circumstances, pointing towards bribery and the laundering of corruption money, have to trigger notification. Additionally, banks would be able to do more in specific areas, such as project financing, where they typically receive far more details about the recipients of funds. The new Wolfsberg paper on corruption is, therefore, just as much a statement of intent as an effort at expectation management.

4   Critical appraisal

Most self-regulatory mechanisms are confronted with three types of criticism.[35] First, they have to prove that they are effective, as they do not usually foresee stringent evaluation mechanisms or dispute settlement procedures. Second, they are typically under suspicion of being undemocratic, especially if a group of self-elected members is able to impose rules on others. Linked with this criticism is a third concern: self-regulatory groups are 'black boxes', they traditionally lack transparency. Again, this would pose a problem if they were to influence rules imposed on third parties.

4.1   Effectiveness

It is true that the Wolfsberg Group does not police its own constituency. However, the area in which the group members are active is one of the most heavily regulated by the public sector. Deficits in the AML or CFT systems have been severely sanctioned, including sanctions against Members of the Wolfsberg Group.[36] Sometimes, the Wolfsberg Principles are quoted as 'best practices' in regulatory decisions. An additional internal monitoring procedure does not seem necessary.

4.2   The multistakeholder approach

Multinational corporations, as is well known, may have a turnover exceeding the GDP of small states. In a globalized world, a group of competitors with a combined share of the market well beyond 50% worldwide, acting as a lobbying group in regulatory matters, could, potentially, challenge the remains of sovereign power in this field.

It is, therefore, crucial to understand that Wolfsberg is not a mere lobbying group for industry interests: on the one hand, it is recognized that it acts as a partner within a context of co-regulation together with the public sector. Academics have termed this form of standard setting 'hybrid

---

[35] Black 2001, 103 et seq.; Delmas-Marty 2004, 260; Jenkins 2001, 1 et seq.; Minogue 2001, 1 et seq.
[36] Recently, sanctions by the US Federal Reserve Bank against ABN AMRO.

regulation' or 'regulation at a distance'.[37] On the other hand, its specific concept of involving members of civil society and academics in all deliberations lends the group credibility far beyond that of a mere industry organization. Discussions within the group are frank and direct, a particular advantage of the **multistakeholder approach**.

Obviously, the representatives of civil society who participate in the process do not have any specific democratic legitimation but they happen to be the participants who proposed the creation of the group and assisted in setting it up.

4.3 The Wolfsberg Forum

As soon as the Wolfsberg process had gained recognition by regulators, more banks wanted to become members. After long discussions it was decided not to expand the original group in order to preserve the effective peer dynamics. However, an event aimed at a wider circle of participants, the **Wolfsberg Forum**, was organized in 2003 and has taken place annually ever since.

4.3.1 The Forum

Whereas the Wolfsberg Group itself meets three to four times a year, the Forum takes place annually in June, back-to-back with the group's summer meeting at Wolfsberg itself. A special day is allotted to a meeting with regulators, law-enforcement agencies (including FIUs) and international bodies like the FATF and the Basel Committee on Banking Supervision. On the following day, delegates of roughly 50 of the world's largest banks are invited to participate in an event, combining the discussions of all new draft papers of the Wolfsberg Group including keynote speeches and talks with entities involved in AML and CFT (most recently the US Under-Secretary for Enforcement or the Executive Director of the FATF). This flexible format allows for the integration of further participants without reducing the dynamics of the original group.

4.3.2 The Forum network

Several of the more technical texts mentioned above were prepared by working groups with the cooperation of Forum participants who are not members of the core group. This approach is particularly effective where specialist knowledge is required (project financing, commodity financing, card banking).

4.3.3 The Wolfsberg Academy

Wolfsberg has, in the past, organized a variety of training sessions on a more applied level for its own specialists, as well as two outreach seminars in Russia and China. Efforts are under way to intensify such outreach activities under the heading of the '**Wolfsberg Academy**'.

5 Conclusion

Most of the activities listed above evolved over time and were not originally planned. They must, however, be regarded as efforts to pre-empt some of the potential criticism leveled at self-regulatory instruments in other areas (e.g. the pharmaceutical industry). So far – in my view – Wolfsberg has managed to maintain its genuine multistakeholder approach by inviting further players at appropriate stages.

---

[37] Black 2001, 103 et seq.

Addresses

The Wolfsberg Group
Contact person: Tracy Paradise
tracy.paradise@ubs.com
www.wolfsberg-principles.com/

Basel Institute on Governance
Contact person: Gretta Fenner
gretta.fenner@baselgovernance.org
www.baselgovernance.org/

Basel Committee on Banking Supervision
www.bis.org/bcbs/

Financial Action Task Force on Money Laundering
www.fatf-gafi.org/

Bibliography

Black, J.: 'Decentring Regulation: Understanding the Role of Regulation and Self Regulation in a "Post-Regulatory" World', in Freeman, M. (ed.): Current Legal Problems, Volume 54, Oxford University Press, Oxford, 2001: 103–146.

Clark, A./Burrell, P. (eds): A Practitioner's Guide to International Money Laundering Law and Regulation, City & Financial Publishing, Surrey, UK, 2003.

Delmas-Marty, M.: Le relatif et l'universel, les forces imaginantes du droit, Éd. Du Seuil, Paris, 2004.

FATF 40/1996, The Forty Recommendations of the Financial Action Task Force on Money Laundering 1990, revised 28 June 1996.

FATF 40/2003, The Forty Recommendations of the Financial Action Task Force on Money Laundering 1990, revised 20 June 2003.

Freeman, M. (ed.): Current Legal Problems, Volume 54, Oxford University Press, Oxford, 2001.

Jenkins, R.: 'Corporate Codes of Conduct: Self-Regulation in a Global Economy', Business Responsibility for Sustainable Development, Paper No. 2, UN Research Institute for Social Development, Geneva, 2001.

Minogue, M.: 'Governance-Based Analysis of Regulation', Working Paper Series, Paper No. 3, University of Manchester: Centre on Regulation and Competition, Institute for Development Policy Management, Manchester, 2001.

Pieth M./Aiolfi, G.: 'The Private Sector Becomes Active: The Wolfsberg Process', in Clark, A./ Burrell, P. (eds): A Practitioner's Guide to International Money Laundering Law and Regulation, City & Financial Publishing, Surrey, UK, 2003: 267–280.

Pieth, M./Aiolfi, G.: A Comparative Guide to Anti-Money Laundering: A Critical Analysis of Systems in Singapore, Switzerland, the UK and the USA, Edward Elgar Publishing, Cheltenham, UK/Northampton, USA, 2004.

The Wolfsberg Group, 'Global Anti-Money-Laundering Guidelines for Private Banking', 30 October 2000, updated in 2002.

The Wolfsberg Group, 'Anti-Money Laundering Principles – Questions & Answers on "High-Risk Activities"', 7 May 2002.

The Wolfsberg Group, 'Anti-Money Laundering Principles for Correspondent Banking, 21 October 2002.

The Wolfsberg Group, 'Frequently Asked Questions ("FAQs") on Correspondent Banking', 2006.

The Wolfsberg Group, 'Frequently Asked Questions ("FAQs") on Selected Anti-Money Laundering Issues in the Context of Investment and Commercial Banking', 2006.

The Wolfsberg Statement, 'The Suppression of the Financing of Terrorism', 11 January 2002.

The Wolfsberg Statement, 'Guidance on a Risk Basel Approach for Managing Money Laundering Risks', March 2006.

The Wolfsberg Statement, 'Anti-Money Laundering Guidance for Mutual Funds and Other Pooled Investment Vehicles', March 2006.

'Wolfsberg Group Pledges Anti-Terrorism Support', Press Statement, 5 October 2001.

Wolfsberg Working Group Paper, 'Card Based Banking, Principles and Typologies, Working Session I-C', Graham Hooper-Barclays, 1 June 2006.

Wolfsberg Working Group Paper, 'Cross-Border Wire Transfers, Issues and Best Practices, Working Group Session I-B', 1 June 2006.

COUNTRIES

THE AMERICAS

John W. Moscow is one of the nation's most experienced white-collar criminal attorneys, with particular expertise in banking regulation and financial crimes. Mr Moscow received a B.A. from the University of Chicago in 1969, and a J.D. from Harvard Law School in 1972. Mr Moscow spent 30 years with the New York County District Attorney's Office. As the highest ranked white-collar prosecutor, Mr Moscow focused on international bank and tax fraud, securities fraud, theft and fraud on governmental entities, and developed an expertise in money laundering. Mr Moscow's current practice is in white collar defense, and advising and representing financial institutions in various civil and criminal litigation and regulatory matters. Mr Moscow frequently lectures and publishes in the fields of banking regulation and financial crime. Mr Moscow is admitted to practice in New York and before the Court of Appeals for the Second Circuit, and the United States District Courts for the Southern and Eastern Districts of New York.

At **Rosner, Moscow & Napierala, LLP**, our mission is to provide our clients with the best representation possible. Often clients seek our services when critical matters – matters involving their rights and reputations – are at stake. We represent them with skill, expertise and dedication. Each of our attorneys has expertise in a unique area of law, enabling us to provide top-level representation in a variety of legal areas, such as litigation and corporate and regulatory issues. Our attorneys have extensive trial and appellate experience, having briefed and argued appeals before the highest state and federal courts.

U S A

John W. Moscow

Partner

Rosner, Moscow & Napierala, LLP
26 Broadway, 22nd Floor
New York, NY 10004-1808
USA

Tel +1 212 785 2577 (main)
    +1 212 785 4380 (direct)
Fax +1 212 785 5203
jmoscow@rmnllp.com
www.rmnllp.com

Anti-Money Laundering: International Law and Practice.
Edited by W.H. Muller, C.H. Kälin and J.G. Goldsworth
© 2007 John Wiley & Sons, Ltd

Contents – USA

1   Overview

During the 1980s narcotics were a major problem in the United States. The United States' legal and regulatory response was focused in large part on keeping currency, accumulated in the street sales of narcotics, from being deposited into the banking system without records being accurately created and maintained showing the identity of all persons making cash deposits or withdrawals of $10 000 or more.

The focus of that initial anti-money laundering effort has broadened immensely over the past 25 years. The anti-money laundering statutes are far more draconian than they were, and the effort that the regulators and law enforcement personnel are putting into anti-money laundering efforts is far greater and far more sustained than it was. That broader focus is due to a great expansion in the numbers and scope of the evils which anti-money laundering efforts are supposed to combat, or even to defeat.

During the 1980s and 1990s the initial anti-narcotics money laundering concept expanded, as new situations arose, involving:

- wholesale thefts from nations by their rulers,

- a major increase in tax evasion, involving both other nations' taxes concealed in the United States, and United States income concealed through off-shore companies, and more recently, a huge increase in efforts to combat terrorist financing.

In terms of anti-money laundering efforts a concept gained acceptance, especially in the last 10 years, among United States lawmakers, regulators and law enforcement personnel that the value transfer systems of the United States, including the money transfer systems and the securities transfer systems, should not be utilized by anonymous persons seeking to move value without attribution to themselves. That concept was not adopted into law until after the terrorist attacks on September 11, 2001, when Congress passed what it termed the USA Patriot Act.

While the proposals that were adopted in the Patriot Act were being discussed, another concept was gaining acceptance; persons and nations hostile to the United States, even those who were fully and accurately identified, should not stand to benefit from the use of the value transfer systems in the United States. Economic embargoes, which had been utilized on limited occasions, have become more and more common; the lists of names have become voluminous.[1] These matters are handled by the Office of Foreign Asset Control, known as OFAC.

Both concepts are currently accepted as guiding principles among lawmakers, regulators and law enforcement. Put simply, the AML/BSA philosophy in the United States is that the identity of persons using the value transfer systems of the country, no matter where those persons may be located, should be recorded and ascertainable. In addition the United States forbids the use of its value transfer systems to send, transmit or receive value from specified persons, countries and

---

[1] There is a problem with the lists in that more than one person may have the same name. In the West, with names, dates of birth, social security numbers and addresses, there are databases which financial institutions can utilize to cut the number of false positives yielded in an OFAC search. In dealing with Arab names, no dates of birth, no social security number and addresses that may be looser than we are used to there are multitudes of 'false positives'. In one search there were 1000 transactions in the name of a terrorist; further work disclosed that there were three people involved, none of them terrorists, in wildly divergent parts of the globe.

regions, whose interests are deemed inimical to those of the United States. The statutes, rules and regulations[2] adopted over the past few years in the United States on their face:

- require that financial institutions know their customers, including their identities, their business, and the source of their funds; and

- require the filing of reports if a transaction, or a structured set of transactions, involves $10 000 or more in currency, or monetary instruments, or if it is otherwise suspicious; and

- forbid American financial institutions from handling the proceeds of crime, including tax crimes, whether the crimes were committed in the United States or elsewhere; and

- in practice require that financial institutions (as defined) utilize computerized systems with effective filters to stop prescribed transactions.

These rules are part of the anti-money laundering part of American jurisprudence. The anti-terrorist financing part is structured very differently.

The anti-terrorist financing portion of American jurisprudence is an out-growth of the second concept mentioned above – that persons whose conduct, whose causes, whose nations or whose regions are deemed sufficiently inimical to the United States will be publicly named and barred from the use of the United States' value transfer systems, whether as transmitters, receivers or third-party beneficiaries. Money already in the dollar transfer system when a person or country is named is supposed to be frozen; money outside the system is supposed to be blocked from entering the system.

The statutes, rules and regulations[3] forbid institutions from transferring value to:

- designated persons, including companies and associations, either because they are perceived to be involved in the narcotics business, because they are perceived to be involved in nuclear proliferation, because they are perceived to be involved in terrorism, or because they are associated with a nation which has been designated for some other reason of American foreign policy (e.g. Cuba);

- designated countries; and

- designated regions.

These rules are part of the OFAC system, barring designated persons, entities and countries from receiving any value through the American value transfer system.

The OFAC system, as an arm of diplomacy, has been used as the legal basis for sanctions against various nations over the years, including Iran, Iraq, Cuba, Libya and South Africa. Since 2001 it has gained a great deal of importance as a weapon against terrorist financing. Obeying that law is complex and difficult, as is discussed below. The number of names of persons and entities on the list is in the thousands, with many of the names similar to each other. But the prescriptions

---

[2] See Appendix A to the *Bank Secrecy Act Anti-Money Laundering Examination Manual* of the Federal Financial Institutions Examination Council, made up of the Board of Governors of the Federal Reserve System, the Federal Deposit Insurance Corporation, the National Credit Union Administration, and the Office of the Controller of the Currency, available at www.ffiec.gov/pdf/bsa_aml_examination_manual2006.pdf.

[3] See the website of the Office of Financial Assets Control (OFAC) at www.treas.gov/offices/enforcement/ofac/programs/terror/terror.shtml for a list of the statutory powers and authorizing legislation on which their activities are based.

of OFAC must nonetheless be obeyed for transactions in dollars wired through the United States and for transactions involving United States currency.

Substantial fines and extended incarceration are the penal sanctions for violations of the anti-money laundering laws and of the OFAC regulations. In addition, the government can seek forfeiture of funds, or substitute funds, which have been moved in violation of certain of the statutes.

2   Who is covered by the laws?

The scope of the various laws differs. The anti-money laundering laws are written to cover all financial institutions, as defined. They include:

- an insured bank as defined in 12 USC 1813(h)
- a commercial bank or trust company
- a private banker
- an agency or branch of a foreign bank in the United States
- any credit union
- a thrift institution
- a broker or dealer registered with the Securities and Exchange Commission *(15 USC78a et seq.)*
- a broker or dealer in securities or commodities
- an investment banker or investment company
- a currency exchange
- an issuer, redeemer or cashier of traveler's checks, checks, money orders, or similar instruments
- an operator of a credit card system
- an insurance company
- a dealer in precious metals, stones or jewels
- a pawnbroker
- a loan or finance company
- a travel agency
- a licensed sender of money **or** any other person who engages as a business in the transmission of funds, including any person who engages as a business in an informal money transfer system or any network of people who engage as a business in facilitating the transfer of money domestically or internationally outside of the convention financial institution system[4]

---

[4] In New York, through which the vast bulk of international wire transfers flow, it is a New York State felony to engage in the business of transmitting money or receiving it for transmission without a license if the amount involved exceeds $250 000 a year. Bank accounts, without an office, established by an out-of-country business and used to transmit money and receive it for transmission as a business, themselves violate the law; the people controlling those accounts may themselves be called to account even if they have never been in New York. A person dealing, directly or indirectly, with such a business faces criminal liability.

- a telegraph company

- a business engaged in vehicle sales, including automobile, airplane and boat sales

- persons involved in real estate closings and settlements

- the United States Postal Service

- an agency of the United States government or of a state or local government carrying out a duty or power of a business described in this list

- a casino, gambling casino or gaming establishment with an annual gaming revenue of more than $1 000 000 which

  - is licensed as a casino, gambling casino or gaming establishment under the laws of any state or of any political subdivision of any state; or

  - is an Indian gaming operation conducted under or pursuant to the Indian Gaming Regulatory Act other than an operation which is limited to class I gaming as defined[5]

- any future commission merchant, commodity trading advisor or commodity pool operator registered, or required to register, under the Commodities Exchange Act, 7 USC 1

- any business or agency which engages in any activity which the Secretary of the Treasury determines, by regulation, to be an activity which is similar to, related to, or a substitute for any activity in which any business listed here is authorized to engage

- any other business designated by the Secretary of the Treasury whose cash activities have a high degree of usefulness in criminal, tax or regulatory matters.

Although accounts managed by accountants and attorneys are not designated, for these purposes, as financial institutions, professionals handling other people's money normally keep those funds in banks, which are governed by the law, and the professionals themselves are personally required to fill out both Currency Transaction Reports and Suspicious Activity Reports under the appropriate circumstances.

2.1   What are financial institutions required to know?

Financial institutions are required to know their customers. They are expected to know the identity of their customers, what they do, and whether the financial transactions in which they engage are normal for their business. Although that standard had been touted as best practice for 20 years, it was only in 2001 that the standard was adopted by Congress. The question of what it means to 'know your customer' is still open in real-world situations involving unanticipated complications. Given the complexity of the world financial system, the question of who is whose customer raises a host of questions.

2.2   KYC at the retail level

At the retail level the standard 'know your customer' can be simple. A financial institution is required to know who the customer is. When the account is opened evidence must be

---

[5] Note that unlawful gambling operations are not covered by the statute, unlike unlicensed money transmission businesses. Unlawful gambling establishments are already subject to prosecution and the proceeds are subject to forfeiture, so using one as a financial institution carries certain collateral risks.

obtained proving that the person opening the account is who he says he is, not someone else. Likewise the institution should know the source of funds in an account, whether it be bi-weekly salary deposits or something more complex. When a financial institution opens an account it should generate a profile for the account, so that it can take comfort that the account is behaving normally. If the account is a simple retail account that may suffice, but experience teaches that accounts can change their nature over time. A local ice-cream store in a residential section of Brooklyn, New York seemed to be harmless enough, but over time the ice-cream store started to accept wire deposits and transmit them overseas to terrorists. The Carnival ice-cream store became the Carnival ice-cream and money laundering store, without the bank's noticing a change in the nature of Carnival's business. Had the bank manager, or a bank computer system, noticed that the ice-cream store made the same substantial deposits in the winter, when no ice-cream is sold, as the store made in the summer, when ice-cream is a huge seller, the major bank involved would have avoided major regulatory and prosecutorial problems.

2.2   KYC at the business level

KYC at the business level can be more complex, because the question arises as to who controls the account, for whose benefit it exists, as well as what the source of funds is. The financial institution is required to know the answer to those questions. Business accounts can be simple proprietary businesses, treated like personal accounts. They can purport to be 'trust' accounts, though financial institutions need to be careful that the word 'trust' is not used to conceal both ownership, control, and the source of funds. Or business accounts can be the accounts for partnerships, limited liability partnerships, corporations, and all forms of joint economic activity. The financial institution needs to know whose account it is, what they do for a living, and what the source is for their funds.

2.2.1   Trust accounts

When accounts are alleged to be trust accounts the financial institution should obtain copies of the trust documents **and it should have someone knowledgeable about trusts read the documents.** The trustee may be known to the financial institution, which satisfies KYC as to control of the account, but the identity of the beneficiary of the account must also be known. If the trust is one of a myriad of documents appearing superficially to be a trust, but not adequately identifying the trustees and the beneficiaries, there may be a problem. So an institution which opens an account for a professional whom they know may find that he has been substituted for as trustee, and that someone, possibly not even the grantor, has the right to change beneficiaries.

2.2.2   Corporate accounts

When the accounts are corporate accounts (including partnerships, associations, and all the other legal forms by which people can act other than individually) the financial institution needs to verify that the corporation is not a shell, but that it is a functioning legal entity whose business can be learned and known. If the corporation is a shell the financial institution needs to learn and document the ownership, control and purpose of the shell. As mentioned above the purpose is to create a paper trail demonstrating the control and beneficial ownership of funds.

2.3   Correspondent financial arrangements

More complex than dealings with trusts and businesses are the questions which involve correspondent financial arrangements. The Patriot Act defines a correspondent account to be 'an account established to receive deposits from, make payments on behalf of a foreign financial institution, or handle other financial transactions related to such institution'. Almost any financial dealing, including a simple placement of funds, if it comes from a foreign financial institution, is covered. See 31 USC 5318A(e)(1)(B). Although the financial institution does not have to know the customers of its correspondent it does have to satisfy itself that the correspondent knows its own customers. Certain institutions, such as shell banks, are forbidden from having accounts with American financial institutions.

2.3.1   Accounts for foreign correspondent banks

Financial institutions which maintain accounts for foreign correspondent banks must maintain records in the United States – within the legal jurisdiction of the United States – identifying the owners of the foreign bank, and the name and address of a person (natural or corporate) authorized to accept service of legal process *on the foreign correspondent* for records from outside the United States maintained by the correspondent.

2.3.2   Terminate the relationship

If the correspondent does not comply with, or go to court to challenge the subpoena, the American financial institution may be required to terminate the correspondent relationship, under pain of a $10 000 a day fine until the relationship is ended.

2.3.3   Person to whom process can be served

The statute providing that a correspondent financial institution must have a person within the United States on whom process can be served does not restrict that process to subpoenas from the Attorney General and the Secretary of the Treasury. While violation of their subpoenas can result in the foreign bank being thrown out of the United States, violation of other legal process would simply constitute contempt of court, with different legal sanctions. Again, the theory underlying this is that the United States wants to be able to trace value – money or securities – going through the United States even if the deposits and withdrawals are made abroad.

2.3.4   The freezing of money

The Patriot Act, in a major change from traditional banking, provides that the United States can freeze money held by a foreign correspondent bank in a correspondent account in the United States, up to the value of funds deposited into the foreign bank abroad, even in a non-dollar account, if the funds deposited abroad would be subject to forfeiture if they were in the United States. Specifically the United States could go into a district court and obtain a forfeiture order against funds of Bank X, held at a major United States bank, because Bank X had accepted deposits abroad, in euros hypothetically, as the result of internet gambling winnings from the United States. In that case Bank X could defend itself from the forfeiture order **only by proving that the money was no longer at the bank, or that not all of the money was still there. The**

foreign bank may defend itself only to the extent that it does not have to forfeit money which has already been withdrawn. As to the funds still in the foreign bank, the account holder is the only person permitted to challenge the forfeiture. As to money held at Bank X, even if the account holder is in Europe, and it was euros which were deposited rather than dollars, the dollars Bank X has are the subject of the forfeiture order in the United States. There is no need for the government to trace the money frozen to the proceeds of the crime; it is sufficient to establish the value of the money sought to be forfeited, and to prove that the correspondent bank in the United States has assets which can be frozen. The theory would appear to be that if Bank X knew its customer, and knew his business, and knew that the funds on deposit were the proceeds of crime, Bank X should not be dealing with him.

2.4 Obligation to screen the names of persons and entities

Banks involved in transmitting money have a new burden imposed by the Patriot Act. Banks are not merely required to know their customers, and to create Customer Identification Profiles; they are required to screen the names of persons and entities transmitting money through the bank, even if the person or entity has no account at the institution in question. What this means in practice is that institutions which transmit funds for third parties have to screen all the names that go through the institution's facilities, and report any transactions which are 'suspicious'.

2.4.1 Screening by computer

All money transmissions have to be screened for the identities of the persons and entities involved. A financial institution involved in transmitting funds has to screen, by computer with appropriate software, the identities of people using the institution and destination of the funds. The computer has to have a database identifying all names on the OFAC lists, and providing enough data to avoid inadvertent transactions involving politically exposed persons (PEPS) and other transactions which, in retrospect, appear suspicious. All suspicious transactions have to be reported. (Software vendors offer solutions but care must be taken in assessing how much information is enough, and how much is too much, with too many false positives.)

2.4.2 Exchange of information between financial institutions

To assist financial institutions in ascertaining whether transactions are suspicious there are provisions under which financial institutions may exchange information with each other without civil liability. Institutions ought to register to exchange information, because regulators may not view self-selected isolation as an excuse for not knowing what's happening with a particular account or set of accounts.

3 Responsibility and obligations of financial institutions

Besides requiring that financial institutions develop Customer Identification Programs (CIP) and that they know their customers and the business profiles of their customers (a corollary of the requirement that suspicious activity be reported) the American AML legislation requires that financial institutions do these things in a formalized way.

3.1 Requirement to establish anti-money laundering programs

Financial institutions are required to establish anti-money laundering programs including, at a minimum:

(a) The development of internal policies, procedures, and controls.

(b) The formal designation of a compliance officer.

(c) Creation and implementation of an on-going employee training program.

(d) The establishment of an independent audit program to test the programs established.

3.1.1 Requirement to have an auditing program

It is a violation of the regulations not to have an auditing program even if there are no other violations. It is not enough to get KYC and CIP correct, and not enough to report all suspicious activity. There has to be a formal plan, it has to be adopted by the institution, and it has to include internal policies as to what should happen.

3.1.2 Policy procedures

It also has to include written systems – procedures – for implementing the policies. Pious words are not enough. The system has to appear to be effective; if it is ineffective the regulators will be unhappy.

3.1.3 Compliance officer

A compliance officer has to be designated. This is important. If a compliance officer has additional duties, the regulators and law enforcement will be unsympathetic to complaints that he was over-worked. Compliance is, under the AML system the United States has adopted, a rapidly growing area with huge responsibilities, and, frequently, inadequate resources to deal with the tasks assigned.

3.1.4 Training program

The training program should be good; a chain is only as strong as its weakest link, and an AML program is no stronger than its weakest link.

Teaching employees who deal in wire transfers about Currency Transaction Reports with which they do not deal in their work is unlikely to persuade regulators that the institution is serious about combating money laundering. Training has to be appropriate to the work done; it is the institution which is at risk if the training is inadequate or misdirected. The fact that training programs are available for simple anti-drug money laundering does not mean that they are appropriate for the institution now.

3.1.5 Audit program

The audit program is an opportunity to catch mistakes before they are made. Whether audit programs are worth the money is an open question, but if money must be spent on them, and it must, by law, the audit program should be utilized. AML is an area where, if there is a problem, senior management can find itself in trouble. Middle management may want to conceal mistakes in an AML program and may yield to a temptation to keep the audit costs down, and to limit the work that the auditors do. That may not be the way to go.

4   Evaluation of risk

Evaluation of accounts for risk is an art, not a science, but it is an art that financial institutions are now required to learn. Institutions need to know about their customers, their correspondent accounts, and the persons using their value-transmitting services. Not everything can possibly be known, so that the procedures designed to fight money laundering must be risk-based, that is, there needs to be an articulable reason for looking at what gets scrutinized and omitting to check the rest.

- Knowing the profile of an account, and knowing the identity of the account holder are key steps to minimizing the risk of certain accounts. The ice-cream store in Brooklyn, New York, mentioned above, should have had a profile in which large cash deposits during the winter raised questions. The procedure should have called for someone to check the basis of the ice-cream store's business activity when it was cold out.

- The ice-cream store started accepting cash deposits, and transmitting them on to a Middle Eastern country in volumes too great to be remittances home from workers at the store. Again, procedures should have been in place to alert the management of the financial institution that a customer was far outside the profile one would expect from his business.

- In dealing with more complicated customers than ice-cream stores customer identification profiles can be difficult, but if the customer is known and the profile, once constructed, is consistent, the risk may be low.

- In dealing with correspondent institutions, one financial institution cannot 'know' its customer's customer, but it does have two clear obligations. It must satisfy itself that its own customer knows its customers, and it must do name checks on the entities using its facilities to transfer value to ascertain that there is nothing suspicious, using public data bases, about the transactions as the institution sees them, or can see them by cooperating with another institution. In dealing with AML aspects of the American system names must be checked to see whether suspicious activity reports need to be filed – e.g. a well-known public servant, brother to his nation's President, depositing 500 years, salary in six years' should have engendered suspicion.

5   OFAC (Office of Foreign Assets Control)

If AML risk assessment is an art, OFAC compliance is not. It is mandatory. The steps that must be taken to avoid OFAC violations include screening all bank activity by computer, checking all OFAC names against every name that goes through the institution to ascertain that the name listed and the person doing business with the financial institution are not the same. Computers cannot do all the work; human intelligence is needed, and that means that a substantial staff is needed, as well as computers, to ascertain when there is a 'hit' on an OFAC name, that the person at your institution is not the person listed on the OFAC list, even if the names are identical.

5.1   OFAC lists

OFAC maintains lists of Specially Designated Nationals and Blocked Persons ('SDN'), Specially Designated Terrorists ('SDT') and Specially Designated Narcotics Traffickers ('SDNT'). As mentioned above there are thousands of names on the lists. Computer screening of all transactions (see below) for those names is required as a practical matter, and once the system is in place for that screening, the system should also be able to screen for politically exposed persons, and for people whose activity, when analyzed on public databases, is suspicious.

5.1.1   Freezing

The OFAC regime is supposed to freeze assets and block transactions involving targeted persons and entities. No judgment is required in one sense, because if a person or a corporation is listed, no business can be done with them, and the assets have to be frozen. As mentioned above, a major problem comes with identity of names, and the resulting false positive that arises when an innocent person with the same name as a culpable one finds his assets are frozen.

5.1.2   Necessity of computerized screening

Why is computerized screening necessary? Because transmission of money is a real-time operation, and running through the names would take far too many man-hours of work without computers.

5.1.3   Activities of a financial institution

Consider the activity that a financial institution may engage in. There are checks and cash, handled by tellers. There are wire transfers, handled by the wire room. There are loans, and there are letters of credit. And there are transfers through the SWIFT system, which in the summer of 2006 is a very sensitive area indeed.

5.2   OFAC rules and requirements

Without listing the individuals or business entities on the OFAC list, it is worth noting that at one point the countries on the list included Cuba, North Korea, Libya, Iraq, Angola, Federated Republic of Yugoslavia, Sudan and Syria. Companies located in Cuba, North Korea, and certain areas of Bosnia and Herzegovina were also included. To complicate matters, subsidiaries of blocked companies are also covered by the prescription of OFAC. That means that the computerized screening system has to include all the names of businesses owned by companies who are subject to OFAC blocking.

- OFAC lists have to be kept up-to-date. Since names are frequently added, and since nations may be taken off the list, checking the OFAC website is an absolute necessity.

- OFAC describes a transaction in which a teller must block a transaction between two non-blocked persons, because the bank against which a check is drawn is owned by a nation on the OFAC list. To accomplish that the tellers must be sensitive to OFAC requirements, which sensitivity requires a training program. Note how the certainty of OFAC ties into the art of the AML program.

- OFAC urges that the wire transfer department review all fields of out-going wire transfer instructions before funds are wired. If any of the fields contains a listed name, the transaction must be stopped until there is a decision as to whether the name is that of the person sought, or if it involves a different person with the same name.

- For letters of credit a financial institution has to ascertain that no one involved, not merely the persons with whom the institution is in privity, but no one standing to benefit, directly or indirectly from the LC, is on the list. Less obviously, if any bank involved in the transaction is a blocked bank the entire transaction must be blocked.

- One of the practical problems with letters of credit and related trade finance is that the OFAC rules run contrary to traditional bank thinking in the area. The OFAC rules require that the entire transaction be scrutinized to ascertain that none of the parties involved is OFAC-sensitive. Traditionally a bank would honor a letter of credit if the terms were met, without question. Now, if honoring terms means paying a subsidiary corporation owned (even indirectly) by a foreign state whose assets are blocked, the money must not be paid. Instead it must be put into a blocked account, and OFAC must be notified.

- Similarly, in connection with loans, a financial institution has to check to see if the borrower, obligor, guarantor or co-signer is blocked.

All these transactions must be screened by computer, with software that is current and aggressive.

6   International wire transfers and SWIFT

The United States implemented a rule that all domestic wire transfers have to list the originating party, the ultimate beneficiary, and the intermediary institutions. The information on those computer screen fields makes scanning for OFAC, and even for AML SAR activity, relatively easy. But there has been no such rule for international wire transfers, or for funds transmitted with SWIFT messages. In trying to close loopholes in the area of economic sanctions, however, a major problem has surfaced, with SWIFT.

- Assume that a German bank wants to pay dollars to a Cuban bank for sugar. Money can be wired through New York in the form of a bank-to-bank transaction, from the German bank to a Venezuelan bank which reflects nothing about a transfer to Cuba. The SWIFT message to the Venezuelan bank may well reflect that money should be paid to a Cuban entity, with none of that information being received in New York.

- That transaction is unlawful, even if it is undiscoverable initially. A transaction that should have been blocked is not blocked and the financial institution involved is liable. What changes, if any, will be adopted in rules about wire transfers is not clear, although changes are clearly being proposed.

- The underlying rule, again, is that the United States does not want its value transfer system used for the benefit of designated persons, companies, nations and regions hostile to the

United States, and does not want its systems used by persons acting anonymously or through the use of fronts.

7 Paperwork

Both the AML and OFAC components of the anti-money laundering and anti-terrorist regimes in the United States have paperwork requirements which require effort regardless of the benefit. A financial institution cannot decide that certain paperwork is worthless and therefore will not be done; the regulatory bodies are, in that regard, quite formalistic.

7.1 Currency Transaction Reports (CTRs), Suspicious Activity Reports (SARs)

For AML regulation the paperwork consists of Currency Transaction Reports (CTRs), Suspicious Activity Reports (SARs), and the documentation of the AML program, including its audit, referred to above.

7.1.1 CTRs

CTRs must be filed when a person deposits or withdraws $10 000 or more, in one or a series of structured transactions. In certain geographically targeted areas (GTOs) the amount can be lowered to $3500. Structured transactions include all ways in which a person can get currency into a bank so it can be wired or transferred by check or otherwise. Although CTRs must be filed, there is no necessary reason for anyone to be suspicious about the transaction if it is engaged in without subterfuge or deceit. A jeweler depositing $50 000 in cash after the sale of diamonds is not suspicious in itself. Seven people, going to different teller windows of a bank to deposit $3000 each into the same account requires a CTR and possibly an SAR.

7.1.2 SARs

SARs must be filed when there is something suspicious about a transaction. SARs are secret; banks cannot be required to disclose whether they have filed them, and no one is permitted to subpoena them. In the case of SARs the regulations are a great deal stronger than the statute, and the courts have upheld the regulations.

7.1.3 Suspicion

The reason is that SARs are at the heart of the idea that financial institutions are the first line of defense in the war against narcotics or terrorism. Financial institutions are required to tell FINCen (whose data banks are available to law enforcement) when they are suspicious; financial institutions are not required to accurately identify crimes. Mere suspicion that a transaction is not what it should be, or is not appropriate, may occasion a SAR. And it is better to be safe, and file, than not to file. But, to be helpful, a SAR should start off articulating why the institution is suspicious – e.g. ice-cream stores don't generate a lot of cash in the wintertime, so if a store is depositing a lot of cash it may not be from the sale of ice-cream. Bankers know why a transaction is aberrant much better than do the police officers who review the SARs (and now, some years after the program started, it is the case that SARs are reviewed). If the banker takes a moment to articulate the reason for the suspicion, he makes his report something of value.

7.1.4 Filing within 30 days

SARs have to be filed within 30 days of an institution being 'suspicious.' That artificial deadline generates a lot of euphemisms about 'suspicion', because institutions investigating a transaction may need more than 30 days to determine what the purpose was of the transaction.

7.1.5 Decision that a transaction is not suspicious

A paper record must also be maintained when the decision is made that a transaction is not suspicious, and an audit trail of who made that decision has to be maintained as well.

7.2 OFAC paperwork

OFAC paperwork is similar in structure. All transactions that the institution engages in have to be screened to be certain that no OFAC-listed entity is a participant in the transaction. If there is a name that comes up, it is called a 'hit'. Records of all OFAC 'hits' on computer screening have to be maintained, as does a paper record of who overrules the hit to permit a transaction to go through. Those records are examined closely by bank regulators during examinations. It is not enough to decide that a transaction should go through; a paper record must be created and maintained justifying the action.

7.2.1 Freezing

When an institution discovers that it has OFAC-list related accounts, it must freeze the funds and notify OFAC.

7.2.2 Contacting OFAC

When there is an OFAC hit, and the institution does not know whether the funds should be blocked or not, it can call or e-mail OFAC at numbers listed on the OFAC website. Although different people have different experiences with OFAC, that organization tries really hard to be 'user friendly'. All communications with OFAC should be kept as part of the records of OFAC compliance.

8 Conclusion

The volume of regulations in the United States is exceedingly large. They are changing all the time, and the possibilities of error are quite high. Observance of the general principles, however, will tend to keep your institution out of trouble.

It is important to bear in mind that the regulators and prosecutors want the law followed; they are not playing games. They will assist if you have questions – hopefully before the transaction at hand has gone through. Use the websites, and call OFAC with questions when you have them.

Addresses

Office of Foreign Assets Control
U.S. Department of the Treasury
Treasury Annex
1500 Pennsylvania Avenue, NW
Washington, DC 20220

SEC Headquarters
Office of Investor Education and Assistance
100 F Street, NE
Washington, DC 20549

**Board of Governors of the Federal
Reserve System**
20th Street and Constitution Avenue NW
Washington, DC 20551

Federal Reserve Bank of New York
33 Liberty Street
New York, NY 10045

Superintendent of Banks
New York State Banking Department
One State Street
New York, NY 10004-1417

Comptroller of the Currency
Administrator of National Banks
Washington, DC 20219

Abbreviations

AML	Anti-Money Laundering
BSA	Bank Secrecy Act
CIP	Customer Identification Program
CTR	Currency Transaction Report
FinCEN	Financial Crimes Enforcement Network
KYC	Know Your Customer
LC	Letter of Credit
OFAC	Office of Foreign Asset Control
SAR	Suspicious Activity Report
SDN	Specially Designated Terrorists
SWIFT	Society for Worldwide Interbank Financial Telecommunication

Nancy J. Carroll is a partner with McCarthy Tétrault LLP's Financial Services Group in Toronto, Canada. Ms Carroll specializes in transactional and regulatory work for Canadian and international financial institutions. She represents banks and insurance companies on significant mergers and acquisitions, divestitures and demutualizations. Ms Carroll advises financial institutions on a broad range of regulatory matters including compliance with anti-money laundering and anti-terrorist financing, privacy, document retention, e-commerce and financial services laws. She advises on the creation and operation of Canadian banks and insurance companies and the establishment and business of Canadian operations for global banks and insurance companies. Ms Carroll has a JD (University of Toronto), MA (Queen's University), and Hons. BA (Mount Allison University).

Barbara McIsaac is a partner with McCarthy Tétrault LLP's Litigation Group in Ottawa, Canada. Ms McIsaac conducts litigation before all Courts in the areas of Commercial Law, Administrative and Public Law and Intellectual Property Law. Ms McIsaac was Senior Counsel to the Somalia Inquiry and is the Senior Counsel for the Government of Canada for the Arar Inquiry. Ms McIsaac is co-author of The Law of Privacy in Canada (Carswell). She was appointed Queen's Counsel in 1990, is a Director of the Advocates' Society, and a member of the Canadian Bar Association and the Carleton County Law Association. Ms McIsaac is a Fellow of the American College of Trial Lawyers. She attended Queen's Law School and was called to the Bar of Ontario in 1975.

Firm's profile

McCarthy Tétrault LLP, Canada's premier law firm, is internationally known for the depth and range of its financial services practice. McCarthy Tétrault has leading expertise in complex inter-national business transactions, banking, insurance, reinsurance, financial institutions regulatory matters, mergers and acquisitions, secured lending, project finance and securitizations. McCarthy Tétrault delivers integrated business law, tax, real property, employment and litigation services nationally and globally through eight offices across Canada and in London, UK.

www.mccarthy.ca

Canada

Nancy Carroll and Barbara McIsaac

Partners

McCarthy Tétrault LLP
Suite 4700
Toronto Dominion Bank Tower
Toronto, Ontario, Canada
M5K 1E6

Tel (416) 601-7733
Fax (416) 868-0673
ncarroll@mccarthy.ca
www.mccarthy.ca

McCarthy Tétrault LLP
The Chambers Suite 1400
40 Elgin Street
Ottawa, Ontario, Canada
K1P 5K6

Tel (613) 238-2105
Fax (613) 563-9386
bmcisaac@mccarthy.ca
www.mccarthy.ca

Anti-Money Laundering: International Law and Practice.
Edited by W.H. Muller, C.H. Kälin and J.G. Goldsworth
© 2007 John Wiley & Sons, Ltd

Contents – Canada

1   Introduction

Canada has implemented a comprehensive national initiative to combat money laundering and terrorist financing. The *Proceeds of Crime (Money Laundering) and Terrorist Financing Act* (*Act*) provides the legislative framework to deter and detect money laundering and terrorist financing activities in Canada. The *Act* sets out reporting and record-keeping requirements for suspicious transactions, large cash transactions, international electronic funds transfers and terrorist property. The *Act* also establishes requirements for client identification, retention of records and implementation of a compliance regime by financial entities and other reporting persons.

Canada's financial intelligence unit, the *Financial Transactions and Reports Analysis Centre of Canada* (*FINTRAC*), was created under the *Act* as an independent agency of the federal government. *FINTRAC*'s mandate is to collect, analyze and assess information related to money laundering and terrorist financing activities and to disclose certain information to law enforcement and intelligence agencies to assist in the detection, prevention and deterrence of these criminal activities.

2   Criminal Code

2.1   Money laundering

Money laundering is an offence under the *Criminal Code* in Canada. It is an offence to use, transfer the possession of, send or deliver to any person or place, transport, transmit, alter, dispose of or otherwise deal with in any manner any property or proceeds of property with the intent to conceal or convert such property or proceeds, knowing or believing that all or a part of such property or proceeds was obtained directly or indirectly as a result of the commission in Canada of a terrorism offence or an act[1] or omission outside Canada that, had it occurred in Canada, would have constituted a terrorism offence. The *Criminal Code* authorizes law enforcement agencies to search, seize and restrain property that is believed to be the proceeds of crime.

2.2   Terrorist activity

The *Criminal Code* defines '**terrorist activity**' as an action, either within or outside Canada, that:

- is an offence under one of the UN anti-terrorism conventions and protocols; or

- is taken for political, religious or ideological purposes with the intention of intimidating the public with regard to its security including economic security; or

- compels a government or person to do something, by intentionally killing, seriously harming or endangering a person, causing serious risk to public health and safety, causing substantial property damage that is likely to seriously harm people or by seriously interfering with or disrupting an essential service, facility or system.

It is an **offence** under the *Criminal Code* to knowingly:

- collect or provide funds, directly or indirectly, to carry out terrorist activities;

---

[1] See s.83.02 of the *Criminal Code of Canada*.

- participate in, contribute to or facilitate the activities of a terrorist group;

- instruct anyone to carry out a terrorist activity on behalf of a terrorist group;

- harbor or conceal a terrorist;

- collect, provide, use, possess, or make available property or financial or other related services for the purpose of facilitating a terrorist activity or for the benefit of a terrorist group;

- deal in any property that is owned or controlled by or on behalf of a terrorist group, or to enter into any such transaction; or

- provide any financial or other service in respect of such property for the benefit of a terrorist group.

A list of terrorist groups is published in the *Regulations Establishing a List of Entities* made under the *Criminal Code* (**Listed Entities**). The *Criminal Code* requires anyone in Canada and any Canadian outside Canada to disclose to the *Royal Canadian Mounted Police* (*RCMP*) and the *Canadian Security Intelligence Service* (*CSIS*) the existence of any property in their possession or control they know is owned or controlled by or on behalf of a terrorist group.

Financial institutions, including authorized foreign banks (in respect of their business in Canada), also have an obligation to report monthly to their regulator, the *Office of the Superintendent of Financial Institutions* (*OSFI*), if they are in possession or control of property that is owned or controlled by a listed entity. An institution that reports having such property in its possession or control is immune from criminal or civil proceedings for having made such a report. Failure to do so is an offence punishable by up to 10 years in prison.

3 United Nations conventions and resolutions

3.1 United Nations Act

The *United Nations Act* ('*UN Act*') provides a vehicle by which orders and measures taken by the *United Nations* can be implemented in Canadian domestic law. The *UN Act* permits the executive branch of the Canadian Government to make any orders or regulations it deems necessary to give proper effect to *United Nations* conventions and resolutions.

Canada supports the work of the *United Nations* in the global fight against money laundering and terrorist financing, including the *United Nations Suppression of Terrorism Resolutions*. The *Government of Canada* has signed and ratified all *UN Conventions* and *Protocols* relating to money laundering and terrorist financing and has taken steps to give effect to such conventions and resolutions in Canadian law.

3.2 Regulations establishing lists of terrorists

Like the *Regulations Establishing a List of Entities* under the *Criminal Code*, Canada's *Regulations Implementing the United Nations Resolution on the Suppression of Terrorism* and the *United Nations Al-Qaida and Taliban Regulations* also provide for lists of individuals and entities believed to be involved in or associated with terrorist activity **(Listed Entity)**. It is an offence for anyone in Canada, or any Canadian outside Canada, to provide or collect funds if they know these would be for use by anyone on such lists. It is an offence for anyone in Canada, or any Canadian outside Canada, to deal in any way with property if they know it is **owned** or **controlled** by anyone on such lists. Canadian financial institutions are required to determine on a continuing basis whether they are in **possession** or **control** of property **owned** or **controlled** by or on behalf of anyone on such lists, and to report monthly to *OSFI* if they are in **possession** or **control** of such property. In addition, anyone in Canada and any Canadian outside Canada is required to disclose to *FINTRAC*, the *RCMP* and the *CSIS* the existence of any property in their **possession** or **control** they believe is **owned** or **controlled** by or on behalf of anyone on such lists.

4 Proceeds of Crime (Money Laundering) and Terrorist Financing Act overview

4.1 Purposes

The purposes of the *Act* are to:

- Implement specific record-keeping and reporting measures to detect and deter organized criminal money laundering activities and financing of terrorist activities.

- Facilitate the investigation and prosecution of money laundering and terrorist financing offences in Canada and by Canadians outside Canada.

- Meet Canada's international commitments to fight multinational crime and terrorism.

4.2 Content of the Act

Part 1 of the *Act* requires **financial entities** and others to comply with customer **identification, due diligence** and **record-keeping** standards and to report **suspicious** and **prescribed** transactions relevant to the identification of money laundering, terrorist financing and the possession of terrorist property. Part 2 of the *Act* is administered by the *Canada Border Services Agency* (*CBSA*) and requires the reporting of the importation and exportation of cash and monetary instruments. Part 3 of the *Act* established *FINTRAC* as Canada's financial intelligence unit to receive reports from reporting entities, analyze those reports for information relevant to money laundering and terrorist financing, and provide identifying information about the account holder, transaction amount and date to Canadian law enforcement agencies such as the *RCMP* and to other agencies including *CSIS*, *CBSA* and *Canada Revenue Agency* (*CRA*) in specific circumstances. The administrative detail for compliance with the *Act* is set out in *Regulations* made pursuant to the *Act*.

---

[2] On October 5, 2006 the Canadian Government introduced Bill C-25 in Parliament. The Bill, which is expected to become law in 2007, will make a number of amendments to the Act. The Bill received Royal Assent on December 14, 2006 but requires an order of the Governor in Council before it becomes law. The proposed amendments include measures to enhance information sharing between FINTRAC, law enforcement and other domestic and international agencies as well as measures to create a registration regime for money services businesses, to enable enhanced client identification measures and to implement an administrative and monetary penalties' regime to better enforce compliance.

4.3 Reporting entities under the *Act*

The *Act* places reporting requirements on the following entities:

- financial entities including banks, credit unions and caisses populaires, trust and loan companies;
- crown corporations that take deposits;
- life insurance companies, brokers and agents;
- securities dealers, portfolio managers and investment counselors;
- money services businesses;
- foreign exchange dealers;
- accountants and accounting firms;
- real estate brokers and sale representatives;
- casinos;
- individuals or entities transferring large amounts of currency or monetary instruments into or out of Canada.

Originally the *Act* was intended to also impose reporting requirements on lawyers and notaries. The *Canadian Government*, however, repealed the *Act*'s application to the legal profession following a constitutional challenge by the *Federation of Law Societies of Canada* (*Federation*) to the application of the *Act* and *Regulations* to the legal profession. The *Federation* has endorsed a model rule prohibiting lawyers and law firms from accepting more than CDN$7500 in cash in a single matter with limited exceptions. The *Canadian Government* has indicated that it intends to amend the *Act* to provide for a regulatory regime for the legal profession that better takes into account the duties of client confidentiality and solicitor–client privilege, thereby closing what has been identified as significant gap in Canada's anti-money laundering and anti-terrorist financing regime.

4.4 What must be reported

Reporting entities are required to report the following:

- Suspicious transactions where there are reasonable grounds to suspect that the transactions are related to the commission of a money laundering or terrorist financing offence.
- Possession or control of terrorist-owned or controlled property.
- International electronic funds transfers of CDN$10 000 or more.
- Large cash transactions of CDN$10 000 or more.
- Cross-border currency transfers of CDN$10 000 or more.
- Customs seizure reports.

When they submit suspicious transaction and other financial transaction reports and terrorist property reports to *FINTRAC* in good faith, reporting entities are protected from criminal and civil legal proceedings.

4.5 Record keeping and client identification obligations

4.5.1 Requirements for financial entities

Financial entities including banks, credit unions, caisses populaires and trust and loan companies, are required to comply with specific requirements with respect to identifying the parties with whom they conduct transactions and to keep certain records after conducting specified transactions. These requirements include the following:

- When conducting a large cash transaction, requirements to keep large cash transaction records, identify clients, determine whether the person providing the cash to the financial entity is acting on the instructions of a third party and keep records related to the third party.

- When opening an account, requirements to keep specified account opening records, identify clients and determine whether the account is to be used by or on behalf of a third party who will give instructions to deal with the funds in the account.

- When creating account operating agreements, debit or credit memos, client credit files, and operating accounts, requirements to keep certain records and client statements.

- When conducting electronic funds transfers of CDN$3000 or more, requirements to identify the client.

- When conducting foreign exchange transactions, requirements to identify the client and keep foreign exchange transaction tickets.

- When conducting certain transactions of CDN$3000 or more with non-account holders, requirements to identify the individual and keep records.

4.5.2 Requirements for trust companies

In addition to the requirements set out above, trust companies are required to keep copies of trust deeds and records of the settlor's name, address and principal business or occupation.

4.5.3 Requirements for life insurance companies, brokers and agents

Life insurance companies, brokers and agents, when conducting a large cash transaction, are required to keep a large cash transaction record, identify the individual giving them the cash, determine whether the individual giving them the cash is acting on the instructions of a third party and keep records of information relating to the third party. When a client pays a life insurance company, agent or broker CDN$10 000 or more, whether or not in cash, for an annuity or other life insurance policy, the life insurance company, agent or broker is required to keep a client information record, identify the client, determine whether the client is acting on the instructions of a third party and if so keep records of information relating to the third party.

4.6 Penalties for non-compliance

The *Act* provides for a maximum fine of CDN$2 million and a maximum jail term of 5 years for failure to report a suspicious transaction, and a maximum fine of CDN$1 million for failure to report a prescribed transaction.

5 Proposed far-reaching amendments to the *Act*

5.1 Proposed amendments

The *Act* provides for a review of anti-money laundering and terrorist financing legislation after being in force for its initial period of 5 years, and amendments are expected to provide for an ongoing Parliamentary review every 5 years. To keep pace with evolving international standards set by *FATF*, to address recommendations in the *2004 Report of the Auditor General of Canada* and to address concerns of law enforcement and security agencies, in June 2005, the *Department of Finance* published a *Consultation Paper* entitled *Enhancing Canada's Anti-Money Laundering and Anti-Terrorist Financing Regime,* outlining proposed changes to the *Act*. Key proposals in the *Consultation Paper* include:

- expanding client identification, due diligence and record-keeping requirements;
- introducing requirements to report suspicious attempted transactions;
- providing for information sharing to detect and deter terrorist financing through charities;
- improving compliance, monitoring and enforcement, including the establishment of a registration regime for money services businesses and creating an administrative and monetary penalty regime to promote compliance with statutory requirements;
- strengthening *FINTRAC*'s ability to provide intelligence;
- enhancing coordination of Canada's efforts to combat money laundering and terrorist financing.

The Canadian Government introduced legislation in 2006 to amend the *Act* to largely implement the proposals in the *Consultation Paper*. This legislation, Bill C-25, is expected to become law in 2007.

5.2 Balancing law enforcement objectives with privacy rights

Privacy safeguards on Canada's anti-money laundering and anti-terrorist financing regime include:

- The independence of *FINTRAC* from law enforcement and other agencies to which *FINTRAC* discloses information.
- Criminal penalties for any unauthorized use or disclosure of personal information under *FINTRAC*'s control.
- The requirement for law enforcement and security agencies to obtain a court order to obtain further information from *FINTRAC* beyond the limited information specified in the *Act*.
- The application of the *Privacy Act* to *FINTRAC*.

Canada's regime to detect and deter money laundering and terrorist financing seeks to strike a balance among the following objectives:

- strengthening law enforcement;
- protecting the privacy of personal information as provided in the *Personal Information Protection and Electronic Documents Act* and protect privacy rights under the *Canadian Charter of Rights and Freedoms*;
- supporting international efforts to combat money laundering and terrorist financing.

With the proposed changes to the *Act*, the balance appears to be shifting to give greater weight to strengthening law enforcement in Canada and internationally.

6 Supervision of anti-money laundering and anti-terrorist financing compliance regime

Several government departments and agencies are directly involved in Canada's national initiative to combat money laundering and terrorist financing.

6.1 Financial Transactions and Reports Analysis Centre of Canada (*FINTRAC*)

The *Financial Transactions and Reports Analysis Centre of Canada* (*FINTRAC*) is Canada's financial intelligence unit. *FINTRAC* is an independent Canadian government agency that operates at arm's length from Canadian law enforcement agencies. *FINTRAC* collects information from financial entities, financial intelligence units of other countries, law enforcement agencies and government institutions and agencies. *FINTRAC* is responsible for ensuring that financial entities and other reporting entities comply with the reporting, record-keeping and client identification requirements of the *Act* and *Regulations*.

FINTRAC analyzes the data it receives and discloses information to law enforcement agencies to help detect, prevent and deter money laundering and the financing of terrorist activities in Canada and internationally.

FINTRAC discloses information to the *RCMP* and provincial local law enforcement agencies. *FINTRAC* may only disclose information to law enforcement agencies when *FINTRAC* determines there are reasonable grounds to suspect that the information would be relevant to investigating or prosecuting a money laundering or terrorist activity financing offence. In such cases *FINTRAC* discloses only designated information to law enforcement agencies, limited to key identifying information such as name, address, date of birth and citizenship, and certain information about the transaction such as the name and address of the place of business where the transaction occurred, the date of the transaction, the amount and type of currency or value of funds and account number. Law enforcement agencies are required to obtain a court order if they seek to obtain additional information from *FINTRAC*.

The *2004 Report of the Auditor General* noted that disclosures by *FINTRAC* to law enforcement and security agencies may contribute to ongoing investigations. However, given their existing case loads and limited resources, law enforcement and security agencies normally find the information *FINTRAC* discloses is too limited to generate new investigations. The *Auditor General* recommended that the Government broaden the kinds of information *FINTRAC* may disclose, within limits that respect the privacy rights of Canadians.

Once *FINTRAC* has determined that it has information relevant to investigating or prosecuting a money laundering or terrorist activity financing offence, *FINTRAC* may disclose certain information to the following agencies and departments:

- *Canada Revenue Agency*, when *FINTRAC* also determines that the information is relevant to a tax or duty evasion offence.

- *Department of Citizenship and Immigration*, when *FINTRAC* also determines that the information would, pursuant to the *Immigration and Refugee Protection Act*, promote international order and justice by denying the use of Canadian territory to persons who are likely to engage in a criminal activity.

- Foreign agencies or financial intelligence units with mandates similar to *FINTRAC*'s and with which *FINTRAC* has entered into agreements to exchange information.

If *FINTRAC* determines there are reasonable grounds to suspect that information it has would be relevant to threats to Canadian security, *FINTRAC* may disclose designated information to the *Canadian Security Intelligence Service* (*CSIS*). *CSIS* is required to obtain a court order if it seeks to obtain additional information from *FINTRAC* beyond key identifying information.

6.2 Office of the Superintendent of Financial Institutions

The *Office of the Superintendent of Financial Institutions* (*OSFI*) works closely with *FINTRAC* to ensure compliance with the *Act* and *Regulations* by all federally regulated financial institutions including banks, insurance companies and trust and loan companies for which *OSFI* has oversight responsibility. *OSFI*'s *Guideline No. B-8 Deterring and Detecting Money Laundering and Terrorist Financing* identifies the steps Canadian federally regulated financial institutions should take to comply with legal requirements to deter and detect money laundering and terrorist financing and to minimize the possibility that financial institutions could become a party to such activities. For example, the boards of directors and management of federally regulated financial institutions are responsible for the design, development, documentation, approval, implementation and ongoing review of specific policies and procedures to detect and deter money laundering and terrorist financing activities and to demonstrate to *OSFI* that they have implemented appropriate policies and that their staff are applying them as intended. Each federally regulated financial institution is required to designate an officer responsible for corporate-wide measures for the financial institution and all of its Canadian and foreign subsidiaries and branches to combat money laundering and terrorist financing. The officer is required to report directly to senior management and the board of directors on a regular basis. Financial institutions are required to establish internal compliance reporting processes to demonstrate compliance with all legal requirements, an annual self-assessment program, and a system of independent procedures testing. Emphasis is placed on ensuring that front-line employees are given sufficient training to recognize money laundering and terrorist financing activities, and to understand and properly apply the financial institution's policies and procedures to deter and detect money laundering and terrorist financing.

The provincial regulatory bodies that have oversight responsibility for provincially regulated financial services providers are also involved in anti-money laundering and anti-terrorist financing initiatives.

6.3 Department of Finance Canada

The *Department of Finance* is responsible for leading and coordinating Canada's anti-money laundering and anti-terrorist financing initiatives, including heading the Canadian delegation to the *Financial Action Task Force* (*FATF*). The Department is also responsible for the *Act* and *Regulations* and has published a *Consultation Paper* recommending a significant updating of Canada's legislation which is expected to be implemented in 2007. The Minister of Finance is responsible for *FINTRAC* and *OSFI* and for evaluating Canada's initiatives in detecting and deterring money laundering and terrorist financing.

6.4 Solicitor General of Canada

The *Solicitor General of Canada* plays a national role in coordinating efforts to combat organized crime and monitors how the *RCMP* and *CSIS* respond to *FINTRAC* disclosures relating to money laundering, terrorist financing and national security.

6.5 The Royal Canadian Mounted Police

The *RCMP Integrated Proceeds of Crime Unit* (*IPOC*) receives and acts on information prepared by *FINTRAC*. The purpose of *IPOC* is to effectively investigate and prosecute criminals and major organized crime groups operating in Canada. In addition to disclosures from FINTRAC, the *RCMP* also receive money laundering and terrorist financing intelligence in relation to cross-border currency reporting incidents from *CBSA* and from other law enforcement agencies. Upon receipt of each intelligence, the *RCMP* does an assessment to determine if a criminal investigation is warranted.

In addition to the RCMP, provincial and municipal law enforcement agencies in Canada also play a critical role in enforcing Canada's laws against money laundering and terrorist financing.

6.6 Canadian Security Intelligence Service

The *Canadian Security Intelligence Service* (CSIS) plays a leading role in investigating and reporting on threats to Canada's national security, including terrorist threats. *CSIS* receives and acts on information prepared by *FINTRAC*.

6.7 Canada Border Services Agency

Part 2 of the *Act* which requires the reporting of the importation or exportation of cash or monetary instruments is administered by the *Canada Border Services Agency* (*CBSA*). The *Act* and *Regulations* require persons to report to Canadian customs officers the importation and exportation of currency and monetary instruments in amounts of CDN$10 000 or more brought across borders by the importer or exporter himself or herself or imported or exported by mail, courier or any other means. These reports are forwarded to *FINTRAC*.

The *CBSA*'s customs officers also examine baggage, question and search individuals for unreported or falsely reported currency and monetary instruments. When a customs officer suspects on reasonable grounds that currency and monetary instruments may be proceeds of crime or terrorist financing, they may seize the currency or monetary instruments and alert the *RCMP*.

6.8 Canada Revenue Agency

If *FINTRAC* discloses information suspected of being relevant to the investigation or prosecution of a money laundering or terrorist financing offence to the *RCMP* and also determines that the information is relevant to an offence of evading or attempting to evade paying taxes or duties, *FINTRAC* will disclose the information to *Canada Revenue Agency* (*CRA*) taxation investigators, as well.

6.9   Citizenship and Immigration Canada

Citizenship and Immigration Canada (*CIC*) may deny entry into Canada to non-citizens who pose a security threat to Canada. *FINTRAC* discloses information to *CIC* to assist in assessing non-citizens for admission into Canada under the *Immigration and Refugee Protection Act*.

6.10   Department of Justice

The *Department of Justice* Canada prosecutes money laundering and terrorist financing offences under the *Criminal Code* and offences under the *Act* and *Regulations* for failure to report suspicious transactions.

6.11   Attorney General

The *Attorney General* seeks court orders for disclosure of additional information from *FINTRAC* to the *RCMP* and *CSIS* where warranted.

6.12   Public Safety and Emergency Preparedness Canada

Public Safety and Emergency Preparedness Canada plays a leadership role under Canada's *National Agenda to Combat Organized Crime*, in coordinating the development of policies to counter money laundering and terrorist financing, and in monitoring the activities of the *RCMP*, *CSIS* and *CBSA*.

7   International cooperation

7.1   Financial Action Task Force

Canada seeks to consistently be at the forefront of global efforts to combat money laundering and international terrorist financing. As a founding member of the *Financial Action Task Force* (*FATF*), the international standard-setting body, Canada's proposed legislative amendments are aimed in part at implementing *FATF*'s revised *Forty Recommendations* and *Nine Special Recommendations* to combat money laundering and terrorist financing. Canada is currently chairing *FATF* for a one-year period which commenced 1 July 2006.

7.2   Egmont Group

As Canada's financial intelligence unit (*FIU*), *FINTRAC* is a member of the *Egmont Group*, the group of FIUs which meets regularly to cooperate on information exchange, training, and development of expertise and best practices in combating money laundering and terrorist financing globally. The permanent Secretariat of the *Egmont Group* is located in Toronto, Canada.

Abbreviations

Act	*Proceeds of Crime (Money Laundering) and Terrorist Financing Act*
CBSA	Canada Border Services Agency
CIC	Citizenship and Immigration Canada

CRA	Canada Revenue Agency
CSIS	Canadian Security Intelligence Service
FATF	Financial Action Task Force
Federation	*Federation of Law Societies of Canada*
FINTRAC	Financial Transactions and Reports Analysis Centre of Canada
FIU	financial intelligence unit
IPOC	RCMP Integrated Proceeds of Crime Unit
OSFI	Office of the Superintendent of Financial Institutions
RCMP	Royal Canadian Mounted Police
Regulations	*Regulations* pursuant to the *Act* including: *Cross-border Currency and Monetary Instruments Reporting Regulations*; *Proceeds of Crime (Money Laundering) and Terrorist Financing Suspicious Transaction Reporting Regulations*; *Proceeds of Crime (Money Laundering) and Terrorist Financing Regulations*, *Regulations Implementing the United Nations Resolutions on the Suppression of Terrorism*; *United Nations Al-Qaida and Taliban Regulations*; and the following *Regulations* pursuant to the *Criminal Code: Regulations Establishing a List of Entities.*

Bibliography

About Business Crime Solutions Inc.: The National Initiative to Combat Money Laundering: Year Three Evaluation, Toronto, 14 February 2003.

Department of Finance Canada: Enhancing Canada's Anti-Money Laundering and Anti-Terrorist Financing Regime Consultation Paper, Ottawa, June 2005, www.fin.gc.ca.

Ekos Research Associates Inc.: Year Five Evaluation of the National Initiatives to Combat Money Laundering and Interim Evaluation of Measures to Combat Terrorist Financing Final Report Submitted to Finance Canada, 30 November 2004.

Financial Transactions and Reports Analysis Centre of Canada: FINTRAC's Guidelines, Ottawa, updated 2006, www.fintrac.gc.ca.

Office of the Superintendent of Financial Institutions: Guideline B-8 Deterring and Detecting Money Laundering and Terrorist Financing, Ottawa, revised November 2004, www.osfi-bsif.gc.ca.

Office of the Auditor General of Canada: Report of the Auditor General of Canada to the House of Commons, Chapter 2, Implementation of the National Initiative to Combat Money Laundering, Ottawa, November 2004, www.oag-bvg.gc.ca.

Ricardo M. Alba, a citizen of Panama, studied Economics, Statistics and Banking and has participated actively in implementation of legal and professional rules regarding money laundering, tax evasion and other economic crimes. Mr Alba has written extensively on the defense of international services of Panama and particularly on the prevention, control and repression of money laundering, in articles, books and interviews in specialized publications. He has delivered lectures, seminars and technical advice in those fields to financial institutions and authorities of several countries including Panama, the United States and other countries in Europe, South America and the Caribbean and is a member of professional associations related to the prevention and control of money laundering in several countries. In 1985 he was awarded the Presidential Order of the Panama's Banking Association and in 2001 the Order of Manuel Amador Guerrero by the Government of the Republic of Panama.

Eloy Alfaro de Alba is a citizen of Panama and a graduate of Columbia College (BA 1969), Columbia University School of Law (J.D. 1972) and Columbia University School of Business (MBA 1974). A partner at the law firm of Tapia, Linares & Alfaro in Panama, he served as President of the Banking Law Association of Panama (1984–1986) and of the International Lawyers Association (founding President 1994–1996). He was appointed to the High Level Presidential Commission for Policy Against Money Laundering in 1994 and participated in drafting legislation to prevent money laundering. From 1997 to 1999 he served as Ambassador of Panama to the White House and is currently serving on the Board of Directors of the Panama Canal Authority.

Firm's profile

The law firm, **Tapia, Linares & Alfaro**, founded in 1949, has an extensive practice in advising banking, shipping and commercial clients, in a wide field of legal endeavors including corporation, trust and foundations, off-shore corporation registration and management, ship registration and financing, admiralty, banking and insurance, mergers and acquisitions, securities transactions and litigation. talial@talial.com

www.talial.com

Panama

Ricardo Manuel Alba

Partner

P.O. Box 0819-08907
Panama, Republic of Panama

Tel +507 260 5427
rmalba@pty.com

Eloy Alfaro de Alba

Tapia, Linares & Alfaro
P.O. Box 0816-02984
Plaza 2000 Building
Avenue Gral. Nicanor A.
de Obarrio (50th street)
Panama, Republic of Panama

Tel +507 263 6066
Fax +507 263 5305
ealfaro@talial.com
www.talial.com

Anti-Money Laundering: International Law and Practice.
Edited by W.H. Muller, C.H. Kälin and J.G. Goldsworth
© 2007 John Wiley & Sons, Ltd

Contents – Panama

1   Introduction

The Republic of Panama adopted since 1984 legislation, both in acts and ordinances, to prevent, control and repress the laundering of money or capital, covering the following aspects:

- Money laundering from drug trafficking is typified as a crime.
- Money laundering is extended to cover other underlying crimes.
- International character of drug and money laundering crimes.
- Precise identification of individuals and owners of juridical entities.
- International judicial cooperation.
- 'Due diligence' is established as a legal obligation and is regulated.
- Obligation to exert 'due diligence' is extended by law and regulations to financial activities, to certain non-financial activities, and to commercial activities.
- Supervisory and control organisms are established for entities subject to application of due diligence.
- Administrative responsibility of juridical persons.
- Intervention of accounts.
- Provisional seizure of assets.
- Confiscation of assets.
- Agreements for international distribution of confiscated assets.
- Corporate responsibility.
- Adoption of prevention programs.
- New dimensions of 'know your client' requirement.
- Conservations of books and records on transactions and clients.
- Reporting cash and monetary instrument transactions to authorities.
- Recording and reporting suspicious transactions to authorities.
- Legal protection to institutions reporting suspicious transactions.
- Establishment of financial intelligence unit.
- International exchange of information among Financial Intelligence Units.
- Limitations to bank secrecy, reserve or confidentiality.
- Undercover operations.
- Simulated drug deliveries.
- Reversal of the burden of proof in laundering of assets from drug trafficking.

- Reduction of sanctions for cooperation with authorities.

- Declaration of cash and securities upon entering the national territory.

The basic elements of Panama laws and regulations applicable to money laundering and to terrorism financing are described hereunder.

2 Legislation for the prevention, control and repression of money laundering and terrorism financing

2.1 Act 23 of 1986–13 of 1994

- Definition of 'drug' (Art. 3).

- Extra-territorial nature of drug crimes (Art. 7).

- Seizure of instruments, securities and assets used in drug crimes (Art. 9).

- Definition of 'transactions' (Art. 14).

- Obligation to maintain confidentiality until judgment is final (Art. 19).

- Undercover operations by the Department of the Public Prosecutor (Art. 25).

- Filming and recording telephone conversations and communications (Art. 26).

- Reduction of sanctions for cooperating with authorities (Art. 28).

- Provisional seizure of instruments, securities and assets (Art. 29).

- Place to maintain on deposit monies, securities and assets (Art. 30).

- Compensation of credits with seized monies, securities and assets (Art. 30).

- Reversal of burden of proof (Art. 32).

- Confiscation of instruments, securities or assets (Art. 35).

2.2 Cabinet Ordinance No.10 of 1994

Every person entering the national territory must complete and submit a declaration of cash, under oath, providing information relative to the cash and cash equivalent assets being brought with him into the country (Art. 1).

2.3 Executive Ordinance No. 16 of 1994

Every person who enters the national territory must submit a declaration of cash or other assets convertible into cash being carried into the country in excess of US$10 000 (Art. 2).

2.4 Executive Ordinance No. 468 of 1994

The ordinance establishes responsibility of the resident agent of a corporation (Art. 1). Resident agents are required to know their clients, to obtain from them and maintain sufficient information to identify clients; in the case of drug traffic and money laundering crimes, to provide authorities upon request (through proceedings that must be initiated in Panama or under Legal Mutual Assistance Treaties) information relative to identity of clients. Pursuant to the ordinance, information provided by resident agents under the ordinance does not constitute violation of professional secrecy or ethics.

2.5 Executive Ordinance No. 136 of 9 June 1995

The Financial Analysis Unit for the Prevention of the Crime of Laundering Money Produced by Drug Traffic, was created as a financial intelligence unit under the Public Security and National Defense Council.

2.6 Act No. 41 of 2 October 2000

- Defines the crime of money laundering as the receipt, negotiation, conversion or transfer of moneys, titles, securities, assets and other financial resources with knowledge that they are the product of activities related to drug trafficking, qualified embezzlement, traffic of human beings, traffic of illegal weapons, kidnapping, extortion, embezzlement, corruption of civil servants, robbery, international vehicle contraband, acts of terrorism and acts against intellectual property (Art. 3).

- Defines qualified embezzlement as the crime committed by whoever through deceit obtains for himself or for a third party illicit gains injuring another, and sanctions it with prison from 1 to 4 years and 50 to 200 days fine (Art. 2).

- Establishes concealment, transactions in banking establishments and other financial institutions, providing false information, use of function or position to facilitate the crime, the use of illicit proceeds for political campaigns and the alteration or destruction of evidence of crimes as crimes concomitant to Money laundering (Art. 3).

- More directly with reference to professionals in banking and other occupations, includes among money laundering activities the 'use of their functions, positions, employment, office or profession to authorize or permit the laundering of capitals', providing for a sanction of imprisonment for 3 to 8 year terms.

- Money laundering and concomitant crimes are subject to sanctions of imprisonment and day-fines (Art. 3).

- Capitals of illegal origin are subject to seizure and confiscation (Art. 5).

- A Special Fund for Retirees and Pensioners is created as destination for confiscated funds, except in case of funds originating in drug crimes (Art. 7).

2.7 Act 50 of 2 July 2003

The law act defines crimes of terrorism and financing of terrorism rendering them autonomous crimes under Panamanian law.

3   Provisions for regulated activities

3.1   Act No. 42 of 2 October 2000 'which provides measures for the prevention of the crime of money laundering'

- Banks, fiduciary enterprises, currency exchange or transfer houses or individuals, financiers, savings and loans associations, stock exchanges, stock centers, stock clearing houses, stock brokers and investment administrators are 'obligated to maintain due diligence and care' (Art. 1).

- Those persons are subject to the obligations of maintaining adequate client identification, filing periodic reports to the Financial Analysis Unit through their respective supervision and control entities, carefully examining transactions that may be linked to money laundering and reporting them to the Financial Analysis Unit, establishing internal procedures to prevent the crime and training their staff in such procedures, and maintaining documents and records of their operations for a minimum period of five years (Art. 1).

- Obligated persons and supervision and control organizations are authorized to provide to the Financial Analysis Unit information related to the crime whenever requested to do so by that entity (Art. 2).

- Obligated persons as well as their directors or officials are exempted from civil or criminal liability for providing information to the Financial Analysis Unit or to the authorities (Art. 3).

- Public officials are subject to the obligation of maintaining confidentiality of information they receive from obligated persons, and are subject to sanctions for violation thereof (Art. 4)

- Supervision and control organizations are authorized to supervise compliance with prevention and control procedures established by the respective obligated persons (Art. 5).

- 'Informing entities' such as companies operating in the Colon Free Zone, other free zones and processing zones, the National Lottery of Beneficence, Casinos and other gambling establishments, Real Estate promoters and brokers, Insurance and Re-insurance companies and Insurance Brokers are obligated to render periodic reports on cash and near cash transactions to the Financial Analysis Unit (Art. 7).

- Supervision and control organizations, ex-officio or at the request of the Financial Analysis Unit, are authorized to impose fines varying from US$5000 to US$1 000 000 for failure to comply with the applicable laws and regulations and establishes a Financial Analysis Unit account as depository destination for those funds (Art. 8).

- A juridical entities is imputed with responsibility for acts of its officers and directors acting on its behalf (Art. 8).

- The immobilization of securities is required as a prerequisite for security transactions in an organized public market (Art. 9).

3.2   Agreement No. 9-2000 of the Superintendence of Banks of October 23, 2000, on the Prevention of Unlawful Use of Banking Services

- Banks are required to maintain proper client identification both in their data and filing systems.

- The notion of client includes individuals and legal entities, regardless of whether they are direct or indirect clients.

146

- Inter-banking operations are exempted from the application of the Agreement.
- Identification of clients, whether individuals or legal entities must be made pursuant to precise criteria.
- Banks must also file reports on cash and near cash transactions pursuant to specific criteria.
- Banks are obligated to maintaining under confidentiality information on the identity of beneficial owners of accounts.
- Successive transactions in proximate dates must be recognized pursuant to criteria provided by the Agreement.
- For purposes of the Agreement, the concept of a 'bank' is defined as the set of branches of a bank establishment that operates in the Republic of Panama.
- Banks are obligated to identify investors, agents and security intermediaries.
- Banks are required to establish a 'profile' of clients with a contractual business relationship in excess of Ten Thousand US Dollars (US$10 000.00).
- Banks are required to maintain, and periodically up-date, a manual on the policy of 'know your client'.
- Banks are also required to maintain transaction documents during a minimum period of five (5) years, counted from the end of its business relationship with the client.
- Suspicious transactions must be identified, recorded and reported pursuant to criteria provided by the Agreement, which also provides examples of suspicious transactions.
- The Superintendence of Banks is authorized to report to the Financial Analysis Unit suspicious transactions of which it becomes aware during inspections to banks.
- Having provided notice to the Financial Analysis Unit of a suspicious transaction, a Bank is prohibited from closing the account until three (3) months have lapsed since the date of the corresponding notice to said unit.
- Banks are obligated to train their staff against the unlawful use of banking services.
- Failure to comply with the provisions of the agreement and failure to comply with the instructions of the Superintendence are subject to sanctions.

3.3 Agreement No. 10-2000 of the Superintendence of Banks of December 15, 2000, on Compliance Officers

- All banks must maintain compliance programs pursuant to guidelines provided by the agreement.
- Banks are obligated to appoint a 'compliance officer' whose professional requirements, general responsibilities, administrative location and field of competence, and specific functions are provided by the agreement.
- Every bank employee is allowed to inform the compliance officer of irregularities in compliance with laws and regulations.
- Banks must inform the Superintendence of Banks of the appointment and replacement of compliance officers.
- Compliance officers are required to provide evaluations on compliance to bank management.

3.4 **Agreement 1-2005 of February 3, 2005 of the National Securities Commission** by means of which new provisions are adopted with reference to obligated persons (self-regulated organizations, security houses, security brokers, and investment administrators) to prevent the use of their services for money laundering and financing of terrorism, and to facilitate the flow of information to authorities with respect to presumed criminals and funds of unlawful origin

3.5 **Agreement 12-2005 of December 14, 2005 of the Superintendence of Banks, by means of which Agreement 9-200 is updated and amended,** with the following content

- Every bank and trust services provider is required to comply with provisions contained in laws and regulations related to the prevention of money laundering and financing of terrorism (Art. 1).

- A client of a bank or trust services provider is defined as the individual or legal entity with a contractual business or trust relationship with the bank or trust services provider (Art. 2).

- Inter-bank operations of banks located in Panama with banks located abroad are subject to the provisions of the Agreement (Art. 3).

- The concept of due diligence is extended to apply to bank clients and to their resources (Art. 4).

- And the concept of due diligence is made applicable to clients of fiduciary enterprises and to their resources (Art. 5).

- All banks and trust services providers must report to the authorities all transactions in cash and monetary instruments in excess of US$10 000 (Art. 6).

- All banks and trust services providers must maintain for at least five years files of reports and other documents and records related to their relationship with clients (Art. 7).

- All banks and trust services providers are required to have a manual on 'know your client' policies and procedures (Art. 8).

- All banks and trust services providers must select and supervise carefully all employees, particularly those in charge of cash transactions and direct relationship with clients (Art. 9).

- All banks and trust services providers must record all suspicious transactions related to money laundering, financing of terrorism or other crimes included in the Agreement (Art. 10).

- Examples of suspicious transactions are provided (Art. 11).

- The Superintendence of Banks is required to report to the Financial Analysis Unit all suspicious transactions of money laundering of which it becomes aware in the course of inspections carried out by it to banks and trust services providers (Art. 12).

- Banks and trust services providers, on the basis of their own criteria, may close accounts related to suspicious transactions previously reported by them to the Financial Analysis Unit (Art. 13).

- Banks and trust services providers are required to update, at least once a year, their policies, procedures and documents aimed at the prevention of money laundering, and to provide training for employees in these up-dated procedures (Art. 14).

- Sanctions for violations to the Agreement (Art. 15) and for contempt (Art. 16) are established by the Agreement as summarized in the chart provided.

3.6 Other ordinances issued by supervisory and control organisms applicable to other regulated activities

3.6.1 Savings and loan cooperative associations

The Panamanian Autonomous Cooperative Institute issued in February of 2001 its *'Ordinance on compliance with Act 42 of October 2, 2000 for Savings and Loans Cooperative Associations.*

3.6.2 Colon Free Trade Zone enterprises

The Board of Directors of the Colon Free Zone issued *Ordinance JD-2-2001 of April 3, 2001* 'adopting procedures for the application of provisions on the prevention of money laundering in the areas under Colon Free Zone administration'. On the same date, it also issued *Ordinance JD-3-2001*, 'by means of which it is ordered that two clauses be incorporated into all contracts authorizing the operation of enterprises in the Colon Free Zone'. These two clauses refer to compliance with the provisions issued by the Administration of the Colon Free Zone to combat money laundering and the obligatory reading of the Ethics Regulations issued by the Association of Users of the Colon Free Zone.

3.6.3 Financial enterprises

The Bureau of Financial Enterprises of the Ministry of Commerce and Industry issued *Ordinance No. 14 of March 12, 2001*, adopting provisions necessary for the prevention of money laundering of financial enterprises.

3.6.4 Casinos, gambling and games of chance

The Board of Control of Games of the Ministry of Economy and Finance approved on 15 May 2001 Ordinances No. 018, No. 019, No. 020 and No. 02, by means of which regulations of casinos and coin rooms, bet booking agencies, bingo rooms and horse racing activities, are adapted to comply with principles and provisions established by *Act No. 42 of 2000* to prevent money laundering.

4 Regulations

4.1 Ordinance No. 163 of 3 October 2000

- Provides the fundamental objective of the Financial Analysis Unit, which refers to the wider concept of the laundering of capitals rather than the laundering of money (Art. 1).

- The functions of the Financial Analysis Unit, includes the exchange of information with similar organisms abroad, direct communication of the result of its analysis to the Office of the Public Prosecutor and reciprocal assistance and exchange of information with the Superintendence of Banks and the Office of the Public Prosecutor (Art. 2).

- Officials of the Financial Analysis Unit are subject to the obligation of confidentiality regarding information obtained in the exercise of their functions (Art. 3).

- Note: By means of *Executive Ordinance No. 78 of 4 June* 2003, the scope of the Financial Analysis Unit was extended to cover the prevention of financing of terrorism.

4.2   Executive Ordinance No. 1 of January 3, 2001

- Establishes the obligation of supervision and control organizations to oversee compliance regarding reporting of cash and cash-equivalent transactions, and to carry-on inspections to confirm adequate maintenance of records on the part of reporting entities. Furthermore, it empowers them to impose fines on reporting entities for failure to comply with those obligations, either on their own initiative or at the request of the Financial Analysis Unit (Art. 1).

- Identifies supervisory and control organizations for the respective reporting entities (Art. 2):

   Supervision and Control Organizations: The Superintendence of Banks, the Ministry of Commerce and Industry, The Autonomous Panamanian Cooperative Institute ('IPACOOP'), the National Securities Commission, the General Manager of the Colon Free Zone, The National Lottery of Beneficence, the National Gaming Control Board of the Ministry of Economy and Finances, the Superintendence of Insurances and Re-Insurances of the Ministry of Commerce and Industry.

   Reporting Entities: Banks, fiduciary entities, currency exchange or transfer agencies, natural or juridical persons engaged in exchange or transfer of currency activities, whether or not as their principal activity, finance companies, savings and loan associations, stock exchanges, security, stock centers, stock clearing houses, stock brokers and administrators, enterprises operating in the Colon Free Zone, in other free zones and processing zones, the National Lottery of Beneficence, casinos and other establishments engaged in gambling and games of chance, real estate brokers and promoters, insurance and re-insurance companies and brokers, and savings and loans associations.

   - Indicates the procedure for preparing, and filing with the Financial Analysis Unit, reports on cash and near-cash transactions (Art. 3).

   - Provides a glossary of terms used in the decree, such as: supervisory and control organisms, reporting entities, successive or proximate transactions, near cash and clients (Art. 4).

4.3   Executive Ordinance No. 26 of March 2, 2001

- Creates the High Level Presidential Commission Against Money Laundering as a permanent ad-honorem advisory board, to advise the President of the Republic.

- The term 'laundering of money from drug trafficking' is replaced by 'laundering of capitals'.

- Note: the scope of activities of the Commission was subsequently extended to cover the prevention of terrorism financing.

4.4   Sanctions and measures provided by laws and regulations of Panama applicable to violations or non-compliance with provisions contained in laws or regulations for the prevention of money laundering

Crime or Aspect of Prevention	Article	Sanction or Measure
A. *Act No. 9 of 1998* 1. Illegal, negligent or fraudulent operation in a banking institution.	95	Intervention of the Bank.
B. *Act 23 of 1986–13 of 1994*		
Instruments, assets and securities used in the commission of drug crimes.	9	Seizure or Confiscation (1).
Demonstration of the unlawful origin of funds subject to provisional seizure for drug crimes.	32	Burden on the Accused.
Bond for bail to detainees of drug crimes.	22	Not Applicable.
C. *Act 41 of 2000*		
Receipt, deposit, negotiation, conversion or transfer of capitals originating in money laundering crimes.	3	5 to 12 years of prison and 100 to 200 days fine.
Concealment of the origin of assets from drug crimes.	3	5 to 12 years of prison and 100 to 200 days fine.
Carrying on money laundering.	3	5 to 12 years of prison and 100 to 200 days fine.

Providing false information for transactions with moneys of drug crimes and other money laundering crimes.	3	5 to 12 years of prison and 100 to 200 days fine.
Facilitate money laundering using a function, employment or profession.	3	3 to 8 years of prison.
Use of money from money laundering to finance political campaigns.	3	5 to 10 years of prison and disablement.

D. *Act 42 of 2000*		
Failure to comply with provisions of the Law or of Regulations.	8	Fine of US$5000 to 1 000 000 to the Bank.
Acts and conduct of Directors, Officers, Executives, and Administrative or Operations Personnel of a Bank.	8	May be attributed to the Bank. In addition Civil and Penal Sanctions to individuals involved.

E. *Ordinance No. 136 of 1995*		
1. Revealing information by a current or former official of the UAF.	6	Dismissal from public office and Art. 170 and 171 of the Penal Code (2)

F. *Agreement 12-2005 of the Superintendence of Banks* (3)		
Failure to Comply with Agreement.	15	Fine of US$5000 to 1 000 000.
Contempt.	16	Up to US$10 000 per day.

(1) Until a finance sentence is issued. In case of a guilty sentence, confiscation ensues.

(2) Establishes sanctions of 10 months to 2 years or of 30 to 50 days fine, and disablement of exercising of functions when a victim has pressed charges.

(3) Without prejudice to the additional application of the fines applicable pursuant to Act 45 of 4 June 2003, on Financial Crimes (Ley 45 de 4 de junio de 2003, sobre Delitos Financieros).

Addresses

Colon Free Zone
16th Street, Colon
P.O. Box 1118 Colon
Republic of Panama
Tel 433-9500
zonalibre@zolicol.org
www.zonalibredecolon.com.pa

The Superintendence of Banks
HSBC Bldg., 1st Floor
Samuel Lewis Avenue
P.O. Box 0832–2397 WTC
Panama City, Republic of Panama
Tel 206-7800
www.superbancos.gob.pa

The Superintendence of Insurances and Re-insurances
51st Street, Campo Alegre
Panama City, Republic of Panama
Tel 214-7484

The National Securities Commission
P.O. Box 0832–2281 WTC
Bay Mall Bldg., 2nd Floor, Office 206
Balboa Avenue, Panama City
Republic of Panama
Tel 501-1700
info@conaval.gob.pa
www.conaval.gob.pa

The National Gaming Control Board of the Ministry of Economy and Finances
Peru Avenue, 35th Street East
Panama City, Republic of Panama
Tel 207-7974
www.mef.gob.pa

The Autonomous Panamanian Cooperative Institute ('IPACOOP')
El Paical, Urb. Los Angeles
Panama City, Republic of Panama
Tel 501-4400
ipacoopdaf@cwp.net.pa

Ministry of Commerce and Industry
Plaza Edison Bldg., 2nd Floor
Ricardo J. Alfaro Ave
Panama City, Republic of Panama
Tel 360-0600
www.mici.gob.pa

The National Lottery of Beneficence
Peru Ave., 25 Street
Panama City, Republic of Panama
507-6800

Bibliography

- Official Gazettes of the Republic of Panama.

- Website of the Superintendence of Banks of the Republic of Panama www.Superbancos.gob. pa.

- Website of the National Securities Commission of the Republic of Panama www.Conaval.gob. pa.

- *Alba, R.M.:* Uniform Program and Manual for the Prevention and Control of Money Laundering in Panama, 3rd ed, Panama, August 2001.

Sebastián Soler joined Marval, O'Farrell & Mairal in 1995 and became a partner of the firm in 1998. His practice at the firm focuses on finance and banking regulations. Before joining the firm, Mr Soler practiced law in New York as an associate at Jones Day (1990–1993) and Kaye Scholer (1993–1995), where he specialized in securities law. He has been admitted to the New York State Bar since 1991. At the firm, he has been instrumental in developing innovative products, such as the use of financial trusts as vehicles for the placement of structured securities linked to Argentine bonds, and derivatives as finance vehicles for Argentine counterparties. Following the December 2001 Argentine economic crisis, he has advised clients on the implications of the Argentine government's debt default and the reinstatement of foreign exchange controls. Mr Soler holds a law degree from the University of Rosario and a Master of Laws (LL.M.) from Harvard Law School, where he has also worked as a visiting researcher.

Firm's profile

Marval, O'Farrell & Mairal was founded in 1923, and is the largest (with over 300 attorneys) and one of the oldest law firms in Argentina. The firm has played a leading role in most of the major transactions arising out of the deregulation and privatization of the Argentine economy and, following the 2001 Argentine economic crisis, in most major debt restructurings. It is also the country's foremost patent and trademark agency. The firm's lawyers can communicate effectively with clients not only in English and Spanish, but also in French, German, Portuguese and Italian.

Argentina

Sebastián A. Soler

Partner

Marval, O'Farrell & Mairal
Av. Leandro N. Alem 928
1001 Buenos Aires
Argentina

Tel 54-11-4310-0100
Fax 54-11-4310-0200
sas@marval.com.ar
www.marval.com.ar

Anti-Money Laundering: International Law and Practice.
Edited by W.H. Muller, C.H. Kälin and J.G. Goldsworth
© 2007 John Wiley & Sons, Ltd

Contents – Argentina

1 Overview of Argentine anti-money laundering laws

The basic legal framework is set forth in *Act 25,246, as amended by Act 26,087 (the Anti-Money Laundering Act*, which was originally enacted on 5 May 2000 for the purpose of preventing, detecting and punishing money laundering activities in Argentina.

As discussed in more detail below, the *Anti-Money Laundering Act* broadened the definitions of 'money laundering' and 'concealment' already existing in the *Argentine Criminal Code (Criminal Code; Código Penal)*, created the *Financial Information Unit (Unidad de Información Financiera)* and made it responsible for monitoring compliance with the *Anti-Money Laundering Act* (with a special emphasis on the prevention of money laundering related to drug traffic, weapon smuggling, child prostitution and pornography, corruption, and racially or politically motivated crimes), and indicated which types of individuals and entities are required to report suspicious transactions and implement 'know-your-customer' procedures.

The *Anti-Money Laundering Act* has been implemented through several decrees of the *Executive Branch (Poder Ejecutivo)* and ordinances of the *Financial Information Unit*. In addition, other agencies, including the *Argentine Central Bank (Central Bank; Banco Central de la República Argentina)*, the *National Securities Commission (Comisión Nacional de Valores)* and the *Argentine Insurance Superintendence (Superintendencia de Seguros)* have issued their own ordinances addressing money laundering prevention within their own jurisdictions.

The *Financial Information Unit* is a 'Financial Intelligence Unit' under the recommendations of the *Financial Action Task Force (FATF)* and the *Financial Action Group of South America (Grupo de Acción Financiera de Sudamérica or GAFISUD)*, and meets the definition of the *Egmont Group*.

2 Definition of money laundering in the Criminal Code

2.1 Definition of 'money laundering'

Since the adoption of the *Anti-Money Laundering Act*, the *Criminal Code* defines the crime of 'money laundering' as the exchange, transfer, administration, sale, pledge or any other use of money or other assets with an aggregate value of more than A\$50 000 (approximately US\$16 181.22, at the current exchange rate in Argentina of US\$1 = A\$3.09) obtained through a crime, by a person who did not take part in such crime if the possible consequence of the conduct of such person is to grant to the money or assets the appearance of having been obtained through legitimate means.

2.1.1 Money laundering of less than A\$50 000

If the value of the money or assets involved is less than A\$50 000, the person responsible is subject to the lower penalty applicable to the crime of concealment described below.

2.2 Definition of 'concealment'

The *Criminal Code* defines the crime of 'concealment' to include helping a criminal to keep safe the proceeds of a crime and acquiring, receiving or concealing money or other assets obtained through a crime perpetrated by another person, when the person granting such help or acquiring, receiving or concealing such assets did not participate in that crime.

2.3   Location of the original crime

The *Criminal Code* provisions regarding money laundering and concealment will apply even if the original crime that gave rise to them took place outside Argentina, provided that it is deemed a crime under the laws of the jurisdiction where it occurred.

2.4   Penalties and fines

In the case of money laundering, the *Criminal Code* penalties range from two to ten years imprisonment and fines worth two to ten times the value of the assets laundered. The minimum imprisonment is increased to five years if the perpetrator performs money laundering activities regularly or as part of an organized band formed for such purpose. If the range of penalties applicable to the original crime is less, that lower range applies to the corresponding money laundering too. The courts may seize any laundered assets.

In the case of concealment, *Criminal Code* penalties range from six months to six years. Those minimum and maximum terms are doubled if the original crime is subject to a minimum imprisonment sanction of three years, the person who carries out the concealment does it regularly or for profit.

A person who is found guilty of money laundering or concealment in connection with discharging his or her duties as a public officer or performing an activity that requires a special license may not hold public office or may have that license revoked, respectively, for a period of three to ten years.

In addition to the *Criminal Code* penalties described above, the *Financial Information Unit* may impose a fine on any individual who, acting on his or her own behalf or on behalf of an entity, does not comply with the reporting obligations of one to ten times the value of the undisclosed assets or transaction. The entity on whose behalf the individual should have acted is subject to the same fine.

3   Information requirements

In general, the *Financial Information Unit* may request information or documentation that it deems useful for the performance of its mission from any public or private entity or individual, and may ask a government prosecutor to request a search warrant or a document subpoena from a court. If, after analyzing the relevant information concerning a suspicious transaction, the *Financial Information Unit* concludes that there are sufficient elements to confirm its suspicious nature, the *Financial Information Unit* must report it to government prosecutors in order for them to determine whether to press charges.

3.1   Special information requirements applicable to certain entities and individuals

In addition, the *Anti-Money Laundering Act* requires certain types of companies and individuals to report suspicious transactions to the *Financial Information Unit* and implement 'know-your-customer' procedures.

The following is a list of the entities and individuals that are subject to those special information requirements:

- Financial entities.
- Pension fund managers.
- Foreign exchange traders.
- Entities and individuals that exploit a gambling business.
- Securities and other market brokers.
- Investment fund managers.
- Government registries of corporations, real estate, automobiles and pledges.
- Dealers of art, antiques and other luxury items.
- Exporters, importers and manufacturers of jewels, precious metals and stones.
- Insurance companies, brokers, agents and appraisers.
- Credit card and traveller check companies.
- Postal service companies that wire or transport currency.
- Public notaries.
- Savings plan companies.
- Export and import agents.
- *Central Bank.*
- *Federal Administration of Public Revenues (Administración Federal de Ingresos Públicos).*
- *National Superintendence of Insurance (Superintendencia de Seguros de la Nación).*
- *National Securities Comisión.*
- *Public Registry of Commerce (Inspección General de Justicia).*
- Public accountants.
- Entities that receive donations from third parties.

3.1.1 Duty to report suspicious transactions

The *Anti-Money Laundering Act* defines 'suspicious transaction' as any transaction that, based on the experience and expertise of the reporting entity or individual and taking into account customary practices for that type of transactions, is unusual, lacks economic or legal justification or involves unjustified complexity.

The entities and individuals listed above have an obligation to report a suspicious transaction to the *Financial Information Unit* regardless of the amount involved (i.e., even if the transaction involves less than the A$50 000 minimum required for the existence of a money laundering crime), unless a special ordinance of the *Financial Information Unit* applicable to the relevant sector provides for a minimum amount.

Individuals and entities that are required to report suspicious transactions (other than the *Federal Administration of Public Revenues*, the federal tax agency, which is subject to the special treatment described below) cannot excuse themselves from meeting their reporting obligations (both the affirmative duty to report a suspicious transaction and the duty to provide information upon request of the *Financial Information Unit*) on grounds of legal or contractual confidentiality commitments (including banking and professional secrecy). The *Federal Administration of Public Revenues* can only disregard its legal duty of confidentiality concerning tax matters in the case of a suspicious transaction that the *Federal Administration of Public Revenues* itself has reported and only with respect to the individuals and entities that are directly involved in that transaction, or in compliance with a court order.

Good faith compliance with the reporting obligations cannot give rise to civil, commercial, criminal or any other kind of liability.

3.1.2 'Know-your-customer' requirements

In general, the *Anti-Money Laundering Act* requires the entities and individuals listed to (i) obtain from its customers documentation that proves their identity, domicile and other basic data determined by implementing ordinances issued by the *Financial Information Unit* for each sector, and (ii) store such customer data in the manner and for the period determined in such ordinances.

3.1.3 Duty of secrecy

The entities and individuals listed must abstain from disclosing to their customers and third parties any information concerning suspicious transactions and related proceedings.

The *Financial Information Unit* must keep secret the information received and the identity of those that reported it until it decides to press charges through a government prosecutor.

4 Special information requirements applicable to financial entities

With a few exceptions, the *Financial Information Unit* has issued a special ordinance applicable to each type of reporting entity or individual listed, indicating examples of transactions which are deemed suspicious in that sector and providing further directives on reporting requirements and 'know-your-customer' controls. In the case of financial entities, the *Central Bank* has issued a similar ordinance covering mostly the same ground. While the scope of this chapter does not allow a detailed description of those ordinances, this section highlights their key provisions.

4.1 Examples of suspicious transactions in the financial sector

The *Financial Information Unit Ordinance 2/2002* provides a list of more than 50 examples of transactions that are deemed potentially suspicious and may need to be reported by the financial entity. The list, which is not exhaustive and is intended only as a guideline of the kind of transactions that merit a higher level of scrutiny, is arranged in seven categories: (i) cash transactions, (ii) bank account transactions, (iii) export/import transactions, (iv) investment transactions, (v) international transactions, (vi) lending transactions and (vii) other transactions. The complete list may be found in *Annex II of Financial Information Unit Ordinance 2/2002*. In addition, the *Central Bank* provides an extensive list of 44 factors that trigger heightened scrutiny to determine that a transaction is not related to the financing of terrorism. That complete list may be found in *Central Bank Communication 'A' 4,521*, which may be consulted at the website of the Central Bank www.bcra.gov.ar.

4.2   'Know-your-customer' requirements applicable to financial entities

Financial entities must obtain from all their customers the following information:

- Basic personal (or corporate) data, evidence of registration as taxpayers, and contact information, including, in the case of companies, similar information about their legal representative and controlling shareholders, and, in the case of individuals, that of their spouses.

- Valid identity document (such as a national identity document or passport), in the case of individuals, and a copy of the by-laws, in the case of companies.

In the case of customers who are considered regular clients, financial entities must also request the following:

- Statements of current and extraordinary revenues, assets and liabilities, accounts and investments in financial entities, and, if any financial statements are prepared, those of the last three fiscal years audited by an external auditor.

- Two outside references that confirm the information supplied by the customer.

- An affidavit about the source and legality of the funds and supporting documentation.

In the case of customers who are considered occasional clients (those who do not have an account at the financial entity), financial entities must instead request the following:

- If a transaction (or the sum of all related transactions) exceeds A$50 000, an affidavit of the source and legality of the funds.

- If a transaction (or the sum of related transactions) exceeds A$200 000 (approximately US$64 724.91), such affidavit must include supporting documentation.

If a customer is not acting on its own behalf or there are doubts as to whether it is, the financial entity must take reasonable measures to obtain equivalent information about the entity or individual on whose behalf the customer is acting.

4.3   Storage of documentation about customers and transactions

The *Central Bank* requires financial entities to keep a database for each customer with information about every transaction involving an amount of at least A$30 000 (approximately US$9708.73). The *Financial Information Unit* imposes a similar requirement for transactions involving an amount of at least A$10 000 (approximately US$3236.24), but, as a practical matter, financial entities tend to follow the *Central Bank* rule. Lists of the minimum data required for each such transaction are found in *Annex III of Financial Information Unit Ordinance 2/2002* and in *Central Bank Communication 'A' 4,459* .

The financial entity must deliver any information contained in its database to the *Financial Information Unit* and the *Central Bank* within 48 hours of its request.

Documentation regarding the identity of each customer and each transaction must be kept for at least five years after the relation with the customer has finished and the transaction has closed, respectively.

4.4   Monitoring and reporting suspicious transactions

In order for financial entities to monitor transactions effectively to detect those that are suspicious, they must do the following:

- Obtain the information about their customers and transactions indicated above.

- Verify that their customers are not included in the lists of terrorists and terrorist organizations distributed by the *Ministry of Foreign Relations (Ministerio de Relaciones Exteriores, Comercio Internacional y Culto)*.

- Learn the business of their customers, the financial products used by them and the reason for their choice, the estimated volume of their transactions, and their attitude towards providing the information requested (which information must be verified and updated at least every six months).

- Analyze each transaction to determine whether its risk level conforms to the profile of the customer.

- Update the customer's information in the event of an unusual or significant transaction, a significant change in the manner the accounts are used, or as deemed necessary in light of the risk standards applied by the financial entity.

Financial entities must take into account the following signs as critical for detecting suspicious transactions:

- A determination that a transaction is not viable in light of the profile of the customer.

- The customer refuses to provide the information requested, attempts to reduce to a minimum the information it is willing to provide, or provides information that is misleading or difficult to verify.

- Any fact that lacks economic or legal justification.

Once the financial entity detects a suspicious transaction, it must report it to the *Financial Information Unit* and deliver any supporting documentation within 48 hours.

4.5   Internal organization of the financial entity

Financial entities must establish internal written policies for the prevention of money laundering that, at a minimum, provide the following:

- Establishment of internal compliance procedures.

- Appointment of a member of its Board of Directors to serve as officer responsible for implementing anti-money laundering policies and handling information requested by the *Financial Information Unit* and the *Central Bank*.

- Appointment of a special committee responsible for devising policies and compliance, formed by at least the officer responsible mentioned above, another member of the Board of Directors, and a senior officer who serves in the financial intermediation area.

- Creation of a training program for all the employees of the financial entity.

- Implementation of periodic external audits of the anti-money laundering program.

Address

Financial Information Unit
Cerrito 264, piso 3
Buenos Aires
Argentina
Contact persons: Alberto Rabinstein, Carlos Del Rio and María José Meincke
Tel 54-11-4384-5981
institucionales@uif.gov.ar
www.uif.gov.ar

Bibliography

Barral, J.: Legitimación de bienes provenientes de la comisión de delitos: análisis de la Ley 25.246 de Encubrimiento y Lavado de Activos de Origen Delictivo, Editorial Ad-Hoc, Buenos Aires, 2003.

Durrieu (h), R.: El lavado de dinero en la Argentina, Librería Editorial Histórica Emilio J. Perrot, Buenos Aires, 2006.

Rodríguez, V.P.: Prevención del lavado de dinero en el sector financiero, Editorial Ad-Hoc, Buenos Aires, 2001.

Eliana Maria Filippozzi is a lawyer in Brazil and Portugal; solicitor of the Supreme Court of England and Wales. Education: University of São Paulo Law School; Queen Mary and Westfield College and College of Law, University of London. Author: 'Direito Bancário Internacional – Captação, Securitização e Seguros' (International Banking Law – Financing, Securitization and Insurance). Co-Author: 'Legal Guide: Doing Business in Brazil' and 'Cross Frontier Insolvency of Insurance Companies'. Co-Author and Coordinator: 'Legal Guide: Public–Private Partnerships in Brazil'. Member: Brazilian Bar; Portuguese Bar; Law Society of England and Wales (Solicitor); Union Internationale des Avocats, Paris, France (President Bank Law Commission). Councillor of the Brazilian Chamber of Commerce in Great Britain. Partner, Banking Department of Noronha Advogados. Languages: Portuguese, English and Italian.

Robert Ellis Williams was educated at University of Lancaster (Accounting and Finance). Associate of the Institute of Chartered Accountants in England and Wales, 1986. Partner, International Tax Department of Noronha Advogados. Languages: English and Portuguese.

Firm's profile

Noronha Advogados is a full service law firm, founded in 1978, with professionals who are licensed in Brazil, England and Wales, Portugal, Argentina, USA and People's Republic of China. We are the only Brazilian law firm with own branches in the locations indicated above. Every professional in the firm speaks at least two languages in addition to his or her native tongue, which permits the firm to provide services in Portuguese, English, French, German, Italian, Spanish and Mandarin Chinese. No other law firm in Brazil has such structure or a similar experience and expertise in international matters, where we can fully represent the interests of our clients, which we can understand much better than any other law firm without such a consolidated international presence.

Other Offices: Rio de Janeiro, Brasília, Curitiba, Porto Alegre, Lisboa, Miami, Los Angeles, Buenos Aires, Shanghai.

Brazil

Eliana Maria Filippozzi

Partner of the Banking
Department

Noronha Advogados
4th Floor,
193/195 Brompton Road
London, SW3 1NE
UK

Tel +44 20 7581 5040
Fax +44 20 7581 8002
emf@noronhaadvogados.com.br
www.noronhaadvogados.com.br

Robert Ellis Williams

Partner of the International
Tax Department

Noronha Advogados
Rua Alexandre
Dumas,1630
04717-0004 – São Paulo
SP-Brazil

Tel +55 11 5188 8090
Fax +55 11 5184 0097
rew@noronhaadvogados.com.br
www.noronhaadvogados.com.br

Anti-Money Laundering: International Law and Practice.
Edited by W.H. Muller, C.H. Kälin and J.G. Goldsworth
© 2007 John Wiley & Sons, Ltd

Contents – Brazil

1   Introduction

Brazil, pursuant to the international commitments assumed with the signature of the Convention of Vienna of 1988, approved its *Money Laundering Act – Law no. 9.613* on 3 March 1998, which was subsequently amended by Law no. 10.701 of 9 July 2003.

The purpose of this law is to combat crimes related to money laundering (as the hiding or camouflaging of the nature, origin, disposition, movement or ownership of assets, rights or amounts) and to detect and punish all and any attempts to legalize the assets generated by such crimes.

Additionally such law created, under the jurisdiction of the *Ministry of Finance*, the *Council for the Control of Financial Activities* (*COAF; Conselho de Controle de Atividades Financeiras*) a collegiate decision-making body, whose main objective is to issue anti-money laundering rules, as well as to examine, identify and investigate suspicious money laundering operations, and apply administrative sanctions.

Brazil is a member of the *FATF* and *GAFISUD* and is fully compliant with the **Forty Recommendations** and the **Nine Special Recommendations on Terrorist Financing.**

2   The Money Laundering Act (MLA)

2.1   Definition of money laundering

Article 1 of the MLA defines money laundering as follows:

Art. 1 – To conceal or disguise the true nature, origin, location, disposition, movement or ownership of assets, rights and valuables that result directly or indirectly from the following crimes:

I – illicit trafficking in narcotic substances or similar drugs;

II – terrorism and the financing of terrorism;

III – smuggling or trafficking in weapons, munitions or materials used for their production;

IV – extortion through kidnapping;

V – acts against the Public Administration, including direct or indirect demands of benefits on behalf of oneself or others, as a condition or price for the performance or the omission of any administrative act;

VI – against the Brazilian financial system;

VII – acts committed by a criminal organization.

3   The scope of application of the MLA

3.1   Entities subject to the MLA

The **record keeping and reporting obligations** set out in the MLA apply to any legal entity that engages on a permanent or temporary basis, as a principal or secondary activity, together or separately, in any of the following activities:

- The reception, brokerage, and investment of third parties' funds in Brazilian or foreign currency.

- The purchase and sale of foreign currency or gold as a financial asset.

- The custody, issuance, distribution, clearing, negotiation, brokerage or management of securities.

Such obligations are also extended to the following:

- Stock, commodities, and futures exchanges.

- Insurance companies, insurance brokers, and institutions involved with private pension plans or social security.

- Payment or credit card administrators and '*consórcios*' (consumer funds commonly held and managed for the acquisition of consumer goods).

- Administrators or companies that use cards or any other electronic, magnetic or similar means, that allow fund transfers.

- Companies that engage in leasing and factoring activities.

- Companies that distribute any kind of property (including cash, real estate, and goods) or services, or give discounts for the acquisition of such property or services by means of lotteries or similar methods.

- Branches or representatives of foreign entities that engage in any of the activities referred to in this article, which take place in Brazil, even if occasionally.

- All other legal entities engaged in the performance of activities that are dependent upon an authorization from the agencies that regulate the stock, exchange, financial, and insurance markets.

- Any and all Brazilian or foreign individuals or entities, which operate in Brazil in the capacity of agents, managers, representatives or proxies, commission agents, or represent in any other way the interests of foreign legal entities that engage in any of the activities referred to in this article.

- Legal entities that engage in activities pertaining to real estate, including the promotion, purchase and sale of properties.

- Individuals or legal entities that engage in the commerce of jewelry, precious stones and metals, works of art, and antiques.

- Individuals or legal entities that trade luxurious goods or those with high value or carry out activities that involve large amounts in cash.

3.2   Duties imposed under the MLA

The MLA provides that the legal entities and individuals mentioned above are subject to the following **duties**.

3.2.1 Customer identification and record keeping

- Identify their customers and maintain updated records in compliance with the provisions set forth by the competent authorities.

- Keep up-to-date records of all transactions, in Brazilian and foreign currency, involving securities, bonds, credit instruments, metals, or any asset that may be converted into cash, that exceed the amount set forth by the competent authorities, and which shall be in accordance with the instructions received by these authorities.

- Provide *COAF*, upon judicial order, with requested information and documents.

3.2.2 Reports of financial transactions

- Report to the competent authorities, within 24 hours and without giving notice to the client, transactions, or proposed transactions, whenever they give rise to suspicion of money laundering crimes.

3.3 Delegation of authority to regulatory agencies

It can be seen from above that the responsibility for the creation of specific and detailed regulations and instructions on record keeping and the reporting of suspect transactions are delegated under the MLA to the 'competent authorities', which are essentially the regulatory agencies governing the activities of the respective legal entities. Thus, financial institutions would be regulated by the *Central Bank of Brazil* (BACEN; *Banco Central do Brasil*); stockbrokers would be regulated by the *Securities and Exchange Commission* (CVM; *Comissão de Valores Mobiliários*); insurance companies and brokers by the *Superintendency of Private Insurance* (SUSEP; *Superintêndencia de Seguros Privados*); and the pension funds by the *Complementary Pension Secretariat* (SPC; *Secretaria de Previdência Complementar*). In relation to legal entities that are not regulated by specific agencies, the detailed regulations and instructions are issued by *COAF*.

4 Obligations of financial institutions

4.1 Record keeping and reporting requirements

Pursuant to *Circular Letter* (*Carta Circular*) 2.852 issued by *BACEN* on 3 December 1998, financial and other institutions authorized to operate by *BACEN* shall:

- Maintain updated records, to be kept for a minimum of five years, of their respective customers.

- Maintain consolidated internal controls and records that make it possible to verify, not only the precise customer identification, but also the compatibility among the respective customer's fund transfers, economic activity, and financial standing.

- Maintain records, as established by *BACEN*, of transactions involving Brazilian and foreign currency, securities, metals, and any other assets that may be converted into cash.

- Report to *BACEN*, transactions, or proposed transactions, that, due to the features concerning the parties, amounts, forms of execution and instruments used, or the absence of economic or legal grounds, may indicate or be related to money laundering crimes.

- Develop and implement internal control procedures to detect transactions that suggest the occurrence of money laundering crimes, such procedures including adequate staff training.

- Inform to *BACEN* the director or manager, as the case may be, who will be responsible for the implementation of, and compliance with, the provisions set forth in said *Circular Letter*.

4.2   Suspicious transactions

BACEN Circular Letter (Carta Circular) 2.826 of 4 December 1998 lists, without limitation, situations deemed to be suspicious for the purposes of the Brazilian anti-money laundering regulations, and as such, must be reported to *BACEN*, as follows.

4.2.1   Situations related to cash or traveler's checks transactions

- Transactions with amounts that exceed the limit established of R$10 000 (ten thousand *reais*) or with lower amounts which, due to their customary character and form, suggest a scheme to avoid reaching said limit.

- Withdrawals with insufficient funds, which are covered on the same day.

- Transfers made by individuals or legal entities, whose transactions or businesses are normally settled by means of checks or other forms of payment.

- Substantial increases in the volume of deposits of any individual or legal entity, with no apparent cause, especially when such deposits are subsequently transferred, within a short period of time, to a destination not previously related to the customer.

- Deposits made in several parts, so that each separate deposit is not significant, but the total amount is.

- Exchange of large quantities of small denominations bank notes for high denomination ones.

- Proposals for the exchange of large amounts of Brazilian currency for foreign currency and vice versa.

- Deposits containing counterfeit bank notes, or made with falsified documentation.

- Deposits of large amounts using electronic means or other means that avoid direct contact with the bank personnel.

- Purchases of traveler's checks and banker's checks, drafts, and other instruments in large quantities (separately or in group), regardless of the amounts involved, without evidence of a clear purpose.

- Fund transfers in places located on the country's borders.

4.2.2   Situations related to the maintenance of current accounts

- Fund transfers in amounts not compatible with the customer's net worth, economic activity, professional occupation, or presumed financial standing.

- Resistance to provide the information needed to open an account, the provision of false information or information that is difficult or expensive to verify.

- Customary activities on behalf of third parties or which do not disclose the true identity of their beneficiaries.

- Numerous accounts for deposits in the name of the same customer, so that the aggregate balances of deposits result in a significant amount.

- Accounts that do not seem to derive from a customer's normal activity or business, since they are used to receive and pay significant amounts with no clear indication of purpose or relation to the account holder or to his/her business.

- The existence of a regular procedure for the consolidation of funds coming from accounts maintained in different financial institutions in the same location, prior to the requests for their corresponding transfers.

- Withdrawals of a significant amount from an account which was previously not very active or from an account that received an unusual deposit.

- Simultaneous and joint uses of separate bank tellers for the performance of large cash or foreign exchange transactions.

- Preference for the use of vaults, bank-closed packages of money for deposits and withdrawals, or the systematic use of safe-deposit boxes in banks.

- Refusals of certain rights, interests, or profitable advantages, such as credit facilities, high yield interests for large balances, or of other special bank services which, in normal circumstances, would be valuable for any customer.

- Sudden and apparently unjustified changes in the form of fund transfers and/or in the type of transactions used.

- Unexpected payments of a problematic loan with no apparent explanation for the origin of funds.

- Frequent requests for higher limits to make some transactions possible.

- Actions which have the purpose of inducing an employee of the institution not to keep files or specific reports on some transaction performed.

- Receipts of funds and the immediate purchase of traveler's checks, drafts, or other instruments to make payments to third parties.

- Receipts of deposits in checks and/or in cash, from different locations, transferred to third parties.

- Transactions involving non-resident customers.

- Requests to facilitate the granting of loans (especially those related to real estate) when the customer's source of income is not clearly identified.

- The opening of or transactions with an account by means of a power of attorney or other proxy instrument.

- The opening of an account in a bank branch located in an international passenger facility (airport, bus central station, or port) or in points of tourist attraction, unless such account belongs to the owner, partner, or employee of a company regularly operating in such facility.

- Proposals for opening a current account by presenting identification documents and inscription number in the Natural Persons Registry (CPF, taxpayer identification number) issued in a border region, or by a person resident, domiciled, or who has any economic activity in bordering countries.

- Transactions between current accounts that display credits and debits that, due to their customary character, amount and form, suggest a scheme to avoid the identification of the persons responsible for the deposits or beneficiaries of the withdrawals.

4.2.3   Situations related to international activities

- Transactions or proposed transactions, either directly or indirectly, in which the foreign person is a resident, domiciled or has his/her main office in a region considered to be a fiscal haven, or in places where the crimes mentioned in the MLA are customary.

- Requests for unusual or undue arrangements for the trading of foreign currency.

- Transactions on behalf of a person who has no prior relationship with or is unknown to the bank and has banking and financial relations in another city.

- Import and export prepayments by a company with no history in the market or whose financial evaluation is not compatible with the amounts traded.

- Transactions in gold by dealers with no history in this trade.

- The use of credit card in amounts not compatible with the cardholder's financial condition.

- Frequent unilateral transfers or unilateral transfers of high amounts, especially as donations.

4.2.4   Situations related to the institutions' employees and their representatives

- An unexpected change in the lifestyle or behavior of an employee or representative.

- An unexpected change in an employee's or representative's operating results.

- Any transaction performed by an employee or representative (whenever the identity of the final beneficiary is unknown) which is contrary to the normal procedure for this type of transaction.

4.3   Internal compliance

Pursuant to *BACEN's* 'Banking Supervision Manual', financial and other institutions authorized to operate by *BACEN* must develop and implement a program that assures and monitors the compliance of the rules of the MLA other anti-money laundering regulations. An effective internal program that complies with anti-money laundering regulations must be written and approved by the high administration of the institution, and include:

- A system of internal control that assures permanently compliance with regulations.

- Co-ordination and daily monitoring of the aforementioned system of internal control by the compliance staff.

- Staff training.

Such program must be tested by internal and external auditors and must take into consideration, *inter alia*, the following principles.

4.3.1 Internal controls

The high administration of the institutions regulated by BACEN is responsible to implement a system with effective internal controls to detect and prevent money laundering activities and it must demonstrate its commitment to comply with the law and regulations, by means of:

- Establishment of procedures for the adequate identification of clients, to detect and communicate to the Central Bank of Brazil operations that are considered suspicious.

- Requesting information about the execution of the procedures, control weakness, actions taken and audit reports. The internal control system must permit that the high administration assures permanent compliance with laws, rules and regulations.

- Ensuring that individual responsibilities are clearly demarcated through job descriptions.

4.3.2 Knowing the client

The institutions regulated by *BACEN* must adopt policies that determine the adequate identification of their clients, and monitoring their operations in order to detect suspicious activities. They must implement adequate controls and systems, adopt diligent procedures to open bank accounts, and monitor their financial movement. Regardless of the method used to open bank accounts, institutions regulated by BACEN must establish standards of identification determined by the risk presented by the client.

4.3.3 Compliance staff

The high administration of the institutions regulated by *BACEN* must appoint the staff responsible for the prevention and combat of money laundering. This staff must have power and resources to manage effectively the program of compliance.

4.3.4 Training

The institutions regulated by *BACEN* must take reasonable care to provide appropriate anti-money laundering training for its staff who handle, or are managerially responsible for the handling of, transactions which may involve money laundering.

4.3.5 Auditing

The **internal and external auditors** of the institution regulated by *BACEN* have the following functions:

- Assess the global integrity and efficiency of the internal control systems and compliance with anti-money laundering regulations.

- Assess the adequacy of transactions.

- Assess the level of awareness amongst staff in connection with the requirements of the anti-money laundering regulations.

- Review staff training to assess its adequacy.

5 Obligations of non-financial institutions

5.1 Record keeping and reporting requirements

As noted above the MLA delegates the responsibility for the creation of specific regulations and instructions to the competent regulatory authorities and in the absence of the same, to COAF. **In this regard COAF has issued a number of resolutions setting out the procedures to be adopted as regards (i) customer identification and record keeping; (ii) transaction registration; (iii) reporting obligations; and (iv) a list of transactions or proposed transactions deemed suspicious. Resolutions have been issued by COAF covering the following business activities:**

- Legal entities that engage in activities pertaining to real estate.

- Factoring companies.

- Entities that carry out the distribution of property by means of lotteries or similar methods.

- Individuals or entities that engage in the commerce of jewelry, precious stones, and metals.

- Legal entities that operate bingo and/or similar games.

- Credit card and payments card administrators.

- Commodity exchanges and their brokers.

- Legal entities that engage in the commerce of works of art and antiques.

- Non-financial legal entities that provide cash transfer services.

Please note that there are no regulations governing the operation of casinos since they are illegal in Brazil.

In addition appropriate regulations have been issued by the following competent authorities:

- *SUSEP* – relating to Insurance Companies, Capitalization Companies, Private Pension Funds, Insurance Brokers, Capitalization Brokers, Private Pension Fund Brokers, Local Reinsurers, Representative Offices of Authorized Reinsurers, and Reinsurance Brokerage Houses.

- *CVM* – relating to entities that engage in the custody, emission, distribution, liquidation, negotiation, intermediation, or administration of securities, stock exchanges, over-the-counter organized entities, futures and commodities exchanges.

6 COAF

6.1 Objectives and structure

COAF is the principal regulatory authority created under the MLA to implement and regulate the same. COAF is subordinate to the Ministry of Finance and is headquartered in Brasilia, the capital of the Federative Republic of Brazil. Its purpose, pursuant to its by-laws, is to discipline, apply administrative penalties, receive, examine and identify the suspicions of illegal activities referred to in the MLA with no prejudice to the competence of other offices and entities. Whenever COAF finds evidence of the commission of crimes defined in law or other illicit activities it must notify the competent authorities so that the appropriate legal measures may be taken.

COAF's structure comprises a Chairperson, appointed by the President of the Republic and a Council, supported by an Executive Secretariat. The Council is comprised of one representative from each of the following agencies or entities:

- *BACEN*;
- *CVM*;
- *SUSEP*;
- *General-Attorney Office for the National Treasury*;
- *Federal Revenue Office*;
- *Intelligence Division of the Military Department of the Presidency*;
- *Federal Police Department*; and
- *Ministry of Foreign Relations.*

Pursuant to the by-laws of *COAF* all the pertinent agencies and authorities represented on its Council will collaborate and exchange information to enable *COAF* to accomplish its objectives.

6.2 Administrative penalties

Upon due investigation and notwithstanding any criminal proceedings that may be initiated by the Public Prosecution authorities, the administrative sanctions that may be applied, together or separately, for a breach of the regulations are:

- a warning;
- a fine up to R$200 000 (two hundred thousand *reais*);
- a ban from holding a managerial position for up to 10 years; and
- cancellation of an entity's authorization to operate.

7 Criminal penalties

The penalty applied to money laundering crimes is from 3 (three) to 10 (ten) years imprisonment, and a fine. The same punishment is applied to anyone who acquires, receives, exchanges, negotiates, hides or conceals the proceeds of crimes defined by the MLA.

In case the crime is committed on a regular basis, or with a criminal organization as an intermediary, the fine is increased from one to two thirds of the penalty. The MLA establishes a legal innovation within the Brazilian legal system: the author or co-author of the crime will be able to receive a pardon or have its fine reduced between one and two thirds if he collaborates, voluntarily, with the investigations, rendering clarifications that lead to the verification of the crimes and the localization of the goods.

All the crimes established in the MLA are non-bailable. Any convicted person will be subject to the provisions under the Brazilian Criminal Code and will forfeit, in favor of the Union, the goods, rights and values object of the crime (the rights of the victim or *bona fide* third person being safeguarded). Moreover, convicted individuals will not be allowed to occupy public office of any nature, the position of director or member of a board of directors, or management of the legal entities used for the practice of the crime.

During investigations or judicial proceedings, upon request made by the prosecutor or the competent police authority and with sufficient evidence, the judge may order the seizure or detention of assets and valuables belonging to the individual accused under the MLA.

In the case of a money laundering crime committed abroad, if the relevant country has a treaty or international convention signed with Brazil, and upon request from the competent foreign authority, the judge shall determine the arrest or seizure of the goods, rights or values originating from the crime. The same shall occur when, in the absence of any treaty or international convention signed with Brazil, the other country's government promises reciprocity to Brazil. In the case of non-existence of a treaty or international convention signed with Brazil, the goods, rights or values arrested or seized, or the resources deriving from their disposal, shall be equally divided between the petitioning country and Brazil (the rights of the victim or *bona fide* third person being safeguarded).

Addresses

CVM
Rua Sete de Setembro, 111
2°, 3°, 5°, 6° (parte), 23°, 26° ao 34°
Andares - Centro
Zip code - 20050-901
Rio de Janeiro, RJ – Brazil
Tel +55 21 3233-8686

BACEN
SBS Quadra 3 Bloco B – Ed. Sede
PO Box: 08670
Zip code - 70074-900
Brasília, DF – Brazil
Tel + 55 61 3414-1414

SUSEP
Rua Buenos Aires, 256 – Centro
Zip code - 20061-000
Rio de Janeiro, RJ – Brazil
Tel +55 21 3806-9800

COAF
Ministério da Fazenda
Esplanada dos Ministérios – Bloco P
Zip code - 70048-900
Brasília, DF – Brazil
Tel +55 61 3412-2000/3000

SPC
Esplanada dos Ministérios - Bloco F, 6 floor
Zip code - 70059-900
Brasília, DF – Brazil
Tel +55 61 3433-5260/5261/5774
spc.gab@previdencia.gov.br

Abbreviations

BACEN	*Central Bank of Brazil (Banco Central do Brasil)*
COAF	*Council for the Control of Financial Activities (Conselho de Controle de Atividades Financeiras)*
CVM	*Securities and Exchange Commission (Comissão de Valores Mobiliários)*
FATF	*Financial Action Task Force on Money Laundering (Grupo de Ação Financeira sobre Lavagem de Dinheiro– GAFI)*
GAFISUD	Financial Action Task Force of South America against Money Laundering (*Grupo de Ação Financeira da América do Sul contra Lavagem de Ativos*)
MLA	*Money Laundering Act*
SPC	Complementary Pension Secretariat (*Secretaria de Previdência Complementar*)
SUSEP	*Superintendency of Private Insurance (Superintêndencia de Seguros Privados)*

Bibliography

Lavagem de dinheiro: legislação brasileira, Conselho de Controle de Atividades Financeiras, Federação Brasileira de Bancos, 2nd edn rev, Brasília: COAF, São Paulo, FEBRABAN, 2005.

Fabián Rivero was born in the United States on October 5, 1981. Fabián received his education at the Montevideo Law School (Uruguay). He is a member of the Commercial Law Chair at the Montevideo Law School and a Junior Associate at Pereda Rossini & Asociados. With Estudio Bergstein (May 2005-December 2006), he was a senior legal assistant at the law firms Corporate Group. Fabian speaks Spanish, English (both native) and Italian.

Ady Beitler was born on August 28, 1981. Ady received his education at the University of Montevideo (Uruguay) and Hamline University School of Law (USA). He is a member of the Constitutional Law Chair at the University of Montevideo and an Associate at Ferrere Attorneys at Law. With Estudio Bergstein (September 2005–June 2006) he worked in the Corporate and M&A Department. Previously, also with Ferrere Attorneys at Law (June 2002–June 2005) he worked in the Complex Litigation Department. Ady is the author of several articles. His last one is named 'Justice as Fairness of the Uruguayan Social Security Financing System', published in The Jurist Magazine in 2006. Ady is a member of the American Society of International Law. He speaks Spanish, Hebrew, English and Portuguese.

Firm's profile

Estudio Bergstein is one of the most prominent law firms in Uruguay, with a strong reputation for combining sophisticated legal service of the highest standard with personalized attention. The vast majority of the firm's professionals are active in academia, and several of them have international academic and professional experience. Estudio Bergstein provides advice in all areas of the law with a diversified client base, including national and multinational clients alike. For a number of international clients Estudio Berstein serves as permanent outside counsel for Latin America.

Uruguay

Fabian Rivero

Associate

Estudio Bergstein
Av. 18 de Julio 841 – Piso 2
11.100 Montevideo
Uruguay

Tel +598 2 487 1076
fabianrivero19@hotmail.com

Ady Beitler

Advocate

Arturo Prat 3760 Apto. 303
11.300 Montevideo
Uruguay

adybeitler@hotmail.com

Anti-Money Laundering: International Law and Practice.
Edited by W.H. Muller, C.H. Kälin and J.G. Goldsworth
© 2007 John Wiley & Sons, Ltd

Contents – Uruguay

1   Introduction

Because of its status as one of the main financial centers of South America, Uruguay has traditionally been an active participant in the struggle against 'money laundering' and the financing of terrorism. Indeed, Uruguay has ratified the key international legislation on this matter,[1] is a member of **CICAD ('Inter-American Drug Abuse Control Commission')** and **GAFISUD ('South American Financial Action Group')**, and has internally implemented the highest standards of control.

The first AML/CFT regulations were enacted in the early 1990s, and the shape-up process finished in 2004. Nowadays Uruguay has regulations and regulatory agencies in AML/CFT matters in all the major economic activities in which these offenses may be involved. All regulatory agencies and private institutions subject to their supervision are periodically trained by the *Uruguayan Center of AML Training.*

There follows next an overview of the AML/CFT regulations under Uruguayan Law.

2   Scope and regulation under criminal law

2.1   Money laundering

2.1.1   Predicate offenses

Money laundering was introduced to Uruguayan Law by the **Anti-Drugs Act 17.016** of 22 October 1998 **('ADA')**. That is why the initial criminal offense on money laundering was limited to drug-related predicate offenses.

The scope of the predicate offenses was progressively broadened thereafter, by influence of the successive amendments to the CICAD's Model Regulations Concerning Laundering Offenses Connected to Illicit Drug Trafficking and Other Serious Offenses (**'CICAD Model Regulations'**), the 2003 amendment to the *FTAF's Recommendations*, and the local evaluation conducted by the *GAFISUD* on May 2002.

On 23 December 1998, *the Anticorruption Act 17.060* penalized money laundering connected with public corruption, and on 25 May 2001, Act 17.343 extended the list of predicate offenses to: terrorism; smuggling superior to US$20 000; illicit trafficking of weapons, explosives, munitions and materials destined to their production; illicit trafficking of organs, textures and medicines; illicit trafficking of men, women or minors; extortion; kidnapping; procurement; illicit trafficking of nuclear substances; illicit trafficking of artwork, animals and toxic materials.

Finally, **the Money Laundering and Terrorism Financing Prevention and Control Enhancement Act of 23 September 2004** (the **'Enhancement Act'**) added the predicate offense of swindle, when committed by any individual, agent or employee of an entity subject to the regulatory control of the **Central Bank of Uruguay ('CBU')** (and in occasions by other persons as well,

---

[1] Uruguay has ratified the *United Nations Convention Against Illicit Traffic in Narcotic Drugs and Psychotropic Substances (1988), Inter-American Convention Against Corruption (1996), Inter-American Convention Against the Illicit Manufacturing of and Trafficking in Firearms, Ammunition, Explosives, and Other Related Materials (1997), The International Convention for the Suppression of Terrorist Bombing (1997), and the International Convention for the Suppression of the Financing of Terrorism.*

such as casino-gaming institutions).[2] Furthermore, *the Enhancement Act* provided that the place of commission of the predicate offenses is irrelevant for purposes of its application.

2.1.2 Strictu sensu money laundering and instrumental offenses

Under the *ADA*, the offense of **strictu sensu** money laundering is defined as the **conversion or transfer** of goods, products or instruments that proceed from any of the predicate offenses described above. This provision has been broadly interpreted, and deemed applicable to any form of incorporating to the licit market all proceeds obtained in connection with the predicate offenses.

Additionally, the *ADA* provides for other related felonies that are deemed instrumental, in the sense that they prohibit concrete activities that facilitate, and are an integral part of, the money laundering process. These felonies are:

(a) To acquire, possess, utilize, or do any type of transaction, over goods, products or instruments that proceed from any of the predicate offenses.

(b) To hide, substitute, alter the circumstantial evidence of, or to impede the real determination of, the nature, origin, location, destination, movement or property of such goods or products, as well as of their connected rights, that proceed from any of the predicate offenses.

(c) To assist the agent/s of the delinquent activity in the predicate offenses in securing the success of the activity, to hamper the actions of the judicial system, to avoid the consequences of the law, or to provide any type of help, assistance or assessment.

Unlike some international instruments, such as the *CICAD* Recommendations, no reference is made to the need for actual or potential knowledge of the illicit origin of the goods. However, by virtue of *Art. 22 of the Uruguayan Criminal Code* – which provides that factual mistakes over the constitutive elements of an offense are exempted from punishment unless the offense specifically punishes negligence – money laundering under Uruguayan Law requires that the person convicted had effective knowledge of the illicit origin of the goods. Exception is made of directors, officers and agents of financial entities subject to the *CBU*'s control, as the *ADA* poses upon them a duty to take all necessary measures to prevent money laundering within their institutions.

2.2   Terrorism

In compliance with its international obligations under the **UN** *International Convention for the Suppression of the Financing of Terrorism of 2003, the Enhancement Act* declares of terrorist nature all criminal offenses that are committed with the intention of causing death or grave bodily injuries to a civilian or any other person that does not directly participate in hostilities in an armed conflict, when the purpose of such act, as judged by its nature or context, is to intimidate the population, or to force a government or an international organization to do or abstain from doing something.

---

[2] Entities subject to the *CBU* control are: Banks, Credit Institutions, Investment Banks, Bureaus de Change, Insurance Companies, Pension Funds Administrators, Investment Funds Administrators, Stock Markets, and Securities Brokers.

The *Enhancement Act* also deems of terrorist nature to anyhow administer, provide or collect funds intended to be utilized to finance terrorist activities, even when these activities would not take place in Uruguayan territory.

Even though terrorism was regulated as an independent felony only in 2004, money laundering from proceeds of terrorist activities was criminalized as per *Act No. 17.343* of May 25, 2001. For this specific purpose, the definition of terrorism before the *Enhancement Act* was enacted, was that included in *the Rome Statute of the International Criminal Court*, ratified by Uruguay in 2002.

2.3   Powers of investigation

Under Uruguayan Criminal Law both the investigation and the decision of a criminal case is entrusted to criminal judges. Subject to certain constitutional limitations, such as the prohibition of searching domiciles at night and all those comprised under the scope of the Principle of Due Process of Law, the Uruguayan *Code of Criminal Procedures* (**'Código de Procedimiento Penal'**) vests judges with the most ample powers of investigation and evidence collection.

In addition, for the specific cases of money laundering investigation, *Articles 9 to 12 of the Enhancement Act* authorize a special proactive investigative technique of money laundering, which is the controlled delivery of illicit substances. These provisions are based on Spain, France, Germany, and Luxembourg legislations, and the *United Nations Convention Against Illicit Traffic in Narcotic Drugs and Psychotropic Substances of 1988*, and seek compliance with the *United Nations Convention against Transnational Organized Crime of December 2000*, and CICAD's Recommendation 17.

The *Enhancement Act* defines 'controlled delivery' as the technique that permits the delivery of illicit substances under the predicate offenses, or delivery of money, precious metals or other monetary instruments connected with traffic of illicit substances under the predicate offenses, for purposes of identifying the persons and organizations involved in money laundering or for purposes of collaborating with foreign authorities in AML/CFT investigations.

Specifically, *Art. 9 of the Enhancement Act* authorizes Criminal Judges to allow the circulation of money, precious metals, drugs, toxic substances or other goods prohibited under the predicate offences, for purposes of investigation, and subject to the strictest confidentiality. This authorization must be granted on a case-by-case basis, in the light of its special convenience for that particular case – according to the importance of the offense – the possibility of controlling the operation, and the effectiveness of international cooperation.

3   The duty to report suspicious operations

3.1   Prior regulation and the need for the Enhancement Act

The duty to report suspicious operations connected with money laundering was regulated by means of administrative ordinances since 2000 (*Central Bank Circular 1.722* of 21 December 2000), and imposed such duty upon all entities subject to the control of the *CBU*. However, this duty lacked enforceability in practice, because entities subject to it had a hierarchically superior duty of confidentiality. This situation was observed by *GAFISUD* in its May 2002 report.

Art. 10 of the Uruguayan Constitution provides for the Legality Principle, under which no individual may be mandated to do anything that a formal legislative act does not provide. Furthermore, *article 25 of the Financial Intermediary Act* sets forth so-called 'banking secrecy protection', i.e. professional banking confidentiality duty. Hence, based on normative hierarchical reasons, financial institutions were initially reluctant to comply with AML/CFT regulations that were enacted by administrative ordinances, because they lacked the power to oblige individuals under *Art. 10 of the Constitution*, nor could they supersede their legal duty of confidentiality concerning clients' information.

In this field, the *Enhancement Act* was enacted seeking to overcome these limitations, and settled the mandatory nature of the AML/CFT obligations. Hence, the Enhancement Act responded to the need to fully comply with the international standards set forth by the *UN Security Council Resolution 1373*, the amended 2003 FATF Recommendations, and the increasing pressure put by the Multilateral Credit Institutions (World Bank, International Monetary Fund and Inter-American Development Bank).

In general, the Enhancement Act regulates a statute of report of suspicious operations, and enhances the powers conferred to the authority that receives and investigates such reports: the Division of Information and Financial Analysis of the *CBU ('DIFA')*.

3.2   Duty to report suspicious operations

3.2.1   Obligations upon financial entities subject to the control of the CBU

Under *Art. 1 of the Enhancement Act*, for purposes of preventing money laundering and the financing of terrorism, all banking institutions and non-banking financial institutions subject to the regulatory authority of the *CBU*, are obliged to report to the *DIFA* the following transactions:

(i) those that, according to the custom of each activity, either result unusual, are presented without evident legal or economic justification, or are presented with an unusual or unjustified complexity; and

(ii) financial transactions over assets of suspected illegal origin.

Non-compliance with this provision is subject to administrative liability.

This obligation incorporates *FTAF's Recommendation 13* and *Special Recommendation IV*, as well as the recommendations made to Uruguay in the report corresponding to the *GAFISUD's* first mutual evaluation of May 2002.

Financial institutions subject to the control of the *CBU* also have an obligation under *Art. 17 of the Enhancement Act* to inform the *DIFA* about the existence of goods linked to persons that: (i) have been identified as terrorists or belonging to terrorist organizations by the United Nations; or (ii) have been declared terrorists by judicial decision (either in Uruguay or overseas).

Finally, under *Art. 19 of the Enhancement Act*, all entities subject to the *CBU*'s control that transport money, precious metals or other monetary instruments over Uruguay's national borders, must communicate such circumstance to the *CBU*.

3.2.2   Obligations upon other entities not subject to the administrative control of the CBU

The obligation to report to the *DIFA* transactions that, according to the custom of each activity, result unusual, are presented without evident legal or economic justification, or are presented with an unusual or unjustified complexity, and financial transactions over assets that are suspected to have illegal origin, is also posed upon certain enterprises not subject to the general control of the *CBU*. These are: casinos; money and value remitters; real estate agents; antiques, artwork and precious metals traders; and, any individual who engages in financial transactions or participates in the administration of business organizations as an agent of third parties, when such business organization does not belong to a consortium or economic group.

Non-compliance with this obligation is sanctioned with fine established by the Executive Branch, up to approximately US$1 900 000.

This extension of the entities subject to duties to report, incorporates the *FTAF's Recommendations 12 and 16*, the recommendations made to Uruguay in the report corresponding to the *GAFISUD's* first mutual evaluation of May 2002, and the report of the *Second Round of Multilateral Evaluation Mechanisms of CICAD/OAS of 2001–2002.*

Furthermore, under *Art. 19 of the Enhancement Act*, all individuals carrying money, precious metals or other monetary instruments over Uruguay's national borders must declare such circumstance to *the National Direction of Customs*.

Finally, the *Enhancement Act* mandates that all persons who operate within the Uruguayan territory, and provide services of business administration, accounting or data processing to entities that engage in financial activities overseas, must register with the *CBU*.

3.2.3   Content of the report

Under *Art. 3 of Decree 86/005* of 24 February 2005, all communications reporting unusual or suspicious transactions under the *Enhancement Act* must contain:

(a) An identification of the persons or entities involved.

(b) A description of the transactions that are presumed unusual or suspicious, indicating if they were effected, its dates, amount involved, type of operation, and in general, any information that is deemed relevant to these effects.

(c) A detailed description of the circumstances that suggested the reporter that the operation was unusual or suspicious of being connected with money laundering or terrorism financing, attaching, when possible, copy of the analytical work effected in that regard.

3.3   Confidentiality

Under *Art. 3 of the Enhancement Act*, reports made to the DIFA are confidential. Therefore, no individual may communicate to any person – including clients of financial institutions – the existence of an AML/CFT investigation over his/her assets.

Finally, under *Art. 4 of the Enhancement Act*, information provided in compliance with the Act shall not be deemed a breach of bank secrecy obligations, nor of professional confidentiality duties. This article settles the problem that in the past impeded the effectiveness of the administrative ordinances that provided for the obligation to report.

4 AML/CFT authorities

Under *Decree 86/005* of 24 February 2005, the *Ministry of Economy and Finance* is entrusted with the general supervision of the AML/CFT regulations, in coordination with the *DIFA*. Nonetheless, the most relevant supervisory activities are performed by the *DIFA*.

The *DIFA* is the head agency within the *CBU* in charge of the Uruguayan AML/CFT system. It is composed by members of all the Superintendences and regulatory divisions of the *CBU*: Superintendence of Financial Intermediaries, Superintendence of Insurance and Reinsurance, The Pension Funds Control Division, and the Area of Securities Market Control.

The *DIFA* is in charge of: (i) receiving, soliciting, analyzing and forwarding all AML/CFT reports made under the *Enhancement Act*, to the appropriate prosecuting authority; (ii) making – through the competent public entities and within the limits of national law – requests for international cooperation; and (iii) providing advice in all matters requested by competent authorities, especially to the *Uruguayan Center of AML Training*.

DIFA could be characterized as an *Egmont Group FIU*, although up to the present it is not a member of such group. In the past the main observations that the *DIFA* received were those concerning the mandatory nature of the obligation to report posed upon financial entities, and the lack of provisions concerning international cooperation. Accordingly, one of the goals of the *Enhancement Act* of 2004 was to obtain the *DIFA's* membership in the *Egmont Group*.

Concerning its function as reports receptor under the *Enhancement Act*, the *DIFA* is also entrusted with the task of instructing the person who filed the report, about the conduct to be followed with respect to the applicable transactions and the relationship with the client.

With respect to *DIFA's* powers to request any information connected with AML/CFT investigations, *Art. 5 of the Enhancement Act* provides that such information may not be denied under privilege or confidentiality duties. This provision incorporates *FTAF's Recommendation 26* and *GAFISUD*'s observations of May 2002.

Furthermore, *Arts. 6 and 18 of the Enhancement Act* provide that the *DIFA* shall have the power to demand from financial institutions to freeze operations in which persons suspected of money laundering or of being terrorists (according to UN lists or judicial decisions) are involved, for a maximum of 72 hours. This decision must be immediately communicated to a Criminal Judge, who will rule over the continuity of the course action taken by the financial institution.

The *DIFA* is also authorized to exchange material information on a money laundering investigation, with the competent authorities of other States who conduct similar functions, and as long as the request is duly grounded. To this end, the *DIFA* is expressly authorized to enter into Memoranda of Understanding.

For the *DIFA* to provide information to international authorities, the following requirements must be cumulatively met:

(a) The information must be utilized by the recipient for the sole purpose of analyzing whether money laundering has been committed.

(b) The information must be subject to the same confidentiality duty that the *DIFA* has vis-à-vis the information it receives.

(c) The information must be utilized only in criminal or administrative proceedings in the country that received the information, subject to a local Criminal Judge's prior and express authorization.

5 Administrative regulations

This chapter refers to those obligations specifically addressed to the entities subject to the control of the *CBU*. This section does not include the obligation to report operations that appear to be involved in money laundering or terrorism financing activities, as they were discussed above.

5.1 Obligations upon financial intermediaries

Financial intermediaries are the entities subject to the strictest administrative regulations concerning AML/CFT, provided in the *Rules for Prevention of Usage of Financial Institutions to Legitimate Assets Obtained in Delinquent Activities*, enacted in 2000. By their virtue, financial intermediaries are mandated to implement an integral system to prevent money laundering or terrorism finance within their institution.

This preventive system must be based on the following components:

(a) *Intense prevention and detection policies and procedures*. This is a **Know Your Client** obligation type. Institutions must adopt reasonable measures to obtain, update and save information about the true identity of the beneficiaries of the accounts and/or transactions, and about the adequate justification over the origin of the clients' funds.

Special emphasis must be placed in identifying persons or entities that engage in operations of currency or precious metals conversion into checks, transfers, deposits, securities or other values of easy operation, when the amount of those operations are of at least US$10 000 or the equivalent in other currencies. A registry of these operations is mandatory, and must assure easy access to the authorities.

(b) *Adoption of a Code of Conduct*. This Code must reflect the AML/CFT institutional policies implemented within the institution, and must reflect the customary ethical and professional rules that govern their activity. The Code of Conduct must be communicated to the shareholders and all employees.

(c) *Policies and procedures with respect to the personnel*. These policies must: (i) ensure a high level of integrity of all the institution's personnel, based on personal precedents; and (ii) provide the personnel with permanent update in AML/CFT regulations and procedures. The entity in charge of such updates is the *Uruguayan Center of AML Training*.

(d) *Appointment of a Compliance Official*. The Compliance Official of an institution is responsible for the implementation, follow up and supervision of the adequate functioning of the AML/CFT of the institution, and is the official contact of the institution with public authorities in AML/CFT matters. For purposes of preventing potential conflicts of interests, Compliance Officials are impeded from joining the Internal Auditing Committee of the institution.

(e) *Intervention and evaluation by the Internal Auditing Area*. The head of the Internal Auditing Area of a financial intermediary must present to the Auditing Committee an annual auditing plan that contemplates the AML/CFT procedures. This auditing plan must be submitted and approved by the board of directors of the institution, and such approval must be recorded in the board of directors ledger.

Moreover, the Internal Auditing Area is obliged to prepare bi-annual reports evaluating the AML/CFT system implemented by the institution. These reports must contain a description of the specific tasks performed, control evaluations, the level of compliance with the projected results, the deficiencies observed, their effect over the internal auditing structure of the institution, as well as all recommendations to counteract these deficiencies. These reports must be included in the internal control ledger of the institution.

(f) *Prohibition to process transactions connected with money laundering.* Financial intermediaries are expressly commanded to refrain from engaging in transactions that raise motives to believe that they are connected with money laundering or terrorism financing.

The applicable rules provide for circumstantial evidence of money laundering, which require special scrutiny by the institutions: (i) to intend to open an account without providing the required information; (ii) to request conversion of foreign low-denominated currency into currency of higher denomination, checks, wire transfers or other values of easy operation; (iii) to frequently constitute deposits in a certain account and almost immediately request a wire transfer, leaving a minimum amount in the account, when this activity is incompatible with the business or background information of the client; and (iv) when usual transfers of funds are effected, provided that these funds do not fully correspond with the individual's economic activities.

(g) *Obligation to diligently cooperate with the competent authorities.* This obligation posed upon financial intermediaries require full availability of information and active cooperation in money laundering investigations, as well as the strictest denial of any type of assistance to the institutions' clients who wish to avoid being investigated by the AML/CFT authorities.

(h) *Annual report from external auditors.* Financial intermediaries are mandated to retain external auditors, who elaborate and submit several periodical reports to the *CBU*. In that context, external auditors of financial intermediaries are mandated to elaborate and submit to the *CBU* an annual report evaluating the AML/CFT system implemented by the audited institution. This report must contain an evaluation of the functioning of the system and its efficiency in preventing money laundering and terrorism financing, an indication of the system's material deficiencies, and specific recommendations to counteract those deficiencies.

5.2   Obligations upon other entities subject to the CBU control

Credit institutions are mandated to: (i) implement rules that allow the adequate knowledge of each of their clients, and to maintain easily accessible registries of all the transactions effected with them; (ii) refrain from granting loans to individuals who do not provide complete identification information, and to refrain from entering into transactions that raise motives to believe that they are connected with money laundering or terrorism financing; (iii) enact policies and procedures that ensure a high level of integrity of all the institution's personnel and provide the personnel with permanent update in AML/CFT regulations; (iv) actively cooperate in money laundering investigations, as well as refrain from providing any type of assistance to the institutions' clients who wish to avoid being investigated by the AML/CFT authorities; (v) to retain external auditors, who shall elaborate and submit to the *CBU* an annual report evaluating the AML/CFT system implemented by the audited institution.

Bureaus de change are subject to the same set of rules applicable to financial intermediaries, as applicable.

Insurance and reinsurance companies are mandated to: (i) declare and justify the origin of the funds utilized for capitalizations and shares acquisitions; (ii) implement policies and procedures to prevent money laundering; (iii) enact policies and procedures that ensure a high level of integrity of all the institution's personnel and provide the personnel with permanent update in AML/CFT regulations.

Pension funds are obligated to: (i) declare and justify the origin of the funds utilized for capitalizations and shares acquisitions; (ii) implement policies and procedures to prevent money laundering; (iii) maintain a registry of all operations which involve US$10 000 or more; (iv) implement an internal auditing system that contemplates the AML/CFT procedures, and to prepare semester reports evaluating the AML/CFT system implemented by the institution, which must be included in the internal control ledger of the institution.

Securities intermediaries and investment funds administrators are obliged to: (i) implement policies and procedures to prevent money laundering, including procedures to obtain material knowledge of the client, to hold a registry of the transactions effected with them; (ii) hire and maintain a Compliance Official, who will be responsible for the implementation and supervision of the anti-money laundering system of the institution, and will be the official contact person with the AML/CFT authorities; (iii) to diligently cooperate with the competent authorities, including full availability of information and active cooperation in money laundering investigations, as well as the strictest denial of any type of assistance to the institutions' clients who wish to avoid being investigated by the AML/CFT authorities; (iv) submit an annual report from external auditors: evaluating the AML/CFT system implemented by the audited institution. Obligations (iii) and (iv) also apply to stock market operators.

6 International cooperation

All requests of international criminal cooperation made by foreign authorities in compliance with their municipal laws on AML/CFT investigations, that refer to assistance in evidence collection, injunctive relief, confiscation, arrest, or transfer of goods, shall be directed to the *Direction of International Juridical Cooperation and Justice of the Ministry of Education and Culture (the 'DIJCJ')*. In conformity with municipal and international law, the *DIJCJ* shall promptly refer the requests to the competent national administrative or judicial court, in order to enforce the requested cooperation.

The competent national courts that are assigned to meet the request for international cooperation, shall benefit from the assistance of the *Public Ministry*[3] and shall verify that: (i) the request has been appropriately grounded; (ii) the foreign authority requesting the cooperation is sufficiently identified; and (iii) that, when applicable, the request is officially translated into Spanish.

In case of requests for international criminal cooperation, their efficacy is subject to the condition that the conduct that motivates the request is a criminal offense under Uruguayan Law. In cases of requests of information contained in registries, or requests to pierce the banking secret, declare

---

[3] The *Public Ministry* is a body composed by criminal prosecutors and advisors of the Judiciary in civil matters.

an attachment, confiscation or delivery of goods, the court shall accept the request if it contains complete evidence of its foundation.

As a general exception, the court may reject any request that may seriously and apparently affect the public order, the security or other essential interests of Uruguay.

Uruguayan courts responding to a request for international criminal cooperation are also allowed to request from the foreign authority any clarifications that local courts may deem appropriate, via the *DIJCJ*. In cases of cooperation denial, the decision must be communicated to the foreign authority via the *DIJCJ*, providing appropriate and complete foundation for the decision.

Bibliography

Adriasola, G.: La Ley 17.835 Sobre Lavado de Activos y Financiación del Terrorismo, LJU, T. 131, 2005.

Adriasola, G.: Lavado de Activos, Cuadernos de Fundación de Derecho Penal, No. 5, 2005.

Costa, L.: Nuevas Tendencias Internacionales en Materia de Prevención Contra los Paraísos Fiscales y el Lavado de Dinero, Revista Tributaria, T. 29, No. 167, 2002.

Etlin, E.: Uruguay en la Lucha Contra el Tráfico Ilícito y Lavado de Dinero, Metales Preciosos y Otros Bienes, LJU, T. 122, 2000.

Lanzón Cuñarro, M.: Informe Sobre el Proyecto de Ley de la República Oriental del Uruguay Modificativa de la Ley de Estupefacientes Vigentes, Revista Judicatura, No. 37, 1994.

Reta, A.: Consideraciones Acerca del Llamado Lavado de Narcodólares, Revista del Colegio de Abogados del Uruguay, Tomo 20, 1991.

Cristóbal Eyzaguirre B. LL.M., Harvard Law School, 1994; J.D., Catholic University of Chile, 1991. He joined Claro y Cia. in 1988 and left in 1997 to work with Citigroup and he rejoined Claro y Cia. as Partner in 2004 . He specializes in corporate, banking and financing matters and litigation, including mergers and acquisitions, syndicated loans, capital markets, project financing, debt restructuring, bankruptcy, private equity investments, antitrust and commercial arbitration and litigation. He is Professor of the Master in Business Law at Los Andes University and of Civil Law at the Catholic University and is a member of the Chilean Bar Association in Chile. His native language is Spanish and he is fluent in English.

Felipe Dalgalarrando LL.M., The University of Chicago Law School, 2002; Academy of American and International Law, Southwestern Legal Foundation, Texas, 2001 (Victor C. Folsom Fellowship); J.D., Pontificia Universidad Católica de Chile, 1997. He joined Claro y Cia. in 1998. He concentrated his practice in corporate finance, project finance, capital markets, and M&A transactions. He is a member of the American Bar Association and the New York State Bar Association and Professor of Commercial Law at the Pontificia Universidad Católica de Chile. He was admitted to practice in Chile (1997) and New York (2003). His native language is Spanish and he is fluent in English and French.

Patricio Middleton LL.M., University of Chicago Law School, 2004; J.D., Universidad Adolfo Ibáñez, 1999; 1997 Recipient of Best Licentiate and Valparaiso Bar Association Awards (highest GPA of generation and highest bar exam grade). He joined Claro y Cia. in 2000. His practice has focused in corporate finance, banking, project finance, securities and M&A, including financing of infrastructure projects (i.e. toll roads and power and oil plants), and filings before Chilean securities authorities. Negotiated and drafted legal documents for cross-border M&As and several financing documents. Handled corporate issues related to equity and debt restructuring. He lectures in Commercial Law at Universidad de Los Andes and is a member of the bar in Chile. His native language is Spanish and he speaks fluent English.

Firm's profile

Claro Y Cia. was founded in 1880, it is one of the oldest and most prestigious full service law firms in Chile. The firm takes pride for representing clients in every civil and commercial legal field. Distinct are its M&A and banking and finance practices as well as its litigation department which is widely known for its ground-breaking practice. The firm's international practice concentrates mainly in representing multinational clients doing business in Chile. Claro & Cia. is a member of Lex Mundi and the Ibero-American section of the Club de Abogados. It is also associated with The Bomchil Group.

Main areas of practice include M&A Corporate, Banking & Finance, Securities, Litigation & Arbitration, Energy & Public Utilities, Mining, Natural Resources & Environmental, Tax and Intellectual Property.

Chile

Cristóbal Eyzaguirre

Felipe Dalgalarrando
Patricio Middleton

Partner

Associates

Claro y Cía.
Apoquindo 3721 13th Floor
Santiago – 6760352
Chile

Tel (56-2) 367- 3000
Fax (56-2) 367-3003
cristobal.eyzaguirre@claro.cl
www.claro.cl

Anti-Money Laundering: International Law and Practice.
Edited by W.H. Muller, C.H. Kälin and J.G. Goldsworth
© 2007 John Wiley & Sons, Ltd

Contents – Chile

1 Introduction

1.1 Legislative evolution

The first legislative regulation of AML transactions in Chile was included in **Law No. 19,366 of 1995**, in the context of illegal trafficking of narcotic drugs and psychotropic substances. Such law allowed the *State Defense Council* (*Consejo de Defensa del Estado*), prior authorization of the relevant court, to request from banks, securities entities, insurance companies and other entities participating in the financial markets, to provide forthwith all information or documentation regarding checking accounts, deposits and other transactions subject to bank secrecy laws, pertaining to persons or entities subject to investigation of illicits related to such law.

Such legislation also imposed criminal and administrative sanctions on those who (i) participate in the use, profit and destination of all assets deriving from the commission of any drug-related crimes; (ii) refuse to provide required information as described above; and (iii) fail to report any drug-related crime to which they became aware by reason of their position or job.

During 2002, such law was amended in order to grant authority to investigate drug-related illicits upon the *Public Prosecutors* (*Ministerio Público*), and they were additionally empowered to take all necessary actions abroad in order to gather information regarding the source of the assets, securities, monies, profits or benefits derived from the commission of any drug-related crimes.

Finally, in 2005 such law was replaced by **Law No. 20,000** (currently in force), which provides that the Public Prosecutors may request from the courts, without prior notice to the affected person and even before formalizing the investigation of any drug-related crimes, the adoption of any precautionary measure necessary to prevent the use, exploitation, benefit or destination of any asset, securities or monies derived from such drug-related crimes, including without limitation: (i) to prohibit execution of certain acts or contracts as well as their registration in any registries; (ii) to retain and freeze deposits of any kind in banks and financial institutions; (iii) to stop stock and bonds transactions; and (iv) in general to take any action to prevent that the proceeds of such illicit activities are covered in apparent legal transactions.

1.2 The creation of the Financial Analysis Unit

But it was not until 2003 that a comprehensive legislative regulation of AML transactions was implemented in Chile. **Law No. 19,913 of 2003** broadened the scope of the AML crimes to other illicits different from those related to drug trafficking. It also created the *Financial Analysis Unit* (*'FAU'*, *Unidad de Análisis Financiero*), a supervisory governmental entity with the specific purpose of preventing and thwarting the utilization of the financial system and other areas of the economy, for the commission of any AML-related crimes.

Some provisions of **Law No. 19,913** were objected by the *Constitutional Court* (*Tribunal Constitucional*) as they were considered violations of the constitutional rights relating to privacy. The foregoing motivated a bill of amendment that was passed into law as **Law. No. 20, 119** on August 31, 2006, which broadened the FAU powers and established some jurisdictional controls to its actions, which is explained below.

1.3 The GAFISUD and the Egmont Group

Chile is a member of the International Financial Action Task Force of South America (*'GAFISUD'*, *Grupo de Acción Financiera Internacional de Sudamérica*), which is the regional equivalent to the Financial Action Task Force (*'GAFI/FAFT'*).

The *GAFISUD* has adopted the '**40+9 Recommendations**' issued by the *GAFI/FAFT* and is currently evaluating the Chilean legal and financial system in light of the international AML/CFT standards.

In addition, the FAU is one of the financial intelligence units that are part of the *Egmont Group*.

2 General AML supervision – the Financial Analysis Unit

2.1 FAU duties and powers

The *FAU* is a supervisory governmental entity with the specific purpose of preventing and thwarting the utilization of the financial system and other areas of the economy, for the commission of any of the following crimes:

(1) To hide or cover the illicit source of specific assets, knowing that they derive from, directly or indirectly, the commission of any of the following crimes, or hide or cover such assets knowing that they have such illicit source:

- trafficking of narcotic drugs and psychotropic substances;

- terrorist conducts;

- violations to the regulations and controls on manufacturing, testing, distribution and storage of firearms and explosives;

- securities fraud;

- banking fraud;

- prevarication by the courts and judicial officials;

- public funds embezzlement, fraud, illegal exaction and bribery by government officials;

- kidnapping, child abductions and sexual abuses.

(2) To acquire, possess, hold or use such assets, with the intention to obtain a profit, knowing their illicit source at the time such assets are obtained.

In general, the main role of the *FAU* is to gather information about suspicious financial activities from all reporting parties, analyze such information and forward it to the Public Prosecutors when the *FAU* considers that any of the above-mentioned crimes may have been committed. In turn, the Public Prosecutors may require the *FAU* to remit any information that may be necessary for any investigations of AML operations they may carry out, whatever the status or phase of such investigations.

The *FAU* also has access to all information contained in databases of governmental entities as such information is considered necessary to develop or complete the analysis of a suspicious transaction previously reported to the *FAU* or detected by the *FAU* in exercising its powers.

In addition, the *FAU* is empowered to exchange information with foreign financial intelligence units. In this regard, the *FAU* has to ensure that such information shall not be used for purposes different from those of AML/CFT and that the requesting entity shall exercise reciprocity in case the *FAU* requests information.

Furthermore, the *FAU* Director is authorized to impose administrative sanctions, such as warnings and fines up to 5000 *Unidades de Fomento* (equivalent to app. **US$170 000**), which may be trebled in case of repeated violations, to any person or entity that does not comply with the obligations and duties imposed by the *Law No. 19,913*. In imposing such sanctions, the Director shall particularly consider the economic capacity of the violator and the seriousness and consequences of the violation.

The affected persons may appeal to the *Court of Appeals* sitting in the domicile of such affected person. The *Court of Appeals* resolutions are appellable before the *Supreme Court.*

2.2   Reporting duty

The following persons and entities are required to report to the *FAU* any suspicious acts, transactions or activities they become aware of in the ordinary course of their businesses:

- banks and financial institutions;
- factoring companies;
- financial lease companies;
- securitization companies;
- general managers of funds and managers of investment funds;
- the *Foreign Investment Committee* (*Comité de Inversiones Extranjeras*);
- money exchange houses and other entities entitled to receive foreign currency;
- issuers and operators of credit cards;
- carriers of money, funds and bearer securities;
- exchanges;
- brokers and dealers;
- insurance companies;
- managers of mutual funds;
- futures and options broker-dealers;
- managers and users of duty-free zones;
- casinos, gambling houses and racetracks;
- customs agents;
- auction houses;
- realtors and real estate companies;
- notary publics and real estate registrars;
- pension funds;
- professional sports corporations.

'**Suspicious activity**' shall mean any act, operation or transaction which, according to usage and common practice in the relevant activity, is apparently unusual or unjustified in economic or legal terms, whether it is made on a one-time or repeated basis. The *FAU* shall determine, on a case by case basis, the circumstances that must be particularly considered as indicative of a suspicious activity.

All such reporting persons shall appoint a responsible officer who will have the duty to deal directly with the *FAU*.

Any person who carries cash or bearer negotiable instruments from and into Chile for an amount exceeding **US$10 000** or its equivalent into any other currencies, shall have to report such to the customs authorities, which shall convey such information to the *FAU*. In case of violation of this duty, the *FAU* Director may impose a fine up to 3000 *Unidades de Fomento* (equivalent to app. **US$102 000**). The *FAU* Director shall specially consider the amount of the non-declared instruments and in any case the imposed fine shall not exceed 30% of such amount.

The reporting entities mentioned above are also required to keep in their records for at least 5 years all information relating to any cash transaction exceeding 450 *Unidades de Fomento* (equivalent to app. **US$15 300**) or its equivalent into any other currencies. Violation of such obligation may result in a 3000 *Unidades de Fomento* (equivalent to app. **US$102 000**) fine imposed by the *FAU* Director.

All such reporting entities as well as their employees shall not disclose to the affected party or third parties that the *FAU* has required information or that such reporting party has provided information to the *FAU* relating to such affected party, and shall not provide to them any other information related thereto. The same prohibition applies to the non-reporting persons that are required to disclose supplementary information as explained in Section 2.4 below and to any person that renders services of any type to the reporting entities and/or their employees and have become aware of the request or disclosure of information to the *FAU*.

Violations of the duties described in the preceding paragraph are punished with up to 5-year imprisonment and a fine of up to 400 *Unidades Tributarias Mensuales* (equivalent to app. **US$24 200**). Same sanctions apply to any person required to disclose information to the *FAU* according to the *Law No. 19,913* who willfully destroys, alters or hides any required information or documentation or provide any false information or documentation.

2.3   Confidentiality and secrecy laws. Liability

All secrecy, confidentiality and reserve provisions with respect to any transaction and activity contained in all laws, regulations and contracts shall not prevent the due performance of this reporting duty, which includes the obligation to provide the *FAU* with all documentation considered by the reporting person in reporting the relevant suspicious activity. Consequently, all bank secrecy obligations applicable to commercial banks and the *Central Bank of Chile* (*Banco Central de Chile*) do not affect this reporting duty.

If the relevant reporting person provides in good faith all required information pursuant to the applicable law, it shall be exempted from any subsequent legal liability that may arise in connection with the disclosure of such information.

The *FAU* is empowered to request from the reporting persons described in Section 2.2 above, all information that is deemed necessary to develop or complete the analysis of a suspicious transaction previously reported to the *FAU* or detected by the *FAU* in exercising its powers as well as all information requested by foreign financial intelligence units with which the *FAU* has cooperative agreements for the exchange of information.

If such supplementary information is protected by secrecy or reserve, the *FAU* request shall be previously approved by a judge from the *Santiago Court of Appeals* appointed by lottery by the President of such court.

Both the *FAU* request for information protected by secrecy or reserve and the resolution of the judge shall be based on '**specific facts**' that justify making an exception to the secrecy or reserve protection. As held by the *Constitutional Court*, the judge shall make a thorough and detailed examination of the background related to the suspicious transaction in order to verify that the *FAU* request is effectively founded in the need to prevent and thwart the utilization of the financial system and other areas of the economy for the commission of the crimes described in Section 2.1 above.

If the *FAU* request is rejected by the judge, the *FAU* may appeal before the *Court of Appeals* in a summary proceeding. The docket will be secret and shall be returned in its entirety to the *FAU* once the appeal process is completed.

Any person who is under professional secrecy obligations shall not be required to disclose any information specifically related to such secrecy.

If during the investigation of the AML crimes described in Section 2.1 above, disclosure of information protected by secrecy or reserve actually takes place and no further information arise that would enable the *Public Prosecutor* to carry out activities aimed at clarifying the facts, the *Public Prosecutor* may temporarily archive the investigation until new and better details emerge.

2.4 Non-reporting parties may also be forced to report

Section 2 paragraph b) of Law No. 19,913 provides that the *FAU* is also empowered to request supplementary information as described in Section 2.3 above from persons who do not have reporting duties. Such request is subject to the same procedure and substantive requirements described in Section 2.3 above for requests of information protected by secrecy or reserve.

3 AML supervision in banking

3.1 The Superintendency of Banks and Financial Institutions ('SBFI', *Superintendencia de Bancos e Instituciones Financieras*) compilation of rules

Chapter 1–14 of the SBFI Compilation of Rules, as amended in March 2006, provides guidelines for the banks to set up an AML/CFT prevention system applicable in their ordinary course of business, which must take into consideration the volume and complexity of their transactions, including their affiliates and supporting entities, and their international presence.

On July 20, 2006 the *SBFI* made applicable these guidelines to the leasing and factoring companies that are bank affiliates.

Such system shall include the following.

3.1.1 Know your customer policies

Any bank shall identify and be acquainted with their clients especially in terms of their riskiness. Banks must set up identification and acceptance policies and procedures from the first engaging transaction with the relevant customer, which shall include, among others, the following factors: (i) the customer's background; (ii) its profile of activities; (iii) amount and source of the funds involved; (iv) the source country and if such country meets the minimal required standards of acceptance; (v) its relations with companies and entities; and (vi) any other risk factors. If the customer is an international public figure, its acceptance must be approved by the senior management of the bank.

Customer profiles must be prepared using the information obtained from the customers and estimations must be made on the prospective volume and type of transactions such customer may execute in the future.

In case of unusual transactions or customers with international political exposure or occasional customers, the bank shall require an affidavit from the customer along with all supporting documentation on the source of the funds in case the transaction exceeds the lower of (x) 400 *Unidades de Fomento* (equivalent to app. **US$13 600**) and (y) any threshold provided in such bank's internal regulations.

The banks shall keep their customers' information duly updated. customers must be warned about their obligation to update their information at least once a year. All provided customer information shall be verified by the bank through appropriate means.

3.1.2 Manual of policies and procedures

The banks shall have a manual of procedures with all applicable policies and procedures in order to avoid being involved in, or serve as a mean for the facilitation or performance of, any money laundering and financing of terrorism transactions.

Such manual shall include policies on '**know your customer**', supervision methods and relationships with correspondent banks. Bank personnel roles and responsibilities shall be clearly identified in the manual.

The manual shall be updated to cover new products and services offered by the bank. Also guidelines regarding the analysis of the transactions of their customers should be contemplated, particularly when they are not consistent with the known unpredicted activity or business of the same, due to, among others, the amounts involved, frequency, consignees or originators, of such transactions.

On the other hand, in case of detection of transactions that seem suspicious, specific procedures should be established to ensure cautious handling and gathering of the information and the steps and deadlines to report such transactions.

Also customer tracking procedures should be included according to their different risk levels. Special tracking procedures shall be set up for customers with international political exposure and customers that due to their profile are exposed to be used to facilitate money laundering.

With respect to their relationships with correspondent and transnational banks, the manuals shall ensure that the financial institutions: (i) gather sufficient information about such banks to fully understand the nature of their businesses and verify their reputation and supervision quality; (ii) know all controls implemented by such banks to prevent money laundering and financing of terrorism transactions; and (iii) determine and document the duties of each bank under such relationship, if applicable.

3.1.3 Compliance Officer

Each institution shall designate a Compliance Officer who shall be a trustworthy employee, independent from the risk taking, operative and internal auditing areas, who shall be at the management level and whose main duty and responsibility shall be to maintain the internal coordination to ensure duly surveillance of the customers' transactions with the institution and its affiliates, the observance of the instructions set forth in the manual of procedures, the investigation of any suspicious cases and reporting thereof to the AML/CFT Committee.

3.1.4 AML/CFT Committee

Each bank, depending on its size, shall have an AML/CFT Committee composed of at least one member of the Board of Directors (not applicable to foreign banks' branch offices), the chief executive officer, at least one chief officer of any area, the in-house counsel and the Compliance Officer of such bank.

The AML/CFT Committee's duties are: (i) planning and coordinating activities aimed at compliance with the currently in effect AML/CFT policies and procedures within the relevant bank; (ii) supervising of the Compliance Officer's work and analysis of transactions; and (iii) implementation of any improvements to the control mechanisms proposed by the Compliance Officer.

3.1.5 Mechanisms for detection, monitoring and reporting of unusual activities

Each institution shall have all necessary technological tools to develop red-flag systems to identify and detect unusual operations. Such instruments shall be capable to monitor all customer transactions throughout all the bank's products, particularly cash transactions, considering such customer's risk level and products.

Each bank shall provide all personnel that interact directly with customers a red-flag list to identify unusual transactions. Any rejection of a customer or potential customer transaction due to unusual activity or any other suspicious characteristics, shall be reported to the responsible control unit of the bank.

Any unusual transaction must be reported to the responsible control unit of the bank. There shall be a specifically-designed form to make such reports. Any analysis of such transactions shall be duly documented.

Once identified a transaction as suspicious, the relevant bank must report such transaction to the *FAU*.

3.1.6 Selection of personnel, training programs and Internal Conduct Code

Each bank shall have rules and policies governing selection of personnel and its conduct when dealing with customers. Such conduct rules shall be contained in the Internal Conduct Code, which shall prevent and address any conflict of interest that may arise in dealing with customers.

Also each bank shall develop training programs for its personnel regarding all applicable AML/CFT rules and procedures and their practical implementation. Such programs shall include all bank's personnel, including its affiliates and supporting entities', and shall be periodic and different for each group of employees depending on whether such employees have been recently hired, their compliance duties, operative unit and direct relationship with customers.

3.1.7 Internal Auditing Committee

The AML/CFT system of each bank shall be periodically evaluated by the internal audit unit of such bank, according to procedures approved by the senior management of such bank.

In this regard, *Chapter 1–15 of the SBFI Compilation of Rules* provides that each bank shall have an Auditing Committee that supervises the efficiency of the internal control systems within the bank, whose duties shall include, among others: (i) to be acquainted with and resolve all conflicts of interest; (ii) to investigate all suspicious conducts and frauds; and (iii) to evaluate compliance with any AML/CFT policies and their compliance.

3.1.8 SBFI evaluation and supervision

The sufficiency and efficacy of the AML/CFT policies and procedures adopted by the institutions, shall be considered in the supervision, management and performance evaluation and rating procedures carried out periodically by the SBFI.

Also the *SBFI*, as part of its supervisory authority upon banks, shall permanently keep a list of all bank depositors of the banks subject to its supervision, including the taxpayer ID number of each depositor.

3.2 Bank secrecy laws

Section 154 of Law No. 252 (the '*Banking Act*') provides that deposits and other repayable funds of any type whatsoever received or taken by banks are subject to strict banking secrecy and no information or data in connection therewith may be disclosed or furnished to any person except for the depositor or customer itself, its agents or representatives or such other persons expressly authorized to access or receive such data by the customer or such agents or representatives. Contravention to such secrecy constitutes a criminal offense punished with imprisonment.

Section 154 further provides that all other banking transactions are subject to '**reserve**', which is a form of confidentiality of lesser degree, which contravention does not constitute a criminal offense. However, these other banking transactions may be disclosed by the banking institutions to any third parties showing a **legitimate interest** thereon, provided that there is no reason to believe that knowledge of the same by such third parties may result in pecuniary damage to the customer. Detailed disclosure of these other banking transactions may be made to professional firms engaged in the evaluation of the relevant bank, but such firms are also subject to the same confidentiality duty.

Pursuant to the same provision, Chilean Courts may order the disclosure or audit of specific transactions directly related to the pertinent trial facts, about deposits or other repayable funds of any type carried out by persons being a party to, or being charged or indicted at, the relevant civil or criminal proceedings.

Pursuant to the same provision, Chilean Courts may order the disclosure or audit of specified transactions in the course of a civil or criminal action directly related therewith.

Also, the Bank Checking Accounts and Checks Act specifically provides that banking institutions shall keep in '**strict reserve**' vis-à-vis third parties all of the information relating to checking accounts maintained by their customers and may only disclose information related therewith to the account holder or to such persons expressly authorized by the latter. However, Chilean Courts may order the disclosure of specific entries or movements of a banking account in the course of civil or criminal actions affecting the account holder.

Those that fail to comply with or violate the bank's secrecy duty may be criminally prosecuted and together with the bank itself may be held liable for damages, if any. Disclosure of information or data subject to mere '**bank reserve**' may also result in civil liability to the concerned bank. Moreover, the relevant bank may be subject to administrative sanctions.

4 AML/CFT supervision in securities and insurance markets – Superintendency of Securities and Insurance ('SSI', *Superintendencia de Valores y Seguros*) rules

SSI Circular No. 1809 of 2006 contains AML/CFT provisions that are applicable to:

- insurance companies;

- securities intermediaries (brokers and dealers);

- general managers of funds;

- managers of mutual funds;

- managers of investment funds;

- securitization companies.

4.1 Principles to be held in consideration in this matter

SSI Circular No. 1809 provides that the following principles need to be held in consideration in this matter by the above-mentioned regulated entities:

- **Due diligence in transactions**. The transactions between the regulated entities and their clients, as well as the transactions undertaken by such entities for the benefit of their clients, require to be adequately identified through an appropriate follow-up process in order to determine, to the extent possible, whether such transactions are to be considered unusual operations in accordance with past practice.

- **Knowledge of the customer**. The entities referred to above shall implement a customary practice with the goal of obtaining an adequate knowledge of their customers, the activities that generate the funds used in such customers' transactions, and the most relevant features of the operations their customers carry out, in order to be able to prevent money laundering and terrorism financing activities. By the same token, such entities shall procure obtaining information that allows them to explain or understand the transactions that are not in accordance with the background of the applicable customer, or those operations that seem unusual by their volume, repetition, counterparty or amount.

- Within the indicated framework, the financial entities shall obtain the approval of their senior management in order to have commercial relationships with clients considered as **Politically Exposed Persons**. In addition, during the life of such relationship an intensified scrutiny shall be carried out.

- In this connection, for 'client' it shall be understood all entities or individuals with which the regulated entities create, establish, maintain, intend to create, execute or fail to create a commercial relationship with the goal of providing to the client a service or product offered within the scope of activities of the regulated entity, being such relationship either an occasional, sporadic, one-time, repeated, frequent or permanent relationship.

- For 'Politically Exposed Persons' it shall be understood the individuals that hold or have held important public positions in Chile or abroad, including, among others, chiefs of state or government; political leaders; governmental, judicial or armed forces officers of high rank; top managers of estate-owned companies; or important members of political parties.

- **Implementation of suspicious operations detection tools**. The entities subject to this regulation shall create and constantly update a set of tools that allow them to detect, control and convey to the relevant authorities the operations that qualify as suspicious activities, according to the definition of suspicious activities indicated below.

- **International recommendations**. The prevention of money laundering and terrorism financing activities has been structured in accordance with a set of international regulations on the subject, mostly contemplated in the recommendations issued by the International Financial Action Task Force.

- **Domestic regulatory framework**. The laws and rules applicable to the entities subject to this regulation are the Securities Market Act and its complementary and special laws, the regulations issued by *the SSI, Law No. 19,913* (which created the *FAU*) and the regulations issued by the *FAU*.

- **Suspicious activities**. For suspicious activities it shall be understood all the activities described in *Section 3 paragraph 2 of Law No. 19,913*, i.e. those described in Section 2.2. above.

- **Report to the *FAU***. Once a suspicious activity is identified, it shall be reported to the FAU.

- **These principles constitute a *de minimis* requirement**. The instructions and recommendations contained in SSI Circular No. 1809 constitute a *de minimis* requirement in connection with money laundering and terrorism financing prevention.

4.2 Operations that shall be subject to scrutiny in order to prevent money laundering and terrorism financing

SSI Circular No. 1809 provides that special attention shall be given to the unusual, irregular or abnormal operations in connection with the activities of any given client or of any other person participating in them, and/or that appear to be suspicious by its origin, structuring, financial design, presentation, supporting documentation, amendment of registered information, submitted information or lack thereof, reiteration or amount of the same or the unusual participation of third parties or unknown parties.

In addition, the regulated entities shall adopt the appropriate measures in order to maintain, either in physical or electronic format, the information regarding the following operations, which are considered as relevant operations for purposes of *SSI Circular No. 1809*:

(a) Operations carried out by individuals or entities of any kind, which entail the payment to the regulated entities of an amount in cash, either in Chilean pesos or foreign currency or in negotiable bearer instruments, that exceed the equivalent of 450 *Unidades de Fomento* (equivalent to app. **US$15 300**).

(b) Operations carried out by individuals or entities that may qualify as suspicious operations.

The information that should be kept by the regulated entities shall include, among others, the following:

(i) The nature of the transaction and copy of all supporting documents and records.

(ii) The names, taxpayer ID number or equivalent for non-resident aliens, nationality, occupation, business, domicile, telephone number and e-mail address of the relevant investor, customer or parties to the transaction; copy of the power of attorney in case the relevant party acts on behalf of a third party, or in the absence of such power, the entity shall ascertain that the party acts on behalf of a third party and shall obtain the contact information of the third party necessary in order to get in contact with the latter; in case of entities, copies of their organizational documents and identification of their representatives.

(iii) Documentation that allow to determine the scope of relations that a company may have with others, i.e. documentation that allow to determine whether such company is part of a group of companies having a specific purpose, together with documentation which allow the identification of the other members of the group.

(iv) Immediate origin of the funds with which the relevant transaction is carried out to the extent the amount of such transaction exceeds 450 *Unidades de Fomento* (as indicated under item (a) above).

Furthermore, the above indicated information needs to be easily accessible, either by the name of the client or investor, its taxpayer number, amount of the operation, its nature or by any other objective criteria. The foregoing is aimed at responding to the requests that may be made in connection with certain operations and persons.

In the event the information about a specific client is obtained by a third entity, the regulated entity shall procure to obtain said information within three business days.

4.3   Manual of Procedures

Each regulated entity shall have a Manual of Procedures regarding the rules and guidelines that each of them must follow in order (i) to prevent, detect and avoid the facilitation and performance of money laundering and terrorism financing activities through it, and (ii) fully know its clients and investors and the activities they carry out, especially if such activities differ from their known activities.

4.4   Compliance Officer

The regulated entities shall appoint a compliance officer in order to coordinate all surveillance, detection, prevention and reporting activities relating to suspicious activities. To the extent possible such compliance officer shall be independent from the business, audit and risk areas of the regulated entity.

4.5 Selection of personnel, training programs and Internal Conduct Code

The regulated entities shall establish objective criteria for the selection of personnel that prevent the hiring of employees connected to organizations involved in money laundering and/or terrorism financing activities.

By the same token, the regulated entities shall implement permanent training and continuing education programs that instruct the personnel in money laundering and terrorism financing techniques which they could face when dealing with clients' operations. The aforementioned programs shall be given to employees that are in direct contact with the clients, and to operators of money desks, stock traders, auditing personnel and to those in charge of following up the operations that could have been done in furtherance of money laundering or terrorism financing purposes.

The entities shall have a personnel conduct code, that could be part of the Manual of Procedures referred to in Section 4.3 above. The conduct code shall contain the principles determined by each entity regarding the relations and operations that must be undertaken with investors, clients or parties to the operations, with the goal of assuring a behavior within an ethic framework that avoids the realization or facilitation of money laundering activities. In addition, the tasks that each of the employees and officers of the regulated entities must carry out in detecting and reporting suspicious activities shall be precisely determined in the conduct code.

4.6 Board of Directors' supervision

The Board of Directors or senior management of each regulated entity shall approve the manual of procedures and the conduct code as well as evaluate at least once in a calendar year all procedures and policies established in the same, their actual compliance and effectiveness. The foregoing applies both to the transactions routinely made by the entity and to the transactions made with new instruments or structures.

The conclusions reached by the Board of Directors or senior management in connection with the above shall be recorded in minutes which need to be kept in the records of the entity as to allow their further exam by the *SSI*.

5 Antiterrorism legislation

5.1 Criminal offense in antiterrorism law

Law No. 18,314 of 1984, as amended in November 2003 (the '*Antiterrorism Act*') provides a specific criminal offense in addition to those previously described, which sanctions the solicitation, collection or provision of funds, directly or indirectly by any means, with the purpose of facilitating the commission of any of the illicits defined as '**terrorist crimes**' in the *Antiterrorism Act*. Such criminal offense is punished with imprisonment.

Addresses

Unidad de Análisis Financiero
Teatinos 950, piso 14
Santiago–8340084
Chile
Tel (56-2) 439-3000
Fax (56-2) 439-3005
www.uaf.cl

Ministerio Público de Chile
General Mackenna 1369
Santiago, Chile
Tel (56-2) 690-9100
www.ministeriopublico.cl

Consejo de Defensa del Estado
Agustinas 1687
Santiago, Chile
Tel (56-2) 675-1800
Fax (56-2) 675-1816
www.cde.cl

Superintendencia de Bancos e Instituciones Financieras
Moneda 1123
P.O. Box 15-D
Santiago, Chile
Tel (56-2) 442-6200
Fax (56-2) 441-0914
www.sbif.cl

Superintendencia de Valores y Seguros
Av. Libertador Bernardo O'Higgins 1449
Santiago 8340518
Chile
Tel (56-2) 473-4000
Fax (56-2) 473-4101
Call center (56-2) 600-473-8000
www.svs.cl

Consejo Nacional para el Control de Estupefacientes (CONACE)
Agustinas 1235, piso 9
Santiago 8340422
Chile
Tel (56-2) 510-0800
Fax (56-2) 697-4973
informacionesconace@conace.gov.cl
www.conacedrogas.cl

BAHAMAS, BERMUDA AND CARIBBEAN

Craig MacIntyre is a partner with Conyers Dill & Pearman's Trust and Private Client Department. Craig is also a director of Codan Trust Company Limited, a licensed trust company affiliate of the firm. Craig's practice area is in private and commercial trusts and his clients include local and international individuals and families, private and family-owned companies, private trustee companies, as well as publicly owned trust companies, banks, insurance companies and other multi-national companies. Craig is also a member of the firm's Employment Law Group and advises local and international employers on Bermuda law issues pertaining to their retirement and employee benefit structures.

Firm's profile

Conyers Dill & Pearman is an international offshore law firm that specializes in company & commercial law, commercial litigation and private client matters. Established in 1928, the firm advises on the laws of Bermuda, British Virgin Islands and Cayman Islands, and has a presence in multiple jurisdictions across the globe. Its global network of licensed trust companies (Codan Trust) undertakes a broad range of trust establishment and administration services.

Bermuda

Craig MacIntyre

Partner
Trusts & Private Client Department

Conyers Dill & Pearman
Barristers & Attorneys
Richmond House
12 Par-La-Ville Road
Hamilton HM 11
Bermuda

Tel 1 (441) 299 4907
Fax 1 (441) 298 7849
craig.macintyre@conyersdillandpearman.com
www.conyersdillandpearman.com

Anti-Money Laundering: International Law and Practice.
Edited by W.H. Muller, C.H. Kälin and J.G. Goldsworth
© 2007 John Wiley & Sons, Ltd

Contents – Bermuda

1 About Bermuda

Bermuda has earned a reputation as a world-class centre of commerce, featuring a business-friendly environment, a stable and growing economy, and an unmatched collection of talent and intellectual capital in key sectors, including insurance, financial services and, more recently, electronic commerce.

Bermuda's regulatory and legal systems have evolved over the years, not only facilitating business, but allowing it to flourish. The island is a well-regulated jurisdiction, with a common law legal system based on English law. Bermuda offers international companies a sophisticated high-tech infrastructure and is rich in intellectual capital.

Bermuda's telecommunications infrastructure and high technology backbone provide maximum bandwidth with full redundancy to the island, enabling Bermuda to accommodate rapidly growing global electronic commerce and communication services.

The island's geographic location between the United States and Europe offers a desirable time zone and efficient access to and from major international airports on both sides of the Atlantic Ocean. Being some 700 miles off the coast of North Carolina (its nearest neighbor), Bermuda is well placed to service and access major US and European markets.

2 Introduction

2.1 The legislation

The (i) *Proceeds of Crime Act 1997* [as amended by the *Investment Business Act 1998*, the *Banks and Deposit Companies (Consequential Amendments) Order 1999*, the *Proceeds of Crime Amendment Act 2000*] (together the 'Act') and (ii) the *Proceeds of Crime (Money Laundering) Regulations 1998* (the 'Regulations'), (together referred to as the 'Legislation') comprise the central framework for Bermuda's anti-money laundering regime. In addition, *Bermuda's National Anti-Money Laundering Committee* (*'NAMLC'*) has issued certain Guidance Notes (the 'Guidance Notes').[1] The Legislation and Guidance Notes together comprise a cohesive and comprehensive code aimed at the prevention, discouragement, detection and prosecution of money laundering offences in Bermuda.

The Act is primarily aimed at preventing offences relating to the proceeds of drug trafficking, serious crimes and other defined money laundering activities in Bermuda. In addition to creating offences relating to money laundering (or the giving of assistance in such activities), the Act also confers expansive information-gathering powers on the police relating to investigations into drug trafficking and whether a person has benefited from criminal conduct. The Act also contains provisions empowering the Court to make confiscation orders with respect to the proceeds of drug trafficking or other relevant offences and permits the enforcement of foreign confiscation orders in certain circumstances.

---

[1] See http://www.namlc.bm/.

2.2   What is money laundering?

The term 'money laundering' is described in the Guidance Notes as all procedures which seek to conceal the true origin and ownership of property obtained through illegal means in order to give the appearance that it has originated from legitimate sources.

Under the Act, if the funds represent proceeds of 'criminal conduct', as defined, then the crime committed will bring the transaction within the ambit of the anti-money laundering provisions of the Act. 'Criminal conduct' is defined as drug trafficking or any relevant offence. 'Relevant offence' is defined as (a) any indictable offence in Bermuda other than a drug trafficking offence; or (b) any act or omission which, had it occurred in Bermuda, would have constituted an indictable offence other than a drug trafficking offence.

Tax offences *may* give rise to a money laundering offence in the same way as any other criminal conduct. A hybrid offence (meaning an offence punishable either by summary conviction or indictment, at the discretion of the Crown) of evading taxation is created by the *Taxes Management Act 1976* and as such, tax evasion could amount to 'criminal conduct' for anti-money laundering purposes. As regards conduct outside Bermuda, the test is whether such conduct, had it occurred in Bermuda, would have constituted the offence of criminal tax evasion.

2.3   The specific money laundering offences

As noted above, money laundering covers all procedures that seek to conceal the origin of proceeds of crime so that they appear to have originated from a legitimate source. The three common features of this type of criminal conduct involve:

- An intention to conceal the true ownership and origin of criminal proceeds.

- Maintaining control over such proceeds.

- Changing the form (i.e. laundering) of those proceeds.

For the purposes of the Act, it is irrelevant whether the act or omission took place outside Bermuda.

The Act provides a list of specific money laundering offences, a summary of which follows.

Offence	Summary
Concealing, Disguising, Converting or Transferring the Proceeds of Crime (section 43)	Where a person conceals, disguises, converts or transfers from Bermuda property which the person knows or has reasonable grounds to suspect is directly or indirectly the proceeds of crime. Includes assisting another in avoiding prosecution for drug trafficking, a relevant offence or a confiscation order.

Assisting Another to Retain Criminal Proceeds (section 44)	Where a person enters into or is concerned in an arrangement to facilitate the retention or control of another's proceeds of crime, or the proceeds of crime are used to secure funds placed at the wrongdoer's disposal or to acquire investments for the wrongdoer's benefit.
	No offence is committed if the person discloses in good faith to a police officer or the Reporting Officer a suspicion or belief that any funds or investments are derived from or used in connection with criminal conduct. The disclosure must be made before doing any act concerned with the arrangement and be done with the consent of the police officer or if the disclosure is made after he does the act but is made on his initiative and as soon as it is reasonable for him to make the disclosure. Such disclosure made in these circumstances will not result in any liability for a breach of confidentiality.
Acquisition, Possession or Use of the Proceeds of Crime (section 45)	Where a person knows that any property is in whole or in part directly or indirectly the proceeds of another person's criminal conduct and he acquires, uses or has possession of that property.
	No offence is committed if there was adequate consideration.
	It is a defense if the person makes the appropriate disclosure about the proceeds of criminal conduct to a police officer or to the appropriate person in accordance with procedures established by the person's employer.

Failure to Disclose Knowledge or Suspicion of Laundering Proceeds of Drug Trafficking (section 46)	Where a person knows or suspects a person is engaged in laundering the proceeds of drug trafficking, and the information comes to his attention in the course of his trade, profession, business or employment and he fails to disclose this information to a police officer as soon as is reasonably practicable after it comes to his attention.
	No offence is committed if a legal adviser fails to disclose information which has come to the lawyer in circumstances subject to legal professional privilege but does not extend to information which is given in order to carry out or assist criminal conduct.

Tipping Off (section 47)	Where a person knows that an investigation is proposed or pending into money laundering, or disclosure has been made to a police officer under the Act, and he discloses information to any other person which is likely to prejudice the proposed or pending investigation.

2.4   Client confidentiality

The Act specifically provides that no liability will be incurred for breach of client confidentiality when reporting suspicions of money laundering. It is generally a defense to the offences, where it can be shown that a person becoming aware of money laundering activity made or intended to make disclosure to a police officer or to an appropriate person in the person's place of employment (e.g. the reporting officer).

The Act does not impose an obligation to disclose any information which is disclosed to an attorney in privileged circumstances, nor can attorneys be liable for tipping off when disclosing privileged information.

3   Regulated institutions

The Regulations and Guidance Notes apply to 'regulated institutions', which are defined as:

- An institution licensed as a bank or deposit company.

- A person licensed under the *Investment Business Act 1998*.

- An undertaking licensed under the *Trust (Regulation of Trust Business) Act 2001*.

- A company or society registered under the *Insurance Act 1978* to the extent that it is carrying out certain long-term insurance business.

- A registered credit union.

- A person processing subscriptions or redemptions related to a collective investment scheme.

- A trading member of the *Bermuda Stock Exchange* resident, or, in relation to a body corporate, with a place of business in Bermuda.

- A trading member or futures commission merchant of the *Bermuda Commodities Exchange*, or a member of the *Bermuda Commodities Exchange Clearing House*, resident, or in relation to a body corporate, with a place of business, in Bermuda.

- A person authorized by the *Bermuda Monetary Authority* (the '*BMA*') to offer currency exchange services.

- A person or entity who has applied for and been accepted as a voluntary regulated institution.

Regulated institutions are required, among other things, to ensure that their employees are periodically trained on the Act, the Regulations, and the procedures instituted in order to ensure compliance with the duties imposed thereunder.

3.1 Implications for regulated institutions

The Regulations impose a duty of vigilance on regulated institutions and their employees which requires the following:

- Verification of the identity of the client (or 'know your client').

- Monitoring, recognizing and reporting of suspicious transactions.

- Keeping of certain records for the time period prescribed.

- Training of employees and staff.

Further, a regulated institution will be required to appoint a reporting officer to whom reports should be made and who shall have responsibility to make reports to the *Financial Investigation Unit* (the '*FIU*', being the division of the police department responsible for enforcement of the Act) when suspicious circumstances require.

3.2 Particular regulated institutions

Since the introduction of the Regulations, certain practical and/or legal issues have arisen in the day to day business of several regulated institutions. Of particular concern to numerous Bermuda companies is how to determine whether in fact they do meet the definition of regulated institution. It is not always clear. This question has been an issue for a number of insurance companies and companies which may (or may not) be 'processing subscriptions or redemptions in collective investment schemes'.

3.2.1 Insurance companies

The definition of regulated institution includes a company or society registered under the Insurance Act 1978 'to the extent that it is carrying out long-term insurance (but not reinsurance) business within the meaning of that Act, other than life insurance or disability insurance'. Each license granted to a company or society registered under the Insurance Act 1978 will specify whether or not the company is registered as a long-term insurer. In considering whether an insurance company which issues annuity policies is caught by the Regulations, the question is whether such annuity business is 'life insurance'. There is no definition of 'life insurance' in the Insurance Act 1978 but it is defined in the Life Insurance Act; which includes virtually all forms of annuity business.

It is our view that insurance companies which issue policies against lives in being are not caught by the definition of regulated institution. However, insurance companies engaged in 'annuity business' not involving lives will be caught. Typically, annuity policies will provide certain defined rights to the owner of the annuity including rights of withdrawal before annuitisation. The intent of the Regulations (notwithstanding the legal definitions) is aimed at regulating such annuity business. As a result, we generally would advise such businesses to comply with the Regulations.

3.2.2 Processing subscriptions or redemptions in collective investment schemes

A person 'processing subscriptions or redemptions related to a collective investment scheme ...' is a regulated institution. This definition may be applicable to Bermuda exempted companies who act as managers or administrators of mutual funds which are in receipt of investors' funds for the purposes of participating in mutual funds.

4   Verification procedures

4.1   General

Client verification is perhaps the most important aspect of the anti-money laundering regulatory measures applicable to regulated institutions. Verification procedures will primarily affect those employees who are involved in business acceptance procedures or account opening matters and business development.

In Bermuda, these procedures are particularly relevant to banks, trust companies and fund administration companies who process subscriptions and redemptions for mutual funds.

4.2   When to verify?

Verification is required:

- For all new clients, individuals or corporate, seeking to establish a 'new business relationship' with a regulated institution.

- For one-off transactions for new clients with a value of $10 000 or more (such transactions may, in addition to cash transfers, include, for example, the creation of a trust or a company).

- For two or more one-off transactions which appear to be linked with a total value of more than $10 000.

- Where there is any other suspicion, notwithstanding that verification may not otherwise be required (for example, if an existing client proposes a new substantial transaction and the regulated institution is unsure of the legitimacy of the source of the funds).

4.3   Verification means know your client

The core intent of the Regulations is to require that a regulated institution is able to verify the identity and bona fides of its applicants for business who are defined in the Regulations as 'verification subjects'. Essentially, the rules require a regulated institution to know the identity of the principal client and any other relevant verification subjects; there can be no anonymous principals involved.

The verification process does not apply to those persons who were, as of 19 January 1998 (the effective date of the Act), already clients of the regulated institution.

A 'verification subject' will include:

- the named settlor of and, if different, the provider of funds to settle a trust;

- individual or corporate trustees;

- individuals who hold powers or control over the trust or its underlying companies (for example, possibly a protector);

- beneficial owners of shares of a company, or interests in a partnership; and

- intermediaries who introduce the client.

Generally, verification is required for those holding interests of 5% or more in the entity in question. There are some exceptions, which will be discussed below.

Where a regulated institution (such as a licensed trust company or one of the banks) is dealing with a trust as a client (where the trustees are a regulated or foreign regulated institution), the regulated institution should obtain written confirmation from the trustees of the trust that they are themselves aware of the true identity of the underlying principals (i.e. the settlor(s) and principal beneficiaries).

Where there are intermediaries acting for underlying principals (for example, the use of a nominee company acting on behalf of an individual principal), the true nature of the relationship between the principals and the intermediaries must be established and appropriate enquiries carried out in respect of all parties.

4.4   Identification procedures

Any new potential client who is applying to do business with a regulated institution should be required to produce satisfactory evidence of his, her or its identity as soon as practicable after first making contact with the regulated institution or its agents or representatives. Accordingly, new clients should be asked to complete a personal declaration in the form attached hereto as Schedule 1 and to provide satisfactory evidence in accordance with the Client Verification Checklists attached hereto as Schedule 2 (for individuals) and Schedule 3 (for companies).

In general, verification procedures should be properly completed prior to signing off on client acceptance, opening an account, creating of a trust or company, or carrying out of any other transaction. In exceptional circumstances, the acceptance of the client, or proceeding with a transaction may take place prior to completing verification, but only with the approval of a senior level relevant employee, provided that funds are not transferred to a third party until verification is completed.

If the potential client's failure to provide the information necessary to complete the verification process itself raises suspicion, a report should be made to the regulated institution's reporting officer, who should then consider whether a report should be made to the FIU or alternatively whether to seek guidance from the FIU on how to proceed.

4.5   References from other regulated institutions

The Guidance Notes provide that 'verification of the institution is not needed when the applicant for business is a regulated institution or foreign regulated institution in a jurisdiction specified in Appendix A to the Notes'. Further, where an applicant for business is introduced to a regulated institution by another regulated institution (for example, one of the local banks) or a foreign regulated institution (for example a UK bank), the regulated institution may rely on a written assurance (in the form suggested in the Guidance Notes) from the introducing institution to the effect that evidence of the identity of the applicant has been obtained and recorded and the proper verification procedures have been followed by the introducing institution. Such written assurance will be treated as 'satisfactory evidence of identity'. In any event, it is good practice for the regulated institution in these circumstances to confirm background details by obtaining, for example, a passport and resume/curriculum vitae for an individual, or the latest annual report in the case of a new corporate client.

When receiving a written assurance from a foreign institution, it should be confirmed firstly, that the institution is in a jurisdiction recognized for its money laundering regulation (see Schedule 4); and secondly, that the foreign institution is regulated (e.g. in some jurisdictions law firms may be regulated while in other jurisdictions they may not).

Where a client is referred to as a regulated institution by another group entity or affiliate, these references may be considered 'reliable introductions' for the purposes of the Regulations. This would mean that verification by the regulated institution in Bermuda is not needed. However, it is suggested that an introduction letter substantively in the form of Appendix B to the Guidance Notes should be delivered by the group entity giving the 'reliable introduction'.

4.6   Corporate clients listed on foreign stock exchanges

The Guidance Notes provide that 'unless a company is quoted on a *recognized stock exchange* or is a subsidiary of such a company, steps should be taken to verify the company's underlying beneficial owner(s)'. 'Recognized stock exchange' is not defined in the Act, the Regulations or Guidance Notes. It is suggested that those jurisdictions listed in Appendix A of the Guidance Notes and any stock exchange which is listed as an Appointed Stock Exchange pursuant to section 2(9) of the Companies Act 1981, should be considered as recognized stock exchanges.

The rationale behind this exception to the verification requirements is that a company listed on a recognized stock exchange is already subject to sufficient regulation by competent authorities.

Any trading member of the Bermuda stock exchange resident or, in relation to a body corporate, with a place of business, in Bermuda is a regulated institution for the purposes of the Regulations. Consequently there is no need to undertake verification where the applicant for new business is a member of the Bermuda stock exchange.

5   Recognition and reporting of suspicious transactions

5.1   Suspicious transactions

Regulated institutions are *required* under the Guidance Notes to be alert to unexpected and unexplained changes in the pattern of transactions relating to a trust or underlying companies. The time to detect a money laundering transaction is typically: (a) at the point of introduction of a new client who is establishing a trust or a company; or (b) where a substantial financial transaction is to take place involving an existing trust or company and new funds are introduced.

Where there appears to be no obvious commercial purpose for a particular transaction, suspicion may arise. Appendix E of the Guidance Notes describes several types of transactions which 'may give rise to opportunities for money-laundering', and while much of this list applies to banks, as opposed to trust companies, the list is informative (although not intended to be exhaustive).

5.2   Employees' responsibility to report

All employees of a regulated institution are under a legal responsibility to be vigilant in complying with the Regulations and Guidance Notes. If they know or have reason to suspect any money laundering activity is proposed or is being carried out, they must report their concerns or suspicions to the regulated institution's reporting officer (internal procedures of a regulated institution may provide for reports to be made to a 'line manager' as a first point of contact). By making such a report, an employee has a defense under the Act or the Regulations as regards any money laundering offence.

All employees of regulated institutions and 'relevant employees' are required to 'know enough about a customer's business to recognize that a transaction or series of transactions are unusual'.

The Guidance Notes provide a pro forma Internal Report of Suspicion.

5.3   Reporting officer's responsibilities

Every regulated institution must appoint a reporting officer who should be familiar with the Guidance Notes and the types of transactions handled by the regulated institution. The Regulations provide:

> a regulated institution shall institute and maintain internal reporting procedures which include provision for identifying a person ('the reporting officer') to whom a report is to be made *of any information or other matter which comes to the attention of an employee and which in the opinion of that employee gives rise to a knowledge or suspicion that another person is engaged in money laundering.* (emphasis added)

Accordingly, the principal responsibility of the reporting officer is to act as a focal point for receiving reports of knowledge or suspicions of money laundering from employees of the regulated institution.

Upon receipt of a Report of Suspicion, the reporting officer should investigate the matter to consider whether or not a report should be made to the FIU. The reporting officer is responsible for considering any report received from employees in the regulated institution 'in light of all other relevant information for the purpose of determining whether or not the information . . . gives rise to such a knowledge or suspicion'. If the reporting officer believes the suspicion of money laundering is substantiated, disclosure should be made promptly to the FIU (a pro forma report for the FIU is included in the Guidance Notes and set out in Schedule D). If the reporting officer is uncertain as to the substantiation of the suspicion, a report should be made to the Financial Investigation Unit.

If the reporting officer decides the information does not substantiate a suspicion of money laundering, there is no obligation to report to the FIU, although the reporting officer should record fully his reasons for not proceeding.

Where a report is made to the FIU, acknowledgment should be promptly made by the FIU, who will also provide their consent for the regulated institution to continue operating the account and/or proceeding with the transaction pending the investigation. In rare cases (e.g. where an arrest is imminent) such consent may not be given. Upon receipt of a report of a suspicious transaction, the FIU will seek to investigate the reported individual(s).

The reporting officer must maintain a register of all reports made to the FIU which should include the date of the report, the person who made the report, the person(s) to whom the report was forwarded and a reference by which supporting evidence is identifiable.

Generally, a reporting officer should be a senior officer involved in compliance or financial control matters for the relevant business. The reporting officer should, if possible, be a resident of

Bermuda, but this is not a strict requirement. The important aspect is that such person should be involved in the running of the business of the regulated institution. The Guidance Notes provide that the reporting officer 'should be well versed in the different types of transaction that the regulated institution handles and which may give rise to opportunities for money laundering'. The Regulations do not require a reporting officer to be a sole individual or located in Bermuda. A reporting officer may therefore be a committee or other body corporate, partnership or association which may or may not be in Bermuda.

The regulated institution must enable the reporting officer to have access to any other information which may be of assistance when considering a report of suspicion. Although neither the Regulations nor the Guidance Notes expressly require it, a reporting officer should ensure that the regulated institution complies with the record keeping procedures required under the Regulations. The reporting officer should also be satisfied that the regulated institution is implementing sufficient procedures to comply with the training requirements of the Regulations. For example, employees should generally be made aware of the legislation and their duty of vigilance under the Regulations.

6   Record keeping requirements

The Regulations require a regulated institution to have in place sufficient record keeping procedures to assist the FIU in their investigations. The FIU will normally confine its investigation to the previous five years.

Regulated institutions must maintain the following records:

- Entry Records. Account opening records and verification document references for five years after the account or matter is closed.

- Ledger Records. Details of transactions for five years from the date the transaction is completed.

- Supporting Records. Including credit and debit slips and cheques for five years from when the transaction is completed.

Where an investigation by the FIU is pending, the FIU may request a regulated institution to retain certain records notwithstanding the time for retention has elapsed.

The Regulations require regulated institutions to keep for the 'minimum retention period' such records or copies 'containing such details relating to its business as may be necessary to assist in an investigation into suspected money laundering'. Records will need to be retained relating to verification and transactions (customer, beneficial owners of accounts or products, buyer, seller and other parties).

In particular, transactions relating to securities and investments should contain details on the nature of the investment, valuation and price, source(s) of funds, bearer instruments and custody.

All relevant records should be kept in a 'readily retrievable' form – i.e. original hard copy, microfilm or microfiche or electronic data.

Regulated institutions should maintain a register of all enquiries made of it by the FIU or other local or foreign authorities.

7   Training

All regulated institutions are required to implement training procedures to ensure their employees, and in particular relevant employees, are aware of the Legislation, the requirement of vigilance and related procedures, recognition and handling of suspicious transactions and their personal obligations under the law.

Each regulated institution should decide for itself how to meet the requirement for training procedures for employees. The Guidance Notes indicate appropriate programs which should be implemented for new employees and specific categories of staff. Examples of the latter will include, in the case of banks, cashiers, foreign exchange operators and dealers who should have particular training in the recognition and reporting of suspicious transactions.

Account opening and new business staff should have particular training and understanding of the verification and internal reporting procedures. Administrative supervisors and managers should have a higher level of instruction encompassing all aspects of vigilance policy and internal procedures.

Reporting officers should receive in-depth training in all aspects of the Legislation, vigilance policy and procedures together with initial and continuing instruction on validation and reporting of suspicious transactions and liaising with the FIU.

Regulated institutions should provide for updating and refresher training at regular intervals.

8   Confiscation orders

8.1   Local

Local confiscation orders may be granted in respect of property which is (or is presumed to be) the proceeds of drug trafficking or a 'relevant offence'.

8.2   Foreign/external confiscation orders

External confiscation orders are defined as orders by a court in a designated country for recovering the proceeds of drug trafficking or from any offence which would be an 'indictable offence . . . if committed in Bermuda'.

The Guidance Notes clarify that 'indictable offences' could include foreign tax offences (since Bermuda law includes tax evasion offences), and accordingly it could be open to a foreign authority to seek enforcement in Bermuda of a foreign confiscation court order based on a tax offence in the foreign country. However, there is well established case law which prohibits enforcement of foreign tax claims in Bermuda.

In order to enforce an external confiscation order, the foreign authority must register the order in the Bermuda Supreme Court. The Supreme Court will only enforce an external confiscation order if (i) at the time of registration, the order is in force and is not subject to appeal; (ii) the defendant was given notice of the foreign proceedings; and (iii) enforcing the order in Bermuda would not be contrary to the interests of justice.

English case-law suggests 'interests of justice' includes enabling persons to exercise important legal rights, and not just to avail themselves of a legislative procedure.

9   Lawyers and other professionals

Lawyers and law firms in Bermuda are not regulated institutions. However, they must be keenly aware of their obligations under the Act. To some extent, the Act intends to impose a 'policing' role on 'professionals' working in international business. Particular care will be required by lawyers when considering the scope of their liability under the Act for 'knowing assistance of another in the retention of proceeds of crime'.

The concept of 'knowing assistance' traditionally arises in the context of the civil law cases on constructive trusts and duty of care, in which parties to a relationship, such as trustees, can be liable for a breach of duty to third parties. In civil cases, liability for 'knowingly assisting' a breach of duty can arise where a person recklessly disregards circumstances or facts known to him which would give rise to actual knowledge or suspicion of a dishonest breach of trust. The cases suggest that such recklessness is practically 'dishonest' vis à vis the relevant duty. Accordingly, the concern is whether a similar approach would be applied by the courts when considering whether a person 'knows or suspects' that a person he is assisting has been involved in or benefited from criminal conduct.

It could be difficult for a lawyer to argue he did not know or suspect misconduct if, on an objective basis, the court could find that an honest and reasonable advisor in a similar position with similar experience would be put on notice or would have had a suspicion. In such circumstances, the lawyer involved could be found guilty of 'assisting' a money launderer. In short, as in the civil context, 'turning a blind eye' or not making appropriate enquiries will probably undermine a successful defense.

Addresses

National Anti Money
Laundering Committee
Ministry of Finance
30 Parliament Street
Hamilton HM 12
Bermuda

The Financial Investigation Unit
Police Headquarters
PO Box HM 530
Hamilton HM CX
Bermuda

Abbreviations

BMA   Bermuda Monetary Authority
FIU   Financial Investigation Unit. The FIU is a *'Financial Intelligence Unit'* under the recommendations of the *FATF* and meets the definition of the *Egmont Group*
NAMLC   Bermuda's National Anti-Money Laundering Committee

Schedule 1

PERSONAL DECLARATION

IF THE ANSWER TO ANY OF THE FOLLOWING QUESTIONS IS YES PLEASE PROVIDE DETAILS IN WRITING IN RESPECT OF THAT ANSWER.

		Yes	No
1.	Do you have any interest in any company or partnership registered or formed in Bermuda?	[ ]	[ ]
2.	Have you ever been refused consent to register a company or form a partnership in Bermuda?	[ ]	[ ]
3.	Have you ever been convicted of a criminal offence involving fraud or dishonesty?	[ ]	[ ]
4.	Has fraud or dishonesty been proven against you in any civil proceedings?	[ ]	[ ]
5.	Have you ever been the subject of a judicial or other official civil or criminal enquiry?	[ ]	[ ]

I hereby certify that the information in this Declaration is true to the best of my information, knowledge and belief.

Signed   _____

Date   _____

Schedule 2

CLIENT VERIFICATION CHECKLIST
FOR INDIVIDUAL CLIENTS

		Yes	No
1.	Verification Required:		
	a) Forming a new business relationship	☐	☐
	b) One-off transaction of $10 000 or more	☐	☐
	c) Two or more one-off transactions	☐	☐
	d) Any other suspicion	☐	☐
2.	Full name:	☐	☐
3.	Date and place of birth:	☐	☐
4.	Nationality:	☐	☐
5.	Current Permanent Residential Address:	☐	☐
6.	Telephone and fax number:	☐	☐

			Yes	No
7.	Occupation:		☐	☐
8.	Name and address of Employer:		☐	☐
9.	Personal Introduction from Existing Client:		☐	☐
10.	Details of Introducer:		☐	☐
11.	Interview of Client Held (see attached Interview Report)		☐	☐
12.	Documentation received:			
	- Passport		☐	☐
	- Client Declaration Form		☐	☐
	- Resume/Curriculum Vitae		☐	☐
	- Drivers License with photo*		☐	☐
	- Birth Certificate*		☐	☐
	- Identity Card*		☐	☐
	- Business Card*		☐	☐
	*Not strictly necessary			
13.	Verification in home country from another regulated institution or other institution:		☐	☐
14.	Any third party verification received. If so, describe.		☐	☐
15.	Any other comments:		☐	☐

Signed:_____

Schedule 3

Client Verification Checklist For Companies (including corporate trustees)
For [Regulated Institution]
pursuant to The Proceeds of Crime Act 1997

The Proceeds of Crime (Money Laundering) Regulations 1998: Regulation 4
(Identification Procedures)

		Yes	No
1.	Verification Required:		
	a. Forming a business relationship	☐	☐
	b. One-off transaction of $10 000 or more	☐	☐
	c. Two or more one-off transactions	☐	☐
	d. Any other suspicion	☐	☐
2.	Verification of all bank account signatories	☐	☐
3.	Certificate of Incorporation	☐	☐
4.	Names and Addresses of Beneficial Owners of the Companies (i.e. 5% or more ownership)	☐	☐
5.	Memorandum of Association and Bye-laws	☐	☐
6.	Certificate of Incumbency	☐	☐

7.	Powers of Attorney given by Directors	☐	☐
8.	Directors statement as to the Company's business	☐	☐
9.	Latest annual report/financial statements	☐	☐

Signed:_____

Schedule 4

Foreign Regulated Institutions

Regulation 2(2)(c) provides: 'foreign regulated institution' means a person or entity subject to regulation in any other jurisdiction which is at least equivalent to these Regulations.

The countries and territories listed below may be treated as jurisdictions in which anti-money laundering regulations is at least equivalent to Bermuda's Proceeds of Crime (Money Laundering) Regulations 1998.

Argentina	Australia	Austria
Bahamas	Belgium	Bermuda
Brazil	British Virgin Islands	Canada
Cayman Islands	Denmark	Finland
France	Germany	Greece
Guernsey	Hong Kong/China	Iceland
Ireland	Isle of Man	Italy
Japan	Jersey	Liechtenstein
Luxembourg	Mexico	Kingdom of the Netherlands
New Zealand	Norway	Panama
Portugal	Singapore	Spain
Sweden	Switzerland	Turkey
United Kingdom	United States	

(a) Regulated institutions in Bermuda are reminded of the provisions of paragraph 5 of the Guidance Notes which require them to ensure that their branches, subsidiaries and representative offices operating in other jurisdictions observe standards at least equivalent to the Guidance Notes. It follows that regulated institutions may regard introductions from such sources in jurisdictions outside the above list as reliable introductions.

(b) In seeking to identify foreign regulated institutions, reference should be made to lists published from time to time by regulators or supervisors of licensed or authorized financial institutions in the jurisdictions mentioned above. Such lists are commonly issued by Central Banks, Securities Commissions or other equivalent Authorities.

(c) The acceptance of business from an institution in a jurisdiction outside the above list is not precluded but, except as outlined in paragraph (a) above, an introduction from an institution in such a jurisdiction may not be treated as a reliable introduction.

(d) A suggested format for a reliable introduction is given in Appendix B to the Guidance Notes

Bibliography

Biggs, S./Farrell, S./Padfield, N.: The Proceeds of Crime Act 2002, Butterworths, 2002.

Millington, T./Sutherland. W.M.: The Proceeds of Crime, Law and Practice of Restraint, Confiscation and Forfeiture, Oxford University Press, 2003.

Tanya Cecile McCartney was born in Nassau, Bahamas and was educated in the Bahamas as well as the United Kingdom. Tanya McCartney read law at the University of Reading, UK, where she obtained a Bachelor of Laws Degree with Honours. She was admitted to the Bahamas Bar and the Bar of England and Wales in 1995, having successfully passed the UK Bar Finals Examination with Honours. Miss McCartney is a member of The Honourable Society of Lincoln's Inn. She completed postgraduate studies at the London School of Economics and Political Science, University of London, UK, where she obtained a Master of Laws Degree with Merit (LLM) in 1996, specializing in commercial and corporate law. A founding member of the Bahamas Association of Compliance Officers she currently serves as President.

Cheryl E. Bazard is a sole practitioner in the law firm of Cheryl E. Bazard Law Chambers and Compliance Consultant and Anti-Money Laundering Trainer. Mrs Bazard has been a compliance professional since 1998. In 2002, when CIBC merged with Barclays Bank in the Caribbean, Mrs. Bazard became Regional Director of Compliance with responsibility for compliance in 16 countries in the Caribbean. Mrs Bazard served as Counsel in the Office of the Attorney General as well as Acting Magistrate in Civil and Traffic Courts. Mrs Bazard read law at the University of Buckingham, UK. She was admitted to the Bahamas Bar and the Bar of England and Wales in 1991. Mrs Bazard sits on the Education Loan Authority, the Disciplinary Committee of the Bahamas' Securities Commission and tutors civil procedure at the Eugene Dupuch Law School in The Bahamas. She is the founding President of The Bahamas Association of Compliance Officers.

Firm's profile

Cheryl E. Bazard Law Chambers is a Bahamian-based law firm that provides a comprehensive range of professional legal services. The principal areas of practice include: Corporate & Commercial Law, Family Law, Personal Injury Litigation, Real Property Law & Immigration. Cheryl E. Bazard Law Chambers is also able to provide a full range of corporate administrative & management services as it is a Bahamian licensed Financial & Corporate Service Provider. The firm also provides an extensive training in Compliance, Corporate Governance and Anti-Money Laundering Issues.

The Bahamas Association of Compliance Officers

BACO was formed on 26 April 1999 to promote professionalism and a better understanding of the role of the compliance officer in the Bahamas within financial institutions and the community at large. The stated mission of BACO is to serve respective financial service organizations and the Bahamian marketplace by seeking to enhance the role of compliance within the Bahamas environment, thereby enhancing public trust in and to better ensure the integrity of the Bahamas financial services industry. The main focus of the organization is the training and education of compliance officers in the Bahamas. The international Compliance Association (ICA) has listed the BACO as an approved Association.

Bahamas

Cheryl E. Bazard

Cheryl E. Bazard Law Chambers
Unwala House Annex
East Street North
Nassau, The Bahamas

Tel +1 242 326-0126/7
Fax +1 242 326-0128
bahlawyer4you@yahoo.com;
bazardlaw@gmail.com

Tanya McCartney

President

**Bahamas Association
of Compliance Officers**
P.O. Box G.T. 2037
Nassau, The Bahamas

Tel +1 242 557 2329

tmccartney@coralwave.com

Anti-Money Laundering: International Law and Practice.
Edited by W.H. Muller, C.H. Kälin and J.G. Goldsworth
© 2007 John Wiley & Sons, Ltd

Contents – Bahamas

1 Financial legislation overview

When **The Financial Action Task Force** (FATF) issued its list of Non Cooperative Countries or Territories in 2000, the Bahamas found itself on this list. Moreover, The **Organisation for Economic Co-operation and Development** (OECD) labeled it a harmful tax jurisdiction. The government of the Bahamas took swift action to ensure that legislative and regulatory measures were put in place to enshrine what was already best practice to a large extent. The end result was a compendium of legislation which shall be discussed in this chapter.

The Bahamian law as it relates to money laundering prevention and combating the financing of terrorism can be found in the following pieces of legislation:

- The Proceeds of Crime Act, 2000 (POCA).
- The Financial Transactions Reporting Act 2000.
- The Financial Transactions Reporting (Amendment) Act, 2001.
- The Financial Transactions Reporting (Amendment) Act, 2003.
- The Financial Transactions Reporting Regulations, 2000.
- The Financial Transactions Reporting (Amendment) Regulations, 2001.
- The Financial Transactions Reporting (Amendment) Regulations, 2003.
- The Financial Intelligence Unit Act, 2000.
- The Financial Intelligence Unit (Amendment) Act, 2001.
- The Financial Intelligence (Transactions Reporting) Regulations, 2001.
- The Anti-Terrorism Act, 2004.

There are also directions and best practices to be found in:

- The Central Bank's Guidelines for Licensees on the Prevention of Money Laundering & Countering the Financing of Terrorism.
- The Financial Intelligence Unit's Guidelines on the Reporting of Suspicious Transactions for Banks and Trust Companies, the Securities Industry, the Insurance Industry, Licensed Casinos, Cooperatives and Financial Service Providers.

1.1 Definition of money laundering

Under section 40 of POCA, a person is guilty of an offence of money laundering if knowing, suspecting or having reasonable grounds to suspect that any property in whole or in part directly or indirectly represents, another person's proceeds of criminal conduct, he uses, transfers, sends or delivers to any person or place that property; or disposes of or otherwise deals with in any manner by any means that property with the intent to conceal or disguise such property. The offence of money laundering is punishable under summary conviction to a term of imprisonment of 5 years and/or a fine of (Bahamian) B\$100 000.00 and on conviction on information to a term of imprisonment of 20 years and/or an unlimited fine.

1.2 Confiscation of assets

Under section 9 of the POCA, upon conviction for one or more drug trafficking offences, a person shall be liable at the time of sentencing in respect of that conviction to have a confiscation order made against him relating to the proceeds of drug trafficking including any property representing such proceeds and all gifts made under section 6(1). Under section 6(1) a gift derived from drug trafficking including a gift made before the commencement of the Act is caught by the Act if it was made by the defendant at any time since the beginning of the period of six years ending when the proceedings for the drug trafficking offence were instituted against him, or where no such proceedings have been instituted, when an application for a restraint order or a charging order is made.

1.3 Terrorist financing

Terrorism is defined in section 2 of the Anti-Terrorism Act 2004 as any act which is intended to intimidate the public or coerce a government or international agency to comply with the demands of terrorists and which is intended to cause death or serious bodily harm to a person, or a serious risk to public health or safety, or damage to property or interference with or disruption of essential services or systems.

Under the Anti-Terrorism Act, 2004, the financing of terrorism is criminalized. Persons who have reasonable grounds to suspect that funds or financial services are related to or are to be used to facilitate terrorism have a duty to report their suspicions to the Commissioner of Police. Failure to make a report is an offence and carries a penalty of imprisonment for a term of 5 years and a fine of B$250 000.00 on conviction on information.

The Anti-Terrorism Act has provisions which empower the Attorney-General to freeze, forfeit and dispose of funds used to facilitate terrorism. Where either an offence of terrorism or providing or collecting funds for criminal purposes is committed by a person responsible for the management or control of an entity located or registered in the Bahamas or in any way organized under the laws of the Bahamas while acting in that capacity, that entity is guilty of an offence and is liable to a fine of B$2 million on conviction on information.

2 The scope of the application of the Anti-Money Laundering Act

2.1 What is a financial institution?

Under section 3(1) of the Financial Transactions Reporting Act, the term 'financial institution' means any of the following:

Bank – 3(1)(a):	A bank or trust company, being a bank or trust company licensed under the Banks and Trust Companies Regulation Act, 2000.
Insurance – 3(1)(b):	A company carrying life assurance business as defined in section 2 of the Insurance Act.
Casino – 3(1)(e):	A licensed casino operator within the meaning of the Lotteries and Gaming Act.

2.2 Non-banking sector

- A co-operative society registered under the Co-operative Societies Act.
- A friendly society enrolled under the Friendly Societies Act.
- A broker-dealer within the meaning of section 2 of the Securities Industry Act.

- A real estate broker, but only to the extent that the real estate broker receives funds in the course of that person's business for the purpose of settling real estate transactions.

- A trustee or administration manager or investment manager of a superannuation scheme.

- A mutual fund administrator or operator of a mutual fund within the meaning of the Mutual Funds Act, 1985.

- Any person whose business or a principal part of whose business consists of any of the following:

  (a) borrowing or lending or investing money;

  (b) administering or managing funds on behalf of other persons;

  (c) acting as trustee in respect of funds of other persons;

  (d) dealing in life assurance policies;

  (e) providing financial services that involve the transfer or exchange of funds, including (without limitation) services relating to financial leasing, money transmissions, credit cards, debit cards, treasury certificates, bankers draft and other means of payment, financial guarantees, trading for account of others (in money market instruments, foreign exchange, interest and index instruments, transferable securities and futures), participation in securities issues, portfolio management, safekeeping of cash and liquid securities, investment related insurance and money changing; but not including the provision of financial services that consist solely of the provision of financial advice;

  (f) a counsel and attorney, but only to the extent that the counsel and attorney receives funds in the course of that person's business for the purposes of deposit or investment; for the purpose of selling real estate transactions; or to be held in a client's account;

  (g) an accountant, but only to the extent that the accountant receives funds in the course of that person's business for the purposes of deposit or investment.

3 Obligations of the financial intermediaries

3.1 Obligations of due diligence

All financial institutions have a legal obligation to implement policies and procedures to identify unusual activity and prevent money laundering activity and the financing of terrorism within its financial institution. Staff must be trained in these policies and procedures and there is also a duty to report suspicious activity

3.2 Verification of the contracting party

Pursuant to section 6 of the Financial Transactions Reporting Act, where any request is made to a financial institution for a person to become a facility holder (whether in relation to an existing facility provided by that financial institution or by means of the establishment, by that financial institution, of a new facility), that financial institution shall verify the identity of that person. Under section 6(2), the verification of the identity must take place before that person becomes a facility holder in relation to that facility. Section 11 of the Financial Transactions Reporting Act lays down the procedures for the verification identity and notes that verification shall be done by means of such documentary or other evidence as is reasonably capable of establishing the identity of that person, including official documents and structural information in the case of corporate entities.

Regulations 3 to 6 of the Financial Transactions Reporting Regulations spell out the documentation necessary for verifying the identity of a facility holder. Initially, these regulations laid out a prescriptive approach to the procurement of documents necessary for the identification of facility holders. The recent amendments contained in Regulation 3(2) of the Financial Transactions Reporting (Amendment) Regulations, 2003 now give a prescriptive as well as an indicative or risk-based approach to identification. In essence, the legislation now looks at the true identity of the facility holder through the full and correct name/names used; the correct permanent address including postcode, if appropriate, the date and place of birth; and the purpose of the account and the nature of the business relationship. Financial institutions are called upon to identify the source of funds, the normal and expected transactions of the facility holder through the financial institution and the monitoring of customer transactions to detect and identify activity inconsistent with the customer profile.

Identification documents include a passport, driver's licence, voter's card, national identity card, or such other identification document bearing a photographic likeness of the individual as is reasonably capable of establishing the identity of that individual. Clause 34 of the Central Bank's Guidelines for Licensees on the Prevention of Money Laundering & Countering the Financing of Terrorism notes that where satisfactory evidence of identity is required, a Licensee should 'suspend' the rights attaching to the transaction pending receipt of the necessary evidence. Documents of title should not be issued, nor income remitted (though it may be reinvested) in the absence of identity.

3.3   Identification of the beneficial owner

Beneficial owners should also be identified as laid down in sections 8 and 9 of the Financial Transactions Reporting Act. Failure to verify the identity of facility holders may result in the case of an individual, a fine of B$20 000.00 and in the case of a body corporate, a fine of B$100 000.00

3.4   Renewed verification and identification

Once verification of identity of a facility holder has been completed no further verification of identity is necessary as long as the facility is used by the facility holder on a regular basis. (Reg. 9 of the FTRR)

3.5   Information from an introducer or intermediary

A financial institution in the Bahamas can get information or verification from a foreign financial institution for foreign clients which is regulated by a body having equivalent regulatory and supervisory responsibilities as the Central Bank, Securities Commission, Registrar of Insurance or the Gaming Board or a financial institution regulated by the Central Bank, the Securities Commission, The Registrar of Insurance or the Gaming Board for domestic clients. However, pursuant to clause 119 of the Central Bank Guidelines, there must be receipt of clear and legible copies of all documentation in their possession within 30 days of receipt of the written confirmation. There must be certification that any photocopies forwarded are identical with the corresponding originals and this certification must come from a senior member of the introducer's management team. If the documents are not obtained within the 30 day period, the account should be suspended and if after a further reasonable period the documents are not received, the business relationship must be terminated. Following consultation with industry representatives, The Central Bank of Bahamas in 2007 advised all licensees that the application of the "30 day rule" **may** be waived **only** where licensees provide company incorporation or registered agent/office services to eligible introducers, subject to certain conditions.

3.6   Training procedures

Pursuant to Regulation 6 of the Financial Intelligence (Transactions Reporting) Regulations, 2001, a financial institution shall take appropriate measures from time to time for the purpose of making all relevant employees aware of the anti-money laundering legislation and of the procedures maintained by the institution in compliance with duties imposed under those pieces of legislation. This training must be at least once per year and must cover the recognition and handling of transactions carried out by or on behalf of any person who is, or appears to be, engaged in money laundering. Failure to train results in a fine of B$10 000.00 on summary conviction and on conviction on information, a fine of B$50 000.00 for a first offence and B$100 000.00 for a second or subsequent offence.

Failure to have policies and procedures as required by Regulation 8 of the Financial Intelligence (Transactions Reporting) Regulations makes one liable on summary conviction to an imprisonment term of 3 years or a fine of B$50 000.00 or both and on conviction on information, to a prison term of 10 years of an unlimited fine or both.

4   Obligations to report suspicions

Under section 14 of the Financial Transactions Reporting Act, there is a duty to report or to disclose knowledge or suspicion of money laundering. The reporting is to be made as soon as practicable after the suspicion is formed. Reporting is to be made by the Money Laundering Reporting Officer to the Financial Intelligence Unit. Persons making reports are protected from civil, criminal or disciplinary proceedings pursuant to section 16 of the Financial Transactions Reporting Act. At the same time, legal professional privilege is retained under section 17 with respect to privileged communication. Failure to report creates a liability on summary conviction to a fine not exceeding B$20 000.00 in the case of an individual and B$100 000.00 in the case of a body corporate. There is also a duty not to disclose that a suspicious transaction report has been made or is in contemplation of being made (s. 18(1) FTRA). Regulation 5 of the Financial Intelligence (Transactions Reporting) Regulations 2001 sets out the reporting procedure within a financial institution.

5   Record keeping

Under section 23 of the FTRA there is an obligation to keep transaction records for a period of not less than 5 years after the completion of the transaction to enable that transaction to be readily reconstructed by the Financial Intelligence Unit. There is also an obligation to keep verification records pursuant to section 24 for a period of not less than 5 years. The records are to be kept either in written form in the English language or so as to enable the records to be readily accessible and readily convertible into written form in the English language. The records should detail the nature of the transaction, the amount of the transaction and the currency, the date on which the transaction was conducted, the parties to the transaction and where applicable, the facility through which the transaction was conducted. Failure to provide such information as requested by the FIU is an offence and the penalty is a fine not exceeding B$50 000.00 or imprisonment for a term not exceeding 2 years or both imprisonment and fine. Failure to retain the records is an offence and on summary conviction, an individual is liable to a fine not exceeding $20 000 and a body corporate is liable to a fine not exceeding $100 000.00. Record keeping with respect to wire transfers is governed by Regulation 8 of the Financial Transactions Reporting Regulations and provides for the maintenance of records of all wire transfers inclusive of information as to the original source, the fields for the ordering and final destination of the funds together with names and addresses.

6   Monitoring of accounts

Accounts should be monitored for the first year of operation pursuant to Regulation 9(2) of the Financial Transactions Reporting Regulations. This is to ensure consistency with the facility holders stated account purposes and business and the identified potential account activity. Regulation 8 of the Financial Transactions Reporting (Amendment) Regulations further notes that there is a duty to continue verification of accounts where there is a material change in the way the facility is operated. The Central Bank Guidelines for Licensees on the Prevention of Money Laundering & Countering the Financing of Terrorism notes that material change is one which is inconsistent with a facility holder's account profile.

6.1   Duty to appoint a Compliance Officer

Pursuant to Regulation 5(e) of the Financial Intelligence (Transaction Reporting) Regulations, the financial institution shall identify and appoint a senior officer as a compliance officer who shall ensure that a regulated institution is in full compliance with the laws of the Bahamas.

6.2   Duty to appoint a Money Laundering Reporting Officer

Pursuant to Regulation 5(a) of the Financial Intelligence (Transaction Reporting) Regulations, the financial institution shall identify and appoint a person ('the Money Laundering Reporting Officer' who shall be registered with the Financial Intelligence Unit) to whom a report is to be made of any information or other matter which comes to the attention of an employee and which in the opinion of that employee gives rise to a knowledge or suspicion that another person is engaged in money laundering.

7   AML/CFT supervision

7.1   The system's components and their coordination

In the Bahamas there is no 'super-regulator' as in the United Kingdom where there is the Financial Services Authority. There is more than one regulator involved in the fight against money laundering and terrorist financing.

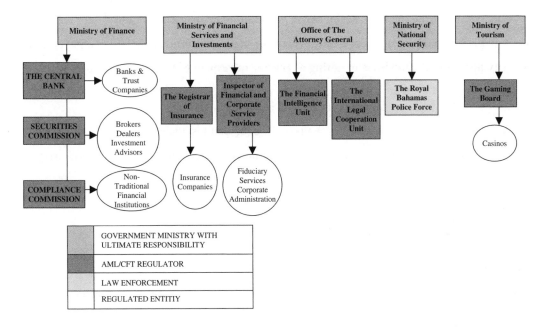

	GOVERNMENT MINISTRY WITH ULTIMATE RESPONSIBILITY
	AML/CFT REGULATOR
	LAW ENFORCEMENT
	REGULATED ENTITIY

7.2   The regulators

The Central Bank of the Bahamas (www.centralbankbahamas.com)

The Central Bank of the Bahamas regulates its Licensees, namely banks and trust companies ('traditional' financial institutions).

The Securities Commission of the Bahamas (www.scb.gov.bs)

By virtue of The Securities Industry Act, 1999, the Securities Commission of the Bahamas has powers to regulate the securities market.

The Compliance Commission (www.bahamas.gov.bs)

The Commission is an independent statutory authority responsible for enforcing compliance with the anti-money laundering rules and regulations *by designated financial institutions which are not otherwise regulated for this purpose* ('non-traditional' financial institutions).

- **Co-operative Societies**.

- **Friendly Societies**.

- **A real estate broker**, but only to the extent that he receives funds in the course of his business to settle a real estate transaction, i.e. any matter involving work that can only be done by or under the supervision of a lawyer pursuant to section 22 of the Legal Profession Act, 1992; or by a current licence holder under the Real Estate (Brokers and Salesmen) Act, 1995.

- **Trustees**, administration managers or investment managers of a superannuation scheme within the meaning of the Superannuation and other Trust Funds (Validation) Act.

- **Any person in the business of borrowing or lending or investing money**.

- **Any person in the business of administering or managing funds** on behalf of other persons.

- **Any person in the business of acting as trustee in respect of funds of other persons**.

- **A counsel and attorney,** where he receives funds in the course of his business to deposit or invest, settle real estate transactions, or hold in a client's account;

- **An accountant,** where he receives funds in the course of his business to deposit or invest.

- **Any person in the business of providing financial services that involves the transfer or exchange of funds,**

The Registrar of Insurance

Regulates and supervises entities and persons involved in the insurance industry

The Inspector of Financial and Corporate Service Providers

The Inspector of Financial and Corporate Service Providers (FCSP) regulates companies engaged in the provision of 'financial and corporate services', which is:

the provision of financial and corporate services for profit or reward in or from within The Bahamas and includes:

(a) the conduct or the carrying on of financial services in or from The Bahamas, including on-line financial services;

(b) the registration or management and administration of international business companies incorporated or existing under the International Business Companies Act, 2000;

(c) the provision of registered agent services and registered office services for companies mentioned in paragraph (b);

(d) the provision of directors or officers for companies mentioned in paragraph (b);

(e) the provision of nominee shareholders for companies mentioned in paragraph (b);

(f) the provision of partners for partnerships registered and existing under the Exempted Limited Partnership Act, 1995; and

(g) the provision of registered agent services and registered office services for partnerships registered and existing under the Exempted Limited Partnership Act, 1995.

The Gaming Board

The Gaming Board is responsible for the licensing and regulating of casinos, which are financial institutions for the purposes of AML/CFT Supervision in the Bahamas.

7.3   Delegation of duties

Section 46 of the Financial Transactions Reporting Act, 2000 provides that:

The [Compliance] Commission may from time to time after consultation with the Inspector, The Bahamas Bar Council, The Bahamas Institute of Chartered Accountants, the Financial Intelligence Unit and such other bodies and organizations representative of such financial institutions as are required to be regulated under this Act, issue such codes of practice as the Commission thinks necessary

(a) for the purpose of providing guidance as to the duties, requirements and standards to be complied with and the procedures (whether as to verification, record-keeping, reporting of suspicious transactions or otherwise) and best practices to be observed by financial institutions;

(b) Generally for the purposes of this Act.

Although the Registrar of Insurance and the Inspector of FCSP are ultimately responsible for regulating their respective licensees with respect to AML/CFT, the Compliance Commission by virtue of this provision, has been given jurisdiction over AML/CFT for both the insurance sector and financial and corporate service providers. The Compliance Commission reports its findings to The Registrar of Insurance and The Inspector of Financial and Corporate Service Providers.

8 The Financial Intelligence Unit

Financial Intelligence Unit Act, 2000 establishes the Financial Intelligence Unit of the Bahamas. It is a member of the Egmont Group.

8.1 Purpose of the Financial Intelligence Unit (FIU)

Section 4(1) of the Act empowers the FIU to act as the agency responsible for receiving, analyzing, obtaining and disseminating information which relates or may relate to the proceeds of offences under the Proceeds of Crime Act, 2000. The FIU receives suspicious transaction reports.

8.2 Functions and powers of the Financial Intelligence Unit

The FIU may:

- Receive all disclosures of information required to be made pursuant to the Proceeds of Crime Act, 2000.

- Receive information from any Foreign Financial Intelligence Unit.

- Order in writing any person to refrain from completing any transaction up to a maximum period of 72 hours.

- Freeze a person's bank account for a maximum period of five days upon receipt of a request from a foreign FIU or law enforcement authority including the Commissioner of Police of the Bahamas.

- Require the production of information (except information subject to legal professional privilege) which it considers relevant to fulfill its functions.

- Share information relating to the commission of an offence under the Proceeds of Crime Act, 2000 with the local law enforcement agency including the Commissioner of Police.

- Provide information to foreign FIUs relating to the commission of an offence under the Proceeds of Crime Act, 2000.

- Enter into any agreement or arrangement in writing with a foreign FIU for the discharge or performance of the functions of the FIU.

- Inform the public and financial and business entities of their obligations under measures that have been or might be taken to detect, prevent and deter the commission of offences under the Proceeds of Crime Act, 2000.

- Retain a record of all information it receives for a minimum of five years after the information is received.

8.3   The Financial Intelligence (Transactions Reporting) Regulations, 2001

The FIU has been given the power to issue Guidelines on suspicious transactions and anti-money laundering and has done so for a number of the financial institutions as defined in the FTRA, 2000. (http://www.lexbahamas.com/FBanks_and_Trust_Money_Laundering_Guidelines_FIU.pdf)

9   Law enforcement

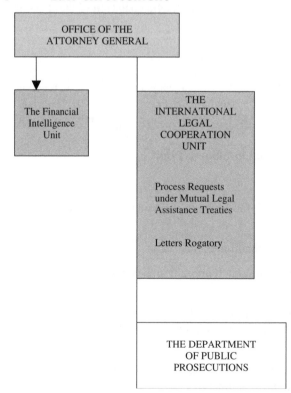

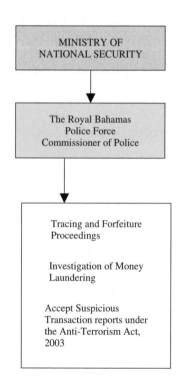

10 International cooperation

A handbook entitled The Information Sharing and Regulatory Cooperation Handbook has been prepared by The Group of Financial Services Regulators (the GFSR) in the Bahamas to provide an overview of the regulatory information-sharing processes and procedures. It is a useful guide to the international cooperation arrangements in the Bahamas. It is available on the website of The Central Bank of Bahamas (http://www.centralbankbahamas.com/public/GFSRIH30.06.05.pdf). The handbook outlines in detail the laws and procedures associated with international cooperation in the context of financial services.

There are two avenues for international cooperation:

(a) judicial; and

(b) regulatory.

10.1 Judicial assistance

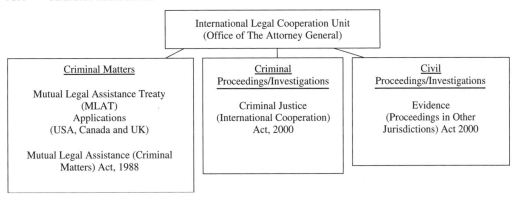

The Competent Authority is the Attorney General under the following pieces of legislation.

- **Mutual Legal Assistance (Criminal Matters) Act, 1988**.

- **Criminal Justice (International Cooperation) Act, 2000**.

- **Evidence (Proceedings in Other Jurisdictions) Act 2000**.

Requests must emanate from the Competent Authority in the Requesting State and addressed to:

The Director of Legal Affairs
Office of the Attorney General
Post Office Building
East Hill Street
P.O. Box N-3007
Nassau, N.P.
Bahamas

10.2 Regulatory assistance

Overseas regulatory agencies may make a request for assistance to its corresponding regulatory agency in the Bahamas (i.e. that exercises the same function as the overseas regulatory agency). The following Regulatory Agencies render assistance:

(a) The Central Bank of The Bahamas.

(b) The Securities Commission of the Bahamas.

(c) The Compliance Commission.

(d) The Registrar of Insurance.

(e) The Inspector of Financial and Corporate Service Providers.

Requests should be made directly to the relevant agency in writing and in English. Practitioners should consult the Information Sharing and Regulatory Cooperation Handbook.

Addresses

**The Central Bank of the Bahamas
c/o The Inspector of Banks and Trust Companies**
Frederick Street
P.O. Box N-4868
Nassau, Bahamas
Tel 242-322-2193
Fax 242-356-3909
www.centralbankbahamas.com

The Compliance Commission
Sir Cecil Wallace Whitfield Building
P.O. Box CB 10980
Nassau, Bahamas
Tel 242-327-5826
Fax 242-327-5806

Ministry of Financial Services & Investments
Goodman's Bay Corporate Centre
West Bay Street
P.O. Box N-7770
Nassau, Bahamas
Tel 242-356-5956
Fax 242-356-5990

The Financial Intelligence Unit
Frederick Street
P.O. Box SB 50086
Nassau, Bahamas
Tel 242-356-9808
Fax 242-322-5551

Bibliography

The Statute Laws of the Commonwealth of the Bahamas

- The Proceeds of Crime Act, 2000 (POCA).

- The Financial Transactions Reporting Act, 2000.

- The Financial Transactions Reporting (Amendment) Act, 2001.

- The Financial Transactions Reporting (Amendment) Act, 2003.

- The Financial Transactions Reporting Regulations, 2000.

- The Financial Transactions Reporting (Amendment) Regulations, 2001.

- The Financial Transactions Reporting (Amendment) Regulations, 2003.

- The Financial Intelligence Unit Act, 2000.

- The Financial Intelligence Unit (Amendment) Act, 2001.

- The Financial Intelligence (Transactions Reporting) Regulations, 2001.

- The Anti-Terrorism Act, 2004.

There are also directions and best practices to be found in:

- The Central Bank's Guidelines for Licensees on the Prevention of Money Laundering & Countering the Financing of Terrorism.

- The Financial Intelligence Unit's Guidelines on the Reporting of Suspicious Transactions for Banks and Trust Companies, the Securities Industry, the Insurance Industry, Licensed Casinos, Cooperatives and Financial Service Providers.

The Information Sharing and Regulatory Cooperation Handbook prepared by The Group of Financial Services Regulators (28 June 2005).

Martin Livingston qualified as a Barrister and Solicitor in New Zealand in 1994 and is admitted as a Cayman Islands attorney. He currently heads up the Maples and Calder Regulatory Financial Services Group in the Cayman Islands. Martin advises international financial institutions on anti-money laundering, asset tracing, risk management, corporate governance, licensing and regulatory matters. In his current position, he also advises on duties of confidentiality and information exchange. These clients have included most of the top 40 global investment banks, as well as numerous fund managers, administrators and insurance companies. As President of the Cayman Islands Compliance Association he is part of the Cayman Islands Private Sector Consultative Committee that assists the Cayman Islands government to determine and develop policy and laws. Martin is also on the Cayman Islands Guidance Notes Committee for the drafting of Cayman Islands anti-money laundering guidelines.

Firm's profile

Maples and Calder, the world's leading offshore law firm, provides clients with multi-jurisdictional legal capability from its offices in Cayman, BVI, Dublin and Jersey. The firm also has offices in London, Hong Kong and Dubai, which provide greater proximity to the firm's European, Asian and Middle Eastern client base and enables the firm to provide time zone sensitive advice. The firm now has over 500 lawyers and staff worldwide and advice is given to leading international and domestic law firms, major financial institutions and high net worth clients.

Cayman Islands

Martin Livingston

Attorney

Maples and Calder
Cayman Islands

Tel +001 345 949 8066
Fax +001 345 949 8080
martin.livingston@maplesandcalder.com
www.maplesandcalder.com

Anti-Money Laundering: International Law and Practice.
Edited by W.H. Muller, C.H. Kälin and J.G. Goldsworth
© 2007 John Wiley & Sons, Ltd

Contents – Cayman Islands

1 Introduction

As one of the world's leading financial centres, the Cayman Islands have regarded the issue of money laundering with the utmost seriousness. In common with other financial centres in the world, the Cayman Islands have continued to enact legislation that is aimed at preventing and detecting money laundering and, more recently, combating the **financing of terrorism**.

The government and financial sector has been acutely aware of the negative perceptions and commentaries in relation to secrecy and **money laundering**. For over 20 years, the Cayman Islands have been actively organising a strict anti-money laundering regime and, when necessary, have implemented additional legislation to bolster the pre-existing anti-money laundering framework so as to keep pace with or exceed international expectations and standards. Legislation has been specifically tailored to provide depth to the Cayman Islands' anti-money laundering provisions and to address concerns relating to confidentiality and tax.

The Cayman Islands were a founding member of the Caribbean Financial Action Task Force ('CFATF'), which is an observer body to the Financial Action Task Force ('FATF'). The Cayman Islands have also recently undergone assessment by the IMF, using a common methodology, including the FATF 40 + 9 recommendations on **anti-money laundering** and combating of the **financing of terrorism**, and have been found to be largely compliant with most recommendations.

2 Legislative background

The Cayman Islands have had legislation specifically dealing with **money laundering** since 1989. The Cayman Islands were amongst the first countries to introduce drug trafficking laws with the enactment of the Misuse of Drugs Law ('MDL') in 1973 and amended the legislation in 1989 to address the elements for **anti-money laundering**. The Cayman Islands were also one of the first **offshore jurisdictions** and the first British Overseas Territory in the Caribbean to introduce all-crimes anti-money-laundering laws, pursuant to the Proceeds of Criminal Conduct Law 1996 ('PCCL'). The PCCL was largely based on the UK Criminal Justice Act 1993 and served as model legislation for other Caribbean nations.

The PCCL is the primary anti-money laundering legislation in the Cayman Islands. It was supplemented by a Code of Practice (the 'Code') in March 2000 and amended in July 2000 to enable subordinate legislation to be issued in the form of binding regulations. The Money Laundering Regulations (the 'Regulations'), initially enacted in April 2000, forms **the secondary level of anti-money laundering legislation.**

The Code and the Regulations co-existed until 26 April 2001 when the Guidance Notes on the Prevention and Detection of Money Laundering in the Cayman Islands (the 'Guidance Notes') were issued jointly by the Cayman Islands Monetary Authority ('CIMA') and local professional industry associations to supersede the Code. Although the Guidance Notes do not carry the force of law and are not mandatory, their aim is to provide transparent guidelines or best practice for the interpretation and implementation of the Regulations.

Each of the MDL, PCCL, the Regulations and Guidance Notes have since been amended and/or revised and, as at the date of drafting, the latest versions are MDL (2000 Revision), PCCL (2005 Revision), Regulations (2006 Revision) and Guidance Notes, last updated September 2003.

3   The PCCL

The PCCL is modelled on equivalent UK legislation but with some very important differences for the protection of clients and professional service providers and tailored to the requirements of an offshore jurisdiction.

The PCCL can be conveniently divided into four parts. In summary, these are:

(a) **Court powers to freeze and confiscate certain property** relating to domestic crimes, i.e. those committed in the Cayman Islands.

(b) **Money laundering offences** committed in the Cayman Islands.

(c) **International cooperation** by the enforcement of certain foreign criminal compensation orders.

(d) Supplementary powers of search and seizure, the establishment and empowerment of the Cayman Islands Financial Reporting Authority (the 'Reporting Authority'), and access to information in the investigation of crime.

3.1   The money laundering offences

There are essentially four categories of offences relating to money laundering which have been introduced by the PCCL. There are separate existing offences under the MDL relating to drug trafficking that are similar in scope (but somewhat narrower).

The money laundering offences are, in summary:

(a) **Providing assistance** to another in an arrangement that helps them to retain or control the benefits of their criminal conduct. Assistance in an arrangement is not defined and is very broad in scope. In practice, it will include almost all services given by financial service providers.

(b) **The acquisition, possession or use (even temporary) of property** knowing that it represents the proceeds of criminal conduct.

(c) **Concealing, transferring or removing** from the Cayman Islands **proceeds of criminal conduct** to assist another to avoid prosecution or a confiscation.

(d) **Disclosing information to ('tipping off') the target of an investigation** or proposed investigation into money laundering or a third party of anything that is likely to prejudice the investigation.

For the purposes of these offences it is not necessary that the original offence from which proceeds stem was committed in the Cayman Islands if the conduct would also constitute an indictable offence had it taken place within the Islands.

These offences carry a maximum penalty of 14 years imprisonment and an unlimited fine except tipping off which carries a maximum of 5 years imprisonment. No prosecution may be brought without the consent of the Attorney General.

The offences most likely to concern the **financial service provider** are those at (a) and (d) above. The guilty mind required before conviction of the offence at (a) above is knowledge or **suspicion** that the person whose funds are dealt with is or has been involved in crime or has benefited from it. This, in contrast to other jurisdictions, is a **subjective test**. The mental state of a company will probably be deemed to be that of the person in a position to be regarded as its directing mind in relation to a particular transaction.

A prosecution for a specific offence cannot be brought where a suspicion about the offence has been reported.[1] Employees who make an internal report in accordance with established internal procedures are also protected. Such a report will not give rise to any civil liability and means that the person making the report cannot be sued, at least in the Cayman Islands, for any **breach of confidentiality**. Unlike other jurisdictions, the service provider who has made a report is not then placed in the position of being unable to continue with the transaction; i.e. they do not have to wait for the consent of the police or the Reporting Authority.

However, the Reporting Authority does have the power to:

(a) Order, with the approval of the Grand Court, any person to refrain from dealing with a bank account for a period not in excess of 21 days.

(b) Request the provision of further information for the purpose of clarifying or amplifying the information previously disclosed.

The PCCL differs from the UK legislation in that there is specific provision to permit access to legal advice without exposure to a tipping off offence. As disclosure to a third party such as, for example, a parent company by its subsidiary may be regarded as tipping off, it is recommended that legal advice is sought whenever there is suspicion about a transaction or client.

3.2   Compulsory reporting of suspected money laundering

An amendment to the PCCL in 2000 imposed a positive legal requirement on a person to report if they know or suspect that another person is engaged in money-laundering and makes it a criminal offence to fail to do so. The key features to note are that the person:

(a) must know or suspect that another person is engaged in money-laundering;

(b) must have become aware of this during the course of his trade, profession, business or employment;

(c) must report the suspicion to the Reporting Authority as soon as reasonably practicable, otherwise they commit an offence;

(d) if an employee, may make their report to the relevant reporting/compliance officer appointed for that purpose by his or her employer, and the internal report will constitute a defence in any subsequent prosecution for that employee.

3.3   'Knowledge' or 'suspicion'

Unusually for the criminal law, but in accordance with the UK standard, **the requisite threshold for most of the money-laundering offences is established at the level of 'suspicion'** which is a lower standard than belief, knowledge or proof.[2]

---

[1] No such defence is provided for the offence of concealing or transferring the proceeds of criminal conduct.
[2] The offence of 'concealing', etc. includes the mental element of 'knowing or having reasonable grounds to suspect' that any concealed property is or represents the proceeds of criminal conduct.

In practical terms, however, **the 'suspicion' threshold must incorporate 'wilful blindness'**. A prosecutor will allege that a service provider who should have had some kind of suspicion but who deliberately or negligently did not undertake the appropriate due diligence to enable him to determine whether or not a reason to suspect exists in fact commits an offence of failure to report.

3.4 What constitutes criminal conduct?

Section 32(10) of the PCCL provides that "In this Law 'criminal conduct' means conduct which constitutes an offence to which this Law applies [which Section 6(7)(c) specifies as indictable (i.e. serious) offences (other than drug trafficking offences, as they are subject to a separate regime)] or would constitute such an offence if it had occurred in the Islands".

This requires the service provider to hypothesise that the relevant conduct which is the origin of the proceeds now sought to be laundered took place in the Islands and then to assess whether that conduct is criminal under the laws of the Cayman Islands and in terms of constituting a crime to which the PCCL applies. (This is sometimes colloquially referred to as a **'dual criminality'** test.)

The test applies to the conduct, not to the crime it constitutes as a matter of law. It is possible that the same conduct may as a matter of law constitute different crimes in different jurisdictions.

4 The Regulations and the Guidance Notes

The Regulations were made pursuant to powers conferred under the PCCL and therefore have the force of law. The Guidance Notes, in contrast, have been issued by CIMA, jointly with a number of professional associations and are not legally binding. Nevertheless financial services providers who are subject to the Regulations are recommended to take the Guidance Notes into account. This is because in determining whether or not a person has complied with any of the requirements of the Regulations, the courts of the Cayman Islands may take into account any relevant supervisory or regulatory guidance that applies to that person.

4.1 How do the Regulations and the Guidance Notes apply?

The Regulations apply to anyone forming a business relationship or carrying out a one-off transaction while in the course of relevant financial business carried on in or from the Cayman Islands. What constitutes 'relevant financial business' is set out in Regulation 4(1) and includes the following:

(a) Banking or trust business carried on by a person who is licensed under the Banks and Trust Companies Law.

(b) Acceptance by a building society of deposits (including the raising of money from members of the society by the issue of shares).

(c) Business carried on by a co-operative society within the meaning of the Co-operative Societies Law.

(d) Insurance business and the business of an insurance manager, an insurance agent, an insurance sub-agent, or an insurance broker within the meaning of the Insurance Law.

(e) Mutual fund administration or the business of a regulated mutual fund within the meaning of the Mutual Funds Law.

(f) Company management business as defined by the Companies Management Law.

(g) Activities falling within Schedule 2 of the Regulations, which broadly include those activities annexed to the First European Union Money Laundering Directive, as well as the services of listing agents and broker members of the Cayman Islands Stock Exchange and the conduct of securities investment business (as defined under the Securities Investment Business Law).

4.2 Mandatory anti-money laundering procedures

Regulation 5(1) requires that a financial services provider must maintain the following procedures as are appropriate for forestalling and preventing money laundering: (i) client identification and verification ('KYC and due diligence'); (ii) record keeping; (iii) internal reporting (including, where applicable, the appointment of a money laundering reporting officer ('MLRO')); (iv) internal controls and communication; and (v) (if staffed) anti-money laundering **training and awareness**.

4.3 Client identification

Unless an exception applies (see below), the Regulations require that a person carrying on relevant financial business in or from the Cayman Islands obtains satisfactory evidence of the identity of the 'applicant for business' when any one-off transaction is to be carried out or business relationship is to be formed. What constitutes satisfactory evidence of identity is not definitively set out in the Regulations.

The Guidance Notes provide greater detail on the information appropriate to establish the identity of an applicant for business depending on whether the applicant is an individual, a corporation, a partnership, a trust or fiduciary client. The Cayman Islands will shortly be adopting a more risk-based approach to performing due diligence in line with international adoption of similar principles.

4.3.1 Verification of the client ('due diligence')

'KYC' or 'Knowing your client' means **not only identifying your client but also verifying that your client is who they claim to be and usually includes obtaining sufficient information on the nature of the business** that the client expects to undertake and any expected or predictable pattern of transactions.

Beyond meeting the client face to face or visiting them at their premises, other methods of verification of identity and purpose of business may include references (business and personal), reviewing electoral registers, or telephone directories, conducting credit reference searches and observing residential bills of service.

It is important that if the financial service provider views or obtains copies of evidential documentation, then such copies be certified accordingly by a suitable certifier.

4.3.2 Retrospective due diligence on existing clients

By amendment to the Regulations in 2000, financial service providers were obliged to conduct due diligence to current (i.e. post-2000) standards on all relationships pre-existing the introduction of the Regulations. The deadline for completion of **the retrospective due diligence** exercise was extended to September 2003. If any relationships remained non-compliant at that date, financial service providers were expected to actively pursue the outstanding information and closely monitor the relationship, compile and report aggregate statistics of non-compliant relationships to CIMA on a regular basis and, if necessary, (and not in contravention of contractual obligations) terminate the relationship.

To date, the Cayman Islands are the only offshore jurisdiction that has completed the exercise of retrospective due diligence in accordance with regulatory requirements. Other offshore jurisdictions have initiated the exercise, but have not prescribed a completion date.

4.3.3 Exceptions to full due diligence

The Guidance Notes acknowledge that the requirements of the Regulations could in some cases involve unnecessary duplication, or be commercially onerous and of no real assistance in the identification of, or the subsequent investigation into, money laundering, particularly where the transaction involves a party regulated in a Schedule 3 country (as listed below).[3] As a consequence, certain exceptions to the maintenance of KYC and due diligence have been recognised and the Regulations and Guidance Notes specify the following cases of exception (listed below) where a financial service provider is not obliged to conduct its own verification of identity of an applicant for business.

4.3.4 Exempted clients

The Guidance Notes recognise certain classes of clients as exempted including, governments and governmental bodies, CIMA regulated entities, broker members of the Cayman Islands Stock Exchange ('CSX'), Schedule 3 'Financial Institutions' (which is defined to include most regulated entities and the main global clearing systems), entities quoted or listed on the CSX or any other CIMA recognised exchange (which includes all US, Canadian and European Union licensed exchanges, as well as World Federation of Exchanges members based in a Schedule 3 country), and subsidiaries (or a company that has common ownership) of any of the foregoing.

The following categories of activity will also be exempted.

4.3.5 One-off transactions

Where a one-off transaction (whether single or in aggregate over a year) is less than CI$15 000 (approximately US$18 300).

4.3.6 Insurance exceptions

Where a premium for insurance business is payable in a lump sum not exceeding CI$2 000 and where periodic premiums for insurance business are payable not exceeding CI$800 in aggregate in a calendar year.

4.3.7 Payment through specified bank account

Importantly, it is not necessary for the financial service provider to undertake verification of identity if the applicant for business is to make a payment and it is reasonable in all the circumstances for the payment to be sent by post or delivered by hand or by any electronic

---

[3] Countries listed in Schedule 3 to the Regulations include those jurisdictions regarded as having anti-money laundering legislation equivalent to the Cayman Islands.

means where the payment is made from an account in the applicant's name at (i) a bank licensed under Cayman Islands law or (ii) a bank regulated and either based or incorporated in a Schedule 3 country.

This exception does not apply where the financial service provider suspects money-laundering or the payment is made to open a relevant account (a bank account through which payments can be made) with a bank licensed under Cayman Islands law, or where payment is to be made in such a way that it does not result in the reinvestment on behalf of the applicant with the same institution, or repayment directly to the applicant for business.

4.3.8 Eligible introductions

As much offshore financial business is effected either by intermediaries or following an introduction from a reputable source, the Regulations and Guidance Notes recognise that **if a reputable source has carried out due diligence on a client in accordance with their own rules and wishes to introduce them to a financial services provider, the relevant due diligence can be relied upon and need not be duplicated.**

The following categories of person are recognised as being eligible to introduce an applicant for business to the Cayman Islands' financial service provider; Corporate group member (notwithstanding their domicile, as long as they adhere to Group policy which is of a Schedule 3 standard), a Cayman regulated entity, a Schedule 3 Financial Institution and Schedule 3 Professional intermediaries, which broadly include lawyers and accountants or firms thereof.

Where a person acts as an **'eligible introducer'** it is a requirement that the financial services provider obtain from them a signed 'Eligible Introducer's Form' (in the form annexed to the Guidance Notes, or its functional equivalent), confirming that they will have obtained verification evidence of the identity of the client(s) whom they are introducing and that they will supply such evidence (or a certified copy) to the financial services provider on request.

4.4 Record keeping procedures

Financial services providers must keep appropriate evidence of client identification, account opening and new business documentation for a period of five years following the closing date at the end of the transaction or the termination of the business relationship. Records to be retained by the financial service provider include such documentation pertaining to the verification of client identity, transactional activity, staff training (e.g. Attendance register and workshop/test materials) and internal reports, as well as any enquiries made by or disclosures made to the Reporting Authority.

4.5 Internal reporting of suspicious activity

The Guidance Notes suggest that a person carrying on relevant financial business in the Cayman Islands should establish a written internal procedures manual, identify a suitable qualified and experienced MLRO and ensure that all staff engaged in the business of the financial service provider are aware of the identity of the MLRO and the procedures to follow when making a suspicious transaction report.

The MLRO must be a natural person, autonomous, independent and of sufficient seniority to be able to access all information necessary to determine whether a suspicion exists. The Guidance Notes also suggest appointing a deputy to cover for the absence or unavailability of the MLRO.

4.6 Internal controls and communication

The Guidance Notes suggest that systems and controls be implemented by financial service providers to monitor the profile of the client on an ongoing basis. All staff of the financial service provider should understand the controls in order to be able to determine whether an activity or transaction is unusual or irregular.

4.7 Training and awareness

Where staffed, financial services providers must ensure that all appropriate staff, in particular new employees, receive training on money laundering prevention on a regular basis, ensure all staff are aware of and fully understand the procedures and their importance, and that a criminal offence may be committed if they contravene the provisions of the legislation.

All relevant staff need to be appropriately educated in the 'know your customer' requirements for the prevention of money laundering. Training should therefore cover not only the need to know the customer's true identity but also, where a business relationship is being established, the need to know enough about the type of business activity expected in relation to the customer at the outset (and on an on-going basis).

4.8 Sector specific guidance

The Guidance Notes provide further detailed explanation for particular areas of business. These areas cover the industries of Mutual Funds, Banking, Company Formation and Management, Trust Administration, Insurance and Real Estate. A section on Money Service Businesses will also shortly be added.

The sector specific guidance does not seek to extend the principles under the main body of the Guidance Notes and in some places modifies the application for certain circumstances; e.g. the alternatives to the reporting function for un-staffed mutual funds.

4.9 Delegation of maintenance of anti-money laundering procedures

The Guidance Notes allow **a managed financial service provider** to **delegate the maintenance** of their anti-money laundering procedures to a suitable party (whether within or outside of the Cayman Islands). Although the maintenance of these functions may be delegated, the ultimate responsibility for compliance with the Regulations remains with the financial service provider.

Pursuant to the Guidance Notes, a financial service provider is permitted to delegate to a suitable counterpart on the conditions that:

(a) CIMA may access the written details and evidence of the suitability of the counterpart to perform the functions.

(b) A clear understanding exists between the financial service provider and the delegate as to the functions to be performed.

(c) Customer identification must be made available to CIMA upon request or the Reporting Authority or other law enforcement authority in accordance with relevant procedures.

(d) The financial service provider regularly satisfies itself as to the reliability of the delegate's procedures.

If the functions have been delegated to a counterpart located and regulated in a Schedule 3 jurisdiction, CIMA regard compliance with the delegate's own regulatory requirements as constituting compliance with Caymans requirements. In other words, if the conditions are met, the delegate can apply their own rules and they are not required to implement any additional standards.

In line with recent international initiatives and **FATF typology** reporting, the Guidance Notes are revised regularly. More recently, sections were added dealing with 'not-for-profit' associations, politically exposed persons, high-risk countries and electronic payment and message systems. The Guidance Notes Committee is currently considering the introduction of a more 'risk-based' approach to anti-money laundering, along the lines adopted by other financial centres and endorsed by the FATF.

5   Combating the financing of terrorism

In response to the events of 11 September 2001 and the introduction of the FATF Special Recommendations on Terrorist Financing, the Cayman Islands Government has implemented legislation to give effect to restrictions imposed by the UN Securities Council Resolutions **to combat terrorism and terrorist financing in the Cayman Islands.**

In 2003 and 2004, the Cayman Islands passed comprehensive legislation to **fully implement Union Nations Security Council Resolution 1373** and give domestic effect to the 1999 *UN Convention for the Suppression of the Financing of Terrorism.* The Terrorism Law 2003 was also enacted and provides for the forfeiture of terrorist funding, prohibition of terrorist activity, money laundering, and mandatory disclosure of information using existing confidential channels (i.e. reporting to appropriate authorities on the same lines as anti-money laundering), among other issues.

6   Conclusion

The introduction of a broad and effective legislative and regulatory regime for anti-money laundering and combating the financing of terrorism strikes a balance between the rights of individual privacy, the practical needs of an offshore financial industry and the obligations to co-operation in the suppression of international crime. In particular, the PCCL has been structured to address legitimate concerns for privacy (e.g. by limiting the dissemination of information) and to provide the financial service industry with the opportunity to produce practical and sensible guidelines for the continuing operation of business (by the Regulations and the Guidance Notes).

The PCCL, Regulations and Guidance Notes fully satisfy the obligations of the Cayman Islands as a member of the CFATF and comply with the most recent FATF recommendations. A number of money laundering actions have been brought in the Cayman Islands since the introduction of the PCCL, the most recent of which resulted in a successful prosecution.

7 Schedule 3 jurisdictions

Argentina	Gibraltar	Netherlands
Australia	Greece	New Zealand
Austria	Guernsey	Norway
Bahamas	Hong Kong	Panama
Bahrain	Iceland	Portugal
Barbados	Ireland	Singapore
Belgium	Isle of Man	Spain
Bermuda	Israel	Sweden
Brazil	Italy	Switzerland
British Virgin Islands	Japan	Turkey
Canada	Jersey	United Arab Emirates
Denmark	Liechtenstein	United Kingdom
Finland	Luxembourg	United States of America
France	Malta	
Germany	Mexico	

Addresses

Cayman Islands Monetary Authority
P.O. Box 10052 APO
Elizabethan Square
80e Shedden Road
George Town
Grand Cayman
Cayman Islands
Contact: RJ Berry, Head of Compliance
Tel (1345) 949-7089
Fax (1345) 945-6131
CIMA@cimoney.com.ky
www.cimoney.com.ky

Financial Reporting Authority
P.O. Box 1054
Dr. Roys Drive
George Town
Grand Cayman
Cayman Islands
Contact: L. Cacho, Managing Director
Tel (1345) 945-6267
Fax (1345) 945-6268

Abbreviations

CFATF	Caribbean Financial Action Task Force
CIMA	Cayman Islands Monetary Authority
CSX	Cayman Islands Stock Exchange
FATF	Financial Action Task Force
KYC	Know Your Customer (or Client)
MDL	Misuse of Drugs Law (2000 Revision)
MLRO	Money Laundering Reporting Officer
PCCL	Proceeds of Criminal Conduct Law (2005 Revision)

British Virgin Islands

Craig MacIntyre

Partner
Trusts & Private Client Department

Conyers Dill & Pearman
Barristers & Attorneys
PO Box 3140
Romasco Place
Wickhams Cay 1
Road Town, Tortola
British Virgin Islands

Tel 1 (441) 299 4907
Fax 1 (441) 298 7849
craig.macintyre@conyersdillandpearman.com
www.conyersdillandpearman.com

Anti-Money Laundering: International Law and Practice.
Edited by W.H. Muller, C.H. Kälin and J.G. Goldsworth
© 2007 John Wiley & Sons, Ltd

Contents – British Virgin Islands

1   About the British Virgin Islands

The British Virgin Islands ('BVI') is a small group of islands at the northeast end of the Leeward Islands in the Caribbean. The BVI is a British Overseas Territory which has successfully established a thriving international business industry. The legal system is based on English common law and the islands have developed an expertise in personal holding companies which entirely belies the size of the jurisdiction.

The financial industry in the BVI is regulated by the *financial services commission*. The commission provides guidance to the financial services industry, in addition to administering and enforcing the law. As a result, the BVI has a thriving and sophisticated financial industry, including an extensive mutual fund and insurance industry.

2   Introduction

2.1   The legislation

The *Proceeds of Criminal Conduct Act 1997* (the '*Proceeds Act*') is the primary piece of legislation in the BVI, that deals with anti-money laundering. The Proceeds Act contains provisions broadly similar to those which are found in the laws of the majority of the sophisticated common law jurisdictions throughout the world. It is closely modelled on the *UK's Criminal Justice Act 1993*, but incorporates requirements that are specific to an offshore jurisdiction. The purpose of the Proceeds Act is to deter any and all forms of money laundering in the BVI and it also requires financial service providers to report transactions that are suspicious to the *Reporting Authority*. The *Reporting Authority* is the financial intelligence unit that has been established by the Proceeds Act to receive suspicious financial transaction reports.

The Proceeds Act is supplemented by the *Anti-Money Laundering Code of Practice 1999* (the '*Code of Practice*') and the *Guidance Notes on the Prevention of Money Laundering* (the '*Guidance Notes*'). The overall effect is that the BVI are materially equivalent to Bermuda in terms of money laundering regulations.

The *Proceeds Act* provides for the recovery of the proceeds of any action which amounts to, or would if it were committed in the BVI amount to, an indictable offence under BVI law. It covers a broad spectrum of offernces but does not include drug trafficking offences, which are covered under the *Drug Trafficking Offences Act 1992*. The *Proceeds Act* is designed to deprive offenders from enjoying the spoils of their illegal activities.

The *Code of Practice* supplements existing anti-money laundering legislation, particularly the *Proceeds Act*, the Drug *Trafficking Offences Act 1992*, the *Criminal Justice (International Co-operation) Act 1993* and the *Mutual Legal Assistance (United States of America) Act 1990*.

The *Code of Practice* provides practical guidance on the requirements of the *Proceeds Act* and clearly defines the standards required for record keeping, 'know your client' rules, training and other relevant matters. The *Code of Practice* represents a mandatory legislative regime with monetary sanctions for non-compliance. It mandates the appointment of a Compliance Officer and a Money Laundering Reporting Officer (which role may be undertaken by the Compliance Officer) for ensuring compliance with the *Code of Practice* and all other related anti-money laundering laws.

The *Code of Practice* also requires that 'relevant persons' submit identification, record keeping, internal reporting and internal control and communication procedures required above to the *Reporting Authority* for their approval.

Under the *Code of Practice*, the Director of Financial Services or a person designated by him, is authorised to conduct an inspection of any relevant person to determine compliance by that person with the requirements of the *Code of Practice* and any other law or directive relating to money laundering. The Director of Financial Services post has been replaced due to the *Financial Services Commission Act 2001*, which established the *British Virgin Islands Financial Services Commission ('FSC')* as an autonomous regulatory authority responsible for the regulation, supervision and inspection of all financial services in and from within the BVI. Such services include insurance, banking, trustee business, company management, mutual funds business as well as the registration of companies, limited partnerships, intellectual property and ships. As a result, the *FSC* now oversees all regulatory responsibilities previously handled by the government through the *Financial Services Department*. The *FSC has* also been tasked with new responsibilities including promoting public understanding of the financial system and its products, policing the perimeter of regulated activity, reducing financial crime and preventing market abuse.

The *Legal and Enforcement Division* provides legal support to the Board and the *FSC*'s operating divisions and ensures that the *FSC's* international cooperation policies and practices comply with BVI laws. This division conducts or causes to be conducted enforcement action against any entity in violation of relevant regulatory and anti-money laundering laws.

The *Code of Practice* is complemented by the *Anti-Money Laundering Guidance Notes* (the '*Guidance Notes*'), which have been published by *the BVI Joint Anti-Money Laundering Co-ordinating Committee*. The *Joint Anti-Money Laundering Co-ordinating Committee* is a broad based multi-disciplinary committee established in 1999 to co-ordinate all the BVI anti-money laundering initiatives. The *Code of Practice* states that in the preparation of the relevant procedures required to be maintained in accordance with *Code of Practice*, relevant persons may adopt or have regard to the *Guidance Notes*. The *Guidance Notes*, although not mandatory, will be used by the *FSC* and possibly the *BVI Courts*, in determining whether or not a BVI financial services provider acted diligently in preventing, detecting and reporting money laundering.

2.2   Who is subject to regulation

The *Code of Practice* defines 'regulated persons' as those carrying on:

- A banking business or trust business within the meaning of the *Banks and Trust Companies Act, 1990.*

- Insurance business within the meaning of the *Insurance Act 1994.*

- The business of company management within the meaning of the *Company Management Act, 1990.*

- Business as a mutual fund or providing services as manager or administrator of a mutual fund within the meaning of the *Mutual Funds Act, 1996.*

- Any activity involving the remittance of the *Telegraph Money Order* under the *Post Office (Telegraph Money Order) Rules, 1934.*

- Any activity involving money transmission services or cheque encashment facilities.

- Any activity in which money belonging to a client is held or managed by an Attorney-at-Law, an accountant or a person who, in the course of business, provides accountancy services.

- The business of acting as company secretary of bodies corporate.

A 'relevant person' is someone who is engaged by way of business in a business or transaction with a regulated person.

2.3   Exemptions

The *Code of Practice* also allows for certain categories of persons to be exempt from the regulations. These people are referred to as 'qualifying relevant persons' and include:

- Individuals carrying on relevant business as sole traders, who do not employ any staff.

- Companies that do not employ any staff in the Virgin Islands and whose relevant business is managed by another relevant person in the Virgin Islands.

- Funds registered under *Part II of the Mutual Funds Act 1996*.

- Funds recognized under *Part III of the Mutual Funds Act 1996*.

- Managers or administrators licensed under *Part IV of the Mutual Funds Act 1996*.

Examples of companies whose relevant business is managed by another relevant person in the BVI include companies that hold restricted trust licenses issued under the *Banks and Trust Companies Act 1990*, companies that hold a general trust license under the *Banks and Trust Companies Act 1990* but do not have a physical presence in the BVI and companies that have a license issued under the *Insurance Act 1994* but do not carry on domestic business within the meaning of *section 31 of that Act*.

2.4   Introduction of business

Where a relevant person is referred business through an 'introducer' they can rely on the introducer to conduct due diligence on the client, as long as the requirements under the *Code of Practice* are met.

The Code *of Practice* does not require the relevant person to verify or maintain satisfactory evidence of the new client's identity, so long as the 'introducer' is:

- a regulated person; or

- an authorized financial institution in a country or territory which is a member of the *FATF* or the *Caribbean Action Task Force ('CATF')* which has anti-money laundering laws and procedures at least similar to BVI; or

- an Attorney-at-Law or an accountant where the relevant person is satisfied that the rules of their profession embody requirements equivalent to the *Code of Practice*.

Additionally, if the relevant person and the new client are within the same corporate group, i.e. subsidiary or holding company, then there is no requirement for identity verification.

If there are reasonable grounds for believing that the introducer is engaged in a business outside of the BVI which is regulated by a regulatory authority, and it is based in or incorporated under the law of a country that is a member of the *FATF* or *CATF* which has anti-money laundering laws and procedures at least similar to the BVI, and that the Introducer will comply with the 'written terms of business' set out below, then the relevant person does not have to verify the new client's identity.

2.4.1 Written terms of business

Such terms shall require the introducer to verify the identity of the new client that they introduced to the relevant person in accordance with the *Proceeds Act* and the *Code of Practice*. The introducer must also maintain a record of the evidence of verification of identity and all transaction records for at least 5 years, in accordance with record keeping requirements below. If requested by the relevant person the Introducer must supply evidence of verification of identity and inform the relevant person if they are not required or have been unable to verify the identity of the new client.

As stated above, where satisfactory evidence of identity cannot be obtained or produced by the Introducer then in order to comply with the *Code of Practice*, the transaction must not proceed any further.

2.5 Offences

The *Proceeds Act* creates four types of offence:

(i) Assisting another to retain the benefit of the proceeds of criminal conduct (having actual knowledge or suspecting that the property is the proceeds of criminal conduct). It is a defence if the financial service provider discloses to the *Reporting Authority* the suspicion that the transaction may involve the proceeds of criminal conduct. After making the report, the financial service provider is able to continue with the transaction without fear of breaching the Act.

(ii) Acquisition, possession or use of the proceeds of criminal conduct (having actual knowledge that the property is the proceeds of criminal conduct). It is a defence if the financial service provider discloses to the *Reporting Authority* the suspicion that the transaction may involve the proceeds of criminal conduct. It is also a defence if the property was acquired for adequate consideration.

(iii) Concealing or transferring the proceeds of criminal conduct (knowing or having reasonable grounds for suspecting that the property is the proceeds of criminal conduct).

(iv) Tipping off. It is an offence to tip-off the target of a pending or proposed investigation into money laundering or to provide any other person with information likely to prejudice the outcome of an investigation. If the financial services provider continues to have dealing with the client while an investigation is under way, they must be careful to ensure that they do not contravene this provision. Prosecution of this sort of offence can only be undertaken with the consent of the Attorney General.

It is not an offence if any person who does an act in contravention of the *Proceeds Act* makes a disclosure either before or after the commission of the act. If such disclosure is made to the *Reporting Authority* after the fact, then the person must do so of their own initiative and as soon as practicable to do so.

A person who fails to comply with the requirements of the *Code of Practice* or any directive relating to money laundering issued thereunder commits an offence and is liable on summary conviction to a fine not exceeding US$5000 and on conviction on indictment (for a first offence) to a fine not exceeding US$10 000 or (for a second or subsequent offence) to a fine not exceeding US$15 000.

2.6   Client confidentiality

The *Proceeds Act* is careful to ensure that no liability will be incurred for breach of client confidentiality when reporting suspicions of money laundering to the *Reporting Authority*.

The *Reporting Authority* shall not disclose information regarding a report of a suspicious transaction, without the consent of the *Attorney General*. The *Attorney General* when deciding whether to give his consent shall take into account the purpose for which disclosure is to be made and the interests of third parties. If he gives his consent, he may impose such conditions on the further disclosure as he sees fit.

The above consent does not apply to information that the *Reporting Authority* discloses to any person or institution in the Territory.

The *Reporting Authority*, subject to the requirement of consent, may disclose any information received in relation to criminal conduct to law enforcement agencies in the Territory or in any other country in order to report the possible commission of an offence, to initiate a criminal investigation in regard to a matter reported, to assist with any investigation or criminal proceedings in relation to a matter reported or to generally give effect to the purpose of the *Proceeds Act*.

3   Verification procedures

3.1   General

The *Code of Practice* states that regulated persons are not to form business relationships or carry out one-off transactions with or for another person unless they:

- maintain the following procedures (details of which are set out below):
    - identification procedures;
    - record keeping procedures;
    - internal reporting procedures;
    - internal controls and communication procedures which are appropriate for the purposes of forestalling and preventing money laundering; and
- take the appropriate measures from time to time for the purpose of making employees aware of:
    - the procedures maintained under the above;
    - the provisions of the Act, and Regulations made thereunder, the *Code of Practice* and any directives issued thereunder; and
- provide training for employees to assist them:
    - in the recognition and handling of transactions carried out by, or on behalf of, any person who is, or appears to be, engaged in money laundering;
    - in dealing with customers where such transactions have been reported to the *Reporting Authority* in accordance with the provisions of the Act.

The *Code of Conduct* applies to business relationships or one-off transactions that were formed or carried out prior to the coming into force of the *Code of Conduct*, where such relationship or transaction is subsisting.

3.2   Identification procedures

A relevant person is required to establish and maintain identification procedures, which as soon as contact is made with an applicant for business, require the applicant to produce satisfactory evidence of his identity or have procedures in place that will produce satisfactory evidence of his identity.

Such identification procedures will not apply if the applicant for business is:

- a regulated person; or

- an authorized financial institution in a country or territory which is a member of the *FATF* or *CATF* which has anti-money laundering laws and procedures at least similar to the Territory; or

- an Attorney-at-Law or an accountant where the relevant person is satisfied that the rules of their profession embody requirements equivalent to *the Code of Practice*.

If there are reasonable grounds for believing that the applicant for business is engaged in a business outside of the Territory which is regulated by a regulatory authority, and it is based in or incorporated under the law of a country that is a member of the *FATF* or *CATF* which has anti-money laundering laws and procedures at least similar to the Territory, then the relevant person does not have to verify the applicant's identity. In order for the country to be deemed to have anti-money laundering laws and procedures equivalent to those of the Territory, it must be so recognized by the *Joint Anti-Money Laundering Co-ordinating Committees*.

The above identification procedures apply equally to continuing transaction as well as one-off transactions.

Such procedures should also provide that if satisfactory evidence of identity cannot be obtained then the business and transaction shall not proceed any further.

4   Record keeping requirements

The *Code of Conduct* and the *Guidance Notes* require relevant persons to maintain a record of (a) the evidence of verification of identity and (b) all transactions carried out by or on behalf of regulated persons. The records should be sufficient to identify the source and recipient of payments so that the investigating authorities can compile an audit trail for suspected money laundering. Such records shall be maintained for at least 5 years from (i) when all activities relating to a one-off transaction or a series of transactions has ended, (ii) when the business relationship has formally ended or (iii) if the business relationship has not ended when the last transaction was carried out. However, where a report has been made to the *Reporting Authority*, or the relevant person has reason to believe, knows or believes the matter to be under investigation, such person shall retain all records for so long as required by the *Reporting Authority*.

All records that are required to be maintained under the *Code of Conduct* must be capable of retrieval in a legible form without undue delay. A relevant person may rely on the records of a third party, in respect of transactions and payments provided they are satisfied that the third party person is willing and able to retain such records and produce copies of them in a legible form if required.

A relevant person is also required to maintain a register of all enquiries made of it by the *Reporting Authority* and the law enforcement authorities, acting under the *Proceeds Act*, the *Code of Conduct* or any regulations.

5 Training

A relevant person is required to provide education and training to all persons involved in its management such as directors or partners and to all key staff, who are staff that at anytime in the course of their duties have or may have access to any information which may be relevant in determining if any person is engaged in money laundering.

Such training must ensure that they are aware of:

- The provisions of the *Proceeds Act*, any Regulations made thereunder and the *Code of Conduct*.
- Their personal obligations under the above.
- The manual of compliance procedures and the internal reporting procedures discussed below.
- The procedures maintained by the relevant person (either the Compliance Officer or the Reporting Officer).
- Their personal liability for failure to report information or suspicious activity in accordance with their internal procedures.

All new key staff should be given the appropriate training as soon as practicable after their appointment.

As well as the training above, employees such as senior staff and specialist staff, require a greater level of training on its policies and procedures to prevent money laundering, its customer identification, record-keeping and other procedures and how to recognize and handle suspicious transactions.

Once a year, refresher training should be given to key staff to make them aware of any changes in the legislation and the internal procedures and to remind them of their responsibilities under the legislation.

6 Compliance Officer

It is a requirement under the *Code of Practice* that each organization that is engaged in business with regulated persons appoints a member of staff to be the Compliance Officer. The Compliance Officer must be a senior member of staff, with suitable qualifications and experience that will allow him to respond to enquiries relating to the conduct of the organisation's business. They will also be responsible for establishing and maintaining a manual of the company's compliance procedures and their internal reporting procedures, as required by the *FSC*. The Compliance Officer is also responsible for ensuring that staff comply with the provisions of the *Code of Conduct* and any other money laundering law.

The Compliance Officer also liaises with the *FSC* and prepares written reports for the *FSC* on the organization's compliance with the relevant laws, in such form as the *FSC* requires.

7 Procedure Manual

Each company must have written internal reporting procedures that:

- Enable all staff involved in the management of the business and all key staff to know to whom any knowledge or suspicion should be reported.

- Ensure there is a clear reporting chain, so that suspicions of money laundering will be passed to the appropriate person, the Reporting Officer or the Compliance Officer, as the case may be.

- Identify the Reporting Officer, to whom any knowledge or suspicion of money laundering activity should be reported to.

- Require the Reporting Officer to consider the report in light of all other relevant information to determine if such information gives rise to such a suspicion.

- Ensure that the Reporting Officer has reasonable access to any other information necessary to make such a determination

- Ensure that the Reporting Officer promptly discloses information received in reports to the *Reporting Authority* where he knows or suspects that someone is engaged in money laundering.

A register of all reports made to the *Reporting Authority*, referred to above, should be kept. It should include details such as the date the report was made, the person who made the report and details of the relevant documents.

8 Confiscation Orders

Where a person is convicted of a criminal conduct and it is thought that he has benefited from such criminal conduct, the court can make a range of orders including confiscation orders, charging orders, restraint orders and an order for bankruptcy. A person will have benefited from an offence if he obtains property as a result of or in connection with the commission of the offence, and the benefit is the value of the property so obtained.

9 External Orders

The *Proceeds of Criminal Conduct (Designated Countries and Territories) Order 1999* (the '*Order*') made pursuant to the *Proceeds Act* extends the *Proceeds Act* to external confiscation orders and proceedings that have been or are to be instituted in 'designated countries' and which may result in external confiscation orders being made there. The Order designates certain countries and territories as 'designated countries and territories' (specifically, *Belgium, Cyprus, Denmark, Germany, Iceland, Italy, the Netherlands, Norway, Portugal, Spain, Sweden* and *the United Kingdom*).

The *Proceeds Act* applies in respect of orders made by the courts of designated countries and territories for the purpose of recovering payments or other rewards received in connection with criminal conduct, an external confiscation order, and proceedings which have been or are to be instituted therein which may result in an external confiscation order being made.

The *Proceeds Act* defines an external confiscation order as an order made by the court in a designated country for the purpose of recovering property obtained as a result of or in connection with conduct corresponding to an offence to which the *Proceeds Act* applies, recovering the value of the property so obtained or depriving the person of a pecuniary advantage so obtained.

Where an application is made to the *Attorney General* on behalf of the *Government* of a designated country, the *High Court* may register an external confiscation order if:

- It is satisfied that at the time of registration the order is in force and not subject to appeal.

- It is satisfied that if the person against whom the order was made did not appear in the proceedings, that they had adequate notice of the proceedings and ample time to defend them.

- It would not be contrary to the interests of justice if the order were enforced in the Territory.

The *High Court* will not register an external confiscation order if the *Attorney General* has issued a certificate to the effect that the order is contrary to the public interest of the Territory.

The registration of an external confiscation order will be cancelled by the *High Court*, if it appears that the order has been satisfied by payment of the amount due or the person against whom it was made is serving imprisonment in default of payment.

10   Other relevant legislation

The *Financial Services (International Co-operation) Act 2000* enhances the present ability of regulators to access information by providing an administrative procedure which factors in a role for the courts. The Act is essentially assistance-oriented and designed to provide assistance to recognised foreign regulatory authorities to obtain information in respect of persons in the BVI in relation to any 'regulatory function'. The definition of 'regulatory functions' expressly excludes the functions of 'assessing, imposing or collecting taxes'.

Under this Act, the *Director of Financial Services,* now the *FSC* is empowered to request, of any person, the production of information or documents with respect to any matter relevant to an inquiry to which a request under the Act relates. Failure to comply may lead the Director to apply to the court for an order of compliance against the subject person or to have that person examined under oath. In order to ensure confidentiality of information, the Act makes provisions for restricting the disclosure of information.

The *Offshore Legislation (Delegation of Functions and Powers) Act 2000* confers power on the *Director of Financial Services* or other senior public officers to perform certain functions which were previously vested in the *Governor*, the *Governor in Council*, or a *Minister of Government*, having the effect of making the *Financial Services Department* independent of government and facilitating a more orderly and efficient dispatch of routine business.

The *Mutual Legal Assistance Treaties* allow generally for the exchange of evidence and information in criminal and ancillary matters. The *Mutual Legal Assistance (United States of America) Act, 1990*, gives effect in the BVI to the *Mutual Legal Assistance Treaty* concerning the

Cayman Islands agreed between the *UK* and the *USA* in 1986 ('the *Treaty*'). The Act facilitates the provision, on a reciprocal basis, of legal assistance in criminal matters between the *USA* and the BVI, with the objective of enhancing the investigation, prosecution and suppression of criminal offences and allows for the sharing of assets with that country. Virtually identical legislation is in place in the other Caribbean Overseas Territories.

For the purposes of *the Treaty*, a criminal offence is either conduct which satisfies the dual criminality test, that is, it is conduct which is punishable by imprisonment of more than one year in both the BVI and the USA, or it is one of a number of specific listed offences which include insider trading and fraudulent securities practices. With the exception of certain civil and administrative proceedings relating to narcotics, *the Treaty* does not extend to civil matters. Conduct which relates directly or indirectly to the regulation, imposition, calculation or collection of taxes is excluded from the Treaty with the exception of tax fraud and the wilful or dishonest making of false statements to government tax authorities (for example, by submitting a false tax return).

Association of Registered Agents Code of Conduct

In 1996 the Association of Registered Agents passed a voluntary Code of Conduct for the self regulation of the industry, providing for minimum know your client requirements for Trust and Management Companies operating within the BVI. Under the Code of Conduct, BVI licensed service providers are required to ensure that all business referred to them by overseas professionals has been subject to due diligence and 'know your client' principles.

Address

The British Virgin Islands Financial Services Commission
Pasea Estate, Road Town
Tortola
British Virgin Islands
Tel 284-494-1324
Fax 284-494-5016
commissioner@bvifsc.vg

Abbreviations

CFATF   Caribbean Financial Action Task Force
FATF   Financial Action Task Force
FSC   The BVI Financial Services Commission

Carolyn Hanson has been in the Compliance/AML field for the last 15 years, mostly in the international banking area, and has worked in a number of jurisdictions including the UK, Isle of Man, Bahamas and Barbados, whilst dealing with many other offshore locales such as the Channel Islands, Malta, Gibraltar, Monaco and 14 sites in the Caribbean. Having experience in the insurance, banking and investment industries Carolyn established compliance regimes for four major areas of the Barclays group, acted as the Regional Compliance Manager and Regional Money Laundering Reporting Officer for the Caribbean and Bahamas Region. Carolyn is a founder member of the Barbados Association of Compliance Professionals and a Fellow of the International Compliance Association.

Organisation's profile

The Barbados Association of Compliance Professionals (BACP) is committed to serving the Barbados financial services industry. While maintaining its professional independence it is intended that the association will work alongside the following regulatory bodies and other local organisations to develop industry best practice and procedures:

- Central Bank of Barbados;

- Anti-Money Laundering Authority;

- Bank Card Fraud Task Force;

- Barbados Institute of Banking & Finance;

- Barbados Bankers Association;

- other government agencies where appropriate.

In addition, the association will benefit from relationships with the International Compliance Association and regional sister associations, particularly those in the Bahamas, Cayman Islands, Bermuda, BVI and Nevis.

Barbados

Carolyn Hanson

Representing the Barbados Association of
Compliance Professionals (BACP)

Tel +001 246 233 0707
chanson@sunbeach.net
www.bacp.info

Anti-Money Laundering: International Law and Practice.
Edited by W.H. Muller, C.H. Kälin and J.G. Goldsworth
© 2007 John Wiley & Sons, Ltd

Contents – Barbados

1   Introduction

Situated at the far easterly end of the chain of Caribbean islands, Barbados is approximately 3 hours from Miami by plane and has a population approaching 267 000. Barbados became an independent nation in 1966 and has a common law legal system, based on that of the UK, with an independent judiciary. The court of last resort for Barbados is the *Judicial Committee of Her Majesty's Privy Council in London.*

The *Government of Barbados* and the financial sector operating on the island are committed to the prevention of money laundering and terrorist financing. Negative commentary on some islands within the region has not been without impact on Barbados, although **the island itself was never present on the *FATF Non Cooperative Countries and Territories (NCCT)* listing,** sometimes referred to as the blacklist.

Barbados has representation within the following major regional and international bodies:

- The Basel Committee.

- The International Association of Insurance Supervisors.

- The International Association of Securities Commissions.

- The **Caribbean Financial Action Task Force (*CFATF*)**.

- The Caribbean Association of Regulators of International Business.

- The International Tax and Investment Organisation.

- Commonwealth Association of Tax Administrators.

- Organisation of American States/Inter-American Drug Abuse Control Commission.

- The **Egmont Group**.

- The Offshore Group of Banking Supervisors.

Barbados respects principles of confidentiality but also exchanges information of both a civil and a criminal nature under a variety of international agreements.

Barbados has both domestic and offshore financial services sectors. The *Central Bank of Barbados (CBB)* regulates domestic, merchant and offshore banks, trust and finance companies.

The *International Business Unit* within the *Ministry of Economic Affairs & Development* regulates local and exempt insurance companies and pension plans via the Supervisor of Insurance and Pensions. Investments are regulated by *Securities and Exchange Commission* housed within the same Ministry.

Currently corporate service providers and credit unions are not regulated but do fall under the ambit of the money laundering legislation as Financial Institutions '**FIs**'.

The Barbados financial services sector includes, at the time of going to press:

Domestic	Offshore
6 commercial banks & 2 merchant banks	53 offshore banks
14 trust and finance companies	413 exempt insurance companies
38 credit unions	4635 international business companies
1 money remitter	

2 Legislative background

Barbados was a founder member of the *Caribbean Financial Action Task Force (CFATF).*

In 2005 Transparency International ranked Barbados 24 out of 158 countries in their Perception Corruption Index with a rating of 6.9.

The primary legislation in Barbados dealing with issues related to **money laundering** and **financing of terrorism** has evolved as follows:

- *Drug Abuse (Prevention and Control) Act 1990.*
- *Proceeds of Crime Act 1990 (POCA).*
- *Money Laundering (Prevention and Control) Act 1998.*
- *Money Laundering and Financing of Terrorism (Prevention and Control) Act 2001.*
- *Anti-Terrorism Act 2002.*

The Drug Abuse (Prevention and Control) Act 1990 was the first piece of legislation enacted specifically aimed at drug trafficking. The *POCA* criminalises any transaction involving, or possession or concealment of, money or property that is the proceeds of any crime punishable by at least one year imprisonment, meaning that **Barbados is subject to an 'All crimes' money laundering regime.**

The *Money Laundering (Prevention and Control) Act, 1998-38 (MLA)* established the *Anti-Money Laundering Authority (AMLA)* and was the first specific AML legislation in Barbados.

Established under section 5 of the *MLA*, the *AMLA* supervises *FIs* in an effort to prevent money laundering.[1]

The *AMLA* has the responsibility of supervising *FIs* regarding anti-money laundering, making it the principal supervisory entity in the fight against money laundering in Barbados.

---

[1] www.barbadosfiu.gov.bb.

The *AMLA* is made up of nine members, drawn mainly from the key public sector agencies that relate directly to anti-money laundering activity.

The *AMLA* receives reports of **suspicious or unusual transactions** from *FIs*. These reports are then analysed and directed in accordance with the findings of the *AMLA*'s financial analysts.

The executive functions of the Authority are carried out by the *Financial Intelligence Unit (FIU)*. This unit is headed by a Director and is responsible for the day-to-day work of the *AMLA*.

The *MLA* was amended in 2001 to include the prevention of terrorism and some additional aspects. At this time the title was revised to the *Money Laundering and Financing of Terrorism (Prevention and Control) Act, 2001 (MLFTA)*.[2]

The *MLFTA* is now the primary legislation in Barbados dealing with anti-money laundering and the prevention of terrorist financing. In 2001 **the burden of proof was shifted to the accused**, requiring that they demonstrate that the property in their possession or control is derived from a legitimate source. **In the absence of such proof the presumption is that such property is derived from the proceeds of crime**.

The *AMLA* has the ability to freeze bank accounts for a period not exceeding 5 days and to prohibit transactions without need for a specific court order (but upon application to a Judge in chambers) for a limited period of 72 hours.

In 2001 the *Central Bank of Barbados*, in partnership with the *AMLA*, issued guidelines for *FIs*[3] such as commercial banks, credit unions, international business, stock brokers, mutual funds and insurance companies.

Other entities such as financial service providers and consultants, money exchange houses, money transmission services, bookmaking and gaming services, dealers in motor vehicles, jewellery, art and antiques, professional accountants, lawyers, post offices, management services including investment management, company registration and trust services and real estate agents were also encouraged to consider the issues within the guidelines.

The *AMLA* and the *Ministry of Economic Development* issued guidelines for fiduciary services and business investment in 2001.

Section 8(f) of the MLFTA requires that every *FI* complies with the guidelines issued by the Authority, changing the status of these guidelines from voluntary to mandatory.

The *Central Bank of Barbados* issued revised guidelines in October 2006. The revised guidelines include:

- Introduction of a risk-based approach to AML/CFT programmes, enhanced **due diligence** for high-risk customers, trusts, non-profit organisations, non-face-to-face customers, introduced business, professional service providers, politically exposed persons, corporate vehicles and correspondent banking.

- The inclusion of **terrorist financing** reflecting local legislation since 2001 and the *FATF special recommendations*.

---

[2] www.barbadosfiu.gov.bb/pdf/Money%20Laundering%20and%20Financing%20of%20Terrorism%20.pdf.
[3] www.centralbank.org.bb/Financial/KnowYourCustomerGuidelines_March2001.pdf

- More detailed guidance on identification requirements.
- Added focus on the responsibilities of directors and senior management.
- The need for retrospective due diligence and ongoing monitoring.
- Minimum standards for training and awareness.

2.1   Scheme of the MLFTA

The *MLFTA* is modelled on the UK legislation and is divided into four parts:

- Part I – Money laundering – definitions of the offences.
- Part II – Anti-money laundering provisions – establishing the *AMLA* and identifying its powers, identifying the *FI*'s responsibilities with respect to customer identification and other duties.
- Part III – Freezing and forfeiture of assets.
- Part IV – Miscellaneous – covering investigations and the liability of officers and bodies corporate.

2.1.1   The money laundering offences

The money laundering and terrorism offences are identified in the following table:

Area	Description of offence	Description of fine	Section of legislation
Reporting obligations	Failure of licensee to make a suspicious transaction report to the AMLA	BDS$100 000 on directors jointly and severally	Section 8 (4) MLFTA
	Failure of a licensee to maintain business transaction records	BDS$100 000 on directors jointly and severally	Section 8 (5) MLFTA
	Failure to report that a person **receives** more than BDS$10 000 (or foreign equivalent) from outside of Barbados without	Summary conviction – BDS$10 000 or 2 years imprisonment On conviction on indictment – BDS$200 000 or 5 years imprisonment	Section 8A(6) MLFTA

	Exchange Control permission		
	Failure to report that a person **transfers** more than BDS$10 000 (or foreign equivalent) without Exchange Control permission	Summary conviction – BDS$10 000 or 2 years imprisonment On conviction on indictment – BDS$200 000 or 5 years imprisonment	Section 8A(6) MLFTA
Interference in the line of duty	The obstruction, hindrance, molestation or assault to any member of the Authority, constable or other person in performing duties under the Act	BDS$50 000 or 2 years imprisonment or both	Section 16 MLFTA
Money laundering offences	Engagement in money laundering	Summary conviction – BDS$200 000 or 5 years imprisonment or both Conviction on indictment – BDS$2 000 000 or 25 years imprisonment or both **Forfeiture of licence for FI**	Section 20 (1) MLFTA Section 12
	Providing assistance to engage in money laundering	Summary conviction – BDS$150 000 or 3 years imprisonment or both On conviction on indictment – BDS$1 500 000 or 15 years imprisonment or both	Section 20(2) MLFTA
	A body of persons (corporate or unincorporated) whether as a director, manager, secretary or other similar officer	Subject to trial and punishment accordingly	Section 21 MLFTA

	engaging in a money laundering offence		
Disclosure of information (tipping off)	Disclosure of information on a pending money laundering investigation Falsifying, concealing, destruction or disposal of information material to an investigation or order	BDS$50 000 or 2 years imprisonment or both	Section 22(4) MLFTA
	Disclosure or publication of the contents of any document, communication or information in the course of duties under this Act	BDS$50 000 or 5 years imprisonment or both	Section 22A (2) MLFTA
Terrorism offences	Provision or collection of funds or financial services to persons to be used to carry out an offence as defined in the listed treaties	Conviction on indictment to 25 years imprisonment	Section 4(1) Anti-Terrorism Act (ATA)
	Provision of assistance or involvement in the conspiracy to commit a terrorist offence	Conviction on indictment and principal offender punished accordingly	Section 3 of ATA
	A terrorist offence committed by a person responsible for the management	BDS$2 000 000 notwithstanding that any criminal liability has been incurred by an individual	Section 5 of ATA

	or control of an entity located or registered in Barbados, or otherwise organised under the laws of Barbados	directly involved in the commission of the offence or any civil or administrative sanction as imposed by law	

[4]*Source*: CBB Guidance Notes, October 2006. *Note*: All amounts are in Barbados dollars – the set exchange rate is pegged at BDS$2 to US$1.

Any act committed outside of Barbados can constitute an offence in Barbados if the act would fall under the definition of the above offences. Indictable offences are deemed to include similar offences committed abroad.

An *FI* is probably most concerned with the providing assistance and **tipping off** offences. The guilty mind *(mens rea)* required for the providing assistance offence[4] is knowledge or reasonable **suspicion** that the property is derived directly or indirectly from some form of unlawful activity. This is a subjective test and the standard of proof is stated within the legislation as being 'on a balance of probabilities'.

'Where a body of persons commits the offence (whether corporate or unincorporated) every person acting in an official capacity at the time of the offence (whether as a director, manager, secretary or other similar position) is also guilty of the offence and will be tried and punished accordingly.'

The mental state of a company will probably be deemed to be that of the person in a position to be regarded as its directing mind in relation to a particular transaction and once again the standard of proof is likely to be based on a balance of probabilities.

An action will not be brought against an *FI* or employee of the institution for a specific offence where a suspicion has been reported to the *AMLA*. This is the 'Safe Harbour' clause. **Employees who make internal reports in accordance with established internal procedures would also be protected**. This protection would also extend to any civil liability and means that the person making the report cannot be sued in Barbados for any breach of confidentiality. There is no process requiring receipt of 'consent' from the *AMLA* after a suspicion is reported. The *AMLA* has the ability to freeze accounts for up to 5 days or prohibit transactions for 72 hours and would generally apply these provisions should there be appropriate grounds.

The *AMLA* has the power to request the provision of further information for the purpose of clarifying or amplifying the information provided in a report.

2.1.2 Compulsory reporting of suspected money laundering

The *MLFTA* imposes a duty on every *FI* to report to the *AMLA* if they have reasonable grounds to suspect that a transaction:

---

[4] Aiding, abetting, counselling or conspiring to commit money laundering, being in receipt/possession/concealment/ disposal of or bringing into or sending out of Barbados any money or other property that is the proceeds of crime.

(i) involves the proceeds of crime;

(ii) involves the financing of terrorism;

(iii) is of a suspicious or an unusual nature.

Section 8(4) of the MLFTA makes it a criminal offence, on the part of the directors of the institution, if there is a **failure to report** such transactions. All directors will be jointly and severally liable, on conviction on indictment, to a fine of BDS$100 000.

The key features to note are that the person:

- must know or suspect that another person is engaged in money laundering;

- must have become aware of this during the course of his trade, profession, business or employment;

- must report the suspicion to the *AMLA* as soon as reasonably practicable, otherwise they commit an offence;

- if an employee, may make their report to the relevant **compliance officer** appointed for that purpose.

2.1.3   'Knowledge' or 'suspicion'

The money laundering offences are based on 'knowledge or suspicion', which is a lower standard than belief, knowledge or proof.

An individual could also be charged with '**wilful blindness**' if he fails (without reasonable excuse) to take reasonable steps to ascertain whether or not the property he is dealing with is from some form of unlawful activity. The same concept would apply to an *FI* that has failed to take reasonable steps to implement or apply procedures to control or combat money laundering.

An *FI* is guilty of an offence if they should have had some kind of suspicion but deliberately or negligently did not undertake the appropriate due diligence (either specifically for a client or systemically, i.e. had no or inadequate AML procedures in place) to enable them to determine whether or not a reason to suspect existed.

2.1.4   What constitutes unlawful activity?

Section 2(1) of the MLFTA provides that "In this Act '**unlawful activity**' means any activity which under any law anywhere is a crime and is punishable by death or imprisonment for a period of not less than 12 months". This means Barbados applies a 'single criminality' test.

2.2   The Guidelines

The current guidelines are issued by the *AMLA* jointly with the *CBB*[5] and the *Ministry of Economic Development*.[6] *FI*s subject to the Regulations must take the guidelines into account when constructing and operating their AML programmes. The courts will take into account any relevant supervisory or regulatory guidance that apply to an organisation.

---

[5] www.barbadosfiu.gov.bb/guidelines.asp.
[6] www.barbadosfiu.gov.bb/international_business.asp.

2.2.1 How do the Act and the guidelines apply?

Although the *MLFTA* applies to all persons and business in Barbados, additional administrative requirements are placed in *FIs*. According to *Section 2(1) of the MLFTA*[7] an *FI* means:

- Any person who carries on business under the *Financial Institutions Act 1996 – 16 (FIA)* and includes:

- deposit-taking institutions;

- money transmission services, investment services or any other services of a financial nature;

- credit unions;

- building societies;

- friendly societies;

- insurance businesses;

- offshore banks;

- exempt insurance companies;

- international business companies;

- societies with restricted liability (SRLs);

- foreign sales corporations (*FSC*);

- mutual funds, mutual funds administrators and mutual fund managers;

- international trusts.

2.2.2 Mandatory anti-money laundering procedures

Section 8(1) sets out the duties of *FIs* designed to prevent money laundering and terrorist financing. These include:

(i) Establishment and maintenance (for a period of 5 years) of

    (a) records of all business transactions over BDS$10 000

    (b) records indicating the nature of the identification evidence obtained, i.e. know your customer documentation

(ii) Reporting of **suspicious transactions**.

(iii) Compliance *AMLA* instructions regarding investigations.

(iv) Allowing the *AMLA* access to records/allowing copies to be made regarding investigations.

(v) Development and application of internal policies, procedures and controls to combat money laundering.

(vi) Development of audit functions to evaluate policies, procedures and controls.

---

[7] www.barbadosfiu.gov.bb/legislation.asp.

(vii) Compliance with AML/CFT training requirements.

(viii) Compliance with guidelines issued by the *AMLA*.

(ix) Monitoring and reporting all currency exchanges of BDS$10 000 or more and all instructions for transfers of international funds of BDS$10 000 or more where the transaction appears to be of an unusual nature.

2.2.3   Client identification

For personal clients, as a minimum the following information should be obtained/ascertained:

• Full name and aliases	• Reason for opening the account
• Permanent address	• Nature and place of business/occupation
• Date and place of birth	• Expected account turnover and source of funds
• Nationality	• Any other information deemed appropriate by the institution

Valid photo-bearing identification should be obtained preferably via one of the following:

• Passport	• Drivers licences, and where the applicant is non resident
• National Identity Card	• Social security number

For legal entities, the following should be obtained:

• Certificate of incorporation	• Certificate of good standing
• Certificate of continuance and certificate of registration	• By-laws
• Memorandum and articles of association	• Partnerships Agreement

The *FI* must

• Verify the identity of the directors, shareholders, officers, account signatories and beneficial owners.

For **trusts**, nominees and fiduciary customers:

- the nature and purpose of the **trust** must be ascertained, and

- the identity of the **trustees**, settlor, protector, etc. must be verified.

The 2001 guidelines stated 'In **instances where original documents are not available copies should only be acceptable where certified by a notary public (e.g. justice of the peace)'.** This statement has caused some confusion. Local *FI*s generally have been taking this to mean taking reasonable steps to ensure copy documents are certified by appropriate persons with the background of those persons being verified.

The 2006 Guidance Notes provides a **list of possible 'eligible persons' for certification purposes** – this is currently under discussion and it has been recommended by the industry that the list be widened to include equivalent persons in other jurisdictions.

The 2006 Guidance Notes recommend that a risk-based approach to performing *KYC* be undertaken in line with international changes and that this is applied to existing clients although again on an overall risk-based basis.

2.2.4 Retrospective due diligence on existing clients

The 2006 Guidelines advise that *FI*s **should reassess their requirements pertaining to identification records** to ensure that all customer records conform to the current stated standards.

2.2.5 Exceptions to full due diligence

Section 7(5) of the MLFTA only allows an exception regarding the evidence of identification where the applicant is itself a *FI* subject to *Part II of the Act*. Or where a series of transactions occur in a business relationship where satisfactory evidence of identity has already been produced.

The institution is expected to document those instances where it is relying on this provision and the *CBB* guidelines provide a specimen Identification Exception form, although this is not necessarily a mandatory format.

Where due diligence has been completed by a branch or banking subsidiary or affiliate of the Barbados *FI* and that process meets the criteria of the Barbados guidelines, then copies of the relevant documentation must be obtained before the account is opened.

In the case of an international bank engaged in group treasury operations, written confirmation of the source of funds must be obtained from the parent company.

2.2.6 Exempted clients

The Barbados Guidelines exempt only those institutional applicants that are themselves subject to the *MLFTA*.

The Fiduciary Services and Business Investment Guidelines also exempt 'small one-off trans-actions' although seemingly do not provide a definition of what constitutes such a transaction, leaving service providers to use their own 'reasonableness test' in this area.

2.2.7 Eligible introductions

The AML legislation does not recognise introductions or referrals in whole or in part as an alternative to proper identification procedures. The onus remains on the institution to separately verify the identity of the customer. The guidelines state that an account holder's identity should not be established solely on the basis of a referral.

2.2.8 Record keeping procedures

*FI*s are required to maintain all business transaction records for a minimum of 5 years for all transactions exceeding BDS$10 000. The main aim of this provision is to ensure FIs can quickly comply with any requests for information from the *AMLA*. Records may need to be retained for longer periods in some circumstances, such as where there has been a report of a suspicious transaction or there is an ongoing investigation.

Business transaction records must be kept in a form that permits them to be reconstructed in full detail in case they are required as evidence in a criminal prosecution.

Institutions must retain customer identification records, account files and business correspondence since it may be necessary to establish the financial profile of a suspected arrangement.

To satisfy this requirement additional information such as the following should be available:

- volume of funds flowing through the arrangement,
- origin of the funds;
- form in which the funds were offered or withdrawn (e.g. cash/cheque);
- identity of the person undertaking the transaction;
- form of instruction and authority; and
- name and address of the counterparty.

*FI*s are also required to document a formal AML policy including areas such as audit of the programme and training of staff in relevant AML issues.

All documentation should be retrievable within a reasonable time in order to comply with instructions issued by the *AMLA*, courts or regulators.

2.2.9 Internal reporting

Subsections 6(a) and 8(1)(c) of the MLFTA require *FI*s to submit reports to the *AMLA*. As part of its internal control system a *FI* should at a minimum, introduce reports appropriate to its operations that cover the following areas:

- cash transactions;
- wirer transfers by country;
- transactions secured by cash;
- large transactions, i.e. those exceeding BDS$100 000 or equivalent;
- suspicious transactions.

2.2.10 Internal controls and procedures

Section 8(1) of the MLFTA requires *FI*s to develop and document an AML programme appropriate to the size and nature of the business and will include:

- Adequate internal policies, procedures and controls with respect to account opening and documentation requirements.

- Designation of a **Compliance Officer** at management level to co-ordinate and monitor the AML programme, receive internal reports and issue external reports to the *AMLA*.

- Management information/reporting systems.

- Screening procedures for new staff and maintain these on an ongoing basis.

- An ongoing employee training programme.

- An effective risk-based audit function to test and evaluate the programme.

2.2.11 Training and awareness

An appropriate AML/CFT training programme must be developed in line with the size and nature of the business. This training programme should be formally documented and form part of the overall AML policy document. It is a legal requirement under *section 8(1)(f) of the MLFTA* for *FI*s to comply with this requirement. All training should be on a regular basis at least once per annum for staff and twice per annum for Compliance Officers. The training programme should at a minimum contain the following:

- Details and contents of the training programme
- Names of staff receiving training
- Dates of training sessions
- Assessment of the training

Training programmes should be tailored to various activities such as (but not limited to):

- Front line staff
- Wire transfer employees
- Loans officers
- Senior Management and directors
- Accounting staff
- Internal Audit
- Compliance Officers
- New employees

Training topics should generally cover:

- Laws and guidelines
- Policies and procedures
- Know your customer requirements
- Know your business relationships
- Reporting procedures
- The identification of possible types of suspicious activities
- Case studies of typologies and trends
- Personal obligations under the MLFTA

Compliance Officers should receive in-depth training on all aspects of the legislation and regulatory framework and specific training on all areas of the AML regime.

2.2.12   Sector specific guidance

Currently the only sector specific guidelines are those issued by the *Central Bank of Barbados* and the *Ministry of Economic Affairs*. The Supervisor of Insurance and Pensions is currently working on sector specific guidelines for the insurance industry however a publication date for these is not yet available.

2.2.13   Delegation of maintenance of anti-money laundering procedures

The 2001 AML guidelines did not make reference to outsourcing of any part of the AML programme, however the 2006 Guidelines issued by the *Central Bank of Barbados* in October 2006, specifically mention outsourcing of the compliance function as follows:

> Section 9.0 Compliance and Audit

> The Bank recognizes, however, that the designation of a compliance officer or the creation of an Internal Audit department may create difficulties for some small licensees. Where the licensee is part of a larger regulated financial or mixed conglomerate, the Group Compliance Officer or Group Internal Audit can perform the compliance and/or internal audit services.

> Where this is not possible, a licensee may, subject to the Bank's agreement, outsource the operational aspects of the compliance or internal audit function involved in the auditing or accounting functions of the licensee.

It should however be noted that the ultimate responsibility for compliance with the *MLFTA* would still remain with the financial service provider even if outsourcing was utilised.

3   Combating the financing of terrorism

In response to the events of 11 September 2001 and the introduction of the *FATF Special Recommendations on Terrorist Financing*, the Barbados Government has implemented legislation to give effect to restrictions imposed by the *United Nations Security Council Resolutions* and to combat terrorism and terrorist financing in or through Barbados.

Barbados passed the *Anti Terrorism Act 2002-6 (ATA)* to fully implement *UN Security Council Resolution 1373 on terrorism*. The *ATA* provides for the forfeiture of terrorist funding, sharing of forfeited funds, prohibition of terrorist activity and mandatory disclosure of information using existing confidential channels (i.e. reporting to appropriate authorities on the same lines as anti-money laundering), among other issues.

The specific offences under the *ATA* are shown below:

Terrorism offences	Provision or collection of funds or financial services to persons to be used to carry out an offence as defined in the listed treaties	Conviction on indictment to 25 years imprisonment	Section 4(1) Anti-Terrorism Act (ATA)
	Provision of assistance or involvement in the conspiracy to commit a terrorist offence	Conviction on indictment and principal offender punished accordingly	Section 3 of ATA
	A terrorist offence committed by a person responsible for the management or control of an entity located or registered in Barbados, or otherwise organised under the laws of Barbados	BDS$2 000 000 notwithstanding that any criminal liability has been incurred by an individual directly involved in the commission of the offence or any civil or administrative sanction as imposed by law.	Section 5 of ATA

4   Conclusion

Barbados has sought to ensure that its regulatory and supervisory practices are consistent with the highest international standards and the government is very much aware of its international obligations and also of the need to ensure that the jurisdiction maintains its reputation as one of quality and integrity and is not used for money laundering or terrorist financing purposes.

In line with international initiatives the *AMLA* aims to ensure that the Guidelines are keeping pace with international developments as the 2006 Guidance Notes show.

The laws and guidelines satisfy the obligations of Barbados as a member of the *CFATF* and comply with the most recent *Financial Action Task Force recommendations*. A number of money laundering actions have been brought in Barbados although few have reached final conclusion and there have, to date, been no Terrorist Financing cases.

Addresses

Central Bank of Barbados
Tom Adams Financial Centre
Spry Street, P.O. Box 1016
Bridgetown, Barbados
Tel (246) 436-6870
Fax (246) 427-9559 (Secretariat)
(246) 427-1431 (Research)
cbb.libr@caribsurf.com
www.centralbank.org.bb

The Supervisor of Insurance
2nd Floor, Weymouth Corporate Centre
Roebuck Street
St. Michael
Barbados
Tel (246) 426-3815
Fax (246) 436-2699
sofi@caribsurf.com

Anti-Money Laundering Authority
Post Office Box 1372
Bridgetown, St Michael
Barbados
Contact: The Director
Tel (246) 436-4734/5
Fax (246) 436-4756
amla@sunbeach.net

The Securities Commission
Tom Adams Financial Centre
Spry Street
Bridgetown
Barbados
Contact: Virginia Mapp – General Manager
Tel (246) 437-3924
mail@seccom.com.bb

Abbreviations

AMLA	Anti-Money Laundering Authority
ATA	Anti-Terrorism Act 2002-6
CBB	Central Bank of Barbados
CFATF	Caribbean Financial Action Task Force
FIs	Financial Intermediaries Institutions
MLA	Money Laundering (Prevention and Control) Act 1998-38
MLFTA	Money Laundering and Financing of Terrorism (Prevention and Control) Act 2001
NCCT	Non Cooperative Countries and Territories
POCA	Proceeds of Crime Act 1990

Aede Gerbranda studied law at Utrecht University and at New York University. He has worked as a lawyer since September 1984. He has been a partner of STvB since 1993. He is Netherlands Antilles counsel to many large companies, including a number of Netherlands Antilles companies listed at the NY Stock Exchange, the NASDAQ and the Singapore Stock Exchange. In addition he counts prominent accounting firms, tax advisors and law firms among his clients as well as banks, finance companies, mutual funds, insurance companies and other companies and wealthy individuals that use the Netherlands Antilles or Aruba in their international operations. He is the author of many publications on Netherlands Antilles company, finance and banking law.

STvB Advocaten ('STvB'), formerly Smeets Thesseling van Bokhorst, is a leading Netherlands Antilles law firm that was founded in 1938 by Antonius A.G. Smeets. The firm specializes in international transactions and over the years has been instrumental in the development of new financial products such as finance companies, off-shore investment funds and private foundations.

Netherlands Antilles and Aruba

Aede Gerbranda

Member of

STvB Advocaten
Concertgebouwplein 5
1071 LL Amsterdam
The Netherlands

Tel +31 20 577 60 80
Fax +31 20 577 60 88
stvb@stvb.nl
www.stvb.nl

Anti-Money Laundering: International Law and Practice.
Edited by W.H. Muller, C.H. Kälin and J.G. Goldsworth
© 2007 John Wiley & Sons, Ltd

Contents – Netherlands Antilles and Aruba

1 Introduction

This survey will only refer to those laws and regulations that relate directly to the fight against money laundering and financing of terrorism in the *Netherlands Antilles*. It will not give a specific survey of all Netherlands Antilles' laws and regulations in this field. The survey will address aspects of international treaties and the guidelines of the *Financial Action Task Force on Money-Laundering* (*FATF*) which are incorporated in Netherlands Antilles law.

1.1 International law and treaties

The *Netherlands Antilles* are a member of the *FATF*. The regulations of the *FATF* are contained in 40 recommendations, providing the framework for the global standard for anti-money laundering systems. After 11 September 2001, the *FATF* extended its mandate to include the combating of the financing of terrorism.

Although the recommendations have no binding force under international law, a number of them are embodied in the provisions of existing multilateral conventions and therefore are legally binding. For the *Netherlands Antilles* the recommendations of the *FATF* were adopted by the *Caribbean Financial Action Task Force* (*CFATF*). During a meeting of the council of the *CFATF* in 1992, 19 additional recommendations were produced to be implemented in local legislation. In order to give the *CFATF* a solid legal basis, the *CFATF* has decided that its members had to enter into a *Memorandum of Understanding*. The *Memorandum of Understanding* became legally binding in October 1996 and as of that date the recommendations of the CFTAF became binding in the Netherlands Antilles.

1.2 Netherlands Antilles' anti-money laundering laws

The Netherlands Antilles' laws or executive decrees relating to money laundering and terrorist financing are:

- 1993 *National Ordinance on penalization of money laundering of 24 May 1993.*
- 1996 *National Ordinance on the reporting of unusual transactions of 10 February 1996.*
- 1996 *National Ordinance on identification of clients when rendering financial services of 10 February 1996.*
- 2002 *National Ordinance on the obligation to report cross-border money transportation of 25 March 2002.*
- 2001 *Ministerial Decree indicators unusual transactions of 4 April 2001.*

In 2001 and 2002 four other Ministerial Decrees have been issued, containing the indicators for certain specific transactions that serve to assist when determining whether or not these transactions must be deemed as unusual.

Hereafter we shall under Sections 2, 3 and 4 address the abovementioned Ordinances.

2 Penalization of money laundering

Money laundering is penalized under the *National Ordinance on penalization of money laundering of 24 May 1993.*

2.1   Terminology

The laundering of **money** in the Netherlands Antilles will be penalized as a criminal act. The word **money** in this context also refers to monetary securities and claims.

2.2   Penalization clauses

There are several actions on the basis of which a person may be deemed guilty of intentionally laundering money. The person who acquires, has at his disposal or transfers money derived from criminal acts, whilst this person knew or should have known that such money was derived from criminal acts, is guilty of laundering money, and may be punished with imprisonment of up to 12 years or a money fine of up to ANG 1,000,000, or both. A similar punishment may be imposed on a person who intentionally reaps a profit from the proceeds of money derived from criminal acts.

2.3   Committers of the crime

Money laundering can be committed by individuals and legal entities. If the criminal act is committed by a legal entity, criminal proceedings and the punishments may be instituted and the punishments and measures may be imposed on the legal entity. In addition it is always possible to proceed against the individuals and legal entities who have ordered the act committed and those who have actually given direction to the illegal actions.

If criminal proceedings are initiated against a legal entity, the legal entity has to be represented during the proceedings by a managing director.

3   Reporting of unusual transactions

3.1   The unusual transaction reporting center

To prevent money laundering, there is an ***unusual transactions reporting center*** (*meldpunt ongebruikelijke transacties*). This center is co-operating under the responsibility of the Minister of Finance and is headed by an independent director.

According to the law the tasks of the reporting center are:

- To collect, register, process and analyze the data obtained by the reporting center.

- To furnish data in conformity with the stipulations laid down in or pursuant to the *National Ordinance on the reporting of unusual transactions*.

- To notify the party having reported, whether data have been furnished: laid down in or pursuant to the *National Ordinance on the reporting of unusual transactions*.

- To investigate developments in money laundering.

- To make recommendations, after having heard the *Central Bank of the Netherlands Antilles* (*Bank van de Nederlandse Antillen*), as regards the measures to be taken to prevent the use of branches of business for money laundering purposes.

- To give information with regard to the phenomenon and the prevention of money laundering.

- To yearly render a report of its activities and its plans for the next year.

3.2   The register

The unusual transaction reporting center keeps a **register**, this register contains all the data necessary for the prevention of money laundering. The Minister of Finance is the administrator of the register. There are only a few occasions in which the data from the register can be examined by third parties. The furnishing of data to authorities outside the Kingdom of the Netherlands can take place only on the basis of a treaty. Certain specific data of the register can be examined by the authorities and officials of the Netherlands Antilles who are in charge of the detection and prosecution of criminal offences.

3.3   The obligation to report

Anyone who renders financial services by virtue of his profession or in the ordinary course of his business is bound to report any unusual transaction that is being carried out or that is proposed, to the reporting center.

3.3.1   The indicators

The Minister of Finance and the Minister of Justice have jointly laid down certain indicators to judge whether a transaction must be considered as unusual. Any act mentioned in these indicators in principle must be regarded as an unusual transaction. The ministers are only allowed to so lay down the indicators for a period of six months. After that period, the indicators will only remain in effect, if they are approved and continued by a national decree.

3.3.2   Financial services

The **financial services** in or from the *Netherlands Antilles* rendered by persons that trigger an obligation to report, as laid down in the *National Ordinance on the reporting of unusual transactions* of 10 February 1996, consist of the following services:

- To take into custody securities, paper currency, coins, currency notes, precious metals and other valuables.

- To open an account, on which a balance may be kept in money, securities, precious metals or other valuables.

- To rent a safe-deposit box.

- To effect payment in connection with the cashing in of coupons or comparable documents of bonds or comparable securities.

- To enter into a life insurance contract as referred to in article 1, first paragraph sub a. of the *National Ordinance on the supervision of the insurance industry* (*Landsverordening toezicht verzekeringsbedrijf*), or to render assistance in connection therewith.

- To make a distribution on account of such a life insurance contract.

- To credit or debit an account, or to cause this to be done, on which account a balance may be kept in money, securities, precious metals or other securities.

- To exchange *Netherlands Antilles'* guilders or foreign currencies.

- To provide other services which are designated by national decree, containing general measures.

Furthermore the following services are designated as a financial service in the *National Decree on the designation of financial services for reporting unusual transactions* (*Landsbesluit aanwijzing financiële diensten melding ongebruikelijke transacties*):

- Entering into an obligation for payment, on behalf of a holder of a credit card to the person who has accepted such manner of payment by being shown such credit card, to the extent that it does not concern a credit card which can only be used with the company or institution that issued the credit card or with a company or institution belonging to the same economic entity through which the legal persons and companies are connected.

- Receiving of moneys or monetary values as part of a money transfer, in order to make such moneys or monetary values payable or have them made payable in the same form or in another form elsewhere, or paying or making payable moneys or monetary values as part of a money transfer after such moneys or monetary values have been made available in the same form or in another form elsewhere.

- Offering prizes and premiums that can be competed for against payment of a value in excess of ANG 20,000 or its equivalent in any other currency, in the context of the national or international operation of gaming and lotteries.

- Rendering fiduciary services, which services shall also be taken to include: rendering of administrative services in or from the *Netherlands Antilles* for and on behalf of international companies, including providing natural or legal persons as directors, representatives or other officers on behalf of international companies; establishing an international company or causing it to be established or winding up an international company or causing it to be wound up by order but for the account of third parties.

The Decree further provides that financial services consisting of the receiving of moneys do not include: (a) receiving these in the context of premium payment pursuant to an insurance agreement, to an institution that has been licensed to carry out its activities as an insurance business in the *Netherlands Antilles* pursuant to the *National Ordinance on the supervision of the insurance industry*; or (b) paying in the context of a distribution under an insurance agreement, by such an institution that has been licensed to carry out its activities as an insurance business.

3.3.3 The report

Anyone who renders financial services must report any unusual transaction so encountered. The report contains data of the customer. His identity, the nature and the number of his proof of identity; the nature, time and place of the transaction and its magnitude. In case of a financial service which involves the crediting or debiting of an account and on which account a balance may be kept in money, securities, precious metals or other securities, the allocation and the origin of all of these valuables involved in the transaction and the circumstances on the basis of which the transaction is considered to be unusual must also be reported.

The *unusual transactions reporting center* is authorized to ask further data or information from the party having reported and also from the party involved. The party from whom these data or information has been requested will be bound to furnish the reporting center with this information in writing, and also, in cases deemed urgent in the discretion of the reporting center within the term, stated by the reporting center.

The persons who are involved with the procedure of the unusual transactions reporting center and the party who makes a report of an unusual transaction, are generally prohibited from making further or other use of data and information so furnished or received.

3.4   The guidance committee

There is a *guidance committee* for the reporting center. The committee consists of up to 12 members with representatives of the Minister of Finance, the Minister of Justice, the branches of business to which the anti-money laundering rules apply, the supervising authority for the branches of business to which the anti-money laundering rules apply and the public prosecutor. The members are appointed and dismissed by the Minister of Finance on the motion of all of these mentioned representatives. The appointment will be for three years. A representative of the Minister of Finance presides over the committee.

The guidance committee has determined its own method of operation. The tasks of the committee are to guide the reporting center and the functioning thereof and to make the know-how and expertise of the committee available to the reporting center. Another task of the guidance committee is to advise the ministers when determining the indicators for unusual transactions.

3.5   Right to inspect

A person will be notified, at such person's request, by or on behalf of the administrator of the register of the reporting center within a month whether and what personal data concerning such person have been entered in the register. This notification shall not be made insofar as this may be necessary for the proper discharge of the task of the reporting center or if weighty third party interests so require. If the request is not complied with, the party involved may address a petition to the *Court of First Instance* (*Gerecht van Eerste Aanleg*) within two months from his receipt of the refusal of the request.

3.6   Internal control with respect to unusual transactions

Administrators of investment institutions and self-administered investment institutions, both as defined in the *National Ordinance on the supervision of investment institutions and administrators* (*Landsverordening toezicht beleggingsinstellingen en administrateurs*), have to develop an internal procedure to detect and report proposed or completed unusual transactions. Such procedure should facilitate the recognition, documenting and reporting of unusual transactions.

The *Central Bank of the Netherlands Antilles* has made a list with examples of suspicious investment-related transactions. In case a transaction mentioned in this list takes place, the staff must be alert. The list concerns for example large or unusual settlements of transactions in cash or bearer form, buying and selling of shares in an investment institution with no discernible purpose or in circumstances which appear unusual. Furthermore, the list refers to clients who are willing to take more risk than a normal investor, clients who often turn around their investments or indulge in early surrender of their participating interests into the investment institution, despite penalties or exit charges.

If the administrator or self-administered investment institution decides that a business relationship with a potential client will not be established or that a existing relationship will be ended as a consequence of the policy to guard against money laundering and terrorist financing, it is important to provide an audit trail for suspicious funds, beside the duty to report the unusual transaction to the reporting center.

3.6.1   Internal review and authorization by senior management

Each administrator and self-administered investment institution should designate at least one senior officer who will be in charge of the deterrence and detection of money laundering and terrorist financing. His tasks and responsibilities are set out in the guidelines of the *Central Bank of the Netherlands Antilles*, and this should all be included in the job description. The job description should be signed off and dated by the officer, indicating the acceptance of the entrusted responsibilities.

In all cases that a report must be drawn up by the administrator or the administrative investment institution to be sent to the reporting center, the senior management has to review and authorize the report with the existing regulations. If the senior management does not authorize the report, all documents relevant to the transaction including the reasons for non-authorization should adequately be documented, signed off by the designated officer and senior management and kept by the reporting institution.

There should be an adequately resourced and independent audit function to test compliance with their policies procedures and controls. This should be tested at least annually by the internal audit department or by an outside independent party. The scope of the testing and the results should be documented. If there are any problems this has to be reported to the senior management, the Board of Directors and the officers with a request for a response to take prompt corrective actions.

3.6.2   Screening of employees, training programs

The business of the administrator and self-administered investment institution must be conducted at a high ethical standard. In addition each administrator and each self-administered investment institution should screen their employees on criminal records. A training program must be developed for personnel who handle the susceptible transactions. There should be a training program for all new and existing employees who are dealing with clients, irrespective of their level of seniority. A higher level of instruction should be provided to those with the responsibility to supervise or manage the staff. After an indefinite period of time, the training should be repeated. Also the records of the training documentation should be maintained at the office.

4   Identification when rendering financial services

Anyone who renders financial services by virtue of his profession or in the ordinary course of his business, a **service provider**, shall be under the obligation to establish the identity of a customer before rendering any financial service to such **customer**. A customer means anyone to whom a financial service is rendered, the party who pays the premium and the person to whom the distribution of a life insurance contract is made.

4.1 Establishing the identity of the customer

The identity of a customer shall also be established by the service provider at the time that it is not known what amount will be involved by rendering services in respect of a transaction or if the financial service relates to a transaction that, based on the **indicators** of the *National Ordinance on the reporting of unusual transactions* must be deemed to be unusual. Even when the amount of the transaction is less than the amount stipulated by the indicators, the identity of the customer should be established, if the service provider knows or reasonably presumes that the transaction to which the financial service relates forms part of a totality of related transactions, involving various institutions. The obligation for the service provider to establish the identity of a customer will not apply to entering into, or mediating at the effecting of, a life insurance contract at a premium or making a distribution on account of a life insurance contract, insofar as a pension insurance offered by a life insurance business is concerned, unless such insurance is surrendered or serves as security.

4.1.1 Natural persons

If the customer is a natural person, the identity of the customer must be established using a driver's license; an identity card issued by the local authorities; a travel document or passport or any other document to be designated by the Minister of Finance. The documents have to be valid in the country where they have been issued. If the natural person is residing abroad it will be sufficient to have a copy of one of the aforementioned documents, with the condition that the copy shall be accompanied by a certified extract of the civil registry of births, deaths and marriages of the customer's place of residence.

If the service provider knows or reasonably presumes that the natural person appearing before him is not acting for himself, the service provider shall take measures in order to discover the identity of the customer for whom such natural person is acting. In the event of a customer being represented by a third party, measures should be taken to establish the identity of such representative. This shall not apply if the natural person is a service provider or is acting on behalf of a service provider in respect of whom an exemption or a release applies, on the condition that such service provider has established the identity of the third party for whom such natural person is acting. This has to be done in the same way as establishing the identity of any other customer.

4.1.2 Legal persons

If the customer is a legal person, its identity shall be established by using a certified extract from the register of the *Curaçao Chamber of commerce and industry* (*Kamer van koophandel en nijverheid Curaçao*) or an equivalent institution in the country where the customer has its registered office or using an identification document to be drawn up by the service provider. The service provider is responsible for the correct identification data. If it appears that the data is no longer valid, the service provider shall be obliged to amend this.

For certain specific services mentioned in the *National Decree on designation of financial services, identification of financial services* (*Landsbesluit aanwijzing financiële diensten identificatie bij financiële dienstverlening*); the credit or debit card number, expiration date or the check number and corresponding bank account number are also designated as the provided information.

Furthermore there is an obligation towards the *Central Bank of the Netherlands Antilles* to establish the identity of the directors and other persons authorized to represent the customer towards the service provider, and the beneficial owners holding a direct or indirect holding equal to or exceeding 5% of the nominal capital of the legal entity. Beside the names and addresses of the individual beneficial owners, their occupation and date of birth are also required to be established.

When there is a **significant shareholder**, holding 25% or more of the shares, and this significant shareholder is a legal person, corporate information should be sought from the company, regarding the ultimate beneficial ownership of that particular company.

When the customer is an **institutional investor**, for example a pension fund, charity or local authority, there must be a reference to appropriate sources to check the identity. The existing business practice will generally be sufficient, most important is the availability of documentary evidence and the evidence of the identity of the representatives of the institutional investor. If it is a pension fund of a listed company or of a government agency, no further steps are required to establish the identity of the customer.

When the investor is a partnership a certified extract from the *Curaçao Chamber of commerce and industry (Kamer van koophandel en nijverheid Curaçao)* or a similar document being the original or certified copy of the certificate of establishment, a certified copy of the partnership agreement or the articles of partnership and the identities of all partners having authority to represent the partnership and identification of all of those authorized to issue instructions and represent the partnership are necessary. The regulations for individuals or corporate entity will also apply, if the partners are individuals or a corporate entity.

In case of a redemption or surrender of an investment, the service provider has to take reasonable measures to establish the identity of the investor where payment is made either: to the registered owner of the investment by means of a cheque crossed 'account payee' or to a bank account held in the name of the registered owner of the investment with a financial institution by any electronic means effective to transfer funds.

The obligation to establish the identity of the customer will be fulfilled when the service provider uses the data determined by him earlier when rendering financial services to such customer.

4.2   Exemptions

There are certain exemptions from the obligation to establish the identity of a customer. These exemptions mainly concern customers who are an enterprise or institution registered pursuant to the *National Ordinance on the supervision of banking and credit institutions* or a life insurance business as in the *National Ordinance on the supervision of the insurance industry*.

4.3   Required information

The service provider shall be under the obligation to have available the data of its customers in such a manner that they shall be accessible.

The service provider shall be under the obligation to keep these data for five years.

The service provider shall be prohibited from rendering a financial service if the identity of the customer has not been established in the prescribed manner.

4.4   Punishment

Any breach or act in contravention of the obligation to identify the identity of a customer is a punishable act. To the extent that such breach or act occurs intentionally, it shall be a criminal offence that may be punished either with imprisonment of up to four years, or with a fine of up to ANG 500,000, or both. To the extent that this breach or act occurs unintentionally, it shall be an offence and may be punished with imprisonment of up to one year, or with a fine of up to ANG 200,000, or both.

Address

Bank van de Nederlandse Antillen
Simon Bolivar Plein 1
Willemstad, Curaçao
Netherlands Antilles
Tel +599 9 434 5500
Fax +599 9 461 5004
www.centralbank.an

Bibliography

Association of International Bankers of the Netherlands Antilles (IBNA), the Curaçao Bankers Association (CBA) and the Curaçao International Financial Services Association (CIFA): Anti-money laundering and anti-terrorist financing regulations of the Netherlands Antilles, Curaçao, 2004.

Bank van de Nederlandse Antillen: Provisions and guidelines on the detection and deterrence of money laundering and terrorist financing for administrators of investment institutions and self-administered investment institutions, Curaçao, 2005.

Shawna Lake is the director of the Marketing and Development Department in the Ministry of Finance in St. Kitts. She has held this position for the last five years. She was formerly Crown Counsel in the Attorney General's Chambers for five years. Towards the end of her term at the Attorney General's Chambers she was asked to start up and head the Marketing and Development Department. Shawna is an attorney at law. She obtained her LLB from the University of the West Indies in 1994 and graduated from the Norman Manley Law School in Jamaica in 1996 with the Legal Education Certificate (LEC). Shawna also holds an MBA (Finance) from the University of Leicester in the United Kingdom.

Idris Fidela Clarke is the Director General and Regulator of the Financial Services Department in St. Kitts, and serves as a Commissioner on the Federation's Financial Services Commission. The Financial Services Department is responsible for licensing and supervising on and offshore companies, trusts and foundations. In addition, the Financial Services Department conducts anti-money laundering and terrorist financing inspections on all non-bank financial institutions and Authorized Service Providers. Ms Clarke is a Certified Public Accountant, and holds an MBA with a concentration in Finance. In addition, she holds a postgraduate diploma in offshore finance and administration and is a Certified Anti-Money Laundering Specialist.

St. Kitts and Nevis

Shawna Lake

Director Marketing and
Development Department

Ministry of Finance
Rams Building
Liverpool Row
Basseterre, St. Kitts, WI

Tel +1 869 465-1153
Fax +1 869 465-1154
directormd@sisterisles.kn
www.skbfinancialservices.com

Idris Fidela Clarke

Director General Financial
Services Department

Ministry of Finance
Pelican Mall
Basseterre, St. Kitts, WI

Tel +1 869 466-5048
Fax +1 869 466-5317
skanfsd@caribsurf.com
www.skbfinancialservices.com

Anti-Money Laundering: International Law and Practice.
Edited by W.H. Muller, C.H. Kälin and J.G. Goldsworth
© 2007 John Wiley & Sons, Ltd

Contents – St. Kitts and Nevis

1   Introduction

The **Federation of St. Kitts and Nevis** is a twin-island Commonwealth nation in the center of the Caribbean chain of islands between North and South America. There is a Federal Government, which is based in the capital of Basseterre in St. Kitts, however Nevis has its own local government referred to as the Nevis Island Administration.

Both St. Kitts and Nevis are involved in the international **financial services** sector with Nevis launching into this sector in 1984 and St. Kitts in 1996. St. Kitts and Nevis have their own separate legislation providing for the formation of companies, trusts, foundations, international business companies, etc. They have their own marketing and promotion offices to deal with the promotion of their individual products and services.

In 2000 the Federation was placed on the **FATF** blacklist as a result of deficiencies in the anti-money laundering regulatory regime, particularly on the island of Nevis, which was the much larger center with almost 30 000 **international business companies** on its register at the time. The two islands worked together to develop comprehensive **anti-money laundering legislation** and systems that resulted in **the removal of the Federation from the FATF blacklist in June 2002**. At the time of removal the Federation met none of the 25 negative non-cooperative country criteria and the country received special commendation from the FATF president on this huge accomplishment in such a short period of time.

The remainder of this chapter will focus on the anti-money laundering/counter-financing of terrorism regulatory infrastructure in the Federation and the legislation and supporting guidelines that form the foundation of this infrastructure.

The text of the legislation, regulations and guidelines referred to in this chapter may be found in the 'Law Library' section of the website www.skbfinancialservices.com.

2   Anti-money laundering legislation

2.1   Proceeds of Crime Act, 2000 (No. 16 of 2000)

The cornerstone of the **anti-money laundering legislation** for the Federation of St. Kitts and Nevis is the ***Proceeds of Crime Act, 2000.*** This Act provides for the freezing, forfeiture and confiscation of the proceeds of crime and more importantly defines money laundering and makes it a specific offence. It provides for the regulation of certain business activities that are outlined in the Schedule to the Act. These include banking business under the Banking Act, offshore banking, trust business, finance business carried on under the *Financial Services Regulations Order, 1997* of St. Kitts, money brokering, gaming, insurance business and other businesses that may be used to launder the proceeds of criminal activity.

The Act provides for the making of regulations to facilitate the regulation and supervision of the regulated businesses under the *Proceeds of Crime Act*. The *Anti-Money Laundering Regulations, 2001* were therefore made under this Act on the 22 May 2001.

2.1.1   Anti-Money Laundering Regulations, 2001 (SR&O No. 15 of 2001)

The *Anti-Money Laundering Regulations* were made pursuant to *section 67 of the Proceeds of Crime Act*. The regulations define more clearly the requirements of regulated businesses to:

- Maintain identification procedures in relation to new and continuing business relationships. Regulated businesses are required under *section 4(2) of the Regulations* to obtain satisfactory verification of the identity of any person with which it is conducting any new, continuing or one-off transactions. They are also specifically prohibited by *section 4(4) of the Regulations* from operating anonymous accounts or accounts which are in fictitious names.

- Maintain identification procedures of applicants introduced to them by third parties. Regulated businesses are to obtain satisfactory evidence of the identity of the applicant from the introducer as soon as reasonably practicable after contact is first made (sec. 6).

- Maintain records of **verification of identity** of all their clients (sec. 7).

- Maintain a record of all transactions (sec. 8).

- Maintain all evidence of identity and records of transactions for at least five years (sec. 9).

- Maintain a register of money laundering enquiries (sec. 11).

- Appoint a compliance office who shall be responsible for establishing and maintaining a manual of compliance procedures for the business, act as liaison for the regulated business with the regulator and prepare written reports for the regulator on the business and compliance in compliance with the regulations.

- Provide for the establishment of procedures for recognizing and reporting suspicious transactions to the **Financial Intelligence Unit** (sec. 14–15).

It is an offence to breach any of the requirements of the anti-money laundering regulations and persons that fail to comply are liable on summary conviction to a fine not exceeding EC$50 000.00 (approximately US$20 000.00)

The Regulations make provision for issuing of directions to regulated businesses by the Financial Services Commission which regulated businesses are required to follow when carrying out business activities.

2.2 Financial Services Commission Act, 2000 (No. 17 of 2000)

This Act provides for the establishment of the *Financial Services Commission*, which is the ultimate regulatory body for St. Kitts and Nevis. The function of the Commission is to receive reports from the regulator for St. Kitts and the regulator for Nevis, interact with the international community with respect to regulatory and supervisory issues, give general advice to the regulators, take necessary steps for the development and effective regulation of finance business in St. Kitts and Nevis, and be responsible for enforcement of the anti-money laundering regulations.

The Commission comprises of a commissioner appointed by the *Federal Minister of Finance* in St. Kitts, a commissioner appointed by the *Premier of Nevis*, a commissioner appointed by the *Federal Minister of Finance* with the concurrence of the *Governor of the Eastern Caribbean Central Bank*, the regulator for Nevis and the regulator for St. Kitts.

2.2.1 St. Christopher and Nevis Guidance Notes on the Prevention of Money Laundering and Terrorist Financing

These Guidance Notes are developed and issued by the *Financial Services Commission* to all regulated businesses. They comprise of guidelines to assist regulated businesses to prevent their businesses being used for money laundering or terrorist financing. The Guidelines are not legislated however, compliance with the Guidelines is a defense to action being brought against a regulated business for money laundering or terrorist financing.

The Guidance Notes contain information ranging from **know your customer** procedures, to hiring protocols, training guidelines for staff on anti-money laundering and counter financing of terrorism.

2.2.2 Financial Services Commission (Exchange of Information) Regulations, 2002 (SR&O No. 15 of 2002)

These regulations were developed pursuant to *section 16 of the Financial Services Commission Act* to provide for cooperation with **foreign regulatory authorities** directly by the regulators of St. Kitts and Nevis. The regulations provide for the matters that must first be taken into consideration before information is provided to a foreign regulatory authority, for example whether the assistance is for regulatory functions, the nature and seriousness of the matter, that assistance cannot be obtained by other means or that the relevant country has enacted similar laws with regard to information exchange.

Regulatory functions are defined in the Regulations as 'statutory functions of a regulatory authority, not being functions of assessing, imposing or collecting taxes'.

2.3 Financial Intelligence Unit Act, 2000 (No. 15 of 2000)

This Act provides for the establishment of the *Financial Intelligence Unit for St. Kitts and Nevis*. The function of the *Financial Intelligence Unit* is to collect, receive, analyze and act upon suspicious transaction information; disseminate information on suspicious transactions to competent authorities (if necessary), establish a database for the purpose of detecting money laundering and liaise with money laundering intelligence agencies outside of St. Kitts and Nevis. The Unit is an administrative body and is required to discreetly analyze suspicious activity information passed on to it in order to determine whether or not it should be passed on to the police for a full money laundering investigation.

3 Counter-financing of terrorism legislation

3.1 Anti-Terrorism Act, 2002 (No. 21 of 2002)

The *Anti-Terrorism Act* was passed in October 2002 to give effect to several United Nations Conventions and Protocols on the suppression and elimination of international terrorism and other incidental matters. **The main purpose of the Act is to define terrorist financing and to make it a specific offence**. It also makes it an offence to raise funding for terrorist activities, to possess and use property for terrorist purposes, to engage in money laundering for terrorist purposes. It also makes it an offence for persons who fail to disclose information relating to a person who has committed terrorist financing. This offence is punishable by imprisonment for up to 14 years or to a fine or both.

3.2 Organized Crime (Prevention and Control) Act, 2002 (No. 22 of 2002)

This Act was passed to give effect to the '*Convention Against Transnational Organized Crime*'. It creates the offences of organized crime, corruption and obstruction of justice. It also provides for the establishment of a criminal assets recovery fund, which would consist of money derived from the confiscation and forfeiture of money, which is the proceeds of criminal activity.

4   Regulatory structure of St. Kitts and Nevis

As previously mentioned, St. Kitts and Nevis are both members of a twin-island Federation, however, they are independent international financial centers, and therefore compete against each other. This presents an unusual situation with regards to the regulatory structure of the Federation. In order to ensure proper supervision of the financial sector, a supervisory regime which addresses the peculiarities of both islands had to be implemented.

The *Financial Services Commission* was established in 2000, as the ultimate regulatory body for financial services in St. Kitts and Nevis. In order to ensure that the Commission was able to accomplish this task, competent persons with significant experience in the finance industry from both St. Kitts and Nevis were appointed to serve as Commissioners. The *Financial Services Commission Act, 2000* established the position of a **Regulator** and such a person is responsible for the regulation of the financial services sector in St. Kitts and in Nevis. In turn, both Regulators report to the Commission, and are responsible for conducting anti-money laundering and counter-terrorist financing examinations. Therefore, one would find a supervisory unit headed by a Regulator on each island. The Examiners employed at each department are responsible for researching, analyzing and monitoring economic, financial and technological developments that may affect the Financial Services Sector in the Federation as well as conducting off-site surveillance and on-site examinations/inspections of non-bank financial institutions.

The *Eastern Caribbean Central Bank* which is responsible for supervising all commercial banks of the **Eastern Caribbean Currency Union (ECCU)** (Anguilla, Antigua and Barbuda, Dominica, Grenada, Montserrat, St. Kitts and Nevis, St. Lucia and St. Vincent) is headquartered in St. Kitts. Similarly, the **Eastern Caribbean Securities Exchange**, which is responsible for facilitating the buying and selling of financial products for the ECCU territories, is also headquartered in St. Kitts. The presence of these two well-established regulatory bodies therefore compliments the existing domestic financial services regulatory framework in the Federation.

4.1   Single regulatory unit

At present, the regulation of the financial sector in St. Kitts and Nevis is fragmented. The international financial sector is regulated by the *Financial Services Commission*, the commercial banks are regulated by the *Eastern Caribbean Central Bank*, the credit unions and other Cooperatives are regulated by the *Ministry of Agriculture*, the gaming industry is regulated by the *Gaming Board of St. Kitts–Nevis*, and the insurance sector is regulated by the *Ministry of Finance*. **However, the *Federal Government of St. Kitts–Nevis* has recently approved the establishment of a single regulatory unit, which would supervise the international financial sector as well as the domestic sector**. This unit will be responsible for licensing and supervision of non-bank financial entities such as insurance companies, money remittance businesses, credit unions and the international financial sector. **The remainder of this chapter will outline the functioning of the existing regulatory system** and not the proposed single regulatory unit as there is no official implementation date for this system as yet.

5 AML/CFT supervision of the financial sector

5.1 St. Kitts licensing procedure

Each *Financial Services Supervisory Department* is responsible for analyzing applications made from competent persons/institutions to obtain a license to conduct finance business. At present there are six types of licenses which may be obtained under the *Financial Services Regulations Order, 1997*, in order to conduct international finance business. They are Deposit Taking, Investment, Insurance, Assurance, Trust and Corporate.

In order for an application to be considered complete, the following documents should be submitted to the *Director General of the Financial Services Department:*

- A list of each shareholder controller and indirect controller of the applicant containing with respect to each: name, address and nationality.

- A statement explaining, in respect of each person on the list, nature and size of controlling interest.

- A list of directors, chief executive and managers of the applicant, containing in respect of each: name, address and nationality.

- A statement explaining, in respect of each person on the list, any contractual arrangements with the applicant.

- To be attached in respect of each person on the list.

    - A police affidavit of no criminal record.

    - Two letters of reference, one from a bank and the other from a reputable professional.

    - A resume with emphasis on the category of finance for which authorization is sought.

- Name and address of lawyer, if any, accompanied by confirmation from such lawyer.

- Name and address of the auditor, with confirmation from such auditor.

- Submission of an undertaking to maintain at all times, the relevant minimum financial resources–net assets of:

Deposit taking	–	unrestricted	US$500 000
		restricted	US$50 000
Investment	–	unrestricted	US$400 000
		restricted	US$40 000
Insurance	–	long term and general	US$300 000
	–	long term and not general	US$200 000
	–	general but not long term	US$$100 000
Trust	–	unrestricted	US$200 000
		restricted	US$20 000

For persons/entities seeking to conduct other finance business, net assets of US$100 000 should be maintained, or professional indemnity insurance for US$100 000 obtained. The applicant may also consider providing a guarantee in the minimum amount of US$100 000, which expressly states that its validity and rights and obligations of the parties to it are governed exclusively by the law of the Federation.

The applicant should submit audited accounts for the past three years preceding the date of application, or an audited balance sheet showing the net assets of the applicant at the end of the month immediately preceding the date of the application, where the applicant has not carried out any business previously. Should the application be for authorization to carry on either deposit taking business, investment business or insurance business, a business plan must be submitted for five years following the date of the application.

Background checks are to be performed on controllers, directors and managers before the granting of the license at a cost of US$2500 per person. The below-mentioned information is required in order for background checks to be completed:

Social Security Number; Passport Number (as well as certified copy of information pages); Date of issuance, Place of issuance; Present address; Date of birth and Place of employment.

Other domestic non-deposit-taking or non-bank financial institutions such as insurance companies, money remittance businesses and credit unions will be required to obtain a license from the supervisory unit as soon as the single regulatory unit has been established.

5.2   Nevis licensing procedure

Persons interested in obtaining a license must complete an application form for registration as a management company and submit it together with a proposal (or letter of intent) and US$555.56, to the *Nevis Financial Services Department*. The proposal should contain information on the proposed **directors** and their qualifications, the market that the company intends to target as well as the amount of local persons to be employed. The company may request a five-year tax exemption on corporate profits and may request exemption of customs duties on office equipment. In addition, due diligence checks at a cost of at least US$1200.00 per person, will have to be conducted on the principals and directors of the company and the *Minister of Finance* will peruse all documents to determine if the license should be granted. A license as a management company may enable a person/entity to register trusts, IBCs, LLCs and foundations, at a cost of US$185.19 per type of license (US$740.75 to provide all of the above-mentioned services).

If approval is granted, a license will be issued from the *Nevis Island Government* after the payment of all prescribed fees. The applicant will be required to incorporate a local company and ensure that it has paid-in capital of at least US$185 185.19 as prescribed in Sec 17(g) of the Nevis Business Corporation Ordinance.

5.3   AML/CFT onsite inspections

The Regulators of both islands are responsible for supervising the international financial sector which comprises of **offshore banks**, investment business, **fiduciary services**, **corporate business** and international insurance schemes. Onsite inspections are planned in order to determine if licensed service providers are in compliance with the local laws and international best practices. During these inspections, due diligence audits are conducted and compliance with the *Guidance Notes on the Prevention of Money Laundering and Counter Terrorist Financing* is assessed as well.

The Examination team adopts a risk-based approach towards the inspections. All authorized service providers are assigned a rating based on the type of authorization received as well as the volume of business conducted. In addition, other related incidents such as pending litigation, non-compliance with major laws or negative press may influence the Examiners' assignment of a particular risk weight. Therefore those entities which are considered to be of significant risk to the financial services sector are closely monitored, and onsite inspections conducted on an annual basis. Those which prove to be less risky are also monitored. However, onsite inspections are conducted on an 18-month basis.

As with any other type of inspection, the Examiners have to determine the adequate sample size of the accounts/companies to be inspected. During the actual onsite inspection, the proper identification of all beneficial owners must be obtained. In order to do this, the Examiners are requested to peruse each sample file in order to determine if the required documentation has been acquired and if such documents are current. The financial transactions are also analyzed, with particular attention paid to those which are slightly under the currency reporting threshold, or considered to be substantial for the transactions slated for such a customer in his/her profile.

At the end of the examination, the authorized person will be given the opportunity to respond to the inspection findings during an exit interview. The report will subsequently be sent to the board of directors for their perusal and appropriate action.

6 Obligations of financial intermediaries

All licensees are required to ensure that they employ vigilant systems which would allow them to detect and prevent money laundering and terrorist financing. These systems should ensure that they are able to verify the true identity of each customer and beneficial owner (proper documentation of this should be kept by the financial intermediary and should be made available to the Regulator at his/her request); be able to recognize suspicious customers/transactions; properly report suspicious activity; keep records for the proper period of time (five years) and ensure that staff members are adequately trained with regards to AML/CFT issues. The aforementioned Guidance Notes on the Prevention of Money Laundering and Financing of Terrorism should serve as a guide to practitioners, and provide sector specific information with regards to the AML/CFT requirements established by law and best practices.

7 Money laundering reporting authority for St. Kitts and Nevis

The Financial Intelligence Unit is the official money laundering and counter financing of terrorism reporting authority for St. Kitts and Nevis. This is provided in the *Anti-Money Laundering Regulations, SR&O No. 15 of 2001*. Regulated businesses that suspect that there is a suspicious activity occurring should report the activity to the Financial Intelligence Unit. The Unit does discreet investigations and analyzes the information received in order to determine whether or not the matter is in fact a money laundering matter. If the Unit finds that there is insufficient information collected to determine whether the matter is a money laundering matter, the data is filed and retained until possible follow up information is obtained. If the Unit finds that the matter does merit further investigation it is referred to the police for a full investigation.

It must be noted that persons or regulated businesses that transmit information or a report in good faith to the *Financial Intelligence Unit* are not liable to have any civil or criminal proceedings instituted against them based on *section 8 of the Financial Intelligence Unit Act* and *section 19(7) of the Anti-Terrorism Act*.

8   Law enforcement

The *St. Christopher and Nevis police force* is responsible for carrying out any full money laundering or terrorist financing investigations that have been referred to it by the *Financial Intelligence Unit* or in the case of terrorist financing by persons other than regulated businesses under the *Proceeds of Crime Act*. They are required to obtain any necessary search warrants to investigate financial records. The police, the customs department and the *Financial Intelligence Unit* work very closely to gather intelligence about potential money laundering or terrorist financing threats and they also coordinate with regard to any money laundering or counter financing of terrorism investigations passed on to the police authorities by the *Financial Intelligence Unit*.

9   International cooperation

9.1   Mutual Assistance in Criminal Matters Act, 1993

This Act provides the foundation for mutual assistance in criminal matters between St. Kitts and Nevis and other Commonwealth countries. Information required by St. Kitts or Nevis to facilitate a criminal investigation in St. Kitts or Nevis may be requested from another Commonwealth country and vice versa through the designated central authority of the country. Assistance may also be sought in tracing property, locating or identifying persons, obtaining evidence, serving documents, arranging the attendance of a person to give evidence, or transferring of a prisoner. However nothing in the Act authorizes the arrest or detention with a view to extradition of any person.

9.2   Financial Intelligence Unit Act and the Financial Services Commission (Exchange of Information) Regulations

As outlined above, these pieces of legislation also provide for international cooperation. The *Financial Intelligence Unit Act* provides a gateway for requests for information from other financial intelligence units and designated competent authorities in foreign countries pursuant to *section 4(2)(f) of the Financial Intelligence Unit Act*.

The *Financial Services Commission (Exchange of Information) Regulations* provides for direct regulator to regulator cooperation and exchange of information provided that certain requirements are met and matters taken into consideration before information is exchanged. These regulations do not extend to the exchange of information in tax matters.

Addresses

St. Kitts Financial Services Department
P.O. Box 898
The Pelican Mall
Bay Road
Basseterre
St. Kitts, West Indies
skanfsd@sisterisles.com

Nevis Financial Services Regulation and Supervision Department
P.O. Box 689
Charlestown
Nevis, West Indies
nevfin@sisterisles.com

The Financial Intelligence Unit
P.O. Box 1822
St. Johnstons Avenue
Basseterre
St. Kitts, West Indies
sknfiu@thecable.net

The Financial Services Commission
P.O. Box 846
Charlestown
Nevis, West Indies
fscomm@caribcable.com

Bibliography

Birks, P.: Laundering and Tracing, Clarendon Press, Oxford, 1995.

Bruton, W.F.: 'Money Laundering: Is It Now a Corporate Problem?', Dickinson Journal of International Law, Vol. 17, No. 3, 1999.

Drayton, F.R.: 'Dirty Money, Tax and Banking: Recent Developments Concerning Mutual Legal Assistance and Money Laundering "Harmful" Tax Competition and the Future of Offshore Financial Centers', Journal of Money Laundering Control, Vol. 5, No. 4, pp. 302–317, 2002.

EUROPE

Judith Schmidt is the deputy head of the Swiss Anti-Money Laundering Control Authority, which is the anti-money laundering/countering the financing of terrorism supervisory authority for the non-banking/non-insurance sector, and a member of the Swiss delegation to the Financial Action Task Force on Money Laundering FATF. She holds a law degree from the University of Bern and an LL.M. from the University of Michigan, and is admitted to the bar in Switzerland. She gained professional experience as an in-house lawyer of a renowned Swiss bank and specialized in banking law and capital market transactions when practicing law with major law firms in Switzerland and the United States. She also holds graduate degrees in international relations and security policy and has worked extensively for the UN, the OSCE and the Swiss Ministry of Foreign Affairs in the fields of human rights and democratization in post-conflict and transition countries and in Switzerland. She is also a certified mediator.

Switzerland

Judith Schmidt

Deputy Head

Anti-Money Laundering Control Authority
Christoffelgasse 5
CH-3003 Bern
Switzerland

Tel +41 31 324 34 05
Fax +41 31 323 52 61
judith.schmidt@efv.admin.ch
www.gwg.admin.ch

Anti-Money Laundering: International Law and Practice.
Edited by W.H. Muller, C.H. Kälin and J.G. Goldsworth
© 2007 John Wiley & Sons, Ltd

Contents – Switzerland

1 Introduction

Switzerland is a major international financial center, with some 420 banks and securities dealers maintaining offices there. In addition, approximately 6500 entities function as non-banking financial institutions. *Switzerland's* long tradition of private banking, the wide range and sophistication of the financial services available and its monetary stability attract a large amount of financial business. However, these very same factors also make *Switzerland* a potential target for money launderers.

Switzerland attaches great importance to maintaining its healthy financial center and is committed to ensuring that the financial center is not abused for criminal purposes, in particular for money laundering or the financing of terrorism. *Switzerland* firmly supports international efforts to combat financial crime and actively cooperates in the most important international bodies dealing with such matters.

Switzerland possesses a solid and extensive set of measures designed to combat money laundering. The Swiss AML/CFT system is a complex body consisting of regulatory preventive components under administrative law, repressive components under criminal law as well as provisions on law enforcement and international cooperation.

Switzerland has been a **member** of the *FATF* and played an active role in its activities since its creation in 1989. In 2005, the Swiss AML/CFT system was assessed by the *FATF* in the third round of mutual evaluations. The experts came to the conclusion that *Switzerland* has an extensive and effective strategy which, to a large extent, satisfies the *FATF Recommendations*. Nonetheless, the implementation of these standards will necessitate some legislative amendments, which are currently under preparation.

2 Criminal provisions and implementation of international sanctions

Switzerland has ratified and implemented the 1988 *UN Convention against Illicit Traffic in Narcotic Drugs and Psychotropic Substances (Vienna Convention)*, the 1990 *Council of Europe Convention on Laundering, Search, Seizure, and Confiscation of the Proceeds from Crime*, and the 12 *UN Conventions against terrorism*, among them the *UN International Convention for the Suppression of the Financing of Terrorism* as well as the 2000 *UN Convention against Transnational Organized Crime (Palermo Convention)*. Preparatory works are under way to enable *Switzerland* to ratify and implement as well the 2005 revised version of the *Council of Europe Convention on Laundering, Search, Seizure, and Confiscation of the Proceeds from Crime and on the Financing of Terrorism*.

The *Swiss Criminal Code (Schweizerisches Strafgesetzbuch; Code pénal suisse)* includes a number of provisions criminalizing money laundering, terrorist financing, or related behavior. These provisions are an integral part of the Swiss AML/CFT system as is the provision allowing for the confiscation of assets proceeding from a crime.[1]

---

[1] The relevant articles of the *Swiss Criminal Code* referred to in this section are: *Art. 305bis* (money laundering), *Art. 305ter* (insufficient diligence in financial transactions), *Art. 260ter* (criminal organization), *Art. 260^{quinquies}* (financing terrorism), *Art. 102* (criminal liability of legal entities) and *Art. 69-72* (confiscation).

2.1   Money laundering

The offence of money laundering was included in the *Swiss Criminal Code* in 1990. It criminalizes an act that is aimed at frustrating the identification of the origin, the tracing or confiscation of assets, which the perpetrator knows or must assume originate from a **serious crime**.

More than 80 crimes covered by Swiss criminal law fall into the category of serious crime,[2] including participation in a criminal organization, the financing of terrorism, drug trafficking, arms trafficking, corruption, fraud, extortion and hostage taking. There is no explicit provision on terrorism as such, but in practice, terrorist acts are tackled by the application of a combination of serious crimes provisions, covering the various elements of such acts. Fiscal offences do not constitute serious crimes and are thus not predicate offences to money laundering. Due to the generally applicable **principle of dual criminality**, *Switzerland* lacks the legal basis to grant mutual legal assistance to foreign states where money laundering is based on such offences. However, mutual legal assistance is possible for the underlying tax fraud.

A **conviction for the predicate offence is not required** for the applicability of the provision on money laundering. The perpetrator is **also punishable if** the **predicate offence** has been **committed abroad** and the principle of **dual criminality** is fulfilled. The *Federal Supreme Court (Bundesgericht; Tribunal fédéral)* has held that the **conviction of the perpetrator for the predicate offence does not exclude his additional conviction for money laundering.**

The maximum penalty for money laundering is a custodial sentence of up to three years, in serious cases of up to five years combined with a monetary penalty of up to 500 daily penalty units.

2.2   Insufficient diligence in financial transactions

A second provision of the *Swiss Criminal Code* supplements the money laundering provision and states that anyone who, on a professional basis, accepts or holds in custody assets belonging to third parties or assists in investing or transferring these (i.e. a financial intermediary), and fails to ascertain the identity of the beneficial owner of the assets with the care required in the circumstances, is punishable by a custodial sentence of up to one year, or to a monetary penalty. The **assets need not be the proceeds of a crime** for this provision to be applicable. As is true for money laundering, the act of insufficient diligence in financial transactions has to be committed **intentionally**.

2.3   Criminal organization

As organized crime is closely linked to money laundering, it is worth mentioning that the *Swiss Criminal Code* also criminalizes **participation in,** or **support of, a criminal organization**. Financial contributions to such organizations, even if consisting of clean money, are considered 'support' in the sense of this provision. Thus, even before the introduction of the separate provision criminalizing the financing of terrorism, such behavior was already largely covered by the provision on criminal organizations. **No link** is **required between** the **support and a criminal act** by the organization. **Terrorist organizations** are **considered to be criminal organizations** and are covered by this article. If a terrorist act has not been completed, the perpetrator or the participant can be prosecuted for attempt, instigation or complicity, as appropriate. Preparatory

---

[2] A serious crime (felony) is defined as a criminal act punishable with a custodial sentence of more than three years.

acts are covered by a separate provision. The maximum penalty that may be imposed is a custodial sentence of up to five years.

2.4 Terrorist financing

The provision specifically covering the offence of terrorist financing criminalizes the **collection or provision of funds with a view to financing a violent crime intended to intimidate the public or to coerce a state or international organization into carrying out, or failing to carry out an act**. The penalty is a custodial sentence for up to five years or a monetary penalty. **No causal relationship** is **necessary** between the collection or provision of funds and a terrorist act.

2.5 The criminal liability of legal entities

A legal entity may be held liable under Swiss criminal law if in the course of business of that entity an offence has occurred and the individual perpetrator of the offence cannot be identified due to **insufficient organizational measures** on the part of the legal entity. If the offence concerns **money laundering, criminal organizations, the financing of terrorism, active corruption in respect of a foreign official or corruption in the sense of the** *Federal Act on Unfair Competition (Bundesgesetz gegen den unlauteren Wettbewerb; Loi fédérale contre la concurrence déloyale)*, the legal entity incurs **primary criminal liability** in parallel to that of the actual perpetrator and independent of the latter's penal liability, **provided the entity has not taken all the appropriate and necessary precautions** to avoid such an offence. The penalty is a fine of up to Sfr. 5 million.

2.6 Confiscation of assets

Assets derived from crime may be confiscated. If the assets subject to confiscation are no longer available, compensatory assets of an equal amount will be confiscated. Assets can also be confiscated from a third party unless they have been acquired *bona fide* by the third party and against an adequate consideration or in case the confiscation would excessively burden the *bona fide* third party. A legal entity may also be subject to confiscation. Confiscation comes **in addition to the other penalties, but can also be ordered if no indictment can be brought**. As a precautionary and provisional measure, the confiscation of assets may be preceded by a seizure or other conservatory measures.

2.7 Prospects

The implementation of the new FATF standards will necessitate some amendments to the Swiss criminal law in order to make counterfeiting of goods, product piracy, and serious smuggling offences as well as insider trading and share manipulation predicate offences to money laundering. These amendments are currently under preparation. Migrant smuggling is criminalized in the *Federal Act on Foreign Nationals (Bundesgesetz über die Ausländerinnen und Ausländer; Loi fédérale sur les étrangers)* which has been accepted in a public vote on 24 September 2006 and will probably enter into force on 1 January 2008.

2.8 Implementation of specific international sanctions

2.8.1 United Nations Sanctions

Switzerland implements the **economic sanctions** of the *United Nations Security Council* against individuals and entities belonging or related to *Usama Bin Laden*, the *Al-Qaida Group* or the

Taliban[3] on the basis of the *Ordinance on measures against persons and organizations with ties to Usama Bin Laden, the 'Al-Qaida' group or the Taliban (Taliban Ordinance)*. The **assets and economic resources** belonging to, or controlled by, any of the listed natural or legal persons, groups or organizations, are **frozen** and it is prohibited to transfer assets to these persons, groups and organizations or to otherwise provide them with funds and/or economic resources, directly or indirectly. The assets remain frozen until such time as the ordinance is modified accordingly.

According to the practices of the AML/CFT supervisory authorities, business relationships with, and transactions for or on behalf of, such persons or entities are also subject to the suspicious transaction reporting requirements of the *Anti-Money Laundering Act (Geldwäschereigesetz; Loi sur le blanchiment d'argent)*.

2.8.2   Support to sanctions of other countries

On the basis of *UN Security Council Resolution 1373*, dated 28 September 2001, which aims at countering terrorism and boosting international cooperation on this matter, the *USA* transmits to other countries **nationally compiled lists** of persons and entities deemed to be **terrorists**, with the request that the receiving country also consider the listed persons and entities as terrorists and take measures against them.[4]

In *Switzerland* these lists are generally transmitted to the financial intermediaries through their respective supervisory authorities with the order that **enhanced due diligence** be applied. Consequently, the financial intermediary checks its business relationships against this list, undertakes special clarification procedures in case one of the listed persons or entities figures among its business relations and files a **suspicious transaction report** with the *financial intelligence unit, the Money Laundering Reporting Office Switzerland (MROS; Meldestelle für Geldwäscherei; Bureau de communication en matière de blanchiment d'argent)* in the event that the overall assessment gives rise to a **founded suspicion** in the sense of the *Anti-Money Laundering Act*. In this case, the **assets** related to the report have to be **frozen**.

2.8.3   FATF measures

At the *FATF's* request, *Switzerland* has also implemented *measures* in connection with the *FATF* initiative on *non-cooperative countries and territories (NCCT)*. This meant that business relationships and transactions with natural and legal persons from the concerned country were subject to special clarifications and, in the case of *additional counter-measures*, to an extended control and verification of the identity of the contracting party and of the beneficial owner.

3   The Anti-Money Laundering Act

3.1   Overview

The 1997 *Federal Act on the Prevention of Money Laundering in the Financial Sector (Anti-Money Laundering Act, AMLA; Bundesgesetz zur Bekämpfung der Geldwäscherei im Finanzsektor*

---

[3] S/RES/1267 (1999) amended by 1333 (2000), 1363 (2001), 1390 (2002), 1455 (2003), 1526 (2004) and 1617 (2005).
[4] As these lists are based on a decree issued by President Bush (Executive Order 13224 of 23 September 2001), they are commonly called 'Bush lists'.

(Geldwäschereigesetz, GwG); Loi fédérale concernant la lutte contre le blanchiment d'argent dans le secteur financier (Loi sur le blanchiment d'argent, LBA)) is a **supervisory law regulating the behavior of financial intermediaries** in order to prevent money laundering.

While the criminal provisions of the *Swiss Criminal C*ode provide the tools to prosecute related criminal behavior, the purpose of the *Anti-Money Laundering Act*, which is part of the body of administrative law, is to prevent proceeds of crimes from entering the legal financial system. To achieve this goal, the *Anti-Money Laundering Act* imposes certain obligations – mainly **due diligence obligations** – on persons offering financial services, i.e. on financial intermediaries. The fulfillment of this set of operative provisions is subject to supervision, and deficient or **non-fulfillment** is **penalized**.

Customer identification provisions, developed through self-regulation and guidelines set out by the *Swiss Federal Banking Commission (SFBC; Eidgenössische Bankenkommission; Commission fédérale des banques)* to thwart money laundering had been applicable to the banking sector long before the enactment of the *Anti-Money Laundering Act*, but these rules were not anchored explicitly in a law. The *Anti-Money Laundering Act* provided this legal basis and extended the application of such obligations from the banking sector to the whole of the financial sector, and in particular to the **non-banking sector**, thereby subjecting the latter to **regulation for the first time.** This regulation requires that financial intermediaries in the non-banking sector be **authorized** by the *Anti-Money Laundering Control Authority (AMLCA; Kontrollstelle für die Bekämpfung der Geldwäscherei; Autorité de contrôle en matière de lutte contre le blanchiment d'argent)* **or that they be affiliated to a S***elf-Regulating Organization (SRO)*, recognized and supervised by the *AMLCA.*

The *Anti-Money Laundering Act* **sets out the fundamental principles** of the financial interme-diaries' obligations and foresees that the **supervisory authorities** implementing the Act **specify in detail the rules** for the implementation of these obligations. This allows the authorities to adapt the detailed rules to their sector.

The *Anti-Money Laundering Act* also **introduced** the financial intermediary's **obligation to report suspicious business relationships or transactions**. Prior to the *Anti-Money Laundering Act* coming into force, Swiss legislation only provided for a right to report, which had been anchored in the criminal law in 1994, as a legal justification for breaching professional secrecy.

On the institutional side, the *Anti-Money Laundering Act* created the *AMLCA* as the supervisory authority for the non-banking sector and vested it with the necessary powers for the execution of its tasks. The Act also provided for the alternative of controlled self-regulation for financial intermediaries in the non-banking sector. The supervisory authorities for the other financial intermediaries were created by other acts and at other points in time. The *Anti-Money Laundering Act* also established the *MROS*, the Swiss *financial intelligence unit.*

The *Anti-Money Laundering Act* provides for **fines** under administrative criminal law in the event of its provisions not being upheld. These fines concern in particular the **exercising of activities subject to the *Anti-Money Laundering Act* without authorization or affiliation to a *SRO* and** the **violation of the obligation to report**. A clear distinction should be made between this and the crime of money laundering and the offence of insufficient diligence in financial transactions, provided for in the *Swiss Criminal Code.*

3.2   Prospects

The *Anti-Money Laundering Act* will have to be adapted to recent developments. The bill under preparation will take particular account of the **extension** of the *FATF Recommendations* **to** cover also the combating of **financing and terrorism**; the **extension of the obligation to report** to include specific situations in which negotiations are discontinued before a business relationship is established. It will also include a **better legal protection** against reprisals **for the reporting financial intermediary** and some additional points. A number of individual measures intended to be part of the revision package are still in the process of consultation. They include, among other points, the **assistance** on the part of the **customs authorities** in the AML/CFT prevention scheme as far as **cross-border transportation of currency** is concerned, the formal introduction of the obligations to verify identification of representatives or agents of legal entities and to **establish the purpose and nature of the business relationship** desired by the customer.

4   The scope of application of the Anti-Money Laundering Act

The *Anti-Money Laundering Act* applies to financial intermediaries. It stipulates a few exemptions for entities such as the central bank, tax-exempted pension funds and financial intermediaries providing services exclusively to financial intermediaries subject to prudential supervision or to foreign financial intermediaries who are subject to a supervision equivalent to theirs. Whether or not the foreign supervision may be considered as being equivalent lies in the judgment of the financial intermediary. The supervisory authorities have not established a list of jurisdictions the supervisory regimes of which they consider to be equivalent.

4.1   Banks, insurance companies and casinos

Art. 2 (2) AMLA defines the scope of application of the Act to a particular group of financial intermediaries, regarded as 'typical' professionals of the financial sector, and to casinos. One common element is that they are all subject to **complete (prudential) supervision** and each type of these financial intermediaries is defined and regulated by a separate act to which the *Anti-Money Laundering Act* refers. In a very generalized and untechnical manner, the term 'banking sector' is sometimes used to refer to all of them, in particular to distinguish the whole group from the non-banking sector, which is subject only to limited supervision.

These financial intermediaries are:

- Banks as defined in the *Banking Act (Bankengesetz; Loi sur les banques)*.

- Fund managers as defined in the *Federal Act on Collective Investments (Bundesgesetz über die kollektiven kapitalanlagen, Loi fédérale sur les placements collectifs de capitaux)* insofar as they keep unit accounts and themselves offer or distribute shares in a collective capital investment scheme.

- Investment companies with a variable capital, limited partnerships for collective investments, investment companies with a fixed capital as well as asset managers within the meaning of the Collective Investments Act, if they themselves offer or distribute shares in a collective capital investment scheme.

- Life insurance companies as defined in the *Insurance Supervision Act* and insurance institutions that offer or distribute shares in a collective investment scheme.

- Securities dealers as defined in the *Stock Exchange Act (Börsengesetz; Loi sur les bourses)*.

- Casinos as defined in the *Gaming Act (Spielbankengesetz; Loi sur les maisons de jeu)*.

4.2   Non-banking sector

4.2.1   The legal provision on the scope of application in the non-banking sector

The scope of application of the *Anti-Money Laundering Act* in the non-banking sector is set out in *Art. 2 (3) AMLA*. This article uses **two different approaches** to define the scope of application, namely a **general clause and** a **list**. According to the catch-all provision, financial intermediaries include **persons who, on a professional basis, accept or hold in custody assets belonging to third parties or assist in investing or transferring these.** The ensuing non-exhaustive list of examples enumerates activities which lawmakers particularly wanted to see covered. Supervision is limited to compliance with the obligations of the *Anti-Money Laundering Act*.

In the non-banking sector, the applicability of the *Anti-Money Laundering Act* does **not** directly relate to specific **professions or sectors, but** instead to certain **activities** susceptible to misuse for money laundering purposes.

4.2.2   The interpretation of the legal provision on the scope of application

At the end of 2004, the AMLCA, the supervisory authority of the non-banking sector, published a **consolidated text** on its interpretation of, and practice concerning, the **personal and geographic applicability of the *Anti-Money Laundering Act* in the non-banking sector** (www.gwg.admin.ch/f/dokumentationen/publikationen/gwg_auslegung/pdf/34481.pdf)[5].

In a nutshell, in the non-banking sector, the *Anti-Money Laundering Act* is generally applicable to asset managers[6] and credit institutions, particularly those offering financial leasing, commodities brokers (in the case of stock exchange trading for third parties), traders in banknotes, coins and precious metals, bureaux de change, money and value remitters, securities dealers not subject to the *Stock Exchange Act*, formal and actual executive organs of non-operative companies (i.e. domiciliary companies and similar vehicles such as trusts) established under the laws of *Switzerland* or of a foreign country, as well as lawyers engaging in financial intermediation unrelated to the traditional activities of their profession.

The applicability of the *Anti-Money Laundering Act* is limited to the financial sector. However, lawmakers as well as the *AMLCA* have construed this notion extensively, so that in practice it covers certain activities, which strictly speaking are not part of the financial sector. Thus, *Switzerland* has defined as financial intermediation, and consequently made subject to the full regime of the *Anti-Money Laundering Act*, certain activities that the *FATF* in its revised **Forty Recommendations** considers to be part of the designated non-financial businesses and

---

[5] The full text of the *AMLCA's* website is available in German, French and Italian. The English website is a somewhat reduced version. References in this chapter to the *AMLCA's* website are to the English version, if available, and to the French version otherwise.

[6] To date, independent asset managers are not subject to a prudential supervision in Switzerland.

professions, with the consequence that *Switzerland* applies to these activities, the (higher) financial sector standards.

4.2.3 Financial intermediation on a professional basis

The *AMLCA* has set out the **criteria for distinguishing between non-professional and professional activities** in its implementing *Ordinance on Financial Intermediation in the Non-Banking Sector as a Commercial Undertaking (Verordnung der Kontrollstelle für die Bekämpfung der Geldwäscherei über die berufsmässige Ausübung der Finanzintermediation im Nichtbankensektor; Ordonnance de l'Autorité de contrôle en matière de lutte contre le blanchiment d'argent concernant l'activité d'intermédiaire financier dans le secteur non banciare exercée à titre professionel)*, which defines **alternatively applicable** and clearly verifiable criteria. If one of the following thresholds is crossed, the activity is deemed to be conducted on a professional basis (i.e. as a commercial undertaking), whereby only the gross revenue criterion applies to financial intermediation among close relatives:

- gross revenue of over Sfr. 20 000 in a calendar year, or

- permanent business relations with more than 10 contracting parties in a calendar year, or

- a total transaction sum amounting to more than Sfr. 2 million in a calendar year, or

- asset management for third parties amounting to more than Sfr. 5 million at any given moment.

As far as **credit activities** are concerned, **two thresholds** have to be crossed **cumulatively**: the **gross revenue** has to be more than **Sfr. 250 000** in a calendar year and the total of **outstanding credits** has to be more than **Sfr. 5 million** at any given time. **Specific types** of credit activities are **exempted** from the scope of the *Anti-Money Laundering Act*, namely credits between employer and employee, company and controlling shareholders and relatives up to a certain degree.

Additionally, money exchange activities carried out as an accessory business qualifies as activity on a professional basis if the financial intermediary carries out or is prepared to carry out one or several interlinked exchange operations amounting to more than Sfr. 5000.

The **ordinance** also **defines rules for changing from a non-professional to a professional activity**.

5 Obligations of the financial intermediaries

Art. 3 to 10 AMLA define the **basic obligations** natural persons or legal entities have under the *Anti-Money Laundering Act*. These obligations contain the **due diligence obligations** and the **obligations to report suspicions** if they are based on reasonable grounds and **freeze the assets** related to the suspicious transaction report.

5.1 Obligations of due diligence

5.1.1 Verification of identity of the contracting party

Prior to commencing business relationships, the financial intermediary must identify the contracting party on the basis of an evidential document. In the case of one-off transactions with a contracting party that has not yet been identified, the duty of identification exists only if one or more transactions that appear to be inter-connected exceed a considerable amount defined by the supervisory authority concerned. In general this amount is Sfr. 25 000.

5.1.2   Identification of the beneficial owner

The financial intermediary must identify the beneficial owner in every case and obtain from the contracting party a written declaration as to the latter's identity whenever:

- the contracting party is not identical to the beneficial owner or when doubt exists in this regard,

- the contracting party is a domiciliary company,

- a one-off transaction of considerable amount is undertaken.

In the case of collective accounts or collective custody accounts, the financial intermediary must require that the contracting party produces a complete list of the economic beneficiaries and that every change to the list is reported without delay.

5.1.3   Renewed verification and identification

Should doubts arise during the course of the business relationship as to the identity of the contracting party or beneficial owner, the financial intermediary must renew the verification of the identity of the contracting party or of the identity of the beneficial owner.

5.1.4   Special obligation to clarify the economic background and purpose

The financial intermediary has a special obligation to clarify the economic background and the purpose of a transaction or a business relationship if:

- The transaction or business relationship appears unusual, unless its legality is apparent.

- Indications exist that assets originate from a crime or that a criminal organization exercises a power of disposition there over.

5.1.5   Obligation to draw up and retain documents

The financial intermediary must draw up documents concerning the transactions undertaken and concerning the clarifications in such a manner that the supervisory authorities, the *SROs* and the prosecuting authorities can gather the necessary information which allows a reliable judgment to be made regarding the transactions and the business relationship as well as the compliance with the obligations relating to the *Anti-Money Laundering Act*. The financial intermediary must retain the documents for at least 10 years after the cessation of the business relationship or after execution of the transaction.

5.1.6   Organizational measures

Financial intermediaries must take the internal organizational measures necessary to prevent money laundering. These measures must be commensurate with the size of the financial intermediary and nature of its activities. They must ensure in particular that their personnel are adequately instructed.

5.2   Obligations to report suspicions and freeze assets

The obligation to immediately make a report to the *MROS* is incumbent upon any financial intermediary who knows or has a well-founded suspicion, i.e. reasonable grounds to suspect that the assets implicated in a transaction or a business relationship originate from money laundering, are the proceeds of a serious crime in accordance with the *Swiss Criminal Code* or that a criminal organization has a power of disposition over them *(Art. 9 AMLA)*.

Concurrently with the filing of the report, the financial intermediary must **freeze the assets under its control that are in connection with the report** and this until it receives a freezing order from the competent judicial authority. If no such order is received, the freezing of the assets ends after a period of five working days. During this period the 'no tipping off' rule applies, i.e. the financial intermediary may inform neither those affected nor third parties of the report.

The financial intermediary who makes a report and freezes assets may not be prosecuted for violation of official, professional or commercial secrecy nor made liable for breach of contract if it has acted with due care dictated by the circumstances.

5.3   The implementing regulations

5.3.1   The implementing regulations of the supervisory authorities and of the SROs

The *Anti-Money Laundering Act* provides that the supervisory authorities specify in detail the rules for the implementation of the obligations set out in the Act for the financial intermediaries under their supervision. **Each of the supervisory authorities** (i.e. the *SFBC*, the *FOPI (Federal Office of Private Insurance; Bundesamt für Privatversicherungen; Office fédéral des assurances privées)*, the *SFGB (Swiss Federal Gaming Board; Eidgenössische Spielbankenkommission; Commission fédérale des maisons de jeu)* and the *AMLCA*) has **issued an ordinance with implementing regulations**. The *SROs* of the non-banking sector **also issue implementing rules** for their members, which are set out **in their respective regulations**.

As far as verifying the identity of the contracting party and establishing the identity of the beneficial owner is concerned, the *SFBC* has declared the pre-existing and periodically revised *Agreement on the Swiss banks' code of conduct with regard to the exercise of due diligence* (presently *CDB 03*, as it was last revised in 2003; *Vereinbarung über die Standesregeln zur Sorgfaltspflicht der Banken (VSB 03); Convention relative à l'obligation de diligence des banques (CDB 03))* made between the Swiss Bankers Association and the banks and approved by the *SFBC*, as binding minimum standards for the financial intermediaries under its supervision. Consequently, the **implementing regulations** to the *Anti-Money Laundering Act*, applicable to **the financial intermediaries supervised by the *SFBC*** are contained in the ***SFBC Anti-Money Laundering Ordinance*** *(EBK Geldwäschereiverordnung; Ordonnance de la CFB sur le blanchiment d'argent)* and the ***CDB 03***.

5.3.2   Second generation implementing regulations

The implementing regulations for financial intermediaries supervised by the *SFBC*, the *FOPI*, the *AMLCA* and all *SROs* are in their second generation and reflect some of the reforms of the revised *FATF* standards. Compared with the first generation regulations, they have been harmonized as far as is practicable.

The *SFBC Anti-Money Laundering Ordinance,* the *AMLCA Anti-Money Laundering Ordinance (Geldwäschereiverordnung Kst; Ordonnance de l'AdC sur le blanchiment d'argent),* the *CDB 03* as well as all of the *SRO* regulations codify a **risk-based approach to client identification and transaction monitoring**, and put in place a *Know Your Customer (KYC)* risk management program. The regulations require different levels of due diligence depending on the risk involved. While all clients still need to be identified as before, in the case of higher-risk business relationships, the financial intermediary must carry out additional investigations, for instance into the origins of the assets. This means that they must first define risk categories for their particular business activity and use them to identify and flag all existing and new higher-risk business relationships. For such higher-risk business relationships, the financial intermediary must verify more than merely the client's identity and go beyond establishing a client profile. Where necessary, additional investigations must be carried out, checked for plausibility and documented. As far as banks are concerned, the program is global and includes their branches and subsidiaries abroad. The decision to commence a relationship with politically exposed persons must be taken with senior executive body involvement. All cross-border wire transfers must now contain details about the funds remitters.

Among other provisions, the *SFBC* ordinance makes computer-based transaction monitoring systems mandatory for all but the smallest financial intermediaries. It also addresses Swiss supervision of subsidiaries belonging to a consolidated group of financial intermediaries and all provisions apply to correspondent banking relationships as well.

The *AMLCA's* ordinance provides for different regimes to apply to the internal organization of the financial intermediary depending on the latter's size. For financial intermediaries employing fewer than five people with AML/CFT responsibilities, the requirements regarding the internal organization are greatly simplified. A competence center for combating money laundering will have to be established by all financial intermediaries, but may be outsourced to competent external persons.

5.3.3   Prospects

The anti-money laundering ordinance of the *SFGB* is currently in the process of being revised and will incorporate as far as is practicable, the reforms already included in the ordinances of the other supervisory authorities. The revised ordinance is expected to enter into force in 2007.

6   AML/CFT supervision

6.1   The system's components and their coordination

Financial intermediaries are supervised in the performance of their obligations under the *Anti-Money Laundering Act* by their respective supervisory authority. The *SFBC* is entrusted with the autonomous supervision of banks, securities dealers, stock exchanges, collective capital investments and mortgage bond issuers. The *FOPI* monitors the business activities of private insurance institutions subject to state supervision, that is to say life, accident and property insurers and reinsurers. The *SFGB* supervises the casinos. In the non-banking sector, the *AMLCA* supervises the *SROs* and the financial intermediaries directly subordinated to it, and the *SROs* supervise their affiliated members.

Also part of the preventive side of the AML/CFT system is the *MROS, Switzerland's financial intelligence unit* whose primary role is to act as a hub between financial intermediaries and the criminal prosecution authorities.

An important aspect in the implementation of the system at the supervisory level is good and extensive coordination and cooperation between the different bodies. The *Anti-Money Laundering Act* makes provisions in this respect and generally speaking ensures constructive dialogue between the authorities on the one hand, the *AMLCA* and the *SROs* on the other hand, as well as between the financial intermediaries and the supervisory authorities.

In addition to the bilateral contacts, the supervisory authorities, the *MROS* and the law enforcement bodies have established a coordinating committee. Further coordination bodies exist between the *AMLCA* and the *SROs* and among the *SROs*.

6.2 Types of financial intermediary supervision

6.2.1 Complete supervision

The *SFBC*, the *FOPI* and the *SFGB* administer the specific supervisory acts governing their sectors and instituting complete supervision, and **regulate authorization and all activities** by financial intermediaries in these sectors. In the phrasing of the *Anti-Money Laundering Act*, the *SFBC*, the *FOPI* and the *SFGB* are referred to as *supervisory authorities established by special acts*.

The **obligations** of the financial intermediaries under the *Anti-Money Laundering Act* and the implementing ordinances issued by the *supervisory authorities established by special acts* **come in addition to the regulations of the special acts** governing the banking and insurance sectors and the casinos. *Anti-Money Laundering Act* authorization and supervision of these sectors' financial intermediaries is not conducted separately, but as part of the general authorization and complete supervision procedures that these financial intermediaries have to undergo. To redress violations of the *Anti-Money Laundering Act*, the *supervisory authorities established by special acts* may take such measures as are generally at their disposal under the special acts or those specified in the *Anti-Money Laundering Act*.

6.2.2 Supervision limited to the Anti-Money Laundering Act

In contrast, the *AMLCA* is established and governed by the *Anti-Money Laundering Act* itself. **Authorization and supervision** of financial intermediaries in the non-banking sector are **regulated exclusively by the *Anti-Money Laundering Act* and the implementing regulations**. The authorization concerns only their financial intermediation activities and the **supervision is limited** to compliance with the obligations of the *Anti-Money Laundering Act* and the implementing regulations.

6.3 Supervision in the non-banking sector

Lawmakers provided for a **choice of supervision regimes in the non-banking sector**, consisting of **direct state supervision** or **controlled self-regulation**. Financial intermediaries not supervised by one of the three *supervisory authorities established by special acts* may choose one of the following regimes:

- they may seek affiliation to one of the *SROs* recognized and supervised by the *AMLCA;* the *SRO* will henceforth be in charge of the intermediary's supervision as the sole authority, or

- place themselves under the authorization and direct supervision of the *AMLCA*.

There is an exception in the case of lawyers and notaries, who have to join a *SRO* and do not have the option of being directly subordinated to the *AMLCA* on the grounds of professional secrecy.

6.3.1   Affiliation to a SRO

Affiliation to a *SRO* recognized by the *AMLCA*, which constitutes membership of a body under private law, gives **the financial intermediary the right to engage in financial intermediation**. The regulations to which the affiliated financial intermediary has to adhere are the obligations of the *Anti-Money Laundering Act* and the implementing regulations set out by the *SRO*. The *SROs* supervise their members' fulfillment of the AML/CFT obligations. Provision is made for *AMLA*-audits to be carried out with the affiliated member on site on a regular basis.

6.3.2   Direct subordination to the AMLCA

The *AMLCA* fulfils the same tasks with regard to the financial intermediaries directly subordinated to it as the *SROs* do with regard to their affiliated members.

The *AMLCA* grants authorization as soon as the financial intermediary fulfils all the requirements of the *Anti-Money Laundering Act* and the related implementation provisions. The on-going compliance with the authorization conditions is assessed through a periodic *AMLA*-audit conducted by one of the audit agencies accredited by the *AMLCA* and chosen by the financial intermediary or conducted by the *AMLCA* itself. The *AMLCA* has an influence on the auditing process by providing the appropriate documentation and detailed requirements with regard to the *AMLA* audit report.

6.3.3   Similarities and differences between affiliation and direct subordination

In the affiliation proceedings, most *SROs* require practically the same documents and information that are set out in the published checklist (www.gwg.admin.ch/f/dokumentationen/publikationen/wegleitungen/pdf/27137.pdf) and that are required by the *AMLCA* in processing an application for direct subordination. The examination of the application is made based on the same information and comparable procedures.

Compared to the *AMLCA's* authorization procedure, the biggest differences when joining a *SRO* lie in the details that financial intermediaries have to provide on the internal organization for the implementation of the AML/CFT measures.

The *AMLCA* issued minimum standards for an audit concept that provides for **individual, risk-oriented control intervals** from **between one to a maximum of three years**, according to the risk classification of the financial intermediary concerned. The financial intermediaries directly subordinated to the *AMLCA* may apply for risk-oriented control intervals to apply to them. Some *SROs* have adopted it for all their members.

In contrast to the *AMLCA*, a *SRO* **may impose a fine** on a financial intermediary in the event of a breach of duty. If a *SRO* discovers that a financial intermediary is not adhering to its AML/CFT obligations, as a rule the financial intermediary is **expelled**. The financial intermediary then comes under the direct supervision of the *AMLCA*, which can then take action against it.

When the *AMLCA* discovers that an authorized financial intermediary no longer respects the conditions of authorization or violates its AML/CFT obligations, the ***AMLCA* may take the necessary measures to restore legality**, whereby it must observe the principle of proportionality. In extreme cases, this can lead to the **liquidation** of the financial intermediary.

6.4   The SROs

Lawmakers conferred a significant role on the *SROs* in the implementation of the *Anti-Money Laundering Act*. The Act took the principle of **self-regulation** strongly into account by allowing the intermediaries to set up their own *SROs*. However, the **supervisory power of the *SROs* is restricted** to setting out implementing rules to the obligations specified in the *Anti-Money Laundering Act* and to the affiliation and supervision of the financial intermediaries. As far as other questions are concerned, e.g. the applicability of the Act to the non-banking sector, only the *AMLCA* is competent to deal with these.

SROs are generally associations set up for the purpose of carrying out *AMLA* supervision of their members. When it affiliates itself to a *SRO*, a financial intermediary places itself under ***SRO* jurisdiction** and commits itself to observing the statutes and internal regulations.

There are currently **11 *SROs*** recognized by the *AMLCA* (www.gwg.admin.ch/e/institut/PDF/sroliste.pdf). These *SROs* basically cover the Italian, German and French-speaking regions, although there is no *SRO* in the Italian-speaking part of *Switzerland* serving all financial intermediaries. The **vast majority** of financial intermediaries in the non-banking sector have become **affiliated to a *SRO***. Of the some 6500 financial intermediaries, only about 400 are directly supervised by the *AMLCA*.[7]

6.5   The Anti-Money Laundering Control Authority (AMLCA)

In its function as the supervisory authority for the non-banking sector, the *AMLCA* authorizes and supervises the financial intermediaries directly subordinated to it and recognizes and supervises *SROs* and has indirect control over the financial intermediaries affiliated to these *SROs*. It approves the regulations set out by the *SROs* as well as any modifications made thereto, and ensures that the *SROs* enforce them. Supervision is based on an annual report drawn up by the *SROs* and on an annual audit of the *SROs* conducted by the *AMLCA*.

In the event that a *SRO* no longer fulfils the conditions for recognition, or violates its legal obligations, the ***AMLCA* may withdraw the *SRO's* recognition**. In such a case, the financial intermediaries affiliated to the *SRO* in question come under the direct supervision of the *AMLCA*, unless they join another *SRO* within a period of two months.

In principle, any *SRO* is entitled to recognition by the *AMLCA* as long as it fulfils the conditions laid down by the *Anti-Money Laundering Act* and has a sufficient number of qualified staff to carry out its tasks without incurring a conflict of interests. The *SRO* must guarantee that the financial intermediaries affiliated to it will observe their legal obligations at all times.

---

[7] In addition, about 160 financial intermediaries of the non-banking sector located in Switzerland and belonging to a banking group and being included in the group's consolidated financial statements have opted to be supervised for purposes of the *Anti-Money Laundering Act* by the *SFBC*.

The *AMLCA* also has to fulfill other tasks, such as **market supervision**. In this respect, the *AMLCA* identifies **financial intermediaries engaging in their activities illegally**. When an illegally operating financial intermediary is discovered, the *AMLCA* takes the necessary measures to **restore legality**. However, market supervision is limited to determining whether or not an activity falls under the scope of application of the *Anti-Money Laundering Act*, and consequently whether or not such activity should be authorized. It does not focus on the way in which the financial intermediaries provide their services or honor their obligations in relation to their clients.

In response to individual requests, the *AMLCA* **provides information on whether a particular financial intermediary is authorized by it or affiliated to a *SRO*** and, if so, to which one. However, individual non-disclosure applications have to be reserved under the *Data Protection Act (Bundesgetz über den Datenschutz; Loi fédérale sur la protection des données)*.

6.6 Prospects

A **bill for** the establishment of **an integrated financial market supervisory authority 'FINMA'**, that should bring the *SFBC*, the *FOPI* and the *AMLCA* under one roof is presently before the Parliament. The effects of such a project will be primarily on the institutional side. The provisional target date for operation is 1 January 2009.

7   Money Laundering Reporting Office Switzerland (MROS)

The *MROS* is *Switzerland's financial intelligence unit*. It has its legal basis in the *Anti-Money Laundering Act*, and was established in 1998 as part of the Services Division of the *Federal Office of Police (fedpol; Bundesamt für Polizei; Office fédéral de la police)*. It has neither the status of a prosecuting authority, nor that of the police but is designated as an **administrative authority.**

It is the task of the *MROS* to **analyze the suspicious transaction reports** submitted by the financial intermediaries. In order to determine the subsequent action to be taken, it carries out research, including consulting its own database and various other databases normally at the disposal of the police. The processing of a report is conducted within the extremely limited time frame of five working days set down in the *Anti-Money Laundering Act*. If a **suspicion is confirmed**, it **forwards the reports to** the appropriate **prosecuting authority**. Depending upon the jurisdiction, this is either the *Office of the Attorney-General* of *Switzerland (Bundesanwaltschaft; Ministère public de la Confédération)* or a cantonal prosecuting authority. About 30% of cases fall under federal jurisdiction.

Should a report contain **references to connections abroad**, for instance the nationality of the persons or the domicile of the companies implicated, not to mention events related to acts of money laundering or terrorist financing that have taken place abroad, the *MROS's* status as a member of the *Egmont Group* enables it to **request information from its foreign colleagues**.

To enhance procedural efficiency and rapidity, a **form for the filing of suspicions** has been placed at the disposal of financial intermediaries **on the *MROS* website** (www.fedpol.ch/e/themen/geld/formular-e.pdf). It is an absolute requirement that this questionnaire be completed.

8 Law enforcement

In *Switzerland*, law enforcement is generally organized on a cantonal level. In order to enhance law enforcement in complex cases, jurisdiction was transferred to the federal authorities. The law now confers the *Federal Criminal Police* (*Bundeskriminalpolizei; Police judiciaire fédérale*) and the *Office of the Attorney-General* with the authority to take over cases that have an international dimension, involve several cantons, or which deal with money laundering and terrorist financing, organized crime, corruption, and white collar crime. In function with this, the *Federal Office of Police* set up a Division within the *Federal Criminal Police* to tackle terrorist financing, economic crime and money laundering. Additionally, the *Service for Analysis and Prevention* (*Dienst für Analyse und Prävention; Service d'Analyse et de Prévention*) was reinforced with specialists working on money laundering and other crimes investigated by the *Office of the Attorney-General* and *Switzerland* has established a *Federal Criminal Court* (*Bundesstrafgericht; Tribunal pénal fédéral*).

9 International cooperation

Switzerland provides support to foreign authorities by means of legal or administrative assistance according to the applicable law. It is important to point out that Swiss banking secrecy rules are not applicable when mutual legal assistance is to be provided in connection with the fight against serious crime.

Abbreviations

AMLA	Anti-Money Laundering Act
AMLCA	Anti-Money Laundering Control Authority
AML/CFT	Anti-Money Laundering/Countering the Financing of Terrorism
CC	Classified Compilation of the Federal Law
CDB 03	Agreement on the Swiss banks' code of conduct with regard to the exercise of due diligence
FATF	Financial Action Task Force on Money Laundering
FIU	Financial Intelligence Unit
FOPI	Federal Office of Private Insurance
MROS	Money Laundering Reporting Office Switzerland
NCCT	Non-Cooperative Countries and Territories
SBA	Swiss Bankers Association
SFBC	Swiss Federal Banking Commission
SFGB	Swiss Federal Gaming Board
SRO	Self-Regulating Organization
UN	United Nations

Weblinks

AMLCA	www.gwg.admin.ch
CC	www.admin.ch/ch/d/sr/sr.html
Egmont Group	www.egmontgroup.org
FATF	www.fatf-gafi.org
FOPI	www.bpv.admin.ch
MROS	www.fedpol.admin.ch/fedpol/de/home/themen/kriminalitaet/ geldwaescherei.html
SFBC	www.ebk.admin.ch
SFGB	www.esbk.admin.ch
SBA	www.swissbanking.org

Bibliography

Cassani, U.: Commentaire du droit pénal suisse, Partie spéciale, Volume 9: Crimes ou délits contre l'administration de la justice, art. 303 – 311 CP, Editions Staempfli+Cie SA, Bern, 1996.

Graber, C.: GwG, Gesetzesausgabe mit englischer Übersetzung, Ausführungserlassen und Anmerkungen, Schulthess, Zurich, 2003.

Nobel, P.: Schweizerisches Finanzmarktrecht, Einführung und Überblick, Stämpfli Verlag AG, Bern, 2004.

Nobel, P.: Swiss Finance Law and International Standards, Staempfli Publishers Ltd/Kluwer Law International, Bern/The Hague – London – Boston, 2002.

Schmid, N. (ed.)/Ackermann, J.-B./Arzt, G./Bernasconi, P./de Capitani, W.: Kommentar Einziehung, Organisiertes Verbrechen, Geldwäscherei, Band I/Band II, Schulthess, Zurich, 1998/2002.

Thelesklaf, D./Wyss, R./Zollinger, D.: GwG, Geldwäschereigesetz, Kommentar zu GwG, GwV-EBK, StGB (Auszug), sowie die einschlägigen Verordnungen und Texte von UNO, FATF, Balser Ausschuss und Wolfsberg-Gruppe, Orell Füssli Verlag AG, Zurich, 2003.

Thévenoz, L./Zulauf, U.: BF–Blanchiment, Réglementation et autoréglementation de la lutte contre le blanchiment et le financement du terrorisme en Suisse, Schulthess, 2004.

Thévenoz, L./Zulauf, U.: BF – Geldwäscherei, Regulierung und Selbstregulierung zur Bekämpfung der Geldwäscherei und der Terrorismusfinanzierung in der Schweiz, Schulthess, 2004.

Dr. iur. Johannes Gasser LL.M., 1970

Attorney at law, Partner
Liechtenstein and Austrian Citizen
University of Innsbruck (Dr. iur. 1995)
Admitted to the Liechtenstein and Austrian bar
Academic expert on European law (Schloss Hofen)
Area of practice: corporate, litigation, real estate, tax law, white collar crime
Foreign languages: English, French and Spanish

Mag. iur. Markus Schwingshackl, 1973

Attorney at law
Italian Citizen
University of Bologna, Italy
University of Innsbruck (Mag. iur. 2001)
Admitted to the Liechtenstein Bar
Austrian Bar Exam (2006)
Areas of practice: litigation, civil law, corporate law, international tax law and white collar crime
Foreign languages: Italian, English and Spanish

Firm's profile

For 50 years, domestic and international clients of the law office **Dr. Dr. Batliner & Dr. Gasser** have relied on it for sustainable and long-term solutions which are developed with a team of experienced attorneys trained in different jurisdictions and especially committed to transnational issues, which require a high level of foreign language proficiency and a sound financial and business understanding. As a law firm offering purely forensic services, it is not only one of the oldest but also the largest law firm in Liechtenstein.

Liechtenstein

Dr. Johannes Gasser, LL.M.

Mag. Markus Schwingshackl

Advokaturbüro Dr.Dr. Batliner & Dr. Gasser

Marktgass 21

9490 Vaduz

Principality of Liechtenstein

Tel +423 236 04 80

Fax +423 236 04 81

lawoffice@batlinergasser.com

www.batlinergasser.com

Anti-Money Laundering: International Law and Practice.
Edited by W.H. Muller, C.H. Kälin and J.G. Goldsworth
© 2007 John Wiley & Sons, Ltd

Contents – Liechtenstein

1   Introduction

The Liechtenstein *Due Diligence Act* (*Sorgfaltspflichtgesetz*, Act of 26 November 2004 on Professional Due Diligence in Financial Transactions) and the *Due Diligence Ordinance (Sorgfalt-spflichtverordung)*, which are governing the application of due diligence in professional financial transactions and serve to combat money laundering, organized crime and the financing of terrorism, were totally revised in the year 2005 and today satisfy the highest international standards. They also serve to implement the Directive 91/908/EEC of the Council in the version of Directive 2001/97/EC of the European Parliament and the Council of 4 December 2001 on prevention of the use of the fiscal system for money laundering (Second Money Laundering Directive). At the same time the *Due Diligence Act* takes into account the newest international standards in the field of the prevention of money laundering as in particular the reviewed and updated Forty Recommendations of the *Financial Action Task Force on Money Laundering (FATF)*.

2   Money laundering

According to §165 *Criminal Code (Strafgesetzbuch)* whoever conceals proceeds of a serious crime (i.e. any intentional act or omission punishable with more than three years' imprisonment), the financing of terrorism, certain corruption offences or offences according to the *Narcotic Act (Betäubungsmittelgesetz)* or disguises their source, in particular by making false statements in legal transactions as to the origin or true nature of such assets, their transfer or whereabouts, commits the criminal offense of **money laundering**. Concealing means any activity that may thwart or impede the discovery of such proceeds by defrauded persons, other victims of related crimes or law enforcement authorities. Punishment in such case may rise up to three years' imprisonment.

Also covered by the criminal offense of money laundering are the acquisition of assets derived from any serious crime, the financing of terrorism, bribery or drug offense committed by another person as well as the safekeeping, administration and management, conversion and exploitation of such assets and their transfer to a third party. Such offense may be punishable up to two years' prison term. Should the amount exceed Sfr. 75 000, courts may extend the term to five years.

3   Personal and substantive scope of application of the Due Diligence Act

3.1   Personal scope of application

The following legal and natural persons are subject to the *Due Diligence Act:*

- **Banks** and finance companies holding a license pursuant to the *Banking Act* (*Bankengesetz*), e-money institutions holding a license pursuant to the *E-Money Act* (*E-Geldgesetz*), as well as Liechtenstein branches of foreign banks, finance companies, and e-money institutions.

- Liechtenstein branches of foreign securities companies.

- Investment undertakings holding a license pursuant to the *Investment Undertakings Act* (*Gesetz über Investmentunternehmen*).

- Insurance undertakings holding a license pursuant to the *Insurance Supervision Act* (*Versicherungsaufsichtsgesetz*) which offer direct life insurance, as well as equivalent Liechtenstein branches of foreign insurance undertakings.

- The Liechtenstein Postal Services (limited company).

- Casinos.

- Natural and legal persons holding a license (*Treuhänderbewilligung*) pursuant to the *Professional Trustees Act* (*Gesetz über die Treuhänder*).

- Natural persons holding a confirmation (*Bestätigung zur Übernahme von Verwaltungsmandaten*) pursuant to Article 180a *Law on Persons and Companies* (*Personen-und Gesellschaftsrecht*).

- Exchange offices (*Wechselstuben*).

- **Lawyers** admitted to the Bar in accordance with the *Lawyers Act* (*Gesetz über die Rechtsanwälte*), and legal agents.

- Natural and legal persons holding a license pursuant to the *Law on Auditors* (*Gesetz über die Wirtschaftsprüfer und Revisionsgesellschaften*) and Auditing Companies as well as auditing offices subject to special legislation.

- Real estate agents.

- Dealers in high-value goods and auctioneers.

Legal and natural persons that do not fall within the scope of the above mentioned subjects are nevertheless subject to the *Due Diligence Act* if they carry out financial transactions on a professional basis.

3.2　Substantive scope of application

The *Due Diligence Act* applies to the professional conduct on **financial transactions**. The following transactions are considered financial transactions or equivalent or financial transactions:

- Every acceptance or safekeeping of the assets of third parties, as well as assistance in the acceptance, investment, or transfer of such assets.

- Establishing a legal entity on the account of a third party that does not operate commercially in the domiciliary State or acting as an organ of such a legal entity. A legal entity that does not operate commercially in the domiciliary State is, in particular, a legal person, company, trust or other association or asset entity – regardless of its legal structure – which does not conduct any trade, manufacturing, or other commercial operation in the domiciliary State.

- Transactions by dealers in high-value goods and by auctioneers if payment is made in cash and the amount exceeds Sfr. 25,000, regardless of whether the transaction is made in a single step or in several steps that obviously appear to be linked.

- The granting of admission to a casino to visitors, regardless of whether the visitor actually takes part in gaming activities or buys or sells gaming tokens.

Business relationships of lawyers and legal agents are not considered as financial transactions, unless the lawyer or legal agent contributes to the planning and execution of financial or real estate transactions for his client, beyond forensic activities, with respect to:

- The purchase and sale of real estate or enterprises.

- The management of money, securities, or other assets of the client.

- The opening or management of accounts, deposits or safe deposit boxes.

- The obtaining of the means necessary for the formation, operation, or management of legal persons, companies, trusts, or other associations of asset entities.

- The establishment on the account of a third party of a legal entity that does not operate commercially in the domiciliary State or the performance of activities as an organ of such a legal entity.

4 Obligations of due diligence

4.1 Identification of the contracting party

4.1.1 The obligation to identify the contracting party

The **contracting party** is any natural person and/or legal entity that enters into a financial transaction in the above outlined meaning with a person subject to due diligence and must be identified by means of documentation with probative value when entering into a business relationship.

There is no obligation to identify the contracting party if:

- A spot transaction is made that does not exceed the maximum amount of Sfr. 25 000, regardless of whether the transaction is made in a single step or in several steps that obviously appear to be linked.

- Remittances or transfers are made which do not exceed the maximum amount of Sfr. 5000, regardless of whether the transaction is made in a single step or in several steps which obviously appear to be linked.

- The amount of a periodic insurance is less than Sfr. 1500 per year.

- A one-time insurance premium is less than Sfr. 4000, or less than Sfr. 4000 is paid into a premium deposit.

- The account in question is a rental deposit account for rental property located in an EEA Member State or in Switzerland.

- The account in question is an account for payment under subscription of capital during formation or for increase in capital of a legal person or partnership to be entered or already entered in the Public Register.

- The contracting party is a legal person admitted to official quotation at a stock exchange.

- The contracting party has already been identified in an equivalent way within the same group or enterprise, in such case, copies of the documents used for the original identification shall be included with the due diligence files.

- An application for insurance has been accepted by a person subject to due diligence which has already identified the contracting party in connection with other financial transactions. In such case, the person subject to due diligence shall include copies of the documents used for the original identification with the due diligence files.

4.1.2   The documents for identification

When initiating a business relationship by personal contact, the Liechtenstein parties are required to identify the other contracting party and to conduct due diligence enquiries to establish the identity of that other party by inspection of a document with probative value (i.e. original copy of a document that can be used in a court of justice for evidence, e.g. the passport) of that party and by collecting and documenting the following information:

- For natural persons: last name, first name, date of birth, address of residence, state of residence and citizenship.

- For legal persons, companies, trusts, other associations and asset entities: name or firm name, address of domicile, domiciliary state, date of formation, and, if applicable, place and date of entry into the Public Register.

When initiating a business relationship by correspondence the contracting party must be identified by obtaining the original or certified copy of the document with probative value and confirmation of the required information by signature or electronic signature.

For natural persons, a document with probative value shall be a valid official identity paper with a photograph, in particular passport, identity card, or driving license. If the contracting party is not in the position to provide such document from his home country, a confirmation of identity shall be provided by the authority responsible in its domicile.

For legal persons, companies, trusts, other associations and asset entities registered in the Public Register, a document with probative value shall be:

- An extract from the Public Register issued by the Public Register Authority.

- A written extract from a database maintained by the Public Register Authority.

- A written extract from trustworthy, privately managed registers and databases.

If they are not registered in the Public Register, a document with probative value shall be:

- An official certificate issued in Liechtenstein.

- The statutes, the formation documents, or the formation agreement.

- A certification of name or firm name, address of domicile, domiciliary state and date of formation by the chosen auditor of the annual accounts.

- An official license to conduct its activities.

- A written extract from a trustworthy, privately managed register or equivalent database.

The certificate on the authenticity of a copy of a document with probative value may be issued by:

- A branch or corporate affiliate of institutional persons subject to due diligence.

- Another institutional person subject to due diligence, a lawyer, a professional trustee, an auditor, or an asset manager subject to Directive 91/308/EEC in the version of Directive 2001/97/EC or an equivalent regulation and subject to appropriate supervision.

- A notary public or other public office that normally issues such certificates of authenticity.

If a business relationship is initiated by correspondence, the persons subject to due diligence must include the original of a certified copy of the document with probative value with the due diligence files. If a business relationship is initiated by personal contact, it shall be sufficient if the persons subject to due diligence make a copy of the original document or the certified copy, confirm on the copy that they have inspected the original or certified copy, put the date and their signature on the copy, and include it with the due diligence files. The documents necessary for identification must reflect the current circumstances. Certificates of authenticity, extracts from registers, and certificates by the chosen auditor of the annual account may not be older than 12 months.

4.2   Identification of the beneficial owner

4.2.1   The beneficial owner

The **beneficial owner** is the person who ultimately holds the economic rights to the assets in question. A legal entity which does not operate commercially in the domiciliary State can only be beneficial owner to the extent that:

- Its purpose is the safeguarding of the interests of its members in joint and mutual assistance or it is statutorily and actually pursuing political, religious, scientific, artistic, charitable, entertainment, or similar purposes.

- Is a holding company which serves as an instrument to form an operative group.

In the case of revocable structures such as an revocable trust, the effective founder is considered to be the beneficial owner. In case of insurance contracts, the person effectively paying for the insurance contracts is considered to be the beneficial owner.

4.2.2   The obligation to identify the beneficial owner

When entering into a business relationship the beneficial owner must be identified with care that is appropriate to the circumstances. In doing so, the assumption that the contracting party is identical to the beneficial owner is allowed. If, however, doubts arise whether this assumption is correct a written statement identifying the beneficial owner must be required from the contracting party.

Doubts concerning the assumption, that the contracting party and the beneficial owner are identical, are reasonable in particular if:

- A person who does not have sufficiently close relation to the contracting party possesses power of attorney.

- The financial situation of the contracting party is known and the assets presented or the insurance applied for are recognizably beyond the financial reach of the contracting party.

- The contact with the contracting party results in other unusual findings.

A written statement is always required if:

- A spot or insurance transaction or a remittance or transfer is made that exceeds the amount which triggers to obligation of identification of the contracting party.

- The business relationship is initiated with a natural person by correspondence.

- The contracting party is a legal entity that does not operate commercially in the domiciliary state.

4.2.3 Exceptions to the obligation to identify

There is no obligation to identify the beneficial owner:

- In cases where there is no obligation to identify the contracting party.

- If the beneficial owner is a legal entity that does not operate commercially in the domiciliary state and is admitted to official quotation at a stock exchange.

- For banks and postal institutions, in the case of accounts or deposits maintained in the name of lawyers admitted in an EEA Member State or in Switzerland on the account of their clients in the course of forensic activity or in their capacity as executors, escrow agents, or in a similar capacity.

- For institutional persons subject to due diligence, namely a bank, a postal institution, an investment undertaking, or an insurance undertaking, if the contracting party is either another institution of that kind domiciled in Liechtenstein or abroad or a securities trader subject to Directive 91/308/EEC in the version of Directive 2001/97/EC or an equivalent regulation and subject to appropriate supervision.

- If the contracting party is an occupational pension institution that is exempt from taxation.

The obligation to identify the beneficial owner is further eased if the contracting party is the representative of a collective form of investment or an associated company with more than twenty beneficial owners as investors. In such case, only the beneficial owner who alone or in joint agreement are entitled to at least 5% of the contributed assets must be established. If the number of beneficial owners does not exceed twenty, all beneficial owners must be identified. The obligation to identify the beneficial owners shall be waived entirely in the case of collective forms of investment admitted to official quotation at a stock exchange.

4.2.4 Repetition of identification

The persons subject to due diligence must repeat the identification of the contracting party or of the beneficial owner if any doubts arise concerning the identity of the contracting party or the beneficial owner in the course of the business relationship. They may discontinue the business relationship if doubts about the information supplied by the contracting party persist despite a repetition of identification. They shall be prohibited from discontinuing the business relationship it the preconditions are met for the reporting obligation to the *Financial Intelligence Unit (FIU)*.

If, in an existing insurance contract, the insurance holder is replaced by another insurance holder, the contracting party shall be identified anew and, if applicable, the beneficial owner shall be identified anew. When a business relationship is discontinued because of persisting doubts about the information supplied by the contracting party the persons subject to due diligence must sufficiently document the outflow of assets.

4.3 The monitoring

It must be ensured that long-term business relationships are monitored in a way adequate to the risks involved. For this purpose, the persons subject to due diligence must establish criteria indicating higher risks and issue international instructions on how such risks are to be limited and monitored. Banks with branches abroad or which lead a financial group with foreign companies must, at a global level, assess, limit, and monitor their risks connected with money laundering, organized crime, and the financing of terrorism.

4.3.1 The profile

For each long-term business relationship a profile must be compiled and kept updated. It shall contain the following information:

- the contracting party and the beneficial owner,
- authorized parties,
- the economic background and origin of the assets presented,
- the profession and business activity or the beneficial owner or the effective founder, and
- the intended use of the assets.

The degree of detail to the information shall take into account the risk involved in the business relationship.

4.3.2 The inquiries

Simple inquiries. If in the context of long-term business relationships circumstances or transactions arise which derivate from the profile or which meet the established risk criteria simple **inquiries** with appropriate effort must be carried out. Such simple inquiries serve to access the plausibility of circumstances and transactions. In this context, the person subject to due diligence should obtain, evaluate and document the information that is suited to make the background of circumstances or transactions plausible and understandable.

Special inquiries. Special inquiries must be carried out if in the context of long-term business relationships circumstances or transactions arise which generate the suspicion that assets might be connected with money laundering, a predicate offense of money laundering, organized crime or the financing of terrorism. The results of the inquiries must be documented in the due diligence files. The person subject to due diligence shall obtain, evaluate and document the information that is suited to dispel or corroborate any arising suspicion.

4.4 The FMA Guideline 2005/1

The *Financial Market Authority* (*FMA*) in its Guideline 2005/1 has issued binding risk criteria which apply to all persons subject to due diligence. They may not misuse their foreign branches and foreign associated companies to circumvent the Guideline and must ensure that the FATF recommendations which apply to them are adhered to by associated companies and branches in countries which are not members of the FATF, except insofar as local regulations prevent them from doing so.

4.4.1 The risk criteria

Risk criteria are in particular:

- Physical presentation of assets to the equivalent value of more than Sfr. 100 000 in one step or stage when the business relationship is established.

- Business relationships with politically exposed persons as persons holding prominent public positions abroad: heads of state and heads of government, high-level politicians, high-level officials in administrative bodies, the courts, the military, and political parties, the highest decision-makers in state-owned enterprises, and enterprises and persons who are recognizably close to such persons.

- Indicators for money laundering according to the Annex of the Guideline. In their internal instructions, the persons subject to due diligence must specify the threshold amounts above which enquiries are obligatory, insofar as the indicators are measurable. They may specify different maximum values for differentiated risk categories.

4.4.2 The scope of the enquiries

In cases where inquiries are required, persons subject to due diligence are requested to obtain the information which enables them to evaluate the background adequately, and verify the plausibility of such information. The results of the inquiries must be documented in a report which must be kept in the due diligence files.

Depending on the circumstances of the individual case, information must be obtained and documented in particular on the following points, insofar as these points are not already covered by the profile of the business relationship:

- The purpose and nature of a given transaction.

- The financial circumstances of the contracting party or beneficial owner, insofar as the person subject to due diligence has knowledge of these circumstances.

- The professional or business activities of the contracting party, the beneficial owner, or the effective founder of a legal entity that does not operate commercially in the domiciliary state.

- The origin of the assets invested or deposited.

Obtaining of information from third parties and consultation of experts when conducting inquiries concerning the background is expressly permitted. Declarations of the client concerning the background of such transactions can not always be accepted at face value, but must be verified with respect to plausibility.

4.4.3 Action once inquiries have been carried out

Once inquiries have been carried out for the person subject to due diligence may face the following situations.

4.4.4 Continuation of the business relationship where no doubt exists

If the circumstances or transactions which are subject to simple or special inquiries can be explained in a plausible manner, the business relationship may be continued unchanged.

4.4.5 Continuation of the business relationship subject to special monitoring

If the person subject to due diligence continues the business relationship despite having doubts, but without a suspicion of a connection with money laundering, a predicate offense of money laundering, organized crime or the financing of terrorism the course of the business relationship must be monitored in more detail.

4.4.6 Discontinuation of the business relationship

If there are doubts, but not a suspicion of a connection with money laundering, a predicate offense of money laundering, organized crime or the financing of terrorism and therefore the person subject to due diligence discontinues the business relationship, it may only allow the assets to be withdrawn in a form which enables the prosecution authorities, if necessary, to continue to follow the paper trail; no money may be paid out in cash or no securities and precious metals may be released, unless the contracting party has fulfilled its obligations in full. The business relationship may not be discontinued and the withdrawal of large amounts may not be allowed if there are concrete indications that action by the authorities is imminent.

4.5 The reporting obligation

4.5.1 The obligation to report to the Financial Intelligence Unit (FIU)

If, as a result of simple or special inquiries or in connection with short-term business relationships by other means, the suspicion arises that a connection with money laundering, a predicate offense of money laundering, organized crime or the financing of terrorism exists, a report in writing must be immediately submitted to the *FIU*.

Until the conclusion of special inquiries or if the preconditions for the **reporting obligation** apply, the business relationship may not be discontinued. An unjustified report shall trigger no liability under civil or criminal law, unless there was intention. In the same way there shall be no civil liability for not discontinuing a business relationship even though the contracting party expressly wishes a discontinuation or termination of the business relationship. Until an order from the responsible prosecution authority arrives, but at most until the conclusion of five business days from receipt by the *FIU* of the above mentioned report, all actions that might obstruct or interfere with any orders issued to seize assets which may be subject to forfeiture or absorption of enrichment are prohibited, unless such actions have been approved in writing by the *FIU*.

The persons subject to due diligence may not inform the contracting party, the beneficial owner, or third parties that they have submitted a report to the *FIU*, until an order from the responsible prosecution authority arrives, but at most until the conclusion of twenty business days from receipt by the *FIU* of the report.

Lawyers and legal agents as well as auditors, auditing companies, and auditing offices subject to special legislation are not required to submit a report to the *FIU* if they have received the information from or through a client in the course of assessing a legal situation for such client, or if they have received the information in the course of their activity as defense attorney or representative of that client in or concerning court proceedings, including advice on the pursuit or prevention of proceedings, before or after such proceedings, or during such proceedings.

4.5.2　The right to report to the FIU

If in connection with preparations for a business relationship, but without one actually being entered into, the suspicion arises that a connection with money laundering, a predicate offence of money laundering, organized crime, or the financing of terrorism exists, a report in writing may be submitted to the *FIU*. An unjustified report shall trigger no liability under civil or criminal law, unless there was intention.

5　Supervision

The execution of the *Due Diligence Act* is supervised by the ***Financial Market Authority (FMA)*** which carries out ordinary inspections on a regular, spot-check basis. Such inspections include both formal inspection concerning compliance with the documentation obligation as well as material inspection concerning the plausibility of the due diligence measures taken. The records and data of such inspection must be processed and stored exclusively in Liechtenstein and may be used for the sole purpose of combating money laundering, predicate offenses of money laundering, organized crime, and the financing of terrorism within the meaning of the *Criminal Code (Strafgesetzbuch)*. Inspections may also be carried out by auditors, auditing companies and auditing offices subject to special legislation mandated by the *FMA*.

Address

Financial Intelligence Unit
Äulestrasse 51
9490 Vaduz
Principality of Liechtenstein
Tel +423 236 61 25
Fax +423 236 61 29
info@sfiu.llv.li

Abbreviations

EEA	European Economic Area
FATF	Financial Action Task Force
FIU	Financial Intelligence Unit
FMA	Financial Market Authority

Bibliography

Beat, P.: Geldwäscherei Abwehr und berufliche Sorgfaltspflicht im Fürstentum Liechtenstein, Librarium Verlag, Werdenberg, 2001.

Breuer, M.: Die Bekämpfung der Geldwäsche im Völkerrecht, in der Europäischen Union und im Fürstentum Liechtenstein, ex jure Verlagsanstalt, Vaduz, 2003.

Gasser, J.: Die strafrechtliche Verantwortlichkeit von Vorgesetzten für Geldwäscherei ihrer Mitarbeiter, in: Liechtensteinische Juristen Zeitung, 2002.

Heiterer, T./Gassner, A. et. al.: SPG samt Nebenerlassen, GMG Verlag, Schaan, 2005.

Ochsner, S./Süssli, D.: Sorgfaltsplichten bei Tätigkeit als Organ einer Sitzgesellschaft, in: Marxer & Partner, Aktuelle Themen zum Finanzplatz Liechtenstein, Liechtenstein Verlag, 2004.

Dr Thomas Schirmer, **LL.M. (Tulane)** is a lawyer and partner of Binder Grösswang Recht-sanwälte. He studied law at, and graduated from, the Law School of the University of Innsbruck (Austria) and holds an economics degree of the Innsbruck Business School. After an LLM program at Tulane University Law School, Thomas Schirmer joined Binder Grösswang Rechtsanwälte in 1995 as an associate. He has been admitted to the Viennese Bar in 1998. His main areas of practice include mergers and acquisitions, corporate law, banking law and structured finance. He contributed to a number of international publications, amongst others to Neate Ed., 'Bank Confidentiality' (3rd edn, Butterworths, 2003). He is a member and officer of the International Bar Association (Committee E – Banking Law, Committee G – Business Organisations) and a member of DACH Europäische Anwaltsvereinigung.

MMag. Markus Uitz studied law at, and graduated from, the Law School of the University of Graz (Austria) and the Institut d'Etudes Politiques (Sciences-Po) in Paris. He also holds a master degree in History and Philosophy of the University of Graz. He joined Binder Grösswang Rechtsanwälte in 2006 as an associate after having gained experience in banks, industry and NGOs such as the European Training and Research Center for Human Rights and Democracy. His main areas of practice include mergers and acquisitions, corporate law, banking law and structured finance.

Firm's profile

Binder Grösswang Rechtsanwälte is an independent full-service Austrian law firm with substantial international practice and has ranked among the leading business law firms in Austria for almost 50 years. The firm acts across the full spectrum of business activities in a wide range of business sectors with a strong focus on M&A and financing transactions, major arbitration and litigation and advice on corporate, commercial, banking, tax, public procurement, competition, IP, labor and real estate law.

Austria

Dr. Thomas Schirmer, LL.M. (Tulane)
MMag. Markus Uitz

Binder Grösswang Rechtsanwälte
Sterngasse 13
1010 Vienna
Austria

Tel +43 1 534 80
Fax +43 1 534 80 8
bg@bgnet.at
www.bgnet.at

Anti-Money Laundering: International Law and Practice.
Edited by W.H. Muller, C.H. Kälin and J.G. Goldsworth
© 2007 John Wiley & Sons, Ltd

Contents – Austria

1 Current situation in Austria

Old habits die hard. Even though Austria has made **impressive improvements** to anti-money laundering (AML) and countering the financing of terrorism (CFT) legislation, a recent study by the University of Utrecht classes Austria in the same category as the Cayman Islands with respect to offshore financing centers.[1] Granted, Austria abolished banking secrecy and implemented OECD directives and the FATF recommendations very late compared to other countries, but it now has been done. Further, Austria's reputation is not fostered through its geographic situation which makes the country a turntable for financial transactions. But, at least in the financial community, the image is already rectified as proven by an IMF laud in 2004.

One of the difficulties underlying the **lack of awareness** about Austrian efforts in AML and CFT is caused by the lack of communication of the real impulses for AML and CFT legislation for the larger public. Even in Austrian criminal law, the provisions on money laundering appear right after the provision about concealment of stolen goods and belong to the category of so-called *Vermögensdelikte* (crimes against other person's patrimony), to which they most certainly do not belong.

In this overview, we will try to show that although Austria has not enjoyed a favorable reputation in the past, there is in fact strong AML and CFT legislation in place. Therefore, we will first give a short introduction to the structure of the competent authorities, followed by an overview of Austrian AML and CFT provisions.

2 Structure of the competent authorities in Austria

Due to the overlapping nature of the underlying transactions, **several Austrian authorities** are responsible for taking measures against money laundering and against the financing of terrorism. They are embedded in a **complex system** involving different ministries, as well as their detached bodies. Generally speaking, one could distinguish the authorities responsible for the administration of criminal justice (*Federal Criminal Police* and *Ministry of Justice*) and the regulating bodies for different sectors in which money laundering attempts are likely to occur (*Ministry of Finance, Financial Market Authority* and *National Bank*).

2.1 Federal Criminal Police Office at the Ministry of Interior

The main **investigative power** lies within the *Federal Criminal Police Office* (*Bundeskriminalamt*) within the *Ministry of Interior* (*Bundesministerium für Inneres*). It was newly created in 2002, with the intention of centralizing the previously divided nine provincial bureaus. An '*Austrian Financial Intelligence Unit*' is situated within this authority as '*Bureau 3.4*' and is staffed by one director, nine police officers and a secretary. It is a member of the Egmont Group (www.egmontgroup.org). Another financial intelligence unit is situated within the EDOK group, Austria's organized crime squad, and focuses on CFT.

Unlike other countries, where this role is located within the National Bank, Austria's police serves as the **contact point** for public suspicions as well as for professionals who are required to notify

---

[1] Rawlings/Unger, Competing for Criminal Money, Tjalling C. Koopmans Research Institute Discussion Paper Series no. 05–26, publicly available under http://www.uu.nl/content/05-26.pdf.

certain money laundering-related activities of their clients. To this end, a 'Registration Office' (*Geldwäschemeldestelle*) has been set up. In 2005, around 2000 notifications were registered at this office, a number which kept constant over the past years.

2.2   Federal Ministry of Justice

The Federal Ministry of Justice combines **two different tasks**. Firstly, their members coordinate the police work, carried out either by the State Attorneys responsible for prosecution, or the Courts responsible for bringing suspects to trial. The second role of the Ministry is to provide the legislature with expert opinions and in so doing help to adapt the legal environment to new threats from money laundering and the financing of terrorism.

2.3   Federal Ministry of Finance

A **hybrid** in the dichotomy explained above **between crime fighting and regulatory authorities**, the *Federal Ministry of Finance* (*Bundesministerium für Finanzen*) is mainly responsible for taking appropriate measures in the development of the relevant legal Acts, for example the *Austrian Banking Act* (*Bankwesengesetz*), the *Insurance Supervision Act* (*Versicherungsaufsichtsgesetz*) and the *Securities Supervision Act* (*Wertpapieraufsichtsgesetz*). These Acts assign the concrete tasks relevant in AML and CFT to other bodies.

2.4   Financial Market Authority

One of these outsourced bodies, and a **new pillar** in the Austrian banking sector landscape, is the *Austrian Financial Market Authority* (FMA; *Finanzmarktaufsicht*). Founded on 1 April 2002, the FMA's main obligation involves the **supervision** of credit institutes, insurance companies and financial services providers, a function for which it has also been granted investigative powers. The FMA's task also extends to informing supervised undertakings about new developments in AML and CFT.

2.5   Austrian National Bank

Even though the FMA has been established as the overarching authority for controlling banks, the *Austrian National Bank* (NB; *Österreichische Nationalbank*) remains a strong player in this field as it is competent for **on-the-spot investigations** in connection with market and credit risks. Additionally, the NB can be assigned investigative power by the FMA. Reciprocal information flow between NB and FMA is guaranteed by mutual cooperation provisions. Further, the NB is responsible for the implementation of restrictions in international money transactions.

2.6   Others

In addition to the bodies mentioned above, a number of other Austrian institutions are also engaged in AML and CFT. Their contribution lies mainly in preparing recommendations for legal amendments taking into consideration new developments. These bodies include, in particular, the *Ministry of Economics and Labour* (*Bundesministerium für Wirtschaft und Arbeit*), the *Ministry of Foreign Affairs* (*Bundesministerium für Auswärtige Angelegenheiten*), the *Chamber of Attorneys* (*Rechtsanwaltskammer*), the *Chamber of Chartered Accountants* (*Kammer der Wirtschaftstreuhänder*) and the *Chamber of Notary Publics* (*Notariatskammer*).

3 Austrian legislation

3.1 System of AML provisions

No separate AML and/or CFT Act exists in Austria and AML and CFT provisions are included in a **wide variety of Acts** such as the *Criminal Act*, the *Banking Act* and the *Trade License Act*. However, the basis for all such provisions is the definition of money laundering contained in the Criminal Act, from which all other provisions derive (although at times not employing the exact wording). The consequences thereof are **terminological differences** in the different acts. Whereas the *Criminal Ac*t uses the term *'Geldwäscherei'*, the *Banking Act* uses *'Geldwäsche'*. The *Trade License Act* even uses both terms but parliamentary discussions have explicitly suggested the synonymic use by the legislator.

Apart from legislation, AML and CFT are influenced by **soft-law**, e.g. several circular letters from the FMA setting out guidelines for credit institutions, financial service providers and insurers. Of course, both Acts and soft-law are deeply influenced by the three EU-AML-Directives and international soft-law initiatives such as the FATF guidelines.

The **measures** foreseen under Austrian law can be seen **in a certain hierarchy**. The basis is a duty for care and diligence. The next level is the identification of a client, then the more restrictively employed duty to investigate. The severest measure is the notification of a transaction at the Registration Office.

These measures are safeguarded through the obligation to retain documents (custody duties) and organizational obligations. All identification criteria and all transaction documents have to be preserved for at least five years and appropriate measures have to be taken to guarantee compliance with AML/CFT provisions.

This scheme is maintained throughout all provisions regarding the regulation of professions. After an overview of AML and CFT provisions in criminal law, we will therefore provide a survey of AML and CFT related provisions in relation to professional duties including banks, investment service providers, liberal professions and other money related activities comprehending trade licenses, gambling, the stock market and insurance companies.

3.2 Criminal basis

Money laundering is dealt with in section 165 of the *Austrian Criminal Act* (CA; *Strafgesetzbuch*) which was amended in 1993 to reflect the increased international awareness in relation to money laundering and the subsequent relocation of crime fighting initiatives to the use of criminal money. The section was significantly altered in 1998, again as a consequence of international developments.

3.2.1 Money laundering

Money laundering is punishable with up to two years detention for

- concealing or covering up the provenance of assets originating from certain criminal acts (in this connection the term 'concealment' includes every act exacerbating the detection of the asset), or

- acquiring, administering, assigning to third parties, placing, storing, transforming or utilizing such assets.

In order for an act of money laundering to occur, it is necessary that the assets have been acquired as a **result of criminal offences**. Criminal offences are defined as all offences punishable with more than three years of imprisonment. In addition, certain other criminal offences (such as forgery of documents, bribery, financing of terrorism, civil disorder and certain financial offences) are explicitly included on the list of possible preparatory acts for money laundering. **Exculpation reasons** for the preparatory act **do not exclude punishment** of the money launderer.

All assets, including claims or other immaterial rights can be subject to money laundering. It is sufficient that the asset was acquired through a **preparatory criminal offence**, was given in return for the preparatory act, or if the asset represents the value of the initially acquired/gratified asset, e.g. something bought with money of the sale of an asset acquired by a criminal offence. Under current Austrian criminal law and the discussions thereto, it is not clear whether such assets remain 'contaminated' following a transaction with a third party carried out in good faith.

Money laundering constitutes a general offence, meaning that anybody can commit this crime. The prerequisite for punishment is intent, even though contingent intent (*dolus eventualis*) is sufficient. As a consequence, the money launderer must be aware of the criminal origin of the asset which is being concealed. All other acts require the **intention degree** of knowledge (*Wissentlichkeit*): the offender must want to realize those above mentioned cases. Knowledge must include the preparatory act.

Punishment for an offense of money laundering is aggravated if the concerned asset is worth more than €50 000 or if the asset belongs to a criminal or terrorist organization. Under those circumstances, a prison term of between six months and five years must be imposed.

3.2.2   Financing of terrorism

The financing of terrorism was considered as assistance or participation in a terrorist act itself until the creation of a separate provision (section 278 d) governing the offence in the CA. The crime consists of **providing assets to or collecting assets for a terrorist organization**, which is defined as union of two or more persons for a longer period of time with the aim of committing terrorist crimes.

The CA sets out **ten criminal acts** which **are deemed to be terrorist crimes**: murder, mayhem, coercion, threat, damage to property, offences constituting a public danger, hijacking of an aircraft, willful endangering of aerial security, offences against the Firearms Act and the War Material Act. Such offences must be committed with the intention of:

- intimidating the population,

- forcing public or international organizations to act or refrain to act in a certain way, or

- convulsing or destroying the constitutional, economic or social structures of a country.

Further, the act must be sufficient to provoke a grave or long-lasting disruption of public life or business.

To be classified as financing terrorism, the money used must not necessarily be of criminal origin. The use of legally acquired money can also lead to a conviction, as **no criterion for the origin of assets** is set forth in the CA.

3.2.3 Responsibility of legal entities

As a result of an amendment to the CA, i.e. the *Responsibility of Legal Entities Act* (*Verbandsver-antwortlichkeitsgesetz*), criminal **offences can also be committed by legal persons** and certain other legal constructs such as business partnerships, if two preconditions are fulfilled:

- A decision maker or employee of the legal entity (who must be a natural person) must have carried out a criminal act.

- The act must be imputable to the legal entity. This is generally the case if the action was carried out for the advantage of the legal entity, or if an obligation of the entity was violated through the criminal act.

The **sanction is a pecuniary penalty,** to be determined on a daily rate basis in relation to the profits of the company (*Tagsätze*). The daily rate is limited to a maximum of €10 000; and a maximum of 180 daily rates may be imposed.

3.2.4 Active regret

Active regret (*Tätige Reue*) for money laundering crimes is structured differently than other active repentance provisions under Austrian law. The difference is especially notable in contrast to other money related crimes: there is **no need for compensation of the victims,** but in order to enjoy exemption from punishment there is an **obligation to secure the assets**. If an offender compensated the victims of the preparatory crime instead of providing the police with the assets, an analogous interpretation of other provisions is still under discussion in legal literature. The scope of the assets to be secured is still discussed, but reasonably, at least the essential parts of the laundered assets must be provided. The same is true for active repentance after committing the crime of financing terrorism.

3.3 Banks – ABA

As mentioned under Section 3.1, all professionals working in money-related areas have similar duties with regard to the prevention of money laundering. Therefore, in this overview the corresponding duties of banks will be treated more in detail and the focus will be placed on diverging rules for other professions.

Money laundering and financing of terrorism are treated in sections 39 to 41 of the *Austrian Banking Act* (ABA; *Bankwesengesetz*). These provisions were amended with effect from 1 January 1994, shortly after the corresponding provisions in the CA. Section 39 ABA sets out **general diligence principles** for credit and financing institutes (CIFI; *Kreditinstitute und Finanzinstitute*). Generally, managers have to apply the due care of a 'diligent director' within the meaning of the *Austrian Stock Corporations Act* (*Aktiengesetz*). **Certain transactions still require an enhanced standard** which has to be complied with by every employee and not only the directors. Those general principles are substantiated in the sections 40 and 41 ABA.

3.3.1 Scope of ABA

The ABA, and thus the AML and CFT provisions therein, are applicable to CIFI. **Credit institutions** are institutions authorized to transact those banking activities which set down in section 1 of the ABA; **financing institutions** are authorized to carry out certain other bank-related activities, such as the entering into leasing contracts or the over-the-counter purchase of foreign means of payment.

3.3.2 Identification duty

All money flowing through CIFI should be transparent in order to avoid money laundering. The basic principle is 'know your customer'. Therefore, the CIFI have the duty to identify their clients:

- when entering into a continuous business relationship, or

- for all transactions with a value of at least €15 000 (if more than one transaction is involved, the value has to be aggregated under prerequisite of a connection between them).

No connection to money laundering or suspicions are required for these two prerequisites to apply. In addition, customers need to be identified if CIFI have **substantiated suspicions** that a client being involved in money laundering or the financing of terrorism.

Further, since 1 July 2002, for every **payment into or out of a saving account** over a threshold of €15 000, the individual behind the transaction must be identified.

Identification must be made in such way that ensures that the **customer is unambiguously identified**, i.e. name and birth date for natural persons, as well as name and registered office in case of juridical persons. Supporting documents must be provided.

The rules on personal identification still apply to remote transactions which can be made via electronic signatures or courier under certain circumstances. Due to the higher risk of malpractice through these communication methods, the duty of care of the involved banks is heightened.

3.3.3 Investigation duty

Three cases can be distinguished in which CIFI have investigation duties:

- where the identity of a client is established by a representative or is supported by foreign documentation,

- where the CIFI are in doubt as to whether a client is in fact acting on his own accounts,

- where CIFI already have suspicions which need to be substantiated.

The duty to investigate must not be overstretched, e.g. it would not be necessary to employ private detectives. Generally speaking, the CIFI must not substitute the work of the investigating authorities but use their **professional and extra-professional knowledge** of their clients to evaluate transactions with regard to potential money laundering attempts. The exact scope is to be determined on an individual case basis.

3.3.4 Notification duty/disclosure duty

CIFI must inform the Registration Office without delay if:

- a transaction which has already occurred, is in progress or is about to occur is for the purpose of money laundering, or

- a customer has not disclosed the information requested.

Following such notification by the CIFI and until the Registration Office has made a decision, no further processing in the transaction can be carried out, except where delay would complicate or obstruct the investigation of the case. Where the Registration Office does not respond by the end of the following banking day, the transaction may be executed.

In addition, the **Registration Office may request all information** deemed necessary to prevent or prosecute money laundering and may request that transactions in progress are provisionally stayed, under the precondition of reasonable suspicion that the concerned transaction serves the purpose of money laundering.

3.3.5 Banking secrecy

The above outlined principles of banks' duties in relation to AML/CFT efforts stand in conflict with an Austrian bank's duty of confidentiality (*Bankgeheimnis*), guaranteed by section 38 ABA.

Credit institutions as well as connected persons such as shareholders, are not allowed to disclose secrets which arise solely as a result of a business relationship. The same is true for the NB, in which case the secret becomes an official secret. There is **no time limit on the duty of confidentiality**. The only exception is made for a notification to the Registration Office in case of substantiated suspicions.

To comply with AML and CFT standards, the provisions on bank secrecy have been amended and **anonymous accounts prohibited**. For all existing anonymous accounts, temporary arrangements have been set: As of 30 June 2002 savings accounts with still unidentified holders have to be labeled by the bank. Until the holder is identified, no payments into the accounts or withdrawals from such accounts are permissible.

3.4 Securities

The above outlined provisions for CIFI are **equally binding for investment service providers** regulated in the *Austrian Securities Supervision Act* (*Wertpapieraufsichtsgesetz*) by way of reference to the provisions of the ABA. The provisions are complemented by the duty imposed on the FMA to inform the Registration Office in case of substantiated suspicions that transactions serve money laundering purposes.

3.5 Liberal professions

3.5.1 Attorneys-at-law

According to the professional duties set out in the *Attorneys-at-Law Act* (ALA, *Rechtsanwalt-sordnung*), lawyers are obliged to carefully **scrutinize all businesses** whose nature suggests a connection to money laundering or the financing of terrorism <u>and</u> in which the lawyer:

- plans or conducts the purchase or the sale of real property or undertakings;
- administers money, commercial papers or other property values;
- opens or administers banking, saving or commercial paper accounts;
- founds, conducts or administers trusts, companies or similar structures including the procurement of the assets necessary to found, operate or administer such structures; or
- conducts financing or real property transactions in the name of his clients.

In the opinion of the legislator, these are the only cases where lawyers could become involved in money laundering in their professional work. It is not yet clear under Austrian law, whether a lawyer has an active duty of investigation.

Other provisions regarding AML and CFT are similar to the ABA. In the above mentioned cases and if:

- the transaction involves more than €15 000;

- the lawyer enters into continuous business relations with his client; or

- there are substantiated suspicions

the lawyer must carry out an **obligatory identity check**. The identity check is not necessary if the concerned party is a CIFI complying with the EU-money-laundering-directive 2001/97/EC or, in case of a third country based CIFI, if similar obligations apply.

To ensure the possibility to practice the law despite a duty of notification for lawyers that resemble those of banks, a lawyer does not have to notify the Registration Office if the client informed him in the course of a consultation or if such information was brought up during a trial (both cases are to be interpreted broadly). The only exception to this exception would be the case in which the consultation of a lawyer itself serves money laundering purposes.

3.5.2 Notary publics

Notary publics are subject to similar regulations as attorneys-at-law and as such the provisions outlined above will also apply to notaries. Details can be found in the *Notary Publics Act* (*Notariatsordnung*).

3.6 Money-related activities

3.6.1 Trade licences

The relevant provisions of the *Austrian Trade Licence Act* (*Gewerbeordnung*) relating to AML and CFT refer to persons **dealing with high-grade goods** such as gemstones, precious metals or works of art, as well as to accountants and estate agents. If transactions by such persons are paid for in cash (or e-cash) and involve more than €15 000, regulations similar to those in the ABA and the ALA apply. They comprise identification duties, custody duties, diligence and investigation duties, as well as organizational duties.

3.6.2 Gambling

Pursuant to section 25 of the *Austrian Gambling Act* (*Glücksspielgesetz*), every visitor to a casino has to be identified by means of photo identification. This serves three completely **different purposes**, namely:

- to control and enforce the age limit (18 years);

- to comply with the casino's duty to carefully check each gambler's habits in order to stop him from gambling if he endangers his personal situation; and

- to comply with identification duties with respect to AML legislation.

Casinos have to keep those records of each visitor for a period of 5 years.

In case of grounded suspicion that

- a gambler's transaction does serve money laundering purposes;
- a gambler belongs to a terrorist organization; or
- the transactions of a visitor to the casino serve financing of terrorism purposes

the concessionaire of a gambling house has to immediately inform the Federal Criminal Police. All such **transaction must be stopped** until a decision of the Police has been taken.

As with other professionals cited in this overview, the concessionaire of a gambling house has to undertake suitable internal controls and notification measures to prevent and foreclose transactions in connection with money laundering. Further, he has an obligation to train his employees in this regard.

3.6.3 Stock market

One particularity of the stock market is the duty to install an **automated surveillance system** for complete gathering of data relating to trading of the stock. Due to this prerequisite, AML and CFT efforts can easily be put in place as all transactions, in principle, remain traceable. Therefore, section 25 of the *Austrian Stock Market Act* (*Börsegesetz*) allocates the responsibility for taking measures against money launderers to the exchange operating company, and not to direct business partners involved in transaction. The duties imposed again largely resemble those already described.

If such automatic systems, however, are not sufficient, it falls within the competence of the FMA to decide which specific amendments to the trading systems have to be made by the exchange operating company, under penalty of a fine within an adequate period of time. Further, the FMA has power to make use of the automated trading surveillance system when carrying out investigations.

3.6.4 Insurance companies

For the **life insurance businesses** in Austria, section 18a of the *Austrian Insurance Surveillance Act* (*Versicherungsaufsichtsgesetz*) stipulates identification duties where:

- the annual premium of the insurance contract is higher than €1000;
- the one-time premium is higher than €2500; or
- the annual premium is increased to more than €1000 during the contractual period.

There are two general clauses which complete the AML and CFT legislation in this regard. All business partners must further be identified if there is reasonable suspicion:

- that the policyholder participates in money laundering or terrorist financing transactions, or
- that the policyholder belongs to a terrorist organization.

Exceptions are made for insurance policies in connection with employment contracts or professional activities. Back-up provisions to guarantee compliance with and enforceability of those rules resemble the duties for other sectors.

4 Outlook

Austria has made substantial progress with regard to AML and CFT legislation. One important international innovation remains to be tackled. The concept of **politically exposed persons** (PEP) has not yet been introduced into Austrian law. However, the implementation of the third EU-AML-directive will amend Austrian law in this regard. It remains an interesting question, as to how this often discussed issue will find its way into the Austrian legal system.

Addresses

Registration Office
Josef Holaubek-Platz 1
1090 Vienna
Austria
Tel +43 (1) 24 836 8529
BMI-II-BK-3-4-2-FIU@bmi.gv.at
www.bmi.gv.at/meldestellen

Austrian National Bank
Otto-Wagner-Platz 3
1090 Vienna
Austria
Tel +43 (1) 404 20-0
Fax +43 (1) 404 20-2399
www.oenb.at

Financial Market Authority
Praterstraße 23
1020 Vienna
Austria
Tel +43 (1) 249 59-0
fma@fma.gv.at
www.fma.gv.at

Abbreviations

ABA	Austrian Banking Act (*Bankwesengesetz*)
ALA	Attorney-at-Law Act (*Rechtsanwaltsordnung*)
AML	Anti-Money Laundering
CA	Austrian Criminal Act (*Strafgesetzbuch*)
CFT	Countering the Financing of Terrorism
CIFI	Credit Institutes and Financing Institutes
FATF	Financial Action Task Force
FMA	Austrian Financial Market Authority (*Finanzmarktaufsicht*)
IMF	International Monetary Fund
NB	Austrian National Bank (*Österreichische Nationalbank*)
OECD	Organisation for Economic Co-operation and Development

Bibliography

Bogensberger, W.: Bekämpfung der Geldwäsche, Verlag Dr. Otto Schmidt, Köln/Schulthess, Zürich, 2002.

Diwok, G./Göth, P.: Bankwesengesetz Kommentar, Verlag Österreich, Wien, 2005.

Fremuth, W./Laurer, R./Linc, S./Pötzelberger, L./Strobl, J.: Bankwesengesetz samt den wichtigsten Nebengesetzen, Manzsche Verlags- und Universitätsbuchhandlung, Wien, 1999.

Hausmaninger, C.: The Austrian Banking Act, Manz, Wien, 1999.

Höpfel, F./Ratz, E.: Wiener Kommentar zum Strafgesetzbuch, Manzsche Verlags- und Universitätsbuchhandlung, Wien, 2005.

Insam, A.: Verdacht auf Geldwäsche, Im Kreuzfeuer internationaler Sorgfaltspflichten. Liechtenstein – Österreich – Deutschland – Schweiz, NWV Neuer Wissenschaftlicher Verlag Wien–Graz, 2006.

Klippl, I.: Geldwäscherei, Bank-Verlag/Verlag Orac, Wien, 1994.

Tades, H./Hoffmann, K.: Rechtsanwaltsordnung, Manzsche Verlags- und Universitätsbuchhandlung, Wien, 2005.

Peter Burrell specialises in contentious regulatory work including investigations by the FSA, SFO, HM Revenue & Customs, DTi, Inland Revenue and the police. Consequently, he has significant experience in advising on the practical and legal implications of conducting investigations, both for regulatory and for purely internal purposes. He is the firm's expert on advising banks and other financial institutions on compliance with the relevant money laundering provisions and is a member of the Law Society Task Force on 'Money Laundering and Financial Crime'. He has advised a number of clients, including investment banking institutions subject to supervision and enforcement visits from the FSA, including on issues arising out of investigations in respect of market abuse, mis-selling and breaches of the FSA Money Laundering Rules.

Kate Meakin is an assistant solicitor in Herbert Smith's litigation and arbitration division. She has experience of SFO investigations, as well as regulatory and disciplinary investigations. She advises clients on a variety of money laundering matters, including reporting issues. She has an LL.B. with First Class Honours from Bristol University and passed the Legal Practice Course with Distinction at Nottingham Law School.

Firm's profile

Herbert Smith is a leading and full-service international legal practice with a 1100-lawyer network across Europe and Asia. Herbert Smith is acknowledged as being in the top tier in each of its main areas of work: transactions, projects and disputes. As well as offices in Europe and Asia, Herbert Smith's international capability is enhanced by its alliance with Gleiss Lutz and Stibbe, two leading Western European law firms.

United Kingdom

Peter Burrell

Partner Litigation &
Arbitration Division

Kate Meakin

Associate Litigation &
Arbitration Division

Herbert Smith LLP
Exchange House
Primrose Street
London EC2A 2HS
UK

Tel 020 7374 8000
Fax 020 7374 0888
peter.burrell@herbertsmith.com
kate.meakin@herbertsmith.com
www.herbertsmith.com

Anti-Money Laundering: International Law and Practice.
Edited by W.H. Muller, C.H. Kälin and J.G. Goldsworth
© 2007 John Wiley & Sons, Ltd

Contents – United Kingdom

1   Introduction

The United Kingdom has a broad framework to combat money laundering which goes beyond the scope of the first, second and, indeed, third *EC Money Laundering Directives*. This flows from its role as an important financial centre. It also stems from recent risk assessments produced by the newly formed *Serious Organised Crime Agency ('SOCA')*. It concluded that the overall threat to the UK remained high, the scope and complexity of the various activities conducted by serious organised criminals was increasing and the criminal networks were becoming more fluid, extended and flexible which was in part due to the use of specialist 'service providers' to assist with money laundering.

The anti-money laundering regime has, in effect, four separate pillars which closely inter-relate. First are the requirements imposed by the *Money Laundering Regulations 2003 ('the Regulations')*. In summary, they require businesses which conduct 'relevant financial business' to maintain systems and controls to prevent money laundering including client identification, record-keeping, training and reporting of suspicious activity. Secondly, there are high-level requirements imposed by the *Financial Services Authority ('FSA')*, the principal regulator for the financial services industry, which require most sectors of the financial services industry to have systems and controls to forestall money laundering. The *FSA* therefore has the ability to reinforce the requirements imposed by *the Regulations* and, by and large, is the statutory body which maintains compliance with *the Regulations*. Thirdly, the *Proceeds of Crime Act 2002 ('POCA')* (as amended) imposes broad obligations on all sectors of society, including business, to report where suspicious that they may be involved in assisting money laundering. Fourthly, the *Terrorism Act 2000* and various other subordinate pieces of legislation prohibit all forms of terrorist financing and fund raising as well as laundering of the proceeds of terrorist activity. It also imposes reporting obligations both on the financial services sector and society at large.

The UK was last assessed against *FATF*'s *Forty recommendations* in 1996/1997. The *FATF* commented that 'the United Kingdom anti-money laundering system is an impressive and comprehensive one, which has been subject to consistent review and improvement'. Whilst *FATF* suggested a small number of changes, the UK framework met the *FATF Forty recommendations* at that time. Since then, a number of changes have been made to the system both to respond to points raised by *FATF* and also to ensure that reports generated by the financial institutions were of greater relevance. For example, it is no longer necessary under the UK regime for financial institutions to make reports about suspected money laundering where the underlying conduct, whilst criminal if assessed in accordance with English law, was lawful where it occurred and where it is not serious.[1] *FATF* also commented on the ability of the *National Criminal Intelligence Service ('NCIS')* which was the *FIU* to process suspicious activity reports it received. *NCIS* has now been incorporated within the newly formed *Serious Organised Crime Agency ('SOCA')*, which has also incorporated parts of *HM Revenue & Customs* dealing with drug trafficking and criminal finance and the relevant part of the UK immigration service dealing with organised crime. In addition to being responsible for receiving and analysing suspicious activity reports, *SOCA* also has an investigation division and has been given wide ranging compulsory powers to obtain information to assist it with its enquiries. It is suspected that with these greater resources, *FATF*'s criticisms will have been addressed.

---

[1] Section 102 Serious Organised Crime and Police Act and Proceeds of Crime Act 2002 (Money Laundering: Exceptions to Overseas Conduct Defence) Order 2006 (SI 2006/1070).

The United Kingdom will undergo a third round **mutual evaluation** by *FATF* in 2007, the results of which are due to be released in June 2007. It is likely that the UK regime will still meet the *FATF Forty recommendations*.

2 Scope of the anti-money laundering regime

As explained above, there are four different, but interacting and supporting elements to the UK anti-money laundering framework. Their scope and requirements are set out in more detail below.

2.1 Money Laundering Regulations 2003 ('the Regulations')

The Regulations implement the requirements of the Second *EC Money Laundering Directive*. However, their requirements also go beyond the Second Directive and, to a degree, implement certain aspects of the Third *EC Money Laundering Directive*, in particular in relation to their scope. For example, *the Regulations* apply to those who provide, by way of business, services in relation to the formation or operation or management of a company or trust.[2] Another principal difference with the Second and Third *EC Money Laundering Directives* is that *the Regulations* also apply to the activity of dealing in goods of any description by way of business (including dealing as an auctioneer) whenever a transaction involves accepting a total cash payment of €15 000 or more.[3] To that extent, the regime is not limited simply to those who deal in goods of a particular description.

Otherwise, the scope of *the Regulations* reflects the *EC Directives*, applying to certain regulated financial services businesses, bureau de change, money transmission providers, estate agents, casinos, insolvency practitioners, accountants and tax advisers, the legal profession (to the extent to which it involves participation in a financial or real property transaction) and, in addition, those carrying out any of the activities mentioned in points 1 to 12 or 14 of Annex 1 to the *Banking Consolidation Directive* when carried on by way of business.[4] It should also be noted that the *the Regulations* apply to that part of a firm's business which falls within *the Regulations*, even if that is not the principal business of that firm or institution, for example, ad hoc lending.[5]

The Regulations require those who carry on relevant business to maintain:

- identification procedures;[6]

- record-keeping procedures;[7]

- internal reporting procedures;[8] and

- procedures to ensure that relevant employees are made aware of the provisions of *the Regulations* and relevant provisions of the *Proceeds of Crime Act 2002* and the *Terrorism Act 2000*, as well as being given training in how to recognise and deal with transactions which may be related to money laundering.[9]

---

[2] Money Laundering Regulations 2003 (SI 2003/3075) Regulation 2(2)(m).
[3] *Ibid* Regulation 2(2)(n).
[4] *Ibid* Regulation 2(2)(e).
[5] *Ibid* Regulation 2(2) and Schedule 1.
[6] *Ibid* Regulation 4.
[7] *Ibid* Regulation 6.
[8] *Ibid* Regulation 7.
[9] *Ibid* Regulation 3(c)(i) and (ii).

Whilst no proceedings have been brought to date for breach of *the Regulations*, it is a criminal offence to fail to comply with them punishable by a term of imprisonment of up to two years or to a fine.[10]

The Government is currently consulting on how to implement the other provisions of the *Third Money Laundering Directive* into English law and is consulting on revisions to the *2003 Money Laundering Regulations* to achieve that effect.[11] That consultation is due to close at the end of October 2006 with revised draft regulations to be published by the end of 2006.

As can be seen, and consistent with the *EC Money Laundering Directives*, the requirements of *the Regulations* are at a relatively high level and are not prescriptive. For example, the identification procedures require that those subject to *the Regulations* must, as soon as is reasonably practicable after contact is first made with the relevant customer, require the customer to produce satisfactory evidence of his identity with increased attention where the customer is not physically present when being identified.[12] *The Regulations* therefore do not specify how a person should be identified or what constitutes 'satisfactory evidence'.

Recently this has led to criticism, from within the United Kingdom, of the approach taken by the financial services sector to identification with the development of a 'box ticking' culture and an over-rigorous and inflexible approach. As a result, and with support from both Government and the *Financial Services Authority,* the UK now champions a much more 'risk-based approach'. This was encapsulated in the 2005 edition of the *Joint Money Laundering Steering Group Guidance* which is produced on behalf of various trade groups and which is used by, in particular, the financial services sector as a means of developing a practical approach to compliance with *the Regulations* as well as the requirements imposed by the *FSA* (see below). Whilst the guidance is produced by the trade bodies, it was reviewed by Government and the *FSA* prior to its publication. It also has official status since a firm's compliance with the guidance must be taken into account by a court in assessing that firm's compliance with *the Regulations*.[13] Some of the principal changes brought about by the new Guidance and the 'risk-based' approach is reliance upon single identification documents and less need to obtain certified copies of identification documents in lower risk cases.[14]

However, whilst the Guidance has official status and assists firms to implement their own systems of internal control to ensure compliance with *the Regulations*, they are not prescriptive and a wide degree of judgement can be applied in how they are implemented within any particular firm.

2.2 The Financial Services Authority ('FSA') anti-money laundering rules

Until recently, the *FSA* had its own detailed rules imposed on a wide range of financial services firms requiring them to maintain systems and controls to forestall money laundering.[15] Broadly, these closely followed the requirements in *the Regulations* and required firms to have:

- arrangements to ensure compliance with the FSA rules, including the appointment of a Money Laundering Reporting Officer;

---

[10] *Ibid* Regulation 3(2).
[11] Implementing the Third Money Laundering Directive: a consultation document – July 2006 – HM Treasury.
[12] Money Laundering Regulations 2003 (SI 2003/3075) Regulation 4(3)(b).
[13] *Ibid* Regulation 3(3).
[14] *JMLSG* Guidance, para. 5.4.19.
[15] FSA Money Laundering Sourcebook.

- procedures to identify the client;

- reporting procedures;

- procedures to train and make staff aware of their obligations; and

- procedures to ensure that the MLRO monitored the day-to-day operation of the firm's anti-money laundering policies and procedures.

However, consistent with the move towards a more 'risk-based' approach, the *FSA* has withdrawn its detailed *Money Laundering Source Book* and instead has included a range of high level systems and controls which firms are required to have to forestall money laundering. These include:

- Arrangements to enable a firm to identify, assess, monitor and manage money laundering risk, which are comprehensive and proportionate to the nature, scale and complexity of its activities.[16] The controls should include appropriate training for employees, an (at least) annual report by the MLRO to the governing body and senior management; appropriate documentation of risk management policies and risk profile; appropriate measures to ensure the money laundering risk is taken into account in day to day operations; and measures so that customers who cannot reasonably produce detailed evidence of identity are not unreasonably denied access to the firm's services.[17]

- Regular assessments of the adequacy of the systems and controls to ensure continued compliance.[18]

- The appointment of an individual as Money Laundering Reporting Officer.[19]

- The allocation to a director or senior manager (who may also be the MLRO) of overall responsibility within the firm for the establishment and maintenance of effective anti-money laundering systems and controls.[20]

Under the former regime, the *FSA* had taken action against a number of firms for failure to comply with its detailed rules. Fines meted out were significant, in the highest case a fine of £2 million was levied on Abbey National plc for failure to identify its customers adequately and failure to ensure that internal suspicious activity reports were promptly considered and reported to *NCIS*. The *FSA* has stated that removal of its detailed rules should not be seen as a sign that it places less emphasis on anti-money laundering compliance. One of its statutory objectives is the reduction of financial crime, including reducing the extent to which it is possible for business carried on by a regulated person to be used for a purpose connected with financial crime.[21] The *FSA* also recognises that any anti-money laundering compliance regime will not be a 'zero failure' regime, i.e. that on occasions firms will fail to comply and that this will not necessitate enforcement action. The author's view is therefore, in future, the *FSA* will look to systemic breaches of its rules and a failure to implement the *JMLSG* Guidance before bringing enforcement action.

In addition to the requirements imposed by the *FSA*, other professions, such as the legal profession and the accountancy profession are subject to the rules and requirements of their own professional

---

[16] SYSC3.2.6A.
[17] SYSC 3.2.6G.
[18] SYSC 3.2.6C.
[19] SYSC 3.2.6I.
[20] SYSC 3.2.6H.
[21] Section 2(2)(d) of the Financial Services and Markets Act 2000 and section 6(1) of that Act.

bodies. For those carrying on money service business or who are dealers in high value goods, they are required to be registered by the *Commissioners for Customs & Excise* and are subject to oversight by *HM Revenue & Customs*.

2.3   Proceeds of Crime Act 2002 ('POCA')

POCA came into effect on 23 February 2003 replacing the existing legislation prohibiting money laundering of the proceeds of drug trafficking and serious crime.[22] The new regime is an 'all crimes' regime applying to any crime no matter how minor.[23] To that extent, it is a significant departure from, and extension of, the Second and Third *EC Money Laundering Directives*. It therefore applies to serious crimes such as drug trafficking, corruption and all forms of financial crime through to a number of regulatory offences such as failure to comply with Health & Safety and Environmental legislation.

POCA has two facets to it. First, there are a number of offences which apply to all members of society. Secondly, there are additional, specific requirements on those falling within the 'regulated sector' which broadly follow the ambit of *the Regulations*.[24] Taking each of those facets in turn:

2.3.1   The concealing, arrangements and possession offences

These three offences apply to all members of society and apply to criminal property. This is defined in *POCA* as a person's benefit from criminal conduct or property which represents such a benefit (in whole or part and whether directly or indirectly).[25] Criminal conduct is similarly broadly defined as any conduct which would constitute an offence in any part of the United Kingdom or which would constitute an offence in any part of the United Kingdom if it occurred there (i.e. it applies to overseas conduct as well).[26] With those two definitions in mind, the offences proscribe the following activities:

- Concealing, disguising, converting, transferring or removing criminal property from England and Wales or from Scotland or Northern Ireland.[27]

- Entering into or becoming concerned in an arrangement which you now suspect facilitates (by whatever means) the acquisition, retention, use or control of criminal property by or on behalf of another person.[28]

- Acquiring, using or possessing criminal property.[29]

In all cases, the offender has to know or suspect that criminal property is involved.

To avoid committing an offence, the person has to make a disclosure to a Police officer, a Customs officer or a nominated officer, being someone nominated by the employer to receive disclosures and to pass them on to the relevant *FIU, SOCA*.[30] However, simply making a report is not sufficient.

---

[22] Criminal Justice Act 1988 and the Drug Trafficking Offences Act 1986.
[23] Section 340(2) of POCA.
[24] Schedule 9 to POCA.
[25] Section 340(3) of POCA.
[26] Section 340(2)(b) of POCA.
[27] Section 327 of POCA.
[28] Section 328 of POCA.
[29] Section 329 of POCA.
[30] Section 338 of POCA.

The UK anti-money laundering regime encapsulates a 'consent regime'. This means that having made a disclosure, the individual has to wait for consent from the authorities before continuing with the act.[31] Deemed consent is given seven working days after a disclosure is made unless the authorities refuse consent.[32] In those cases where consent is refused, the authorities then have a further 31 calendar days from the date of that refusal in order to restrain the criminal property.[33]

The consent regime under *POCA* has created a number of practical difficulties and has given rise to civil claims against banks by customers whose funds have been frozen. It can also lead to tensions with the provisions described below in relation to tipping off. It was recently recommended[34] as part of the review of *SOCA*'s operations for the consent regime to be re-considered.

In addition to the ability to make reports before committing one of the above mentioned acts, the regime also provides a defence if a report is made afterwards and there is a good reason for the failure to make a disclosure beforehand and the disclosure is made on the person's own initiative and as soon as it is practicable for him to make it. Finally, there is a further defence available where the person intended to make a disclosure but had a reasonable excuse for not doing so, for example, because of threats of physical harm.

Since the reporting regime applies to professionals who are subject to obligations of confidentiality, the regime provides that a disclosure of information under *POCA* will not constitute a breach of confidentiality or any other restriction on the disclosure of information howsoever imposed.[35] There are specific rules relating to disclosures by the legal profession since the fundamental right of a client to consult with a lawyer in confidence is recognised within the regime. However, that right falls away where the client is using the lawyer in furtherance of a crime and in those circumstances, the lawyer will be free to make a disclosure.[36]

The maximum sentence for committing one of these offences is a term of imprisonment for up to 14 years, an unlimited fine or both.[37]

2.3.2 The failure to disclose offence for the 'regulated sector'

In addition to the requirements above, where a firm or individual within the regulated sector knows or suspects or has reasonable grounds for knowing or suspecting that another person is engaged in money laundering and that information has come to them in the course of a business in the regulated sector, they are required to make a disclosure as soon as is practicable after the information or other matter has come to their attention.[38] If they fail to do so, they are guilty of an offence unless they have a reasonable excuse for that failure or they are a professional legal adviser and the information or other matter came to them in 'privileged circumstances'.[39]

The penalty for failing to make a disclosure is a term of imprisonment for up to five years or an unlimited fine or both.

---

[31] Section 335 of POCA.
[32] Section 335(3) and (5) of POCA.
[33] Section 335(4) and (6) of POCA.
[34] Stephen Lander Review.
[35] Section 338(4).
[36] *R v Cox & Railton* (1884) 14 QBD 153.
[37] Section 334.
[38] Section 330.
[39] Section 330(6) and (10).

As can be seen, the scope of the regime is very broad giving rise to some 200 000 suspicious activity reports in the last year. There have been a number of minor amendments made to the regime including changes to the 'single criminality test', such that it is no longer necessary to make reports about the laundering of property derived from overseas conduct which is lawful where it occurred and which is not treated as serious under English criminal law (i.e. it would be punishable with a term of imprisonment of less than one year if committed in England and Wales). Secondly, where the money laundering is occurring overseas and is lawful there or where the discloser cannot identify the person engaged in money laundering or the whereabouts of the laundered property, and he does not believe, and there are not reasonable grounds for him believing, that the information he has will assist in identifying the money launderer or the whereabouts of any of the laundered property, it is not necessary to make a report.

2.3.3   Tipping off offence

POCA also contains two offences to ensure that investigations by law enforcement are not prejudiced. Each has slightly different trigger points but broadly they make it an offence to make a disclosure which is likely to prejudice an investigation which is being or might be conducted.[40] The maximum sentence for committing a tipping off offence or prejudicing an investigation is a term of imprisonment not exceeding five years or an unlimited fine or both.[41]

The one important exemption to both the tipping off and prejudicing an investigation offences is the ability of a professional legal adviser to make a disclosure to a client in connection with the giving by the legal adviser of advice to the client or to any other person in connection with legal proceedings or contemplated legal proceedings.[42]

2.4   Anti-terrorism provisions

Similarly to *POCA*, the anti-terrorism provisions have two elements. There are a number of offences which apply to all members of society and which therefore impose reporting obligations upon all. Secondly, certain financial sector firms are under additional reporting obligations which require a report to be made at a lower threshold.

In addition to the provisions contained within the *Terrorism Act 2000*, the Government has also enacted a number of pieces of subordinate legislation to give effect to UN sanctions against proscribed organisations. There is also a broad overarching piece of subordinate legislation which makes it an offence to provide 'financial services' to a person on a list of proscribed persons.[43] Most financial institutions therefore as part of the client acceptance process, will ensure that the customer's name does not appear on such a list.

The offences under the *Terrorism Act 2000* are:

- The fund-raising offence – a person commits an offence if they invite another to provide or receive or provide money or other property intending that it should be used or having reasonable cause to suspect that it may be used, for the purposes of terrorism.[44]

---

[40] Sections 333 and 342 of POCA.
[41] Section 334(2) and 342(7).
[42] Sections 333(3) and 342(4).
[43] The Terrorism (United Nations Measures) Order 2001, SI 2001/3365.
[44] Section 15, Terrorism Act 2000.

- The use and possession offence – a person commits an offence if they use money or other property for the purposes of terrorism or they possess money or other property and intend that it should be used, or have reasonable cause to suspect that it may be used, for the purpose of terrorism.[45]

- The funding offence – a person commits an offence if they enter into or become concerned in an arrangement as a result of which money or other property is made available or is to be made available to another and they know or have reasonable cause to suspect that it will or may be used for the purposes of terrorism.[46]

- The money laundering offence – a person commits an offence if they enter into or become concerned in an arrangement which facilitates the retention or control by or on behalf of another of terrorist property by concealment, removal from the jurisdiction, transfer to nominees or in any other way. It is a defence for a person charged with that offence to prove that he did not know and had no reasonable cause to suspect that the arrangement related to terrorist property.[47]

For those members of society outside of the 'regulated sector', and those who receive information in the course of a trade, profession, business or employment, there is a duty to report where they believe or suspect that another person has committed one of the offences set out above.[48] Again, there are exceptions for legal advisers. The punishment for not making a disclosure is a term of imprisonment for up to five years or an unlimited fine or both.[49]

For those who receive such information but not in the course of a business, etc. then if they wish to continue with the arrangement, e.g. the funding or fund raising, they would need to make a disclosure to a constable and would need the express consent of the constable before proceeding.[50]

Finally, in relation to those within the 'regulated sector', there is a reporting obligation if they know or suspect or have reasonable grounds for knowing or suspecting that one of the offences set out above has been committed and the information upon which that knowledge or suspicion, or reasonable grounds for knowledge or suspicion, came to them in the course of a business in the 'regulated sector'.[51] Again, the penalty for not making a disclosure is a term of imprisonment not exceeding five years or an unlimited fine or both.[52]

There are further reporting obligations where the person has information which he knows or believes might be of material assistance in preventing the commission by another person of an act of terrorism or in securing the apprehension, prosecution or conviction of another person, in the United Kingdom, for an offence involving the commission, preparation or instigation of an act of terrorism.[53] The punishment for failing to make such a disclosure is a term of imprisonment not exceeding five years or a fine or both.[54]

---

[45] Section 16, Terrorism Act 2000.
[46] Section 17, Terrorism Act 2000.
[47] Section 18, Terrorism Act 2000.
[48] Section 19, Terrorism Act 2000.
[49] Sections 19(8), Terrorism Act 2000.
[50] Section 20, Terrorism Act 2000.
[51] Section 21A, Terrorism Act 2000.
[52] Section 21A(12), Terrorism Act 2000.
[53] Section 38B Terrorism Act 2000.
[54] Section 38B(5), Terrorism Act 2000.

2.5   Developments

As mentioned above, the UK will undergo a third round **mutual evaluation** in 2007. Despite changes made to the UK regime since the last assessment in 1996/1997, such as the limited exception for overseas conduct, it is likely that the UK regime will still meet the *FATF Forty recommendations*. Further, the third *EC Money Laundering Directive* must be implemented into UK law by December 2007. Whilst some of the provisions of the third Directive are already reflected by the UK regime, the UK Government is currently consulting on how to implement the other provisions and published revised draft regulations in January 2007.[55]

Addresses

Joint Money Laundering Steering Group
Pinners Hall
105/108 Old Broad Street
London EC2N 1EX
UK
Contact person: David Swanney
david.swanney@jmlsg.org.uk

FATF/GAFI
2, rue André Pascal
75775 Paris Cedex 16
France
contact@fatf-gafi.org

Serious Organised Crime Agency
P.O. Box 8000
London SE11 5EN
UK
SAR Helpdesk +44 (0)20 7238 8282

Abbreviations

DTI	Department of Trade & Industry
FATF	Financial Action Task Force
FIU	Financial Intelligence Unit
FSA	Financial Services Authority
JMLSG	Joint Money Laundering Steering Group
MLRO	Money Laundering Reporting Officer
NCIS	National Criminal Intelligence Service
POCA	Proceeds of Crime Act 2002
SFO	Serious Fraud Office
SOCA	Serious Organised Crime Agency

Bibliography

Biggs, S./Farrell, S./Padfield, N.: The Proceeds of Crime Act 2002 – Butterworths New Law Guides, Butterworths Lexis Nexis, UK, 2002.

Financial Services Authority: Financial Services Authority Handbook.

The Joint Money Laundering Steering Group: Prevention of money laundering/combating the financing of terrorism – Guidance for the UK Financial Sector, Parts I & II, January 2006.

---

[55] Implementing the Third Money Laundering Directive: Draft Money Laundering Regulations 2007, January 2007, HM Treasury.

Andrew Le Brun joined the Jersey Financial Services Commission as director of its International and Policy Division on 1 May 2000. He has responsibility for ensuring that the Commission is aware of developing standards set by international standard setting bodies, coordinating internal and external assessments against these standards, and reviewing the regulatory and legislative environment within which the Commission operates. He is currently involved in a review of the Island's anti-money laundering legislation and Anti-Money Laundering Guidance Notes to bring them into line with revised international standards. Immediately prior to this appointment, Andrew was an audit partner at KPMG in the Channel Islands. Andrew is a member of the Institute of Chartered Accountants in England and Wales.

Organisation's profile

The **Jersey Financial Services Commission** is responsible for the regulation, supervision and development of the financial services industry in Jersey. The Commission is a statutory body corporate, set up under the Financial Services Commission (Jersey) Law 1998. The Law establishes the Commission as an independent body, fully responsible for its own regulatory decisions. The Commission is accountable for its overall performance to the States of Jersey through the Minister for Economic Development.

Jersey

Andrew le Brun

Jersey Financial Services Commission
Nelson House
David Place
St. Helier
Jersey JE4 8TP
Channel Islands

Tel +44 1534 822 065
Fax +44 1534 822 001
a.lebrun@jerseyfsc.org
www.jerseyfsc.org

Anti-Money Laundering: International Law and Practice.
Edited by W.H. Muller, C.H. Kälin and J.G. Goldsworth
© 2007 John Wiley & Sons, Ltd

Contents – Jersey

1 Introduction

1.1 Overview

The continuing ability of *Jersey's* finance industry to attract legitimate customers with funds and assets that are clean and untainted by criminality depends, in large part, upon the Island's reputation as a sound, well-regulated jurisdiction. Any financial services business in *Jersey* that assists in laundering the proceeds of crime, or financing of terrorism, whether:

- with knowledge or suspicion of the connection to crime, or

- in certain circumstances, acting without regard to what it may be facilitating through the provision of its products or services

will risk prosecution for **criminal offences**, risk the loss of its licence or other regulatory sanctions (where regulated and supervised), face the loss of its reputation, and damage the integrity of *Jersey's* finance industry as a whole.

Jersey has had in place a framework of anti-money laundering legislation since 1988, and for the countering of terrorism since 1990. This legislation has continued to be updated as new threats have emerged, including legislation to extend the definition of criminal conduct for which a money laundering offence can be committed and to combat international terrorism.

Every financial services business in *Jersey* must recognise the role that it plays in protecting itself, and its employees, from involvement in money laundering and terrorist financing, and also in protecting the Island's reputation for probity. This principle relates not only to business operations within *Jersey*, but also operations conducted by *Jersey* businesses outside the Island.

1.2 Legal and administrative structure

Jersey's main legislative provisions against money laundering and terrorist financing are contained in the:

- *Proceeds of Crime (Jersey) Law 1999* (***Proceeds of Crime Law***).

- *Drug Trafficking Offences (Jersey) Law 1988* (***Drug Trafficking Offences Law***).

- *Terrorism (Jersey) Law 2002* (***Terrorism Law***).

In addition, the *Money Laundering (Jersey) Order 1999* (*Money Laundering Order*) applies additional obligations to financial services businesses (defined later) to establish procedures, controls, and communication, and to take appropriate measures to train and promote an awareness of money laundering and terrorist financing, with the purpose of forestalling and preventing money laundering and terrorist financing.

Additional obligations in the ***Money Laundering Order*** are supported by the *Anti-Money Laundering Guidance Notes for the Finance Sector* (***Guidance Notes***), which were introduced at the same time as the *Proceeds of Crime Law* and issued by the *Jersey Financial Services Commission;* (*Commission*). The *Guidance Notes* have since been supplemented by a number of Anti-Money Laundering Guidance Updates. The status of these *Guidance Notes* is considered later.

2 Criminal provisions and implementation of international sanctions

2.1 Offence of money laundering

Money laundering is defined in Article 1 of the *Proceeds of Crime Law*. It means conduct that is an offence under Articles 32, 33 or 34 of the *Proceeds of Crime Law*, under Articles 30, 37, or 38 of the *Drug Trafficking Offences Law*, or under any of Articles 15 to 18 of the *Terrorism Law*.

Under the provisions set out above, it is an offence in *Jersey* to:

- Conceal or disguise any property, convert or transfer any property, or remove property from *Jersey*, knowing or having reasonable grounds to suspect that the property represents the proceeds of criminal conduct.

- Acquire, use, or possess property, knowing that the property represents another person's proceeds of criminal conduct.

- Become concerned in an arrangement that assists another person to retain the proceeds of criminal conduct, knowing or suspecting that the person has been engaged in criminal conduct or has benefited from criminal conduct.

The definition of money laundering in the *Proceeds of Crime Law* includes terrorist financing offences.

Criminal conduct is defined to cover drug trafficking, terrorist activities, and any other offence in *Jersey* for which a person is liable on conviction to imprisonment for a term of one or more years, and includes conduct that has occurred in another country, which would have constituted an offence had it occurred in *Jersey*.

It is not necessary that a person be convicted of a offence to establish that property represents the proceeds of criminal conduct.

The substantive offences outlined above are punishable by a maximum term of imprisonment of 14 years, or a fine or both.

2.2 Offence of terrorist financing

Articles 15 to 18 of the *Terrorism Law* criminalise the provision and collection of funds and use and possession of property for the purposes of terrorism.

Under the provisions set out above, it is an offence in *Jersey* to:

- Invite another person to provide property, intending that it should be used, or having reasonable cause to suspect that it may be used, for the purposes of terrorism.

- Receive property, intending that it should be used, or having reasonable cause to suspect that it may be used, for the purposes of terrorism.

- Provide property knowing or having reasonable cause to suspect that it will or may be used for the purposes of terrorism.

- Use property for the purposes of terrorism.

- Possess property, intending that it should be used, or having reasonable cause to suspect that it may be used, for the purposes of terrorism.

- Enter into, or become concerned in, an arrangement as a result of which property is made available or is to be made available to another, knowing or having reasonable cause to suspect that it will or may be used for the purposes of terrorism.

- Enter, or become concerned in, an arrangement which facilitates the retention or control by or on behalf of another person of terrorist property.

For the purposes of the *Terrorism Law*, terrorist property includes property that is likely to be used for the purpose of terrorism, the proceeds of the commission of acts of terrorism and proceeds of acts carried out for the purposes of terrorism. Property is deemed to be the proceeds of an act where it wholly or partly, directly or indirectly represents the proceeds of the act.

The substantive offences within the *Terrorism Law* outlined above are punishable by a maximum term of imprisonment of 14 years, or a fine or both.

2.3   Offence of tipping off

Under Article 35 of the *Proceeds of Crime Law* and Article 41 of the *Drug Trafficking Offences Law*, a person is guilty of the offence of **tipping off** if he discloses information to anyone that is likely to prejudice an investigation into money laundering:

- whilst knowing or suspecting that an investigation into money laundering is being, or is about to be, conducted; or

- whilst knowing or suspecting that a suspicious activity report has been made to a police officer; or

- whilst knowing or suspecting that a suspicious activity report has been made to the appropriate internal reporting officer at his place of employment.

The tipping off offence under Article 35 of the *Terrorism Law* contains an objective test, where the information or other matter likely to prejudice an investigation or proposed investigation is disclosed when there is reasonable cause to suspect that either a suspicious activity report has been or is to be made, or that an investigation is underway or proposed.

Tipping off can occur when information or other matter likely to prejudice an investigation or proposed investigation is disclosed to any other person. The information or other matter does not need to be disclosed directly to the customer or individual under suspicion, and disclosure may mean little more than communicating or advising a matter.

However, a person will not have committed a tipping off offence if he is able to prove either of the following:

- that he is a professional legal advisor disclosing the information in connection with, or in contemplation of, legal proceedings or the giving of legal advice (except where there is a view to furthering a criminal purpose); or

- that he did not know or suspect that the disclosure was likely to prejudice the investigation.

No offence is committed where disclosure that a suspicion has been reported would not be likely to prejudice an investigation. For example, where the existence and contents of a disclosure have been revealed in the course of criminal proceedings, it is unlikely that any prejudice would be caused by the subsequent disclosure of the report to the individual concerned.

A person who is guilty of such an offence is liable to imprisonment for a term not exceeding five years, or to a fine or to both.

2.4 Offence of failing to report

Offences arise under Article 40 of the *Drug Trafficking Offences Law* and Articles 20 and 23 of the *Terrorism Law*. Under Article 40 of the *Drug Trafficking Offences Law*, it is an offence for a person to **fail to report** (as soon as is reasonably practicable) knowledge or suspicion of another person's involvement in drug money laundering where that knowledge or suspicion comes to his or her attention in the course of a trade, profession, business or employment. A similar obligation exists under Article 20 of the *Terrorism Law* but does not apply to financial services businesses (defined later), which are subject to Article 23.

Under Article 23 of the *Terrorism Law*, it is an offence for a financial services business to fail to report where there is **knowledge or suspicion**, or where there are **reasonable grounds to be suspicious**, of another person's involvement in either terrorist money laundering or terrorist financing.

This offence is punishable by a maximum term of imprisonment of five years, or a fine or both.

2.5 Offence of failing to have procedures to forestall and prevent money laundering

Article 37 of the *Proceeds of Crime Law* provides for *Jersey's Treasury and Resources Minister* to prescribe procedures, by order, to be maintained by persons who carry on financial services business (defined later) for the purposes of forestalling and preventing money laundering (the *Money Laundering Order*).

If a person carrying on a financial services business contravenes or fails to comply with a requirement that is contained in the *Money Laundering Order*, he shall be guilty of an offence. If the person is a body corporate it shall be liable to a fine. If the person is not a body corporate, he shall be liable to imprisonment for a term not exceeding two years, or a fine or both.

2.6 Freezing, seizing, and confiscating assets

The *Proceeds of Crime Law*, *Drug Trafficking Offences Law*, and *Terrorism Law* provide for the confiscation of proceeds and instrumentalities of criminal conduct. The *Proceeds of Crime Law* and *Drug Trafficking Offences Law* (but not the *Terrorism Law*) also provide for **the confiscation of property of corresponding value**.

These laws also provide for the freezing and seizure of assets subject to confiscation prior to the issuance of a confiscation order where there are reasonable grounds for doing so.

In addition, there are also provisions in *Jersey* to provide for **the civil forfeiture of terrorist cash**.

2.7 The criminal liability of legal entities

The offences of money laundering and terrorist financing may be committed by both legal entities and natural persons by virtue of Article 3 of the *Interpretation (Jersey) Law 1954*.

Also, under Article 37(5) of the *Proceeds of Crime Law* and Article 63 of the *Terrorism Law*, where an offence is committed by a legal entity, such as failure to comply with the *Money Laundering Order*, and is proved to have been committed with the consent or connivance of, or to be attributable to any neglect on the part of, a partner, director, manager, secretary or other similar officer of the legal entity, the person shall also be guilty of the offence.

2.8 Implementation of specific international sanctions

2.8.1 United Nations (UN) sanctions

UN Security Council Resolution 1267 (1999) (and its successor resolutions – *1333 (2000), 1363 (2001)*, and *1390 (2002)*) has been enacted in *Jersey* through the *Al-Qa'ida and Taliban (United Nations Measures) (Channel Islands) Order 2002*.

The *Al-Qa'ida and Taliban (United Nations Measures) (Channel Islands) Order 2002* contains the following offences:

- Making funds available to Usama bin Laden and any person designated by the *UN Sanctions Committee* under *UN Security Council Resolution 1390* (*a listed person*).

- **Failing to disclose information** which causes an institution to know or suspect that a customer or person with whom it has had dealings is a listed person or person acting on behalf of a listed person, or has committed an offence of making funds available to a listed person.

UN Security Council Resolution 1373 has been enacted in *Jersey* through the *Terrorism (United Nations Measures) (Channel Islands) Order 2001*.

The *Terrorism (United Nations Measures) (Channel Islands) Order 2001* contains the following relevant offences:

- **Receiving funds** and intending that they should be used, or knowing or having reasonable cause to suspect that they may be used, for the purposes of terrorism.

- **Making any funds or financial services available** to, or for the benefit of, persons who commit terrorism, control persons who commit terrorism, or act on behalf of persons who commit terrorism, other than under the authority of a licence granted by *Jersey's Chief Minister*.

- **Failing to disclose information** which causes an institution to know or suspect that a customer or person with whom it has had dealings is a person who commits, or attempts to commit an act of terrorism, or who participates in terrorism or has committed an act of terrorism.

2.8.2 Financial Action Task Force (FATF) measures

FATF Recommendation 21 calls on countries to apply appropriate countermeasures to countries that do not apply or insufficiently apply the *FATF* Recommendations.

Where the *FATF* recommends that its members should implement appropriate countermeasures, the *Commission* supports these measures through the *Guidance Notes*.

3 Money Laundering Order

3.1 Overview

Article 2 of the *Money Laundering Order* provides that no person shall, in the course of any financial services business (defined later) carried on, form a business relationship or carry out a one-off transaction unless the person carrying on such business maintains:

- identification procedures;

- record-keeping procedures;

- internal reporting procedures (including the appointment of a reporting officer); and

- such other procedures of internal control and communication as may be appropriate for the purposes of forestalling and preventing money laundering and terrorist financing.

The *Money Laundering Order* also requires appropriate measures to be taken for the purposes of making employees aware of these procedures and enactments relating to money laundering and terrorist financing, and to train employees in the recognition and handling of transactions carried out by or on behalf of any person who is or appears to be engaged in money laundering or terrorist financing.

3.2   Prospects

A number of amendments to the *Money Laundering Order* are under consideration as part of *Jersey's* **response to changes in international standards**. In particular, it is intended that the successor to the *Money Laundering Order* should provide for:

- The application of **a risk-based approach to customer due diligence measures**, and for such measures to clearly extend beyond identification procedures.

- **Clearer identification procedures** to be conducted where an applicant for business or customer is not an individual.

- **Evidence of identity to be reviewed** in cases where a financial services business knows or suspects that a customer is engaged in money laundering or terrorist financing, or where a business knows or suspects that the evidence that it holds is not satisfactory.

- **The appointment of a money laundering compliance officer**, who will be responsible to the business' management for monitoring compliance with requirements to prevent and detect money laundering and terrorist financing, and will be required to be registered with the *Commission*.

- **Maintenance of procedures** that monitor and test the effectiveness of procedures and training.

In addition, it is intended that the successor to the *Money Laundering Order* should more adequately provide for the circumstances in which **it should be possible to rely on another financial services business to have conducted some elements of customer due diligence measures**.

4   Scope of application of the Money Laundering Order

4.1   Schedule 2 to the Proceeds of Crime Law

Special obligations are placed on persons that conduct '**financial services business**'. What is financial services business is set out in Schedule 2 to the *Proceeds of Crime Law*.

Schedule 2 to the *Proceeds of Crime Law* defines financial services business activity as being:

- Any deposit-taking business, as defined in Article 1(1) of the *Banking Business (Jersey) Law 1991 (Banking Business Law)*.

- Any insurance business to which Article 5 of the *Insurance Business (Jersey) Law 1996 (Insurance Business Law)* applies.

- The business of being a functionary of a collective investment fund, as defined in Article 1(1) of the *Collective Investment Funds (Jersey) Law 1988 (Funds Law)*.

- Any investment business as defined in Article 1(1) of the *Financial Services (Jersey) Law 1998 (Financial Services Law)*.

- The business of providing trusteeship services (not being services as a trustee of an occupational pension scheme).

- The business of company formation.

- The business of company administration.

- The business of a bureau de change.

- The business of providing cheque cashing services.

- The business of transmitting or receiving money or any representation of monetary value by any means.

- The business of engaging in any of the activities within the meaning of the Annex to the *Second Banking Coordination Directive (No. 89/646/EEC)* (not being a business specified above, including lending and financial leasing). A full list of such activities can be found on www.jerseylegalinfo.je.

4.2   Prospects

Jersey is currently considering **how to implement *FATF* Recommendations 12 and 16**, which extend requirements to have procedures and measures to 'designated non-financial businesses and professions'. This includes real estate agents, accountants, and lawyers.

5   Obligations imposed on financial services businesses

5.1   Obligation to have procedures of internal control and communication

As already noted, Article 2 of the *Money Laundering Order* provides that no person shall, in the course of any financial services business carried on, form a business relationship or carry out a one-off transaction unless the person carrying on such business maintains certain procedures and takes certain measures. In addition, Article 2(1)(a)(iv) of the *Money Laundering Order* requires a financial services business to have such other procedures of internal control and communication as may be appropriate for the purposes of forestalling, detecting and preventing money laundering.

On 27 January 2006, the *Court of Appeal* upheld a decision made by the *Royal Court* to convict persons for failing to comply with Article 2(1)(a) of the *Money Laundering Order*. The *Court of Appeal* agreed that **the obligation under Article 2(1)(a), to maintain procedures for the purposes prescribed in the *Money Laundering Order*, is an absolute one** and the ruling makes it clear that even a single breach is enough to constitute an offence.

The *Commission's* view is that this case emphasises the importance for financial services businesses to maintain adequate procedures to combat money laundering on an ongoing basis.

5.1.1 Verification of identity of the applicant for business and any parties on whose behalf the applicant acts

Article 2(1)(a) of the *Money Laundering Order* requires a financial services business to establish and maintain customer identification procedures that involve identification and verification of identity in order to form a business relationship or carry out a one off transaction.

Specific requirements for customer identification procedures are contained within Articles 3 to 7 of the *Money Laundering Order*. In particular, Article 5 of the *Money Laundering Order* provides that such procedures must require 'reasonable measures' to be taken for the purpose of establishing the identity of any person on whose behalf an applicant for business is acting, and Article 6 says that identification procedures need not be adopted in certain cases.

Under Article 5, where an applicant for business is a trustee, reasonable measures will generally mean being able to rely on a written assurance from a trustee that: (i) is prudentially supervised; and (ii) located in a country that is considered to have legislation in place to counter money laundering and terrorist financing that is considered to be equivalent to *Jersey's*; (*an equivalent jurisdiction*). Such an assurance must include confirmation that the trustee is aware of the true identity of the underlying principals, i.e. settlors/named beneficiaries, and that there are no anonymous principals. The *Guidance Notes* provide that, ideally, the identity of the underlying principals, in particular those who are supplying and have control over the funds, should be disclosed by the trustee to the business establishing the relationship with the trustee, and the written assurance provided be supported by copies of the documentary evidence of identity held by the trustee.

Where a **trustee** is not regulated or is not based in an equivalent jurisdiction, the *Guidance Notes* state that the identity of the settlor and all of the named beneficiaries should be ascertained by the business establishing the relationship with the trustee.

Inter alia, Article 6 of the *Money Laundering Order* does not require identification procedures to be conducted where there are reasonable grounds for believing that the applicant for business is itself a financial services business in *Jersey* that is bound by the *Money Laundering Order* or is a person covered by the *European Union* Money Laundering Directive (i.e. any member of the *European Economic Area*). This concession is interpreted as extending to establishing the identity of any person on whose behalf the applicant for business is acting, and is relevant to trustees that are supervised by the *Commission*.

5.1.2 Verification of identity in the case of an applicant that is not an individual

Article 3 of the *Money Laundering Order* requires the production by an applicant for business of satisfactory evidence of identity, or the taking of such measures, specified in procedures, as will produce satisfactory evidence of identity.

In the case of an applicant for business that is not an individual, the *Guidance Notes* set out procedures to be applied to identify and verify the identity of the beneficial owners and controllers of the applicant.

5.1.3 Verification of identity in the case of business that is introduced by another financial services business

Article 3 is also relevant in the case of business that it introduced to a financial services business by another financial services business.

In the case of an applicant for business that it introduced by another financial services business, then the *Guidance Notes* provide that, where that other financial services business is: (i) regulated; and (ii) located in *Jersey* or an equivalent jurisdiction, then it will be possible to rely upon a certificate of introduction from that other business, and will not be necessary to duplicate identification procedures.

5.1.4 Obligation to draw up and retain documents

Article 8(1)(a) of the *Money Laundering Order* requires a financial services business to make and retain the following records:

- copies of evidence of identity obtained in accordance with Articles 3 or 5; or

- information as to where a copy of the evidence can be obtained; or

- sufficient information as to enable the details of a person's identity to be re-obtained, but only where it is not reasonably practicable to either obtain a copy of the evidence, or to retain information as to where a copy can be obtained.

Article 8(2) requires a financial services business to retain records in relation to evidence of identity for at least five years from the end of a relationship with a customer (or completion of a one-off transaction).

Article 8(1)(b) also requires a financial services business to make and retain a record containing details of every transaction carried out with or for a customer in the course of financial services business. Under Article 8(2), records relating to transactions must be held for at least five years from the date when all activities relating to the transaction were completed.

5.1.5 Training and awareness

Article 2(1)(b) requires that a financial services business must, in relation to employees whose duties relate to the provision of financial services:

- Take appropriate measures from time to time for the purposes of making them aware of: the identification, record keeping and internal reporting procedures, and such other procedures of internal control and communication as may be appropriate for the purposes of forestalling and preventing money laundering or terrorist financing; and the enactments in *Jersey* relating to money laundering and terrorist financing.

- Provide those employees from time to time with training in the recognition and handling of transactions carried out by, or on behalf of, any person who is or appears to be engaged in money laundering or terrorist financing.

5.2 Reporting procedures

Article 9 requires that a financial services business must establish and maintain reporting procedures which:

- Identify a person to whom a report is to be made – a money laundering reporting officer (*MLRO*).

- Require that a report is made of any information or other matter coming to the attention of any member of staff in the course of their business activity which, in the opinion of that person, gives rise to knowledge or suspicion that another person is engaged in money laundering or terrorist financing.

- Require that a report is considered by the MLRO (or by another designated person) in the light of all other relevant information for the purpose of determining whether or not the information or other matter contained in the report gives rise to knowledge or suspicion of money laundering or terrorist financing.

- Allow the MLRO (or a designated person) to have reasonable access to other information which may be of assistance in considering the report.

- Ensure that the information or other matter contained in a report is disclosed as soon as is reasonably practicable by the MLRO (or designated person) to a police officer, where the MLRO (or designated person) knows or suspects that another person is engaged in money laundering or terrorist financing.

5.3   Guidance Notes

This *Guidance Notes* are issued by the *Commission* pursuant to its powers under Article 8 of the *Financial Services Commission (Jersey) Law 1998* and in the light of provisions of Article 37 of the *Proceeds of Crime Law* and Article 23(6) of the *Terrorism Law*, which anticipate that anti-money laundering and counter-terrorist financing procedures will be prescribed for persons carrying on financial services business.

Failure to comply with the *Money Laundering Order* is a criminal offence under Article 37(4) of the *Proceeds of Crime Law*. In determining whether a financial services business has complied with any of the requirements of the *Money Laundering Order*, the *Royal Court* is, pursuant to Article 37(8) of the *Proceeds of Crime Law*, required to take account of the *Guidance Notes*, as amended from time to time.

Similarly, in determining whether a person has committed an offence under Article 23 of the *Terrorism Law* (the offence of failing to report), the *Royal Court* is required to take account of the *Guidance Notes*.

6   Supervision for compliance with requirements to prevent and detect money laundering or terrorist financing

6.1   Role of the Commission

Compliance with the *Money Laundering Order* and *Guidance Notes* is considered by the *Commission* in the conduct of its supervisory examinations of operators of collective investment schemes, deposit-takers, insurance businesses, investment businesses, and trust company businesses.

The ability of a supervised financial services business to demonstrate compliance with the *Money Laundering Order* and *Guidance Notes* will therefore be directly relevant to its supervised status and the *Commission's* assessment of the fitness and propriety of its principals.

Non-compliance with the *Guidance Notes* may be regarded by the *Commission* as an indication of:

- conduct that is not in the best economic interests of *Jersey* under Article 6 of the *Funds Law*;

- improper conduct under Article 10 of the *Banking Business Law*;

- improper conduct under Article 7 of the *Insurance Business Law*;

- a lack of fitness and propriety under Article 9 of the *Financial Services Law*; and/or

- a failure to comply with certain fundamental principles within the *Insurance Business Codes of Practice* issued pursuant to the *Insurance Business Law*, and the *Trust Company Business* and *Investment Business Codes of Practice* issued pursuant to the *Financial Services Law*.

6.2   Examination visits

The *Commission* conducts three types of examination visit: discovery; risk-themed; and focused. The aim of the *Commission* in conducting risk-themed examinations is to concentrate on a specific area of conduct across a segment of the industry. For example, in 2005, the chosen theme for trust company businesses supervised under the *Financial Services Law* was risk management systems and controls as they relate to the underlying customer base of such businesses. Examinations encompassed an assessment of written risk management policies and procedures and *Commission* officers reviewed, on a sample basis, customer records and files, and held discussions with management and staff involved in operational and compliance matters. Results were then measured against each business' written procedures and what might be considered best practice in this area. The results of this review have been published.

Focused examinations involve the preparation of a self-assessment questionnaire by the business. This questionnaire is intended to provide an overview of a supervised financial services business and the functions that it carries out. Inter alia, the questionnaire used for the examination of trust company businesses requests information on:

- Compliance and risk structure.

- Anti-money laundering training delivered to new and existing members of staff.

- Reviews undertaken by the compliance function, and their frequency.

- Any accounts or customers that are subject to sanctions.

- Suspicious activity reports made to the police and internal reports that did not result in such a report.

The questionnaire also requires a copy of procedures, compliance and money laundering manuals to be provided to the *Commission*.

6.3   Breaches of Money Laundering Order detected by Commission

The present policy of the *Commission* is that, if it should come across an apparent breach of the *Money Laundering Order* in the course of its supervision, including as a result of an onsite examination, the *Commission* will refer it to the *Attorney General* if the breach is considered to be sufficiently serious. It should be stressed, however, that a decision on whether to prosecute a breach of the *Money Laundering Order* will be a matter solely for the *Attorney General*.

The *Commission* will generally regard a breach of the *Money Laundering Order* as sufficiently serious to the extent that it poses a threat to clients or potential clients or to the reputation of the Island and/or where it casts doubt on the integrity, competence or financial standing of the person concerned. It will also be relevant if the breach was deliberate or premeditated rather than accidental, or if the person (individual or body corporate) has failed to report a material breach to the *Commission*.

Failure, inability or refusal to cooperate with the *Commission* to rectify a breach, and a history of past breaches or poor regulatory compliance (which may give grounds to believe that the breach is likely to be repeated and/or is part of a systemic failure), will also be taken into account.

Such a referral took place in 2005, following an examination of a trust company business. The business concerned and one of its directors were ultimately prosecuted, convicted and fined.

The above list of relevant factors is not intended to be exhaustive. But it should be enough to indicate that **referrals to the *Attorney General* by the *Commission* will be judged on their merits on a case-by-case basis** and will not be made on every occasion a breach of the *Money Laundering Order* is identified.

Supervised financial services businesses and their directors should however be in no doubt that they put themselves at potential risk if they do not take adequate steps to ensure that they are compliant with the *Money Laundering Order*. In assessing their compliance with the *Money Laundering Order* they should pay close attention to the *Guidance Notes*.

6.4   Role of the Joint Financial Crimes Unit (JFCU)

Under Article 10 of the *Money Laundering Order*, where the *Commission* (and any person acting in the course of any investigation under regulatory legislation) obtains any information and is of the opinion that the information indicates that any person has, or may have, been engaged in money laundering or terrorist financing, then the *Commission* must disclose that information to a police officer – in practice the *JFCU*–as soon as is reasonably practicable.

The *Commission* also works closely with the *JFCU* at operational level. For example, where a suspicious activity report raises issues at a particular financial services business, then the *JFCU* will discuss those issues with the *Commission*, which will then take appropriate action. Periodically, the *JFCU* also provides details to the *Commission* of those businesses that have failed to submit any suspicious activity reports.

6.5   Prospects

Whilst the most significant part of *Jersey's* finance industry – operators of collective investment schemes, deposit-takers, insurance businesses, investment businesses, and trust company businesses – is overseen for compliance with obligations to prevent and detect money laundering and terrorist financing, there are currently no provisions in place to provide for the oversight of other types of financial services business.

In line with *FATF* Recommendations 23 and 24, consideration will be given as to how *Jersey* might extend its regime for overseeing compliance with special obligations to counter money laundering and terrorist financing to include all financial services business. Plans are already well developed for money services businesses – those in the business of a bureau de change, the business of providing cheque cashing services, or the business of transmitting or receiving money or any representation of monetary value by any means.

7 Law enforcement

7.1 The JFCU

The *JFCU* is a partnership between *the States of Jersey Police Force* and the *States of Jersey Customs and Excise Department*. The *JFCU* receives all suspicious activity reports, maintains *Jersey's* financial intelligence system, and conducts money laundering and terrorist financing investigations.

In 2005, the *JFCU* received 1162 suspicious activity reports (three year average: 1378), and 362 requests for assistance from other jurisdictions (three year average: 488).

7.2 The Law Officers' Department

The *Law Officers' Department* includes Her Majesty's *Attorney General* and Her Majesty's *Solicitor General*.

The *Attorney General* heads the *Law Officers' Department*, and is *Jersey's* senior prosecutor and legal advisor to the government. Inter alia, he has statutory powers for the investigation of fraud, and persecutory powers in respect of money laundering and terrorist financing offences and confiscation. His office acts as the central authority in mutual assistance matters.

8 International co-operation

8.1 Commitment

Jersey places immense importance on providing assistance to other jurisdictions in the fight against crime, and has developed a large arsenal of powers to help foreign authorities.

The *JFCU* is a member of the *Egmont Group* and the *Commission* has concluded a number of bilateral memoranda of understanding with overseas financial services regulators, as well as being a signatory to the *International Organisation of Securities Commissions'* multilateral memorandum of understanding.

8.2 Assistance that can be given

Jersey can provide most forms of **legal assistance** to all countries. However under legislation used to freeze and confiscate proceeds of crime, not every country or territory can currently be assisted. That said, *Jersey* is able to assist around 150 states in respect of the proceeds of drug trafficking and around 40 states in respect of the proceeds of crime.

Legal assistance available includes powers to:

- Ask questions and obtain documents in cases of serious or complex fraud – through the *Investigation of Fraud (Jersey) Law 1991*.

- Obtain documents and witness statements for formal evidence with the option to cross examine witnesses under oath through the *Evidence (Proceedings in Other Jurisdictions) (Jersey) Order 1983* and *the Criminal Justice (International Co-operation) (Jersey) Law 2001 (Criminal Justice Law)*.

- Freeze and confiscate the proceeds of crime and terrorist financing through the *Proceeds of Crime Law*, the *Drug Trafficking Offences Law*, the *Criminal Justice Law* and the *Terrorism Law*.

- Obtain documents (together with search and seizure powers) through the *Proceeds of Crime Law*, the *Drug Trafficking Offences Law*, the *Criminal Justice Law* and the *Terrorism Law*.

Address

Jersey Financial Services Commission
P.O. Box 267
Nelson House
David Place
St Helier
Jersey
Channel Islands
JE4 8TP
Contact person: Andrew Le Brun
a.lebrun@jerseyfsc.org

The *Jersey Financial Services Commission* is responsible for the regulation, supervision and development of the financial services industry in *Jersey*.

The Commission is a statutory body corporate, set up under the *Financial Services Commission (Jersey) Law 1998*.

Abbreviations

Banking Business Law	Banking Business (Jersey) Law 1991
Commission	Jersey Financial Services Commission
Criminal Justice Law	Criminal Justice (International Co-operation) (Jersey) Law 2001
Drug Trafficking Offences Law	Drug Trafficking Offences (Jersey) Law 1988
Equivalent jurisdiction	A country that has legislation in place to counter money laundering and terrorist financing that is considered to be equivalent to Jersey's
FATF	Financial Action Task Force
Financial Services Law	Financial Services (Jersey) Law 1998
Funds Law	Collective Investment Funds (Jersey) Law 1988
Guidance Notes	Anti-Money Laundering Guidance Notes for the Finance Sector
Insurance Business Law	Insurance Business (Jersey) Law 1996
JFCU	Joint Financial Crimes Unit (Jersey's financial intelligence unit)
Listed person	any person designated by the UN Sanctions Committee under UN Security Council Resolution 1390
Money Laundering Order	Money Laundering (Jersey) Order 1999
MLRO	Money Laundering Reporting Officer

Proceeds of Crime Law	Proceeds of Crime (Jersey) Law 1999
Terrorism Law	Terrorism (Jersey) Law 2002
UN	United Nations

Bibliography

Bazley, J./Winch, D.: Money Laundering for Lawyers, LexisNexis Butterworths, 2004.

Biggs, S./Farrell, S./Padfield, N.: The Proceeds of Crime Act 2002, Butterworths LexisNexis, 2002.

Clark, A./Burrell, P.: A Practitioner's Guide to International Money Laundering Law and Regulation, City & Financial Publishing, Old Woking, 2003.

Graham, T.: Butterworths International Guide to Money Laundering Law and Practice, Butterworths LexisNexis, 2003.

How to Combat Money Laundering and Terrorist Financing, Central Banking Publications, London, 2005

IMF and World Bank: Reference Guide to Anti-Money Laundering and Combating the Financing of Terrorism, IBRD and World Bank, Washington, 2004.

IMF and World Bank Group: Financial Intelligence Units – An Overview, IMF, Washington, 2004.

Jersey Financial Services Commission: Draft Handbook for the Prevention and Detection of Money Laundering and the Financing of Terrorism, Jersey, May 2006.

Legal Department – IMF: Suppressing the Financing of Terrorism, IMF, Washington, 2003.

Mark Gerard Ferbrache read law at Cambridge University. He was called to the Bar of England and Wales in 1987 and the Guernsey Bar in 1988. Since 2002 he was head of litigation at another leading Guernsey firm, specializing in international commercial disputes including freezing orders and asset tracing. He regularly advises in relation to complex trust, banking and insurance disputes. His clients include the Guernsey Financial Services Commission. Recent cases include representation of the administrators of Messenger Insurance PCC Ltd. This is the first ever administration of a PCC. This litigation was the largest piece of litigation in both Guernsey and the High Court in 2005/2006. He also advised the Royal Bank of Scotland International in the Equatorial Guinea case which went to the Privy Council. He is a member of: Society of Trust and Estate Practitioners (committee member); Association of Contentious Trust and Probate Specialists; Guernsey Bar sub-committee on trusts; Fiduciary Sector Policy Forum (committee member); Royal Court Civil Procedure Review Committee.

Firm's profile

Ferbrache Richardson Advocates is one of the leading firms in the Channel Islands providing a comprehensive range of legal services to both private individuals and the international business community. We are often at the forefront of innovations in Guernsey Law. The firm represents a wide variety of international institutions and businesses including clearing and investment banks, insurance companies, investment and fiduciary businesses. It also advises and assists lawyers in other jurisdictions on matters of Guernsey law on a daily basis.

Guernsey

Mark G. Ferbrache

Partner

Ferbrache Richardson, Advocates

Le Neuve Charterie
Le Frie-au-Four
St Saviours
Guernsey, GY7 9TG
Channel Islands

Tel +44 1481 723 191 (switchboard)
    +44 1418 734 217 (direct)
Fax +44 1481 700 171 (direct)
ferbrache@guernsey.net

Anti-Money Laundering: International Law and Practice.
Edited by W.H. Muller, C.H. Kälin and J.G. Goldsworth
© 2007 John Wiley & Sons, Ltd

Contents – Guernsey

1   Background

1.1   Introduction

The *Bailiwick of Guernsey's* finance industry is the *Bailiwick's* largest employer and primary generator of income. It enjoys a good international reputation as a modern, well-regulated jurisdiction. To ensure this continues, *Guernsey* has enacted very comprehensive anti-money laundering legislation.

1.2   The Bailiwick

The *Bailiwick* consists of *Guernsey, Alderney* and *Sark*, and several smaller islands. Of these, *Guernsey* is the largest. The majority of the offshore financial business is conducted in *Guernsey*.

The *Bailiwick* has an unusual constitutional status, most particularly with regard to the *European Community*. The islands are dependencies of the British Crown but not part of the *United Kingdom*. Whilst the British Crown bears ultimate responsibility for the good government of the *Bailiwick, Guernsey, Alderney* and *Sark* all have their own elected governments. The *UK* government is responsible for the *Bailiwick's* international relations and for its defense, but does not seek to bind the constituent islands of the *Bailiwick* to international treaties without their prior consent. Although *Guernsey* is neither a separate Member State nor an Associate Member of the *European Community*, *Article 1* of *Protocol No 3* placed the *Channel Islands* within the *Common Customs Area* and *Common External Tariff* of the *European Community*. *Guernsey* ensures that it develops its procedures and regulations consistent with the *European Community* in the area of trade. It also co-ordinates its legislation in matters of immigration.

2   Money laundering legislation

2.1   Point of reference

The *Bailiwick's* anti-money laundering regime comprises various laws, regulations and guidance notes, which are set out in chronological order for the sake of convenience. A good point of reference is the **Guernsey Financial Services Commission's** website: www.gfsc.gg

2.2   Primary legislation

The Criminal Justice (Fraud Investigation) (Bailiwick of Guernsey) Law 1991

The Money Laundering (Disclosure of Information) (Guernsey) Law 1995

The Money Laundering (Disclosure of Information) (Alderney) Law 1998

The Criminal Justice (Proceeds of Crime) (Bailiwick of Guernsey) Law 1999

The Drug Trafficking (Bailiwick of Guernsey) Law 2000

The Criminal Justice (International Co-operation) (Bailiwick of Guernsey) Law 2001

The Terrorism (United Nations Measures) (Channel Islands) Order 2001

The Money Laundering (Disclosure of Information) (Sark) Law 2001

The Al-Qa'ida and Taliban (United Nations Measures) (Channel Islands) Order 2002

The Terrorism and Crime (Bailiwick of Guernsey) Law 2002

2.3 Secondary legislation

The Criminal Justice (Proceeds of Crime) (Bailiwick of Guernsey) (Enforcement of Overseas Confiscation Orders) Ordinance 1999

The Drug Trafficking (Bailiwick of Guernsey) Law (Enforcement of External Forfeiture Orders) Ordinance 2000

The Drug Trafficking (Bailiwick of Guernsey) Law (Designated Countries and Territories) Ordinance 2000

The Royal Court (International Co-operation) Rules 2002

The Drug Trafficking (Designated Countries and Territories) (Amendment) Ordinance 2002

The Criminal Justice (Proceeds of Crime) (Enforcement of Overseas Confiscation Orders) (Amendment) Ordinance 2002

The Criminal Justice (Proceeds of Crime) (Bailiwick of Guernsey) Regulations 2002

2.4 Codes of Practice/Guidance Notes

The Guernsey Financial Services Commission Codes of Practice for Corporate Service Providers, Trust Service Providers and Company Directors 2001

The Guernsey Financial Services Commission Guidance Notes on the Prevention of Money Laundering and Countering the Financing of Terrorism 2002

3 Money laundering and terrorist fund related offences

3.1 Applicable legislation

Money laundering ('ML') offences are created by the ***Criminal Justice (Proceeds of Crime) (Bailiwick of Guernsey) Law 1999*** ('*the 1999 Criminal Justice Law*'), ***Drug Trafficking (Bailiwick of Guernsey) Law 2000*** ('*the 2000 Drug Trafficking Law*') and ***Terrorism and Crime (Bailiwick of Guernsey) Law 2002*** ('*the 2002 Terrorism and Crime Law*'). Terrorism related offences are created by the ***Terrorism (United Nations Measures) (Channel Islands) Order 2001*** and ***Terrorism and Crime (Bailiwick of Guernsey) Law 2002***. The specific offences and selected defenses are set out in more detail below:

3.2 The Criminal Justice (Proceeds of Crime) Bailiwick of Guernsey Law 1999

The *1999 Criminal Justice Law* creates three offences in relation to the proceeds of **criminal conduct**:

3.2.1 Concealing or transferring the proceeds of criminal conduct

Under *s. 38*, a person is guilty of this offence if he:

i. conceals or disguises any property which is, in whole or in part directly or indirectly represents, their own or another's proceeds of **criminal conduct**; or

ii. converts or transfers that property or removes it from the *Bailiwick,*

for the purpose of avoiding the prosecution of themselves or another for **criminal conduct** or the making or enforcement in their case, or the case of another, of a **confiscation order**.

3.2.2   Assisting another person to retain the proceeds of criminal conduct

Under *s. 39*, a person is guilty of this offence if he enters into or is otherwise concerned in an arrangement whereby:

i. the retention or control by or on behalf of another (called in this Law 'A') of A's proceeds of **criminal conduct** is facilitated (whether by concealment, removal from the *Bailiwick*, transfer to nominees or otherwise); or

ii. A's proceeds of **criminal conduct**: are used to secure that funds are placed at A's disposal; or are used for A's benefit to acquire property by way of investment,

knowing or suspecting that A is or has been engaged in **criminal conduct** or has benefited from **criminal conduct**.

3.2.3   Acquisition, possession or use of the proceeds of criminal conduct

Under *s. 40*, a person is guilty of an offence if, knowing that any property is, in whole or in part directly or indirectly represents, another's proceeds of **criminal conduct**, he acquires or uses that property or otherwise has possession of it. It is a defense to show that the person who either acquired the property or had possession of it has given adequate (valuable) consideration.

3.3   Criminal conduct

Criminal conduct' is defined as any conduct, other than drug trafficking (which is covered by the *2000 Drug Trafficking Law*), which constitutes a criminal offence under the laws of the *Bailiwick* and is triable on indictment or which would constitute such an offence if it were to take place in the *Bailiwick*. Thus, it is irrelevant whether the conduct is criminal in the jurisdiction in which it was committed.

3.4   Offence under ss. 39 or 40 of the 1999 Criminal Justice Law

A person will not commit an offence, notwithstanding that his conduct would otherwise constitute an offence under *ss. 39* or *40* of the *1999 Criminal Justice Law*, if: (a) he discloses his knowledge or suspicion to a police officer before he does the relevant act; and (b) the act is done with the consent of the police officer; or (c) the **disclosure** is made after he does the act, but is made on his own initiative and as soon as it is reasonable for them to make it. An employee may instead make the **disclosure** to the appropriate person under his employer's internal reporting procedures (as required by the *2002 Regulations* and the *Guernsey Financial Services Commission* ('*the GFSC*') *Guidance Notes on the Prevention of Money Laundering and Countering the Financing of Terrorism 2002* ('*the Guidance Notes*')).

3.5   The Drug Trafficking (Bailiwick of Guernsey) Law 2000

The *2000 Drug Trafficking Law* creates three offences in connection with the proceeds of drug trafficking:

* Concealing or transferring the proceeds of drug trafficking (s. *57*);

* Assisting another person to retain the benefit of drug trafficking (s. *58*); and

* Acquisition, possession or use of the proceeds of drug trafficking (s. *59*).

These offences are substantively the same as the equivalent offences under the *1999 Criminal Justice Law*, save that they solely relate to the proceeds of drug trafficking.

3.6 The Terrorism (United Nations Measures) (Channel Islands) Order 2001

The Terrorism (United Nations Measures) (Channel Islands) Order 2001 creates five offences in relation to **terrorist funds**:

3.6.1 Collection of funds

Under *Article 4*, it is an offence to knowingly or with reasonable cause to suspect solicit, receive or provide funds for the purpose of **terrorism**.

3.6.2 Making funds available

Under *Article 5*, it is an offence to make funds available to **terrorists**, persons or entities owned or controlled by **terrorists**, or persons or entities acting on their behalf, without a **license** granted by **HM Procureur** (the *Guernsey* equivalent of HM Attorney General).

3.6.3 Breach of freezing order

Under *Article 6*, it is an offence to make funds available in breach of a **freezing order** granted by **HM Procureur**.

3.6.4 Facilitation offences

Under *Article 7*, it is an offence knowingly to facilitate the commission of any of the above offences.

3.6.5 Offences in connection with licenses

Under *Article 8*, it is an offence: (a) knowingly or recklessly to supply false information for the purpose of obtaining a **license**; or (b) having obtained a **license**, to act in breach of any conditions attached thereto.

3.7 The Terrorism and Crime (Bailiwick of Guernsey) Law, 2002

The *2002 Terrorism and Crime Law* creates five offences in connection with **terrorist funds**:

3.7.1 Fund raising

Under *s. 8*, it is an offence to receive or provide, or invite another to provide, money or other property for the purposes of **terrorism**. A person is required to intend (in the case of receiving or inviting another to provide) or know (in the case of providing), or have reasonable cause to suspect, that the property will or may be used for such a purpose.

3.7.2 Use and possession

Under *s. 9*, it is an offence to possess money or other property for the purposes of **terrorism**. A person is required to intend or have reasonable cause to suspect that the property should or may be used for such a purpose.

3.7.3 Funding arrangements

Under *s. 10*, it is an offence to enter into or become concerned in an arrangement as a result of which money or other property is or is to be made available to another for the purposes of **terrorism**. A person is required to know or have reasonable cause to suspect that the property will or may be used for such a purpose.

3.7.4 Money laundering

Under *s. 11*, it is an offence to enter into or become concerned in an arrangement which facilitates the retention or control of **terrorist property** by or on behalf of another. A person is required to know or have reasonable cause to suspect that the arrangement related to **terrorist property**.

3.7.5 Breach of freezing order

Under *Schedule 4 paragraph 7*, it is an offence to fail to comply with a **freezing order** made by the *States Advisory and Finance Committee* or to engage in an activity knowing or intending that it will enable or facilitate the commission by another of such offence. It is a defense if a person proves that they did not know and had no reasonable cause to suppose that they were in breach of such prohibition.

3.8 Disclosure of suspicion

A person will not commit an offence, notwithstanding that his conduct would otherwise constitute any of the above offences under the *2002 Terrorism and Crime Law*, if: (a) they are acting with the consent of a police officer; or (b) after becoming involved in a transaction relating to money or other property, they disclose their suspicion or belief that the money or other property is **terrorist property** to a police officer. An employee may instead make the **disclosure** under his employer's internal reporting procedures.

3.9 The Criminal Justice (Proceeds of Crime) (Bailiwick of Guernsey) Regulations 2002

The *2002 Regulations* were issued pursuant to the *1999 Criminal Justice Law*. They relate solely to financial services businesses. 'Financial services businesses' (singularly, '*FSB*') include businesses providing a wide range of financial and credit services. However, the *2002 Regulations* do not cover circumstances where such services are provided by lawyers, accountants and actuaries and are incidental to the provision of legal, accounting or actuarial services.

3.10 Key features of the 2002 Regulations

The key features of the *2002 Regulations* are that they require any person carrying on an *FSB* in the *Bailiwick* to:

- establish and maintain identification, record keeping and internal reporting procedures in relation to the **FSB**;

- ensure that employees whose duties relate to financial services business are aware of the above procedures and the relevant laws; and

- provide key staff, i.e. all those who deal with customers/clients or their transactions, with comprehensive training in the relevant laws, their personal obligations under the laws, and the anti-ML and anti-financing of **terrorism** policies and procedures in place in the **FSB**.

3.11 The Guernsey Financial Services Commission Guidance Notes on the Prevention of Money Laundering and Countering the Financing of Terrorism 2002

*The **Guidance Notes*** were issued by the ***GFSC*** to assist financial services businesses to comply with the requirements of the relevant laws. *The **Guidance Notes*** state that the court may take account of *the **Guidance Notes*** in any proceedings brought under the relevant laws or in determining whether a person has complied with the requirements of the ***2002 Regulations***, and that they are a statement of the standard expected by the ***GFSC*** of **all** ***FSB***s in the *Bailiwick*. Compliance is therefore essential.

3.12 The Duty of Vigilance/Internal Reporting Procedures

FSBs should be constantly vigilant in deterring criminals from making use of them for the purpose of ML. The duty of **vigilance** consists mainly of the following five elements, which are dealt with in greater detail below:

- Verification

- Recognition of suspicious customers/transactions

- Reporting of suspicion

- Keeping of records, and

- Training.

Each ***FSB*** must have in place systems which enables it to:

- determine (or receive confirmation of) the true identity of customers requesting their services

- recognize and report suspicious transaction to the *Financial Intelligence Service* (***'FIS'***)

- keep records for the prescribed period of time

- train key staff

- liaise closely with the ***FIS*** and the ***GFSC*** on matters concerning **vigilance** policy and systems and

- ensure that internal audit and compliance departments regularly monitor the implementation and operation of **vigilance** systems.

FSBs must appoint a money laundering reporting officer (***'MLRO'***). The ***MLRO*** should be a senior member of staff with the necessary responsibility to ensure compliance with *the **Guidance Notes*** and who has responsibility for **vigilance** policy and for dealing with reports of suspicious transactions.

FSBs should ensure that 'key staff' know to whom their suspicions of **criminal conduct** should be reported and that there is a clear procedure for reporting such suspicions without delay to the *MLRO*. It is for the *MLRO* to investigate the suspicious transaction. If, following that investigation, the *MLRO* remains suspicious, it should promptly submit a report to the *FIS*.

3.13   Verification (know your customer)

An *FSB* should establish to its reasonable satisfaction that every person whose identity needs to be verified actually exists (save for a small number of exceptions). Guidance is given as to the application of this principle to individuals, partnerships, companies (including corporate trustees), other institutions and intermediaries. However, the exact standard of **due diligence** will depend on the exact nature of the relationship and *the Guidance Notes* do not specify what constitutes sufficient evidence of identity.

3.14   Recognition of suspicious customers/transactions

A suspicious transaction will often be one which is inconsistent with a customer's known legitimate business or activities, or with the normal business for that type of financial services product. It follows, therefore, that the *FSB* should know enough about the customer's business to recognize that a transaction, or a series of transactions, is unusual.

3.15   Keeping of records

*FSB*s should:

- retain each original customer verification document for at least 6 years after the day on which a business relationship or one-off transaction ceases or, where customer activity is dormant, 6 years from the last transaction and

- retain each original customer document that is not a customer verification document, or a complete certified copy for at least 6 years after the day on which all activities taking place in the course of the dealings in question were completed.

Where the *FIS* is carrying out an investigation in respect of a customer or transaction, it may request an *FSB* to keep records beyond the usual retention period. If an *FSB* is aware of such an investigation but has not received a request from the *FIS* that records be retained, it should nevertheless not, without the prior approval of the *FIS*, destroy any relevant records, even though 6 years may have elapsed.

3.16   Training

*FSB*s have a duty to ensure that both existing and new 'key staff' receive comprehensive training in:

- the relevant laws

- **vigilance** policy (including related systems)

- the recognition and handling of suspicious transactions and

- the personal obligations of all key staff under the relevant laws.

3.17 The Guernsey Financial Services Commission Codes of Practice for Corporate Service Providers, Trust Service Providers and Company Directors (1 April 2001)

The *Codes of Practice* state that providers of corporate services and trust services, and company directors should comply with the *2002 Regulations and Guidance Notes*.

3.18 Civil remedies

Running alongside the criminal sanctions available under the legislation exists an extensive civil armory. The *Guernsey* courts have embraced and developed the remedies available under *English* law. These include **freezing orders**, restraining orders, and orders for **disclosure**. *Norwich Pharmacal* orders are available when a third party has innocently been caught up in the affairs of an alleged wrongdoer. The Royal Court can, in appropriate circumstances, impose a constructive trust. In short, there is a fully developed and mature civil procedure to ensure that a party's civil rights are fully respected.

4 Disclosure/tipping off offences

4.1 The Criminal Justice (Proceeds of Crime) Bailiwick of Guernsey Law 1999

The *1999 Criminal Justice Law* creates two key **disclosure** offences:

4.1.1 Tipping off

Under *s. 41*, a person is guilty of this offence if he knows or suspects that:

i. a police officer is acting, or is proposing to act, in connection with an investigation which is being, or is about to be, conducted into ML (as defined) or

ii. a **disclosure** under *ss. 39* or *40* of the *1999 Criminal Justice Law* has been made to a police officer or pursuant to an employer's internal reporting procedures

and he discloses to any other person information or any other matter which is likely to prejudice that investigation or any investigation which might be conducted following the **disclosure**.

4.1.2 Prejudicing an investigation

Where, under the *1999 Criminal Justice Law*:

i. a production order has been made or has been applied for and has not been refused or

ii. a warrant has been issued

under *s. 47*, a person is guilty of an offence if, knowing or suspecting that the investigation is taking place, he makes any **disclosure** which is likely to prejudice the investigation.

4.2 Disclosure

It is a defense to a charge of prejudicing an investigation if a person had lawful authority or reasonable excuse for making the **disclosure**. Further, nothing in *ss. 41* and *47* makes it an offence for a professional legal adviser to disclose information in circumstances covered by legal professional privilege.

4.3 The Drug Trafficking (Bailiwick of Guernsey) Law 2000

The *2000 Drug Trafficking Law* creates three **disclosure** offences:

- failure to disclose knowledge or suspicion of money laundering (*s. 60*)
- **tipping off** (*s. 61*) and
- prejudicing an investigation (*s. 66*).

4.4 Failure to disclose knowledge or suspicion

In the case of failure to disclose knowledge or suspicion of money laundering, if a person comes to know or suspect that another person is engaged in drug trafficking, he commits an offence if he does not disclose this knowledge or suspicion to a police officer or under his employer's internal reporting procedures. However, it is not an offence for a professional legal adviser to fail to disclose any privileged information.

4.5 Tipping off

The offences of **tipping off** and prejudicing an investigation are substantively the same as the equivalent offences under the *1999 Criminal Justice Law*, save that they solely relate to the proceeds of drug trafficking.

4.6 The Terrorism (United Nations Measures) (Channel Islands) Order 2001

The *Terrorism (United Nations Measures) (Channel Islands) Order 2001* creates two **disclosure** offences:

4.6.1 Failure to disclose knowledge or suspicion of offences

Under *article 9*, it is an offence for an *FSB* to fail to disclose to **HM Procureur** its knowledge or suspicion that a customer/person with whom it has had dealings since the Order came into force is a **terrorist** or has committed a **terrorist** offence.

4.6.2 Failure to comply with a request for information

HM Procureur can require any person to provide information or documents to secure compliance with or detect evasion of the Order or equivalent measures in the *UK, Jersey, Isle of Man* or *British Overseas Territories*. Under article 10, it is an offence to:

i fail to provide such information

ii knowingly or recklessly provide false information

iii willfully obstruct the request or

iv damage, destroy or conceal any document with intent to evade these provisions.

4.7 The Terrorism and Crime (Bailiwick of Guernsey) Law, 2002

The *2002 Terrorism and Crime Law* creates nine **disclosure** offences:

4.7.1 Disclosure of information likely to prejudice an investigation

Under *s. 40*, it is an offence to prejudice an investigation into **terrorist** offences. The defenses are the same as for the offence of prejudicing an investigation under the *1999 Criminal Justice Law*. However, the mental requirement is different; the person making the **disclosure** likely to prejudice the investigation must know or have reasonable cause to suspect that the investigation is taking place, rather than know or actually suspect.

4.7.2 Interfering with relevant material

Under *s. 40*, it is also an offence to interfere with material which is likely to be relevant to an investigation into **terrorist** offences. It is a defense for a person to prove that they had a reasonable excuse for the interference.

4.7.3 Failure to disclose information concerning offences in connection with terrorist funds: persons not connected with financial services businesses

Under *s. 12*, any person who, based on information which comes to their attention in the course of a trade, profession, business or employment other than an *FSB*, believes or suspects that an offence in connection with **terrorist funds** has been committed is guilty of an offence if without a reasonable excuse they do not disclose this belief or suspicion and the information on which it is based to a police officer, or under their employer's internal reporting procedures. Actual belief or suspicion is required. **Disclosure** by a professional legal advisor or of privileged information or suspicion or belief based on such information is not required.

4.7.4 Failure to disclose information concerning offences in connection with terrorist funds: persons connected with financial services businesses

This offence under *s. 15* is materially the same as the offence under *s*. 12 save that it applies to persons connected with *FSB*s and actual belief or suspicion is not required; only reasonable grounds for knowing or suspecting.

4.7.5 Failure to disclose information about acts of terrorism

Under *s. 38*, any person in possession of information which he knows or suspects might be of material assistance in preventing an act of **terrorism** or in securing the apprehension, prosecution or conviction of another person in the *Bailiwick* for an offence involving the commission, preparation or instigation of an act of **terrorism** is guilty of an offence if they fail without a reasonable excuse to disclose that information to a police officer.

4.7.6 Failure to provide information required under a freezing order

Under *Schedule 4, paragraphs 7* and *8*, a person commits an offence if he fails without reasonable excuse to provide the information or documents sought by a **freezing order** made under the *2002*

Terrorism and Crime Law, or knowingly or recklessly provides information or documents which are false.

4.7.7 Giving a false or misleading explanation of seized or produced material

An appropriate judicial officer (or police officer in limited circumstances) can require a person to provide an explanation of material seized pursuant to a warrant or produced pursuant to a production order issued under the *2002 Terrorism and Crime Law*. Under *Schedule 5, paragraph 6*, it is an offence to give a false or misleading explanation.

4.7.8 Failure to provide an explanation of material seized pursuant to emergency authorization

This is the same as the above offence, save that it relates to cases of emergency under *Schedule 5, paragraph 7*.

4.7.9 Failure to provide financial information

An appropriate judicial officer can make an order in relation to a **terrorist** investigation which authorizes a police officer to require an *FSB* to provide customer information for the purposes of the investigation. Under *Schedule 6, paragraph 1*, failure to comply with this requirement is an offence. It is a defense for the *FSB* to prove that the information required was not in its possession or that it was not reasonably practicable to comply.

5 Account monitoring orders

Under *Schedule 7, paragraph 1* of the *2002 Terrorism and Crime Law*, an appropriate judicial officer may make an account monitoring order for the purposes of a **terrorist** investigation if satisfied that the tracing of **terrorist property** is desirable for the purposes of the investigation and will enhance its effectiveness. This requires the specified *FSB* to provide specified information relating to specified accounts for a specified period of up to 90 days to a police officer.

5.1 Disclosure reports

If an *FSB*'s **MLRO** concludes that a **disclosure** should be made, a report should be sent to the *FIS*. If urgent, initial notification should be made by telephone. To the extent permitted by law, *FSB*s should comply with any instructions subsequently received from the *FIS*, including the provision of further requested information. The *FIS* may give the **FSB** written consent to continue operating the financial services product for the client or, in exceptional cases, such consent may not be given. An *FSB* should maintain a register of all reports made to the *FIS*.

A report to the *FIS* will not be disclosed outside the *FIS* and the client is never approached. In the event of a prosecution, the source of the information is protected.

As well as reporting to the *FIS*, where a **disclosure** has been made under the *Money Laundering (Disclosure of Information) Laws for Guernsey 1995, Alderney 1998* or *Sark 2001*, or *1999 Criminal Justice Law*, the *GFSC* also requires *FSB*s to report to it if: the *FSB* failed to detect the transaction; the transaction may present a significant risk to the reputation of *Guernsey* and/or the

FSB; it is suspected that a member of the *FSB*'s staff was involved; or a member of the *FSB*'s staff has been dismissed for a serious breach of ML controls.

5.2   Production orders and warrants

Under the *1999 Criminal Justice Law*, *2002 Drug Trafficking Law* and *2002 Terrorism and Crime Law*, a police officer may apply to the court for a production order or warrant for the purposes of an investigation into the type of crime covered by the relevant law. Such orders will typically require an *FSB* to deliver up specified categories of documents or other information. The *Criminal Justice (Fraud Investigation) (Bailiwick of Guernsey) Law 1991* ('*the 1991 Fraud Law*') also provides that **HM Procureur** may issue orders for the production and explanation of material without recourse to the courts.

5.3   Disclosure by the authorities of disclosed material

Information obtained under the *1991 Fraud Law* may be disclosed in the interests of justice to any person or body for the purposes of any investigation or prosecution of an offence in the Bailiwick or elsewhere.

Information disclosed to the police pursuant to the *1999 Criminal Justice Law* may not be disclosed by the police or anyone receiving the information from them, save as permitted by statute. In this regard, **disclosure** is permitted within the *Bailiwick* for the purposes of the investigation of crime, or for criminal proceedings, within the *Bailiwick*. **Disclosure** is also permitted for other purposes in the *Bailiwick* to the *GFSC*, **HM Procureur**, a police officer or any other person authorized by **HM Procureur** to obtain that information. **Disclosure** is permitted outside of the *Bailiwick* with the consent of **HM Procureur** for the purposes of the investigation of crime, or for criminal proceedings, outside the *Bailiwick*.

The *2000 Drug Trafficking Law* does not contain equivalent provisions. It does, however, contain provisions for obtaining local evidence for use overseas in connection with criminal investigations and proceedings with respect to drug trafficking. The *Criminal Justice (International Co-operation) (Bailiwick of Guernsey) Law 2001* makes equivalent provisions with respect to criminal investigations and prosecutions generally.

Information and/or documentation disclosed pursuant to a request under *the Terrorism (United Nations Measures) (Channel Islands) Order 2001* may be disclosed to the Crown on behalf of the *UK* government, to the *States of Jersey*, or the government of the *Isle of Man* or any *British Overseas Territories* listed in the *Schedule to the Terrorism (United Nations Measures) (Channel Islands) Order 2001*. It may also be disclosed to the *UN* or the government of any other country for the purpose of monitoring or securing compliance with the Order. In addition, it may be disclosed in connection with proceedings for an offence under the Order in *Jersey* or under equivalent legislation in the *UK*, the *Isle of Man* or any *British Overseas Territory* listed in the *Schedule to the Order*.

5.4   Impact of disclosure on civil liability

The effect of the above-mentioned legislation is that a person who makes a **disclosure** to the authorities concerning what they know, believe or suspect to be the proceeds of **criminal conduct** or **terrorist funds** will not be regarded as having breached any civil prohibition against the **disclosure** of such information (e.g. a banker's duty of confidence to his customer).

6 Enforcement

6.1 The Courts

The relevant *Guernsey* courts are comprised of the Magistrates' Court, the Royal Court and the Court of Appeal. Further right of appeal lies to the Privy Council. *Alderney* has the Court of Alderney and *Sark* has the Court of the Seneschal. The Royal Court deals with the more serious matters in the *Bailiwick*, including charges on indictment. It has power to make **confiscation**, **forfeiture**, **restraint** and **charging orders** and, upon application by **HM Procureur**, to deal with requests for assistance from prosecution and investigatory authorities overseas.

6.2 The Financial Intelligence Service

The *FIS* is a joint customs and police body. It is the central point within the *Bailiwick* for the gathering, collating, evaluation and dissemination of all financial crime intelligence, including **disclosure** reports, and bears responsibility for the investigation of any person suspected of ML.

6.3 The Guernsey Financial Services Commission

The *GFSC* was established in 1988 by the *Financial Services Commission (Bailiwick of Guernsey) Law 1987* and regulates finance business in *Guernsey*. The *GFSC*'s primary stated objective is '*to regulate and supervise financial services in Guernsey, with integrity and efficiency, and in so doing help to uphold the international reputation of Guernsey as a finance centre.*'

The *GFSC* does not exercise an enforcement function and is unable to specifically punish *FSB*s for failure to comply with ML obligations. It is, however, entitled to take such failure into consideration in the exercise of its regulatory and supervisory functions and, particularly, in the exercise of its judgment as to whether the directors and managers are fit and proper persons. Therefore, if an *FSB* does not reach the standards set by *the Guidance Notes*, it is at risk of having its **license** to carry on business within the *Bailiwick* revoked.

6.4 The Law Officers of the Crown

HM Procureur, whose position is equivalent to Attorney-General, and **HM Comptroller**, whose position is equivalent to Solicitor-General, are appointed by the Crown. They are legal advisors to the Crown and the *Bailiwick's* legislatures. The Chambers of the **Law Officers** are concerned with all aspects of the administration of justice. The **Law Officers** bring and supervise all prosecutions in the *Bailiwick* and it is to the **Law Officers** that requests will be made from other jurisdictions for assistance.

7 Restraint and confiscation

- The *1999 Criminal Justice* and *2000 Drug Trafficking Laws* contain provisions for **confiscation**, **restraint** and **charging orders**.

- When a convicted defendant appears for sentencing, the court can make a **confiscation order** if it decides that the defendant has benefited from **criminal conduct**. This need not be the conduct for which he or she has been convicted.

- A **restraint** or **charging order** may be made by the court in order to enforce a **confiscation order**. Restraint orders prohibit any person from dealing with property named in the order (subject to any specified exceptions). A **charging order** can either be a realty charging order or personalty charging order and secures payment to the Crown of all or part of the amount which the defendant has been, or may be, ordered to pay under a **confiscation order**.

- The court may also make **restraint** or **confiscation orders** to enforce **confiscation orders** made in countries or territories designated in an Ordinance issued by the *States of Guernsey*. To be enforceable in the *Bailiwick*, such orders must be registered in the *Bailiwick* by the court.

- Under the *Terrorism (United Nations Measures) (Channel Islands) Order 2001*, **HM Procureur** can freeze funds which he has reasonable grounds to suspect are **terrorist funds** without the need to obtain a court order.

- The *2002 Terrorism and Crime Law* also contains provisions for **forfeiture**, **restraint** and **freezing orders**. The court can make a **forfeiture order** against a person convicted of an offence in connection with **terrorist funds**. The distinction between **confiscation** and **forfeiture orders** is that the former operates *in personam* against the defendant and the latter operates *in rem* against the property to be forfeited.

- A **restraint order** under the *2002 Terrorism and Crime Law* is materially the same as a **restraint order** under the *1999 Criminal Justice* and *2000 Drug Trafficking Laws*. A **freezing order** is an order made by the *States of Guernsey Treasury and Resources Department*, which prohibits persons from making funds available to or for the benefit of a person, or persons specified in the order. It is typically used to restrain funds held by an *FSB* on behalf of the defendant.

- Finally, an immigration or police officer may seize and detain cash if they have reasonable grounds for suspecting that it is **terrorist** cash. The court may order the forfeiture of all or part of the cash if the cash or part is **terrorist** cash. There are also provisions dealing with tracing and mixing property and appeals against forfeiture.

Abbreviations

FIS	Financial Intelligence Service
FSB	Financial Services Business
GFSC	Guernsey Financial Services Commission
ML	Money Laundering
MLRO	Money Laundering Reporting Officer

Relevant Addresses

Financial Intelligence Service
Hospital Lane
St Peter Port
Guernsey
Channel Islands
GY1 2QN

The Law Officers of the Crown
PO Box 96
St James Chambers
St Peter Port
Guernsey
GY1 4BY

Guernsey Financial Services Commission
PO Box 128
La Plaiderie Chambers
La Plaiderie
St Peter Port
Guernsey
GY1 3HQ

Bibliography

Ashton, Dr R.: Money Laundering, The Practitioner's Guide,Keyhaven Publications Plc, England, 2000.

Hellman, S./Dunster, M.: Butterworths International Guide to Money Laundering Law and Practice, Reed Elsevier (UK) Ltd, United Kingdom, 2003.

www.gfsc.gg

David Stokes is a graduate of Oxford University. He qualified as a chartered accountant in 1974 and from 1985 until his retirement in 2002 was a partner in PricewaterhouseCoopers and its predecessor firms, specializing in business restructuring. He has extensive international experience, having been based at various times in his career in Europe, Asia and South America. He is particularly experienced in financial advisory work and corporate change management. Resident in Cyprus since 2002, he is now a consultant to Andreas Neocleous & Co, the leading Cyprus-based international law firm, specializing in business advice.

Firm's profile

Andreas Neocleous & Co. is the largest law firm in Cyprus and the Eastern Mediterranean. Its goal is to offer a world-class service to international clients in all areas of the law, providing individually-tailored business solutions to protect and promote their interests. With offices in Moscow, Bucharest, Kiev, Prague and Brussels the firm has an international outlook and long experience in advising clients wishing to invest in the dynamic economies of Central and Eastern Europe.

Cyprus

David Stokes

Consultant

Andreas Neocleous & Co
199 Archbishop Makarios III Avenue
Limassol
Cyprus

Tel +357 25 362818
Fax +357 25 359262
david.stokes@neocleous.com
www.neocleous.com

Anti-Money Laundering: International Law and Practice.
Edited by W.H. Muller, C.H. Kälin and J.G. Goldsworth
© 2007 John Wiley & Sons, Ltd

Contents – Cyprus

1   Introduction

The principal anti-money laundering legislation in Cyprus is the *Prevention and Suppression of Money Laundering Activities Law Number 61(I) of 1996* (*the Law*). The Law has been amended in order to keep abreast of international best practice and fully conforms with all *EU* directives on the prevention of the use of the financial system for the purpose of money laundering,[1] with the Council of Europe's 1990 Convention on *Laundering, Search, Seizure and Confiscation of the Proceeds from Crime* and with the revised *40 Recommendations* of the Financial Action Task Force (*FATF*).

2   Overview of the Law

The main purpose of the Law is to prevent the laundering of proceeds of serious criminal offences, including terrorist financing and related activities, and to provide for their confiscation. The Law makes money laundering or assisting in it a crime and establishes a Unit for Combating Money Laundering; (*MOKAS*) which is responsible for receiving and analysing **suspicious transaction** reports and for money laundering investigations. The Law is comprehensive in its coverage, extending not only to **banks**, but also to other financial services businesses, **insurance companies**, **lawyers**, **accountants**, real estate agents and dealers in precious metals and stones. Such organizations carrying out 'relevant financial business' (see Section 4 below) are required to take adequate steps to prevent their services being misused for money laundering. They must put in place procedures for **customer identification**, record keeping and internal reporting. They must ensure that their employees are aware of their obligations under the Law and provide adequate **training** to help them identify potential money laundering transactions. They are also required to appoint an appropriate person as Money Laundering Compliance Officer (*MLCO*) to act as a central reference point and as a liaison with *MOKAS*.

The Law contains provisions for the confiscation of assets of persons convicted of a **predicate offence** and for restraining the assets of such persons and of persons reasonably suspected of involvement in money-laundering offences.

3   Offences

3.1   Predicate offences

Predicate offences are defined as all criminal offences punishable with imprisonment exceeding one year from which proceeds in any form were generated that may become the subject of a money laundering offence. It is immaterial whether the **predicate offence** is subject to the jurisdiction of courts in Cyprus.

The *Ratification Law of the United Nations Convention for Suppression of the Financing of Terrorism*, enacted in 2001 based on the *UN Model Law*,[2] makes terrorist financing a

---

[1] *Directive 91/308/EEC* as amended by *Directive 2001/97/EC*
www.europa.eu.int/eurlex/lex/LexUriServ/LexUriServ.do?uri=CELEX:32005L0060:EN:NOT.

Directive 2005/60/EC
www.europa.eu.int/eur-lex/lex/LexUriServ/LexUriServ.do?uri=OJ:L:2005 : 309 : 0015:0036:EN:PDF.
[2] www.imolin.org/imolin/tfbill03.html.

criminal offence punishable with 15 years imprisonment or a fine of C£1 million (approximately US$2 074 000) or both and specifically provides that terrorist financing and related activities constitute **predicate offences** for the purposes of the anti-money laundering legislation.

3.2 Money laundering offences

Section 4 of the Law provides that every person who knows or ought to have known that any kind of property is proceeds from a predicate offence is guilty of an **offence** if he does any of the following:

- Converts, **transfers** or removes such property, for the purpose of concealing or disguising its illicit origin or of assisting any person who is involved in the commission of a **predicate offence** to evade the legal consequences of his actions.

- Conceals or disguises the true nature, source, location, disposition, movement, rights with respect to property or ownership of this property.

- Acquires, possesses or uses such property.

- Participates in, associates or conspires to commit, or attempts to commit and aids and abets and provides counselling or advice for the commission of any of the offences referred to above.

- Provides information with respect to investigations that are being performed for laundering offences for the purpose of enabling the person who acquired a benefit from the commission of a **predicate offence** to retain the proceeds or the control of the proceeds from the commission of the said **offence**.

On conviction, a person knowingly committing such an **offence** is subject to imprisonment for up to 14 years, a fine or both. A person who did not know that the property was proceeds from a **predicate offence**, but ought to have known, is subject to imprisonment for up to 5 years or a fine, or both.

3.2.1 Failure to report

Any person who, in the course of his trade, profession, business or employment, acquires knowledge or reasonable suspicion that another person is engaged in money laundering is required to **report** his knowledge or suspicion as soon as reasonably practical. Failure to do so is punishable by imprisonment for up to 5 years or a fine of up to C£3000 (approximately US$6200) or both.

3.2.2 'Tipping-off'

It is also an **offence**, punishable with imprisonment for up to 5 years, for any person to prejudice the investigation of **money laundering offences** by making a disclosure, either to the person who is the subject of a suspicion or to a third party, knowing or suspecting that the authorities are carrying out such an investigation.

4 Relevant activities

Recognizing that certain business activities are susceptible to misuse for money laundering purposes the Law places stringent requirements on organizations offering them. The list of 'relevant financial and other business' is comprehensive, encompassing not only banking activities and high-value cash transactions, but also consultancy services, as follows:

- Deposit taking.

- Lending (including personal credits, mortgage credits, factoring, financial or commercial transactions including forfeiting (receivables discounting)).

- Finance leasing, including hire purchase financing.

- Money transmission services.

- Issuing and administering means of payment such as credit cards, travellers' cheques and bankers' drafts).

- Guarantees and commitments.

- Trading for own or customer's account in:

  - money market instruments such as cheques, bills or certificates of deposit;

  - foreign exchange;

  - financial futures and options;

  - exchange and interest rate instruments;

  - transferable instruments.

- Underwriting or participating in share issues.

- Consultancy services to enterprises concerning their capital structure, industrial strategy and related issues including the areas of mergers and acquisitions of business.

- Money broking.

- Investment business, including dealing in investments, managing investments, giving investment advice and establishing and operating collective investment schemes. In this context the term 'investment' includes long-term **insurance** contracts, whether linked long term or not.

- Safe custody services.

- Custody and trustee services in relation to stocks.

- **Insurance** policies taken in the General Insurance Sector by a **company** registered in Cyprus either as a resident or an overseas **company**, but which carries on **insurance** business exclusively outside Cyprus.

- Exercise of professional activities by auditors, external **accountants** and tax advisors, including transactions for the account of their customers in the context of carrying on relevant financial business.

- Exercise of professional activities on behalf of independent **lawyers**, with the exception of privileged information, when they participate, whether:

  - by assisting in the planning or execution of transactions for their clients concerning the:

    o buying and selling of real property or business entities;

    o managing of client money, securities or other assets;

- opening or management of bank, savings or securities accounts;

- organization of contributions necessary for the creation, operation or management of **companies**;

- creation, operation or management of trusts, **companies** or similar structures;

  – or by acting on behalf and for the account of their clients in any financial or real estate transaction.

- Investment services described in Parts I and II of Annex One of the *Investment Firms Laws of 2002 to 2003* provided in connection with:

  – transferable securities and units in collective investment undertakings;

  – money-market instruments;

  – financial-futures contracts including equivalent cash-settled instruments;

  – forward interest-rate agreements;

  – interest-rate, **currency** and equity swaps;

  – options to acquire or dispose of the above including equivalent cash-settled instruments. This category includes in particular **currency** and interest rate swaps.

- Transactions in real estate by real estate agents by virtue of the provisions of the Real Estate Agents Laws currently in force.

- Dealings in precious metals and stones whenever payment is made for cash and in an amount of £15 000 or more.

As casinos are illegal in the Republic of Cyprus and only limited-stake gambling on sporting events is allowed, the Law does not encompass gambling.

5 Anti-money laundering procedures

5.1 Overview

The Law requires all persons engaged in **relevant activities** to establish and maintain policies and procedures to guard against their business being used for money laundering. They must implement **customer identification** and record keeping procedures, appoint compliance officers and ensure that their employees receive adequate **training** concerning anti-money laundering responsibilities and procedures. The aim is to facilitate the identification of **suspicious transactions** through the strict implementation of 'know your customer' procedures and to provide an audit trail for law enforcement agencies by ensuring adequate records are available.

It is illegal for any person, in the course of relevant financial and other business, to form a business relationship or carry out a one-off transaction with or for another, unless adequate procedures are in place for:

- Identifying customers and maintaining records in relation to their identity and their transactions.

- Identifying **suspicious transactions** by means of appropriate internal control, communication and detailed examination.

- Making employees aware of the organization's procedures to prevent money laundering and of their responsibilities under the Law and **training** them to recognize and deal with **suspicious transactions**.

- Reporting **suspicious transactions** to a competent person such as an *MLCO*.

5.2   'Know your customer' principles

Organizations carrying on financial business must maintain 'know your customer' procedures in accordance with Sections 62 to 65 of the Law. The identity of all customers must be verified, apart from relevant domestic organizations themselves subject to the Law and **banks** and credit institutions incorporated in countries whose anti-money laundering procedures are, in the opinion of the Central Bank of Cyprus (*CBC*), at least on a par with those applying in Cyprus. Identification must take place before any business relationship is established or any 'one-off' transaction is executed.

While the Law does not explicitly state what constitutes adequate evidence of identity, the *CBC* guidance note sets out the key principles and requirements as follows:

- Accounts must be in the full name of the holder. **Banks** may not open or maintain secret, anonymous or numbered accounts or accounts in fictitious names. Failure or refusal to provide satisfactory identification evidence is grounds for suspicion that the customer may be engaged in money laundering. The relevant organization should not carry out any business for the customer and should consider making a suspicion report to *MOKAS*.

- A risk-based approach should be adopted. The extent and number of checks required to establish a customer's identity will depend on the perceived risk according to the type of service, product or account sought by the customer and the projected turnover of the account.

- Organizations should obtain satisfactory evidence that they are dealing with a real person, whether natural or legal, and obtain sufficient evidence of identity to establish that the prospective customer is who he claims to be.

- Adequate steps should be taken to identify the **beneficial owner** of funds and, in the case of legal persons, to ascertain the ownership and control structure of the customer.

Prior to doing any business, adequate information must be obtained in the following areas in order to construct the customer's business profile:

- The purpose and reason for opening an account or requesting services.

- The anticipated level and nature of the activity to be undertaken.

- The projected turnover of the account or size of transaction, the origin of the funds and the destination of outgoing payments.

- The customer's sources of wealth or income.

- The nature and scale of his business or professional activities.

When a bank becomes aware or has any reason to believe that a prospective customer has been refused a bank account or other services by another bank in Cyprus or abroad, then the bank should treat that customer as a high-risk customer and apply enhanced due diligence measures. Appropriate senior management approval should be obtained for opening the account or providing the service and transactions passing through the account should be subject to especially close scrutiny.

The identity of all parties to a joint account or transaction must be satisfactorily verified. It is not sufficient to identify only a representative.

The best identification documents possible (i.e. documentation from reputable sources that is the most difficult to obtain illicitly) should be obtained. Reference numbers and other relevant details should be recorded and copies should be kept on file. Wherever possible, original documents must be examined. Copy documents may only be relied upon if they bear original certification from a notary, a certifying officer, a lawyer, an embassy or other appropriate authority, whose credentials must, in case of doubt, be verified.

5.3 Identification in practice

5.3.1 Natural persons, present in person

Relevant organizations should hold a personal interview with any prospective customer and obtain all identification details at the time. For natural persons verification of name should be by reference to a document bearing a photograph. Under the *Banking (Amendment) (No3) Law of 2004 (Law 231(I) of 2004)* **banks** are required to use an official identity card or passport submitted by the real owner of the account as proof of identity and this will normally be the standard for all organizations. To safeguard against forgery, secondary evidence of identity should also be obtained.

Separate verification of the customer's permanent address should be carried out, by a home visit, by sight of a recent original utility bill, local authority tax bill, or bank statement or by checking the telephone directory.

5.3.2 Non-residents

For non-residents of Cyprus passports or national identity cards should always be examined and copies made. In the event of any doubt, checks should be made with an embassy or consulate of the country of issue in Cyprus or with a professional intermediary or a reputable credit or financial institution in the prospective customer's country of residence. This procedure will also identify potential customers from countries designated by *FATF* as 'non-cooperative' or subject to United Nations or *EU* sanctions.

5.3.3 Natural persons, not available for personal interview

The same **customer identification** and due diligence procedures should be undertaken in respect of prospective customers who do not present themselves for a personal interview. In addition one or more of the following supplemental measures must be undertaken:

- examination of additional documentary evidence;
- additional verification or certification of the documents supplied;
- obtaining confirmatory certification from an institution or organization operating in another *EU* member state;

- requiring the first payment in the context of the business relationship or series of one-off transactions to be made through an account in the customer's name with a credit institution operating in an *EU* member state.

5.3.4 Partnerships, charities, unincorporated businesses and clubs

In the case of partnerships and other unincorporated businesses whose partners or owners have not been verified in the context of existing business relationships, the identity of the **beneficial owners** and authorized signatories should be verified in the same way as for natural persons. The original or copy certificate of registration should be obtained, together with evidence of the address and activities of the business. The constitution and registration documents of clubs, societies and charities should be examined in order to establish their legitimacy and the identity of all authorized signatories must be verified. For charities, the relevant government department should be contacted to confirm the details supplied at the interview. The capacity of authorized representatives to contract or sign on behalf of the partnership, club or charity should be confirmed by reference to the appropriate documentation.

5.3.5 Corporate bodies

Because of the difficulties of identifying beneficial ownership, **companies** are particularly likely to be used as vehicles for money laundering, particularly when associated with a legitimate trading **company**. Before a business relationship is established, a **company** search and other commercial enquiries should be undertaken in order to confirm that the **company** exists and that it has not been, or is not being, dissolved, struck off or wound-up. Further checks should be made in the event of changes in the **company**'s structure or ownership or in the event of a change in the transactions undertaken.

The following should be verified as a minimum:

- The registered number.

- The registered name and any trading names used.

- The registered address and any separate principal trading addresses.

- The identity of the directors.

- The identity of all persons authorized to transact business on the **company**'s behalf with the organization.

- In the case of private and non-listed public **companies**, the identity of sufficient shareholders to account for 75% of the share capital. Where the registered shareholders act as nominees, the identity of sufficient principal ultimate **beneficial owners** (persons with direct or indirect interests of 5% or more in the **company**'s share capital) must be verified to account for 75% of the share capital.

- The **company**'s business profile.

Originals or adequately certified copies of the documents evidencing this information should be examined and copies made. In addition board minutes should be examined to confirm that the persons purporting to act on behalf of the **company** are duly authorized. The identity of all the individuals concerned should be established as outlined above. Where corporate bodies play a role in the management or shareholding of a prospective customer or client, the procedures must trace back through the various corporate strata until they reach the individuals concerned. Where a material shareholding is held by a trust, the identity of the trustees, settlor and beneficiaries of the trust must be established.

Given the safeguards that exist before **companies** are admitted to listing and the practical difficulties of individually identifying a large group of shareholders, shareholder identity need not be verified in the case of **companies** listed on a recognized stock exchange.

Attention should also be given to identifying the individuals who control the **company**'s business and assets, such as persons who have the power to manage funds, accounts or investments without requiring authorization and who would be in a position to override internal procedures.

5.3.6 Trusts (including occupational pension schemes) and nominees

Where a bank is asked to open an account, or a professional is asked to act, for trustees or nominees, the identity of the trustees, the settlor and the beneficiaries should be verified. Particular care is necessary when the trustees or nominees operate accounts in countries with strict banking secrecy or where the trust is constituted in a jurisdiction without robust anti-money laundering measures.

Lawyers receiving funds on behalf of a trust are required to identify the source of the funds, to ensure that they fully understand the nature of the transaction and that payments are made only in accordance with the terms of the trust and with proper written authorization.

In the case of occupational pension schemes the identity of the principal employer and the trustees should be verified, but it is not generally necessary to verify the identity of individual scheme members.

5.3.7 Non-face-to-face customers

The Law prescribes special measures for identifying customers who are not physically present for identification purposes. For such customers, the relevant organization must either:

- obtain from the customer additional documentary evidence; or
- take supplementary measures to verify or certify the documents supplied; or
- obtain confirmation of identity by an institution or organization operating in a member state of the *EU*; or
- require that the first payment of the transaction or series of transactions is carried out through an account in the customer's name with a credit institution operating in an *EU* member state.

In cases where the major shareholder of a **company** is a trust set up in Cyprus or abroad, the identity of the trustees, settlor and beneficiaries of the trust must be established.

5.4 High-risk business

The Law and the guidelines prescribe special precautions for persons or entities categorized as high risk including:

- **Politically exposed persons,** i.e. those holding public office and their close relatives and associates, particularly in countries with a high degree of corruption.
- **Companies** issuing bearer shares.
- Client accounts opened by **accountants** or solicitors for individual clients.

Banks wishing to open correspondent accounts for **banks** operating in certain jurisdictions must obtain the prior written approval of the *CBC*.

Transactions involving non-cooperative countries and territories must be carefully monitored and reported to *MOKAS* if there is any doubt about their legitimacy.

5.5 Record keeping

Section 66 of the Law requires organizations carrying out relevant financial business to retain records concerning **customer identification** and details of transactions for use as evidence in any possible investigation into money laundering. The retention period is five years from the completion of the relevant business or, if an investigation is undertaken by *MOKAS*, until *MOKAS* confirms that the case has been closed.

To avoid creating an excessive volume of records, retention may be in electronic or other form as long as it allows all relevant information to be retrieved without delay.

5.6 Vulnerable transactions

5.6.1 Electronic transfers of funds

Recognizing the efficacy of electronic funds **transfers** in moving substantial sums quickly across borders, the *CBC* requires all outgoing electronic **transfers** by **banks** in excess of US$1000 to show the name, the account or reference number and address of the originator. For smaller outgoing **transfers** this information need not be included in the transfer but it should be retained and made available to the intermediary or beneficiary bank upon request.

Banks receiving incoming funds **transfers** in excess of US$1000 are required to ensure that the above information in respect of the originator is included in the transfer, and should not execute the transaction without it. The Law protects **banks** from possible claims from their customers for non-execution or delay in applying incoming funds to the credit of their accounts in such an event.

5.6.2 Cash deposits in foreign currency

Banks may not accept cash deposits in foreign **currency** notes in excess of US$100 000 or equivalent per calendar year from any person or group of connected persons unless they have the prior written approval of the *CBC*. Cash deposits below the threshold that form part of a series of linked deposits whose aggregate amount is in excess of US$100 000 require similar approval. To obtain permission, the *MLCO* of the bank concerned must provide full details of the customer and his activities and explain the nature of the transaction and source of the funds. The *MLCO* must also confirm that the bank has fully applied the prescribed **customer identification** and due diligence procedures and that the funds involved are not suspected to be associated with illicit activities, including terrorist finance.

5.7 The Money Laundering Compliance Officer

Organizations are required to institute adequate internal monitoring and reporting procedures including the appointment of an *MLCO* of appropriate experience and stature to discharge the duties of the post and command the necessary authority.

The *MLCO*'s duties will include, as a minimum:

- Receiving information from employees regarding activities or transactions suspected to be connected with money laundering.

- Validating and evaluating any information received. Evaluations must be adequately documented and appropriate records must be retained to provide an audit trail.

- Reporting to *MOKAS* in the event that the employee's initial suspicions are justified.

- Liaising with *MOKAS* throughout any investigation and providing relevant information requested by *MOKAS*.

- Providing advice and guidance to other employees on money laundering issues and raising awareness of money laundering issues and procedures.

- Determining employees' **training** needs in relation to money laundering issues and ensuring that adequate **training** is available.

The *CBC* guidelines include standard forms for the initial report, for the *MLCO*'s evaluation and for the report to *MOKAS*.

The *MLCO* bears primary responsibility for compliance with the requirements of the Law and any guidance issued by the relevant supervisory body, and is therefore required to keep abreast of developments regarding money laundering issues and to ensure that the organization's procedures are robust, up to date and observed in practice.

The *MLCO*s decisions are subject to review by the appropriate supervisory body and he is required to discharge his duties carefully and thoroughly, exercising sound judgement with integrity and in good faith.

In addition to their day to day duties *MLCO*s are required to compile an annual report on their activities and their organization's compliance with its obligations under the Law and any related guidance. The annual report should be prepared within two months of the end of each calendar year and submitted to the relevant supervisory body, as well as to senior management of the organization, who are expected to take appropriate action to deal with any shortcomings.

5.8 Identifying and reporting suspicious transactions or activities

Section 27 of the Law requires that any knowledge or suspicion of money laundering should be promptly reported to a police officer or *MOKAS* and provides the relevant organization protection from any claim for breach of any duty of confidence. The protection extends only to the initial disclosure of the suspicion or belief that funds derive from money laundering, and to the information on which it is based. The Cyprus Bar Association's guidance to members recommends that follow-up disclosures should be made only under a court order. It should also be noted that advocates are not bound to disclose privileged information.

It is envisaged that employees encountering **suspicious transactions** or circumstances will report them to the *MLCO* in the first instance. After due enquiry, consideration and consultation the *MLCO* will, if appropriate, report to *MOKAS*.

Having made a disclosure report, the *MLCO* should liaise closely with *MOKAS* in order to avoid any inadvertent action being taken which might hamper the investigation. For example, if the relevant organization decides to terminate its relationship with the customer, care should be taken not to alert the customer that a disclosure report has been made.

After making the disclosure, relevant organizations are expected to follow any instructions given by *MOKAS*, particularly as to whether or not to execute or suspend a transaction. No liability for breach of any contractual or other obligation attaches to a bank that, on instructions from *MOKAS*, refrains from or delays executing a customer's order.

In addition to ad hoc reporting to *MOKAS*, all **banks** in Cyprus are required to submit a monthly report to the *CBC* of cash deposits in excess of US$10 000 equivalent and incoming and outgoing funds **transfers** in excess of US$500 000 equivalent.

5.9   Educating and training employees

Section 58 of the Law obliges relevant organizations to provide their employees with adequate **training** in the recognition and handling of transactions suspected to be linked to money laundering and to make their employees aware of the money laundering legislation and the organization's policies and procedures. A continuous programme of **training**, tailored to the specific needs of individual groups such as new joiners, customer-facing staff and compliance staff, should be provided. Regular refresher **training** should be provided to ensure that staff are reminded of their responsibilities and kept up to date. An administrative fine of up to C£3000 (approximately US$6200) may be imposed for failure to comply.

6   Confiscation and restraint of assets

Before sentencing any person found guilty of a **predicate offence** the court is obliged to consider whether the accused acquired any proceeds from the **offence** and, if so, the court may make a **confiscation order**. The **confiscation order** covers all the realizable property of the accused, including any gifts or transfers at an undervalue made by the accused.

If criminal proceedings are pending against a person in respect of a **predicate offence** or if *MOKAS* has information that creates a reasonable suspicion that a person may be charged with committing a money-laundering offence, then the court, on the application of the Attorney-General, may make an order freezing the realizable property of the accused.

A receiver may be appointed under either type of order with powers to identify, trace, get in and realize the realizable property.

7   Conclusion

As a major offshore financial centre at the crossroads of Europe, Asia and Africa, Cyprus recognizes the risk that criminals may seek to exploit its services for illicit purposes and has put in place robust measures to safeguard against such activity. The anti-money laundering measures taken in Cyprus have been repeatedly evaluated in the last few years by international bodies including the Council of Europe, the *FATF* and the International Monetary Fund. All evaluation reports have commented favourably on the measures adopted by Cyprus and have concluded that they meet, and in many areas surpass, both international best practice and the standards adopted by larger countries.

Addresses

Central Bank of Cyprus
Supervision of International Banks,
Regulation and Financial Stability
Department
80 Kennedy Avenue
P. Box 25529
1395 Nicosia
Cyprus
Tel +357 22 714100
Fax +357 22 378049
spyrosstavrinakis@centralbank.gov.cy

Unit for Combating Money Laundering ('*MOKAS*')
The Law Office of the Republic
27 Katsoni Street, 2nd & 3rd Floors
CY-1082 Nicosia
Cyprus

Contact person: Mrs Eva
Rossidou-Papakyriakou, Head of *MOKAS*
Tel +357 22 446018
Fax +357 22 317063
mokas@mokas.law.gov.cy

Abbreviations

CBC	Central Bank of Cyprus
FATF	Financial Action Task Force of the OECD
MLCO	Money Laundering Compliance Officer
MOKAS (in Greek MOKAΣ)	Unit for Combating Money Laundering

Bibliography

Central Bank of Cyprus: Guidance Note to banks for the prevention of Money Laundering, issued in accordance with Section 60(3) of the Prevention and Suppression of Money Laundering Activities Law of 1996. www.centralbank.gov.cy/media/pdf/IBCRE_SCI15_151104.pdf

Council of the Bar Association of Cyprus: Money Laundering: Guidance Notes for Lawyers.

Nick Verardi is a Partner and Joint Head of the Commercial department of Dickinson Cruickshank, Advocates. Nick advises a number of local and international companies including financial institutions on a wide range of matters including all regulatory aspects, insurance (captive and life), corporate restructuring, including mergers and acquisitions and management buy-outs; asset financing; e-commerce; directors duties; and shareholders rights. Nick qualified as a Manx advocate in 1994 and has been a Notary Public since 1999. He is also a member of the International Bar Association and a (non-practising) solicitor of the Supreme Court of England and Wales. Nick is also a council member of the Isle of Man Chamber of Commerce.

Mark Conway is an advocate in the Commercial department of Dickinson Cruickshank, Advocates. Mark qualified as an Isle of Man Advocate in January 2006 before joining Dickinson Cruickshank in April 2006. Since joining Dickinson Cruickshank, Mark has gained experience in a broad range of commercial and other matters. Prior to training as an Isle of Man Advocate, Mark worked at a firm of financial advisers in the UK and in the tax department of a firm of chartered accountants.

Firm's profile

Dickinson Cruickshank is one of the leading firms on the Island with legal expertise in all areas including commercial, property, private client and dispute resolution. Established in 1899, the firm has played a significant role in the Island's emergence as an internationally renowned finance centre, but is also an important part of Island society dealing with conveyancing, personal injury, family disputes, planning, trusts, wills and employment law. The firm has played a prominent role in the business life of the Isle of Man. In keeping with the progressive emergence of the Island into the world of international business, and in response to the consequent demand made of its legal profession, Dickinson Cruickshank has expanded acquiring the skills and experience to satisfy that demand, while at the same time retaining the traditional client base offering a comprehensive range of legal services to Island residents.

Isle of Man

Nick Verardi

Partner – Advocate and Notary

Mark Conway

Advocate

Dickinson Cruickshank
Advocates & Notaries
33 Athol Street
Douglas
Isle of Man, IM1 1LB

Tel +44 1624 647 647
Fax +44 1624 620 992
nickverardi@dc.co.im
markconway@dc.co.im
www.dc.co.im

Anti-Money Laundering: International Law and Practice.
Edited by W.H. Muller, C.H. Kälin and J.G. Goldsworth
© 2007 John Wiley & Sons, Ltd

Contents – Isle of Man

1 Background

1.1 Political

The *Isle of Man* is an **internally self-governing Dependency of the British Crown** and, as such, is not part of the *United Kingdom (UK)*. The *Isle of Man* is not a member of the *European Union* although, through a protocol to the Act annexed to the 1972 *Treaty of Accession of the UK*, some *EU* rules apply to the *Isle of Man*. **It is not, however, part of the single market for financial services and, as a result, is not covered by the *EU Money Laundering Directive*.**

1.2 Financial

The *Isle of Man* is an **established low tax financial centre** enjoying total independence from the *UK* on matters of direct taxation. There is low personal tax (including a £100 000 tax cap), a corporate rate of tax of 0% (with limited exceptions) and no capital transfer tax, stamp duties or inheritance tax. As the Island has its own parliament and ability to make its own laws, the *Isle of Man* has been able to flourish as a successful and internationally respected offshore financial centre.

1.3 AML/CFT

The *Isle of Man* has held a **strong stance in relation to AML/CFT** since 1987 when it first enacted AML legislation. The *Isle of Man* led the offshore jurisdictions in relation to AML/CFT at this time, indeed it led most jurisdictions. The *Isle of Man*'s AML/CFT regime includes legislation to curb money laundering from the proceeds of all serious criminal offences and the financing of terrorism.

The *Isle of Man Government*[1] has been, and continues to be, strongly committed to assisting in the global measures to deny terrorist groups access to the financial system and is committed to ensuring that the *Isle of Man* is not abused for criminal purposes. Although the *Isle of Man* is not a member of *FATF*, it follows the organization's procedures and recommendations.

2 Criminal legislation

The *Isle of Man* has a robust arsenal of legislation, regulations and administrative practices to counter money laundering. **The nature of the money laundering offences and the definition of predicates are drawn widely and cover all offences triable on information** (serious offences triable by jury). Overseas offences are included where, had the equivalent conduct occurred in the *Isle of Man*, it would have been a predicate offence.

2.1 Primary legislation

The *Isle of Man* has in place criminal legislation designed to combat money laundering, terrorist financing and related offences, reinforced by strong maximum sentences. **The primary legislation applies to all persons and businesses but the *Anti-Money Laundering Code 1998* (*the Code*) places additional requirements on relevant businesses.**

---

[1] The Government's website can be found at www.gov.im.

The most important statutes are:

- The *Drug Trafficking Offences Act 1987* introduced powers to require the production of information and documents, restrain and confiscate the proceeds of drug trafficking and made it an offence to assist another to retain the benefits of drug trafficking.

- The *Prevention of Terrorism Act 1990* created the offence of assisting in the retention or control of terrorist funds and the concealment of transfer of such funds.

- The *Criminal Justice Act 1990* extended the confiscation powers to all crimes, and allows the *Isle of Man* to assist other jurisdictions.

- The *Criminal Justice Act 1991* allowed the *Isle of Man* to meet the requirements of the *Vienna Convention* and includes powers to enable mutual assistance in criminal matters on the same basis as set out in the *European Convention on Mutual Assistance in Criminal Matters*.

- The *Drug Trafficking Act 1996* consolidated and extended the *1987 Act* to include the offence of failing to disclose the knowledge or suspicion of the laundering of the proceeds of drug trafficking and of prejudicing an investigation by tipping off.

- The *Criminal Justice (Money Laundering Offences) Act 1998* extended the *Criminal Justice Act 1990* to criminalize the laundering of the proceeds of all serious crimes.

- The *Anti-Terrorism and Crime Act 2003* created offences relating to the financing and support of terrorism and includes other provisions to assist the authorities in combating money laundering and terrorist financing.

2.2 Offences

2.2.1 Money laundering and related offences

Money laundering offences appear in several *Acts of Tynwald* (*Tynwald* is the *Isle of Man*'s Parliament) but common themes run throughout the legislation. Related offences include assisting another to retain the benefit of his criminal conduct, failure to disclose knowledge or suspicion of money laundering and tipping off.

The penalties for money laundering and related offences in the *Isle of Man* are severe, with a maximum custodial sentence of 14 years and an unlimited fine for the money laundering and related offences and a maximum custodial sentence of 5 years and an unlimited fine for failing to disclose or tipping off.

It is important to note that any disclosure of a suspicion or belief of money laundering to the authorities shall not be treated as a breach of any restriction imposed by statute or otherwise, such as a breach of client confidentiality.

2.2.2 Terrorist organization and support of terrorism

The *Anti-Terrorism and Crime Act 2003* introduced the offences of raising funds for, or supporting, a proscribed organization. Support is a wide concept and includes inviting support for a proscribed organization and is not simply restricted to the provision of money or other property.

2.3 Possible measures

The legislation provides a number of possible measures in the AML/CFT regime in addition to the strong maximum sentences available to the criminal courts.

2.3.1 Seizure

A constable or customs officer may seize and detain cash if there are reasonable grounds for believing that it is terrorist cash or represents any person's proceeds of criminal conduct or is intended by any person for use in any criminal conduct.

2.3.2 Forfeiture

The authorities (through the *Attorney General*) may make an application for the forfeiture of seized cash to the *High Bailiff* (a stipendiary magistrate). The *High Bailiff* may order the forfeiture if he is satisfied that the cash represents any person's proceeds of criminal conduct or is intended by any person for use in any criminal conduct.

The standard of proof upon the authorities in the proceedings is the civil standard, namely the balance of probabilities.[2]

An order may be made whether or not proceedings are brought against any person for an offence with which the cash in question is connected.

2.3.3 Confiscation of assets

The *Isle of Man*'s legislation includes provisions that if a person guilty of drug trafficking or a prescribed offence has benefited from that offence, **the court can order the defendant to pay an amount that the court determines as the defendant's proceeds of the criminal conduct**. The court determines this amount using certain assumptions set out in the legislation.

The standard of proof used in relation to confiscation orders is again the balance of probabilities and the burden of proof is on the defendant to rebut the assumptions by proving that the property is not from proceeds of his criminal conduct.[3]

Property owned or held by a third party can be confiscated if the third party received the property as a gift made within the previous 6 years or where the defendant has transferred the property to the third party at an undervalue.

The *Isle of Man* also has the power to enforce confiscation orders made in the *UK* or other designated countries.

2.3.4 Freezing orders

An application to the court to restrain property at an early stage in proceedings can be made by or with the consent of the *Attorney General* or, in relation to a drug trafficking offence the *prosecutor*, in order to prevent the dissipation of property and to freeze bank accounts. The court can then make a freezing order which prohibits persons (including financial institutions) from making funds available to or for the benefit of a person or persons specified in the order.

The order applies to all persons in the *Isle of Man*, all persons elsewhere who are either nationals of the *UK* who are ordinarily resident in the *Isle of Man* or are bodies incorporated under the laws of the *Isle of Man*.

---

[2] Accordingly, the authorities must prove that it is more likely than not that the cash represents any person's proceeds of criminal conduct or is intended by any person for use in any criminal conduct.

[3] In this situation, the defendant would need to prove that the chance of the property not being proceeds of his criminal conduct is greater than 50%, or more likely than not.

2.4   Investigative orders

The court can order a financial institution to monitor accounts and supply specified information to an appropriate officer for a specified period of time. It can also order a financial institution to provide customer information to a constable named in the order. Customer information includes, inter alia, a customer's personal details, account numbers, any evidence of a customer's identity and the identity of a person sharing an account with a customer.

2.5   Secondary legislation

The *Isle of Man* also has secondary legislation which imposes requirements on persons undertaking relevant business. These requirements are contained in the *Anti-Money Laundering Code 1998* (as amended by the *Anti-Money Laundering (Amendment) Codes 1999, 2001 and 2005*), the *Anti-Money Laundering (Money Service Businesses) Regulations 2002*, the *Anti-Money Laundering (Online Gambling) Code 2002* and the *Anti-Money Laundering Standards for Insurance Businesses*.

3   The Anti-Money Laundering Code 1998 (as amended)

3.1   Overview

The *Criminal Justice Act 1990* provided that the *Department of Home Affairs* shall make codes for the purposes of preventing and detecting money laundering which is intended to:

- Provide practical guidance with respect to the requirements of any statutory provisions relating to the benefits or proceeds of criminal conduct or drug trafficking.

- Require any person carrying on any business specified in the code to institute and operate such systems, procedures, record-keeping, controls and training as may be specified in the code.

- Require persons carrying on, employed in or otherwise concerned in any business specified in the code to comply with such systems, procedures, record-keeping, controls and training as are required to be instituted.

- Provide that in contravention of the codes, a person guilty of an offence is punishable on summary conviction to a fine not exceeding £5000 or to custody for 6 months or to both and on information to custody not exceeding 2 years or to a fine or to both. There does not need to be any evidence of money laundering provided that there has been a breach of the code.

3.2   Scope

The *Anti-Money Laundering Code* applies to those who conduct **relevant business**. People undertaking relevant business are referred to as a **relevant person**.

Relevant business includes:

- banking business, and any activity deemed to be banking business by the *Financial Supervision Commission (the FSC)* under powers under the *Banking Act 1998*;

- investment business;

- insurance business;

- credit unions;

- local authorities authorized to raise or borrow money;

- money service businesses;

- estate agents;

- bookmakers and casinos;

- the *Isle of Man Post Office Authority* relating to activities undertaken in behalf of the *National Savings Bank*;

- accountants, advocates and registered legal practitioners, who hold or manage client money in the course of their activities;

- the provision of corporate services; and

- the provision of trust services.

3.3   General requirement

The general requirement of the Code is that **a relevant person shall not form a business relationship unless the relevant person complies with the provisions of the Code**.

The relevant person must also ensure that employees are aware of the procedures and the provisions of the money laundering requirements and provide training for employees to assist them in the recognition and handling of transactions carried out by or on behalf of any person who is or appears to be engaged in money laundering, in dealing with customers where such transactions occur and in procedures to be adopted where transactions have been reported to the appropriate law enforcement authorities in accordance with the money laundering requirements.

3.4   Penalty for breach

If a relevant person breaches the Code, the maximum punishment is a fine not exceeding £5000 or custody for a period not exceeding 6 months or both. **There is no requirement for money laundering, terrorist financing or related offences to have occurred**.

If the offence is committed with the consent or connivance of, or to be attributable to neglect on the part of, a director, manager, secretary or other similar officer of the body corporate or a person who was purporting to act in such a capacity, he, as well as the body corporate, is guilty of an offence.

3.5   Guidance notes

The Code is supplemented by **guidance notes**[4] produced by the *FSC* to assist persons undertaking relevant business. The guidance notes explains provisions of the Code and also explains what the *FSC* consider **best practice**. The guidance notes are not legally binding but explain how the *FSC* would expect institutions to fulfil their responsibilities under the AML/CFT legislation.

---

[4] The AML guidance notes can be found at www.gov.im/fsc/handbooks/guides/AML/welcome.xml.

4 Obligations of the Code

4.1 Due diligence

4.1.1. Primary duty

The relevant person shall require an **applicant for business** to produce satisfactory evidence of his identity **as soon as practicable after contact is first made**. The guidance notes provide details on the documents that can be used for identity but it is usual for applicants for business to provide original or certified copies of their passports.

The guidance notes to the Code specify what further information must be obtained from applicants for business and the documentation that should be obtained to **verify the identity and address** of the applicant. It is usual for the applicant for business to provide an original or certified copy of a rates or utility bill.

A **certifier** should be a lawyer, accountant or bank manager or someone similar.[5] The copy document should be signed and dated by the certifier, state the position or capacity of the certifier and state that it is a true copy of the original

If the applicant for business is a corporate entity the relevant person shall also require the **beneficial owner** of the entity to produce satisfactory evidence of his identity.

If another person is appointed as a signatory on an account or directors of a company appoint a non-director as a signatory on an account or grant a power of attorney in favour of an individual, **full due diligence** should be obtained on the new individual.

All documents in a language other than English should be adequately translated into English.

4.1.2 Continuing duty

There is a **continuing duty** to verify identity, especially if transactions are undertaken which are significantly different from the normal pattern of previous business or suspicion arises as to the applicant's true identity or business activities.

4.1.3 Source of funds and wealth

When entering into a **business relationship**, the relevant person is required to make enquiries to ascertain the source of wealth for the applicant for business and this should form part of the know your customer profile. The relevant person should not accept generic descriptions such as 'savings' or 'investments' without further checks.

The enquiries should be sufficient to fully understand the potential customer's circumstances and if the results of the enquiries are unclear, consideration should be given to the appropriateness of entering into a business relationship with the applicant for business.

4.1.4 Corporate clients

In the case of corporate clients, the relevant person must obtain certain information relating to the company itself, the activities of the company and the officers and beneficial owners of the company. The specific requirements of the Code can be found in the guidance notes.[6]

---

[5] This list is not exhaustive and further examples are given in the guidance notes.
[6] The guidance notes can be found at www.gov.im/fsc/handbooks/guides/AML/welcome.xml

4.1.5 Trust clients

In the case of trust clients, the relevant person should obtain and verify the identity of any principal beneficiaries. In cases where this is not practical, **the relevant person should always establish the identity of the beneficiary before any distribution of the trust property is made to the beneficiary**.

Other documentary evidence relating to the trust will also need to be provided to the relevant person.

4.1.6 Exemptions

The Code enables some types of applicants for business to be accepted without detailed identification and verification checks in certain circumstances. There is an **exemption for one-off transactions** subject to certain financial limitations. The *FSC* do not consider that the provision of a company or other structure for a client or the establishment of a mortgage to be an exempted one-off transaction.

There are also exemptions in the case of **acceptable applicants** and **introducers** under the Code. The requirements of these exemptions can be found in the Code and the guidance notes.

4.1.7 Existing business relationships

At present, there is an exemption to obtaining identification papers for business relationships in existence prior to 1 December 1998. However, this provision has been removed from the draft *Anti-Money Laundering Code 2006*.

4.1.8 Ongoing monitoring

The relevant person is under a **continuing duty to monitor the conduct and activities of the relationship/account/client company** to ensure that it is consistent with the nature of business and estimate of turnover stated when the relationship was established. This allows a relevant person to detect **unusual or suspicious activity**.

If a suspicious transaction report is made by the relevant person, there is a separate obligation to continue to monitor the subject of the suspicious transaction report and the institution should report further suspicions without delay.

4.1.9 General rule

The general rule is that if the relevant person does not obtain **satisfactory evidence** of the identity of the applicant for business, the business relationship and the transactions shall not proceed any further.

4.2 Reporting suspicious transactions

4.2.1 Requirement of the Code

The Code requires the relevant person to establish written internal reporting procedures which in relation to his relevant business will, inter alia:

- Identify a **suitably qualified and experienced officer** to be appointed *Money Laundering Reporting Officer (MLRO)* to whom a report is to be made of any information which comes to the attention of the person handling that business which gives rise to a knowledge or suspicion that another person is engaged in money laundering. The FSC also expect a *Deputy MLRO* to be appointed.

- Enable all persons involved in its management and all appropriate employees to know to whom a report should be sent setting out any knowledge or suspicions of money laundering activity.

- Require the *MLRO* to consider all **suspicious transaction reports** he receives in the light of all other relevant information available to him for the purpose of determining whether or not it gives rise to a knowledge or suspicion of money laundering.

- Require that the information contained in a report is disclosed promptly to a constable where the appropriate person knows or suspects that another is engaged in money laundering.

4.2.2 Reports to the authorities

There is no minimum figure to consider when making a suspicious transaction report. Consideration should also be given by the *MLRO* to making a **disclosure** when business has been declined because of suspicions on the part of the institution.

4.2.3 Repeated reports

If staff continue to encounter suspicious activity or transactions which they have previously reported to the *MLRO*, they should continue to make internal reports to the *MLRO* on each occasion of suspicion. **The *MLRO* should then make repeated disclosures to the *Financial Crime Unit (FCU)* where suspicious activities continues**.

4.2.4 Register of reports to the authorities

The relevant person is required to maintain a register of all such reports. The register shall contain details of the date on which the report is made, the person who makes the report, the constable to whom it is made and information sufficient to identify the relevant papers.

4.3 Obligation to keep records

4.3.1 Record of identity

Whenever a relevant person is required to verify the identity of a person, they shall keep a record in the *Isle of Man* which indicates the nature of the evidence obtained. Ideally, this will be a copy of the information, but where this is not reasonably practicable, the record shall contain such information as would enable a copy of the evidence to be obtained.

4.3.2 Record of transactions

The relevant person must also keep a record of all transactions carried out by or on behalf of a client. These records must be sufficient to identify the source and recipient of payments from which investigating authorities will be able to compile an audit trail for suspected money laundering.

4.3.3   Retention of records

All records created and maintained under the Code need to be retained for at least 5 years from the date when all activities formally ended or if the business relationship was not formally ended, when the last transaction was carried out. Where a suspicion report has been made to a constable, that person shall retain all relevant records for as long as required by the constable.

In some limited circumstances (such as under the *Banking (General Practice) Regulatory Code*) records are to be retained for 6 years. If there is any contradiction between provisions, the *Regulatory Codes* takes precedence and the records should be retained for 6 years.

Even if a business relationship is not entered into, the relevant person should retain all documentation for at least 5 years from the relevant date.

4.3.4   Retrieval of records

A relevant person shall ensure that any records required to be maintained are capable of retrieval without undue delay.

4.3.5   Register of enquiries

A relevant person shall also maintain a register of all enquiries made of it by law enforcement or other authorities acting under powers provided by the money laundering requirements. This register shall be kept separate from other records and shall include the date and nature of the enquiry, the name and agency of the inquiring officer, the powers being exercised and details of the accounts or transactions involved.

4.4   Education and training

4.4.1   All staff

The Code requires that a relevant person shall provide training for all persons involved in its management and all appropriate employees to ensure that they are aware of:

- the provisions of the AML requirements;

- their personal obligations under the AML requirements;

- the internal reporting procedures; and

- their personal liability for failure to report information or suspicions in accordance with internal procedures.

4.4.2   Senior and specialist staff

Supervisors, managers and those acting as directors or secretaries of client companies should receive a higher level of training. Accordingly, the relevant person should also provide education and training appropriate to these particular categories of staff in:

- Its policies and procedures to prevent money laundering, including the offences and penalties arising from the relevant primary legislation for non-reporting or for assisting money launderers.

- The procedures relating to dealing with production and restraint orders.

- Its customer identification, record-keeping and other procedures.

- The requirements for verification of identity and retention of records.

- The recognition and handling of suspicious transactions.

4.4.3 MLROs

MLROs and *Deputy MLROs* **should receive in-depth training on all aspects of the primary legislation, the Code and internal policies**. They should also receive extensive initial and ongoing instruction on the validation and reporting of suspicious transactions, on the feedback arrangements and on new trends of criminal activity.

4.4.4 Refresher training

Staff should receive refresher training at regular intervals (not less than annually for key staff) to remind staff of their responsibilities and to make them aware of any changes in the AML requirements and the internal procedures of the relevant person.

4.4.5 Records of training

Records should be kept demonstrating that the relevant person has complied with the provisions of the Code which should include, inter alia, details of the content of the training programmes provided, the names of the staff who have received the training and the date of the training. These records should be retained for a minimum of 6 years.

5 Prospects

5.1 Draft Anti-Money Laundering Code 2006

A new draft anti-money laundering code has been circulated on the *Isle of Man*. At the time of writing, the current position is that the *Anti-Money Laundering Committee* is considering the results of the consultation period which ended in May 2006.

Differences between the draft and the existing Code include:

- Evidence of identity shall not be satisfactory unless reasonable measures have been taken to identify the beneficial owner of the money or property concerned in the relevant transaction.

- The existing business relationship exemption has been removed.

- The introduction of staff screening provisions.

- Maximum punishment for non-compliance increased to custody not exceeding 2 years or to a fine or both.

- The extension of the definition of relevant business to include, inter alia, the provision of legal services which involves participation in a financial or land transaction.

5.2   Companies Act 2006

The *Companies Act 2006* provides for a new type of corporate vehicle (the *NMV*) to exist alongside companies incorporated under the existing legislation. Prima facie, it would appear that the *NMV* would be less effective from an AML/CFT viewpoint as there is no obligation to file the register of members or register of directors at the *Companies Registry*.

However, each *NMV* is required to have a **registered agent** in the Isle of Man, who must hold a license under the *Fiduciary Services Acts* **and only these licensed agents can incorporate a** *NMV*. Accordingly, these licensed entities will be a relevant person for the purposes of the Code and, as such, will be required to comply with the requirements of the Code. **Accordingly, there will be no dilution of the AML/CFT regime**.

6   Supervision

6.1   Financial Supervision Commission[7]

The *FSC* is an **independent statutory body** whose functions include the licensing and supervision of banks, building societies, investment business, corporate and trust service providers and the authorization, recognition and regulation of collective investment schemes.

The *FSC* conducts regular visits to the entities that it licenses to ensure that the required systems to deter and prevent money laundering are in place and that the systems are at the required standard.

The *FSC* have interpreted its practice as follows:

- The purpose of a banking and financial centre is to provide economic benefits to the *Isle of Man*.

- There is nothing to gain from permitting activities which shelter or facilitate criminal activities.

- Institutions and customers benefit from standards of licensing and supervision which reflect best practice and are acceptable to supervisory authorities in other jurisdictions.

The *FSC* has a wide range of powers and sanctions, which it has used regularly. For example, **the *FSC* can wind up companies in the public interest and declare individuals unfit to be directors of *Isle of Man* companies**. In addition, licenses can be suspended or revoked, and specific directions can be placed upon licensees.

6.2   Financial Crime Unit

The *FCU* is the *Isle of Man*'s **financial investigation unit** and is the central reception point for all financial intelligence. This intelligence is evaluated and shared through legal frameworks with other jurisdictions as appropriate.

The *FCU* works closely with the finance sector on the *Isle of Man* and plays a full part in implementing agreed recommendations arising from evaluations of the legal and regulatory

---

[7] The FSC website can be found at www.gov.im/fsc.

frameworks of the *Isle of Man*'s finance sector by various international bodies, such as the *International Monetary Fund and FATF*. The *FCU* is also a member of the *Egmont Group*.

7   International obligations

The *FSC* attaches great importance to ensuring that its policies and procedures conform to internationally accepted best practice. Although not a member of *FATF*, **the *Isle of Man* fully endorses *FATF's* 40 Recommendations and the 9 Special Recommendations on Terrorist Financing**.

The *Isle of Man*'s regulatory authorities can provide information and assistance to other on-Island and off-Island regulators in response to specific requests or on their own initiative.

The *Criminal Justice (Money Laundering Offences) Act 1998* confers a statutory power for information contained in 'all crimes' suspicious transaction reports to be passed on to authorities outside the *Isle of Man*. The information is passed with the permission of the *Attorney General* at the intelligence-gathering and investigation stages.

The *Convention on Laundering, Search, Seizure and Confiscation of the Proceeds from Crime* of 1990 applies to the *Isle of Man*. In the same way as authorities in the *UK*, *Isle of Man* authorities may cooperate with other jurisdictions in the search for and seizure, retention and confiscation of assets if they are linked to crimes punishable both in the other jurisdiction and in the *Isle of Man*.

8   Sanctions

The *Isle of Man Government* is strongly committed to fulfilling its international obligations with regard to sanctions regimes and denying terrorist groups access to the financial system. The *Isle of Man* imposes sanctions determined by the *United Nations (UN)* and the *European Union*.

Sanctions imposed by the *UN* automatically apply to the *Isle of Man* through the *Isle of Man*'s special relationship with the *UK*. Trade sanctions may be imposed in the *Isle of Man* by means of Orders-in-Council or *European Community* customs legislation having direct effect in the *Isle of Man* as a result of the *Isle of Man* being part of the *UK*'s customs area. Other measures, including financial sanctions, may be imposed by either Orders-in-Council or applications orders (the latter used to give effect in the *Isle of Man* to *EU* instruments which do not have direct effect in the *Isle of Man*).

Sanctions have been imposed in relation to a number of jurisdictions including members of the former *Milosevic* regime in *Yugoslavia*, the *Taliban* in *Afghanistan*, *Usama Bin Laden* and *Al Quaida* and the associates of *Saddam Hussein* in *Iraq*.

From time to time, the *Isle of Man Treasury* issues lists of individuals and entities under the above sanctions. These lists are published on the *Isle of Man Government* website (www.gov.im/treasury/customs/sanctions.xml). Financial institutions on the *Isle of Man* are obliged to check whether they maintain accounts for any listed individual, and if so they must freeze the accounts and report their findings to the *Customs and Excise Division* of the *Treasury*.

Addresses

Financial Supervision Commission
PO Box 58
Finch Hill House
Douglas
Isle of Man
IM99 1DT
www.gov.im/fsc

Insurance and Pensions Authority
4th Floor
HSBC House
Ridgeway Street
Douglas
Isle of Man
IM1 1ER
ipa.admin@ipa.gov.im

Financial Crime Unit
PO Box 51
Finch Hill House
Douglas
Isle of Man
fcu@gov.im

Customs and Excise Division Isle of Man Treasury
PO Box 6
Customs House
North Quay
Douglas
Isle of Man
IM99 1AG
customs@gov.im

Isle of Man Courts of Justice
Deemster's Walk
Bucks Road
Douglas
Isle of Man
IM1 3AR

John Handoll is a partner in William Fry's Competition & Regulation unit. He advises on domestic and European Union competition law matters, as well as on a wide range of areas involving European Union and domestic law, including AML/CFT compliance, free movement and public procurement. John graduated from Manchester University with an LLB Degree (Hons.) in 1978. He was awarded a Diploma in European Integration from Amsterdam University in 1979. In 1980 he was called to the English Bar and was admitted as a solicitor (England & Wales) in 1991. He qualified as an Irish solicitor in 1997. John has lived and worked in several European States (Belgium, Ireland, Italy, the Netherlands and the UK). He has written a leading work on the free movement of persons in the EU and various studies on EC competition law, the free movement of capital and legal aspects of Economic and Monetary Union. His book 'Capital, Payments and Money Laundering in the EU' was published by Oxford University Press in 2006.

Firm's profile

With significant involvement in mergers and acquisitions activity, **William Fry** is a leader in the commercial, corporate and financial services sector. In addition, the firm also provides substantial litigation, commercial property and regulatory capabilities through its specialized departments.

As one of Ireland's largest law firms, William Fry advises a substantial number of leading Irish and international companies, covering both the public and private sectors. With a staff of over 300, the firm operates a large international practice and regularly acts in cases involving other jurisdictions, including: the United Kingdom, the United States and a large number of continental European States.

Ireland

John Handoll

Partner

William Fry
Fitzwilton House
Wilton Place
Dublin 2
Ireland

Tel +353 1 639 5000
Fax +353 1 639 5333
johnhandoll@williamfry.ie
www.williamfry.ie

Anti-Money Laundering: International Law and Practice.
Edited by W.H. Muller, C.H. Kälin and J.G. Goldsworth
© 2007 John Wiley & Sons, Ltd

Contents – Ireland

1   Introduction

This chapter outlines the legal framework relating to **anti-money laundering** (AML) and **combating the financing of terrorism** (CFT) in Ireland.

As a member of the European Union, Ireland is bound to implement and apply EU rules in relation to AML and CFT. It has fully implemented the *1991 Money Laundering Directive* as amended in 2001. It is in the course of implementing the *2005 Money Laundering Directive*.

It is also a member country of the *Financial Action Task Force* and is committed to apply the *FATF 40 Recommendations* and the *FATF 9 Special Recommendations*. In February 2006, the *FATF* finalized its *Third Mutual Evaluation Report* of Ireland's AML/CFT regime. Reference can usefully be made to the wealth of information contained in this lengthy (196-page) document.

This chapter addresses:

- the legislative framework for AML/CFT (Section 2);

- the main money laundering and terrorist financing offences (Section 3);

- compliance by designated bodies (Section 4);

- investigation and enforcement (Section 5).

2   AML/CFT: the Irish legislative framework

2.1   The Criminal Justice Act 1994

2.1.1   General

The basic framework for AML/CFT compliance is set out in the *Criminal Justice Act 1994* (as amended) (the 1994 Act).

The relevant provisions address the prevention and detection of **money laundering offences** (as defined in Section 31 of the 1994 Act) and **terrorist offences** (as generally defined in the *Criminal Justice (Terrorist Offences) Act 2005*). Offences are also created in respect of the failure of **designated bodies**, and persons working in these bodies, to observe the **AML/CFT compliance requirements**.

In summary, **financial institutions and other entities** carrying out particular activities which are particularly prone to be used for money laundering or terrorist financing must take steps to **identify their client**, to **retain documentation**, to **adopt appropriate procedures** and, save for a 'legal privilege' exception, to **report suspicions to the *Garda Síochána* (the police service) and to the *Revenue Commissioners*** (the desire to identify tax evaders is a key driver in the operation of the legislation). Failure to observe these requirements can result in **significant fines and periods of imprisonment**.

2.1.2   Designated bodies and activities

Bodies designated under the *1994 Act* or secondary legislation comprise **financial institutions, accountants, auctioneers, auditors, estate agents, tax advisers, solicitors, dealers in high value goods and (although they are illegal in the State) casinos.**

The requirements as to identification, retention of documentation and procedures apply in respect of specific operations and activities specified in the annex to *Council Directive 89/646*, in the *Life Assurance Directive* and in regulations made under the *1994 Act*: these are addressed in relation to the specific designated bodies below.

2.1.3 Identification

The usual rule is that **a designated body must take reasonable measures to establish the identity of any person** for whom it proposes to provide services on a continuing basis, in respect of transactions that, individually or as linked transactions, **amount to at least €13 000, or where it otherwise suspects that a service is connected with the commission of a money laundering or terrorist financing offence**. Where the sum involved is not known at the time of the transaction, the identification requirements are to apply once it is established that the €13 000 threshold has been crossed. Where the designated body knows or believes that the client is itself acting for a third party, it is to take reasonable measures to establish the identity of the third party. Exceptions to these requirements apply, under the limits set out in the *Money Laundering Directive*, to life assurance undertakings (see Subsection 3.3.2, below).

2.1.4 Retention of documentation

Where a designated body has identified a person, it is to **retain a copy of the materials used for identification** for at least five years after the relationship with the person has ended. In relation to **transactions**, the original documents or copies admissible in legal proceedings relating to the relevant transaction are to be **retained for at least five years after execution of the transaction**.

2.1.5 Procedures

A designated body is, in relation to the carrying on of its business, to adopt measures to prevent and detect the commission of money laundering and terrorist financing offences. Such measures are to include:

- **establishing procedures** to be followed by directors, officers and employees;
- giving directions on the application of the *Money Laundering Directive* and of the *1994 Act*; and
- **training directors, officers and employees** in order to enable them to identify transactions which may relate to the commission of a money laundering or terrorist financing offence.

2.1.6 Obligations in relation to other designated bodies

The identification, retention of documentation and procedural requirements do not apply where the designated body provides a service for another designated body in Ireland, or a body corresponding to a designated body in another EU Member State or a prescribed third State or country.

2.1.7 Reporting

A designated body, including a director, officer and employee, who **suspects the commission of a money laundering or terrorist financing offence, or a breach of the AML/CFT compliance**

obligations, in relation to the business of that body is **required to report that suspicion to the** *Garda Síochána* **and to the** *Revenue Commissioners*. The reporting obligation exists not only where the business of the designated body has itself been *used* for laundering by a particular client: it is **widely considered that the reporting obligation exists for all relevant suspicions** formed *in the course of business* of the designated body, even in the case of suspicions relating to third persons.

The *1994 Act* provides for the possibility of an **internal reporting procedure** to be established by a designated body in order to facilitate the operation of these provisions.

In addition, persons legally charged with the supervision of a designated body who suspect the commission by that body of a money laundering or terrorist financing offence, or a breach of the AML/CFT compliance obligations, are also required to report the suspicion to the Garda Síochána and to the Revenue Commissioners.

Information so reported may be used in an investigation for any offence, including but not limited to money laundering and terrorist financing offences.

Section 57 of the 1994 Act, which deals with the disclosure of information, provides that, in determining whether a person has complied with any of the requirements of the Section, '**a court may take account of any relevant supervisory or regulatory guidance which applies to that person or any other relevant guidance issued by a body that regulates, or is representative of, any trade, profession, business or employment carried on by that person**'.

2.1.8 Tipping-off

The *1994 Act* also makes it an **offence to 'tip off'**. Where a report to the *Garda Síochána* and to the *Revenue Commissioners* has been made, a person who makes any disclosure likely to prejudice an investigation arising from the report is to be guilty of an offence.

2.1.9 Penalties

Any **breach of the provisions on identification, record keeping, procedures, reporting or tipping-off will be treated as a serious offence**. Not only the company itself, but also its directors, officers and employees will be liable to **severe penalties**. A person is liable, on summary conviction, to a fine of €1000 and/or up to 12 months imprisonment or, on conviction on indictment, to an unlimited fine and/or imprisonment of up to 5 years. These offences are **arrestable offences** and persons suspected of committing an offence may be arrested without warrant and detained for questioning.

2.2 The financing of terrorism

Ireland is no stranger to the scourge of terrorism and long-established legislation has provided a basis for the **forfeiture of property** of unlawful terrorist organizations (the Irish Republican Army and the Irish National Liberation Army).

With the enactment of the *Criminal Justice (Terrorist Offences) Act 2005* (the 2005 Act), Ireland has strengthened its armoury in the fight against terrorist financing. *Part 4 of the 2005 Act* contains provisions directed at the suppression of financing of terrorism, principally designed to enable ratification by Ireland of the *1999 UN Convention on the Suppression of the Financing of*

Terrorism. There is a new **offence of financing terrorism** (see Section 3.3, below) and provisions on **freezing and confiscation of funds** (see Section 5, below).

3   The main offences

3.1   Money laundering

The **core money laundering offences** are set out in *Section 31 of the 1994 Act* and cover cases where a person who knows or believes that property is or represents the proceeds of criminal conduct, or is reckless as to whether this is the case, without lawful authority:

- Converts, transfers or handles the property or removes it from the State, with the intention of: (a) 'concealing or disguising its true nature, source, location, disposition, movement or ownership or any rights with respect to it'; (b) assisting a person to avoid prosecution for the criminal conduct concerned; or (c) avoiding the making, or frustrating the enforcement, of a confiscation order.

- Conceals or disguises the true nature, source, location, disposition or ownership or any rights with respect to the property.

- Acquires, possesses or uses the property.

'Criminal conduct' is defined as conduct which would constitute a (serious) indictable offence, or, where it occurs outside the State, would constitute such an offence if it had occurred in the State and constitutes an offence under the law of the place where it occurs. Participation in such conduct – for example, as an accessory – is also included.

Criminal conduct is covered whether it occurred **before or after** the commencement of the relevant provisions and whether it was attributable to the person guilty of money laundering or to another.

Broad definitions are given to the concepts of converting, transferring, handling or removing property and it is made clear that **references to converting, transferring or removing any property include the giving of advice and assistance** in relation to these actions.

There are provisions on 'knowledge', 'belief' and 'recklessness' which will give rise to a presumption that a person knew, believed or was reckless unless the court or jury in any trial is satisfied that there is a reasonable doubt as to whether a person so knew or believed or was so reckless. **This brings the onus of proof below the usual standard in criminal cases of proof beyond a reasonable doubt**. A similar approach applies in relation to determining 'intention'.

A person guilty of money laundering is liable, on summary conviction, to a fine not exceeding about €1300 and/or to imprisonment for no more than 12 months. On conviction on indictment, where proceedings are brought by the Director of Public Prosecutions, the person concerned is liable to an unlimited fine and/or to imprisonment for no more than 14 years.

3.2   Terrorist financing

There are **two basic offences of financing terrorism** under the *2005 Act.*

Under *Section 13(1),* which reflects the requirements of the *1999 UN Convention on the Suppression of the Financing of Terrorism,* a person will be guilty of the offence of financing terrorism if, inside or outside the State, he or she by any means, directly or indirectly, unlawfully and wilfully provides, collects or receives funds intending or knowing that they will be used in order to carry out:

- An act that constitutes an offence under the law of the State which is within the scope of, and as defined in, treaties listed in the Annex to the Terrorist Financing Convention.

- Any other act

  (i) that is intended to cause death or serious bodily injury to a civilian or to any other person not taking an active part in the hostilities in a situation of armed conflict, and

  (ii) the purpose of which is, by its nature or context, to intimidate a population or to compel a government or an international organization to do or abstain from doing any act.

Subject to provisions on acts committed outside the State, a person attempting to commit an offence *under Section 13(1)* will be guilty of an offence.

Under *Section 13(2)*, which reflects the requirements of the *2002 EU Framework Decision on Combating Terrorism*, a person will also be guilty of an offence if her or she by any means, directly or indirectly, unlawfully and wilfully provides, collects or receives funds intending that they be used or knowing that they will be used:

- for the benefit or purposes of a terrorist group; or

- in order to carry out a terrorist act (other than one covered by *Section 13(1)*) that is an offence under *Section 6*.

A person who attempts to commit an offence under *Section 13(2)* is guilty of an offence.

An offence may be committed under *Section 13(1) or (2)* whether or not the funds are used to carry out a terrorist act.

A person guilty of an offence under *Section 13* is liable, on summary conviction, to a fine of no more than €3000 and/or up to 12 months imprisonment or, on conviction on indictment, to an unlimited fine and/or imprisonment of up to 10 years. Since the offence is indictable, it is a predicate offence for money laundering purposes.

4 AML/CFT: compliance by designated bodies in Ireland

4.1 Introduction

This section identifies **bodies designated in, or under, the *1994 Act***, outlines specific provisions relating to them and refers to the various applicable *Guidance Notes*.

Designated bodies cover a broad range of financial institutions and a number of non-financial businesses and professions. In addition to identifying the designated institutions, businesses and professions, the legislation also specifies the operations and activities which trigger the AML compliance obligations.

Guidance Notes have been issued for most of the specific categories of designated bodies. Most of these have been issued with the approval of the *Money Laundering Steering Committee* which is composed of representatives of a number of government departments, the *Financial Services Regulator*, the *Garda Síochána* and sectoral representative bodies.

In March 2005, general *Guidance on the Offence of Financing of Terrorism and the Financial Sanctions Regime for designated bodies* was issued with the approval of the *Money Laundering Steering Committee.*

4.2   Designated bodies

The current list of designated bodies is as follows.

Financial Institutions

- banks;
- building societies;
- money-brokers;
- trustee savings banks;
- life assurance undertakings;
- persons providing a service in financial futures and option exchanges;
- An Post (the national postal services operator);
- credit unions;
- persons providing a service in relation to buying and selling stocks, shares and other securities;
- persons providing foreign currency exchange services;
- investment companies;
- management companies of a unit trust scheme;
- general partners of an investment limited partnership;
- insurance brokers or insurance agents;
- persons providing money remittance services;
- administration companies providing services to collective investment schemes;
- investment business firms;
- trustees or custodians of a collective investment scheme where it is regulated in the State;
- electronic money institutions; and
- persons in the State who, as their principal activity, carry out an operation included in numbers 2 to 9 and 11, 12 and 13 of the list annexed to *Council Directive 89/646.*

Non-financial Institutions

- accountants;
- auctioneers;
- auditors;
- estate agents;

- tax advisers;

- solicitors;

- dealers in high value goods;

- casinos (even though illegal!).

4.3   Financial institutions

4.3.1   General

The list of designated financial institutions is set out in Section 3.2.

The AML/CFT compliance provisions apply to these institutions where they carry out prescribed activities. These consist of certain operations listed in *Council Directive 89/646*, activities to which the *Life Assurance Direc*tive applies and other activities prescribed by regulation.

The **relevant operations listed in *Council Directive 89/646*** are as follows:

- lending;

- financial leasing;

- money transmission services;

- issuing and administering payments;

- guarantees and commitments;

- trading, whether for own or customer's account, in: money market instruments, foreign exchange, financial futures and options, exchange and interest rate instruments, or transferable securities;

- participation in share issues and related services;

- advice to undertakings on capital structures, industrial strategy and related questions, and advice and services related to mergers and the purchase of undertakings;

- portfolio management and advice;

- safekeeping and administration of securities; and

- safe custody services.

In relation to **life assurance**, reference should be made to the **activities listed in *Article 2* of the *Life Assurance Directive*** (2002/83).

A number of **other activities have been prescribed by regulation**:

- the acceptance of deposits and other repayable funds from the public;

- the purchase or sale of units or shares of collective investment schemes;

- the provision of services to a person in connection with the purchase or sale of land where payment is in cash and for not less than €13 000;

- the provision of investment services or investment advice;

- the carrying out of trustee or custodian duties for a collective investment scheme;

- the provision of money remittance services.

It should be noted that some of these last activities can also be carried on by designated non-financial institutions.

4.3.2   Identification requirements for life assurance companies

Taking advantage of the possibilities offered by the *Money Laundering Directive*, **life assurance companies are exempted from the identification requirements** in certain cases:

- Where the annual premium of a life assurance policy does not exceed €900, or a single once-off premium does not exceed €2300.

- Where a life assurance policy in respect of a pension scheme is taken out by virtue of a contract of employment or the occupation of the person insured, provided that the policy does not contain a surrender clause and that it is not used as collateral for a loan.

- Where the premium is received from an account held in the name of the policyholder with another designated body (or a corresponding body in another EU Member State or a prescribed third country).

4.3.3   Guidance notes

A number of separate *guidance notes* have been issued for different types of financial institution:

- credit institutions (May 2003);

- financial institutions (*excluding* credit institutions) supervised by the *Irish Financial Services Regulatory Authority (June 2003)*;

- insurance and retail investment products, to be used by life assurance companies and insurance intermediaries (February 2004);

- stockbrokers (February 2004);

- credit unions (July 2004).

4.4   Accountants, auditors and tax advisers

4.4.1   General

Persons in the State who practise as accountants on their own account, auditors or tax advisers are designated bodies for the purposes of *Section 32 of the Criminal Justice Act 1994.*

4.4.2   'Legal privilege' exception

An **accountant, auditor or tax adviser is exempt from the requirement to report suspicious transactions** where he or she receives or obtains information from, or relating to a client:

- in the course of ascertaining the legal position for that client;

- when performing the task of defending or representing that client in or concerning judicial proceedings; or

- when advising that client in relation to instituting or avoiding judicial proceedings.

The term 'client', in relation to an accountant, is not to include a person who employs that accountant under a contract of service.

4.4.3   Guidance

The *Consultative Committee of Accountancy Bodies – Ireland* issued updated guidance documents on AML and AML procedures in September 2005.

The *Irish Taxation Institute* issued Guidelines on the Money Laundering Legislation for Tax Advisers in May 2004.

4.5   Solicitors

4.5.1   General

Persons in the State practising as solicitors are designated bodies where they participate in any of the activities set out in *Article 2a(5) of the Directive*. The obligation to identify clients seems to apply irrespective of the type of work to be carried out. However, the obligation to maintain records, as well as to report suspicious transactions apply only where the solicitor assists in the planning or execution of transactions for a client concerning:

- buying or selling real property or business entities;

- managing client money, securities or other assets;

- opening or managing bank, savings or securities accounts;

- organizing contributions necessary for the creation, operation or management of companies;

- creating, operating or managing trust, company or similar structures.

These document-retention and reporting obligations will also apply where the solicitor acts on behalf of a client in any financial or real estate transaction.

4.5.2   'Legal privilege' exception

A solicitor is exempt from the requirement to report suspicious transactions where he or she receives or obtains information from, or relating to, a client:

- in the course of ascertaining the legal position for that client;

- when performing the task of defending or representing that client in or concerning judicial proceedings; or

- when advising that client in relation to instituting or avoiding judicial proceedings.

4.5.3 'Tipping-off'

A solicitor may **commit the offences of money laundering and 'tipping-off' in respect of all areas of professional activity**. The *Minister for Justice, Equality and Law Reform* has made it clear that he does not regard the fact that a solicitor has ceased acting for a client after making a report is tantamount to 'tipping-off'.

4.5.4 Guidance

The *Law Society of Ireland* issued Guidance Notes for Solicitors on Anti-Money Laundering Legislation in September 2003.

4.6 Estate agents and auctioneers

4.6.1 General

A person practising in the State as an estate agent is a designated body in respect of activities relating to the carrying on of his trade.

An auctioneer practising in the State is also a designated body in respect of activities relating to the carrying on of his trade.

4.6.2 Position of auctioneers

It should be noted that **a dual regime applies to auctioneers** in that, in relation to a real estate transaction, the ordinary threshold of €13 000 will apply for identification purposes whilst, in relation to high value goods, a threshold of €15 000 in cash has been set (see Section 4.7, below).

4.6.3 Guidance

Guidance Notes for Estate Agents and Auctioneers in respect of Land and/or Buildings and High Value Goods were issued in March 2005.

4.7 Dealers in high value goods

Dealers in high value goods, including precious stones, precious metals and works of art are designated bodies where payment is made in cash for a sum of €15 000 or more. With the exception of auctioneers, such dealers are not generally regulated – though some will belong to trade associations – and there is no dedicated regulatory framework for securing their compliance.

There are no guidance notes for dealers in high value goods, save for auctioneers.

4.8 Casinos

Casinos are designated bodies under the relevant legislation. However, casinos are illegal in Ireland and there are therefore no licensed casinos in Ireland and no other body holding itself out as a 'casino'. The Irish regulations nevertheless included casinos, apparently at the instance of the *European Commission* in order to secure full compliance with the *Directive*. Although there are a number of 'private members clubs' offering 'casino-like' facilities, they have not been regarded as casinos and are hence not designated bodies. It is understood that this is being reviewed by the *Department of Justice, Equality and Law Reform* in consultation with the *Attorney-General*.

5 AML/CFT: investigation and enforcement in Ireland

5.1 Investigating bodies

Where **suspicious transaction reports (STRs)** are received, possible money laundering and terrorist financing offences are investigated by the *Garda Síochána* and possible tax offences are investigated by the *Revenue Commissioners*.

Within the *Garda Síochána*, the *Garda Bureau of Fraud Investigation (GBFI)*, which is also designated as the *Irish Financial Intelligence Unit*, receives *STRs*. A unit within the *GBFI*, **the *Money Laundering Investigation Unit (MLIU)* assesses all *STRs*** and handles money-laundering investigations itself or refers them to other *Garda units*. The *MLIU* will handle all terrorist financing investigations in liaison with the *Garda Crime and Security Branch,* which will in turn interact with the security services.

Within the *Revenue Commissioners*, **the *Suspicion of Money Laundering Reports Office* is responsible for investigating money laundering offences in relation to possible tax offences**.

5.2 Prosecution

As seen above (Section 2), the **core money laundering and terrorist financing offences are punishable with substantial fines and/or prison sentences**. This is also the case for failure to comply with AML/CFT compliance rules.

The *Director of Public Prosecutions (DPP)* has the responsibility for prosecuting the most serious crimes – referred to as prosecutions on indictment.

5.3 Confiscation

Ireland has legislation providing for both the **criminal and civil confiscation of the proceeds of crime**.

The *1994 Act* enables a court, on the application of the *DPP*, to require a person convicted of an offence on indictment, to repay any benefit arising from the offence. The **burden of proof required is the civil standard**, on the balance of probabilities, rather than the criminal standard of beyond reasonable doubt. In relation to drug trafficking and terrorist financing offences, the burden of proof will also shift to the defendant to prove that the funds in question are not a benefit arising from the offence.

The 1994 Act also provides for the **seizure of the *instruments* of crime**, including money laundering and the financing of terrorism, as well as of **cash intended to be used in criminal conduct**.

The *Proceeds of Crime Act 1996* enables the **forfeiture of property on a civil law basis, where the *High Court* is satisfied on a balance of probabilities that the property is or represents the proceeds of crime. It may then order the freezing of the property and, after seven years, its disposal for the benefit of the Irish Exchequer. In contrast to the *1994 Act*, there is no need for a prior conviction. The **Criminal Assets Bureau**, which is a multi-agency body, has a **key role in relation to the identification, confiscation, freezing and seizing of assets deriving, or suspected of deriving, from criminal activity**.

5.4 Freezing of terrorist funds

EU Regulations implementing Security *Council Resolutions 1267 and 1373* are directly applicable in Ireland. Statutory instruments made under the 2005 Act create offences for non-compliance and give powers to the *Central Bank and Financial Services Authority of Ireland (CBFSAI)* to give directions or issue instructions. Breach can result in fines not exceeding €10 million or twice the value of the assets in respect of which the offence was committed (whichever is the greater) and/or imprisonment for not more than 20 years.

More generally, the *2005 Act* empowers the *Garda Síochána* to apply to the High Court for **interim or interlocutory orders freezing funds** which are to be used in relation to terrorist offences or an offence of financing terrorism. An order for disposal may be made after an interlocutory order has been in place for seven years. These provisions are designed to mirror provisions in the *Proceeds of Crime Act 1996*.

Since 2005, **the confiscation provisions of the *Criminal Justice Act* have applied in respect of terrorist financing offences**.

Addresses

An Garda Síochána
Garda Bureau of Fraud Investigation
Money Laundering Investigation Unit
Harcourt Square
Harcourt Street
Dublin 2
Ireland
Tel +353 1 666 3712
Fax +353 1 666 3711
mliu@iol.ie

Office of the Revenue Commissioners
Suspicion of Money Laundering Reports Office
Block D
Ashtowngate
Navan Road
Dublin 15
Ireland
Tel +353 1 827 7636
Fax +353 1 827 7636
doconn@revenue.ie

Bibliography

Financial Action Task Force: Third Mutual Evaluation/Detailed Assessment Report – Ireland, 17 September 2006.

Olaf Otting, born 1965, is partner in the Frankfurt office of the German law firm Gleiss Lutz. After a traineeship in a bank, Otting studied law at the universities of Bielefeld and Münster. He joined the Stuttgart office of Gleiss Lutz in 1997. His main practice areas are regulatory issues, especially Banking Regulatory Law, Privatizations, Public Private Partnerships and Public Procurement.

Firm's profile

Gleiss Lutz is one of the leading German law firms. With more than 220 lawyers, and offices in Berlin, Frankfurt, Stuttgart and Munich, Gleiss Lutz advises corporate clients in Germany and abroad, as well as public authorities in various areas of law. In particular, Gleiss Lutz assists its clients in all kinds of corporate restructuring, M&A transactions and corporate financing. Gleiss Lutz is involved in IPOs, bond issues and other capital market transactions. Major corporations regularly seek the firm's advice on all issues of corporate governance and regulatory matters. Gleiss Lutz has an international alliance with UK firm Herbert Smith and the Netherlands firm Stibbe.

Germany

Olaf Otting

Rechtsanwalt

Gleiss Lutz
Mendelssohnstraße 87
60325 Frankfurt am Main
Germany

Tel +49 69 95514-544
Fax +49 69 95514-198
olaf.otting@gleisslutz.com
www.gleisslutz.com

Anti-Money Laundering: International Law and Practice.
Edited by W.H. Muller, C.H. Kälin and J.G. Goldsworth
© 2007 John Wiley & Sons, Ltd

Contents – Germany

1   Introduction

The **central act** governing money laundering in *Germany* is the *Act for the Tracing of Profits from Serious Crime (Gesetz über das Aufspüren von Gewinnen aus schweren Straftaten)*, the so-called *Money Laundering Act (Geldwäschegesetz)*, which came into force on 29 November 1993. With this Act, *Germany* transposed the EU-Directive 91/308/EEC into domestic law. The Act has substantially been amended by the *Anti-Money Laundering Act (Geldwäschebekämpfungsgesetz)* of 15 August 2002, which transposed the second EU-Anti-Money-Laundering-Directive and introduced provisions to fight international terrorism. **The Act lays down identification, recording and notification obligations on credit institutions and other persons falling within its scope to help the *State Prosecution Service (Strafverfolgungsbehörde)* trace profits from serious criminal activities, to combat money laundering and to prevent the introduction of illegal moneys into the finance system.**

Asking enterprises/persons in the private and public sector to assist the *State Prosecution Service* in preventing money laundering by making enquiries and notifications and by recording information is **an important additional source of information on money laundering activities** for the *State Prosecution Service*, especially as the enterprises obligated in the Money Laundering Act could themselves be used by criminals for money laundering purposes.

The **Money Laundering Act** goes **hand in hand** with section 261 of the *Criminal Code (Strafgesetzbuch)* which makes money laundering a criminal offence. This provision came into force on 22 September 1992 and has been amended several times. Section 261 of the *Criminal Code* provides that any person who conceals an object which derives from defined illegal acts, such as robbery, deceit, offences by a criminal ring such as a terrorist group, or covers up its origin, or frustrates or endangers the ascertainment of such object's origin, location, forfeiture, collection or confiscation can be punished with imprisonment from three months to five years. In particularly serious cases, the imprisonment can be from six months to ten years. A person also commits a criminal act if he/she obtains criminal property for himself/herself or a third party, or keeps such property in custody, or uses it for himself/herself or a third party, when such person knew the origin of the criminal property at the time that he/she received it.

Although the Money Laundering Act is also addressed to credit institutions, the Money Laundering Act is not part of the bank regulatory scheme, it is an **independent** act. This makes sense as will be seen from below, in that the Money Laundering Act targets persons and entities other than just credit institutions.

2   The scope of application of the Money Laundering Act

The persons falling within the scope of the Money Laundering Act can be divided into **three main categories**: (1) those in the financial services sector, including the insurance sector; (2) other regulated (or non-regulated) persons and companies whose scope of business can raise money-laundering concerns; and (3) other persons in particular circumstances.

2.1   Enterprises in the financial services sector

Persons obligated under the Money Laundering Act in the financial services sector are **Institutions** as defined in Sec. 1 (4) of the MLA, which are:

- credit institutions

- financial service institutions

- financial enterprises

- investment share companies

- certain insurance companies.

With respect to the definition of these types of institutions, the law refers to the definitions laid down in the *German Banking Act* (*Kreditwesengesetz*). **However, it is important to note that the definition of an 'Institution' under the MLA differs from the definition of an 'Institution' under the German Banking Act.** The MLA definition is much broader as it includes all the types of financial services companies mentioned above.

2.1.1 Credit institutions

Under the German Banking Act, **credit institutions** are **enterprises** which **conduct banking business commercially** or **on a scale which requires a commercially-organized business undertaking**. **Banking business** is any one of the following:

- The acceptance of deposits or other unconditionally repayable funds from the public, provided that the right to repayment is not documented in bearer or registered debt securities, irrespective of whether or not interest is paid (deposit-taking business).

- The business stated in Section 1 (1) sentence 2 of *the Mortgage Bond Act* (*Pfandbriefgesetz*) (pledge business).

- The granting of cash loans and acceptance credits (lending business).

- The purchase of bills of exchange and cheques (discount business).

- The purchase and sale of financial instruments in the credit institution's own name and for the account of others (financial commission as agent business).

- The provision of safe custody and administration of securities for the account of others (securities custody business).

- The carrying out of business specified in section 7(2) of the *Investment Companies Act* (*Investmentgesetz*) (investment fund business).

- The entering into of an obligation to acquire loan receivables prior to maturity (so-called revolving business).

- The assumption of guarantees and other warranties on behalf of others (guarantee business).

- The execution of cashless payments and clearing operations (giro business).

- The assumption of financial instruments for placement at the credit institution's own risk or the assumption of the equivalent by way of guarantee (underwriting business).

- The issuance and administration of electronic money (e-money business).

- The activity of a central counterparty within the meaning of subsection 31.

Insurance companies under private or public law, undertakings who carry out banking business exclusively with its parent company or an affiliated company, and entities that undertake financial commission only in derivatives at a stock exchange for other members of this exchange are exempted from the definition of a credit institution for the purposes of the obligations incumbent on credit institutions pursuant to the Money Laundering Act. The German bank regulator – the *Federal Institute for the Supervision of Financial Services* (*Bundesanstalt für Finanzdienstleistungsaufsicht* [the '*BaFin*']) can order additional exemptions in individual cases.

2.1.2 Financial services institutions

Under German law, **financial services institutions** are **enterprises** which **conduct financial services** for others **commercially** or **on a scale which requires a commercially organized business undertaking**. **Financial services** are any one of the following:

- The brokering of transactions for the sale and purchase of financial instruments or evidence thereof (investment brokerage).

- The sale and purchase of financial instruments in the name of and for the account of a third party (contract brokerage).

- The management of individual portfolios in financial instruments for others with a right of discretion (portfolio management).

- The sale and purchase of financial instruments by way of own account trading for others (own account trading).

- The brokering of deposit business with enterprises domiciled outside the European Economic Area ('EEA') (third state deposit brokerage).

- The execution of payment orders (finance transfer business).

- Trading in currency (currency business).

- Issuing and administration of credit cards and travel cheques unless the card issuer is also the provider of the service underlying the payment process (credit card business).

2.1.3 Financial enterprises

Financial enterprises are enterprises that are **not credit institutions** (2.1.1 above) nor **financial services institutions** (2.1.2 above) and whose **main activity** consists in

- acquiring and holding shareholdings and partnership interests;

- acquiring money receivables for consideration;

- entering into leasing agreements;

- dealing in financial instruments for one's own account;

- providing investment advice in financial instruments (investment advice);

- advising enterprises on their capital structure, industrial strategy or related questions as well as advising in connection with mergers and takeovers of corporations and to offer services; or

- to broker loans between credit institutions (money brokerage).

2.1.4 Branches

The Money Laundering Act is also addressed to **branches** of credit institutions, financial services institutions and financial enterprises which are domiciled in *Germany*, but whose parent is domiciled outside *Germany*. **The Law does not distinguish between parent companies within the EU and those from third countries.** So even if a branch is operated under the 'European Passport' and therefore generally not supervised by the German banking authority, the Anti-Money-Laundering Rules are enforced by the competent German authorities.

On the other hand, **a German institution which is subject to the provisions of the MLA has to make sure that its branches abroad also comply with the requirements of the German Act. If this is not possible due to the legal system of the foreign country the *BaFin* has to be notified within three months after the establishment of the branch abroad.**

2.1.5   Investment share companies

The MLA also applies to **Investment Share Companies** as defined in Sec. 2 (5) of the German *Investment Act (Investmentgesetz)*. These are companies whose purpose is the administration of certain assets for a group of shareholders.

2.1.6   Insurance companies

The Money Laundering Act is addressed to **insurance companies, but only to those which offer life insurance contracts or accident insurance provided the premiums are repayable.** Included under the term insurance companies are also insurance brokers who intermediate the aforementioned insurance contracts.

The companies under 2.1 are hereinafter collectively referred to as '**Institutions**'. Institutions are subject to various duties under the MLA, especially the duty to always identify their contract partner if they enter into a long-term business relationship.

2.2   Other regulated (and non-regulated) companies and persons

The **other group** the Money Laundering Act addresses are:

- Lawyers, legal counsel that are members of a law society, patent lawyers and notaries provided they participate on behalf of their clients in the planning and execution of the following business:
  - purchase and sale of real estate or businesses
  - administration of money, securities and other financial assets of their clients
  - the opening and administration of bank, saving or securities accounts
  - the procurement of resources necessary to form, operate or manage companies
  - the formation, operation or management of trust companies, companies or similar structures
  - if they carry out, in the name and on behalf of the client, finance or property transactions.
- Accountants, sworn bookkeepers, tax advisors and tax agents.
- Real estate brokers.
- Casinos whose customers can buy or sell playing tokens to a value of €1000 or more.

Like institutions the mentioned group of persons and companies will always have to identify its customer.

2.3   Miscellaneous

The **last category** is a sweep up group which covers any

- Other persons carrying on business, to the extent they are acting in the course of their business and are not subject to carry out an identification under the Money Laundering Act (i.e. as they do not fall into a category under 2.1–2.2 above) (see below).

- Persons who manage financial assets for a third party, for consideration, and who are not subject to carry out an identification pursuant to any other provision of the Money Laundering Act.

These companies are not always subject to obligations under the MLA but only under particular circumstances.

Commercial money transportation firms are excluded from this circle of persons falling within the scope of MLA.

3   Obligations of those persons falling within the scope of the MLA

3.1   Obligations of due diligence

3.1.1   Verification of identity of the contracting party on entering into long-term business relationships

An institution must seek **evidence of the identity** of its contracting partner on the entering into of a contract which forms a **long-term business relationship. A long-term business relationship exists, in particular, where an account is to be managed, valuables are to be kept in custody, a pledge is to be taken or a safe deposit box is to be opened. It also applies to the entering into of other contracts, e.g. a leasing agreement.** This duty also applies to those persons designated under 2.2 above. In *Germany*, credit institutions are required to identify their customer if they open an account anyway. This obligation has always been imposed on banks under German tax law. **A bank has to know the person that is entitled to move money on an account.**

With respect to insurance companies falling under 2.1.6 above, the obligation to identify the contracting partner only applies (i) **if the amount of the periodic premiums to be paid during a year exceeds €1000, or (ii) where only a lump sum payment is to be made, if it exceeds €2500 or (iii) if more than €2500 is to be paid into a contribution deposit account.** This rule also applies if the amount of the periodic premiums payable during the course of a year is increased to €1000 or more. This does not, however, apply to insurance contracts which are entered into as part as of an occupational pension scheme on the basis of an employment contract or professional activity of the insured, provided that if the contract is terminated prematurely, there is no redemption value payable and the insurance cannot serve as security for a loan. **If the insurance contract is entered into through an insurance agent or broker or if such is processed through such a broker, then the identification can also be undertaken by the broker.**

3.1.2   Verification of identity of contracting party on accepting cash, securities or precious metals

An institution and those persons under 2.2 above **must also seek evidence of the identity of a person when accepting cash, securities or precious metals with a value of €15 000 or more.**

The person to be identified is the person facing him and handing over the cash, securities or precious metals. This rule, thus, applies to the exchange of foreign currency and payments onto foreign accounts, for example. It does, however, not cover transfers from one account to another, provided that the person has already been identified on the opening of the account. This is because the aim of the Money Laundering Act is to identify new monies coming into the financial system.

A duty to seek evidence of the identity of such person also exists if several individual financial transactions are carried out by a customer which together add up to the value of €15 000, provided there are indications that there is a link between the payments.

The purpose of this rule is to prevent money launderers from circumventing the identification requirements existing at the threshold of €15 000 by making a number of smaller transactions under €15 000 (so-called **smurfing**). The term 'link' has purposely been left abstract as it would be difficult to find a definition to cover all diverse forms of circumvention. A link may be said to exist if a number of transactions are undertaken within a certain period of time which are noticeable due to the similarity in the way they are entered into, the object of the transaction and the way they are settled.

With respect to persons not subject to regular identification requirements (those falling under 2.3 above), these persons are only under a duty to seek evidence of the identity upon accepting cash to a value of €15 000 or more. Again, here, the obligation to identify is vis-à-vis the person facing him/her. This duty to identify also applies to agents appointed by such persons to receive money on their behalf to the extent they are acting in the course of their business.

3.1.3   Identification upon a suspicion

Irrespective of the above obligations to identify, in particular independently of any above-stated thresholds, an institution and other have to identify their customer if there is a **suspicion that a financial transaction serves the purpose of a money laundering crime or serves the financing of a terrorist group**. A financial transaction in this case is any act, 'the purpose or effect of which is to cause a movement of money or other form of displacement of a financial asset'. This covers both cash and non-cash transactions. From the definition, it can be seen that just entering into a contract is sufficient if its purpose is a movement of money.

3.1.4   Meaning of identification

To identify pursuant to the Money Laundering Act **means that on the basis of a valid identity card or passport, the name, date of birth, place of birth, nationality and address**, to the extent contained therein, **of the customer and the type, number and issuing authority of the official ID card or passport have to be determined**. A driver's license, for example, is not sufficient. Foreign official identity documentation, the purpose of which is to allow the owner to be identified can be used to identify non-German inhabitants.

Generally, the customer has to be **physically present** for the identification in order to allow a comparison of the person appearing with the image on the identity card or passport. Identification by post is generally not allowed. However, if for good reason, a personal identification is not possible, then such identification can take place through a so-called 'reliable' third party. Such a reliable third party includes, but is not limited to other Institutions, notaries, the Deutsche Post AG or an embassy or consulate in another EU state. If the identification is performed by a reliable third party, the institution that opens the account nevertheless remains responsible for a proper identification pursuant to the requirements of the MLA. If the address is not on the ID card/passport, this should be obtained by other proof, e.g. electricity bill. The mere giving of a P.O. box is not sufficient.

With respect to the identification of corporate bodies, e.g. a stock corporation or a limited liability company, identification is sufficiently carried out by reference to an official public register, such as the *commercial register* (*Handelsregister*) or the register of associations. The respective excerpt from the register must be made available. The individuals acting on behalf of the corporate, however, must be identified as in the case for natural persons. However, exceptions apply according to a circular issued by the *BaFin*: the identification of individuals representing a company can be waived if the person is registered as the representative of the company in a public register or if more than 5 persons who are registered in such way are already entitled to dispose over the account. A foreign equivalent public register extract will suffice for identifying foreign companies.

In addition, as a number of the above companies are under a duty to establish internal procedures to ensure they cannot be 'misused' for money laundering purposes (see 3.1.8 below), and as all the groups mentioned above have to report to the public prosecution service any facts which result in a suspicion that a transaction is to serve money laundering or the financing of terrorist activities to the criminal authorities (see point 3.2 below), the financial institution should obtain a rather broad picture of its customer, in particular the nature and purpose of the business relationship ('**Know Your Customer Principle**'). The institution should enquire as to the purpose, background and circumstances of the transaction and as far as possible, the institution should try to find out about the source of funds.

3.1.5   Exception to the rule of identification

There is no need to identify the customer, if the customer being identified is **personally known to the person under a duty to identify, and if such customer has been identified at an earlier opportunity, or if the person to be identified is working for a commercial money transport undertaking**. A person may be personally known, for example, because of a long-term business relationship or regular business contact, e.g. daily delivery of business receipts. It is, therefore, not necessary to identify the customer upon every payment or each time a contract is entered into. However, it should be noted that the identifying party still should know who the customer is and his/her address. The identity of the customer should, therefore, be known from another opportunity to identify the customer. This exception, therefore, only applies to the duty to have to show an ID/passport each time that the customer pays in money or enters into another contract.

The duty to identify also does not apply between Institutions themselves.

With respect to insurance companies, the obligation to identify is deemed to be fulfilled, if the insured grants the insurer the authority to withdraw the premium(s) from the account by way of standing order/direct debit, provided that there was a duty to identify the insured upon the opening of the account. If it is not possible to collect the premium by the standing order/direct debit, then the insurer has to carry out the identification subsequently.

In addition, the duty to identify does not apply to owners or staff of an enterprise who regularly pay cash payments onto the enterprise's account. This is to prevent unnecessary bureaucracy. **The duty to identify also does not apply to cash payments made into a night safe.** In both these cases, the Institution should obtain a declaration from the enterprise that it is regularly bringing in business receipts or making payments onto a night safe. If a night safe is kept, the keeper has to obligate the user to only use it for his/her account.

Commercial money transport undertakings are also exempt. This is because the person instructing them will have undertaken sufficient due diligence themselves before commissioning the transport undertaking.

3.1.6   Identification of the beneficial owner

Institutions, and those persons under 2.2 above, have to also enquire of the customer it has **to identify, whether such customer is acting for its own account**. The purpose of this rule is to disclose to the person under a duty to identify in whose economic and legal interests a customer is acting and to prevent dummy transactions. In particular, the covering up of the origin of moneys from serious crime by using trust accounts, is to be hindered by this rule.

If in an individual case, it is clear from the external circumstances that the customer is acting for his/her own account, then no questions need to be asked. However, it should be recorded why this is the case. If the person states that he/she is not acting for his/her own account, the identifying person has to determine the name and address of the person for whom the customer being identified is acting for. This also applies to lawyers, notaries, tax advisors and trustees who open accounts for a client.

If during the course of an existing relationship or when carrying out a transaction there is doubt from the external circumstances that the customer is acting on his/her own behalf, then Institutions and those firms in category 2.3 have to take reasonable measures to determine the identity of the economic beneficiary. If there is still doubt as to the identity of the economic beneficiary, then further questions should be asked and, if necessary, proof of the identity of the economic beneficiary should be obtained.

3.1.7   Obligation to draw up and retain documents

The data obtained in connection with the customer identification must be **recorded. This obligation goes hand in hand with the obligation to identify.** Only if the data is first identified and then recorded can finance transactions and other relationships subsequently be traced. A copy of the identity card or the passport of the customer or a record of the data obtained must be made. If a person is exempt from recording the identity, then the name of person being identified and the reason why the customer is personally known, has to be recorded.

The records have to be kept for six years. The six-year period starts to run in the case of the entering into of an insurance contract at the end of the calendar year in which the contract relationship with the insured ends. Otherwise, the six year period starts to run from the end of the calendar year in which a particular fact was established.

The way of keeping the record is left to the recording company's discretion. Records can, for example, be kept in original paper form, on screen or on other data carriers. However, it has to be ensured that the data ascertained and the data recorded are compatible with each other. In addition, the data must be kept on hand and in a way allowing the firm to establish legibility promptly upon request.

The records may only be used to pursue a money laundering offence. If criminal proceedings are commenced, this circumstance together with the underlying facts also have to be notified to the tax authorities as soon as it is determined that a finance transaction would be of significance for the tax authorities to initiate or carry out tax criminal proceedings. This list for which the records may be used is exhaustive.

3.1.8 Organizational measures

A number of the companies in the groups mentioned above have to take measures to ensure that they are not misused for money laundering. These companies include credit institutions, financial services institutions, auctioneers and casinos. The background to this rule is to request enterprises, whose business may be used for money laundering activities, to help in the prevention of money laundering, by setting up internal control procedures to prevent abuse. In other words, such enterprise is obliged to become active in the fight against money laundering. The management of the company is responsible for the implementation of appropriate measures.

Such measures are:

- **The appointment of a money laundering prevention officer** (*MLPO, Geldwäschebeauftragter*) whose seniority is immediately under the management. Such money laundering prevention officer is the contact person for the *State Prosecution Service*, the *Federal Bureau of Criminal Investigation* (*Bundeskriminalamt*) and the *BaFin*. The appointment of the MLPO has to be notified to the *BaFin*.

- **The development of internal principles**, appropriate business and customer-related security systems and control procedures for the prevention of money laundering and the financing of terrorist groups.

- **To ensure that staff** who are authorized to carry out cash and non-cash finance transactions **are reliable**. This is an important provision. Its aim is to ensure staff do not collude with money laundering criminals and assist in the money laundering themselves.

- **To regularly inform staff** about money laundering methods and the obligations that exist pursuant to the Money Laundering Act.

The money laundering prevention officer has an important function. He has to be in control of all issues relating to compliance with the Money Laundering Act, is responsible for giving binding declarations vis-à-vis the *State Prosecution Service* and must be able to give directions internally. He is, for example, responsible for:

- internal and external reporting of suspicious transactions (see below);

- formulating and updating internal money laundering procedures and policies;

- training employees;

- monitoring a business relationship where money laundering is suspected;

- constant control of compliance with the Money Laundering Act and with the internal regulations for the prevention of money laundering.

He must be entitled to give internal orders to the Institution's employees with respect to Money Laundering issues.

The internal policies and procedures should be laid down in writing. How detailed they are, depends on the size, organization structure, risk situation, customer structure and type of business carried out.

The development of internal principles, appropriate business and customer related security systems and control systems is important as the money laundering will constantly develop new means of money laundering. In particular, staff training is important so that staff are in a position to recognize money laundering. Staff need instruments in place to help them recognize money laundering. The *BaFin* demands that all credit institutions implement IT-bases research systems to prevent money laundering. This includes risk management systems that identify transactions with a potential to be misused for money laundering purposes or to finance terrorist groups.

With regard to the qualification of employees dealing with financial transactions, a person will be regarded as reliable if, given his/her personality, it can be assumed that such person will observe, also from his/her professional expertise, understand and implement, the money laundering laws and the internal procedures and policies of the firm carefully and that he/she himself will not participate in any money laundering offence. The CV, internal reports and references can be used for this purpose.

Finally, if the firm has an internal audit control, this audit should also review that the money laundering is complied with.

3.2   Obligations to report suspicious transactions

Any person falling within the scope of the MLA must **notify** the relevant *State Prosecution Service* and the *Federal Bureau of Criminal Investigation* (*Bundeskriminalamt*) without delay orally, by telephone, by fax or by other electronic means, of the determination of any facts which result in the conclusion that a finance transaction is serving the purpose of money laundering or would if carried out. This is so that the *State Prosecution Service* can start to work on the suspicion immediately. If the notification is made orally, then it has to be repeated in writing.

The duty to notify the *State Prosecution Service* is what gives the Money Laundering Act its teeth. Without such an obligation to notify, the *State Prosecution Service* would lose an important source of knowledge for finding out about money laundering transactions.

There is a central agency, the central agency for suspicious notifications (*Zentralstelle für Verdachtsanzeigen – Financial Intelligence Unit Deutschland, FIU*) within the *Federal Bureau of Criminal Investigation* that has to collect and to analyse all reports of suspicious transactions. In 2005 the *FIU* had to deal with 8241 reports of suspicious transactions.

The person making the report may not inform the customer or any agency other than the *State Prosecution Service* of a notification or any investigation that is initiated. This is so that the customer is not warned in advance causing him/her to evade the *State Prosecution Service* from seizing the monies.

The content of the notification may only be used for criminal proceedings, for tax proceedings and for regulatory purposes by the relevant regulatory body.

After a notification is made, a financial transaction may not be implemented, until the notifying party has received the consent of the *State Prosecution Service* or if two working days have passed since the date of the notification without the transaction being prohibited. This is to give the *State Prosecution Service* time to investigate the suspicion. If it is not possible to postpone the finance transaction on account of its urgent nature, then it may be carried out; the notification has to be made immediately afterwards. An urgent case exists if the customer expressly asks for the transaction to be carried out immediately and not doing so would warn him/her of the suspicion.

The *BaFin* has explained which circumstances may give rise to the suspicion of money laundering. These are, inter alia, that:

- a transaction has no reasonable economic background;

- the amount or kind of assets to be transferred are not in line with the usual living conditions of the relevant customer;

- a transaction is performed in a overcomplicated or cost-intensive manner, without a reasonable economic explanation.

The institution may reject a transaction. However, the obligation to report exists also if the transaction is not performed.

The reports have to be filed to the *State Prosecution Service* by a competent person, usually the MLPO, who deals with all the internal hints and reports. The bank has to make sure internally that all internal reports are transferred to the competent person directly, who is responsible for submitting these to the *State Prosecution Service*.

The institution has to decide if a report is regarded as necessary. If not, the reasons for not filing a report have to be documented. There are a number of formal requirements for the report to the *State Prosecution Service*. Inter alia the report has to include:

- address, telephone number and fax number of the institution;

- the name of the responsible individual (usually the MLPO);

- information if the suspicious transaction has already been performed;

- names and addresses, identification documents of the customer;

- the facts that give rise to the suspicion.

3.3   Offences

The obligations to identify and to report suspicious transactions are strict. Each obligated firm should ensure through their internal organization and working procedures that employees report all cases of suspicion to the relevant money laundering prevention officer. As far as offences of employees are concerned, the following applies:

It is an administrative offence (*Ordnungswidrigkeit*) not to seek evidence of a person's identity as described above nor to record or keep such record of the identification. Both of these can be punished with a fine of up to €100 000.

Any person who does not enquire as to the economic beneficiary of the transaction or does not determine the name and address, informs the customer or a third person other than the *State Prosecution Service* of a notification of a money laundering suspicion to the *State Prosecution Service* or does not inform the *State Prosecution Service* in time, commits an administrative offence, that can be punished with a fine of up to €50 000.

A person who makes a notification pursuant to Section 3.2 above can be held responsible for such a notification, only if the notification was made **knowing** it was **incorrect, willfully** or **due to gross negligence**. The exemption is comprehensive and covers claims under civil and employment laws and tort. The purpose of the exemption is to increase the willingness of persons to make a notification. The caveat is to prevent notifications being made that are unfounded or an abuse of process.

With respect to criminal liability, any person who lets the money laundering transaction take place with his/her consent or as a result of his/her implied acceptance or gross negligence commits a criminal offence under section 261 *Criminal Code*. Prerequisite of such criminal liability is that any asset constituting or representing a person's benefit from certain criminal conduct is concealed or that the identification of the origin or the locating of such asset is frustrated or endangered. The offence can also be committed by acquiring, using or having possession of such asset or by giving or transferring it to any third person.

The offender must know, suspect or hold for possible or frivolously overlook the illegal origin of the property.

Simply accepting funds that derive from the crimes mentioned will suffice for section 261 *Criminal Code* provided that the subjective prerequisites as described above are fulfilled by the person receiving the money. Being particularly careless or deliberately indifferent about the illegal origin of the funds may, thus, lead to criminal liability.

A criminal offence may, thus, be committed by any employee who is involved in customer transactions. Disclosure will protect him/her from prosecution. The disclosure must, however, reach the *State Prosecution Service*. If the money laundering prevention officer does not make a disclosure, he should inform the relevant employee. The employee can then decide himself whether to make a disclosure to avoid prosecution from a possible involvement in money laundering.

4   Supervision of Money Laundering Act

The following authorities are responsible for overseeing the Money Laundering Act:

- For the *bank of reconstruction* (*Kreditanstalt für Wiederaufbau*), the **Federal Ministry of Finance (Bundesministerium der Finanzen)**.

- For all other credit institutions (except for the German Bundesbank), financial service institutions, investment companies, the **Federal Institute for the Supervision of Financial Services (Bundesanstalt für Finanzdienstleistungsaufsicht (BaFin))**.

- For insurance companies, the relevant supervisory body for insurance (which is the *BaFin*), for insurance brokers the *BaFin* as well.

- Otherwise, the responsible authority according to federal or state law.

Credit institutions, financial service institutions, investment companies and insurance companies are primarily supervised under the uniform roof of the *BaFin*. Previously different authorities, e.g. *Bundesaufsichtsamt für das Kreditwesen, Bundesaufsichtsamt für das Versicherungswesen*, carried out the supervision, but these were merged in 2002 to form one authority. The *BaFin* or its predecessor authority have issued detailed rules as to money laundering to be observed by the respective regulated institutions.

According to Sec. 6a of the *German Banking Act* the *BaFin* can freeze money if there are facts that indicate that this money serves the financing of a terrorist group.

The supervision of credit institutions under the Money Laundering Act is closely linked with their general supervision under the German Banking Act. First of all, the same authority (the *BaFin*) is competent. The *BaFin* can make use of its power under the German Banking Act if it comes to the conclusion that a credit institution neglects its obligations under the Money Laundering Act. In this case, e.g. the reliability of the bank's management – which is a necessary requirement for the banking license – could be doubted. The *BaFin* can also issue individual orders based on Sec. 6 (2) of the German Banking Act. In addition the *BaFin* has issued a number of detailed circulars and memoranda that explain the duties and obligations under the Money Laundering Act.

Addresses

Bundesanstalt für Finanzdienstleistungsaufsicht
Federal Institute for the Supervision of Financial Services (the 'BaFin')
Graurheindorfer Str. 108
53117 Bonn
Germany

Tel +49 228-4108-0
Fax +49 228-4108-1550

Lurgiallee 12
60439 Frankfurt

Tel +49 228/4108 -0
Fax +49 228/4108-123

Bundeskriminalamt
(Federal Bureau of Criminal Investigation)
Referat SO 32
Zentralstelle für (Geldwäsche-)
Verdachtsanzeigen
(Central Agency for suspicious notifications)
65173 Wiesbaden

Tel +49-(0)611 55-18615 or
+49-(0)611 55-14545
Fax +49-(0)611 55-45300

Bibliography

Beck, H./Samm, C.-T.: KWG-Kommentar (loose-leaf 02/06).

Boos, K.-H./Fischer, R./Schulte-Mattler, H. (eds): Kreditwesengesetz, 2nd edition, 2004.

Busch, D./Teichmann, H.: Das neue Geldwäscherecht, 2003.

Findeisen, M.: Nationale und internationale Maßnahmen gegen die Geldwäsche und die Finanzierung des Terrorismus – Ein Instrument zur Sicherstellung der Stabilität der Finanzmärkte, Working Paper Series No. 7, 2003.

Fülbier, A./Aepfelbach, R./Langweg, C.: Kommentar zum Geldwäschegesetz, 5th edition, 2006.

Höche, T.: Bekämpfung von Geldwäsche und Terrorfinanzierung, 2003.

Reischauer, F./Kleinhaus, J.: KWG-Kommentar (loose-leaf 02/06).

Schröter, J./Steuer, S. (eds): Bankrecht und Bankpraxis, volume 5, Chapter 16 (loose-leaf 11/05).

Warnitz, H.-B./Janovsky, T. (eds): Handbuch des Wirtschafts- und Steuerstrafrechts, 2nd edition, 2004, Chapter 5.

Philippe Blaquier-Cirelli is a senior partner at Jeantet Associés supervising the litigation group. He represents major French and international clients in complex litigation and arbitration cases. Philippe Blaquier-Cirelli earned his Juris Doctor and Master's degree in Private Law at the University of Lille. He also holds a Master's degree from the Law School of La Sorbonne University in Paris (major international private law). He graduated from The Hague Academy of International Law and from the Institut des Hautes Etudes de Défense Internationale. He has written and lectured on various legal issues relating to French and international law, primarily on international litigation and dispute resolution. In particular, he has been a lecturer at the Institut d'Etudes Politiques of Paris and Assistant Secretary at The Hague Academy of International Law.

Pierre-Yves Couturier is a partner at Jeantet Associés, one of the leading French law firms. He specializes in criminal litigation with emphasis on notorious white-collar cases. He represents major French, European and US companies. Pierre-Yves Couturier received his education at the University of Bordeaux where he earned his Master's degree in corporate law and an Advanced degree in private law. He also holds a Diploma of the Criminology Division at the René Descartes School of Medicine (University of Paris V). He has written and lectured on various legal issues relating to French and international criminal law. He is a member of the International Association of Criminal Law and was appointed Defense Counsel for the International Criminal Tribunals. In 2006, he represented the judges during the highly publicized hearings in front of the Parliamentary Committee investigating the French criminal system.

Firm's profile

Established in 1924, **Jeantet Associés** is a leading independent French law firm recognized for its extensive practice in strategic areas of business law. The firm's distinguished experience and expertise attract a full array of clients ranging from public, private, national and multinational corporations to banking and financial institutions and sovereign and territorial government agencies. Practice areas include mergers and acquisitions, banking and finance, tax, antitrust, competition and distribution, international trade and contracts, labor law, business criminal law, administrative law, bankruptcy, insolvency and restructuring, real estate, energy and natural resources and litigation and alternative dispute resolution.

France

Philippe Blaquier-Cirelli
Pierre-Yves Couturier

Attorneys-at-law
Partners

Jeantet Associés
87–89 avenue Kléber
75784 Paris Cedex 16
France

Tel +33 1 45 05 81 85
Fax +33 1 45 05 82 28
pblaquiercirelli@jeantet.fr
pycouturier@jeantet.fr
www.jeantet.fr

Anti-Money Laundering: International Law and Practice.
Edited by W.H. Muller, C.H. Kälin and J.G. Goldsworth
© 2007 John Wiley & Sons, Ltd

Contents – France

Introduction

Early on, States recognized the need to combat money laundering, or the processing of criminal proceeds in order to disguise their illegal origin. Money laundering can have damaging effects both on the economy and the security of States.

Hence, in the 1980s, national and international bodies expressed their will to combat money laundering. This led to the creation and implementation in France of the appropriate legal and institutional instruments.

1   Relevant legislation

1.1   Chronology

In the early 1980s, the *Council of Europe* urged Member States to ensure that their financial communities adopt measures against the transfer and the safekeeping of funds of criminal origin (*Recommendation of 27 June 1980*).

1.1.1   FATF

That recommendation was the basis for the establishment in French law of the special offense of money laundering (*Act of 31 December 1987*[1]). That was followed less than a year later by the establishment of an offense enabling the French customs authority to combat such practices (*Act of 23 December 1988*). It is worth mentioning that, prior to these developments, the banking sector was already aware of its role and the need to act in this area. More specifically, it was aware of the inherent risk in the transfer and deposit of funds derived from criminal activity (*Basel Statement of Principles of 12 December 1988*[2]).

However, it was not until *the United Nations Convention against drug trafficking of 20 December 1988*[3] that Member States were bound to pass legislation establishing money laundering as an offense (the Convention came into force in France on 31 March 1991). The Convention also provided for the creation of a permanent group to study counter measures against money laundering. *The Financial Action Task Force ('FATF')*, the leading international body on money laundering was set up soon after.

The role of *FATF* is to foresee and recommend anti-money laundering measures, in particular to study the role of the banking system in this field (Forty Recommendations in 1990, since reviewed and updated to take into account the expansion of money laundering schemes and international terrorism). These Recommendations were promptly introduced in France by the *Act of 12 July 1990*[4] and its implementing *decree of 13 February 1991*[5] (codified in 2000 in the *French Monetary and Financial Code*). This legislation created a customer due diligence

---

[1] *Act n° 87-1157* of 31 December 1987.
[2] *Act n° 88-1149* of 23 December 1988.
[3] *The United Nations Convention Against Illicit Traffic in Narcotic Drugs and Psychotropic Substances* adopted in Vienna on 19 December 1988.
[4] *Act n° 90-614* of 12 July 1990 on the contribution of financial institutions to the fight against money laundering in connection with drug trafficking.
[5] *Decree n° 91-160* of 13 February 1991.

requirement (*obligation de vigilance*) for banking sector professionals and an obligation to report transactions suspected of having an illicit origin, or reporting obligation (*déclaration de soupçon*).

1.1.2 European Directives and their implementation in French law

The Recommendations also led to the establishment, by the *Decree of 9 May 1990*,[6] of *TRACFIN*, France's financial intelligence unit, as well as the *OCRGDF*, the central bureau for serious financial crime at the *Ministry of the Interior (Office central pour la répression de la grande délinquance financière)*. TRACFIN is charged with processing reports of suspected money laundering by persons referred to in the *Act of 12 July 1990. TRACFIN* has an automated personal data system, dubbed 'Tracinfo', that stores such data for 10 years (*Order of 30 July 2001*). Moreover, a number of French banks with international networks are already equipped with similar screening mechanisms.

At *European Union* level, the *Council Directive of 10 June 1991*[7] on prevention of the use of the financial system for the purpose of money laundering was the first directive to require Member States to enact laws. Such implementation occurred with the enactment of the *Act of 13 May 1996*,[8] which introduced the general offense of money laundering into French legislation, thus extending the scope of penalties. The system was enhanced by the *New Economic Regulations Act of 15 May 2001*,[9] which reinforced the internal mechanism to combat money laundering. *Article 34 of the Act of 15 May 2001* broadened the obligation to report sums and transactions suspected of having an illicit origin by a change of wording: the latest version of *article L-562-2 of the French Monetary and Financial Code* mandates financial entities as well as the persons referred to in the relevant section to report to *TRACFIN* any sums or transactions involving sums 'that might' have been derived from certain offenses, while *the 1990 Act*[10] required such reporting only when the sums 'seemed to have been derived' from certain offenses. Furthermore, the phrase 'from activities by criminal organizations' was replaced by 'from organized criminal activities'.

A second Directive came into force on 4 December 2001,[11] amending *Council Directive 91/308/EEC* on prevention of the use of the financial system for the purpose of money laundering. In order to combat money laundering more effectively, it broadened the scope of the obligation to report suspicious transactions (*déclaration de soupçon*). *The second Directive* extends the categories of people bound by this obligation and the list of illicit activities that may give rise to money laundering. That led to the enactment of the *Act of 11 February 2004*,[12] which extends the obligation to report suspicious transactions to members of the legal profession. The obligation itself was reinforced by the *Act of 9 March 2004*.[13]

---

[6] *Decree of 9 May 1990* on the establishment of a coordination unit in charge of processing intelligence and taking action against clandestine financial networks (Traitement du renseignement et action contre les circuits financiers clandestins).
[7] *Directive n° 91/308/EEC* of 10 June 1991.
[8] *Act of 13 May 1996 n° 96-392* on combating money laundering and drug trafficking and international cooperation regarding seizure and confiscation of the proceeds of crime.
[9] *Act n° 2001-420* of 15 May 2001 on New Economic Regulations.
[10] See n° 4.
[11] *Directive n° 2001/97/EC* of 4 December 2001.
[12] *Act n° 2004-130* of 11 February 2004 modifying the status of certain legal professionals, court experts, intellectual property advisors and auctioneers.
[13] *Act n° 2004-204* of 9 March 2004 on the adaptation of the judicial system to new trends in crime.

A *third European Directive* was adopted on 26 October 2005,[14] aimed at strengthening the preventive mechanism provided by the previous two Directives. Member States must bring into force the laws, regulations and administrative provisions necessary to comply with the *2005 Directive* by 15 December 2007. Under French law, the latest development in this regard was the publication on 27 June 2006[15] of an *implementing decree for the Act of 11 February 2004* regarding the legal profession as well as the adoption under *French law* of some of the provisions of the *third European Directive*.

1.2   Definition of money laundering

The *Act of 13 May 1996*[16] established the general offense of money laundering while maintaining (i) the special offense of money laundering in connection with drug traffic (*Article 222-38 of the French Criminal Code*) and (ii) a special customs offense (*Article 415 of the French Customs Code*). In addition, there is a special section in the *French Criminal Code* related to money laundering in connection with terrorist activities (*Articles 421-1-6 and 422-2-2 of the French Criminal Code*). The legislative intent was to combat, as broadly as possible, money laundering stemming from illegal activities linked to terrorism, whether the originating funds were obtained illegally or not (*Act of 15 November 2001*[17]).

1.2.1   Nature of the offense

Money laundering is an 'incidental' offense. This means that it must be linked or associated with the main offense. That offense, which must have been committed prior to the money laundering and have generated a direct or indirect benefit, must be either a crime or an offense under the *French Criminal Code* (excluding petty offenses).

The prior existence of a felony or an offense is a necessary but sufficient condition. Therefore, punishment of the person having committed the main offense has no bearing on the money laundering offense. Likewise, the fact that the main offense was committed outside France either by a French national or by a foreigner does not prevent prosecution of the offense. Moreover, the *Criminal Chamber of the French Supreme Court (Cour de Cassation)* held that the same person can be prosecuted and sentenced with respect to both the main offense and the offense of money laundering, which differs from the case law on receiving stolen goods (*recel*). The person who committed an offense can thus be prosecuted for laundering the proceeds derived from that illegal activity (*judgment of the Criminal Chamber of the French Supreme Court of 14 January 2004*).

Money laundering is an 'intentional' offense, which means that it cannot be caused by negligence or carelessness. Thus the person prosecuted for money laundering must have had full knowledge of his or her actions. The *French Criminal Code* requires not only awareness or knowledge of the illegal origin of the proceeds, but also willingness to disguise the origin of the proceeds.

However, knowledge of the main offense by the person who laundered money is sufficient for that person to be prosecuted on the basis of the main offense.

---

[14] *Directive n° 2005/60/EC* of 26 October 2005.
[15] *Decree n° 2006-736* of 26 June 2006 on combating money laundering and amending the Monetary and Financial Code.
[16] See n° 8.
[17] *Act n° 2001-1062* of 15 November 2001 on everyday security.

Money laundering is either ordinary, or aggravated when it is committed (i) habitually or (ii) using facilities offered by the practise of a profession or (iii) when it is committed by an organized gang or (iv) with knowledge of the seriousness of the main offense or (v) when it is committed more than once.

An attempt to commit money laundering is liable to the same penalties as the actual offense.

1.2.2   Definition

Since 1996, the *French Criminal Code* includes a new chapter entitled 'Obligations relating to the Prevention of Money Laundering' (ii) (*Articles 324-1 to 324-9*).

The French legal definition of money laundering can be found under *Article 324-1 of the French Criminal Code*, which reads as follow:

To launder money is to facilitate by any means the falsification of the origin of the goods or income derived by the perpetrator of a felony or an offense that has brought him or her direct or indirect benefit.

Money laundering also includes assistance in investing, concealing or converting the direct or indirect proceeds of a felony or an offence.

1.3   Penalties

Distinctions are made depending on whether the offense was committed by a natural person or by a legal person.

1.3.1   Natural persons

For the general offense of ordinary money laundering misdemeanor, a natural person is punishable by a maximum of 5 years imprisonment and a fine of €375 000 (*Article 324-1 of the French Criminal Code*). Aggravated circumstances exist when the general offense is committed habitually or using facilities offered by the practice of a profession or when it is committed by an organized gang. In those cases, a natural person is punishable by a maximum of 10 years imprisonment and a fine of €750 000. The same penalties apply to the special offense of money laundering.

The fines may be raised to half the value of the property or funds in respect of which the money laundering operations were carried out.

With respect to the special customs offense, a natural person may be punished by imprisonment of 2 to 10 years, the confiscation of the sums obtained illegally or the equivalent amount when seizure cannot be ordered and a fine equal to 1 to 5 times the amount related to the offense or attempted offense.

Money laundering in connection with terrorism is punishable by a maximum of 10 years imprisonment and a fine of €225 000. These penalties may be increased if the aggravated circumstances set forth in *Article 421-3 of the French Criminal Code* are present.

1.3.2   Legal persons

A legal person can only be held criminally liable if it is proven that the offense was committed by a person representing the legal person and on its behalf. The penalties that can be brought against legal persons are:

- A fine equal to 5 times the amount incurred by a natural person, which amounts to €1 875 000 for the general offense of ordinary money laundering or €3 750 000 for the general offense of aggravated money laundering.

- The penalties set forth in *Article 131-39 of the French Criminal Code* (including dissolution, prohibition on practicing directly or indirectly one or more social or professional activities, court supervision of liquidation, permanent closure or closure for up to 5 years).

1.4   Outlook

Considerable progress has already been achieved. As a result of close cooperation between the banking system and *TRACFIN*, the *French Banking Federation* now offers its members a training package on money laundering counter measures, with a view to improving reporting of suspicious activities. The package also improves the requisite internal procedures to enhance monitoring and the capacity to detect signs of money laundering.

1.4.1   Developments under debate

There is growing awareness among representatives of the legal profession of the consequences of their compulsory involvement in combating money laundering. In France, the issue is the subject of fierce debate, particularly with regard to the reporting obligation and the principle of client-lawyer confidentiality. In order to raise lawyers' awareness of the situation, in December 2005 the *National Bar Association* published a booklet of basic recommendations to prevent money laundering.

For many years, French legislation was more stringent than international anti-money laundering requirements. This is no longer the case. In fact, the severity of penalties contrasts surprisingly with the weakness of preventive measures with respect to money laundering, especially regarding the requirement to report on sums or transactions suspected of having an illicit origin.

This gap will partly disappear with the implementation in French law of the *third European Directive*, which broadens the scope of the obligation to report suspicious activities.

1.4.2   A necessary development

The *third Directive* also introduces the concept of 'money laundering risk'. The advantage of the new concept is that specific procedures are applied depending on the type of risk.

Member States must pass domestic legislation to comply with the *third Directive* by 15 December 2007. One of the main features of *the third Directive* is a new monitoring obligation, or customer identification obligation, i.e. the identification of instances of beneficial ownership on the basis of a definition of 'beneficial owner' that supersedes 'financial or economic beneficiary'. In other words, that will lead to the identification of the beneficial owner for which the customer of the financial institution is performing the transaction in order to determine the identity of the agent and the identity of the principal.

This rule alone illustrates the progress accomplished by European law in the field, which is now ahead of French legislation. Nevertheless, most of the provisions of the *2005 Directive*[18] with

---

[18] See n° 14.

respect to monitoring obligations are already contained in the *French Monetary and Financial Code*.

For instance, the Directive recommends the identification of the beneficial owner of a transaction performed by a financial entity. This obligation already exists in French law and was even stepped up by the *Decree*[19] *of 26 June 2006*, which provides a legal definition of 'beneficial owner'.

Finally, attention needs to be drawn to the crucial issue of prosecuting money laundering in an international context. Cross-border offenses entail special difficulties for a French judge in terms of jurisdiction as well as applicable foreign law, since these offenses are by nature harder to identify and punish.

2　Prevention and detection of money laundering

In order to render the mechanism for detecting money laundering as efficient as possible, the French legislator has implemented genuine cooperation between the public authorities (institutional mechanism) and the banking sector (functional mechanism). In order to enhance the effectiveness of the public prosecutor, it was necessary to act upstream. That goal was achieved by the *Act of 12 July 1990*, setting up of a *TRACFIN* Unit as well as adopting the obligation to monitor transactions and to report those suspected of having an illicit origin.

2.1　Institutional mechanism under French law

This mechanism is chiefly embodied by two agencies: *TRACFIN* and the *OCRGDF*.

2.1.1　Overview

TRACFIN is at once an intelligence agency dealing with clandestine financial networks, a center of financial expertise, and an operational unit charged with combating money laundering. In the latter capacity, *TRACFIN*'s primary role is to collect reports of suspicious transactions submitted by professionals bound by a reporting obligation pursuant to the *Act of 12 July 1990. TRACFIN* reports directly to the Ministry of Finance. It analyzes the reports and conducts investigations into the reported transactions suspected of having an illicit origin. It may, where appropriate, exchange information with other agencies such as the *OCRGDF*. It may also cooperate with other national or international entities such as *EUROPOL*, the customs authorities or the supervisory authorities in the sectors covered by the reporting obligation. Where appropriate, *TRACFIN* brings the facts to the attention of the public prosecutor. In turn, the public prosecutor gathers evidence for possible indictment with the assistance of *OCRGDF* staff. The procedure allows the reporting source to remain anonymous: the source itself is not quoted and its initial report is not appended to the prosecution documents (*Article L-562-6 of the French Monetary and Financial Code*).

2.1.2　Mission

To perform its mission, *TRACFIN* has been granted special powers, for example:

- It may oppose the performance of the reported transaction for a maximum period of 12 hours. That period may be extended by the judicial authorities.

---

[19] See n° 15.

- It may ask any member of the professional organizations bound by the reporting obligation to forward all relevant documents relating to the reported operation. This can be done in order (i) to trace the operation or (ii) to cooperate with foreign agencies dealing with the matter. The data received by *TRACFIN* cannot be used for any purposes other than to combat money laundering and terrorist financing. Disclosure of such information is liable to criminal prosecution.

2.2 Functional mechanism: role of financial institutions

Since *the 1980 Council of Europe Recommendation*, the role of the banking sector in combating money laundering has been stressed. Under French law, the *Act of 12 July 1990*[20] took the same approach by establishing a monitoring obligation for the relevant professionals and, most importantly, an obligation to report sums or transactions suspected of having an illicit origin to *TRACFIN*. The special feature of French legislation is that it involves a broad range of professionals from the finance and banking sector and from the accounting and legal professions in combating money laundering.

As of 1991, a number of financial institutions were required to set up internal procedures in order to perform their monitoring and reporting duties introduced by the 1990 Act[21] (Regulation of the Regulatory Committee for the Banking and Financial System ['*CRBF*'] of 15 February 1991[22]).

The same applied regarding internal controls necessary to ensure compliance with those procedures. That obligation has since been broadened by the *Third European Directive*.[23]

For the sake of clarity, the categories of persons that must comply with the reporting and monitoring obligations need to be identified. Hereafter these persons will be referred to as 'the financial institutions and persons listed under *Article L-562-1 of the French Monetary and Financial Code*'. They are:

- financial institutions;

- persons who execute, supervise, or recommend transactions relating to the acquisition, sale, transfer or renting of real property;

- the legal representatives and managers of casinos, groups, clubs and companies that organize games of chance, lotteries or sports, racing and other betting;

- persons who regularly engage in trading in, or organizing the sale of gems, precious materials, antiques and works of art;

- companies entitled to the exemption granted by the *Committee Regulating the Credit Institutions and Investment Funds (CECEI)*;

- notaries, bailiffs, receivers and court-appointed administrators, as well as members of *the French Administrative Supreme Court (Conseil d'Etat)* and of the *French Supreme Court (Cour de Cassation)*, and *counsel of the Courts of Appeal;*

- court-appointed auctioneers and companies effecting voluntary sales of furniture at public auctions;

---

[20] See n° 4.
[21] See n° 4.
[22] *Regulation n° 91-07* of 15 February 1991 of the *Regulatory Committee for the Banking and Financial System*.
[23] See n° 14.

- accountants and auditors;

- authorized intermediaries trading in transferable securities.

In any event, the legislative intent was to cover the broadest variety of situations related to money laundering by making a distinction between facilitating by any means the falsification of the origin of criminal proceeds, and providing assistance in investing, concealing or converting the direct or indirect proceeds of a felony or offense. The detection mechanism therefore needed to be adapted to reflect the variety of situations. This variety can be seen through the prism of reporting and monitoring obligations.

2.2.1   Reporting obligation

The financial institutions and persons listed under *Article L-562-1 of the French Monetary and Financial Code* are subject to the obligation to report sums and transactions suspected of having an illicit origin.

Those persons must report sums or transactions when they have doubt about the legality of those sums or transactions.

The list of transactions can be found under *Article L562-2 §1 and 2 of the French Monetary and Financial Code* (regarding the legal profession, the list of transactions is codified under *Article L562-2-1 of the French Monetary and Financial Code*). The list of transactions was extended by *the Third European Directive* in 2005.[24]

The transactions covered by the reporting obligation involve sums that might have been derived from drug trafficking, fraud against the financial interests of *the European Union*, corruption or organized crime or that might contribute to the financing of terrorist activities.

The reporting obligation must be performed in good faith. In that case, the person reporting the transaction is entitled to immunity from prosecution either civil or criminal (*Article L562-8 of the French Monetary and Financial Code*). Such immunity applies even if the illicit origin of the reported sums or transactions is not established or if the facts in dispute ultimately lead to an acquittal.[25]

This issue of immunity has been ruled upon by the *French Supreme Court*. Following a report, the reporting entity must not divulge the fact that it has made a report or revealed any information about any legal consequences. Under no circumstance may the reporting entity inform its client of the procedure (*Article L574-1 and L574-2 of the French Monetary and Financial Code*).

Persons other than the financial entities or persons referred to under *Article L562-1* who, in the normal course of their business, execute, supervise or recommend transactions that give rise to financial transfers, are required to report to the public prosecutor any transactions they have knowledge of involving sums that they know to be the proceeds of an offense.

This second reporting obligation differs from the obligation to report sums or transactions suspected of having an illicit origin since the person reporting the transaction must have actual knowledge of the illegal fact (*Article L561-1 of the French Monetary and Financial Code*).

---

[24] See n° 14.
[25] Judgment of the *Criminal Chamber of the French Supreme Court* of 3 December 2003.

The reporting obligation breaks down into three types of procedure:

- The procedure concerning persons bound by the reporting obligation (with the exception of the legal profession) – such persons must report sums or transactions suspected of having an illicit origin to *TRACFIN*. In turn, *TRACFIN* refers the matter to the public prosecutor if the information received reveals facts liable to prosecution.

- The procedure concerning the legal profession – this report must be submitted to the *National Bar Association*, which will, if necessary, refer the matter to *TRACFIN*.

- The procedure concerning the persons referred to in *Article L561-1 of the French Monetary and Financial Code* who do not come under the first two categories – these persons must report suspicious operations directly to the public prosecutor.

The public prosecutor will then verify and investigate the matter in order to establish whether the proceeds are of criminal origin. The funds may be seized or confiscated.

In addition to the reporting obligation, financial entities and the persons referred to in *Article L562-1 of the French Monetary and Financial Code*, have a monitoring obligation.

2.2.2 Monitoring obligation

This obligation covers both the general and the reinforced monitoring obligations.

The general monitoring obligation applies independently of any particular suspicion, as a simple precautionary measure (*Article 563-1 of the French Monetary and Financial Code*).

This obligation applies in anticipation of forthcoming audits and it is not linked to particular transactions. It encompasses the obligation for financial entities (and those persons referred to under *Article L562-1 of the French Monetary and Financial Code*) to confirm the identity of regular or occasional customers.

Likewise, upon terminating the contractual relationship with a customer, the financial entity and the persons referred to under *Article L562-1 of the French Monetary and Financial Code* must keep the documents concerning the identity of their regular or occasional customers for a period of 5 years.

The reinforced monitoring obligation requires those professionals bound by the obligation to report to *TRACFIN* to monitor suspicious transactions carefully and to request information about those transactions with respect to their background and purpose (*Articles L563-2 to L563-4 of the Monetary and Financial Code*). The persons subject to this reinforced obligation are the financial institutions and persons referred to *under Article L562-1 of the French Monetary and Financial Code*.

This obligation is triggered by financial thresholds (transactions exceeding a certain amount) and it consists most often in identifying the occasional customer or the beneficial owner of the transaction.

For any transaction involving sums of more than €150 000, where the transactions performed by the customer in question do not usually exceed that amount, the financial entities (or the persons referred to in *Article L562-1 of the French Monetary and Financial Code*) are required to ask the customer about the origin and destination of the sums as well as the purpose of the transaction and the identity of the person benefiting from the transaction.

This reinforced duty applies particularly when the transaction is performed under unusually complex conditions or does not seem to have a financial justification or a legal purpose. In such instances, the details of the transaction must be described in writing and kept for a period of 5 years from the date of the transaction (*Article L563-3 of the French Monetary and Financial Code*).

However, there is a limit to these obligations: the professionals involved cannot overstep their professional duties. In particular, they cannot interfere in the management of their customer's businesses nor encroach upon the policing powers of *TRACFIN* or the judicial authorities.

3 Recent developments

3.1 The Third European Directive

As mentioned earlier, the *Third European Directive*[26] broadens the categories of professionals bound by the reporting requirement and the types of transactions covered by the reporting and monitoring obligations.

The reporting obligation covers all offenses punishable by imprisonment or by a preventive injunction for a period of more than one year.

The monitoring obligation is triggered by new financial thresholds above which verification becomes compulsory. The Directive introduces the concepts of 'occasional customer' and 'beneficial owner' (the definition of these terms was introduced into French legislation by the *Decree of 26 June 2006*, which allows a more precise application of the *French Monetary and Financial Code*).

3.2 Decree of 26 June 2006

The main purpose of this decree is to extend preventive measures against money laundering to new categories of professionals. It introduces a monitoring obligation for 'occasional customers' and also establishes the mechanism for off-site identification of natural persons and the creation and implementation of internal control procedures.

The decree[27] represents the latest anti-money laundering development under French law. It deals primarily with two issues: the extension of the reporting obligation to the accounting and legal professions and the implementation of some aspects of the *Third European Directive*. Regarding the accounting and legal professions, the *Act of 11 February 2004* already required such professionals to report transactions with an illicit origin.

The delay in implementing this legal requirement was caused by debate over the client–lawyer confidentiality principle and the principle of independence of members of the Bar. On 26 April 2006, the *National Bar Association* forwarded a request to members of the European Parliament asking that lawyers not to be included in the categories of persons bound by the reporting obligation or the duty to cooperate with the authorities.[28] As it stands, the reporting obligation for lawyers only applies to their non-judiciary activities and only when they participate directly or on behalf of their clients in a financial or real estate transaction or certain other transactions.

---

[26] See n° 14.
[27] See n° 15.
[28] Recueil Dalloz 2006 n° 26.

The second major contribution of *the Decree of 26 June 2006* is to implement[29] aspects of the *Third European Directive*. The decree focuses on the monitoring obligation. In this respect, it provides a definition of 'occasional customer', defined as any person whose sole purpose is to perform a one-time transaction. A transaction involving sums in excess of €8000 (or linked transactions with a combined value in excess of €8000) makes customer identification compulsory (*Article 563-1-1 of the French Monetary and Financial Code*).

The decree also defines the concept of 'beneficial owner'. A beneficial owner is the person on whose behalf the transaction is performed or requested. There are some exceptions to the duty to identify beneficial owners codified under *Article R563-1-IV-4 of the French Monetary and Financial Code*. The establishment and implementation of internal procedures to detect suspicious transactions became compulsory with the passage of the Third European Directive. The Decree of 26 June 2006 extends the obligation to establish and implement internal procedures to all financial institutions and the persons bound by the monitoring and reporting obligations.[30] This has considerably broadened anti-money laundering procedures and requirements under French law.

4 Penalties

The financial entities (and the persons referred to under *Article L562-1 of the French Monetary and Financial Code*) are not subject to criminal prosecution when they do not comply with their reporting and monitoring obligations. However, they may be subject to disciplinary or administrative sanctions.

4.1 Disciplinary and administrative sanctions

Pursuant to *Articles L563-5 and L563-6 of the French Monetary and Financial Code*, non-compliance by a professional concerned with the two abovementioned obligations may expose that professional to disciplinary or administrative sanctions by his or her supervisory authority (*Banking Commission*, etc.). *The French Supreme Court* has ruled that the victim of a criminal act could not invoke non-compliance with these obligations as grounds for claiming damages from financial entities.[31] That interpretation is currently under debate.[32]

4.2 Disclosure to clients

Sanctions may be applied if the fact that a report has been filed or any information about any legal consequences is disclosed to clients. In this respect, *Article L562-4 of the French Monetary and Financial Code* sets a maximum fine of €22 500. A professional can also be barred from practice for violating the non-disclosure obligation.

Without doubt, anti-money laundering measures have been considerably stepped up in the past few years. The extension of the relevant procedures to professionals of the accounting and legal professions, particularly lawyers who until now under French law were not bound by reporting and monitoring obligations, strengthens this preventive mechanism.

---

[29] *Brigitte Brom & Delphine* Chemin, Lamy Editions, 30 June 2006.
[30] *Chantal Cutajar, J.C.P.* Ed. Générale n° 27, 5 July 2006.
[31] Judgment of 28 April 2004 of *the Commercial Chamber of the French Supreme Court.*
[32] 15th Chamber, section A, of *the Court of Appeal of Paris* of 5 March 2002, n° 2001/03509, SA Crédit Lyonnais vs. SARL Moon & al.

Addresses

Jeantet Associés
87–89 avenue Kléber
75784 Paris Cedex 16
France
Tel +33 1 45 05 81 85
Fax +33 1 45 05 82 28
www.jeantet.fr
Contacts: Philippe Blaquier-Cirelli;
Pierre-Yves Couturier
pblaquiercirelli@jeantet.fr;
pycouturier@jeantet.fr

The TRACFIN Unit
(Treatment of Information and Action
against Clandestine Financial Network)
8 rue de la Tour des Dames
75 436 Paris cedex 09
France
webmaster@tracfin.finances.gouv.fr
www.tracfin.minefi.gouv.fr

The O.C.R.G.D.F. Unit
('Central Office against Aggravated
Financial Crimes')
Direction Centrale de la Police Judiciaire
Sous-Direction des Affaires économiques
et financières
11 rue des Saussaies
75008 Paris
France
Tel +33 1 49 27 49 27; +33 1 40 07 6060

The French Supreme Court
'Cour de cassation'
5 Quai de l'horloge
75055 Paris Cedex 01
France
Tel +33 1.44.32.95.95
www.courdecassation.fr

The French Banking Federation
'Fédération bancaire française'
18 rue La Fayette
75009 Paris
France
Tel +33 1 48 00 52 52
Fax +33 1 42 46 76 40
www.fbf.fr

The National Bar Association
'Conseil National des Barreaux'
22 rue de Londres
75009 Paris
France
Tel +33 1.53.30.85.60
Fax +33 1.53.30.85.61
www.cnb.avocat.fr

The French Public Prosecutor Office
'Procureur de la République'
Tribunal de grande instance de Paris
Pôle financier
4 bd du Palais
75055 Paris RP
France
Tel +33 1 44 32 51 51
www.tgi-paris.justice.fr

The Bar Association of Paris
'Ordre des Avocats à la Cour de Paris'
11 place Dauphine
75053 Paris Cedex 01
France
www.avocatparis.org

Abbreviations

EUROPOL	European Police office
FAFT	Financial Action Task Force
OCRGDF	Office central pour la répression de la grande délinquance financière (central bureau for serious financial crime at the Ministry of the Interior)
TRACFIN	Traitement du renseignement et action contre les circuits financiers clandestins
TRACINFO	Traitement automatisé de l'information mis en œuvre par la cellule *TRACFIN*

Bibliography

Conte, P.: Droit Pénal Spécial, LexisNexis, Paris, 2005.

Cutajar, C.: Blanchiment des profits illicites, Thèmexpress, F. Lefebvre, Paris, 2002.

De Mordant De Massiac, B./Soulard, C.: Code des Douanes, art 415 (CD), LexisNexis SA, Paris, 2006.

Ducouloux-Favard, C./Garcin, C.: Droit Pénal des Affaires, Lamy, Paris, 2005.

Fontanaud, D.: (sous la direction de), La criminalité organisée, Paris, mai 2002.

Godefroy, T./Kletzen, A.: Blanchiment et confiscation, Etudes et données pénales, n°83, Paris 2000, La situation française à travers l'analyse de dossier, Document CESDIP, Centre de recherches sociologiques sur le droit et les institutions pénales, Ministère de la Justice, n°83, Paris, 2000.

Hotte, D./Heem, V.: La lutte contre le blanchiment des capitaux, LGDJ, Paris, 2004.

Jerez, O.: Le blanchiment de l'argent, Banque, 2e éd., Paris, 2003.

Lebailly, B.: La répression du blanchiment en droit français, in Le blanchiment des produits illicites, Presse universitaire de Strasbourg, p. 121, Paris, 2000.

Peillon, V./Montebourg, A.: La lutte contre le blanchiment des capitaux en France: un combat à poursuivre, Rapport Assemblée Nationale, n°2311, Paris, 2002; Le Luxembourg: un paradis bancaire au sein de l'union européenne, obstacle à la lutte contre le blanchiment.

Pelletier, H./Perfetti, J.: Code Pénal, art 222-38; art 324-1 et suivants, LexisNexis SA, Paris, 2006.

Pezard, A.: Code Monétaire et Financier, art L 561-1 à L 564-3 et art L 574.1 à L 574-2, LexisNexis SA, Paris, 2006.

Pradel, J./Danti-Juan, M.: Droit Pénal Spécial, Cujas, Paris, 2005.

Rance, P./De Baynast, O.: L'Europe judiciaire, Dalloz, Paris, 2001.

Stasiak, F.: Droit Pénal des Affaires, LGDJ, Paris, 2005.

Veron, M.: Droit Pénal Spécial, Armand Colin, Paris, juin 2002.

Donald Manasse is licensed to practice law within the State of New York, Connecticut, and in France and is domiciled for such purpose at 2 rue du Congrès, 06000 Nice. He is authorized to practice in Monaco as a legal consultant in international judicial, fiscal and commercial matters and is domiciled for such purpose at 4 boulevard des Moulins, 98000 Monaco. He is a senior lawyer in a general law practice, dealing in matters of private international law with an emphasis on commercial law, real property, intellectual property, litigation, arbitration and sports law. He has written and lectured on various legal issues relating to Monaco, French and international law. In particular, he is the author of the Monaco section in the CCH publication – 'International Offshore Financial Centers', the Monaco and French chapters 'International Real Estate Handbook' (Wiley, 2005) and of various publications dealing with Monaco law in intellectual property and trademarks.

Sophie Marquet is a member of the Bar of the State of New York and is a junior lawyer with Donald Manasse Law Offices, 4 boulevard des Moulins, 98000 Monaco. Mrs Marquet earned her Juris Doctor in Private Law from La Sorbonne University in Paris and her Master's degree in International Business Law at the University of Aix-en-Provence. She holds an LLM from Duke University, Law School.

Firm's profile

Five-lawyer **Donald Manasse Law Offices** possesses undoubted strength in a range of commercial and corporate matters such as M&A and real estate structuring. The firm has a general international practice, with a strong emphasis on real estate transactions. Donald Manasse works in three languages: French, Italian and English. Other lawyers in the firm speak French, English, Spanish and German.

Monaco

Donald Manasse
Counselor at Law

Sophie Marquet
Counselor at Law

Donald Manasse Law Offices
4, boulevard des Moulins
98000 Monaco

Tel +377 93 50 29 21
Fax +377 93 50 82 08
dmm@manasselaw.com

Anti-Money Laundering: International Law and Practice.
Edited by W.H. Muller, C.H. Kälin and J.G. Goldsworth
© 2007 John Wiley & Sons, Ltd

Contents – Monaco

1 Introduction: Monaco and its specifics

The Principality of Monaco is a sovereign and independent State governed by a hereditary and constitutional Monarchy. The Constitution dates to 17 December 1962. His Serene Highness Prince Albert II of Monaco is the head of State representing the Principality in its relations with foreign nations.

The Principality actively collaborates with the investigations of international organizations such as the Financial Action Task Force on Money Laundering (FAFT- GAFI), the European Committee for Criminal Problems of the Council of Europe (MONEYVAL), the Monetary Financial and the Monetary and Financial Systems Department of the International Monetary Fund (IMF). All reports concluded that Monaco complied with international standards regarding anti-money laundering and combating financing of terrorism.

In his accession speech on 12 July 2005, Prince Albert II issued a strong message stressing the importance of the objectives of fighting money laundering and financing of terrorism:

> I intend however that ethics remain the backdrop for all the actions of the Monegasque authorities. Ethics are not divisible. Money and virtue must be combined permanently. The importance of Monaco's financial market will require extreme vigilance to avoid the development of the type of financial activities which are not welcome in our country. To avoid such deviance; Monaco must function in harmony with all those organizations who share the same aim. Monaco must therefore respect the requirements of FATF-GAFI (Financial Task Force on Money Laundering) and the tax authorities and in particular the French and American tax authorities, and respect all the other good practices in the control of financial flows.

The legislative and budgetary powers are exercised jointly by the Prince and the Conseil National (an elected national assembly), while the judiciary powers come under the authority of the Prince and are exercised independently by the courts and tribunals.

The objectives set by Prince Albert II have already led to the enactment of a new provisions that improve available measures in the fight against terrorism (Law n°1.318 of 29 June 2006) and of anti money-laundering (Law n°1.322 of 9 November 2006).

2 Criminal provisions and implementation of international sanctions

2.1 Drugs trafficking related offenses

The first stone in the construction of the legislative and regulatory body of anti-money laundering provisions was the definition of drugs trafficking (Law n°890 of 1 July 1970) on which subsequent anti-money laundering provisions were based.

Any person who illicitly cultivates, employs, detains, offers, offers for sale, transfers, buys, sells, transports, distributes, delivers drugs, whatever the reason, even as a broker, is guilty of drugs trafficking and is liable to be imprisoned.

Subsequently, provisions were added to allow assets acquired with the proceeds of the drugs trafficking to be confiscated (Law n°1.086 dated 20 June 1985), and the financing relating to drugs trafficking was included in the definition of the offense of drugs trafficking, and stronger penalties applied (Law n°1.105 of 20 July 1987), marking the turning point, on the basis of which Monaco could enforce a strong and effective anti-money laundering policy.

The United Nations Convention of Vienna dated 19 December 1988 was made applicable in Monaco (Sovereign Ordinance n°10.201 of 3 July 1991 later changed to Law n°1.157 of 23 December 1992 modifying Law n°890 of 1 July 1970), creating a new offense of money laundering by negligence which introduced sanctions for money laundering in the financing of drugs trafficking and other organized crime. A person will be found guilty of the offence of money laundering even though he did not commit the offense as defined by the law, but he acted in relation thereof or concurred, by misapplication of his professional duties, to an investment, transfer, hiding or conversion of drug trafficking proceeds (as defined by the modified Law n°890 of 1 July 1970) or knowingly detained or acquired for himself or on the account of someone else, the proceeds of drugs trafficking.

In the case law the first well-known case tried in Monaco was *Binyamin c/ Ministère public*, in which a decision was rendered on *16 November 1998*, Mr Binyamin was arrested with US$7 500 000 in cash that had not been previously declared in compliance with exchange control regulations. He admitted having embezzled the sums that had been entrusted to him by persons whom he suspected were engaged in drug trafficking. Mr Binyamin was found guilty of the offense of money laundering since he knowingly detained proceeds of drugs trafficking organized by others.

In a subsequent case, *Ministère public c/ Pédicone (10 October 2000)* Mr Pédicone had made large cash deposits of cash on a bank account from funds remitted by Mr Becerra-Barreracon, known to the American and Italian police as a cocaine trafficker. The court found that Mr Pédicone knew that the money constituted proceeds from drug trafficking and sentenced him to seven years imprisonment.

2.2 Article 218-3 of the Penal Code

2.2.1 Creation of an offence of money laundering in the Penal Code

The second milestone in the development of the Monegasque anti-laundering set of rules came with the creation in the Monaco Penal Code of the offence of 'money laundering' under article 218 and modifying the Code of Criminal Procedure Code regarding confiscation and seizure (Law n°1.161 of 7 July 1993).

Article 218 of the Penal Code provides that guilt of the offence of money laundering is established for anybody who knowingly:

- Acquires, for himself or on the account of someone else, any real or personal property, using directly or indirectly *assets and monies of illicit origin* or who knowingly detains or uses such property.

- Concurs to any operation of transfer, investment, hiding or conversion of *assets and monies of illicit origin*.

- Detains *assets and monies of illicit origin*, without prejudice to the provisions applicable to the reception of stolen goods.

Article 218-3 (as recently modified by the Law n°1.322 of 9 November 2006) defines 'assets and monies of illicit origin' as the proceeds of any offenses punished by more than 3 years of imprisonment and the following offenses:

- Forgery and use of counterfeit currency.

- Corruption of administrators and private employees.

- Procuring.

- Inducement to sexual indecency.

- Inducement to false testimony.

- Destruction of seized assets.

- Bankruptcy and fraudulous bankruptcy.

- Misappropriation of assets by the bankruptcy syndic.

- Abuse of trust.

- Violation of trade secret.

- Commercial fraud on the quality of the goods.

- Violation of trademarks.

- Insider trading.

This recently adopted definition includes much more offenses in the underlying category of crimes the use of the proceeds of which can constitute money laundering. Article 218-1 sets out the rule that the offense of money laundering as defined at article 218 may be constituted even when the underlying offense was committed abroad, subject to the condition that the act be penalized both abroad and in the Principality of Monaco. The double requirement that the offense be penalized in Monaco and abroad prevents that certain underlying offenses committed abroad be punished in Monaco if only penalized abroad.

Article 218-2 sets out the rule that the offense of money laundering may be established where a person acted by negligence in misapplication of his professional duties and participated in any operation to transfer, invest, hide or convert assets and monies of illicit origin.

Concerning confiscation and seizure, the text provided that the prosecutor or the tribunal can order the seizure of property on the advice of the prosecutor. The parties may appeal such decision within 20 hours of its notification.

2.2.2 Recommendations of international organizations

On 23 August 2003 the Monetary and Financial Systems Department of the International Monetary Fund (IMF) issued a report assessing the supervision and regulation of the financial system in Monaco, concluding that Monaco has put into place a comprehensive legal framework supporting a well-regulated financial environment but that this may require strengthening to respond to financial developments. It recommended most notably to (1) include financing of terrorism in the definition of money laundering, (2) increase due diligence for higher risk customers, and (3) modify the legislation for confiscation of assets used in the commission of the crime and assets of equivalent value. The first recommendation was resolved as early as April 2002, before the report was finalized (in 2003). Further details will be given in Section 2.3 below.

Shortly after, on 15 December 2003, the European Committee for Criminal Problems of the Council of Europe (MONEYVAL) assisted by two members of the Financial Action Force Task on Money Laundering (FAFT-GAFI) also issued a report assessing Monaco's provisions regarding anti-money laundering and concluded that Monaco complied with international standards in that respect. Three recommendations however were made to (1) provide for the criminal liability of legal entities, (2) improve financial intermediaries' know-your-client procedures, and (3) adopt a definition of money laundering including all serious crimes rather than a restrictive definition.

The third recommendation of the MONEYVAL/FAFT-GAFI report was recently addressed (Law n°1.322 of 9 November 2006) as detailed in Section 2.2.1 above with the broad definition of money laundering provided in article 218-3.

2.3   Combating financing of terrorism

2.3.1   First CFT provisions

Monaco introduced the first provisions specifically concerning the financing of terrorism, applying the provisions of **United Nations Convention of New York dated 9 December 1999** (Ordinance n°15.320 of 8 April 2002).

'Financing terrorism' is defined as the act of by any means, directly or indirectly, providing, gathering or managing funds, with the intention to use them or knowing that they will be used to commit acts of terrorism, whether or not the funds were used to commit the acts of terrorism. Offenders incur imprisonment of 5 to 10 years.

'Funds' are defined as assets of every kind, whether tangible or intangible, movable or immovable, however acquired, and legal documents or instruments in any form, including electronic or digital, evidencing title to, or interest in, such assets, including, but not limited to bank credits, travelers checks, bank checks, money orders, shares, securities, bonds, drafts, letters of credit.

Procedures to freeze funds relating to the financing of terrorism (Sovereign Ordinance n°15.321 of 8 April 2002) were followed by several ministerial decrees publicizing up to date lists of names of persons concerned by such measures. In substance, all financial institutions, insurance companies, entities or other persons must seize funds of any persons, legal or other entity included in the ministerial decree and may not provide any service to such persons. Moreover, despite the obligations of professional secrecy, they must provide to the Budget and Treasury Department any information necessary to comply with the provisions above mentioned.

2.3.2   Recent developments and compliance with international organizations recommendations

Recently, Monaco addressed (Law n°1.318 of 29 June 2006) (1) the recommendation of the IMF regarding the modification of the legislation for confiscation of assets used in the commission of the crime and assets of equivalent value, and (2) the recommendations of the MONEYVAL/FATF-GAFI report regarding the creation of a criminal liability of legal entities and the adoption of a definition of money laundering including all serious crimes instead of a limited definition.

The main features of Law n°1.318 of 29 June 2006 are as follows:

- Acts of terrorism include, when committed in relation to an individual or collective enterprise directed against the Principality of Monaco or any other State or international organization and of nature, through intimidation or terror, to either threaten political, economical and social structures, damage or destroy them or to cause grave trouble to the public peace, a list of offenses among which feature:

    - the offence of money laundering as defined at article 218 to 218-3 of the Penal Code, and

    - stock market infractions relating to fund management and financial activities (as defined by Law n°1.194 of 9 July 1997).

- Acts of terrorism also include offenses relating to financing of terrorism.

- Legal entities, with the exception of the State of Monaco may be criminally liable for the offense of terrorism, and incur confiscation of their assets, in the same way as individuals.

The provisions above relating to the liability of legal entities do not apply to the offense of money laundering but rather to the offense of acts of terrorism, and therefore do not fully address the first recommendation in that sense of the MONEYVAL/FAFT-GAFI report (see Section 2.2.2 above).

3 The scope of application of the anti-money laundering and combating terrorism provisions

3.1 Financial establishments subject to AML and CFT obligations

3.1.1 Definitions and duties

Law on financial institutions anti-money and combating financing of terrorism efforts (Law n°1.162 of 7 July 1993 as modified by Law n°1.253 of 12 July 2002) states that the following entities – financial institutions – are subject to specific reporting duties:

- Persons engaged on a regular basis in activities of banking or financial intermediary.

- Financial services connected to the postal service.

- Insurance companies.

- Companies authorized to engage in activities of portfolio management under Law n°1.194 of 9 July 1997.

- Stock exchange employees.

- Authorized trustees and co-trustees under Law n°214 of 27 February 1936 as modified and managers and administrators of foreign legal entities.

Financial institutions as defined above must declare to the State Minister (or to the Prosecutor for notaries and jurists and lawyers) all sums and operations held in their account bearing on sums that may proceed from drugs trafficking or criminal organized activities, as well as proceeds of terrorism. As detailed in Section 4 below, the State Minister's responsibilities in receiving declarations are delegated to the Service of Information and Control of Financial Circuits (SICCFIN).

Directors or officers within the financial institutions and other entities who are in charge of the identification procedures must be declared to the SICCFIN and are subject to the legal provisions applicable to persons other than financial establishments as described in Section 3.2. Two cases illustrate how directors may delegate their functions of identification and who is responsible.

In *Fondacaro, Loffredi, Alonzo c/ Ministère public, 4 December 2000*, large deposits of cash were accepted on a bank account in Monaco prior to their transfer to the Bahamas branch of the bank. The assistant director, Mr Alonzo, had only inquired with the Lugano parent branch of the bank which had authorized the deposits in Monaco, while the administrative director, Mr Fondacaro, and the delegated administrator, Mr Loffredi, had not declared the transactions to the SICCFIN. The Court of Appeal ruled that Mr Fondacaro and Mr Loffredi, rather than Mr Alonzo, were responsible for declarations to the SICCFIN. Mr Alonzo would have been responsible for the declarations only if he had received a delegation of power to make them, while Mr Fondacaro and Mr Loffredi would have been discharged of the responsibility. In the absence of any such transfer of responsibility, however, no other person may be held responsible for failing to make a declaration.

In *Ministère public c/ Miani, Lanza, Eliard, Ragot, 7 May 2001*, the suspicious deposits made by Mr Pédicone (see *Ministère public c/ Pédicone, 10 October 2000* in Section 2.1 above) were not declared to the SICCFIN. The general secretary of the bank, its chief executive officer, the assistant general director and the manager of the account on which the deposits were made, were prosecuted for not having declared the transactions. The Court of Appeal ruled that the assistant general director and the account manager did not have any right or duty to make the declarations of suspicious origin, and they were therefore acquitted. The bank's general secretary had been given the responsibility to make declarations of the suspicious origin of funds and was therefore condemned to pay a fine. Together with the chief executive officer who was found to be objectively responsible.

Complex operations exceeding €100 000 without any apparent economic justification must be submitted to scrutiny.

In addition, financial establishments must verify the identity of their clients except when these are themselves financial establishments

In respect of measures to combat the financing of terrorism, **Law n°1.253 of 12 July 2002** complies with the new norms issued by the Financial Action Task Force on money laundering (FATF). It introduced provisions in accordance with the United Nations and FATF recommendations. The main features are as follows:

- Determination of entities and persons subject to the suspicion declaration.

- Extension of the declaration of suspicion to the operations possibly linked to terrorism.

- Substitution of the concept of 'criminal organized activities' to the concept of 'criminal organization activities'.

- Definition of a new terminology explicitly targeting a certain type of behavior or activity rather than the participation in specific organizations.

- Extension of the duty of declaration to the operations of entities established on territories or States where legislation or practice is considered insufficient by the FAFT regarding anti-money Laundering.

3.1.2   Specific conditions of application of Law n°1.162 of 7 July 1993

Law n°1.162 of 7 July 1993 is applied in accordance with the specific application provisions of **Sovereign Ordinance n°11.160 of 24 January 1994** as modified by **Sovereign Ordinance n°15.453 of 8 August 2002**.

Financial establishments must verify the identity of their clients, by requesting identity documents for persons, and an extract of the official register for legal entities. Occasional clients must be identified if they execute an operation bearing on an amount exceeding €15 000 or if they rent a safe (Law n° 1.162 of 7 July 1993).

When a complex operation exceeding €100 000, as described above, is envisioned without any apparent economic justification, financial establishments must issue a report stating the identities, status, professions, addresses of principals and beneficiaries, together with the origin and destination of payments, purpose of transactions and functioning of the accounts (Law n° 1.162 of 7 July 1993).

Financial establishments must also keep written track of internal organization measures put in place in order to comply with the provisions of the law (Law n° 1.162 of 7 July 1993). These measures must concern the following points:

- Diligences regarding activities, information on sums and nature of operations subject to specific scrutiny.

- Procedure to follow for the declaration of suspicion to the SICCFIN.

- Means of registration and keeping of documents and information in order to protect their confidential nature.

- Supervision system allowing verification of these measures.

In addition, Monaco has defined specific obligations of vigilance on the part of credit institutions for checks and credit cards (Ministerial Decree n° 2003-503 of 29 September 2003 as modified by the Ministerial Decree n° 2004–222 of 27 April 2004). In substance, credit institutions must scrutinize checks and credit card transactions in compliance with specific criteria in order to increase their knowledge of clients so as to comply with anti-money laundering and combating financing of terrorism requirements.

3.2   Other persons

All 'other persons' who in the course of their profession, execute, control or advise on operations bearing on the transfer of capital are also subject to very similar reporting duties (Law n° 1.162 of 7 July 1993). The exception is those concerning the specific scrutiny of complex operations exceeding €100 000 without any apparent economic justification.

The exact wording of the law exempts lawyers who, during the exercise of the rights of defense, acquire information relating to the realization, control or advice of operations bearing on transfers of capital (Law n° 1.162 of 7 July 1993).

However, very importantly on **6 March 2001**, in an appeal from the Bar Association of Monegasque Lawyers, the Tribunal Suprême partially annulled **Law n° 1.162 of 7 July 1993**, because the wording of the lawyers exemption was found unclear and therefore it could not with certainty be defined when lawyers were or were not subject to reporting obligations and thus could be sanctioned. The provisions of the **Law n° 1.162 of 7 July 1993** therefore no longer apply to Monegasque lawyers (and this is generally understood to cover only members of the Monaco Bar which is limited to Monaco nationals).

The professionals who are considered as being concerned by the execution, control or advice on operations bearing on capital transfers and subject to specific reporting duties as above mentioned (Sovereign Ordinance n° 14.466 of 22 April 2000) are:

- Auditors, accountants, and insolvency syndics.
- Legal and financial counselors.
- Business agents and estate agents.
- Real estate agents.
- Funds transporters.
- Merchants and persons organizing the sale of gems, precious metals, antiques, art objects and other valuable goods.
- Corporate service providers for foreign companies.
- Persons acting as investors and transferring capital for the account of third parties.

3.3   Casinos

Casinos or gambling clubs are subject to strengthened anti-money laundering provisions: as financial entities, casinos or gambling clubs must declare to the SICCFIN all sums and operations held in their accounts that may be proceeds from drugs trafficking or criminal organized activities, and the proceeds of terrorism (Law n°1.162 of 7 July 1993 as modified by Law n°1.253 of 12 July 2002).

In addition, all clients buying or exchanging chips in amounts exceeding €15 000 for table games and €1 500 for slot machines must be identified and such identification documents kept for five years. The casinos are subject to the same record keeping and verification obligations for their control systems as the financial establishments.

4   The SICCFIN and other supervisors

Monaco's Financial Intelligence Unit, the Service of Information and Control of Financial Circuits (SICCFIN) was created in 1994. It is a specialized administrative structure constituted under the jurisdiction of the Finance and Economy Department. It has three principal missions.

As a preliminary remark, the SICCFIN was entrusted with the missions of the State Minister as far as receiving declarations as detailed above in Section 3 (Sovereign Ordinance n°11.246 of 12 April 1994).

The SICCFIN is the recipient of suspicious transactions declarations. It must analyze them and transfer the information to the judicial authorities when the operations appear to fall within the offenses defined by the laws and regulations. It has the power to suspend the execution of any financial operation for 12 hours which may be continued by a judicial confiscation.

Secondly, the SICCFIN is empowered to verify compliance of the financial operators to the law (Law n°1.162 of 7 July 1993). To that end, the SICCFIN may control documents on site without regard to professional secrecy and can among other things:

- Obtain communication of all documents deemed necessary.
- Gather information necessary for its mission in respect of persons or in its obligations to control financial operators.

- Verify the application of procedures (Sovereign Ordinance n°11.160 of 24 January 1994) of Law n°1.162 of 7 July 1993 (see Section 3.1.2 above).

- Question directors or officers of the financial establishments together with any person likely to provide information on issues at hand.

Thirdly, the SICCFIN participates in the training of all professionals targeted by **Law n°1.162 of 7 July 1993**.

The SICCFIN recommends administrative sanctions such as a warning, a reprimand, the prohibition of certain activities or the withdrawal of an authorization to exercise an activity.

Questionnaires prepared by the SICCFIN are regulated: statements to be completed by February 28 of each year are sent to financial establishment relating to their situation on December 31 of each year (Ministerial Decree n°2004-221 of 27 April 2004). Such statements regard anti-money laundering and combating financing of terrorism provisions, and identify the directors having the responsibility for completing the statements.

An additional committee was created to coordinate the various administrative services controlling financial activities. It is composed of the Director of the SICCFIN, the Governmental Counselor on Finance and Economy and one administrator of his department, the Director of Budget and Treasury, and the Director of Economic Expansion. It meets four times per year to exchange information relating to common interests in the control of activities of banking, investment, insurance, management and administration of foreign legal entities (Sovereign Ordinance n°15.530 of 27 September 2002).

5   International cooperation

Monaco integrated international level anti-money laundering efforts by adhering to the **United Nations Convention of Vienna dated 19 December 1988** that created the new offense of money laundering by negligence, which allowed sanctioning money laundering of drugs traffic financing and organized crimes as described in Section 2.1 above (Sovereign Ordinance n°10.201 of 3 July 1991).

A specific offense regarding the financing of terrorism came to exist through the enactment of the **United Nations Convention of New York dated 9 December 1999**.

The **Council of Europe Convention of Strasbourg of 8 November 1999** concerning money laundering search, seizure and the confiscation of the proceeds of crime was made applicable in the Principality in 2002.

Finally, the Ordinance of 9 August 2002 regarding international cooperation for anti-money laundering seizures and confiscations completed the regulatory framework.

Moreover, as described above, Monaco actively participates in investigations of international groups such as the Financial Action Task Force on Money Laundering (FAFT-GAFI), the European Committee for Criminal Problems of the Council of Europe (MONEYVAL), the Monetary Financial and the Monetary and Financial Systems Department of the International Monetary Fund (IMF) in 2003.

Monaco became in 1995 the seventh member of EGMONT, a group the objectives of which are to reinforce international cooperation between various anti-money laundering terrorism financing units aiming to improve information exchange and expertise.

As far as banking regulations, a cooperation agreement was signed between the **French Banking Commission and the SICCFIN on 8 October 2003** to set the modes of exchange of information between these two entities.

The **bilateral convention with France of 26 December 2001** relating to the introduction of the euro in Monaco contained additional provisions to fight money laundering. More specifically, such provisions concerned the adoption of anti-money laundering provisions equivalent to measures of the European Community and in compliance with FATF-GAFI recommendations.

Finally, bilateral agreements described below have been signed since 1994 with 18 countries in order to improve the exchange of information. The cooperation between countries allows commissions rogatory, by which information is requested by one state's authority to Monaco's SICCFIN, and information is exchanged.

Country	Date of signature	Authority
France	17 October 1994	TRACFIN
Luxembourg	3 April 2001	Parquet du Luxembourg
Great Britain	3 August 2001	NCIS
Switzerland	24 January 2002	MROS
Liechtenstein	5 September 2002	EFFI
Panama	26 November 2002	UAF
Slovenia	29 January 2003	OMLP
Lebanon	20 May 2003	SIC
Italy	16 September 2003	UIC
Ireland	13 November 2003	MLIU
Malta	5 February 2004	FIAU
Principality of Andorra	4 May 2004	UPB
Poland	16 April 2004	GIIF
Mauritius Island	22 June 2004	FIU Mauritius
Slovakia	24 June 2004	UFP-SR
Canada	25 October 2004	FINTRAC
Peru	30 November 2004	FIU UIF
Thailand	4 April 2005	AMLO

6   Conclusion

Legislation and regulations to prevent and sanction money laundering and the financing of terrorism were enacted in four periods, 1985–1987, 1993–1994, 2002 and 2006. As a result of a strong willingness in Monaco that the Principality be a financial center that complies with international standards, as reaffirmed by Prince Albert II on many occasions since taking the throne, Monaco is now equipped with a targeted, efficient and dissuasive arsenal of legislation and regulations that complies with international standards and conforms to the specific recommendations of the FATF-GAFI, MONEYVAL and IMF.

While the means of preventing the financing of terrorism have recently been efficiently updated with the adoption of the new broad definition of money laundering to cover more offenses, further developments addressing recommendations on **money laundering** are expected on: (1) improvement of procedures of 'know your client' for higher risk customers, (2) confiscation of the instruments of the crime and of assets of equivalent value, (3) providing for the criminal liability of legal entities.

Addresses

Service of Information and Control of Financial Circuits (SICCFIN)
13, rue Emile de Loth
MC 98000 Monaco
Tel +377 93 15 42 22
Fax +377 93 15 42 24
www.siccfin.gouv.mc
Contact person: Ms Ariane Picco-Margossian, Director

Monaco Government
Ministère d'Etat
Place de la Visitation
MC 98000 MONACO
Tel +377 98 98 80 00
Fax +377 93 15 82 17
www.gouv.mc

Financial Action Task Force on money laundering (FATF)
www1.oecd.org/fatf

Egmont Group
www.egmontgroup.org

Moneyval Committee
www.coe.int

United Nations
www.un.org

International Monetary Fund (IMF)
www.imf.org

Javier García Sanz is a lawyer in the Madrid office of Uría Menéndez. He joined the firm in 1995 and became a partner in January 2005. Javier represents clients in the various stages of judicial and arbitration proceedings on civil and commercial matters, including company, banking and intellectual property law, human rights, tort and obligatins and contracts. With respect to administrative law, he regularly provides advice to companies and public entities on matters regarding public contracts, authorisations and licences, public assets, punitive proceedings, data protection, energy and telecommunications. His experience includes litigation in contentious-administrative [proceedings as well as human rights protection proceedings before the Constitutional Court.

Guillermo San Pedro is a senior associate in the Madrid office of Uría Menéndez. He joined the firm in 1997. Guillermo focuses his practice on corporate law and in particular on financial and banking law, complaince, insurance law, securities law and capital markets, mergers and acquistions and general commercial law advice. He works both for national and international clients. He has also participated in the negotiation of key transactions in a number of different sectors.

Firm's profile

Uría Menéndez has evolved from the firm established in the 1940s in Madrid by the late Professor Rodrigo Uría González and now has fourteen offices in Europe, the United States and Latin America. It operates mainly in the Iberian Peninsula and Latin America, where it advises on Spanish, Portuguese and European Union law. The firm provides advice in all areas of law relating to the business world and has for many years assisted companies in developing their businesses. URÍA MENÉNDEZ has always been very close to the academic world and frequently provides assistance in humanitarian projects.

Spain

Javier García Sanz / Guillermo San Pedro

Lawyers

Uría Menéndez
Príncipe de Vergara, 187
28002 Madrid
Spain

Tel +34 91 586 06 92
Fax +34 91 586 07 42
jgs@uria.com / gsp@uria.com
www.uria.com

Anti-Money Laundering: International Law and Practice.
Edited by W.H. Muller, C.H. Kälin and J.G. Goldsworth
© 2007 John Wiley & Sons, Ltd

Contents – Spain

1 General overview and regulatory environment

1.1 Development of anti-money laundering regulation in Spain

Traditionally, control was exercised in Spain over money laundering activities through the provisions on exchange control and the criminal regulations. Since the **late eighties**, the implication of Spanish authorities in the fight against money laundering became more intense. This led to the promulgation of new regulations specifically aimed at investigating, preventing and punishing money laundering activities and to new specialized authorities being set up.

The **progressive increase in the number and effectiveness of the measures and regulations** on anti-money laundering in Spain was due to various reasons. First, the international environment, which since the late eighties has been oriented not only to repress crime but also to prevent and prosecute the laundering of the money deriving from crime. Second, the participation of Spain in international organizations, including the accession to the European Community in 1986. And, finally, the development of the Spanish economy, which has led to the increase of those crimes that are usually linked to money laundering.

Spain has made and continues making efforts to implement the international recommendations on anti-money laundering. According to the 2002–2003 self-assessment report published by the Financial Action Task Force on Money Laundering (*FATF*), at the time Spain was in compliance of 26 of the 28 FATF's recommendations requiring specific action and partially complied with the remaining two recommendations.

1.2 Current status of anti-money laundering activities and regulations in Spain

As a result of that process, Spain is currently especially pro-active in the fight against money laundering, as a member of the most relevant **international organizations**. In particular:

- Spain has been a member of the FATF since 1994.

- Spain participates as an observer in the South American Financial Action Task Force Against Money Laundering (*GAFISUD*), the FATF's regional group for South America set up in December 2000, and is one of the most pro-active countries in the task force.

- Spain has participated as an observer in the Caribbean Financial Action Task Force (*CFATF*), the FATF's regional group for Central America and the Caribbean, since 1999.

- Since March 2002, Spain is a member of the *FIU.Net* project for information exchange between Financial Intelligence Units, established upon the initiative of various Member States of the European Union in June 2000.

The Spanish regulations on anti-money laundering are highly influenced by the recommendations of the international organizations (including, apart from those mentioned above, the Basel Committee on Banking Supervision, the International Association of Insurance Supervisors and the International Organization of Securities Commissions) and, especially, by the **European Union Directives** on the subject.

2 Basic regulations on anti-money laundering

The **most relevant regulations** on anti-money laundering currently in force in Spain are contained in the following Acts and ordinances:

- **Act 19/1993, of 28 December 1993, establishing certain rules on anti-money laundering** (*Ley 19/1993, de 28 de diciembre, sobre determinadas medidas de prevención del blanqueo de capitales*). The 19/1993 Act implemented the 91/308/CEE Council Directive in Spain. It was partially amended by Act 19/2003, of 4 July 2003, on the legal regime of movements of capitals and economic international transactions and on certain measures on anti-money laundering (*Ley de Régimen jurídico de los movimientos de capitales y de las transacciones económicas con el exterior y sobre determinadas medidas de prevención del blanqueo de capitales*), implementing the regulation of the 2001/97/CE Directive. As amended, it will be referred to as the '**AML Act**'.

- **Royal Decree 925/1995, of 9 June 1995, implementing the regulations of the AML Act** (*Real Decreto 925/1995, de 9 de junio, por el que se aprueba el Reglamento de la Ley 19/1993, de 28 de diciembre, sobre determinadas medidas de prevención del blanqueo de capitales*). It was partially amended by Royal Decree 54/2005, of 21 January 2005. As amended, it will be referred to as the '**AML Ordinance**' and, together with the AML Act, as the '**AML Rules**').

The AML Rules include administrative and financial (but not criminal) provisions. As will be explained below, they are directed to certain subjects, both within inside and outside the financial system. Although they include administrative infringements and sanctions, their aim is mainly of a preventive nature and provides for the collaboration of both the public and the private sectors to detect any money laundering activities.

- **Act 12/2003, of 21 May 2003, on the prevention and blocking of terrorism financing** (*Ley 12/2003, de 21 de mayo, de prevención y bloqueo de la financiación del terrorismo*), complemented by the Substantive Act (*Ley Orgánica*) 4/2003, of 21 May 2003. It includes certain rules aimed at blocking any use of financial instruments by individuals or entities linked to terrorist activities or organizations. It will be referred to as the '**PBFT Act**'.

In addition to the administrative law provisions, the Spanish Criminal Code qualifies certain activities related to money laundering as criminal offences. The criminal law regulations will be analyzed under Section 5 of this chapter.

3 Anti-money laundering authorities

3.1 Commission for the Prevention of Money Laundering and Monetary Offences (Comisión de Prevención del Blanqueo de Capitales e Infracciones Monetarias)

The *Commission for the Prevention of Money Laundering and Monetary Offences* (the '**AML Commission**') is the public body which ultimately coordinates, directs and promotes the activities for the prevention of the use of the financial system or of enterprises of any other nature for money laundering, as well as for the prevention of monetary offences of a criminal nature and administrative infringements of the regulations on foreign economic transactions.

It is chaired by the Secretary of State of Economy and its members include, among others, representatives of the Public Prosecution Service, of the Police Corps, of some Government offices, of the Financial Regulators – Bank of Spain and *National Securities Market Commission (Comisión Nacional del Mercado de Valores, CNMV)* and of the Autonomous Regions. Its aim is to allow representation of the different authorities and administrative bodies with competences on counter-money laundering.

The AML Commission may act in a plenary session (which usually meets twice a year) or through a **Standing Committee** *(Comité Permanente)*, which meets more regularly. The Standing Committee is composed of a limited number of the members of the AML Commission and performs the duties delegated by the AML Commission. It may also propose the plenary to adopt certain measures.

The **Secretary of the AML Commission**, which corresponds to the *General Subdirectorate of Inspection and Control of Capital Movements (Subdirección General de Inspección y Control de Movimientos de Capitales)* of the Ministry of Economy is in charge of (i) drafting the projects of new regulations on anti-money laundering and (ii) commencing and developing administrative sanctioning proceedings in connection with money laundering, until a proposal for their resolution is drafted.

3.2 Executive Service of the Commission for the Prevention of Money Laundering and Monetary Offences (Servicio Ejecutivo de la Comisión de Prevención del Blanqueo de Capitales e Infracciones Monetarias)

The *Executive Service of the Commission for the Prevention of Money Laundering and Monetary Offences* (commonly known by its Spanish acronym–**SEPBLAC**) is the body that acts as the Spanish Financial Intelligence Unit *(FIU)*.

The SEPBLAC is linked to the Bank of Spain and its personnel come from the Bank of Spain, the Tax Agency and the Police corps. This diverse composition enables the SEPBLAC to be a key body in the prevention of money laundering practices and the application of anti-money laundering legislation.

The SEPBLAC's duties, defined in article 15.2 of the AML Act, include:

- Rendering assistance and reporting to judicial bodies, public prosecution, police and other administrative authorities in connection with money laundering activities.

- Receiving the voluntary and compulsory information on events and transactions that must be submitted to the authorities according to anti-money laundering regulations, analyzing such information and taking the necessary actions. All the information received from individuals or entities subject to the AML Rules as well as from national or international authorities is processed through a computer system known by the Spanish acronym *TAIS (Tratamiento Automatizado de la Información del Servicio – Automated Processing of Service Information)*, which integrates all the information held by the SEPBLAC.

- Monitoring the appropriateness of the measures and bodies implemented by the parties subject to anti-money laundering regulations and proposing corrective measures.

- Supporting the AML Commission and preparing the reports that it may request.

As Spain is a member of the Egmont Group of FIUs, the SEPBLAC is actively involved in the exchange of information with other FIUs.

The SEPBLAC periodically publishes a report, which is a very useful and complete source of information on anti-money laundering activities in Spain.

3.3 Other authorities

Although the AML Commission and the SEPBLAC are the most relevant administrative authorities in Spain on anti-money laundering, there are other bodies that also play an active role in the prevention of money laundering:

- The **Commission for the Surveillance of Terrorism Financing Activities** (*Comisión de Vigilancia de Actividades de Financiación del Terrorismo*) is in charge of enforcing the provisions of the PBFT Act in connection with the financing of terrorism, especially concerning the blocking of financial instruments. This Commission reports to the *Ministry of Internal Affairs* (*Ministerio del Interior*) and its decisions are subject to judicial control. The SEPBLAC helps this Commission to carry out its duties.

- Within their respective areas of supervision, all **administrative authorities** have an obligation to cooperate with the courts, the public prosecution, the AML Commission and the SEPBLAC in connection with anti-money laundering. In particular, the administrative authorities who may discover facts suspiciously linked to money laundering must report them to the SEPBLAC in writing. The role of the Bank of Spain, the CNMV, the *Directorate General of Insurance and Pension Funds* (*Dirección General de Seguros y Fondos de Pensiones*) and the Property and Commercial Registries is especially important in this regard.

- **Special units** have been created in the two Spanish main **Police Corps**, which are the *National Police Corps* (*Cuerpo Nacional de Policía*) and the *Civil Guard* (*Guardia Civil*), to investigate and fight against money laundering. These special units are highly coordinated with the SEPBLAC.

- A special **Anti-corruption Public Prosecution Office** (*Fiscalía Anticorrupción*) was set up in 1995 for economic-related crimes.

4 Analysis of current anti-money laundering rules in Spain

4.1 Definition of money laundering

The AML Rules provide a **broad definition of money laundering**. In this regard, the purpose of both the AML Act and the AML Ordinance is defined in their respective Section 1 as the establishment of legal obligations, acts and proceedings aimed at preventing the use of the financial system, and other economic activity sectors, for the laundering of funds deriving from any type of participation in any crime punished with more than three year imprisonment.

According to the AML Rules, money laundering shall be understood as the acquisition, use, conversion or transfer of goods or assets deriving from any of the illicit activities mentioned in the preceding paragraph, with the aim of concealing their origin, or helping the person who had taken part in the illicit activities to avoid the consequences of his/her acts; as well as hiding the true nature, origin, location, movements or ownership or other rights over such goods or assets.

4.2 Parties subject to anti-money laundering rules

The AML Rules establish two different groups of parties that are subject to the obligations set forth in the AML Act and the AML Ordinance. It is worth mentioning that when individuals performing any of the activities subject to the AML Rules work as employees of a corporation or render services to a corporation, the relevant obligations shall apply to such corporation.

4.2.1 First group of parties

The first group of parties includes the following entities (hereinafter, the '**First Group of Parties**'):

- credit institutions;

- insurance entities authorized to operate in the life line of business,

- securities brokers and dealers (*sociedades y agencias de valores*);

- investment companies (except for entities managed and represented by management companies of collective investment institutions);

- management companies of collective investment institutions and pension funds;

- portfolio management companies;

- credit card companies;

- individuals or corporations engaged in the activity of currency exchange or management of money transfers, regarding the transactions relating to these activities.

Financial credit entities (*establecimientos financieros de crédito*) and foreign individuals or corporations carrying out in Spain, through branches or on a service rendering basis, any of the activities mentioned above shall also be comprised within this group.

4.2.2 Second group of parties

The second group of parties subject to the AML Rules includes those individuals or entities engaged in any of the following professional or business activities (hereinafter, the '**Second Group of Parties**'):

- casinos;

- activities involving real estate promotion and agency or mediation in the purchase and sale of real estate;

- auditors, external accountants and tax advisors;

- notaries, lawyers and court agents (*procuradores de los tribunales*) are also subject to the AML Rules: (i) when they take part in the design, execution or advice in transactions on behalf of clients regarding the sale and purchase of real estate or commercial entities; the management of funds, securities or other assets; the opening and management of checking accounts, savings accounts or securities accounts; the organization of the contributions required for the incorporation, operation or management of companies; or the incorporation, operation or management of trusts, companies or similar structures; or (ii) when they act in the name and on behalf of clients in any financial or real estate transaction;

- activities related to the marketing of jewelry and precious metals and stones;

- activities related to the marketing of works of art and antiques;

- philatelic and numismatic investment activities;

- professional transport of funds;

- international transfers of funds through postal services; and

- marketing of lotteries, regarding the transactions related to payment of prizes.

Auditors, external accountants, tax advisors, notaries, lawyers and court agents are not subject to anti-money laundering obligations in relation to the information that they may receive from their clients or obtain about their clients when they are determining the legal position of the client or when they perform their duty to defend or represent the client in administrative or court proceedings or in connection with those proceedings, including any advice on the commencement or the way to avoid proceedings, irrespective of the moment in which they have obtained the said information.

4.3 Main anti-money laundering obligations

4.3.1 Client identification

The parties subject to the AML Rules must request documents evidencing the identity of clients upon establishing business relationships with them or carrying out any transaction. The documents to be requested from clients vary depending on whether the client is an individual or a corporation.

If the client is an individual, he/she must provide his/her passport, national identity card, or identity document valid in the country of origin, which must contain a photograph of its holder. **If the client is a corporation**, it must provide a document evidencing its name, kind of corporation, corporate address and corporate purpose. In both cases, the powers of attorney of the persons representing the client must also be evidenced to the parties subject to the AML Rules.

For the First Group of Parties subject to the AML Rules, if there is a suspicion that the client is not acting in its own name, the identity of the individuals who are represented must also be also verified. If the client is a corporation, reasonable measures must be taken to know the controlling or shareholding structure of such corporation.

In addition, upon establishing a business relationship with a client, the First Group of Parties must request information about the professional or business relationship of such client, and take measures in order to verify to a reasonable extent the accuracy of such information. These measures shall take into account the risk level of the client. In this regard, the First Group of Parties shall apply additional identification controls in those business areas with a special risk of being associated to money laundering activities, such as private banking, distance banking, correspondent banking relationships, transfers of funds abroad, and any others as determined by the AML Commission.

Notwithstanding the above, the AML Rules set forth two groups of **exceptions** to some of the abovementioned identification requirements:

- In some cases, it is possible to **identify the client after the business relationship is established or a transaction carried out**. In this connection, Section 3.7 of the AML Ordinance allows the First Group of Parties to establish business relationships or executing transactions through electronic, telephonic or telematic means with clients who are not present, in the following cases:

- when the identity of the client is evidenced in accordance with the rules applicable to electronic signatures;

- when the first payment comes from a bank account opened for the same client in Spain or any other country which is not among those blacklisted by the Ministry of Economy; or

- when requirements to be established by the Ministry of Economy are complied with.

In any event, the relevant identification documents must be obtained from the client within one month from the commencement of the business relationship.

- **When the client is a financial institution** domiciled in the EU or in any of the countries listed by the AML Commission as applying similar anti-money laundering requirements to those of the EU, no identification requirements will apply.

- Likewise, no identification obligations will be required, when the transaction consists of (a) **operations below €3,000**, except for certain transfers of funds, or (b) **certain pension plans or life insurance contracts**, provided that such contracts do not include the policy holder's right to request payment of the relevant insurance reserves (*rescate*) and cannot serve as collateral for loans.

4.3.2   Inspection of certain activities

Parties that are subject to the AML Rules must analyze any transaction, irrespective of its amount, that could be linked to money laundering in any way. In particular, any unusual or complex transaction, or transactions without an apparent economic or lawful purpose will be analyzed and the results of the analysis must be stated in writing.

The internal control procedures and measures to be established by the parties subject to the AML Rules (see Section 4.3.6 below) must include a list of suspicious transactions that would need to be carefully analyzed, and the use of software applications suitable for carrying out such analysis, taking into account the type of transaction, business sector and geographic area of activity of the relevant party.

4.3.3   Retention of documents

Any documents and records that evidence the execution of the transactions and business relationships between the clients and the parties subject to the AML Rules, must be kept by the latter parties for a period of **six years**, starting from the date of execution of the relevant transaction. This obligation applies to the First Group of Parties in all cases. As regards the Second Group of Parties it will only apply if the transaction exceeds €30,000, although such threshold is not applicable to auditors, accountants, tax advisors, notaries, lawyers and court agents. Copies of the identification documents that must be requested from clients must also be kept for a period of six years from the date on which the business relationship with a client ends.

4.3.4   Reporting obligations

The parties subject to the AML Rules must **collaborate with the SEPBLAC, and communicate to it**, immediately, any fact or transaction in which there is an indication or the certainty that it is connected to a money laundering activity, as well as any circumstance related with such fact or transaction which may arise thereafter. Any transaction which shows a lack of correspondence with the nature, the volume of the activity, or the preceding activities of the customers must also be reported to the SEPBLAC if no economic, professional or business reason behind it is found.

In any event, the **First Group of Parties** must report to the SEPBLAC, **on a monthly basis**:

- Any transaction which implies physical movement of cash, notes, travel cheques, cheques or other documents payable to the bearer, issued by a credit entity, with the exception of transactions which are paid or charged in the customer account, if the amount exceeds €30,000.

- Any transaction involving individuals or entities resident in a tax haven, as defined by an Order of the Ministry of Economy, and any transactions involving funds being transferred to or from these territories or countries, regardless of the nationality of the parties taking part in the transaction, if it exceeds €30,000.

- Any other transaction that, after a previous proposal from the AML Commission, may be determined by government ordinances.

If there is not a transaction to be communicated, the First Group of Parties must communicate this situation every six months to the SEPBLAC. Exceptionally, the duty of monthly communication referred to above will not apply if the transactions relate to usual clients whose activities are known as lawful by the First Group of Parties.

In July 2005, a telematic communications system to facilitate the exchange of information between the SEPBLAC and credit institutions came into operation.

4.3.5   Refraining from carrying out transactions. Confidentiality duties

The parties subject to the AML Rules must refrain from performing any transaction in which there is an indication or the certainty that it is connected to money laundering, and shall communicate it to the SEPBLAC. However, when the execution of the transaction cannot be avoided or its non-execution could jeopardize the prosecution of the beneficiaries of such transaction, the parties subject to the AML Rules would be allowed to carry it out, communicating the transaction to the SEPBLAC immediately after its execution.

In addition, the parties subject to the AML Rules cannot communicate to their clients that they are being investigated in accordance with such rules.

4.3.6   Internal control measures. Training obligations

If the number of employees of a party subject to the AML Rules is higher than 25, such party must establish **procedures and set up bodies for internal control and communication purposes**, in order to know, prevent and avoid transactions connected to money laundering activities. These proceedings and bodies can be structured for a group of companies and will establish the necessary means to ensure communication with their branches, even if they are in other countries.

The person heading the internal control body will be the **representative** of the entity vis-à-vis the SEPBLAC, and will be in charge of, among other aspects, conducting the information reporting set forth in the AML Rules. The said representative must be appointed by the management body of the entity, have adequate experience and knowledge to perform his/her duties, and his/her appointment must be communicated to the SEPBLAC, which can raise objections if the candidate does not comply with the abovementioned requirements.

If the number of employees of a party subject to the AML Rules is not higher than 25, the person responsible for the activity must carry out the internal control and communication duties described above.

The internal control and communication procedures and bodies referred to above must be **audited** every year by an external expert, who must issue a report describing in detail the existing measures of internal control, assessing their efficiency and proposing amendments, if any. The Second Group of Parties can audit such procedures and bodies every three years, provided that a written internal audit is drafted every year. The external expert's report will include an annex with a detailed description of the professional curriculum of the expert and will be made available to the SEPBLAC for a period of six years. The external expert must be designated by the relevant party subject to the AML Rules, and must be an individual with an academic and professional experience suitable for developing his duties. The expert (considered as the individual, not the firm to which he/she may belong) cannot render any kind of paid services to such party for three years before and after the preparation of the report.

Finally, the parties subject to the AML Rules must **train their employees** so that the latter are made aware of the legal requirements established in the AML Rules, and thus enable them to fulfill all the obligations discussed above.

The SEPBLAC carries out **inspections** over the subject parties in order to verify the existence and effectiveness of their internal control proceedings and to propose recommendations and corrective measures in those proceedings.

4.4 Infringements and sanctions

4.4.1 Very serious infringements and sanctions

According to Section 5 of the AML Act, the following actions shall be deemed as very serious infringements of the AML Rules:

- The breach of the confidentiality obligation which requires not to disclose to the client or any third party the fact that it is being analyzed or that a reporting of a suspicious transaction has been made to the SEPBLAC.

- The breach of the duty to report the specific transactions set out in Government ordinances.

- The breach of the duty to report suspicious transactions to the SEPBLAC when the party subject to the AML Rules had been notified by any of its employees about such suspicious transaction.

- To fail to provide or resist to provide to the SEPBLAC with such information that it may require in writing in accordance with the AML Act.

- Any serious infringement when the relevant party had been previously found guilty of certain crimes, or sanctioned with at least two administrative infringements set forth by the AML Act.

Very serious infringements will be sanctioned with: (a) public reprimand; (b) a fine for a minimum amount of €90,150 and a maximum amount equal to the higher of 5% of the entity's own funds, twice the amount of the relevant transaction or €1.5 million; and (c) the revocation of the administrative authorization of those entities whose activities are subject to previous administrative authorization. The sanction under letter (b) will be imposed in any event, together with one of the sanctions under letters (a) and (c).

In addition, those directors or managers who were responsible for the infringement could be sanctioned with one or more of the following sanctions: (a) a fine to each of them ranging from €60,000 to €600,000; (b) removal from his/her office, and disqualification from carrying out management activities in the same entity during a maximum term of five years; and (c) removal from his/her office, and disqualification from carrying out management activities in any entity subject to the AML Act, during a maximum term of ten years.

The statute of limitations for very serious infringements will be five years from the date on which the infringement was carried out.

4.4.2   Serious infringements and sanctions

The breach of the obligations indicated in Section 4.3 above, with the exception of those breaches which qualify as very serious infringements, will be deemed as serious infringements and sanctioned with: (a) public or private reprimand; (b) a fine for a minimum amount of €6,010 and a maximum amount equal to the higher of 1% of the entity's equity, the amount of the relevant transaction plus 50% of such amount or €150,253. The fine will be imposed in any event, together with either a public or private reprimand.

In addition, those directors or managers who were responsible for the infringement could be sanctioned with one or more of the following sanctions: (a) public or private reprimand; (b) a fine to each of them ranging from €3,000 to €60,000; and (c) temporary suspension from his/her office for a maximum term of one year.

The statute of limitations for serious infringements is three years from the date on which the infringement was carried out.

5   Criminal offences related to anti-money laundering

In addition to administrative penalties, certain money laundering activities may also constitute criminal offences under Spanish Law. The regulation on **criminal offences** related to money laundering is mainly included in **Sections 301 to 304 of the Spanish Criminal Code**.

In particular, Section 301 of the Criminal Code qualifies as a criminal offence the conduct consisting of acquiring, converting or assigning assets, knowing that they derive from a criminal offence, or performing any other act to hide or conceal its unlawful origin or to help the person who has taken part in the offence or offences to elude the consequences of his or her acts. It also considers a criminal offence the hiding or concealment of the true nature, origin, position, destination, movement or rights over assets, knowing that they derive from a criminal offence. The criminal offence from which the assets derive may have been totally or partially committed outside Spain.

These conducts will also be considered criminal offences even if they have not been committed deliberately, but due to gross negligence of their author. Penalties are imposed not only for committing the criminal offence, but also for causing the criminal offence, conspiring to commit it or proposing it, although depending on the circumstances the penalties will be lower than those imposed on the author.

Penalties and other measures which may be imposed as a consequence of this criminal offence include imprisonment, fines, prohibition to exercise one's profession, confiscation of assets, prohibition to obtain public aids or tax benefits, dissolution of companies and compulsory closing of premises. The penalties and measures will be aggravated in certain cases: (i) if the assets derive from drug dealing; (ii) if the criminal offence has been committed by members of an organization that is known to carry out money laundering activities; (iii) if the criminal offence has been committed by members of certain professions such us businessmen, financial intermediaries, public servants, doctors and other physicians, teachers and social workers.

If both administrative and criminal proceedings have been initiated as a result of a particular money laundering activity, the administrative investigations or proceedings will be suspended until the criminal proceedings are definitively terminated.

Abbreviations

AML Act	Act 19/1993, of 28 December 1993, establishing certain rules on anti-money laundering (*Ley 19/1993, de 28 de diciembre, sobre determinadas medidas de prevención del blanqueo de capitales*), as amended
AML Commission	Commission for the Prevention of Money Laundering and Monetary Offences (*Comisión de Prevención del Blanqueo de Capitales e Infracciones Monetarias*)
AML Ordinance	Royal Decree 925/1995, of 9 June 1995, developing the regulation of the AML Act (*Real Decreto 925/1995, de 9 de junio, por el que se aprueba el Reglamento de la Ley 19/1993, de 28 de diciembre, sobre determinadas medidas de prevención del blanqueo de capitales*), as amended
AML Rules	Both the AML ACT and the AML Ordinance
CNMV	Spanish Securities Commission (*Comisión Nacional del Mercado de Valores*)
CFAFT	Caribbean Financial Action Task Force
FATF	Financial Action Task Force on Money Laundering
FIU	Financial Intelligence Unit. In Spain this function corresponds to the SEPBLAC
GAFISUD	South American Financial Action Task Force Against Money Laundering
PBFT Act	Act 12/2003, of 21 May 2003, on the prevention and blocking of the financing of terrorism (*Ley 12/2003, de 21 de mayo, de prevención y bloqueo de la financiación del terrorismo*)
SEPBLAC	Executive Service of the Commission for the Prevention of Money Laundering and Monetary Offences (Servicio Ejecutivo de la Comisión de Prevención del Blanqueo de Capitales e Infracciones Monetarias)
TAIS	Automated Processing of Service Information of the SEPBLAC

Bibliography

Álvarez, D./Eguidazu, F.: La prevención del Blanqueo de Capitales. Editorial Aranzadi, Pamplona, 1998.

Cobo del Rosal, M./Zabala, C.: Blanqueo de Capitales-Abogados, Procuradores y Notarios, Inversores, Bancarios y Empresarios (Repercusión de las Nuevas Directivas de la Comunidad Europea), CESEJ – Ediciones, Madrid, 2005.

Fuentes, G. and others: Prevención y represión del Blanqueo de Capitales. Consejo General del Poder Judicial, Madrid, 2000.

Palicio, I.: El sistema financiero y el blanqueo de capitales. Notas de Estabilidad Financiera n°2, Banco de España, Madrid, 2002.

Very useful information, both in Spanish and English, can also be obtained from the web page of the SEPBLAC (www.sepblac.es).

Alberto Giampieri is a partner both in the Rome and the Milan office of Gianni, Origoni, Grippo & Partners and heads the Department of Banking Law of the firm. He graduated summa cum laude from the law school of 'La Sapienza' University of Rome, Italy, in 1986 and joined the firm in 1990. He attended the City of London Polytechnic in 1990 and the Yale University in 1991. He was admitted to the Rome Bar in 1990 and he has been a member of the International Bar Association since 1993.

Alberto Giampieri practices in banking and finance, structured finance, M&A, project financing, securitization.

Paolo Iemma is a partner in the Milan office of Gianni, Origoni, Grippo & Partners. He graduated in law, summa, from the law school of 'La Sapienza' University of Rome, Italy, in 1991. From 1992 to 1998, he worked as an officer in both the Supervision of Intermediaries' Department and the Legal Department of CONSOB, the Italian public regulator of the securities market. Paolo Iemma joined Gianni, Origoni, Grippo & Partners in 1998. He practices mainly in the areas of banking, investment services, asset management and securities regulation.

Firm's profile

Gianni, Origoni, Grippo & Partners is an award-winning business law firm providing legal advice in all areas of commercial law. In 2006, for the second time in three years, our firm was named 'Law Firm of the Year' at the IFLR European Awards. Thanks to the commitment to excellence of our professionals, today every area of our firm is widely recognized among the top firms in the legal arena: clients recognize our 'special skill in integrating various specialisms successfully under one roof' (Chambers Global 2006). Established in 1988, Gianni, Origoni, Grippo & Partners comprises more than 330 professionals based in Italy (Rome, Milan, Padua, Bologna, Naples and Turin) and abroad (London and New York).

Italy

Alberto Giampieri / Paolo Iemma

Lawyers

Gianni, Origoni, Grippo & Partners
Via delle Quattro Fontane, 20
00184 Roma
Italy

Tel +39 06 47 87 51
Fax +39 06 487 11 01
agiampieri@gop.it/piemma@gop.it
www.gop.it

Anti-Money Laundering: International Law and Practice.
Edited by W.H. Muller, C.H. Kälin and J.G. Goldsworth
© 2007 John Wiley & Sons, Ltd

Contents – Italy

1 Introduction

The anti-money laundering legislation in Italy is not of a recent creation. Although the most significant developments of the *AML* regime have taken place in Italy only throughout the 1990s after the enactment of the *AML Act* (in 1991), specific anti-money laundering provisions had already been enacted several years before.

As a matter of fact, for over 25 years Italy has been following principles and recommendations arising from international working groups and organizations and, in some cases, has anticipated the issue of *AML* provisions at a *EU* level. In 1978, a good 13 years before the adoption of the first *EU* directive *91/308/CEE on prevention of the use of the financial system for the purpose of money laundering*, the new **crime** of money laundering was introduced into the *Italian Criminal Code (**ICC**; Codice Penale)*, followed, in 1990, by a specific provision punishing 'the use of money, goods or proceeds of illegal provenance'.

With the enactment of the *AML Act* in 1991 and the subsequent legislation (which was mainly deriving from *EU* directives), a complete legislative framework on the matter has gradually been formed. In year 2004 the second *EU* directive *2001/97/CE on prevention of the use of the financial system for the purpose of money laundering* was implemented in Italy, while the third one *2005/60/CE on the prevention of the use of the financial system for the purpose of money laundering and terrorist financing* will have to be implemented by the year 2007.

The current Italian *AML* regime, due to the overlapping of several acts and ordinances at a domestic level, particularly in the latest 15 years, derives from a significant number of different legal sources, which, in some cases, are not well coordinated and have suggested the Italian parliament to delegate the government to adopt a unified act in the subject matter in the next future.

2 Anti-money laundering authorities

The Italian **authorities** involved in the *AML/CFT* are a number, with different roles and competences. The general *AML* political strategies are defined by the *Ministry of Economy and Finance (**MEF**; Ministero dell'Economia e delle Finanze)*, while operational supervisions are carried out by the *Italian Exchange Office (**UIC**; Ufficio Italiano dei Cambi)* with the support of the *Bank of Italy (**BOI**; Banca d'Italia)* and the cooperation of other regulators and bodies.

2.1 The MEF

As anticipated, within the *AML/CFT* sector, the **MEF** is basically in charge for *AML* strategies, which are carried out by means of the following functions:

- legislative drafting, contribution to the *EU* legislative procedure, implementation of international standards and *EU* legislation through national laws and regulations;

- policy-making and development of general guidelines;

- representation of Italy in all relevant international fora (G-7, G-8, European Union, *OECD*, *FATF*, etc.);

- coordination of the Italian **authorities** involved in the prevention of money laundering and the financing of **terrorism** by means of two interagency committees: the *AML Committee* and the *Financial Security Committee* (see below).

The *MEF* is also granted sanctioning powers, since it is responsible for imposing administrative **sanctions** for violations of the *AML/CFT* preventive measures.

2.2   The UIC

The primary responsibility in the *AML/CFT* field is on the *UIC*. The *UIC*, established in 1945 and reorganized in 1998, is a public institution, owned by the *BOI* and governed by a five-person board of directors chaired by the *BOI* Governor. The main *UIC* functions are currently related to:

- the balance of payment statistics;

- the management of foreign exchange reserves; and

- *AML/CFT* prevention and contrast.

The *UIC* was charged with *AML* compliance duties since 1991 but only in 1997 was it conferred exclusive responsibility for receiving, analyzing and disseminating *suspicious transactions (STR)* disclosures and, therefore, serves as the Italian *Financial Intelligence Unit (FIU)*.

UIC has access to public and commercial databases such as the *Companies' Register*. The *UIC* has no access to law enforcement information except with regard to criminal records and in the case of foreign *FIU* requests for information, in which event the *UIC* is the contact point to assemble and transmit all appropriate information to the requesting counterpart. It cooperates on an ongoing basis with law enforcement counterparts (*DIA* and the *NSPV* of the *GdF*, see below), and provides a yearly report to the *MEF*. The *UIC* has statutory power to make reports to the *MEF*, to parliamentary committees and to the *National Anti-Mafia Prosecutor* on measures it deems appropriate.

In year 2001, the *UIC* competences and powers were extended to **terrorism** financing offences. Finally, the *UIC* disposes of supervisory powers on *financial intermediaries* carrying out financial services (i.e. *acquiring holdings, granting loans in whatever form, providing money transmission services* and *trading in foreign exchange*) in Italy and, as such, holds the relevant public roll.

2.3   The AML Committee

Created in 1993, the *AML Committee (Comitato Antiriciclaggio)* chaired by the *MEF* and consisting of representatives of the *BOI*, *UIC* and *GdF*, has the role of solving interpretative issues arising from the day-by-day application of *AML* Laws and regulations and proposing amendments and integrations to the *AML* legislation.

As opposed to *UIC* and *MEF*, the *AML Committee* does not have a legislative function (it does not have the power to issue mandatory provisions), but the contribution that it has made so far to solve interpretative issues and to give practical guidelines is unanimously considered crucial and some scholars have proposed that in the future a legislative role will also be attributed to it. To date the *AML Committee* has issued approximately one hundred documents, including legal opinions and general guidelines.

2.4 The Financial Security Committee (FSC)

The *Financial Security Committee (FSC, Comitato di Sicurezza Finanziaria)*, established in 2001, is the main authority in the fight against terrorist financing. The FCS, chaired by the General Director of the *MEF*, includes representatives of the following ministries, agencies and law-enforcement bodies: the *MEF*, the *Ministry of Foreign Affairs (Ministero degli Affari Esteri)*, the *Ministry of Home Affairs (Ministero degli Interni)*, the *Ministry of Justice (Ministro della Giustizia)*, the *BOI*, the *UIC, CONSOB (Stock Exchange Commission; Commissione nazionale per le Società e la Borsa)*, the *GdF*, the Carabinieri corps, the *Anti-mafia National Directorate (Direzione Nazionale Antimafia, DNA)* and the *Anti-mafia Investigative Directorate (Direzione Investigativa Antimafia, DIA)*.

The *FSC* has the role of preventing the Italian financial system from being used by international terrorists to finance their criminal operations; and ensuring international coordination of measures taken by other countries, in particular the G-7 and the *EU*.

One of the *FSC*'s most sensitive activities concerns the **freezing** of terrorists' assets. The *FSC* promotes dialogue and cooperation between different government departments, agencies and law-enforcement bodies with a view to maximizing information sharing. The *FSC* has also created channels of communication with courts of law and the intelligence service. The *FSC* maintains close contacts with its foreign counterparts. It has the power to request information to any public office, also in derogation of the ordinary duty of confidentiality.

2.5 Others

A number of other enforcement agencies and investigative bodies may be involved in the investigations and repressions of crimes and administrative breach in the *AML/CFT* field. Among them, it is worthwhile mentioning the *Ministry of Home Affairs*, in which the two branches named *Central Anticrime Directorate (Direzione Centrale Anticrimine)* and *Central Directorate for Prevention Police (Direzione Centrale della Polizia di Prevenzione)* are operating, the *Financial and Economic Police (Guardia di Finanza, GdF)*, the *Carabinieri* corps, the prosecutorial **authorities**, which include specialized units such as the *Direzione Distrettuale Antimafia (DDA)*, the *Direzione Nazionale Antimafia (DNA)*, the *Italian Revenue Agency (Agenzia delle Entrate)*.

3 The Italian anti-money laundering regime

The *AML* legislation in Italy is based upon the provision of criminal **sanctions** to punish money laundering conducts and both preventive and informative *AML* duties to be complied with by certain categories of *financial intermediaries* and **professionals** (including lawyers and public notaries).

3.1 Money laundering crimes and sanctions

There are two crimes provided for by the *ICC* which relate directly to money laundering activities. The first is that of '**riciclaggio**' (use of money or valuable deriving from an unlawful source), provided for in *Article 648-bis of ICC*, which sets forth that *'save in cases of complicity in the crime, whoever replaces or transfers money, goods or other proceeds of an intentionally* committed **crime**, *or commits other acts in relation to such [money, goods or proceeds] so as to obstruct the identification of their criminal provenance...'* will be guilty of the **crime**. The second specific **crime** is found in *Article 648-ter of ICC*, entitled 'the use of money, goods or proceeds of illegal provenance'. The latter makes it an offence to invest money, goods or other proceeds of **crime** in any economic or financial activity. All the above crimes are applicable to persons who knowingly engage in money laundering.

Money laundering offences are punished by **imprisonment** from 4 to 12 years and a fine from €1,032 to €15,493. Penalties can be increased when the offence is committed in the discharge of professional duties up to a third of the legal maximum and can be reduced when the predicate offence is punished by less than 5 years' **imprisonment**.

Legal persons are not subject to **criminal liability** under Italian law. A system of **administrative liability** was introduced by *Legislative Decree 231 of 2001* as modified in August 2003. **Administrative liability** for crimes is applicable only for certain crimes, including corruption and bribery and **terrorism** financing but does not include money laundering. A draft law was recently submitted to the Parliament to extend the **administrative liability** of legal persons in the case of money laundering. The draft law is expected to be adopted soon.

3.2   Anti-money laundering provisions and sanctions

The *AML Act* sets forth special requirements in order to prevent money laundering transactions. The main principles upon which the *AML Act* is based are:

- **Restrictions on the transfers** of cash and bearer securities for amount exceeding €12 500 if not effected through 'authorised intermediaries' (*Transfer Agents*), a list of which is provided by the *AML Act*. The list includes banks, Poste Italiane S.p.A., electronic money transfer entities, licensed investment firms, asset management companies, open-ended investment undertaking, insurance companies (including Italian branches of *EU* insurers), stockbrokers (agenti di cambio), Italian trust companies (società fiduciarie), companies carrying out the service of collection of taxes.

- **Identification and recording requirements** imposed to the *Transfer Agents* as well as to other entities such as, inter alia, *financial intermediaries*, audit firms, legal or natural entities carrying out additional categories of activities and professions, e.g. high value goods dealers, credit intermediaries, real estate agents, financial agents; cash and securities custody and carriage, credit collection and casinos, persons registered into the roll of the accountants and qualified accountants (ragionieri e periti commerciali), in the roll of the certified auditors (revisori contabili), in the roll of the certified accountants (dottori commercialisti) and in the roll of the labour consultants, public notaries and lawyers when carrying out, in name or on behalf of their clients, any financial or real estate transaction and advising their clients in relation to certain transactions (jointly with the *Transfer Agents*, the *Identifying Entities*).

- **Reporting requirements to the *UIC* of any suspicious transaction** imposed to the *Identifying Entities* above and to the following entities (jointly with the *Identifying Entities*, the *Reporting Entities*) companies managing centralized management systems of financial instruments, management companies of regulated markets or entities managing trading structures and inter-bank funds, companies managing securities settlement systems, companies managing clearing houses, public administration bodies.

3.2.1 Restriction on the movement of cash and bearer securities

In order to limit the use of cash and bearer securities in Italy, the *AML Act* provides that any transfer of cash or bearer securities in Euro or any other foreign currency with a value exceeding €12,500 may only be effected through *Transfer Agents*. Failure to comply with any of the provisions relating to the above transactions is punishable with a fine from 1% up to 40% of the value of the relevant transaction. *Reporting Entities* are subject to the obligation to notify the *MEF* of any breach to the above restriction they become aware while providing their services. Failure to comply with such obligation is punishable with a fine from 3% up to 30% of the value of the relevant transaction.

3.2.2 Identification and recording requirements

The name of any person or entity (i) carrying out transactions involving the transfer or movement of any means of payment of amounts exceeding €12,500; or (ii) opening accounts, deposits or other on-going relationships with an *Identifying Entity*, must be identified by the latter and a number of details concerning the above operation (the '*Data*') must be identified and inserted into the *Computerized Central Records (Archivio Unico Informatico, the 'CCR')* within 30 days and stored for 10 years. On-going relationships are represented by on-going contractual relationships, including the intermediary institutional activities, which can originate more than one deposit transaction, withdrawal or transfer of money or other valuables. A contractual relationship may be deemed to be on-going if it has the potential to originate several transactions, regardless of the number of transactions it actually originates.

The details to be filed with the *CCR* are the following: (a) date; (b) structure (whether it is a sole transaction or is composed of several transactions); (c) detailed reason and relevant code (whose list is published by *UIC*); (d) synthesized reason and relevant *UIC* code; (e) currency (domestic and foreign) and relevant *UIC* code; (f) total amount of single means of payment or bearer securities and the percentage of cash; (g) client's business and relevant economic field; and (h) data of the individual or legal entity on behalf of which the transaction is carried out.

As far as the accounts, deposits and on-going relationship (all together, the 'Relationships') are concerned, *Identifying Entities* shall record (a) opening data; (b) details of the individual or legal entity in the name of which the Relationships are entered into ('*Owner*'); (c) personal data of the individuals entering into the Relationships in the Owner's name; (d) personal data of the individuals authorised to act on the Owner's behalf; (e) Owner's business and relevant economic field; and (f) currency of the Relationships.

As to the *CCR*: (i) they must be established within 30 days from the commencement of the business; and (ii) the information relating to the accounts, deposits and on-going relationships may be kept in a register other than the *CCR*, provided that it remains possible for the *Identifying Entity* to obtain the Data. Within the 10 days following the second month after the month in which a recording is made, the *UIC* shall be provided with an informative file containing the Data extrapolated by the *CCR*; if no recording is made, a corresponding statement must be made.

Identification and recording requirements do not apply to transactions and on-going relationships among *Transfer Agents* (the '*Exemption*'). As far as international operators are concerned, the Exemption applies also to transactions and on-going relationships that banks and other *Transfer Agents* having registered offices or branches in Italy enter into with banks and branches abroad; any movements of cash on hand and bearer securities entails, however, the obligation to record a number of details such as the code (given by *UIC*) of the foreign correspondent of the Italian bank concerned, date, reason, code of the foreign country concerned, amount and portion in cash (in case of transactions). The *MEF* has reserved to itself the power to suspend the Exemption or to impose the identification of entities operating in certain countries and the recording of particular types of relationships and operations.

Failure to set up the *CCR* is punishable with **imprisonment** from 6 to 12 months and a fine from €5,164 to €25,822. Several less serious **sanctions** are provided for less important breaches of the identification and reporting duties by the *Identifying Entities'* staff.

3.2.3 Reporting of suspicious transactions (STRs)

AML Act sets out the procedure to be complied with by the *Reporting Entities* in order to report *STRs*. It provides general guidelines for the reporting procedure, while each *Reporting Entity*, according to its specific corporate structure and characteristics, is required to take the most suitable arrangements in order to prevent *ML* transactions from being carried out and to actually co-operate with the **authorities** concerned (in particular, with *UIC* and any other authority entrusted with the investigation and possibly criminal procedure), both strengthening its system of internal controls and adopting specific programs of staff training on this matter. Pursuant to such provisions, the above reporting is basically carried out at two separate levels:

- the first level refers to managers of the *Reporting Entities'* branches or operating offices;

- the second level refers to the *Reporting Entities'* legal representatives or relevant delegates.

Any person operating at the first level shall promptly inform the other persons operating at the second level of any transaction that, in light of the relevant characteristics, value, nature or any other circumstances known to them by virtue of their task, as well as of the economic capacity of the business carried out by the entity concerned, may suggest that the money or valuables involved in such transaction is likely to derive from any of the criminal offences provided for by the above mentioned *Articles 648-bis* and *648-ter of the ICC*, respectively, the 'money laundering' and 'use of money or valuable deriving from an unlawful source'.

Any person operating at the second level must review the reports which incorporate all the above information and, if satisfied, on the basis of all the elements at his/her disposal, about the reliability of the reports, shall promptly (if possible, before performing the transactions concerned) forward the same to *UIC*, which will start the relevant administrative procedure aimed at ascertaining whether the report is grounded or not. The contents of the above reports may not be disclosed to any involved party or to third parties. The *UIC* may suspend the transaction concerned for 48 hours, provided that this does not affect the ordinary activity of the *Reporting Entities* involved.

Details of persons reporting **suspicious transactions**, as well as of the relevant *Reporting Entities* are kept under strict confidentiality by all public **authorities** concerned. The *Reporting Entities* themselves, however, have to arrange an appropriate procedure to facilitate the above reporting by their personnel and grant the latter a complete anonymity. The suitability of the measures adopted shall be verified by *UIC*.

Failure to carry out the above reporting is punishable – unless the fact represents a more serious **crime** – by a fine from 5% up to 50% of the value of the transaction. Disclosure of the contents of a report to the parties concerned or to third parties is punishable – unless the fact represents a more serious **crime** – with **imprisonment** from 6 months to 1 year or a fine from €5,164 to €51,645.

On January 2001, the **BOI** published a document (the '*Guidelines*') containing guidelines to assist *Reporting Entities* in detecting *STR*. *Guidelines* include:

- Recommendations to correctly comply with the reporting of *STR* obligation. In particular, the operator's task is essentially to detect the **suspicious transactions** in relation to the characteristics of the customers.

- Instructions to achieve the 'know your customer' goal.

- The so-called 'case referenced list', i.e. 38 examples of *STRs*.

4   The combating the financing of terrorism (CFT) regime

The definition of **terrorism** in *Article 270-bis and subsequents* of the *ICC*, entitled '*Associations with terrorist aims including international or for the subversion of the democratic order*', has been widened in year 2005, and includes promoting, constituting, organizing, managing or financing organizations which intend to carry out violent activities, or assisting any individual who participates in such organizations. Pursuant to new articles of the *ICC*, introduced in 2005, it also includes enrolling or training individuals to carry out violent activities if, in view of their nature or context, such activities might cause grave harm to a country or international organization, and are intended to intimidate the population or to constrain the powers of the state or international organizations to carry out or not carry out any activity, or to destabilize or destroy fundamental political, constitutional, economic and social structures of a country or of an international organization. This includes foreign states and international organizations or institutions. This definition is in addition to other acts defined as **terrorism** or as carried out for terrorist purposes in international conventions or laws to which Italy is bound.

Following September 11, 2001, Italy established the **FSC** (see Section 2.4 above). The **FSC** co-ordinates the action of the **authorities** involved in the fight against **terrorism** financing, decides of the names of suspected terrorists to be submitted to the *EU* and the *UN*, collecting also all necessary information to update the lists, acts upon requests by owners of frozen assets to use frozen funds 'for fundamental human needs' and sets up relationships with foreign correspondent units, in order also to co-ordinate the **freezing** mechanisms with other jurisdictions.

As a member of the *EU* the framework for implementation of the *UN* resolutions on the financing of **terrorism** has been devised by EC regulations 881/2002 and 2580/2001. EC regulation 881/2002 states that all funds and economic resources belonging to, or owned or held by a natural or legal person, group or entity designated by the **Sanctions** Committee and listed in annex of the regulation shall be frozen. According to general European law principles, European regulations are immediately effective in Italy without the need for domestic implementing legislation. Controlled institutions are therefore required to directly implement this regulation and, as new names are published on the subsequent lists, financial institutions which identify a customer whose name is on the list should immediately freeze the account. Funds can be notified without prior notification to the persons concerned. In Italy, upon **freezing**, financial institutions should notify the *UIC* through a simple communication. In year 2001, the *UIC* issued an instruction requiring banks and financial institutions: (1) to notify any measure adopted to freeze funds; (2) to report any operation or relation which, according to information available, is traceable to listed individuals or entities; and (3) to promptly notify the *UIC* of any operation and relation connected to the financing of **terrorism**, in order to be able to suspend those activities if necessary.

United Nations Security Council Resolution (NSCR) no 1373 is implemented through *EU* common position *2001/391/CSFP* and *EC Regulation 2580/2001*. The provisions of *EC Regulation 2580* for **freezing** apply only for non-*EU* citizens. For listed persons/entities from within the *EU* ('domestic terrorists'), it is not applicable. However, pursuant to other Italian existing provisions, the power of preventive seizure and confiscation of mafia assets is extended to persons suspected of **terrorism** and therefore allows for confiscation to be ordered outside criminal proceedings. These legal provisions were subsequently extended to international terrorists in 2001.

5 Conclusions

The Italian legislation on *AML/CFT*, whose foundations are on the *AML Act*, despite being subject to amendments and integrations in 1997, 1999, 2004 and 2006, has substantially maintained the original structure, built on few simple elements, and has been completed by a very strong sanction regime.

The results of the efforts of the Italian legislator on *AML/CFT* efforts seem to be, so far, reasonable. The *International Monetary Fund* has recently issued a detailed and complete report on the Italian *AML/CFT* regime, in which it concludes that the current *AML/CFT* framework in Italy is *'extensive and mature, and achieves a high degree of compliance with most of the FATF 40 + 9'* (IMF Country Report No. 06/84). As the IMF pointed out, however, the Italian *AML/CFT* regime needs to be updated and completed. The Italian **authorities** are paying attention to implementing the revised standard and to further strengthening the legislative framework. An act to ratify the *United Nations Convention Against Transnational Organized **Crime** (2000)*, so-called **Palermo Convention**, is under discussion by parliament, provisions to strengthen the terrorist asset **freezing** regime are to be adopted soon and supervisory resources are being increased with respect to the securities sector.

An important step is going to be the forthcoming enactment of the Italian Unified Act on *AML*. Currently, in fact, the legal framework is placed in dozens acts and ordinances, in addition to an increasing number of interpretative circulars and other guidelines of the Italian **authorities**. The consolidation and streamlining of all pertinent legislation in an unified text to improve its clarity and effectiveness was decided by the Italian parliament, which has delegated the Italian government to adopt a consolidated act, which should also implement the so-called third *EU* directive *2005/60/CE*, thus completing the legislative framework on the subject matter.

Addresses

Ministero dell'Economia e delle Finanze (*MEF*)
Via XX Settembre, 97
00187 Roma
Tel +39 06 476111
www.mef.gov.it

Ufficio Italiano dei Cambi (*UIC*)
Via delle Quattro Fontane, 123
00184 Roma
Italy
Tel +39 06 46631
Fax +39 06 4825591
direzione@uic.it
www.uic.it

Abbreviations

AML	Anti-money laundering
AML Act	Italian Law No 197 of 5 July 1991
BOI	Bank of Italy *(Banca d'Italia)*
CCR	Computerized Central Records *(Archivio Unico Informatico)*
CFT	Combating the financing of terrorism
CONSOB	Stock Exchange Commission *(Commissione Nazionale per le Società e la Borsa)*
DDA	District Anti-mafia Directorate *(Direzione Distrettuale Antimafia)*
DIA	Anti-mafia Investigative Directorate *(Direzione Investigativa Antimafia)*
DNA	Anti-mafia National Directorate *(Direzione Nazionale Antimafia)*
EU	European Union
FATF	Financial Action Task Force
FIU	Financial Intelligence Unit
FSC	Financial Security Committee *(Comitato di Sicurezza Finanziaria)*
GdF	Financial and Economic Police *(Guardia di Finanza)*
ICC	Italian Criminal Code *(Codice Penale)*
MEF	Ministry of Economy and Finance *(Ministero dell'Economia e delle Finanze)*
ML	Money laundering
NSPV	Special Unit of Monetary Police within the GdF *(Nucleo Speciale di Polizia Valutaria presso la GdF)*
OECD	Organisation for Economic Co-operation and Development
STR	Suspicious transactions
UIC	Italian Exchange Office *(Ufficio Italiano dei Cambi)*
UN	United Nations

Bibliography

International Monetary Fund, IMF Country Report No. 06/84, Italy: Financial Sector Assessment Program–Detailed Assessment Report on Anti-Money Laundering and Combating the Financing of **Terrorism**, March 2006, available at http://www.imf.org/external/pubs/ft/scr/2006/cr0684.pdf.

Dimitrios K. Karamagiolis was born in Greece in 1970. He studied in the Faculty of Law at the University of Athens (LL.B., 1994) and completed his doctorate degree in the University of Frankfurt am Main, Germany (Dr. Jur., 1999). He is a senior associate of Tsibanoulis & Partners Law Firm and his practice areas are Criminal Law and White Collar Crime, Securities, Derivatives, Civil Litigation. From 2001 until 2005 he was a Lecturer of Law in the Greek Military Academy. He has published a book titled 'The Consequentialistic Structure of the Principles of Imputation' (in German, 2002) and has contributed in journals on issues related with criminal law and legal theory. He is a member of Athens Bar and the International Association for Legal and Social Philosophy (IVR). He speaks German, English, Spanish and Greek.

Firm's profile

Tsibanoulis & Partners Law Firm is a leading law firm in Greece with an exceptional reputation in the areas of banking law and financial services, capital markets regulation, securities law and white-collar crime. The firm has 5 partners and 24 associates, most of them multilingual, and is able to offer to its clients multi-jurisdictional legal experience in addressing globally their needs. Work is conducted in Greek, English, French and German.

Greece

Dimitrios Karamagiolis

Attorney at Law

Tsibanoulis & Partners Law Firm
18 Omirou St.
10672 Athens
Greece

Tel +30 210 36 75 100
Fax +30 210 36 75 164
d.karamagiolis@tsibanoulis.gr
www.tsibanoulis.gr

Anti-Money Laundering: International Law and Practice.
Edited by W.H. Muller, C.H. Kälin and J.G. Goldsworth
© 2007 John Wiley & Sons, Ltd

Contents – Greece

1 Introduction

Money laundering first appeared as a legal issue in Greece in the late 1980s and early 1990s mainly through the participation of Greece in the United Nations proceedings in Vienna and by the **Financial Action Task Force (FATF)**.

In 1988, the **United Nations** held the **Convention Against Illicit Traffic in Narcotic Drugs** in Vienna. Among other, entering states undertook the obligation to penalize drug related money laundering. The Greek Parliament ratified the **UN** Convention embodied in Act 1990/1991 which has since constituted an integral part of the Greek legal framework as stated in article 28 of the **Greek Constitution**. The **FATF** was established by the G-7 Summit held in Paris in 1989 for the development and promotion of national and international policies to combat money laundering and terrorist financing. To meet this objective, in 1990 **FATF** published a report with 40 Recommendations which constituted a comprehensive plan for Greece and the other member countries for the transformation of their legal framework to effectively prevent money laundering.

Nevertheless, Greece did not enact legislation targeting money laundering until 1993. In accordance with the principles prescribed by international initiatives such as the *FATF recommendations of 1989 and Directive 91/308, the Greek Parliament voted for the addition of article 394A to the Penal Code*. Two years later, this article was replaced out of necessity by the **Money Laundering Act** *(Act 2331/1995 as amended, MLA)*, which imposed for the first time in Greece specific obligations for banks and credit institutions.

Furthermore with **Acts 3034/2002 and 3116/2003** Greece ratified international agreements related to action needed to be taken against terrorism and terrorist financing. In accordance to these acts and in compliance with the special recommendations issued *by FATF, Acts 2928/2001 and 3251/2004* were issued which amended the *Greek Penal Code* and imposed specific provisions (e.g. severe punishments, etc.) towards combating terrorism and its financing.

Recently, in compliance with the *new directive concerning money laundering (Directive 2001/97)* and introducing stricter measures, the Greek legislature produced *Act 3424/2005,* which amended in significant issues the *MLA.*

2 The Money Laundering Act (MLA)

2.1 Overview

The *MLA* deals with anti-money laundering policies especially with those related to securing illegal profits which are obtained through organized crime. The Act contains a list of certain '**core crimes**' (below under 2.2.2), such as fraud, corruption, activities of criminal organizations, drug dealing, tax evasion, etc. Prior commission of such crimes is prerequisite for the punishment of money laundering. Banks, credit institutions and financial institutions are obliged to monitor all suspicious transactions performed by their clients and report transactions which are suspicious to constitute money laundering. Severe penalties can be imposed by the courts for breaches of the prescriptions of the *MLA.*

2.2 Criminal provisions

2.2.1 Definition of money laundering

Money laundering constitutes the following intentionally performed activities:

- The conversion or transfer of property knowing that it originates from criminal activities or from participation in such activities, with an intention to concealing or covering its criminal origin or assisting whoever might be involved in these activities, in order for that person to avoid the legal consequences of his actions.

- The concealment or covering of the truth with regard to the nature, origins, disposal or appropriation of property or the place where this property lies or was acquired or the ownership on that property or on relevant to the property rights, knowing that the property originates from criminal activities or from participation in such activities.

- The acquisition, holding or use of property, with knowledge, at the time of the acquisition, that the property originates from criminal activities or from participation in such activities.

- Participation in one of the activities mentioned by the previous cases, the forming of an organization for the commission, the attempt of committing, the assistance, the incitement, the provision of advice to third parties for committing or for facilitating commission of the activity.

2.2.2 Criminal activities ('core crimes')

The criminal activities which produce illegal assets that can be the object of money laundering ('**core crimes**') are defined as follows:

(a) participation in a criminal organization (*article 187 of the Criminal Code*);

(b) committing all kinds of terrorist actions (*article 187a Criminal Code*);

(c) terrorist financing, as envisaged in *paragraph 6 of article 187a of the Criminal Code*. This article was introduced by *Act 3251/2004* (see above) and foresees severe jail sentences as well as further penal and administrative sanctions for persons committing or assisting terrorist acts and/or terrorist financing;

(d) bribery (*article 235 of the Criminal Code*);

(e) human trafficking (*article 323a of the Criminal Code*);

(f) computer fraud (*article 386a of the Criminal Code*);

(g) sexual exploitation (*article 351 of the Criminal Code*);

(h) the actions envisaged in *Act 1729/1987* 'against drug trafficking';

(i) the actions envisaged in *Act 2168/1993* 'on guns, ammunition, explosives, etc.';

(j) the actions envisaged in *Act 3028/2002* 'on the protection of antiquities and of the cultural heritage overall';

(k) the actions envisaged in *Act 181/1974* 'on the protection from harmful radiance';

(l) the actions envisaged in *Act 3386/2005* 'on illegal immigration';

(m) the actions envisaged in *Act 2803/2000* 'on the protection of the financial interests of the *European Communities*';

(n) bribery of a foreign public official, as envisaged in *Act 2685/1998* 'on the containment of bribery of foreign public officials in international business transactions';

(o) bribery of *European Community* or of Member State officials, as envisaged in *Act 2802/2000*;

(p) market abuse either in the form of exploiting competitive informational advantages, or in the form of market manipulation;
and

(q) any other criminal offence, which is punished with imprisonment of over six (6) months and through which a profit was obtained that exceeds €15 000. It must be noted here that the misdemeanors of tax evasion and of omitting the payment of debts to the State, are specifically excluded from the above and are therefore not considered as **core crimes**. The misdemeanors of omitting the payment of employees and of omitting the payment of employer contributions to the social security do not constitute a **core crime** either as long as the amount not paid does not exceed €150 000.

2.2.3   Sanctions

According to Greek Criminal Law, legal entities cannot be held criminally responsible for their acts. It should be noted that employees of legal entities can as natural entities be held criminally liable according to the MLA as follows.

Any person who committed money laundering is punished with a sentence of five (5) up to ten (10) years of incarceration. The person guilty of money laundering is punished with **incarceration** of at least ten (10) and up to twenty (20) years if he committed the crime while acting as an employee of a credit or financial institution and exercised such acts in a professional basis or by being a repeat offender or by acting within the frame of an organized criminal or terrorism band/group or organization. The criminal liability for the main crime does not exclude the punishment of the person guilty of the acts of money laundering as well. If the core crime is punished with up to one (1) year **imprisonment**, the person guilty above or a third party shall be punished, for money laundering, with **imprisonment** of at least six (6) months and up to five (5) years. In case there was a conviction of the person guilty of the core crime, any possible penalty against him or a third party for the crime of money laundering resulting from this main crime cannot exceed the imposed penalty for the performance of the core crime.

In addition to the aforementioned, any employee of credit or financial institutions or any other person under the obligation to report suspicious transactions who intentionally fails to report suspicious or unusual transactions or presents false data, contrary to the relevant legislative, administrative and proscriptive provisions and regulations is punished with up to two (2) years imprisonment.

Furthermore, any person while being examined by the judicial authorities as witness, or by other competent authorities or referring to them, under any capacity, intentionally disguises or conceals the truth regarding the nature, the origin, the dispensation or the circulation of the assets or the place this asset is located, being aware of the fact that this asset derives from criminal activity, is punished with imprisonment of at least six (6) months and up to five (5) years, unless there is reason of imposing greater penalty. Furthermore any person establishing or acquiring a company or constituting an organization aiming at the perpetration of the crime referred to in the first paragraph or consciously participating in such a company or providing to a third party advice for the perpetration of such crime, is punished with imprisonment of at least two (2) and up to (5) years, unless there is reason of imposing a greater penalty.

Finally, when a legal entity obtained a profit through transactions that constitute money laundering, an **administrative fine** can be imposed which reaches ten times the amount of the illegally obtained profit, or between €29 347.02 and €2 934 702.86 in cases where the illegally obtained profit cannot be determined.

2.3 Prospects

According to the provisions of the *MLA* the crime of money laundering can be perpetrated in many ways. Purchasing, concealing, receiving, transferring, selling, donating and taking as lien or chattel real are all forms of money laundering when the property concerned is product of a 'core crime'. The perpetrator should have active knowledge of the property's illegal origin. Additionally, the perpetrator should intend to cover up the above mentioned origin, i.e. it is not sufficient that he supposes or simply accepts the possibility of the property's criminal background. According to the new provisions of *MLA* the perpetrator of the 'core crime' can now be the same person as the perpetrator of the money laundering. The new provision could prove itself to be quite problematic as serious issues arise especially regarding the fact that severe punishment for money laundering could be imposed together with the punishment of smaller crimes. These points were upheld by the majority of academic scholars and judges of Criminal Law.

3 Freezing and confiscation of assets

3.1 Freezing of assets

When a routine investigation is effected for the legalization of profits from criminal activities, the investigating judge has the right, with the concurring opinion of the public prosecutor, to freeze the accounts kept with a credit or financial institution, as well as order the opening of the defendant's treasury, regardless of whether the latter might be joint or shared with other persons, as long as there are substantial suspicions that those accounts or treasuries contain cash or items that originate from the legalization of profits from criminal activities. The same applies when an investigation for criminal activities is effected and substantial suspicions exist that the accounts or the treasuries contain cash or items subject to seizure. In the case of a preliminary examination, or pre-examination, the **freezing of accounts** or the **opening of treasuries** may be ordered by a judicial council. This order of the investigating judge or the judicial council produces the same effect as a seizure report and is issued without any previous hearing of the defendant. The order which freezes assets does not have to refer to a specific account or treasury and is served to the defendant and to the official of the credit or financial institution or to the manager of the branch where the investigating judge or public prosecutor are seated. In case of a joint account or treasury, the order or resolution must also be served to the third party.

The previously mentioned measure is effective as of the moment of service to the financial or credit institution of the order of the examining magistrate or the resolution of the council. From that moment onwards the opening of the treasury is prohibited and any disbursal of funds from the account is void vis-à-vis the State. Any official or employee of a credit or financial institution who intentionally contravenes these provisions, shall be subjected to imprisonment of up to two years and to a fine.

In cases when the inquiry for the legalization of profits from a crime or for the detection of property is conducted by the **MLCA** (under 6.2.1), the freezing of assets or the prohibition of transfer on any other element of property, may under extraordinary circumstances be instructed by its president, under the same terms and conditions envisaged above.

3.2   Confiscation of assets

A property constituting product of criminal activity or obtained in any way from a product of such criminal activity or property being used, totally or partially, for criminal activity is seized and, since there is no possibility of rendering it to the owner, it is obligatory confiscated by the conviction. The **confiscation** is imposed even if the property belongs to a third party, since this third party was aware of the criminal activity at the time he/she obtained the property. In case the property or the product of the 'core crime' exceeds the amount of €4000 and is not practically possible to be seized, elements of property equivalent to the above mentioned property or products are seized and confiscated under the previous terms. In case of conviction for attempting the perpetration of the crimes described as 'core crimes', the property being seized and confiscated is the one the perpetrator was planning to use for the crime.

In case the property was transferred to a third person, the person convicted is obliged to compensation of an amount equal to the value of the property at the time of the action's discussion. The above claim might be also raised against a third party who obtained the property by way of gift, provided that at the time of acquisition he or she was married or related by blood directly to the convicted or his brother or his adopted child. This claim can be as well brought up as against every third party who obtained the property acting in bad faith, and if at the time he obtained the property the third person was aware of the criminal proceedings against the convicted.

4   The scope of application of the MLA

4.1   The scope of the application

The MLA applies to any person or entity who conducts as a business one or more of the following **activities or operations** for or on behalf of a customer:

(a) Credit institutions.

(b) Financial institutions. A financial institution is any business, which does not constitute a credit institution and the main activity of which consists in securities investment or in exercising one or more of the activities permitted to credit institutions, including:

    (i) portfolio investment companies

    (ii) mutual fund companies

    (iii) mutual fund companies in the real estate field

    (iv) real estate investment companies

    (v) firms providing investment services

    (vi) companies providing investment intermediation services.

(c) Companies of financial leasing.

(d) Casinos, internet casinos and companies organizing games of chance.

(e) Factoring.

(f) Venture capital.

(g) Accountants, auditors and external auditors.

(h) Tax consultants and companies of tax consultant.

(i) Estate agents and estate agencies.

(j) Auction places.

(k) Traders of goods of great value and auctioneers when the value of the transaction exceeds the amount of €15 000 no matter if the payment is in full or on installment.

(l) Notaries and lawyers when participating or helping with the scheme or the materialization of the transactions for their clients regarding the purchase or sale of estates or companies, the administration of money, assets or other elements of property of their clients, the opening or the administration of savings bank accounts or assets accounts, the organization of the necessary for the creation, operation or administration of the companies contribution/fees, the incorporation, operation or administration of fiduciary companies or relevant units, either acting on the name and on behalf of their clients within the frame of financial transactions or transactions regarding estates. The provision of legal advice remains subject to the obligation of professional secrecy unless the legal counselor is taking part in money laundering activities, if the legal advice is provided for money laundering purposes, or if the lawyer knows that the client is seeking legal advice for money laundering purposes.

(m) Postal services, only to the extent that they act as interveners for the capitals transfer.

4.2   The interpretation and prospects of the legal provision on the scope of application

As discussed the crime of money laundering can be perpetrated in many ways. Purchasing, concealing, receiving, transferring, selling, donating and taking as lien or chattel real are all forms of money laundering when the property concerned is product of a 'core crime'. The perpetrator should have active knowledge of the property's illegal origin. Additionally the perpetrator should intend to cover up the above mentioned origin, i.e. it is not sufficient that he supposes or simply accepts the possibility of the property's criminal background. According to the new provisions of *MLA* the perpetrator of the 'core crime' can now also be punished for having committed at the same time money laundering. Accordingly a wide range of serious criminal liability for individuals is based and therefore a heavy burden of responsibilities for the **financial intermediaries** is produced. The new provision could prove itself to be quite problematic in its application by the courts as serious theoretical issues arise within the system of the Greek Criminal Law. The amended *MLA* has been heavily criticized by various sides.

5   Obligations of the financial intermediaries

5.1   Obligations of due diligence

5.1.1   Verification of identity of the contracting party

Credit and financial institutions when entering into business agreements, within the frame of any business relation and particularly when opening a savings account of any nature, when offering safe custody facilities and when providing the use of a safe deposit box, as well as when entering an agreement of a mortgage loan, shall require **identification** of their customers by means of supporting evidence. Means of supporting evidence is considered to be the presentation of the identity card or the passport or other public document. From this identification should emerge the present address, the occupation of the covenanter or party and work address. This requirement shall also apply for any transaction with customers other than those referred to above, involving a sum amounting to €15 000 or more, whether the transaction is carried out in a single operation or in several operations which take place the same day or have the same cause.

By way of derogation from those referred to in the preceding paragraphs identification is not required for:

(a) Insurance policies written by insurance undertakings, where the periodic premium amount or amounts to be paid in any given year does or do not exceed €1000 or where a single premium is paid amounting to €2500. If the periodic premium amount or amounts to be paid is or are increased so as to exceed the €1000 threshold, identification shall be required.

(b) Insurance policies in respect of pension schemes taken out by virtue of a contract of employment or the insured's occupation, provided that such policies contain no surrender clause and may not be used as collateral for a loan.

Credit and financial institutions may but are not required to carry out such identification, when the party is a credit or financial institution, legal entity of civil law or institution, 51% of which, at least, belongs to the state.

In the event of doubt as to whether the covenanters or the parties referred to above are acting on their own behalf or where it is certain that they are not acting on their own behalf, the credit and financial institutions shall take reasonable measures to obtain information as to the real identity of the persons on whose behalf those customers are acting.

5.1.2   Identification of the beneficial owner

When the **transacting party** is acting on behalf of a third party, apart from the presentation of his own identity card, he or she must provide information as to the real identity of this third party, person or legal entity, on whose behalf he or she is acting. The credit or financial institution must check this identification, even if the party has not made the above declaration, but there is reasonable doubt of whether the customer acts on his own behalf or it is certain that he does not act on the behalf of a third party. When the transacting party is an **offshore company** the credit or financial institution must obtain information regarding the **beneficial owner** of the company.

5.1.3 Obligation to draw up and retain documents

The information related to the above agreements and transactions and the legal documents are kept by the credit or financial institution for at least five years

(a) when regarding the agreements, after the termination of their relationships with the customers

(b) when regarding the transactions, from the last transaction
except if, in both cases, another law provision imposes a longer period for their keeping.

The credit and financial institutions receiving orders for the cross-border electronic transfer of funds shall include in the relevant messages the name, address and, since the funds to be transferred derive from a savings account kept by the credit institution which carries out the transaction, the number of the account of the mandator.

5.1.4 Obligations to report suspicions and to prevent suspicious transactions

Credit or financial institutions must not conduct transactions for which they know or they substantially suspect that they are connected with the legalization of income from criminal activities, unless there is an **urgent need** for realizing the transaction or this is dictated by its nature, or in case where the non-realization of the transaction might hinder the disclosure of evidence or people which might be involved in the legalization of income. In that case a **report** is immediately submitted following the transaction.

The credit and financial institutions should: (a) closely inspect every transaction which, by means of its nature or by means of data concerning the person or the capacity of the contracting party could be associated with the legalization of income from criminal activities or from the financing of terrorists or terrorist organizations; (b) establish internal control and communication mechanisms in order to forestall and prevent the conduct of transactions connected with the above crimes; (c) evaluate the overall portfolio which is possibly maintained by the contracting party in the context of those crimes so as to ascertain the relevance and compatibility of the transaction considered, with this portfolio; (d) safegaurd these provisions are applied to the subsidiaries and to their foreign branches, unless this is wholly or partly prohibited by the relevant foreign legislation, in which case they shall inform the competent Public Prosecutor and the *MLCA* (under 6.2.1); and (e) take all other necessary action decided by their competent authority for the prevention of the above crimes, including the non-conclusion of the transaction, insofar as the identification and verification terms of the contracting party's identity have not been satisfied, as is specifically prescribed by the relevant authorities.

Credit or financial institutions do not have the right to freeze assets of their clients when they hold suspicion that money laundering is or has occurred. They have the right only not to carry out the **suspicious transaction**. The right to freeze assets is provided exclusively to the judicial authorities and to the *MLCA*.

5.2 Organizational measures

The administrators of the shares, foreign exchange and derivatives markets shall maintain **effective mechanisms and procedures** for the prevention and the immediate detection of potential cases involving the legalization of profits from criminal activities or the financing of terrorism and should report to the *MLCA* (below under 6.2.1), without delay, the instances where the above offences are reasonably suspected to be taking place, by disclosing all the relevant information and data and by granting all help necessary for their inquiry.

Each credit or financial institution should prescribe one official to which other officials and employees shall report every transaction deemed suspicious concerning the legalization of profits from criminal activities and every incident that they come across in the context of their capacity and which could form evidence of criminal activity. In the case of branches this report is immediately made to the branch manager who immediately reports to the competent official, if the branch manager shares the suspicions. If the branch manager or his substitute is prevented, denies, neglects, or does not share the suspicions of the reporting employee, then the employee reports to the competent official. The latter informs by telephone and by means of a confidential document the *MLCA*, by simultaneously providing all necessary information and facts, if, following the investigation he conducts, he deems that the information and the existing evidence constitute signs of criminal activity.

Each financial group appoints an official, within the group's largest company, as coordinator for safeguarding the observance of the obligations of the group's separate companies. In view of that, the official shall cooperate and exchange information with the abovementioned officials of the group's separate companies, he is informed of any potential reports of those companies to the competent authority and may himself submit reports to the *MLCA*.

6 Supervision and enforcement

6.1 The MLA supervision system's components

6.1.1 BOG/HCMC

The ***Bank of Greece (BOG)***, pursuant to the provisions of its Statute and of *Act 2076/92* regarding mainly the supervision of credit institutions having their head office in Greece and the mutual recognition of the supervision regime governing *EU*-based banks, supervises credit institutions having their head office in Greece, including their branches abroad. The *Bank of Greece* is also the authority responsible for the implementation by credit institutions of the provisions of this law, regarding prevention and suppression of money laundering.

The ***Hellenic Capital Market Commission (HCMC)*** is an independent decision-making body, in the form of a Public Law Legal Entity operating under the supervision of the ***Ministry of National Economy***. It is established in Athens and the *Acts 148/67, 1969/91, 2166/93, 2324/95 and 2396/96* regulate its operation. *HCMC* is the authority responsible for the implementation by financial institutions (as defined above under 4.1) of the provisions of this law, regarding prevention and suppression of money laundering.

Both the *BOG* and the *HCMC* have issued a series of regulations and circulars with which the *MLA* is implemented.

6.1.2 The MLA supervision system authorities

The **anti-money laundering supervision** authorities are:

(a) The ***Bank of Greece*** for credit institutions, leasing companies, factoring companies, postal services, only to the extent that they act as interveners for the capital transfers and credit and financial institutions, foreign exchange companies, loan and lending offices and companies which act as intermediaries in capital transfers.

(b) The *Hellenic Capital Market Commission (HCMC) for financial institutions* as defined above (under 4.1).

(c) The *Private Insurance Supervision Committee* for insurance companies.

(d) The *Committee of Accounting Standardization and Control for accountants, auditors, external auditors and auditorial companies*.

(e) The *Ministry of Finance* directly for venture capital companies, tax consultants and companies of tax consultants, on-line casinos, real estate agents, and real estate agencies, auction houses and traders of goods, the last when the value of the transaction exceeds the amount of €15 000 no matter if the payment is in full or on installment.

(f) The *Ministry of Justice* for lawyers and public notaries.

(g) The *Supervision and Control Committee for Gambling for casinos and gambling companies*.

The *BOG*, the *HCMC*, the *Private Insurance Supervision Committee* and the *Committee of Accounting Standardization and Controls* each form a special unit with a view to supervising the compliance of the companies supervised by them for the fulfillment of their obligations that are prescribed by the provisions of the first chapter of the present law. Those special units are assisted by employees of the competent authorities and especially by those supervising, directly or indirectly, the supervised companies. Those competent authorities shall submit semi-annually a detailed report to the *Ministry of Finance (MoF)* concerning the evaluation of companies and any penalties or measures imposed on them. The submission of the above reports to the *MoF* is conducted by deviating from any specific provision of banking, capital markets and professional confidentiality.

6.2 Law enforcement

6.2.1 The Money Laundering Control Authority *(MLCA)*

An Independent Administrative Authority is established under the name *'National Authority for Combating the Legalization of Income from Criminal Activities'*, which has the function of the *'Financial Intelligence Unit'*, in the sense of the *Egmont Group*. The Authority has its seat in Athens and is administrative independent.

The Authority has the following responsibilities:

(a) It gathers, inspects and evaluates the information transferred to it and which is connected with suspicious transactions for the legalization of profits from criminal activities.

(b) It receives, inspects and evaluates all information relevant to the transactions for the legalization of profits from criminal activities, which is transmitted to it from foreign authorities with which it cooperates for the provision of any assistance possible.

(c) It has access to all kinds of files of any public authority responsible for the keeping and processing of data. Taxing confidentiality does not apply within the context of the above investigations.

(d) It conducts financial controls under critical, in its opinion, circumstances, on any public authority or organization or public enterprise, without prior notification of any other Authority.

(e) During the conduct of the above controls, it asks for data concerning the circulation of bank accounts or accounts of other credit and financial institutions.

(f) It asks for the cooperation of departments and organizations of any form and for the provision of data, even from judicial authorities, on the occasion of the control and the inquiry on criminal activities of legalization of income originating from the core crimes mentioned above.

(g) It informs in writing or by secure electronic means the conveyor of the information that the latter has been received and shall provide the conveyor with other relevant data without however breaching the confidentiality of its pre-examining activities and without impeding the exercise of its duties.

It evaluates and investigates information and reports transmitted to it by competent authorities of our country or by the competent bodies of international organizations and which concern the financing of terrorism.

The *MLCA* has direct subordination to the *MoF*.

6.2.2   Other authorities

The task of law enforcement of *MLA* is mostly carried out by the ***Authority of Special Controls (ASC)*** which is directly subordinated to the *MoF*. The competences of this body are designed for the combat of economic crime in general and include the investigation of money laundering cases. For this purpose the *ASC* has the right to conduct investigations in conveyances, stores, warehouses and other places where commodities can be located and can, under certain circumstances, arrest and interrogate suspects, confiscate books, documents, commodities and bank accounts. For the purposes of combating money laundering the *ASC* collaborates closely with the *BOG*, the *HCMC* and other affiliated organizations as well as with the competent judicial authorities.

Addresses

Ministry of Finance
5–7 Nikis St., Athens
Greece
Tel +30 210 333 2000
www.mnec.gr

Bank of Greece
21 Eleftheriou Venizelou Ave., Athens
Greece
Tel +30 210 32 01 111
www.bankofgreece.gr

Money Laundering Control Authority
207 Pireos Avenue & 92 Alkifronos St.,
Athens
Greece
Tel +30 210 34 26 892
www.sdoe.gr

Hellenic Capital Market Commission
1 Kolokotroni & Stadiou St., Athens
Greece
Tel +30 210 33 77 100
www.hcmc.gr

Abbreviations

ASC	Authority of Special Controls
BOG	Bank of Greece
FATF	Financial Action Task Force
HCMC	Hellenic Capital Market Commission
MLA	The Money Laundering Act
MLCA	Money Laundering Control Authority
MoF	Ministry of Finance

Bibliography

Androulakis, N.: The penal doctrine and its impact in practice, 50 years later, Nomiko Vima 2002, p. 289 ff.

Dionyssopoulou, A.: Legalization of incomes from criminal activities and acceptance of products of crime. A contribution to the matter of the object of legal protection in act 2331/95, Poinika Chronika 1999, p. 988 ff.

Giannopoulos, T.: Legalization of incomes from criminal activities as seen in article 394a of the Greek Penal Code, Poinika Chronika 1993, p. 1238 ff.

Katsios, S.: Money laundering, Sakkoulas Publishers, Thessaloniki 1998.

Katsios, S.: The directive 91/308 for the fighting against legalization of illegal incomes and the non appliance of act 2331/95, Poiniki Dikaiosini 4/2000, p. 349 ff.

Pavlos, S.: Legalization of incomes from criminal activities (art.2 of Law 2331/1995) and specially its differences from acceptance and disposition of products of crime (art.394 of the Greek Penal Code), Iperaspisi 2000, p. 633 ff.

Stergioulis, E.: The competence and the role of Europol in fighting of the legalization of incomes from illegal acts, Poiniki Dikaiosini 4/2000, p.1048 ff.

Symeonidis-Kastanidis, E.: The crime of legalization of incomes from illegal acts – Problems from the application of law 2331/95 up to now, Poiniki Dikaiosini 3/2002, p. 292 ff.

Tragakis, G.: Organized crime and money laundering, Nomiki Bibliothiki Publishers, Athens 1996.

Vasilakopoulos, P.: Money laundering – Critical observations on the penal regulations of law 2331/95, Poinika Chronika 1996, p.1361 ff.

Françoise Lefèvre is a partner in the Litigation and Arbitration department of Linklaters De Bandt Brussels. A specialist in domestic and cross-border litigation, regulatory investigation, white-collar crime, and national and international arbitration, both *ad hoc* and institutional (ICC, LCIA, CEPANI, etc.), she has extensive experience in all forms of urgent injunctive relief, in jurisdictional issues, both civil and criminal, and questions of conflicts of law, and in banking law and construction law. Other areas of expertise include corporate litigation and international sales of goods. Ms Lefèvre was admitted to the Brussels Bar in 1981. She is a member of the Institut de l'Arbitrage International, Paris; the London Court of International Arbitration, London; and CEPANI, Brussels. She speaks French, English and Dutch. Ms Lefèvre is a graduate of the Free University of Brussels, and received her LLM from Trinity College, Cambridge University.

Olivier Praet works in the Litigation and Arbitration department of Linklaters De Bandt Brussels. His experience includes white-collar crime, regulatory investigation and commercial litigation. Mr Praet is a graduate of the Free University of Brussels, both from the School of Law and the Institute of Political Science. He was admitted to the Brussels Bar in 1998. Mr Praet speaks French, English, and Portuguese.

Firm's profile

Linklaters is a law firm which specializes in advising the world's leading companies, financial institutions and governments on their most challenging transactions and assignments. With offices in major business and financial centers, we deliver an outstanding service to our clients throughout the world. The lawyers in Belgium practise under the name Linklaters De Bandt, except for the European law group which practises as Linklaters.

Belgium

Françoise Lefèvre
Olivier Praet

Lawyers

Linklaters
Brederode 13
1000 Brussels
Belgium

Tel: +32 2 501 95 49
Fax +32 2 501 95 83
francoise.lefevre@linklaters.com
olivier.praet@linklaters.com
www.linklaters.com

Anti-Money Laundering: International Law and Practice.
Edited by W.H. Muller, C.H. Kälin and J.G. Goldsworth
© 2007 John Wiley & Sons, Ltd

Contents – Belgium

1   Introduction

Since the early 1990s, like most other European countries, **Belgium developed several tools to fight money laundering through two different approaches**: Belgian authorities enacted **several laws to prevent money laundering** and the Belgian parliament passed **a law making money laundering a criminal offense**.

As will be developed further in the following paragraphs in connection with **prevention**, Belgium, more or less, aligned its legislation with the European directives; the scope of the provision curbing the offence of money laundering is very broad. In less than 20 years, Belgium has succeeded in building up a very complete system to fight against money laundering. However, notwithstanding the results, constant adaptations of the law are required to respond to the challenges.

After a brief history, this presentation aims to provide the reader with only a general overview of the current legal system applicable in Belgium, explaining both the preventive law and the criminal provisions enacted throughout the years and keeping in mind that these laws are constantly reviewed and amended by the lawmakers.

2   Brief history

Belgium had already implemented criminal sanctions against money laundering activities before the entry into force of the 1991 Directive.

The *Law of 17 July 1990* modified Articles 42, 43 and 505 of the *Criminal Code (Code pénal* – hereinafter 'CC') and inserted a new Article 43bis in the CC in order to sanction money laundering. On 7 April 1995, the scope of application of Article 505 CC was extended in order to align the Belgian regulations with the 1991 Directive.

On the other hand, a *Law of 11 January 1993* (*'Loi du 11 janvier 1993, relative à la prévention de l'utilisation du système financier aux fins de blanchiment de capitaux et du financement du terrorisme'* – hereinafter the *'Law of 1993'*) imposed measures aiming to prevent the use of the financial system for money laundering. The Law of 1993 also created the Belgian anti-money laundering control institution, the **CTIF (Cellule de Traitement des Informations Financières)**, which in addition to its national missions acts as the secretariat of the Egmont Group. This law has been modified several times including on *12 January 2004 (Loi du 12 janvier 2004 modifiant la loi du 11 janvier 1993 relative à la prévention de l'utilisation du système financier aux fins du blanchiment de capitaux, la loi du 22 mars 1993 relative au statut des entreprises d'investissement et à leur contrôle, aux intermédiaires financiers et conseillers en placements*), in order to align Belgian legislation with the 2001 Directive. New amendments are in the making in order to adopt the 2005 Directive.

The scope of application of the preventive law and the criminal provisions differ quite substantially. Their respective scopes of applications and interpretations will therefore be reviewed separately below.

3   Prevention of the use of the financial system for money laundering

The *Law of 1993* imposes preventive measures, the violation of which may give rise to administrative sanctions (e.g., fines) with the aim of insuring the efficiency of the anti-money laundering fight through the setting up of an institution which will control financial operations and through a mechanism of reporting suspicious operations to this institution. The *Law of 1993* also aims to fight against the terrorism by curbing its financing.

3.1   Definition of money laundering activities

Article 3 of the Law of 1993 gives the following **definition of money laundering**:

- **Converting or transferring** funds or assets with the view to hiding or disguising their illegal origin or to helping the perpetrator of the **offense** to hide where the funds or assets originate from to avoid the legal consequences of his acts.

- **Hiding or disguising** the nature, the location, the origin, the movement or the ownership of the funds or assets, the illegal origin of which is known.

- **Acquiring, detaining or using** funds or assets, the illegal origin of which is known.

- **Participating in, attempting to help, helping, advising** someone to perpetrate one of the above behaviors, thus facilitating its perpetration.

- A criminal association aiming at committing money laundering.

The definition of money laundering in the *Law of 1993* therefore reflected extensively the definition thereof contained in the 1991 Directive.

The behavior concerned must be intentional.

3.2   The underlying offense

The *Law of 1993* only applies if the funds that are the object of the money laundering activities derive from **a specific list of offenses**. The funds must derive from:

- offenses linked to

  - terrorism and the financing of terrorism

  - organized crime

  - unlawful drug trafficking

  - unlawful arms trafficking

  - unlawful assets and goods trafficking

  - clandestine labor trafficking

  - human trafficking

  - organs and human tissue trafficking

  - exploitation of prostitution

  - illegal use or trade of hormonal substances for animals

  - fraud prejudicial to the financial interests of the European Union

- serious and organized **tax fraud** in which complex mechanisms or processes on an international scale are used

- bribery, both of public officials and of private individuals and misappropriation by public officials

- serious environmental crime

- counterfeiting of goods

- counterfeiting coins or notes

- piracy

- a stock exchange offense

- an irregular public offering

- the supply of unauthorized investment services, currency trade or unauthorized funds transfer

- swindle

- breach of trust

- misuse of company assets

- hostage taking

- violent extortion or theft

- fraudulent bankruptcy.

The Belgian anti-money laundering control institution, the **CTIF (*Cellule de Traitement des Informations Financières*)** has indicated that serious and organized **tax fraud** is serious when forged documents are made or used or when the loss to the Treasury is substantial and it is organized when strawmen, screen companies, or complex legal structures are used for the international transfer of funds.

3.3   Scope of application of the Law ratione personae

The *Law of 1993* **imposes on certain categories of people the duty to identify the clients they work with as well as the duty to report suspicions of money laundering** connected to the abovementioned specified list of offenses.

The Law contains a specific list of persons to whom it applies:

- in general, all Belgian credit, investment, insurance, and banking institutions (including the *National Bank of Belgium* (Banque Nationale de Belgique) and the *Post Office*) as well as the Belgian branches of foreign credit institutions

- bureaux de change

- credit card companies

- leasing companies

- real estate agents

- security companies

- notaries, bailiffs

- auditors, accountants, tax advisors

- casinos

- market operators

- diamond traders

- insurance brokers (life insurance)

- lawyers when

  - they assist their client in the preparation or the realization of transactions relating to

    o purchase and sale of real estate and commercial companies

    o management of funds, bonds, assets belonging to the client

    o opening or managing bank accounts (savings accounts or portfolios)

    o organization of contributions necessary for the setting up, management and direction of companies

    o constitution, management and direction of fiduciary companies, or of similar structures

  - they act in the name of the client and for his account in any financial or real estate transaction.

The lawyers performing the activities listed above must report to the *Head of the Bar* the facts they know or suspect to be linked to money laundering, except if they have obtained the **information** from their client while evaluating the client's position in order to represent and defend the client before the courts, including how to initiate or avoid a procedure (art. 14bis §3).

The *Head of the Bar* checks that the conditions have been fulfilled and transfers the information to the *CTIF*.

Various Belgian Bars have filed before the *Constitutional Court (Cour d'Arbitrage)* a request for annulment of several provisions of the Law, specifically those relating to the obligation to report suspicions of money laundering activities.

On 13 July 2005, the *Constitutional Court* decided to ask a prejudicial question to the *European Court of Justice* in Luxembourg *(Cour de justice des Communautés Européennes)* on whether the inclusion of the lawyers in the list of persons to which the obligations provided for in the 2001 Directive applies *(Article 1.2 of the 2001 Directive)* violates *Articles 6* of the *European Convention on Human Rights (Convention de Sauvegarde des droits de l'homme et des libertés fondamentales)* and 6.2 of the *European Union Treaty (Traité sur l'Union Européenne)*. The Court decision is still awaited.

Considering the extensive list of persons to whom the *Law of 1993* applies, it is estimated that around 30 000 people should report suspicions of money laundering to the *CTIF*.

3.4 Obligation to identify

Pursuant to *Article 4 of the Law of 1993*, the above-listed persons **must identify** their clients and their proxy holders and check their identity, on the basis of documents of which they must keep a paper or electronic copy when:

- they enter into business relationships which will make them usual clients
- the client wishes to realize
  - an operation of €10 000 or more in one or more transactions
  - an operation below €10 000 as soon as there exists a suspicion of money laundering
- for the transfer of funds for which the person giving the instruction to transfer must be identified
- when they have doubts as to the identity of an existing client.

Identification required:

- for individuals, the name, forename and address
- for companies and trusts, the name, the address, the directors, the proxy holders, the object and the nature of the relationship.

Article 5 of the Law of 1993 provides that persons subject to the Law must take all reasonable measures to identify the person for the account of whom the operation is made when:

- the client does not act for his own account or is suspected not to
- the client is a company or a trust, which requires the final economic beneficiaries being identified.

An exception is provided for when the client is a listed company or a company subject to the Law, such as a credit institution, located in Belgium or abroad in an *FATF* Member State (*Article 6*).

Article 6bis of the Law of 1993 provides that special identification measures will be determined by Royal Decree for non face-to-face transactions. Such a Royal Decree has not yet been issued.

However, the **Belgian Banking Commission** (*Commission Bancaire, Financière et des Assurances*) has issued specific regulations applicable to **banks** (see the regulation of 27 July 2004 approved by *Royal Decree of 8 October 2004 (Arrêté Royal du 8 octobre 2004 portant l'approbation du règlement de la Commission Bancaire, Financière et des Assurances relative à la prévention du blanchiment des capitaux et du financement du terrorisme)* as well as *Banking Commission guidelines of 22 November 2004 and 20 July 2005*).

By these various regulations and guidelines, the *Banking Commission* has given to the banks and institutions subject to its control practical indications relating to the obligation to identify and know their clients, to keep identification documents and to structure the internal organization in order to ensure that adequate money laundering provisions are duly implemented.

3.5 KYC principle (know your customer)

***Article 4 §2 of the Law of 1993* requires that all operations should be carefully reviewed in order to make sure that they are consistent with the knowledge of the client, its activities, its**

risk profile and, when necessary, the origin of the funds. The law does not indicate when the identification of the origin of the funds is necessary but the preparatory works reveal that such identification of the origin of the funds is required in case of assets management and operations carried out for politically exposed persons without, however, giving any definition as to whom the politically exposed persons are. The *Banking Commission* regulation has given clear and extensive definition of this category.

Pursuant to *Article 8 of the Law of 1993*, the persons subject to the Law must review all operations they consider particularly likely, by their nature or their unusual relationship with the client's activities, by the surrounding circumstances or by the quality of the parties, to be linked to money laundering.

The practical modalities of identification and of KYC obligations will be determined by the relevant regulatory or disciplinary authorities or by Royal Decree, according to the level of risk of the client or of the operation.

If this identification and vigilance are not possible, it is forbidden to enter into or to maintain a relationship.

3.6 Reporting obligation

Persons covered by the *Law of 1993* must report to the *CTIF* operations they suspect or know to be linked to money laundering (*Article 12*), or to the Head of the Bar in case of lawyers (*Article 14bis*). The Head of the Bar must then verify whether the conditions provided by the law are observed and, in the affirmative, he must immediately report to the *CTIF*.

The *CTIF* has the right to block the transaction during two business days toward credit institutions only and not, for example, toward lawyers and has the right to ask for additional **information** also from third parties such as the police, the State or the receivers in bankruptcy cases or lawyers (*Article 15 §1*).

The *CTIF* will transfer to the Public Prosecutor the cases where there are serious indications of money laundering (*Article 16*) and will report to the *Minister of Finance (Ministre des Finances)* the cases of serious and organized tax fraud (Article 17 §2).

3.7 Tipping off

It is forbidden to inform the client or any third party that a report has been issued to the *CTIF* or that a prosecution for money laundering is ongoing (*Article 19*).

The *Law of 1993* does not provide for any **criminal sanction** *per se* in case of tipping off, but the tipping off could be considered as a sign of aiding and abetting the client in money laundering.

Article 20 of the *Law of 1993* provides for **immunity** from all civil, criminal or disciplinary action against those who reported a suspicion of money laundering in good faith.

3.8 Prohibition of cash payment above €15 000

The *Law of 1993* prohibits cash payment in any commercial transaction concerning a good the value of which is above €15 000 (*Article 10ter*). In addition, the purchase price of real estate can only be paid through a bank transfer or a bank check except if it concerns an amount below €15 000, representing less than 10% of the purchase price (*Article 10bis*).

3.9   Sanctions in case of violation of the obligations

The disciplinary authority may publish the measures it takes and impose an administrative fine ranging from €250 to a maximum of €1 250 000 (*Article 22*). For persons that are not subject to any disciplinary authority, these measures may be imposed by the *Minister of Finance*.

Any breach of the prohibition concerning a cash payment above €15 000 (*Article 10ter*) may be sanctioned by an administrative fine the amount of which cannot exceed 10% of the amount paid cash or €1 250 000. This fine may be imposed by the *Minister of Economic Affairs (Ministre des Affaires Economiques)* (*Article 23*).

4   Curbing money laundering

The *Laws of 17 July 1990 and 7 April 1995* have determined the scope of application of *Article 505 CC* as it specifically relates to the money laundering offense.

4.1   The underlying offenses

Article 505 CC **sanctions a series of behaviors relating to items listed in Article *42, 3 CC*.** Therefore these 2 articles must be read in conjunction: *Article 42, 3* lists the items that are suspectible to become the **object** of the money laundering, where *Article 505 CC* defines which **behavior** qualify as money laundering.

4.1.2   Article 42, 3 CC

Article 42, 3 CC identifies the objects susceptible to be money laundered as being the **patrimonial advantages directly derived** from an offense (the primary advantages), the goods and values which have been **substituted** to these primary advantages and the income derived from **these invested** advantages.

The reference to the goods listed in *Article 42, 3 CC* proves that the legislator has adopted a different approach from that adopted by the European authorities when they drafted the Directives and from the *Law of 1993*. The money laundering offense is not established by reference to a list of specified underlying offenses but by reference to patrimonial advantages produced by the primary offence which become then the object of the money laundering activities.

The money laundering offense is very general in the sense that it relates to the product of any offense, including misdemeanors. The scope of application of *Article 505 CC* is therefore a lot wider than that of the *Law of 1993*, as it covers all the offenses existing in Belgian law.

The illegal assets listed in *Article 42, 3 CC* can be described as follows:

- **The patrimonial advantages directly deriving from the offense**: they are called primary advantages. They consist of goods and assets that the perpetrator of the underlying offense has obtained while committing this offense, whatever the nature of the asset.[1] Quoted as examples of this type of advantage: the blood money paid to a hitman, revenue from arms trafficking or drug trafficking, corruption money, the ransom paid after a kidnapping.[2]

---

[1] C. Meunier, Du neuf dans les pouvoirs de saisie pénale par le juge et dans les possibilités de confiscation pénale, obs. under Corr. Arlon (juge d'instruction), 6 septembre 1996, *J.L.M.B.*, III, 1997, p. 1453.

[2] F. Roggen, Aspects de procédure en matière de blanchiment : les saisies et le référé pénal, in *Acte du Colloque sur le Blanchiment- La situation des entreprises, des organismes financiers et de leur conseillers*, Solvay Business School, Brussels, 4 juin 2003, p. 10.

- **The assets and goods that have been substituted for the primary advantages**: this category relates to the assets that have been purchased with the stolen money or the bonds and shares that the hitman has bought with his blood money.

- **The income from the invested advantages** (either from the primary advantages or from those that have been substituted to these primary advantages): this category relates to the interest produced by the illegal funds deposited in a bank account.[3]

4.1.3   The underlying offense

An underlying offense must therefore have been committed and must have produced funds, values or goods targeted by Article 42,3 CC, which are the object of the behavior sanctioned by *Article 505 CC*. **If the patrimonial advantages are not of an illegal origin, there can be no question of money laundering.** The existence of a money laundering offense that results in a conviction is therefore only possible if an underlying offense has been committed. The case law has debated the question whether or not and up to which point the judge has to demonstrate the existence and the nature of such underlying offense. Indeed, in numerous cases, it is difficult to identify precisely the underlying offense either because it was committed a long time ago, or because the underlying offense was committed abroad and that detailed information is lacking.

From case law it is clear that the judge was not obliged to indicate in all details the nature of the underlying offense that had produced the illegal assets.

On 21 January 2000, the Belgian *Supreme Court (Cour de cassation)* decided that a conviction for money laundering was legally justified if the judge had indicated the existence of the constitutive elements of the offense, including the fact that the perpetrator knew the illegal origin of the assets. It was, however, not required that the judge indicate precisely the crime or the offense that had produced the assets, or the fact that the Belgian judge had jurisdiction over the underlying offense, or if the underlying offense was time-barred or not.[4]

In another decision rendered on 25 September 2001, the *Supreme Court* decided that it was necessary only to indicate that the goods were of illegal origin and the perpetrator knew of that fact, without having to indicate precisely the underlying offense, upon the condition that, on the basis of the factual data, the judge could exclude any legal origin for the funds.[5] In that case, it was decided that it did not matter whether the funds came from drug trafficking, diamond trafficking or stolen art. It is sufficient that the judge states the illegal origin of the funds, without having to indicate which sort of criminal act produced the funds.

Despite the fact that an indictee never has to demonstrate his innocence, it is obvious that, in practice, it will be in his interest to demonstrate that the assets or the goods that he has manipulated could have had or had a legal origin. It will make it more difficult for the judge to exclude any legal origin, as required by the *Supreme Court*.

4.1.4   Tax fraud

It has been hotly debated whether or not tax fraud could constitute an underlying offense in money laundering. Indeed, several authors, mostly tax specialists, have defended the idea that a patrimonial advantage as listed in *Article 42, 3 CC* could not cover the situation of tax fraud, as

---

[3] F. Roggen, *op.cit.*, p. 10.
[4] Cass., 21 juin 2000, *A.C.*, 2000 p. 1165, *J.T.*, 2000, p. 788.
[5] Cass., 25 septembre 2001, *Pas.*, 2001, II, 1480.

the absence of declaration of income in a tax return could, at the most, allow a perpetrator to avoid a debt or an expense, but did not cause the creation of a patrimonial advantage.[6]

However, a substantial number of criminal law specialists are of the opinion that the simple fact of avoiding the payment of a tax in itself constitutes a patrimonial advantage.[7] Such advantage could indeed consist of a reduction of charges.

On 22 October 2003, the *Supreme Court* decided that the avoidance of a tax constituted a patrimonial advantage.[8] Some authors have argued that this decision was rendered in a case of tax fraud and not of money laundering and that it could not be transposed to money laundering because the patrimonial advantages derived from tax fraud could not be specifically localized among the assets of the perpetrator.[9], [10] The *Supreme Court* has not yet had the opportunity to decide on this specific issue but, on 26 February 2004, the *Court of First Instance of Brussels (Tribunal correctionnel de Bruxelles)* decided that *Article 505 CC* did not exclude any underlying offense and that the voluntary avoidance of a tax debt could very well constitute the required underlying offense for the application of *Article 505 CC*. The case concerns the avoidance of inheritance rights.[11], [12]

4.2 The sanctioned behaviors

4.2.1 Article 505, §1, 2 CC

Article 505, §1, 2 CC **penalizes the acts of buying, receiving, possessing, keeping, managing goods of illegal origin (those listed in** *Article 42, 3 CC)* **if the perpetrator knew or should have known the illegal origin of these assets.**

[6] T. Afschrift, Blanchiment et fraude fiscale, *Journal de droit fiscal*, juillet-août 1997, pp. 194 à 224 ; M. Moris, Le blanchiment d'argent provenant d'infractions fiscales, in *Les Paradis fiscaux et l'évasion fiscale*, Bruylant, 2001, Coll. de la Faculté de droit de l'ULB, pp. 241 à 284 ; T. Afschrift et V. De Brauwere, Manuel de droit pénal financier, Kluwer, Brussels, 2001, pp. 331 et 340 ; L. Huybrechts, «Fiscaal strafrecht», A.P.R., Story-Scientia, Gand, 2002, p. 78.

[7] G. Jakhian, 'l'infraction du blanchiment et la peine de confiscation en droit belge', *R.D.P.*, 1991, p. 781 ; L. Cornelis et R. Verstraeten, 'Mag er not witgewassen worden', *T.B.H.*, 1992, p. 181 ; M. Rozie, 'De bijzondere verbeurdverklaring van vermogensvoordelen toegepast op fiscale delicten', in *Fiscaal strafrecht en strafprocesrecht*, 1996, p. 210 and followings; A. De Nauw, 'De verschillende luiken van het wettelijk systeem tot bestraffing en tot voorkoming van het witwassen van gelden en de fiscale fraude', in *Fiscaal strafrecht en strafprocesrecht*, 1996, p. 219 and followings; A. Van Roosbroeck, *Voorkoming en bestraffing van witwassen van geld en illegale vermorgensvoordelen*, E.T.L., Anvers, 1995, p. 265 ; and J. Spreutels et C. Scohier, 'Y a-t-il une interaction entre la lutte contre la fraude fiscale et la lutte contre le blanchiment en droit belge et en droit international?', *Les paradis fiscaux et l'évasion fiscale*, Bruylant, Coll. de la Faculté de droit de l'ULB, 2001, p. 325.

[8] Cass., 22 octobre 2003, R.D.P., 2004, p. 277 with the submissions of the General Attorney J. Spreutels; T. Straf., 2004, p. 167 with the comment of G. Stessens; *J.L.M.B.*, 2004, p. 336, with the comment of F. Roggen; *J.T.*, 2004, p. 354, with the comment of E. Boigelot; *T.F.R.*, 2004, p. 139, with the comments of J. Speecke; *R.D.C.*, 2004, p. 199, with the observations of O. Creplet.

[9] G. Stessens, 'Over de beperkte fiscale roeping van de witwassenwetgeving', *A.F.T.*, 1999, p. 321 and followings; G. Stessens, 'Normaals over de verbeurdverklaring van vermogensvoordelen uit een misdrijf en aanverwante aspecten, zoals de strafbaarstelling van witwassen', *R.W.*, 1999–2000, p. 1073 ; G. Stessens, 'De Belgische strafrechtelijke witwassenwetgeving', *in* X., *Dix ans de lutte contre le blanchiment des capitaux en Belgique et dans le monde,* Acte du colloque international organisé par la CTIF le 14 mars 203, sous la direction de J. Spreutels, Bruxelles, Bruylant, 2003, pp. 64 à 75.

[10] G. Stessens, 'Zwartgeld ten eeuwige dagen in de strafrechtelijke greep van het parket?', observations under Cass., 22 octobre 2003, *T. Straf.*, 2004, p. 182.

[11] J. Speecke, 'Het Hof van cassatie spreekt zich uit over het principe van de verbeurdverklaarde vermogensvoordelen ingeval fiscale fraude en de cumul met de supplementaire aanslag', observations under Cass., 22 octobre 2003, *T.F.R.*, 2004, p. 146, n° 7.

[12] Civ. Bruxelles, 26 février 2004, Fiscaal Strafrecht 2004/84, p. 873.

The judge will have to determine whether the perpetrator may not have known that the assets derived from an offense because the objective circumstances were such that its mistrust should necessarily have been triggered.[13] The parliamentary works quote as examples of objective elements that lead one to infer the knowledge of the illegal origin of the assets:

- the very low purchase price

- the personality of the sellers

- the secret character of the operation

- the place of delivery

- the anonymity of the suppliers

- the lack of invoices

- the abnormal quantity of goods.

The task of the Public Prosecutor in delivering the onus of proof is therefore alleviated, since he does not have to establish the evidence of the subjective knowledge. The judge will have to determine whether the factual circumstances constitute a collection of objective criteria allowing him to conclude that the perpetrator had or should have had knowledge of the illegal origin of the funds.[14] The judge must analyze the facts on the basis of the knowledge that the perpetrator had when the offense was committed and not *a posteriori*, take into account the individual characteristics of the perpetrator, including his experience, his profession, his judicial past as well as all surrounding elements that could have aroused his suspicions.[15]

This measure alleviates the onus of proof but does not remove **the intentional element** from the offense. It does not allow the incrimination of the mere negligence of the perpetrator.[16]

The author of the underlying offense cannot be prosecuted for money laundering pursuant to *Article 505, §1, 2 CC.*

4.2.2   Article 505, §1, 3 CC

Article 505, §1, 3 **prohibits converting or transferring goods of an illegal origin with the view to hiding their illegal origin or to helping a person involved in the committing of the offense to avoid the legal consequences of the offense.**

This new **sanction** was introduced by the *law of 7 April 1995.*

It requires **a special intent** which means that actual knowledge of the illicit origin of the funds needs to be established.

---

[13] Rapport fait au nom de la Commission de la Justice, Document parlementaire de la chambre, 1989–1990, n987/4, p. 8.

[14] Rapport fait au nom de la Commission de la Justice, Document parlementaire de la chambre, 1989–1990, n987/4, p. 8.

[15] T. Afschrift et de V. Brauwere, *op.cit.*, p. 322 ; Trib. 1er instance d'Anvers, 23 février 1993, T.R.V., 1994, p. 195.

[16] T. Afschrift et de V. Brauwere, *op.cit.* ; L. Cornelis et R. Verstraeten, Mag er nog wit worden gewassen, R.D.C., 1992, p. 176 and followings; J.F. Tossens and P. Lambrecht, Le secret bancaire et le contrôle de l'Etat sur les opérations de change et sur les effets délictuels, *in* Blanchiment d'argent et secret bancaire, La Haye, 1996, p. 53.

The author of the underlying offense may also be prosecuted for money laundering under this provision.

4.2.3   Article 505, §1, 4 CC

Article 505, §1, 4 **prohibits the fact of hiding or disguising the nature, the origin, the location, the disposition, the movement or the ownership of the goods of illegal origin, if the perpetrator knew or should have known that they were of illegal origin.** Reference is made to the developments above *Article 505, §1, 2 CC* for the required **intent**.

The behavior can consist of an abstention. A conscious abstention may sometimes favor disguising the nature or the location of goods of illegal origin.[17]

The perpetrator of the underlying offense may be prosecuted for money laundering pursuant to Article 505, §1, 4 CC.

4.2.4   The draft bill

A draft bill is pending before the *Belgian Chamber of Representatives (Chambre des Représentants)*. It has already been approved by the *Commission for Justice (Commission de la justice)* and is awaiting discussion before Parliament. It contains several proposals for amendments to adopt the 2005 Directive and to address some of the criticisms raised by the current system.

The draft bill proposes amending the text of *Article 505, §1, 2 CC* so that the perpetrator of the underlying offense could also be prosecuted for money laundering, as is already possible for the offenses listed *in Article 505, §1, 3 and 4 CC*. Indeed, a *Supreme Court* decision of 8 May 2002[18] has indicated that the present situation contains a loophole in the repressive system: the perpetrator of the underlying offense committed abroad could come and launder his money in Belgium without any risk if he behaves according to *Article 505, §1, 2 CC*.

In addition, it is proposed that the offense described under Article *505, §1, 2 CC* would no longer apply to patrimonial advantages derived from some tax fraud offenses for perpetrators other than the authors or accomplices of these tax offenses. The practical effect of this provision would be that the banks which receive assets of illegal origin derived from a tax offense, could not be prosecuted for money laundering if they only committed acts listed in *Article 505, §1, 2 CC*. However, if they committed acts listed in *Article 505, §1, 3 and 4 CC* or if they had advised their client to commit the tax fraud, they would still remain liable for money laundering.

4.3   Sanctions

4.3.1   Imprisonment and/or a fine

If convicted, the author of a money laundering offense may be sentenced to **imprisonment** of up to five years and/or a **criminal fine** of €550 000.

---

[17] R.Verstraeten et D. Dewandeleer, «Witwassen na de wet van 7 april 1995 : kan het nog witter ?», R.W.,1995–96, p. 700

[18] RG P.02.0021.F.; www.juridat.be, JC 02583_1

4.3.2　Confiscation

In addition, pursuant to *Article 505, §3 CC*, **the assets which were laundered must be confiscated by the State**. This obligation could have been seen merely as a repetition of the possibility offered to the court by *Article 42, 1 CC* if the Belgian legislator had not deprived the court of its power: the **confiscation** must be ordered, even though such confiscation had not been requested by the public prosecutor's office. Moreover, in doing so, the Belgian legislator targeted not the proceeds of the money laundering offense (which the court may always confiscate under *Article 42, 1 CC*), but the proceeds of the underlying offense. Any confiscation ordered pursuant to *Article 505, §3 CC* must be imposed on the money laundered assets themselves and cannot be ordered, by substitution, on other assets found in the ownership of the money launderer.[19]

This follows from the approach taken by the Belgian legislator that, under *Article 505, §3 CC*, a Belgian court may order the confiscation of the proceeds of the underlying crime although it has no jurisdiction to try such crime.

The application of *Article 505, §3 CC* recently led to an issue that divided the French- and Dutch-speaking chambers of the *Supreme Court*.

Pursuant to a decision rendered on 21 October 2003 by the Dutch-speaking Chamber of the *Supreme Court*,[20] it was decided that illegal goods had to be confiscated vis-à-vis each of the perpetrators, even if the illegal money-laundered assets had left the ownership of the perpetrators.

However, in a decision rendered on 14 January 2004 by its French-speaking Chamber,[21] the *Supreme Court* decided that confiscation was not a penalty and could not be imposed on the assets of the perpetrator of the money laundering offense who had handed the illegal goods over to a third party. The French-speaking Chamber of the Court decided that a judge could only confiscate the object of the money laundering offense where it could be located and not against the perpetrator of the money laundering offense if he had relinquished the illegal assets.

With these contradictory approaches by the two Chambers of the *Supreme Court*, a draft bill pending before the *Chamber of Representatives* is aimed at reconciling the two positions and proposes confirming that confiscation is a real penalty and must be applied toward all authors and accomplices of the money laundering offense even if the money laundered assets have already been relinquished. In addition to favoring the more strict option taken by the *Supreme Court*, if voted as such, the draft bill will also reverse the case law which prohibited confiscation of assets equivalent to those obtained as a result of the offense.

However, in order to avoid a disproportional sanction, the draft bill provides that the judge will be allowed to reduce the amount which is confiscated in order not to subject the perpetrator to a cost which is disproportionate to the general value of his assets and the seriousness of the offense.

The proposed amendment will be extremely detrimental to bank and financial institutions because confiscation could be made against their assets as a matter of policy even if they had in the meanwhile relinquished the money laundered assets to third parties.

---

[19] Arrêt de la Cour d'appel de Bruxelles, 30 juin 2003, J.L.M.B., 2004, II, p. 584.
[20] RG P.03.0757.N.; www.juridat.be, JC 03AL 1_1
[21] RG P.03.1185.F; www.juridat.be, JC 041E 1_1

Addresses

Cellule de Traitement des Informations Financières (CTIF)
Avenue de la Toison d'Or, 55 bte 1
1060 Brussels
Belgium
Tel +32 2 533 72 11
Fax +32 2 533 72 00
www.ctif-cfi.be
Contact person: Jean-Claude Delepière, Chairman
info@ctif-cfi_be

Commission Bancaire, Financière et des Assurances (CBFA)
Rue du Congrès 12–14
1000 Brussels
Belgium
Tel +32 2 220 52 11
Fax +32 2 200 52 75
www.cbfa.be
Contact person: Albert Niesten, Secretary General
seg@cbfa.be

Abbreviations

CBFA   Commission bancaire, financière et des assurances
CC   Criminal code
CTIF   Cellule de traitement des informations financières
FATF   Financial Action Task Force (on money laundering)
KYC   Know your customer

Bibliography

Afschrift, T: Blanchiment et fraude fiscale, *Journal de droit fiscal*, 1997.

Afschrift, T./De Brauwere, V.: Manuel de droit pénal financier, Kluwer, Brussels, 2001.

Boigelot, E.: observations under Cass. 22 octobre 2003, in *J.T.*, 2004.

Cornelis, L./Verstraeten, R.: Mag er nog witgewassen worden, in *T.B.H.*, 1992.

Creplet, O.: observations under Cass. 22 octobre 2003, in *R.D.C.*, 2004.

De Nauw, A.: De verschillende luiken van het wettelijk systeem tot bestraffing en tot voorkoming van het witwassen van gelden en de fiscale fraude, in *Fiscaal strafrecht en strafprocesrecht*, Mys en Breesch, Gent, 1996.

Dewandeleer, D./Verstraeten, R.: Witwassen na de wet van 7 april 1995, kan je nog witter, in *R.W.*, 1996.

Huybrechts, L.: Fiscaal strafrecht, in *A.P.R.*, Story-Scientia, Gent, 2002.

Jakhian, G.: L'infraction du blanchiment et la peine de confiscation en droit belge, *R.D.P.*, 1991.

Lambrecht, P./Tossens, J.F.: Le secret bancaire et le contrôle de l'Etat sur les opérations de change et sur les effets délictuels, in *Blanchiment d'argent et secret bancaire*, Den Haag, 1996.

Meunier, C.: Du neuf dans les pouvoirs de saisie pénale par le juge et dans les possibilités de confiscation pénale, in *J.L.M.B.*, III, 1997.

Moris, M.: Le blanchiment d'argent provenant d'infractions fiscales, in *Les Paradis fiscaux et l'évasion fiscale*, Bruylant, Brussels, 2001.

Roggen, F.: Aspects de procédure en matière de blanchiment : les saisies et le référé pénal, in *Acte du Colloque sur le Blanchiment- La situation des entreprises, des organismes financiers et de leur conseillers*, Solvay Business School, Brussels, 2003.

Roggen, F.: observations under Cass. 22 octobre 2003, in *J.L.M.B.*, 2004.

Rozie, M.: De bijzondere verbeurdverklaring van vermogensvoordelen toegepast op fiscale delicten, in *Fiscaal strafrecht en strafprocesrecht*, Mys en Breesch, Gent, 1996.

Scohier, C./Spreutels, J.: Y a-t-il une interaction entre la lutte contre la fraude fiscale et la lutte contre le blanchiment en droit belge et en droit international?, in *Les paradis fiscaux et l'évasion fiscale*, Bruylant, Coll. de la Faculté de droit de l'ULB, Brussels, 2001.

Speecke, J.: Het Hof van cassatie spreekt zich uit over het principe van de verbeurdverklaarde vermogensvoordelen ingeval fiscale fraude en de cumul met de supplementaire aanslag, in *T.F.R.*, 2004.

Speecke, J., observations under Cass. 22 octobre 2003, in *T.F.R.*, 2004.

Spreutels, J./Scohier, C.: Y a-t-il une interaction entre la lutte contre la fraude fiscale et la lutte contre le blanchiment en droit belge et en droit international?, in *Les paradis fiscaux et l'évasion fiscale*, Bruylant, Coll. de la Faculté de droit de l'ULB, Brussels, 2001.

Stessens, G.: Over de beperkte fiscale roeping van de witwassenwetgeving, *A.F.T.*, 1999.

Stessens, G.: Normaals over de verbeurdverklaring van vermogensvoordelen uit een misdrijf en aanverwante aspecten, zoals de strafbaarstelling van witwassen, *R.W.*, 1999–2000.

Stessens, G.: De Belgische strafrechtelijke witwassenwetgeving, *in* X., *Dix ans de lutte contre le blanchiment des capitaux en Belgique et dans le monde*, Bruxelles, 2003.

Stessens, G.: Zwartgeld ten eeuwige dagen in de strafrechtelijke greep van het parket?, *T. Straf.*, 2004.

Stessens, G.: observations under Cass. 22 October 2003, in *T. Straf.*, 2004.

Tossens, J.F./Lambrecht, P.: Le secret bancaire et le contrôle de l'Etat sur les opérations de change et sur les effets délictuels, in *Blanchiment d'argent et secret bancaire*, Den Haag, 1996.

Van Roosbroeck, A.: Voorkoming en bestraffing van witwassen van geld en illegale vermogensvoordelen, in ETL, Anvers, 1995.

Verstraeten, R./Cornelis, L.: Mag er not witgewassen worden, *T.B.H.*, 1992.

Verstraeten, R./Dewandeleer, D.: Witwassen na de wet van 7 april 1995, kan je nog witter, in *R.W.*, 1996.

Enide Perez has been working as a criminal defence lawyer since 1997 and has been involved in a large variety of criminal proceedings, especially in the field of economic criminal law. She has handled environmental, tax and various fraud cases and has defended and advised large publishing houses and journalists, in criminal cases involving the freedom of speech. Until 2002, she worked at the law firm *Sjöcrona Van Stigt* in Rotterdam. She is currently working at the law firm *Stibbe* in Amsterdam. Enide Perez is a member of the *Dutch Association of Defence Counsel* (*Nederlandse Vereniging van Strafrechtadvocaten*).

Max Vermeij has been practicing criminal law since 2000, after two years of practicing tax law. He has defended corporations and individuals in a large variety of (corporate) fraud, tax and environmental cases. His practice also includes defending corporations in cases involving the confiscation of illegally obtained profits. Furthermore, Max Vermeij advises (listed) companies in matters regarding compliance with securities regulations. Max Vermeij is currently working at the law firm *Stibbe* in Amsterdam. He is a member of the *Dutch Association of Defence Counsel* (*Nederlandse Vereniging van Strafrechtadvocaten*).

Firm's profile

Stibbe is an internationally oriented full-service Dutch legal practice, characterized by pragmatic advice and thorough sector and industry knowledge. Stibbe is well positioned for cross-border transactions due to longstanding experience and a dense international network (alliance with Gleiss Lutz and Herbert Smith). Within Stibbe, the Corporate Criminal Law Unit focuses on the specialized field of corporate criminal law, advising clients concerning investigations and lawsuits regarding domestic and international tax, banking and stock exchange fraud cases.

Netherlands

Max J.N. Vermeij and Enide Z. Perez

Criminal defence lawyers

Stibbe
Strawinskylaan 2001
1077 ZZ Amsterdam
Netherlands

Tel +31 20 546 04 28/+31 20 546 04 78
Fax +31 20 546 08 17
max.vermeij@stibbe.com/enide.perez@stibbe.com
www.stibbe.com

Anti-Money Laundering: International Law and Practice.
Edited by W.H. Muller, C.H. Kälin and J.G. Goldsworth
© 2007 John Wiley & Sons, Ltd

Contents – Netherlands

1   Introduction

Both money laundering and the financing of terrorism are criminal phenomena. Although terrorism can be financed with legally obtained funds as well as with illegal funds (which sets it apart from money laundering, where funds are, by definition, illegally obtained), **money launderers and sponsors of terrorism often utilize the same methods to channel funds** to their destination. The criminal prosecution of terrorists and money laundering criminals, client identification and the availability of data concerning suspect financial transactions are important AML/CFT instruments.

In the *Netherlands*, the **first steps** towards client identification were taken with the introduction of the *Identification Financial Services Act 1988 (IFSA 1988; Wet identificatie bij financiële dienstverlening 1988)*. This Act only applied to credit (and comparable) institutions and was based on **self-regulation**, with banks issuing a code of conduct for the identification of their clients.

In 1993, the *Identification Financial Services Act 1993 (IFSA 1993; Wet identificatie bij financiële dienstverlening 1993)* was introduced, in combination with the *Disclosure of Unusual Transactions Act (DUTA; Wet melding ongebruikelijke transacties)*. At first, only **financial institutions** such as banks, life insurance and credit card companies and casinos had to comply with the identification and reporting duties. Gradually, the **scope of the provisions has been widened** to include other service providers, such as dealers in high-value goods (since 2001) and legal professionals (since 2003).

After the terrorist attacks of 11 September 2001, the Dutch government has amended the *Dutch Criminal Code (DCC; Wetboek van strafrecht)* to conform to the framework decree of the *Council of Europe* concerning the combating of terrorism.[1] One of the amendments concerns the implementation of a provision, penalizing the participation in an organization which has the intent to commit terrorist criminal offences.

The Dutch government furthermore accelerated and intensified its efforts in the fields of providing more financial safety and combating the financing of terrorism. Due to the fact that, in some instances, financial flows and terrorist activities may be connected, an important area of attention has been promoting the **integrity of the financial sector**. In a policy document entitled *The integrity of the financial sector and the combat against terrorism*, published in the fall of 2001, the government drew attention to the importance of financial supervisory legislation, legislation targeting unusual and suspect flows of money (such as the *Disclosure of Unusual Transactions Act (DUTA, Wet melding ongebruikelijke transacties)* and the **explicit penalization of money laundering**) and the need for effective enforcement of such legislation.[2]

2   Anti-money laundering provisions

On 14 December 2001, money laundering was separately and specifically penalized in the *DCC*.[3] Prior to that, money laundering had to be prosecuted using provisions that targeted the handling of stolen property.

These provisions were, however, not always sufficient for this purpose. For example, the perpetrator of a crime can, under these older and less specific provisions, not be prosecuted for

---

[1] *Resolution 2002/475/JBZ* of 13 June 2002.
[2] See *Lower House*, 2001–2002, 28106, no. 2.
[3] See *Dutch Bulletin of Acts and Decrees* 2001, no. 606.

the offence of handling the proceeds from that crime. This limitation has disappeared with the introduction of the new anti-money laundering provisions: *Articles 420bis, 420ter* and *420quater* of the *DCC*.

Article 420bis of the *DCC* is the general anti money laundering provision. *Article 420bis, paragraph 1 under a,* states that it is **forbidden to hide or to conceal** the actual nature, **the origin**, the location, the disposal or relocation **of an object or an asset**, or to hide or conceal who is entitled to or has possession of an object or an asset, **while knowing that the object or asset has** – directly or indirectly – **proceeded from a criminal offence**.

Article 420bis paragraph 1 under b of the *DCC* states that it is forbidden to **acquire**, to have in one's possession, to hand over, to convert or to use an object or an asset, while knowing that the object or asset has – directly or indirectly – proceeded from a criminal offence.

This article covers all possible (tangible) objects and assets (including property rights and monies). The term *knowing* also covers *conditional intent (voorwaardelijk opzet)*.

Both crimes (the active *hiding* as well as the *acquisition* of objects or assets) can be punished with imprisonment for a maximum term of 4 years or with a fine of €67 000 for natural persons and €670 000 for legal persons.

Article 420ter of the *DCC* states that **habitual money laundering** (*gewoontewitwassen*) is punishable with imprisonment for a maximum term of 6 years or with a fine of €67 000 for natural persons and €670 000 for legal persons. With the addition of *habitual*, *Article 420ter* of the *DCC* is simply an **aggravated** version of the basic money laundering offence penalized in *Article 420bis*. Simply repeating the crime of money laundering does not constitute a habit; there has to be a connection between the various offences. In this way, habitual money laundering differs from recidivism of the basic money laundering.

Article 420quater of the *DCC* penalizes **negligent money laundering** (*schuldwitwassen*). The only difference between this criminal offence and that of *Article 420bis* is the **degree of guilt**. The latter article requires the higher standard of *knowingly* to have been satisfied, while in *Article 420quater* of the *DCC*, it suffices that one *should reasonably have suspected* that an object or an asset has proceeded from a crime. Negligent money laundering can be punished with imprisonment for a maximum term of 1 year or with a fine of €67 000 for natural persons and €670 000 for legal persons.

3   Provisions targeting (the financing of) terrorism – related criminal provisions

3.1   Financing of terrorism

As the ministerial explanations accompanying the recent amendments to the *DUTA* and the *Identification Services Act* (*ISA; Wet identificatie bij dienstverlening*)[4] also point out, the financing of terrorism can be brought under several provisions of the *DCC*.

Financing terrorism can, for example, be punished as ***preparation*** (*voorbereiding*) of a criminal offence. *Article 46* of the *DCC* penalizes preparation of a criminal offence that can be punished with imprisonment for a term of eight years or more, in case the perpetrator intentionally acquires, manufactures, imports, transports, exports or has in his possession goods, materials, carriers of

---

[4] See *Lower House*, 2004–2005, 29990, no. 8.

information, spaces or conveyances that are apparently intended to commit that criminal offence. Terrorist criminal offences are severely punished and the financing of terrorist criminal offences therefore can be punished as *preparation* under *Article 46*. *Preparation* can be punished with half of the maximum penalty the criminal offence can be punished with. In case the maximum penalty of the criminal offence is a imprisonment for life, preparation can be punished with imprisonment for a maximum term of 15 years.

Of course, the provisions concerning *complicity* and *provocation* can apply to financing terrorism and financing terrorism can also constitute participation in an organization which has the intent to commit terrorist criminal offences, which is a separate criminal provision that will be discussed hereafter.

3.2 The Act on terrorist criminal offences

3.2.1 Material support of a criminal organization

On 10 August 2004,[5] the *Act on terrorist criminal offences* came into force and added several criminal provisions relating to terrorist offences to the *DCC*. Among the provisions added are a new fourth paragraph of *Article 140* of the *DCC*, which states that **providing financial or other material support** to a criminal organization, or raising funds or recruiting members for a criminal organization, is also considered participation in such organization.

3.2.2 Terrorist organization

A new *Article 140a* has been added to the *DCC*, which provides that participation in an **organization which has the intent to commit terrorist criminal offences**, can be punished with imprisonment for a maximum term of 15 years or with a fine of €67 000 for natural persons and €670 000 for legal persons. The *founders*, *leaders* and *directors* of the organization can be punished with imprisonment for a maximum term of 30 years[6] or with a fine of €67 000. Providing financial or other material support to a criminal organization, or raising funds or recruiting persons for a criminal organization, again, is equated with participation in the organization.

3.2.3 Criminal offences with terrorist intent

Finally, the *Act on terrorist criminal offences* has introduced a definition of *terrorist intent* (*Article 83a* of the *DCC*) and has increased the penalties for a number of criminal offences, when committed with terrorist intent.

3.3 Criminal organization

More generally, participation in a criminal organization whose intent it is to commit criminal offences, is a criminal offence under Dutch criminal law (*Article 140* of the *DCC*) and can be punished with imprisonment for a maximum term of 6 years or a fine of €67 000 for natural persons and €670 000 for legal persons. The *founders*, *leaders* and *directors* (*oprichters, leiders en bestuurders*) can be punished with imprisonment for a maximum term of 8 years or a fine of €67 000.

---

[5] See *Dutch Bulletin of Acts and Decrees*, 2004, no. 373
[6] The maximum term of 20 years has been increased on 1 February 2006 to 30 years by the Act of 22 December 2005. See *Dutch Bulletin of Acts and Decrees* 2006, no. 11 and no. 23.

3.4 The criminal liability of legal persons

Under Dutch criminal law, criminal offences can be committed both by **natural** and by **legal persons** (*corporations*; *rechtspersonen*). Corporate criminal liability presupposes an act or omission of an individual. This individual act or omission can lead to a **corporate criminal liability**, if a judge rules that it is *reasonable* to **attribute** the behavior of the individual to a corporate entity. The *Dutch Supreme Court* (*Hoge Raad der Nederlanden*) has ruled that, generally, an act that has been committed *within arm's length* of a company, or *within a corporate setting* (*in de sfeer van de onderneming*), may be *within reason* be attributed to this company.

Only after it has thus been established that a corporate entity has committed a criminal offence, certain natural **persons within the corporation** (*other* than the individual, material perpetrator), of whom it can be proven that they have **directed** (*feitelijke leiding geven aan*) or **ordered** (*opdracht geven aan*) the prohibited conduct, can be held criminally responsible as well.

In a recent judgement,[7] the *Dutch Supreme Court* has given some specific (non-exhaustive) examples of the conditions under which an act can be said to have been committed *within a corporate setting* (and consequently can be *reasonably attributed* to the company under investigation):

- the behavior (or failure to act) was displayed by someone who was working, as an employee or otherwise, *on behalf of* the corporate entity;

- the behavior fitted into the *regular pattern of operations* of the corporate entity;

- the behavior served the corporate entity's *commercial purpose*; or

- the corporate entity could *influence* whether or not the act was committed, and would normally have *accepted* the act.

According to the *Dutch Supreme Court*, acceptance of certain behavior may be equated with *not having taken the precautions* that might be reasonably expected from the corporation in order to avoid the behavior in question.

Of course, a corporation is an immaterial construct. In case a corporation is identified (on the basis of any of the criteria above) as a suspect, it will have to be represented by an individual. This can be a statutory director, or any other person authorized by a director to represent the corporation.

Legal persons can be punished by imposing a fine. Additional punishments can be meted out as well. A legal person, generally, may be confronted with the confiscation of assets, the publication of the court's decision and, particularly in case of an economic offence, the (partial) closing down (for a maximum period of one year) of the enterprise in which the offence took place. Another possible measure against a legal person would be the (partial) deprivation of certain rights or the (partial) withholding of certain benefits (for a maximum period of 2 years), which rights or benefits have been (or could have been) awarded by the government in connection with the business in question.

3.5 Confiscation of illegally obtained profits or advantages

Apart from the imposition of a fine and, possibly, any of the additional penalties mentioned in the preceding paragraph, a (legal) person, convicted for a crime, can be confronted with a

---

[7] *Dutch Supreme Court*, 21 October 2003, *Nieuwsbrief Strafrecht (NbSr)* 2003, 14, nr. 442.

consecutive, separate court procedure, leading to the confiscation of *illegally obtained profits* (*Article 36e* of the *DCC*).

Such a confiscation order is (intended as) a **non-punitive measure**, and can be imposed if the convicted (legal) person has benefited *by means of* or *from*:

- the revenues of the offence for which he has been duly *convicted*;

- the revenues of a *similar* offence, given *sufficient indications* that the person in question also committed this similar offence;

- the revenues of a *serious offence* (i.e. an offence for which a fine of €67 000 can be imposed), again given *sufficient indications* that the person in question also committed this offence;

- the revenues of *any other* criminal offence – not necessarily committed by the person in question – in case a so-called *Criminal Financial Investigation (Strafrechtelijk Financieel Onderzoek)* has made it *plausible* that such revenues were received. This fourth variant requires that the (legal) person in question was convicted for a *serious* offence (i.e. an offence for which a fine of at least €67 000 can be imposed).

4 Obligations of financial institutions

4.1 Introduction

The explanatory notes accompanying the introduction (in 1994) of the *IFSA 1993* and the *DUTA* explicitly referred to the *Forty Recommendations* established by the *Financial Action Task Force on Money Laundering (FATF)* in 1990. Some of the *Forty Recommendations* specifically addressed client identification in relation to financial services. Other recommendations touched upon issues such as the information position of law enforcement (supplying information to financial intelligence units), and the integrity of staff. With the introduction of the *IFSA 1993* and the *DUTA*, the Dutch government implemented both the *Forty Recommendations* and *Council Directive 91/308/EEC* of 10 June 1991 (the first *Money Laundering Directive*) on the prevention of the use of the financial system for the purpose of money laundering.

In the following paragraphs, the essentials of the current *Identification Services Act (ISA; Wet identificatie bij dienstverlening)* which has replaced the *IFSA 1993* and the *DUTA* will be discussed.

4.2 The Identification Services Act (ISA)

4.2.1 Introduction and stated purposes of the ISA

The date of entry into force of the original *IFSA 1993* was 1 January 1994.[8] The Act was amended on several occasions. In 2002, the adjective *financial* and the reference to the year in which the Act was originally proposed (1993) were dropped from its designation, and the Act was continued as the *Identification Services Act*.

The *ISA* has been further implemented by means of the *Designation Order concerning Institutions and Services as meant in the ISA and the DUTA*,[9] and the *Regulations implementing the ISA*.[10]

---

[8] *Dutch Bulletin of Acts and Decrees* 1994, 48.
[9] *Royal Decree of 24 February 2003, Dutch Bulletin of Acts and Decrees* 2003, 94.
[10] *Ministerial Regulation of 20 January 1994, Netherlands Government Gazette*, 1994, 17, last amendment on 13 April 2005, *Netherlands Government Gazette*, 2005, 77.

The main aim of both the *ISA* and the *DUTA*, as stated in the explanatory notes to these respective Acts, was twofold: **prevention and repression of tax fraud and money laundering**. After the introduction of the *ISA*, criminals were expected to be deterred from abusing the financial system, as the **anonymity**, formerly provided to clients of financial institutions, would have **disappeared** as a consequence of the requirement that financial institutions should identify their client under certain conditions and keep records of the identification. In other words: the *ISA* would **conserve the *paper trail*** of (financial) transactions.[11] As regards the *DUTA*, **repression** was an important element as well, as the Act aimed, *inter alia*, to provide law enforcement with operational data.

Since the terrorist attacks of 11 September 2001, an **additional objective** of the identification of clients requesting a (financial) service, has been the combat against (the financing of) **terrorism**. In this respect, important changes (to, for example, the *FATF*'s *Forty Recommendations*) have been the shift to the identification of *ultimate beneficial owners* (the persons behind possible client entities such as trusts) and the introduction of a risk-based approach, which under certain circumstances will have to culminate in customer due diligence efforts by financial institutions.

Originally, the obligation to identify clients only applied to certain *financial* institutions (hence the original designation of the Act, containing the word *financial*). As of 2002, however, the *ISA* also applies to sellers of certain high-value goods (such as cars, yachts, antiques, etcetera). As of June 2003, the *ISA* also applies, under certain circumstances to a limited number of legal professionals.

4.2.2 Outline of the ISA

Definition of key concepts

Article 1 of the *ISA* defines key concepts such as **institution**, **service** and **client**. Clients can be either natural or legal persons. Typical institutions falling within the scope of the *ISA* are, of course, **financial institutions** such as credit institutions (banks), insurance companies and securities institutions. The sellers of high-value goods, mentioned above, were given a separate category in 2002. A catch-all category is provided, which contains certain legal professionals (lawyers, civil law notaries, accountants and tax advisors) insofar as they provide services that border on *advisory work* (*e.g.* financial, economical or tax **advice which does not formally require a legal professional**) instead of being purely concerned with the determination of a client's *legal position*.

The services targeted are:

- the **safekeeping** of securities, money and other valuables;

- the **opening and administration of accounts** (for funds, securities, precious metals or other values);

- the **letting of safe-deposit boxes**;

- the **cashing of coupons** (or their equivalents) of bonds and comparable securities;

- **arranging** life insurance policies;

---

[11] See: Mul V.: Banken en witwassen (doctoral thesis), Gouda Quint, 1999, blz. 156; Broekhuizen, K.W.H./Hillen J.L.S.M.: Wet identificatie bij dienstverlening, in: Tijdschrift voor financieel recht, 2005-1/2, blz. 22.

- **paying out** life insurance policies;

- providing a service related to one or more transactions exceeding a certain **minimum threshold**;

- selling, or acting as an intermediary in the sale of, cars, yachts, antiques and other **high-value goods**; and

- certain **advisory services** provided by (legal) professionals.

The duty to identify a client

Article 2 of the *ISA* requires institutions to identify a client **prior** to rendering a financial service. A limited number of exemptions is available. Unnecessary repetition of client identification is avoided as much as possible: an institution is not required to re-identify a client that had already been identified on a prior occasion by that same institution, unless the identification was done at another branch or office and the value of the repeat transaction exceeds €10 000.

How to identify clients – special provisions for non face-to-face situations

Article 3 of the *ISA* indicates which **identity documents** (e.g. passport, driver's license) are to be used when identifying natural persons, and which procedures are to be followed in case the client is a domestic or foreign legal person.

In many instances, credit and financial institutions do not have face-to-face contact with customers, for example, when credit cards are issued, or in direct banking and direct insurance situations. *Article 4* of the *ISA* applies to identification of clients in case such services are rendered on a non face-to-face basis and provides that (as opposed to the *standard* procedure) the identity of a client who does not appear in person may be established by demanding a *copy* or the *document number* of an official identity document. This, however, is only allowed in case (a) the transaction does not involve cash *and* (b) the first payment related to the service is made to or from an account held with a credit institution based in the *EU* or in certain designated states. An institution that has identified a client using a *copy* or a *document number* is further obliged to verify that the client's identity matches the identity of the client whose account has been debited or credited for the first payment. To complete the circle, it is also required that the identity of the latter (the account holder) has been established in compliance with the *ISA*.

Clients represented by a third party

Article 5, paragraph 1, of the *ISA* addresses identification in case of **representation** of clients. *Paragraph 1* of this article states that an institution should identify, first of all, the natural person, appearing before her and acting on behalf of (the representative of) a client. In connection with this requirement, *Article 5, paragraph 2*, obliges the institution, when dealing with a natural person, to determine whether this person is acting on his own account or on behalf of a third party (i.e. on behalf of a client or on behalf of a representative of a client). The identity of the third party, represented by the natural person appearing before the institution, has to be established as well, using the methods described in the preceding articles of the *ISA*. In case the third party, in his turn, represents yet another third party, the identity of the latter has to be established as well.

Furthermore, *Article 5, paragraph 4*, obliges the institution to make a ***reasonable* effort** towards identification of the ultimate client.

Record keeping

Article 6 of the *ISA* obliges institutions to **record** (and **keep available**) certain data. Apart from obvious client data such as names, date of birth, and address, the institution has to record data pertaining to the identity document that was presented, and data regarding the service that was provided. In connection to this duty, *Article 7* provides that the institution should keep the data accessible for a period of **five years**, starting after the contract or agreement, that formed the basis for the service rendered, was completed.

Administrative sanctions

As a result of the amendments that came into force on 1 May 2006, the supervisory authority can now apply ***administrative* sanctions** in case of non-compliance with the *ISA*. In the past, non-compliance could only be addressed by means of ***criminal* prosecution** of an institution, which was, in many cases, **not in proportion** to the nature of the offence. Now that the supervisory authority is able to impose *administrative* measures such as an *incremental penalty payment* (*last onder dwangsom, Article 8b* of the *ISA*), an *administrative fines* (*bestuurlijke boete, Article 8c et seq.* of the *ISA*) and publication of name, address and residence of a person who has been non-compliant (*Article 8l* of the *ISA*), it is expected that intervention will occur at an earlier stage. The *una via* principle has been embodied in *Articles 8i* and 8*o* of the *ISA*. It follows from these articles that *punitive* administrative measures and criminal prosecution are **mutually exclusive**. So, once an administrative fine has been imposed or a transgression has been publicized, criminal prosecution is no longer possible, and *vice versa*.[12]

Criminal sanctions

Article 8 of the *ISA* explicitly **forbids** an institution to render a service in case the (intended) **client has not been duly identified** on the basis of the Act. Violation of *Article 8* is a criminal offence under the *Economic Offences Act* (*EOA; Wet op de economische delicten*), and can lead, in case criminal intent can be proven, to the imposition of a prison sentence of a maximum of 2 years and/or a (maximum) fine of €16 750 for natural persons (or a maximum of €67 000 in case the proceeds of the crime exceed €4 188) or €670 000 for legal persons.

4.2.3 Further identification requirements applicable to credit institutions and insurance companies

Aritcle 14 of the *Decree regarding prudential rules under the Act on Financial Supervision (Besluit prudentiële regels Wft)*[13] stipulates that credit institutions and insurance companies

---

[12] Unlike administrative fines and publication of a transgression, the imposition of an incremental penalty payment (*last onder dwangsom*) is not considered to be a *punitive* measure (as it is intended to stop and/or to prevent certain behaviour), and therefore does not prevent the authorities from initiating a subsequent criminal prosecution against the transgressor.
[13] *Royal Decree of 12 October 2006, Dutch Bulletin of Acts and Decrees,* 2006, 519. Until 1 January 2007, this requirement could be found in Article 5, paragraph 1, of the *Decree regarding management intergrity for credit institutions and insurance companies (Besluit integere bedrijfsvoering kredietinstellingen en verzekeraars, Royal Decree of 10 October*

(without prejudice to the applicability of the provisions of the *ISA*) should have **internal guidelines**, regulating the manner in which the identity, nature and background of their clients are established. In the *Regulation concerning Customer Due Diligence for credit institutions and insurance companies (Regeling CDD kredietinstellingen en verzekeraars),*[14] the standards to be satisfied are specified.[15]

Credit institutions[16] have to follow the **guidelines** set out in 2002 by the ***Basel Committee on Banking Supervision***.[17] *Sections 2.1 and 2.2* of the *Basel Committee*'s publication deal with general identification requirements and specific identification issues, respectively. Some of these issues regard transactions with corporate entities (the institution should identify **beneficial owners** and those who have control over funds), client accounts opened by professional intermediaries (when opened on behalf of a single client or a group of identifiable clients, these clients should all be identified separately), and non face-to-face transactions (where mitigation of risk is advised, such as requiring that the first payment be carried out through an existing account in the client's name with another bank subject to similar customer due diligence standards). Customer acceptance policies and on-going monitoring of accounts and transactions are addressed as well by the *Basel Committee*. In 2003, the *Basel Committee* issued an attachment to its 2001 publication, entitled *General Guide to Account Opening and Customer Identification*. As regards corporate entities, the *Basel Committee* admonishes banks to always identify those who have **ultimate control** over a client entity.

Article 6 of the *Decree regarding management integrity for credit institutions and insurance companies (Besluit integere bedrijfsvoering kredietinstellingen en verzekeraars)* obliges Dutch credit institutions to investigate, upon request of the *Dutch Central Bank (De Nederlandsche Bank)*, possible integrity risks posed by persons or organizations that are presumed to be engaged in terrorist activities.

4.2.4   Supervision of the ISA

Supervision of compliance with the *ISA* is **not centralized**. For each category of institutions, the supervisory authority that is competent for market conduct also supervises *ISA* compliance. Competent supervisory authorities are the *Dutch Central Bank (De Nederlandsche Bank)* for credit institutions, credit card companies, money transaction offices, casinos and trust offices, the *Pensions and Insurance Supervisory Authority (Pensioen- en Verzekeringskamer)* for insurance companies, the *Authority for the Financial Markets (Autoriteit Financiële Markten)* for securities institutions and financial intermediaries, the *Fiscal Information and Investigation Service and Economic Investigation Service (FIOD-ECD)* for sellers of valuable goods, and the *Financial*

2003, Dutch Bulletin of Acts and Decrees, 2003, 396), in combination with the Regulation concerning Customer Due Diligence for credit institutions and insurance companies (Regeling CCD kredietinstellingen en verzekeraars. The introduction of the Act on Financial Supervision (Wet financial toezicht) and the Royal Decree of 12 October 2006, as of 1 January 2007, have not been intended to cause any material changes as regards existing CDD requirements.

[14] *Regulation of 23 December 2003*, established by the *Dutch Central Bank (De Nederlandsche Bank NV)* and the *Pensions and Insurance Supervisory Authority (Pensioen- en Verzekeringskamer)*.

[15] The *Dutch Central Bank (De Nederlandsche Bank NV)* has also issued guidance in the form of an *Explanation to the Regulation concerning Customer Due Diligence for credit institutions and insurance companies (Nadere toelichting CDD Identificatie*, April 2004) and an *Explanation to the CDD for banks (Toelichting CDD for banks*, current version April 2006).

[16] Our discussion will not address the regulations for insurance companies.

[17] See: *Basel Committee on Banking Supervision*: Customer due diligence for banks, October 2002.

Supervision Office (Bureau Financieel Toezicht) for legal professionals, tax advisers, accountants and real estate agents.

4.2.5 Prospects

In the fall of 2004, the *Ministry of Finance (Ministerie van Financiën)* published a draft legislative proposal, concerning amendments to the *ISA* based on the revised June 2003 version of the *Forty Recommendations* (in which a risk-based approach in implementing the recommendations is allowed). In the draft, no reference yet was made to the (foreseeable) need to implement the third *Money Laundering Directive (Directive 2005/60/EC*, adopted on 26 October 2005), which has led some authors to speculate that the *ISA* will be gradually reduced to the status of a framework law, with separate regulations and decrees implementing the *Third Money Laundering Directive*.[18] The *Ministry of Finance* has also commissioned research regarding the *effectiveness* of identification. This research effort is intended to aid in facilitating the alignment of the requirements mentioned in the new Directive with the day-to-day management of service providers.[19]

4.3 The Disclosure of Unusual Transactions Act (DUTA)

4.3.1 Introduction and stated purposes of the DUTA

The *DUTA* became effective as of 1 February 1994.[20] The Act was amended on several occasions.

The *DUTA* has been further implemented by means of the *Designation Order concerning Institutions and Services as meant in the ISA and the DUTA*,[21] the *Regulations implementing the ISA and the DUTA*,[22] and the *Regulations concerning the Indicators for Unusual Transactions 2005*.[23]

The explanatory notes to the *DUTA* state that the aims of the Act include **strengthening the information position of law enforcement**, by introducing a duty to report certain transactions, while at the same time improving the **integrity** of financial service providers. As regards the actual duty to report, its stated aims are, on the one hand, to **prevent the abuse of the financial system** for money laundering purposes, and, on the other, to actively **combat money laundering**.

4.3.2 Outline of the DUTA

Definition of key concepts

Article 1 of the *DUTA* defines the key concepts *service*, *client*, *transaction* and *unusual transaction*.

---

[18] See: Broekhuizen, K.W.H/Hillen J.L.S.M.: Wet identificatie bij dienstverlening, in: Tijdschrift voor financieel recht, 2005-1/2, blz. 23.
[19] See press release of *De Nederlandsche Bank*, 9 March 2006.
[20] *Dutch Bulletin of Acts and Decrees* 1994, 49.
[21] *Royal Decree of 24 February 2003; Besluit van 24 februari 2003 tot aanwijzing van instellingen en diensten in het kader van de Wet identificatie bij dienstverlening en de Wet melding ongebruikelijke trasnacties, Dutch Bulletin of Acts and Decrees* 2003, 94.
[22] *Ministerial Regulation of 20 January 1994; Uitvoeringsregeling Wet identificatie bij dienstverlening en Wet melding ongebruikelijke transacties, Netherlands Government Gazette*, 1994, 17, last amendment on 13 April 2005, *Netherlands Government Gazette*, 2005, 77.
[23] *Ministerial Regulation of 19 August 2005; Regeling indicatoren ongebruikelijke transacties 2005, Netherlands Government Gazette*, 2005, 164.

The services targeted by the *DUTA* are:

- the **safekeeping** of securities, money and other valuables;

- the **opening and administration of accounts** (for funds, securities, precious metals or other values);

- the **letting of safe-deposit boxes**;

- the **cashing of coupons** (or their equivalents) of bonds and comparable securities;

- **arranging** life insurance policies;

- **paying out** life insurance policies;

- **crediting or debiting** a money, securities or other **account**;

- **exchanging** euros or foreign currency;

- selling, or acting as an intermediary in the sale of, cars, yachts, antiques and other **high-value goods**;

- extra-legal **advisory services** provided by independent legal advisers (lawyers, civil law notaries), tax advisers, accountants, commercial advisers, real estate agents and trust offices.

A *client* is defined as a person (either a natural or a legal person) to whom, or on behalf of whom, a service is provided. A *transaction* is defined as an act or combination of acts carried out by, or carried out on behalf of, a client in connection with one or more services. An *unusual transaction*, then, is a transaction qualified as such on the basis of the **indicators** referred to in *Article 8* of the *DUTA*.

The duty to report unusual transactions – record keeping

Article 9 of the *DUTA* states that **any person who provides a service** on a **professional** or **commercial** basis, is required to report any unusual transaction, performed or planned (in the future) in connection with that service to the *Financial Intelligence Unit Nederland (FIU-NL)*[24]. The report should contain the identity of the client, the type and number of the client's identity document, the nature, time and place of the transaction, the value of the monies, securities, precious metals or other valuable involved in the transaction (and in case the service consists of crediting or debiting an account: also the provenance and destination of the monies, securities, etc.), the circumstances that led to the qualification of the transaction as *unusual*, and (if applicable) a description of the high-value goods that were sold (cars, yachts, antiques, etc.).

These data (contained in the report to the FIU-NL) should be kept for a period of **five years,** commencing after the moment the report is made. A report has to be made within a 14 day period, commencing when the unusual character of the transaction has been established by the service provider.[25]

---

[24] Formerly *Office for the Disclosure of Unusual Transactions (ODUT; Meldpunt Ongebruikelijke Transacties)*.
[25] This requirement can be found in the Appendix to the *Regulations concerning the Indicators for Unusual Transactions 2005* (*Ministerial Regulation* of 19 August 2005, *Netherlands Government Gazette*, 2005, 164).

The Office for the Disclosure of Unusual Transactions

Articles 2 through *7* of the *DUTA* contain provisions regarding the *Financial Intelligence Unit Nederland (FIU-NL)*; a *Financial Intelligence Unit* in the sense of *FATF Recommendation 13*), such as an enumeration of its tasks and its **duty to keep a register**. The **main task** of the FIU-NL is **to process and analyze** the reports that it receives from service providers. In case the FIU-NL comes to the conclusion that a reported *unusual* transaction is **suspect**, the relevant data are transferred to law enforcement. To facilitate this process, *Article 10* gives the FIU-NL the authority to make further inquiries with the person that reported a transaction, or with a person involved with crediting or debiting an account.

Indicators for unusual transactions

Article 8 of the *DUTA* states that the *Minister for Finance* (*Minister van Financiën*) and the *Minister for Justice* (*Minister van Justitie*) jointly, and in consultation with the FIU-NL, will establish the **indicators** by means of which it will be determined whether a transaction is *unusual* or not. The (current) indicators can be found in the *Appendix* to the *Regulations concerning the Indicators for Unusual Transactions 2005* (*Regeling indicatoren ongebruikelijke transacties 2005*).

A basic distinction is made between *subjective* indicators and *objective* indicators.

As regards the **subjective** indicators, it is mandatory to send a report to the FIU-NL if, in the service provider's opinion:

- the transaction is *presumed* to be a *money laundering transaction* or a transaction *connected with the financing of terrorism*; or

- the transaction *gives cause to suppose* that it *may* be *connected* to *money laundering* or the *financing of terrorism*.

The *objective* indicators vary with the nature of the service provider's business. The following indicators apply (current list, applicable as of 1 November 2005):

- For *credit, securities* and *investment institutions* and *money transaction offices*:

  - *exchange transactions* if involving €15 000 or more in cash being exchanged into either a *foreign currency* or *from small to large denominations*;

  - *money transfer transactions* involving €2000 or more in cash;

  - transactions with (legal) persons, established in *certain countries or territories* that have been classified by the Minister for Finance and the Minister for Justice as *posing an unacceptable risk for money laundering or the financing of terrorism*.

- For *life insurance companies* and *insurance brokers*:

  - transactions with (legal) persons, established in *certain countries or territories* that have been classified by the Minister for Finance and the Minister for Justice as *posing an unacceptable risk for money laundering or the financing of terrorism*.

- For *credit card companies*:

  - *cash deposits* of €15 000 or more;

  - the *use of a credit card* in connection with a transaction of €15 000 or more.

- For *casinos*:
  - the *deposit* of coins, bank notes or other value bearers for an amount of €15 000 or more;
  - a *funds transfer* of €15 000 or more;
  - the *sale of chips* for an amount of €15 000 or more in case the client pays with cheques or foreign currency.
- For *dealers in high-value goods*:
  - *cash transactions* involving €15 000 or more.
- For *independent legal advisers, lawyers, civil law notaries, tax advisers, accountants, commercial advisers, real estate agents* and *trust offices*:
  - transactions involving payment (to the service provider in question, or with him acting as an intermediary) of €15 000 or more *in cash, bearer cheques* or *similar* instruments of payment.

The indicators listed above came into force as of 1 November 2005. The current list **departs** rather conspicuously from previous lists. An important reason for changing the list has been the wish to **improve the effectiveness** of the indicator system and to diminish the administrative burden resting upon service providers. As regards the effectiveness: in recent years, the performance statistics of the FIU-NL have shown a considerable gap between the number of reports it received (in 2004: 175 000) and the number of transactions that were subsequently transferred to law enforcement (in 2004: 41 000). In other words: the former system of indicators produced too many hits that were *objectively true* but nonetheless *false* (i.e.: *not relevant*) from a law enforcement point of view. Also, the recent change in the indicator system allowed the implementation of *FATF*'s *Special Recommendation nr. IV*, concerning the requirement that financial institutions should be required to make a report in case they suspect that funds are linked or related to, or are to be used for terrorism, terrorist acts or by terrorist organizations.

To assist service providers in arriving at a *subjective judgment*, the FIU-NL offers **examples** on its web site. When comparing the current list of indicators with previous lists, one also notices that the number of objective (quantifiable) indicators has been decreased, and that the threshold value for exchange, credit card and casino transactions has been increased from €10 000 to €15 000.

In the appendix to the *Instructions regarding Money Laundering (Aanwijzing witwassen)*, issued by the *Board of Procurators General (College van procureurs-generaal)*,[26] a number of **typologies** has been compiled. If a specific case exhibits one or more elements of a typology, the *Instructions* support that a suspicion of money laundering may be warranted. Examples of these typologies include:

- the client is unable to provide a plausible (economic) explanation for the frequency with which various currencies are offered for exchange;
- the magnitude of a transaction bears no relation to the income of the client;
- the client appears not to have counted the money he presents in a cash transaction.

The (objective) indicator targeting transactions with entities in certain countries that pose an unacceptable risk for money laundering or the financing of terrorism is new. The countries

---

[26] Effective as of 1 November 2005, *Netherlands Government Gazette*, 2005, 202.

and territories in question are not necessarily those that the *FATF* has placed on the list of *Non Cooperative Countries or Territories (NCCT)*, but only those among them that show an unwillingness to take measures that would get them off the *NCCT* list.

Indemnities for service providers

Article 12 of the *DUTA* **protects** a service provider, having reported a transaction as *unusual*, **from being himself prosecuted for money laundering**. *Article 13* stipulates that a service provider is not liable for any damages that a third party may suffer as a result of a report that has been made to the FIU-NL, unless the third party makes a plausible case that the facts and circumstances of the case did not reasonably require the service provider to make a report. *Article 19* of the *DUTA* binds to secrecy any person (service provider) that has made a report to the FIU-NL.

Administrative sanctions

As a result of the amendments that came into force on 1 May 2006, the supervisory authority can now apply ***administrative*** sanctions in case of non-compliance with the Act. In the past, non-compliance could only be addressed by means of **criminal prosecution** of a service provider, which was, in many cases, **not in proportion** to the nature of the offence. Now that the supervisory authority is able to impose administrative measures such as an *incremental penalty payment* (*last onder dwangsom, Article 17c* of the *DUTA*), an administrative fine (*bestuurlijke boete, Article 17d et seq.* of the *DUTA*) and publication of name, address and residence of a person who has been non-compliant (*Article 17m* of the *DUTA*), it is expected that (administrative) intervention will occur at an earlier stage. The *una via* principle has been embodied in *Articles 17j* and 17*p* of the *DUTA*. It follows from these articles that *punitive* administrative measures and criminal prosecution are **mutually exclusive**. So, once an administrative fine has been imposed or a transgression has been publicized, criminal prosecution is no longer possible, and *vice versa*.[27]

Criminal sanctions

Violation of the **duty to report**, a *failure* to **supply additional data** to the FIU-NL or a ***breach of confidentiality*** after a report has been made to the FIU-NL are criminal offences under the *EOA*, and can lead, in case criminal intent can be proven, to the imposition of a prison sentence of a maximum of 2 years and/or a (maximum) fine of €16 750 for natural persons (or a maximum of €67 000 in case the proceeds of the crime exceed €4188) or €670 000 for legal persons.

4.3.3 Supervision of the DUTA

Supervision of compliance with the *DUTA* is **not centralized**. For each category of institutions, the supervisory authority that is competent for market conduct also supervises *DUTA* compliance. Competent supervisory authorities are the *Dutch Central Bank* (*De Nederlandsche Bank*) for credit institutions, credit card companies, money transaction offices, casinos and trust offices, the *Pensions and Insurance Supervisory Authority (Pensioen- en Verzekeringskamer)* for insurance companies, the *Authority for the Financial Markets* (*Autoriteit Financiële Markten*) for securities institutions and financial intermediaries, the *Fiscal Information and Investigation Service and*

---

[27] Unlike administrative fines and publication of a transgression, the imposition of an incremental penalty payment (*last onder dwangsom*) is not considered to be a *punitive* measure (as it is intended to stop and/or to prevent certain behavior), and therefore does not prevent the authorities from initiating a subsequent criminal prosecution against the transgressor.

Economic Investigation Service (FIOD-ECD) for sellers of valuable goods, and the *Financial Supervision Office (Bureau Financieel Toezicht)* for legal professionals, tax advisers, accountants and real estate agents.

4.3.4   Prospects

At this time, there are no pending legal proposals to amend the *DUTA*.

5   Law enforcement

In the *Netherlands*, there are 19 court districts, each with its own *Public Prosecutor's Office (arrondissementsparket)*. Given the expertise needed to successfully prosecute money laundering, a considerable degree of **centralization** has taken place. A *National Prosecutor for DUTA Affairs (NPDA; Landelijk officier van justitie inzake MOT-aangelegenheden)* has been appointed. The *NPDA* belongs to the *Functional Public Prosecutor's Office (FPPO; Functioneel Parket)*. Located in The Hague, the *FPPO*'s general aim is to prosecute environmental and economic crime and fraud, which of course includes money laundering. The NPDA has at his disposal a specialised *Bureau (BLOM; Bureau politiële ondersteuning Landelijk Officier van Justitie Wet MOT)*, which, as of 1 January 2006, has been integrated with the former *Meldpunt Ongebruikelijke Transacties* into a project organization called the *FIU-NL*. The new organization will contribute to law enforcement by analyzing and filtering reported *unusual* transactions, and transferring data concerning *suspect* transactions to specialized police investigators. Inversely, a police investigator or a *Public Prosecutor* can submit a request for information regarding possible money laundering transactions to the FIU-NL.

6   International cooperation

The Dutch FIU-NL is a member of the *Egmont Group* and as such has subscribed to the *Principles for Information Exchange Between Financial Intelligence Units for Money Laundering and Terrorism Financing Cases*, adopted on 13 June 2001. One of these principles is **reciprocity** in exchanging information. Within the *Egmont Group*, an online system (*FIU.NET*) is in place through which a number of European *FIU*'s can issue information requests to their peers. On the basis of such information, the FIU-NL is able to check whether persons that are being investigated in the Netherlands are connected with unusual transactions abroad.

Abbreviations

AML	Anti Money Laundering
CFT	Combating the Financing of Terrorism
DCC	Dutch Criminal Code (*Wetboek van strafrecht*)
DUTA	Disclosure of Unusual Transactions Act (*Wet melding ongebruikelijke transacties*)
EOA	Economic Offences Act (*Wet op de economische delicten*)
FATF	Financial Action Task Force on Money Laundering

FIOD-ECD	Fiscal Information and Investigation Service and Economic Investigation Service (*Fiscale Inlichtingen- en Opsporingsdienst en Economische Controledienst*)
FIU-NL	Financial Intelligence Unit Nederland
FPPO	Functional Public Prosecutor's Office (*Functioneel Parket*)
IFSA 1988	Identification Financial Services Act (*Wet identificatie bij financiële dienstverlening 1988*)
IFSA 1993	Identification Financial Services Act 1993 (*Wet identificatie bij financiële dienstverlening 1993*)
ISA	Identification Services Act (*Wet identificatie bij dienstverlening*)
NCCT	Non Cooperative Countries or Territories
NPDA	National Prosecutor for DUTA Affairs (*Landelijk officier van justitie inzake MOT-aangelegenheden*)
ODUT	The former Office for the Disclosure of Unusual Transactions (*Meldpunt Ongebruikelijke Transacties*), now FIU-NL

Bibliography

Basel Committee on Banking Supervision: Customer due diligence for banks, October 2002.

Broekhuizen, K.W.H./Hillen, J.L.S.M.: Wet identificatie bij dienstverlening, in: Tijdschrift voor financieel recht, 2005-1/2, Uitgeverij Den Hollander, Deventer, 2005.

Cleiren, C.P.M./Nijboer, J.F.: Tekst & Commentaar Strafrecht, Kluwer, Deventer, 2004.

Lamp, R.: Identificatie bij dienstverlening: internationale ontwikkelingen en nationale implementatie, Tijdschrift voor Compliance, 2005-3, Uitgeverij Den Hollander, Deventer, 2005.

Mul, V.: Banken en witwassen (doctoral thesis), Gouda Quint, Gouda, 1999.

Raaijmakers, G./Vermeulen, E.: Vennootschaps- en effectenrecht, Ars Aequi Wetseditie, Ars Aequi Libri, Nijmegen, 2005.

Pit Reckinger is 'maître en droit' and holds a DEA in business law. He became a member of the Luxembourg bar in 1990. He has worked with Linklaters & Paines (London) in 1990/1991. He is a partner in the corporate, banking and finance group of the firm since 1994. His areas and expertise focus specifically on mergers and acquisition, shareholders agreements and financing documents, bond and equity listings, bank secrecy, aspects of money laundering and compliance issues for banks. He has published contributions in banking law, recently in the areas of bank confidentiality and the concept of beneficial owner in banking law, in international finance law and tax law. He is fluent in French, German, English and Luxembourgish.

Firm's profile

Elvinger, Hoss & Prussen is a leading Luxembourg law firm, established in 1964, with strong practices in corporate law, corporate finance, mergers and acquisitions, banking and general commercial law, insurance, investment and pension funds, SICARs, asset management, private equity structures, European law, securitisation, intellectual property, administrative law and tax law. The firm provides high-level legal services, both in terms of legal advice and litigation as well as arbitration to local and international financial and industrial groups and financial institutions, Luxembourg investment funds and their service providers.

Luxembourg

Pit Reckinger

Avocat à la Cour

Elvinger, Hoss & Prussen
2, Place Winston Churchill
L-1340 Luxembourg

Tel (+352) 44 66 44 0
Fax (+352) 44 22 55
pitreckinger@ehp.lu
www.ehp.lu

Anti-Money Laundering: International Law and Practice.
Edited by W.H. Muller, C.H. Kälin and J.G. Goldsworth
© 2007 John Wiley & Sons, Ltd

Contents – Luxembourg

Introduction

This chapter sets out in general terms the framework of Luxembourg anti-money laundering laws and regulations. It is not meant to constitute a detailed guide of the rules as applicable to each profession separately and it is not a substitute to specific advice on the subject.

Anti-money laundering rules are of two types: those aiming at repression which consist of the criminal offences punishing anyone who commits or participates in an act of money laundering or financing of terrorism and those aiming at prevention which set out the measures which certain specified professionals[1] more likely through their activity to be involved in money laundering or financing of terrorism have to observe.

The law of 19 February 1973 on the sale of drugs and the fight against drug addiction as amended[2] (article 8-1) and the Luxembourg criminal code (article 506-1 to 506-7) define the concept of 'money laundering'. The definition refers to laundering of money originating from drug trafficking as well as from a large number of serious crimes and extends to the financing of terrorism. Those criminal provisions punish by fines (from €1250 to €1 250 000) and/or imprisonment (from one to five years) anyone who commits or participates knowingly in an act of money laundering.

The legal framework for preventive anti-money laundering obligations is set out by the law of 12 November 2004 relating to the fight against money laundering and against financing of terrorism (the '2004 Law')[3] which implements the second money laundering directive 2001/97/EC of 4th December 2001.[4] The 2004 Law sets out general obligations as applicable in the same manner to a large number of professionals ranging from banks, other professionals of the financial sector, insurance companies and investment funds to lawyers, notaries, auditors, real estate agents and high value goods merchants.

Anti-money laundering rules have historically been closely linked to the development of Luxembourg as a financial sector.

By essence, financial sector professionals are among the most exposed professions to be used to reinject monies of criminal origin into the economy and officially benefit of it thereafter.

Naturally therefore, the first rules relating to the fight against money laundering applied to financial sector professionals. And today the rules fixed by the Commission for the Supervision of the Financial Sector ('*CSSF*') still set the standard for a large range of professionals which are subject to the same duties.

Given the importance of Luxembourg as a financial sector we will thus often focus on obligations applicable to financial sector professionals. For those professionals, their supervisory authority *CSSF* has over time, following changes in law, issued circulars[5] describing in detail the applicable obligations tailored to the specific needs or features of the various professions it regulates.[6]

---

[1] Mainly banks and other professionals of the financial sector but also insurance companies, investment and pension funds, lawyers, notaries, auditors, chartered accountants, real estate agents, casinos, etc.

[2] Law of 7th July 1989 (Mémorial A, p. 923).

[3] Mémorial A, p. 2766.

[4] The present article does not take into account any anticipated changes upon the implementation of the third money laundering directive 2005/60/EC of 26th October 2005.

[5] All circulars on the fight against money laundering issued by the supervisory authority for the financial sector (*CSSF*) are available on www.cssf.lu.

[6] Banks, investment firms, commissioners, investment managers, professionals acting for their own account, UCI distributors, underwriters, financial instrument custodians, transfer agents and registrars, participants in an investor

For most of the other professionals which are subject to anti-money laundering by law, their relevant professional supervisory or regulatory body will have issued rules specific to the particular profession.[7]

Over the years Luxembourg has gradually built up a solid set of measures composed of criminal law rules defining money laundering by reference to an extensive list of underlying crimes (ranging from drug trafficking to serious and organised crime and financing of terrorism), legal provisions set out in the 2004 Law defining preventive professional obligations applicable to a large number of professionals which are completed by a complex set of regulatory and professional regulations. Together they aim at efficiently combating money laundering and financing of terrorism and preserve the good reputation of Luxembourg as a financial sector.

1   The money laundering and terrorist financing offences

The money laundering and terrorist financing offences are defined in the criminal code in article 506-1 to 506-7 and in article 8-1 of the law of 19 February 1973 on the sale of drugs and the fight against drug addiction.

In general terms the offence consists in either (i) helping to justify the untrue origin of the subject or the proceeds of certain criminal activities, or (ii) helping to place, convert or hide the subject or proceeds of such activities, or (iii) acquiring, detaining or using the subject or proceeds of such activities.

The underlying criminal activities concerned are: drugs trafficking, organised crime, kidnapping of minors, sexual offences against minors, prostitution, arms and munitions offences, corruption in public office or in private life, fraud against the financial interests of the state or of international bodies or offences of terrorism or of terrorist financing.[8]

The offence of terrorist financing consists in providing or collecting funds or other property with the intention that they are used, or in the knowledge that they will be used with a view to committing one or more terrorist offences.

The fact to launder money from or linked to any of these underlying criminal activities is punishable by terms of imprisonment of one to five years and/or a fine from €1250 to €1 250 000. Pursuant to these provisions, both the author, the co-author or accomplices are liable to these sanctions.

The legal definition of money laundering which we have summarised above in general terms is broad in scope and refers to a wide range of devices all of which are designed to falsify the source of the property which constitutes the subject or the proceeds of such underlying criminal offences.

As for any other criminal offence the breach of money laundering may only constitute a criminal offence if a 'tangible element' and an 'intentional element' coexist.

---

compensation scheme, investment advisers, brokers, market makers, operators of payment systems or securities settlement systems, exchange agents, claim recovery agents, professional lenders, securities lenders, fund transfer professionals, savings funds administrators, fund managers, domiciliary agents, client communication agents, administrative agents, IT systems and financial communication network operators, trust businesses.

[7] A list of the most important current rules is set out at the end of the chapter.

[8] A precise legal analysis of underlying offences under criminal law would exceed the scope of this article. Professionals will find indications and references in the relevant regulations governing their profession (see the list at the end of the chapter).

The tangible or material element requires that there is evidence of an underlying offence and indication that money which is the subject or the proceeds of the underlying offence was received or used by the professional or that he has benefited therefrom. It is to be noted that the breach of professional obligations referred to under 3.5 below which is separately punishable by a criminal fine does not require the evidence of the underlying offence to money laundering but could exist independently by the mere failure to comply with professional obligations such as identification duties.

As for any criminal offence however it exists only if the participation in the money laundering offence has been made intentionally. The offence will be committed only if there is evidence of intent. A mere negligence therefore does not constitute a criminal offence if the breach was done without the professional being conscious that he was participating in a money laundering activity. The requirement for the prosecutor to bring evidence of the 'intentional element' applies both to the offence of money laundering as well as to the offence consisting of a breach of professional duties referred to under 3.5 below.

The interpretation of what is intentional is left to the courts and may vary according to the different criminal offences existing under Luxembourg law. If it is established that the professional committed the breach knowing that he was committing the criminal offence of money laundering, i.e. having knowledge of the criminal origin of the funds, regardless of the intention or the goal for which the breach was committed, the intention should be duly evidenced and the sanctions will apply.

2   The professionals concerned

Anti-money laundering obligations aimed at prevention (as opposed to the repressive criminal rules referred to above) are solely imposed upon 'professionals'.

Private persons are obviously expected to act honestly but they are not subject to specific obligations when carrying out for example financial transactions. However, they could be liable under the provisions of the criminal code as author or accomplice if they knowingly participate in any punishable money laundering transaction.

The Luxembourg rules aimed at preventing money laundering apply to specific categories of professionals where it is considered that they would be the most likely involved in money laundering activities: among those are mainly regulated professionals but since the 2004 Law also unregulated professionals.

2.1   The regulated professions

The regulated professions are those which are regulated by a specific law which organises the supervision of the professionals concerned, sets out rules of conduct applicable to them and possibly establishes representative bodies which sometimes have the power to apply disciplinary sanctions upon its members.

2.1.1   Banks and professionals of the financial sector

Banks and professionals of the financial sector which are authorised to exercise their activities in Luxembourg on the basis of the 1993 Financial Sector Law. The professions concerned comprise mainly banks, investment managers, investment fund distributors, investment advisers, brokers, broker dealers, underwriters, domiciliation companies, etc.[9]

2.1.2 Insurance companies

Insurance companies authorised to act as such in Luxembourg pursuant to the law of 6 December 1991 relating to the insurance sector but only in respect of life insurance activities.

2.1.3 Pension funds

Pension funds which are subject to the supervision of the insurance commission, persons authorised to manage such pension funds and insurance brokers which are authorised to exercise their activities in Luxembourg.

2.1.4 Undertakings for collective investment ('UCI')

Undertakings for collective investment established under Luxembourg law comprising both those UCIs which are distributed among the public and those UCISs the sale of which is restricted to institutional investors.

2.1.5 Management companies of UCIs

Management companies of UCIs (more commonly referred to as UCITS III investment companies) which have additional activities to the common responsibilities for the management and administration, or which are distributing Luxembourg UCIs.

2.1.6 Pension funds

Pension funds subject to *CSSF* supervision.

2.1.7 Professionals who carry out an activity of the financial sector

Professionals who carry out an activity of the financial sector but who, for a specific reason, are excluded from the scope of the 1993 Financial Sector Law. They comprise inter alia professionals which render financial services exclusively to their parent undertakings or subsidiaries, exclusively to undertakings forming part of the same group, or exclusively consisting in administration of employee-participation schemes.

2.1.8 Independent auditors

Independent auditors (*réviseurs d'entreprises*) within the meaning of the law of 28th June 1984, relating to the organisation of the professional independent auditors.

2.1.9 Chartered accountants

Chartered accountants (*experts comptables*) within the meaning of the law of 10th August 1999 relating to the organisation of the profession of chartered accountants.

---

[9] For a complete list see hereabove footnote 3.

2.1.10 Notaries

Notaries (*notaires*) within the meaning of the law of 9 December 1976 relating to the organisation of the profession of notary.

2.1.11 Lawyers

Lawyers (*avocats*) within the meaning of the law of 10 August 1991 on the profession of lawyers but limited to situations where they act for clients in the preparation or realisation of financial or real estate operations or of transactions such as the sale or purchase of real estate or commercial businesses, asset management opening of bank accounts, creation or management of companies or similar structures. Lawyers are not subject to any such professional obligations where they merely act in a capacity as legal advisers and in particular in relation to the preparation of the conduct of judicial proceedings.

2.1.12 Casinos

Casinos and gambling institutions within the meaning of the law of 20 April 1977.

2.2   The unregulated professions

Unregulated professions are those which are not subject to ongoing supervision even though certain obligations may be imposed upon them by specific laws or the access to the profession may be regulated.

Among those, the following professions are subject to professional obligations in respect of money laundering:

* Real estate agents established or acting in Luxembourg.

* Tax advisers or advisers in economic affairs.

* Merchants in high value goods where payment is made in cash for a sum in excess of €15 000 comprising in particular businesses dealing in jewellery, watches, cars, ships, airplanes, gold, other precious metals, diamonds, art, antiques, furs and carpets, electronic equipment, etc.

Luxembourg law in addition to enumerating those professionals which are subject to anti-money laundering obligations, provides that each of the professionals concerned must make sure that the same obligations as imposed upon them by Luxembourg law are observed within their branches or subsidiaries either in Luxembourg or abroad except if such branches or subsidiaries are subject to equivalent anti-money laundering obligations in their country of establishment. Similarly the law provides that the obligations shall apply to branches in Luxembourg of foreign businesses.

3   The professional obligations

The 2004 Law sets out in general terms professional obligations aimed at avoiding money laundering which, subject to limited exceptions referred to below, equally apply to each of the above referenced category of professionals. They are grouped under three headings: (i) know your customer, (ii) adequate internal organisation and (iii) cooperation with the authorities.

These general obligations which have force of law have, for most of the professions concerned, been separately explained and/or completed by regulations or recommendations setting out in further details what is expected from the professionals. Each of such regulations is referred to in the list set out at the end of the chapter.

3.1 Know your customer

The '*know your customer*' obligation starts with the requirement for a professional to identify his contractual counterpart but goes well beyond this mere identification and extends to the obligation to identify the beneficial owners and the obligation to request further information on the client in particular vis-à-vis specific types of clients or where a suspicion of money laundering arises.

3.1.1 Identification of the client – general

The client is defined by the 2004 Law as the person with whom the professional enters into a business relationship and in particular for certain types of professionals when they open an account or a savings book or offer safe custody services.

Occasional clients are not subject to identification except where the transaction exceeds in value €15 000[10] (regardless of whether the transaction is carried out in a single transaction or in several linked transactions) or where for such an occasional client there is a suspicion of money laundering (see Subsection 3.1.6).

The identification of the client has to be made on the basis of documentary evidence.

For natural persons the professional will normally take a copy of an official document certifying the identity of his clients (although the regulations of the *CSSF* also allow to transcribe the most important elements thereof instead of taking a copy). Specific regulations from certain professional bodies[11] specify further that the professional is obliged not only to take a copy or transcribe the data but also has to ensure that the document produced matches the client by comparing the signature and photos etc. A reasonable verification is required.

Where the client is not physically present, those documents have to be certified by an authority (police, notary, embassy ...).[12]

For legal entities the identification will be made on the basis of the documents establishing the due incorporation and existence of the legal entity mainly through copies of articles of association and proof of registration in a local commercial register. Further, details of the representatives of the legal entity (directors and/or senior management) and in particular of those who have power on the account opened with the professional will have to be identified in the same way as for individuals.

The identification shall be made before business relationship actually starts, i.e. before a transaction is carried out with the relevant client. For banks however it is possible to give clients an account number on which moneys may be received before the identification review is completed but such moneys have to remain blocked in the account and may only be used for banking transactions once the bank has completed its know your customer procedure to its satisfaction.

Although it is not expressly set out in the 2004 Law the mere identification of the client on the basis of documentary evidence is not deemed sufficient to fulfil the '*know your customer*' obligation. The professional rules set out by the specific regulatory bodies in particular the *CSSF*

---

[10] See however in Subsection 3.1.7 for casinos the threshold is lowered to €1000.
[11] See *CSSF* circular 2005/211 or *IRE* circular of 20.06.2006.
[12] See 3.1.2(a) below.

and the circulars issued by the prosecutor leave no doubt that professionals have to go beyond such identification.

In a recent circular which the prosecutor's office has addressed to all merchants in high value goods[13] it is specified that clients have to be interrogated on the origin of the funds and assets which are the subject of the transaction. Where there is doubt on this origin the professional must take reasonable measures to levy all doubt and where the doubt cannot be levied the professional shall not carry out the transaction. Such circular specifically requires the merchant to obtain the address and the profession of each client.

Similarly the *CSSF* circular 05/211 specifies that the professional of the financial sector must make sure to receive complete and satisfactory answers to all his questions which he may ask the client and which relate to the client, the client affairs and the purpose of the business relationship which is sought.

3.1.2 Identification of clients – special cases

For certain types of operations or specific types of clients the 2004 Law or applicable professional regulations impose additional obligations or grant derogations.

(a) Client relationship at distance

Where the client is not physically present at the time when the business relationship is entered into, the 2004 Law requires that the professional must take specific and adequate measures which are necessary to face the increased risk existing in relation to money laundering. In practice the professional has a choice between two possibilities: either the identification documents are certified by a competent authority (embassy, notary, police, etc.) or by a financial institution subject to equivalent money laundering rules or where the professional only receives a copy of the identification document the first payment has to be made in a transaction from an account opened in the name of the relevant client with another financial institution subject to equivalent money laundering obligations. In this respect it is important to stress that it is not sufficient to receive payment from such other financial institution but the professional shall receive proof that the relevant client has an account opened with the financial institution who transferred the money.

The *CSSF* circular 05/211 provides that depending on the risk associated with the relevant type of client or relationship it is recommended that further justifying evidence is received by the professional such as: reference letter from a financial institution, justification of the professional activity of the client, evidence of the origin of funds or confirmation of the address of the client.

(b) Politically exposed persons

Specific measures have to be taken with respect to politically exposed persons. The *CSSF* circular 05/211 provides that professionals must have adequate procedures in place to determine whether the client (or the beneficial owner, see below) is a politically exposed person, i.e. a person who holds or has been entrusted with prominent political public functions including family members and partners[14] (but excluding specifically persons holding only intermediary or lower level

---

[13] Circular to merchants of high value goods of 13.03.2006 by the Luxembourg prosecution office (*Parquet du Tribunal d'Arrondissement*), financial intelligence unit (*cellule de renseignements financiers*).

[14] Heads of State or of Government, Senior Politicians, Senior Government members, members of parliament, senior members of large regional or municipal bodies or organisations, Judicial or Military Officials, Senior Executives of State corporations or important political party officials.

functions). An enhanced verification of the origin of funds must be carried out and such clients must be subject to a special continuous supervision during the business relationship.

Whereas the *CSSF* regulations merely refer to politically exposed persons the recent circular of the prosecutor addressed to all merchants in high value goods goes beyond the politically exposed persons concept and includes among 'sensible clients' even managers of the private sector. Such extension would appear to go beyond the scope which national and international law makers have set. Due to its vagueness it is particularly difficult to apply in practice and professionals will not be easily able to determine who to categorise as 'sensible' client. In reality such provision indicates no more than what the 2004 Law anyhow already provides, i.e. that professionals have to examine with specific attention transactions likely to be linked to money laundering because inter alia of the personality of the client (see hereafter Subsection 3.1.5). Rather than requesting specific vigilance in respect of such types of client, the emphasis should be put on the concept of corruption. It is only where a professional deals with a client and cannot exclude the possibility of corruption which constitutes a primary offence which can give rise to money laundering that the professional obligations as laid down by the 2004 Law in relation to politically exposed persons will apply and may trigger a denunciation to the prosecutor.

(c) Professionals holding third-party moneys

Another category of clients that requires specific attention are those which have a professional activity which implies the transfer of third-party funds where the relevant professional is not a licensed and supervised financial sector professional. This is for instance the case for lawyers or notaries. For such clients the professional must determine whether the relevant client acts for his own account (for example where he receives professional fees on his account) or for account of his own third-party clients (for example where a lawyer or a notary receives money which is used to incorporate a company). In the latter case, the professional must identify not only his client (lawyer or notary) but also the beneficial owner for whom such client acts. In any case the professional must specifically ensure that the relationship is not used for purposes of money laundering or financing of terrorism.

(d) Non-cooperative country clients

Any client from a country which is considered by the *FATF* as a non cooperative territory must be subject to a specific perusal at the time the relationship is entered into and thereafter as long as the relationship exists.[15]

3.1.3   Exemptions from identification obligation

(a) Financial institutions

However where the client is itself a national or foreign financial institution subject to equivalent money laundering obligations no identification must be made at all neither of the client nor of the beneficial owners whose money such client may hold. Nevertheless the professional must make sure that the relevant client is indeed a duly authorised financial institution in a country submitting such professionals to equivalent money laundering rules. All countries which are members of the EU, EEA or *FATF* are recognised as imposing such equivalent obligations

---

[15] For an updated list see http: \\www.fatfgafi.org\index\fr\htm.

to its financial institutions. The equivalent requirements condition is also satisfied in the case of branches or subsidiaries of financial institutions established in one of the aforementioned countries, irrespective of the country in which such branches or subsidiaries are located provided that the financial institutions require their branches and subsidiaries to ensure compliance with the provisions applicable to them, either by virtue of law or group rules.

Even where the professional is exempt from identifying such customer, he has to discharge its monitoring obligations generally and in particular to report on suspicious transactions. It may indeed not be ruled out that even under cover of a licensed professional of the financial sector money laundering activities may be carried out.

(b) Undertakings for collective investments

According to the 2004 Law only those UCIs which market their shares or units are subject to the relevant anti money laundering rules. The *CSSF* Circular 2005/211 specifies that a UCI shall not be subject to the 2004 Law where it markets its shares or units via an intermediary (distributor) who is himself a domestic or foreign financial institution subject to equivalent money laundering obligations (see (d) above). However where the relevant intermediary is not subject to such equivalent obligations or where the UCI markets its shares or units in direct contact to its clients, the responsibility for identification lies with the UCI itself.

3.1.4   Identification of beneficial owners[16]

The 2004 Law obliges the professionals not only to identify their contractual counterpart but also, if different, the person on whose behalf they act.

The requirement to proceed to identifying beneficial owners applies equally to natural persons and legal entities. Where there is any doubt as to whether clients subject to identification procedures are acting on their own behalf or where there is certainty that they are not acting on their own behalf, reasonable care must be taken in order to obtain evidence of the actual identity of the person on whose behalf the customer is acting.

The *CSSF* circular 05/211 specifies that beneficial owner identification is '*a key component of the KYC [know your customer] profile*'.

In its circular, the *CSSF* specifies that where, as part of the exercise of the know your customer obligation, the professional is informed that the client is not himself the beneficial owner he should seek to get confirmation in writing from the beneficial owner directly in support of the statements made by the client. He should further identify the beneficial owner on the basis of documentary evidence in the same way as for the client.

If the client is a legal entity the question arises whether the company could itself be regarded as the beneficial owner or whether the owners of the shares of the company have to be identified.

In this respect *CSSF* circular 05/211 invites the professional to a basic distinction between shell companies which simply act as a screen to preserve the anonymity of the beneficial owners for which identification of the beneficial owners is required and other companies.

In the first case the identification shall be required for persons holding as beneficial owners a controlling interest in the company currently deemed to be more than 25% of the share capital.

---

[16] For an indepth study see Pit Reckinger/Myriam Pierrat 'Le Banquier face à l'ayant-droit économique', Droit bancaire et financier au Luxembourg, ALJB, volume 2, Larcier, 2004.

Where this interest is held indirectly ownership must be traced back to the natural person beneficially owning the interest.

The *CSSF* circular 05/211 specifies that distinguishing features of a shell company include the limited number of shareholders, the absence of a stock market listing and the lack of any trading activity.

A listing is in general a criteria which is used to conclude that the company may be regarded as the beneficial owner. It is however not an absolute guarantee and it should not necessarily be the only criterium to be used by the professional. An analysis should be made on the basis of the entire presentation of the company in particular its commercial activity.

Further difficulties arise in respect of specific types of clients such as trusts where in each case the identification procedure should cover the ultimate beneficial owner, i.e. the beneficiary of the trust. Given that for certain types of trusts the beneficiary may change over time, professionals should also identify the originator and will have to identify the beneficiary at the latest at such time where moneys are paid out to him.

The determination of the beneficial owner may be a time-consuming and delicate exercise. Such is the case in respect of entities which are set up by private equity funds to structure their investments. Although the manager of the private equity fund will be easy to identify, such manager may be reluctant or even sometimes be prohibited under local rules to provide a list of investors in the fund or even more produce identification documents of such persons. Further, a full identification would because of time constraints not allow the transaction to take place within the timeframe required and investment opportunities could be lost. In such cases practical solutions need to be found on a case-by-case basis. Very often the managers of the fund concerned will be subject to equivalent identification requirements as those required by the 2004 Law. A certificate from such person that he has identified all investors in the fund in accordance with applicable money laundering provisions should then be obtained as part of the know your customer exercise.

3.1.5 Delegation of the identification duties

The 2004 Law has introduced the possibility for professionals to delegate (by way of a mandate) to other professionals in Luxembourg or abroad which are active in the same sector of activity and which are subject to equivalent money laundering obligations the duty of identifying clients. Such possibility which existed previously among financial sector professionals has been extended to all professions subject to the 2004 Law. Such delegation is allowed only to the extent that a written agreement exists between the two professionals which guarantees at all times access to the identification documents during the term of the agreement and provided that the Luxembourg professional receives a copy of the documents for each client. Notwithstanding the fact that technical identification duties may thus be delegated, the responsibility for the identification remains with the professional in Luxembourg as if no delegation had taken place.

3.1.6 Careful perusal of certain transactions where a suspicion of money laundering arises

The 2004 Law obliges each professional to examine with particular attention every transaction which is likely to be linked to money laundering because of its nature, the circumstances surrounding it or the personality of the persons involved. In this respect many professional supervisory or regulatory bodies refer to lists setting types of transactions which are deemed suspicious. It is in fact impossible to draw up a complete list of suspect transactions. The most important for every professional will be to exercise a good faith judgment in order to determine whether the transaction is reasonable and to refuse to carry out any transaction which he would not understand or which he could not explain or justify.

3.1.7 Continuous supervision

Although the know your customer obligations must be carried out at the time the business relationship is entered into the 2004 Law imposes on professionals a continuous supervision duty of the relationship with their client and enhanced obligations depending on the degree of risk associated with the relevant clients. In particular the special clients referred to above such as politically exposed clients must be subject to an enhanced supervision.

3.1.8 Retention of documents

The 2004 Law obliges professionals to safekeep underlying documentation to serve as evidence for a period of at least five years starting from the end of the relationship for copies of all identification documents and with respect to the documentation relevant to specific transactions for a period of at least five years starting from the execution of the transaction.

3.2 Obligation to have an adequate internal organisation

Each professional shall have internal control and communication procedures which are adequate to prevent money laundering transactions.

Professionals shall set up written procedures which have to be followed in respect of any client relationship at inception and during the business relationship.

Further, each professional shall take appropriate measures to educate its employees to money laundering provisions and help them to recognise suspicious information and give them appropriate training.

For most professions, regulatory bodies impose that a specific person is designated as the responsible person for money laundering. Such person is responsible vis-à-vis the supervisory authorities and is also designated as the link between the relevant professional and the judicial authorities for purposes of the cooperation. It is that person or his delegate who makes decisions within the organisation whether and when suspicious transactions are notified to the prosecutor.

3.3 Cooperation with the authorities

Professionals, their management and employees are obliged to fully cooperate with Luxembourg authorities in charge of the fight against money laundering and against the financing of terrorism. In that respect any professional secrecy or confidentiality duties to which a professional may be subject to are lifted.

Passively this general obligation obliges professionals to respond to requests from the prosecutor (or its own supervisory authority if such authority has by law the power to intervene) and provide upon request all necessary information in accordance with the procedures applicable by law.

Actively the 2004 Law obliges each professional to inform on its own initiative the prosecutor of any fact which might be in indication of money laundering or financing of terrorism inter alia by reason of the profile of the client, his evolution, the origin of the funds, the nature, the purpose or the proceedings of the transaction.

The transmission of information to the prosecutor is done by the person designated within the professional's organisation as responsible for anti-money laundering. For financial sector professionals a copy must be sent to the supervisory authority. The obligation to inform the *CSSF* may be deemed contrary to the legal prohibition of tipping-off. Indeed, article 5(5) of the 2004 Law provides that no communication may be made to the client or third parties that information was passed to the prosecutor (see 3.4 below). Given that the supervisory authority anyhow has unlimited investigatory powers over professionals it regulates, it is anyhow in a position to request that such information is transmitted to it. The justification of this general request is obviously the need to properly exercise its prudential supervision.

For lawyers a derogatory regime applies as set out below.

In practice banks are frequently faced with a situation where published general information (for example in newspapers) indicate that a client is to some extent involved in a criminal investigation abroad (with often only limited information or details) but where the bank's file on the client and the transactions which were carried out by the client on his accounts have been duly justified and do not show any element which might be an indication of money laundering. The Luxembourg prosecutor has taken the unjustified view that in such case a banker should always proceed to the denunciation of his client.

If however it is found later that the information was wrong and that indeed the suspicion against the client was unfounded, a declaration by the banker to the prosecutor may have caused serious harm to the client. Indeed, for the least the prosecutor may have seized all assets or the account remained blocked for the period of the investigation. Very often however, especially where the client is a resident of another country, the prosecutor will share his findings with the authorities of the country where the client is resident with the risk that the client is thus subject to different proceedings in his home country which may not be considered punishable as money laundering in Luxembourg.

A mere indication of a suspicion of a criminal activity published in a newspaper article cannot, in our opinion, by itself be an element which is sufficient for the denunciation obligation of the professional to come into existence. The lower court and the court of appeal have in a recent case confirmed our view by ruling that such an indication in a newspaper, having regard to the information available to the Bank, was not in itself sufficient to trigger the requirement for a denunciation.

The obligation of denunciation imposed by law exempts the professional from professional secrecy duties.

Not only is the professional (whether a bank, a lawyer, etc.) relieved from professional secrecy he is also exempted from any liability where he has made a denunciation in good faith. Article 5(4) of the 2004 Law provides that a disclosure in good faith to the Luxembourg authorities in charge of money laundering by a professional or an employee or manager of such professional of informations which in their opinion constitutes a suspicion of money laundering may not be deemed to constitute a violation of a contractual restriction to disclose information or of a professional secrecy and does not entail for the person concerned any liability of any sort. In other words where a declaration has been made in good faith on the basis of elements which the professional may reasonably have considered as constituting money laundering but which in fact turned out to be wrong, such professional as well as his employees will not be subject to any liability of any sort, either civil, criminal or disciplinary.

The obligation to inform the authorities even applies when on the basis of an element of suspicion the professional refuses to enter into a relationship with a potential client.

Following an information to the prosecutor, the prosecutor may block and seize funds or assets which are held by the professional for or from the client. An oral instruction from the prosecutor must be confirmed in writing within three days failing which the blocking instruction will cease to have effect on midnight of the third day. Such a measure may not be challenged in civil or urgency courts. However any such blocking or seizure is limited in time for a maximum period of three months.

3.4 No tipping off

Professionals or their managers or employees may not communicate to the client concerned or to any third person that information has been transmitted to the prosecutor or that an investigation has been started.

This does obviously not prevent the professional, where he discovers an element or circumstance which could constitute a suspicion of money laundering to contact the client and ask for explanations or underlying documentary evidence. Where a professional is part of a financial group the question often arises whether there can be discussions or concertations with other group companies or with the internal group controller. Similarly the question arises whether correspondents and auditors (who themselves are subject to own denunciation obligations) may be contacted for additional information or advice. As long as the professional has not with certainty determined whether a suspicion has arisen and is still at a preliminary point in his investigation, any such discussions or requests for clarification remain possible. Conversely, where the auditor as part of its audit mission discovers facts which could result in forming a suspicion but still need further investigation or explanation, he shall consult with his client to form a view. Only, if the professional does not receive the anticipated satisfactory responses and an element of suspicion remains which leads the professional to make a declaration to the prosecutor, does the prohibition to communicate this fact to the client or third parties apply. One formal derogation to the prohibition of tipping off exists under the 2004 Law, allowing a branch or a subsidiary of a financial group to communicate to the internal group auditor that the information has been so transmitted but then only under the express condition that the prior authorisation from the public prosecutor was received.

However, beyond the state of fact searching by the prosecutor where a criminal investigation is commenced by an investigating magistrate and judicial measures are taken such as an official seizure of the assets or documents held by the professional (often in the context of an international rogatory commission), the client must be informed forthwith in order to enable him to take recourse against such a measure. The rights of defence warrant that through receiving the information thereon, the client is put in a position to challenge in court the measures taken.

3.5 Sanctions for breach of the professional obligations

The non observance of the professional obligations set out in the 2004 Law is punished by a fine between €1250 and €125 000.

The breach of professional obligations relating to fight against money laundering is a criminal offence. It is a separate offence to the money laundering offence itself or the underlying offences which may give rise to money laundering. It may be pursued even in the absence of an underlying money laundering offence.

At the time of the discussions on the bill of law which became the 2004 Law there was a very lively debate on the subject whether the criminal offence of non observance of the professional obligations in respect of money laundering would require the intention of the relevant professional or whether such offence would be punishable even where the non observance of the obligation would have been unintentional i.e. where a professional would have unknowingly accepted money derived from criminal activity.

Before the 2004 Law the prosecutor's office considered that the non-observance of the professional rules imposed on the professionals of the financial sector was an unintentional offence where the mere breach of the '*know your customer*' obligation triggered criminal sanctions for the banker.

This position was very much criticised.

The debate was closed by the 2004 Law confirming the position that the offence of non cooperation or a breach of professional obligations as any other criminal offence needed a criminal intent. Today it is clear that only those who intentionally contravene to the professional obligations could be subject to a criminal offence.

The question remains how courts will define the intentional element in respect of a breach of professional obligation. For lack of court cases it is not possible to have certainty on the subject. It is however likely that courts will concentrate their analysis on the question whether a person knew or should have known and is thus deemed to have been knowledgeable that it was breaking its professional duties.

3.6   The legal profession

Notaries are among the professionals subject to know your customer and identification procedures in the same fashion as banks or other professionals of the financial sector.

With respect to the obligation to cooperate with the authorities and in particular inform the prosecutor specific provisions have been introduced in the 2004 Law for the legal profession.

Lawyers are not subject to any obligation to cooperate with criminal authorities with respect to information which they hold from clients as part of the legal consultation or as part of defending their clients and representing them in judicial proceedings. This is a fundamental guarantee for the rights of defense and for the right of every person including criminals to obtain a legal assistance.

Outside this limited exemption where lawyers may become subject to an obligation to denounce certain facts to the prosecutor, such denunciation is made not to the prosecutor directly but to the *Bâtonnier de l'Ordre des Avocats* (the chairman of the Bar) who will verify whether the circumstances are such that a denunciation is compulsory pursuant to the 2004 Law. Only then would the *Bâtonnier* transmit the declaration to the prosecutor.

Again this additional layer is meant to constitute a special guarantee that the rights of defense are preserved.

3.7   The casinos

Casinos are professionals which are specifically exposed to receiving monies originating from criminal activity. It is therefore specified that for every client buying or selling play money in

Casinos the identification obligations apply for an amount of €1000 or more (as opposed to the general threshold of €15 000 applicable to the other profession).

List of important supervisory or professional body rules for specified professionals

Financial sector

CSSF Circular 05/211 relating to the fight against money laundering and terrorism financing and the prevention of the use of the financial sector for the purpose of money laundering and terrorism financing; for undertakings for collective investment (UCI): Recommendation of 17 March 2000 by the ALFI on prevention of the use of UCIs for the purpose of money laundering as well as usages and recommendations by the Luxembourg banking association (*ABBL*) of July 2000.

Life Insurance companies

Circular letter 01/9 of 30 November, 2001 by the Insurance Commissariat relating to the scope of professional duties, to the prevention of the use of the insurance sector for the purpose of money laundering; notification of 9 December 1997 by the *ACA* (Association of Insurance Companies) relating to money laundering; amended law of 6 December 1991 on the insurance sector.

Independent auditors (réviseurs d'entreprises)

Recommendation by the institute of independent auditors (*IRE*) of 20 June 2006 on the legal and professional duties of independent auditors relating to the fight against money laundering and terrorism financing; amended law of 28 June 1984 relating to the organisation of the professional independent auditor.

Lawyers (avocats)

Circular Nr 03 – 2004/2005 (by the Luxembourg bar) and the amended law of 10 August 1991 on the profession of lawyers.

Notaries (notaires)

Amended law of 9 December 1976 relating to the organisation of the notarial profession and circular issued by the chamber of notaries to its members which is not publicly available.

High value goods merchants

Circular for merchants in high value goods by the Prosecutor (financial intelligence unit); article containing explanations on the circular published on page 72, Merkur Nr 5/2006 (monthly by the chamber of commerce).

Addresses

Parquet du Tribunal d'Arrondissement
Cellule de Renseignements Financiers
rue du Palais de Justice
L-1841 Luxembourg
Tel +352 475981 336
Fax +352 470550

**Commission de Surveillance du Secteur
Financier (*CSSF*)**
110, route d'Arlon, L-1150 Luxembourg
Tel +352 262511
Fax +352 26251601
www.cssf.lu

Commissariat aux Assurances
7, Boulevard Royal
L-2449 Luxembourg
Tel +352 226911-1
Fax +352 226910/+352 226911444
www.commassu.lu

Institut des réviseurs d'entreprises (IRE)
7, rue Alcide de Gasperi
L-1020 Luxembourg
Tel +352 2911391
Fax +352 291334
www.ire.lu

Conseil de l'ordre des avocats
1–7, rue St. Ulric,
L-2651 Luxembourg
Tel +352 4672721
Fax +352 225646
www.barreau.lu

Chambre des Notaires du Grand-Duché
50, route d'Esch,
L-1470 Luxembourg
Tel +352 447021
Fax +352 455140
www.notariat.lu

Chambre de Commerce
7, rue Alcide de Gasperi
L-1020 Luxembourg
Tel +352 4239391
Fax +352 438326
www.cc.lu

Abbreviations

1993 Financial Sector Law	Law of 5 April 1993 relating to the financial sector
2004 Law	Law of 12 November 2004 relating to the fight against money laundering and against financing of terrorism
ABBL	Luxembourg Banking Association
ACA	Association of Insurance Companies
CSSF	Commission for the Supervision of the Financial Sector
FATF	Financial Action Task Force (see footnote 8)
IML	Luxembourg Monetary Institute and predecessor of the *CSSF*
IRE	Institute of independent auditors
Mémorial	Official gazette of the Grand Duchy of Luxembourg
UCI	Undertakings for Collective Investment

Valery V. Tutykhin was born in 1973 in Russia. Graduated with honors from the Law Faculty of Moscow State Institute for Foreign Relations in 1995, holds a Candidate degree in Economics (2003). Practiced as lawyer with Watson, Farley & Williams, then Partner at John Tiner & Partners (Moscow). Advocate, Chairman of the bar chambers as of 2003. Author of 4 books and over 70 articles on Russian law and economy. Main practice areas include Finance and Tax Law, Mergers and Acquisitions, Securities, Asset Protection for Russian-based clients.

Firm's profile

John Tiner & Partners was established in 1995 as a joint venture between Russian and foreign lawyers. The firm specializes in Tax and Finance law, M&A, Litigation, Asset Protection and Corporate law.

Russian Federation

Valery Tutykhin

Chairman of the Bar Chambers/Partner

John Tiner & Partners Law Firm
13, St.1, 4/17 Pokrovsky boulevard
Moscow
Russia

Tel +7 495 937 75 76
Fax +7 495 937 75 01
info@russianlaw.com
www.russianlaw.com

Anti-Money Laundering: International Law and Practice.
Edited by W.H. Muller, C.H. Kälin and J.G. Goldsworth
© 2007 John Wiley & Sons, Ltd

Contents – Russian Federation

1   Introduction

Although the *Criminal Code of Russia* contained '*Legalization of criminal proceeds*' as a specific crime since 1 January 1997, this corpus delicti remained virtually untested by Russian courts in the first years of its existence in law. The legislative system of **AML** measures started evolving actively only in early 2000s. In its Review to Identify Non-Cooperative Countries or Territories published in June 2000 **FATF** mentioned *Russia* among non-cooperative countries, citing, among other things, the 'lack of a comprehensive anti-money laundering law and implementing regulations that meet international standards'.

In response to blacklisting, the Russian Parliament adopted the **Federal law No 115-FZ** '*On countering the legalization (laundering) of income received in the criminal manner*' (in force as of 2 February 2002) which was later supplemented with anti-terrorist financing provisions and renamed '*On countering the legalization (laundering) of income received in the criminal manner, and of the financing of terrorism*' ('the *AML Act*'). This *Act* remains the main source of anti money laundering regulation in *Russia*; it was supplemented with more than 30 acts of subordinate legislation in 2002–2006.

Russia was removed from the *FATF* blacklist in October 2002 and became a member of *FATF* in June 2003.

Russia's approach to **AML** largely follows the *FATF* 40 Recommendations, although not all of them have so far been implemented. At the same time the *FATF* guidelines are sometimes given new meaning by the Russian legislators and law enforcement. Significant importance of cash transactions in the Russian economy and widespread tax evasion have caused the shift in **AML** law-making from tracking the pure laundering (i.e. legalization) of assets to making businessmen and institutions accountable for participating in other gray economy phenomena, such as turning non-cash money into physical cash (strictly speaking, the antipode of classic laundering) or assistance in capital flight of business-related earnings.

2   Criminal and administrative offenses

2.1   Criminal Code

The Criminal Code of Russia ('the Criminal Code') devotes two articles to the crime of money laundering. **Article 174** criminalizes '*Legalization (laundering) of monetary means or other property acquired by other persons through criminal means*' which is described as 'knowingly making financial operations and other transactions with monetary means or other property acquired by other persons in a criminal manner ... with intent to give legitimate look to the ownership, use and disposal of the said monetary means or other property' and currently provides for the following punishment, depending on which part of **Article 174** the crime falls under:

- **Part 1.** Without aggravating circumstances – fine up to RUR 120 000 (exchange rate **US$1 = RUR 28**) or in the amount equal to the salary or other income of the convict for the term of up to one year.

- **Part 2.** If the monetary means or other property mentioned above exceeds RUR 1 000 000 – fine from RUR 100 000 to 300 000, or in the amount equal to the salary or other income of the convict for the term from one to two years, or imprisonment for the term of up to 4 years with or without the fine of up to RUR 100 000 or in the amount equal to the salary or other income of the convict for the term of up to 6 months.

- **Part 3.** If the crime as described in Part 2 was committed by a group of persons by prior agreement or by a person using his/her official capacity – imprisonment from 4 to 8 years, with or without the fine of up to RUR 1 000 000 or equal to the salary or other income of the convict for the term of up to 5 years.

- **Part 4.** If the crime as described in Part 2 or 3 was committed by an organized group – imprisonment for the term from 7 to 10 years, with or without the fine of up to RUR 1 000 000 or equal to the salary or other income of the convict for the term of up to 5 years.

Article 174 – 1 entitled *'Legalization (laundering) of monetary means or other property acquired by the person as a result of committing a crime'* deals with situations when a person engages in money laundering for his/her own benefit, to legitimize the proceeds of own crime or uses such proceeds in business or other economic activity. **Article 174 – 1** also has four parts which provide for the following punishment:

- **Part 1.** Without aggravating circumstances – fine up to RUR 120 000, or in the amount equal to the salary or other income of the convict for the term of up to one year.

- **Part 2.** If the monetary means or other property mentioned above exceeds RUR 1 000 000 – fine from RUR 100 000 to 500 000, or in the amount equal to the salary or other income of the convict for the term from one to three years, or imprisonment for the term of up to 5 years with or without the fine of up to RUR 100 000 or in the amount equal to the salary or other income of the convict for the term of up to 6 months.

- **Part 3.** If the crime as described in Part 2 was committed by a group of persons by prior agreement or by a person using his/her official capacity – imprisonment from 4 to 8 years, with or without the fine of up to RUR 1 000 000 or equal to the salary or other income of the convict for the term of up to 5 years.

- **Part 4.** If the crime as described in Part 2 or 3 was committed by an organized group – imprisonment for the term from 10 to 15 years, with or without the fine of up to RUR 1 000 000 or equal to the salary or other income of the convict for the term of up to 5 years.

2.2   Administrative Offenses Code

The Russian Administrative Offenses Code contains one article which punishes money laundering offenses not falling within the spectrum of criminal law. Article 15.27 entitled *'Violation of legislation on countering the legalization (laundering) of income received by criminal means, and the financing of terrorism'* provides that failure by an organization which effects transactions with monetary means or other property, to record, keep and report information about transactions which must be reported, as well as failure to organize internal *AML* controls, is punishable at the level of the responsible officer by an administrative fine from 100 to 200 minimal wages (RUR 60 000–120 000) and at the level of the legal entity by a fine from 500 to 5000 minimal wages (RUR 300 000–3 000 000) or mandatory suspension of activity for the term up to 90 days.

Similar to crimes, administrative offenses may be punished only by a decision of the court. Court decisions may be reversed through the appeal process.

2.3   Limitation of scope

In accordance with **Articles 174** and **174-1** of the *Criminal Code*, the following crimes are not predicate offenses to the crime of money laundering:

- Failure to return hard currency earnings from abroad (**Art. 193**).

- Evasion of customs dues due from natural person or organization (**Art. 194**).

- Evasion of taxes or duties due from a natural person (**Art. 198**).

- Evasion of taxes or duties due from an organization (**Art. 199**).

- Failure to perform the duties of a tax agent (**Art. 199.1**).

- Concealment of monetary means or property of an organization or an individual entrepreneur which must be used to satisfy a tax or duty claim (**Art. 199.2**).

Nevertheless, the practice of Russian prosecuting bodies is such that indictments for tax related crimes are reformulated to contain criminal charges other than tax evasion or the evasion of customs dues. For example, the acts of a company director who minimized taxes on his company by transferring a part of its profits to a dummy legal entity which then sent the money offshore through a specially designed scheme (a frequent practice in **Russia**), would be indicted not only under **Art. 199** of the *Criminal Code* ('Evasion of taxes due from an organization'), but also under **Art. 165** ('*Causing property damage by way of deceit or abuse of trust*' where the victims suffering the damage are the legal entity and its shareholders) and possibly **Art. 173** ('*False entrepreneurial activity*' which covers establishment of a dummy company for illegal purposes). In a number of high profile cases **Art. 159** ('*Fraud*') was also used for indictment of what were essentially tax matters.

In the opinion of the author, the exclusion of fiscal offenses from predicate crimes to the crime of money laundering is likely to be lifted in the coming years. As a sign of moving in this direction, the **FSFM** insisted at the Typologies Seminar of the Eurasian group to counter legalization of criminal income and financing of terrorism (a *FATF*-type regional body established in October 2004 by *Russia, Byelorussia, Kazakhstan, China and Tajikistan*) held on 3–4 November 2005 on recognizing that the reinvestment of illegal gains into the economy through non-resident organizations is indeed a money laundering typology, although it is widely recognized that the primary source of offshore savings of Russian residents is capital flight not linked to crimes other than tax evasion.

2.4   Right to revoke license

The AML Act provides for the right of respective regulatory bodies to revoke licenses of organizations subject to their regulation for not complying with the provisions of the *AML Act*. This right has been widely used since 2004 by the **Central Bank of Russia** (*Tsentralny Bank Rossii*) to discontinue the activity of the banks allowing their businesses to be used for the purposes of illegal foreign transfers, tax evasion and illegally obtaining large amounts of cash.

3 The AML Act

3.1 Overview

The AML Act came into force on 7 August 2001 and since then has undergone four amendments, making it more and more in line with *FATF* 40 Recommendations. The Act establishes a framework of regulation of various persons and organizations in Russia, sets out the record keeping and reporting duties of the regulated subjects, empowers the *President of Russia* to appoint an authority to be the national *AML Authority* and gives the said body the powers to administer compliance with the *AML Act (the 'AML Authority')*.

The scope of regulation of the *AML Act* extends primarily to 'organizations effecting transactions with monetary means and property', but besides that the *Act* imposes a number of duties on other persons including notaries, advocates (Russian qualified lawyers admitted to the bar), accountants, legal consultants and incorporation agents.

3.2 Transactions subject to mandatory control

The AML Act provides a list of transactions which are subject to the record keeping and reporting requirements.

Transactions for the amount exceeding RUR 600 000 (US$21 428.57) are subject to the controls of the AML Act if they fall under any of the following categories:

- Cash withdrawals from, or placement of cash to, the legal entity's bank account, unless it is a customary way of doing the particular business.

- Sale and purchase of hard currency by an individual.

- Purchase of securities by an individual with cash.

- Receipt of cash by an individual against a bearer check issued by a non-resident.

- Exchange of bank notes for those of different denomination.

- Making a cash contribution into the authorized capital of an organization.

- Receiving to, or transferring from, an account of monetary means or making or receiving of a loan or any securities transaction if at least one party to such transaction is an individual or legal entity having its place of residence or registration or maintaining a bank account with a bank located in, a territory/country which is included in the list of territories not participating in international cooperation to fight money laundering and terrorism financing, such list being determined by the *Government of Russia* on the basis of lists established by international organizations in the field of anti-money laundering (currently mirrors the *FATF* list dated 2004).

- Placement of money to the bank account opened to bearer; opening an account for a third party and placement cash thereto; transfer of money abroad to an anonymous account as well as receiving a transfer from such account; operations on the account of a legal entity registered less than 3 months before the operation or if it is the first ever operation on the legal entity's account.

- Placement of securities, precious metals, precious stones, jewelry and scrap thereof or other valuables to pawn-shops.

- Payments of the insurance premium and payments to the insured.

- Receiving or giving property under a financial leasing arrangement.

- Transfers made by non-credit organizations on the instructions of their clients.

- Purchase or sale of precious metals, precious stones, jewelry and scrap thereof.

- Receiving payments (including winnings) from a lottery or totalizator or other game of chance, including those in electronic form.

- Granting by a legal entity not being a credit organization, of a non interest bearing loan to an individual or another legal entity.

Transactions with real estate are subject to controls of *the AML Law* if their amount equals or exceeds RUR 3 000 000 (US$107 142.86), in any currency.

Any transaction is subject to mandatory controls if it is with a person placed on the list of persons suspected in participation in the extremist activity. Such list is compiled and distributed in the manner set forth by the *Government of Russia* (**'Terrorist activity suspects list'**).

3.3   Organizations effecting transactions with monetary means and property

The following types of organizations are deemed for the purposes of the *AML Act* to be 'organizations effecting transactions with monetary means and property' and thus subject to the full scale regulation and controls provided by the *AML Act*:

- Credit organizations (includes banks and non-banking credit organizations).

- Professional participants of the securities market (includes securities brokers, dealers, managers, securities exchanges, depositary/custody service providers and managers/administrators of collective investment schemes).

- Insurance organizations (which includes insurance brokers).

- Leasing companies.

- Organizations of *Federal Postal System*.

- Pawn-shops.

- Organizations dealing in precious metals and stones, jewelry and scrap.

- Organizations managing bookmaking businesses and/or organizing totalizators, lotteries and other games of chance including those in the electronic form (this category covers Internet casinos).

- Organizations managing investment funds and private pension funds.

- Organizations rendering intermediary services in the sale and purchase of real estate.

In accordance with the *AML Act*, the above organizations have to identify their clients, undertake reasonable steps to identify beneficiaries of organizations and transactions, periodically review and update their client/beneficiary records, record and within one day send to the *AML Authority* the details of transactions which fall under the criteria established by the *AML Act* (see 3.2 above) and must respond to the requests of the *AML Authority* for information. Besides that the organizations concerned must inform the AML Authority of any transactions which are considered to be suspicious. Each organization must therefore develop internal control systems to single out such transactions. Officers responsible for the functioning of internal control systems must be appointed within each such organization. The mandatory record keeping term is set at five years.

It is prohibited for any officer of the organization to reveal to their client the fact that a report to the *AML Authority* has been made.

There is currently no requirement in law that the organization suspecting that a transaction may be related to money laundering/terrorist financing shall suspend the transaction and/or freeze the assets in question, although it has been announced that such amendments may soon be introduced into the legislation. Currently the obligation to suspend a transaction exists only for transactions with persons placed on the *Terrorist activity suspects list* and their controlled companies.

Credit organizations may deny account opening to persons not furnishing required information, having no presence at the stated address and to those who are suspected in participating in terrorist activity. The credit organization also has the right to suspend a transaction for which the client has failed to furnish required documentation.

Credit organizations are prohibited from opening correspondent accounts for shell banks and may not open accounts by correspondence or maintain anonymous accounts for any client.

3.4   Obligations of lawyers, notaries and accountants

Advocates, notaries and persons in the business of legal consulting and accounting services are required by the *AML* Act to identify their clients, record and keep information and make reports of suspicious activity to the *AML Authority* only when they do or make preparatory work for any of the following for their client:

- transactions with real estate;
- managing money, securities or any other property;
- managing bank accounts or securities accounts;
- obtaining monetary means for establishment and/or administration/maintenance of organizations, as well as buying and selling organizations.

Paragraph 5 of **Article 7.1** of the *AML Act* provides that information covered by the legislation of *Russia* on ensuring advocate secrecy is exempt from suspicious transaction reporting requirements. The Russian law extends advocate secrecy (legal professional privilege) only to advocates (members of the bar), although the *European Convention on human rights 1950* (Rome, 1950) and the precedents of the *European Court on human rights* which form part of the Russian law in accordance with the *Russian Constitution* and explanatory documents of Russian supreme courts, extends legal professional privilege to any legal advisors.

4   The supervision system

4.1   FSFM being the AML authority

The state body authorized by the *AML Act* to ensure compliance with the *AML Act* of the persons covered by the Act and analyze mandatory and voluntary (suspicious transactions) reports made in accordance with the *Act* is the federal service of the *Russian Federation* on financial monitoring (*FSFM*), formerly *Committee on financial monitoring.*

By its administrative status, *FSFM* is a subdivision of the *Russian Ministry of Finance*. Not being a law enforcement body (such as the *Militia* or the *Federal Security Service*), *FSFM* may not conduct its own criminal investigations. If a transaction is suspected by *FSFM* to be linked to money laundering or terrorist financing, *FSFM* must pass its findings to law enforcement authorities for further investigation. The law enforcement body then takes its own decision whether a criminal case should be initiated or not. This largely limits the investigative powers of *FSFM*, and it is the author's opinion that in the coming years *FSFM* may be reformed into a *Financial Police* or similarly named body with investigative and law enforcement powers.

FSFM currently has the right to make on-site inspections of organizations covered by the *AML Act* to check if they comply with the provisions of the *AML Act*. It also has the right to request the production of any documents which may assist it in determining whether a particular transaction has traits of money laundering. Besides that, through the network of inter-departmental agreements with the *Central Bank of Russia*, the **Tax Service** and a number of other bodies *FSFM* has access to almost any information available in State databases.

4.2 Industry regulators

Industry regulators such as the Central Bank of Russia and the *Federal Service for the supervision of the insurance business* monitor compliance of their subject organizations with the provisions of the *AML Act* and have the right to make on site inspections.

Industry self-regulatory organizations do not play any role in ensuring compliance of their members with provisions of anti-money laundering legislation, this function being solely vested with State bodies.

5 International agreements/cooperation

Russian Federation is party to the following agreements of relevance to the sphere of anti-money laundering and countering the financing of terrorism:

- *The United Nations Convention Against Corruption (UNCAC)* (2003).

- *The International Convention for the suppression of the financing of terrorism* (1999).

- *Convention on laundering, search, seizure and confiscation of the proceeds of crime* (1990).

- *UN Convention against transnational organized crime* (2000).

Besides that, *Russia* has over 15 agreements on mutual assistance in criminal and civil matters which are used by the Russian authorities to obtain information and assistance relevant to anti-money laundering investigations. For example, Russian authorities routinely use the *USA–Russia Treaty on mutual assistance in criminal matters* (2000) to obtain information about *US* registered companies used in money laundering and tax evasion schemes by Russian residents.

FSFM has entered into several agreements with financial intelligence units of other countries (including *Cyprus* and *Venezuela*) and uses them to exchange information with their foreign colleagues for the purposes of its investigations. Similar agreements on mutual assistance in money laundering cases exist between the **Government of Russia** and governments of several countries (*Georgia, Croatia, Bulgaria, Nigeria, Kazakhstan, Uzbekistan, Italy*).

FSFM is a member of The **EGMONT** group and uses the *EGMONT* network to facilitate the exchange of information.

Not being an international financial center and suffering chronically from capital flight, *Russia* stands more on the requesting side of international cooperation than on the performing side. Russian authorities are keen on expanding their international agreements network which would enable them to more efficiently gather information from foreign states.

6   Law enforcement statistics

In accordance with the data published by the Russian Ministry of Internal Affairs in December 2005, in the year 2005, 5388 crimes of money laundering were uncovered, 4424 of them brought to court, and 133 persons were convicted.

Address

Federal Service of Russian Federation on Financial Monitoring
Ctroenie 1,39 Myasnitskaya Street
K-450, 107450, Moscow
Russia
Tel +7 495627 33 97
Fax +7 495 207 60 60
www.kfm.ru
Contact person: Zubkov Victor Alekseevich, Chairman
info@fedsfm.ru

Abbreviations

FATF	Financial Action Task Force
FSFM	Federal Service of the *Russian Federation* on Financial Monitoring
UNCAC	United Nations Convention Against Corruption

Andreas Neocleous & Co was founded in 1965 and is now generally regarded as the leading firm in the Eastern Mediterranean region. The Kiev office of Andreas Neocleous & Co is managed by **Dmytro Korbut** supported by a number of consultants and specializes in corporate and commercial banking and finance, formation and management of corporate entities, taxation, international tax planning, litigation in Ukrainian courts and international arbitration, cross-border investment, private client and trust work. As well as heading the Kiev office, Mr Korbut specializes in litigation, real estate development, the formation and management of corporate vehicles and international tax planning. Prior to joining Andreas Neocleous & Co Mr Korbut was head of the litigation practice of another international firm in Kiev. Mr Korbut was awarded a Chevening Scholarship by the British government in 2001 and graduated from Nottingham University with an LLM in European Law. Prior to that time, from 1997 to 2001 Mr Korbut was Deputy Director of the International Law Department of the Ukrainian Ministry of Justice. In recognition of his services Mr Korbut was awarded the 'Honour of Recognition from the Minister of Justice of Ukraine' for considerable personal input into the process of state legal policy development. Mr Korbut is a co-author of *Doing Business with Ukraine* (second and third edition) by GMB Publishing, 2005.

Ukraine

Dmytro Korbut

Legal Consultant / Head of Kiev Office

Andreas Neocleous & Co

24/7, Institutska Street, Suite 12

Kiev, Ukraine

Tel +38044 2534495

Fax +38044 2534495

dk@neocleous.com.ua

www.neocleous.com

Anti-Money Laundering: International Law and Practice.
Edited by W.H. Muller, C.H. Kälin and J.G. Goldsworth
© 2007 John Wiley & Sons, Ltd

Contents – Ukraine

1 Introduction

Ukraine obtained its independence more then 15 years ago but it is still in the process of transition towards true democracy and a market economy. The process of political and legal reform is occasionally interrupted by setbacks and inevitable conflicts in the choice of direction. The 'orange revolution' in Ukraine in November–December 2004 was the result of the old political regime trying to reverse democratic reforms and falsify the results of the Presidential elections. As a result Viktor Yushchenko became the new President of Ukraine. Two years on, Viktor Yanukovych allegedly accused of falsifying the Presidential elections in 2004 became Prime Minister of Ukraine after his political party won Parliamentary elections in 2006. Notwithstanding these occasional problems, Ukraine shares common values with the rest of Europe and is constantly striving to put in place democratically based Western style legal, financial and banking system. Recognizing the progress achieved by Ukraine in this respect on April 2004 the *Financial Action Task Force (FATF)* removed Ukraine from the *FATF's Non-Cooperative Countries and Territories (NCCT) list*, where Ukraine was previously included due to its inadequate anti-money laundering regime.

2 Overview of Ukrainian anti-money laundering legislation

Ukraine signed *the Council of Europe's 1990 Convention* on *Laundering, Search, Seizure and Confiscation of the Proceeds from Crime* on 29 May 1997 and ratified it on 17 December 1997. The *40 Recommendations* of *the FATF* were incorporated into Ukrainian legislation on 28 August 2001 and Ukraine signed the UN *International Convention for the Suppression of the Financing of Terrorism* on 8 September 2000 and ratified it on 12 September 2002.

However, the principal anti-money laundering legislation was enacted in Ukraine only when the Law *'On Prevention and Counteraction of the Legalization (Laundering) of the Proceeds from Crime'* (hereinafter, the 'anti-money laundering law') was adopted by *the Parliament of Ukraine* on 28 November 2002 and signed by *the President of Ukraine* on 7 December 2002. This law was deficient in several material respects. The system for reporting suspicious transactions was so limited as to be virtually ineffective, and the ability of its financial intelligence unit to share information with law enforcement agencies was in doubt. Following the *FATF's* recommendations Ukraine has addressed the deficiencies. First, the law was amended to explicitly allow the Ukrainian financial intelligence unit to share information with law enforcement agencies and the suspicious transaction reporting thresholds were reduced. Second, the Ukrainian criminal code was amended to criminalize money laundering, the failure to file suspicious transaction reports, and tipping off the subjects of such reports. Finally, the Ukrainian banking and financial services laws were amended to require the full disclosure of beneficial ownership at account opening for all legal entities and natural persons. Under the most recent amendments introduced in December 2005 any financial operation where beneficiary is a person from the terrorists' list must be stopped and reported.

The anti-money laundering regulations were also incorporated into: (1) the principal banking legislation including *the Law of Ukraine 'On Banks and Banking Activity'* of 7 December 2000 No 2121-III (hereinafter, the 'Banking Law') and *the Resolution of the National Bank of Ukraine No. 189 of 14 May 2003 'On Regulation on Financial Monitoring by Banks'*; (2) legislation regulating other financial services including *the Law of Ukraine 'On Financial Services and the*

State Regulation of Financial Services', the *'Regulation on Financial Monitoring on Securities Market' adopted by the Decision of the State Commission on Securities and Stock Exchange No. 93 of 4 October 2006,* and the *Resolution of the Cabinet of Ministers of Ukraine No. 1800 of 20 November 2003 'On procedure of internal financial monitoring of commercial entities which organize and own casinos and other gambling institutions and pawnshops'*. Finally, the Cabinet of Ministers of Ukraine adopted *'The Concept of Developing System of Prevention and Suppression to the Infiltration into the Legal Turnover of the Proceeds from Crime and Financing of Terrorism for the Period of Years 2005–2010'*.

3 Offences

3.1 Predicate offences and proceeds from crime

Under the *Article 1 of the Anti-Money Laundering Law* **Predicate offence** means an act punishable under *the Criminal Code of Ukraine* (the Criminal Code) by imprisonment for three years or more, or an act which is a criminal offence punishable under the criminal law of a foreign state and for which criminal liability is prescribed by *the Criminal Code*, if such act resulted in obtaining the proceeds from crime. Ukraine has ratified *the United Nations Convention for Suppression of the Financing of Terrorism* and financial or any other support of terrorist activity is punishable under the Criminal Code and defined as a predicate offence. Two certain types of criminal offences are specifically excluded from the list of predicate offences, namely: (1) violation of foreign currency control procedures (prohibiting outflow of capital from Ukraine) punishable under *Article 207 of the Criminal Code*; and (2) tax evasion punishable under *article 212 of the Criminal Code*.

Proceeds from crime mean any economic benefit resulting from the commitment of an illegal act that precedes the legalization (laundering) of proceeds consisting of material property, securities, movable or immovable property, or documents of title to such property or a share in it.

3.2 Money laundering offences

According to *the Anti-Money Laundering Law*, **the legalization (laundering) of proceeds** includes any acts taken to conceal or disguise the illegal origins of money or any other property, or possession thereof, titles to such money and property, their sources, location or movement. It also covers the acquisition, possession or use of money or any other property provided a person realizes that they were the proceeds of crime.

Article 209 of the Criminal Code establishes criminal liability for the laundering of funds, including the following activities:

- financial operations with proceeds from crime;

- acts taken to conceal or disguise the illegal origins of proceeds from crime (money or any other property), or possession thereof, titles to such money and property, their sources, location or movement;

- acquiring, possessing or using the proceeds of crime.

These offences are punishable by imprisonment, by disqualification from holding certain positions or performing certain business activities and by confiscation of property (both the proceeds of crime and any other property owned by the offender). The periods of imprisonment and disqualification vary according to the severity of the offence. The basic sentence is between 3 and 6 years, with a disqualification period of 2 years. For repeat offences, offences involving groups of persons or sums in excess of approximately US$208 000 the prescribed period of imprisonment is increased to between 7 and 12 years and the disqualification period is increased to 3 years. For offences committed by organized criminals or involving an amount in excess of approximately US$625 000 the prescribed period of imprisonment is between 8 and 15 years and the disqualification period 3 years.

3.2.1 Failure to act

Under *the Code of Administrative Offences of Ukraine (part 1 of Article 166-9)* the following acts of any responsible employee of any institution of primary financial monitoring will be considered as administrative offences: (1) violation of customer identification; (2) failure to register financial operation subject to primary financial monitoring; (3) failure to report, late report or reporting false information concerning financial operation subject to primary financial monitoring; (4) violation of record keeping procedures (information and documents concerning identification of person performing financial operation or concerning financial operation subject to primary financial monitoring). Any such administrative offence is punishable with a fine from 50 to 100 times the amounts of minimum tax exempted incomes of Ukrainian citizen (from US$168.00 to 337.00).

Repeated failure to report or providing false information concerning financial operations subject to primary financial monitoring are criminal offences under *the Criminal Code*, punishable by a fine of up to approximately US$6800 or by imprisonment for up to 2 years and disqualification for 3 years from holding certain positions or undertaking business activities.

3.2.2 Disclosure (tipping-off) of information

The Code of Administrative Offences of Ukraine (part 2 of Article 166-9) also provides that (1) disclosure (tipping-off) of information, reported to the State Committee for Financial Monitoring, or (2) disclosure of the fact of reporting such information to *the State Committee for Financial Monitoring* will be considered as administrative offences punishable with a fine of up to approximately US$1000. If the offence relates to information obtained in the course of the offender's professional duties, it is treated as a criminal offence and punishable with a fine of up to approximately US$10 100 or by imprisonment for up to 2 years and disqualification for 3 years from holding certain positions or undertaking business activities.

4 Relevant activities

According to the *Article 1 of the Anti-Money Laundering Law* the scope of this law encompasses financial transactions (relevant activities) involving the processing or securing of any payment through a primary financial monitoring entity, including:

- making or withdrawing a deposit;
- transferring funds between accounts;
- currency exchange;
- services related to the issuing, purchase or sale of securities and other kinds of financial assets;

- granting or receiving a loan or a credit;

- insurance (reinsurance);

- provision of financial guarantees and liabilities;

- trust management of securities portfolio;

- financial leasing;

- issue, circulation, payment (dissemination) of the state and other kinds of cash lottery;

- services related to the issue, purchase, sale or servicing of checks, bills of exchange, credit cards, postal money transfer orders and other payment instruments;

- opening of an account.

In addition financial monitoring of casinos and other gambling activities is established by the *Resolution of the Cabinet of Ministers of Ukraine No. 1800* of 20 November 2003 'On procedure of internal financial monitoring of commercial entities which organize and own casinos and other gambling institutions and pawnshops'.

5 Anti-money laundering procedures

5.1 The system of financial monitoring in Ukraine

According to *the Anti-Money Laundering Law* the national financial monitoring system in Ukraine comprises of two levels:

- The primary level, including banks, insurance and other kinds of financial institutions; payment organizations, members of payment systems, acquiring and clearing institutions; commodity, stock and other exchanges; professional operators in securities market; joint investment institutions; gambling and pawn institutions and legal entities holding any kinds of lottery; enterprises, institutions that manage investment funds or non-governmental pension funds; communication companies and associations, other non-crediting institutions that transfer funds; other legal entities that process financial transactions according to law.

- The state level, including the *National Bank of Ukraine (the 'NBU'), the State Commission on Securities and Stock Exchange (the 'SCSSE') and the State Commission Regulating the Financial Services Markets (the 'SCRFSM')* which, pursuant to the law, regulate and supervise the activity of legal entities engaged in financial transactions; and *the State Committee for Financial Monitoring (the 'SCFM')* the specially authorized executive agency for financial monitoring reporting to the Cabinet of Ministers.

The system of financial monitoring in Ukraine is based on a division of responsibilities between each participant. Detection, reporting and recordkeeping are the responsibility of the primary level, which is supervised and monitored by the relevant State Organs. The *SCFM* collates and analyses information reported at the primary level, initiates criminal investigations, coordinates activity on the State level of financial monitoring and provides guidance to all participants.

The *Anti-Money Laundering Law* sets out the following responsibilities for participants at the primary level:

- To identify the person engaged in the financial transaction subject to financial monitoring pursuant to the Law; or the person who opens an account (including a deposit account) on the basis of documents submitted in accordance with the established procedure or if there are reasons to believe that the information regarding person's identification should be clarified.

- To detect and register financial transactions subject to financial monitoring pursuant to the Law.

- To submit to *the SCFM* the requisite information on financial transactions subject to compulsory financial monitoring within three working days from the transaction.

- To co-operate with *the SCFM* in analysis of transactions subject to compulsory financial monitoring.

- To provide, according to the laws, additional information at *the SCFM's* request related to any financial transactions that have become the object of financial monitoring, including confidential and commercial information, within three working days from the moment of receiving the request.

- To assist the entities of state financial monitoring in analysing financial transactions subject to monitoring.

- To take measures to prevent disclosure (including disclosure to persons whose financial transactions are being checked) of information that is submitted to *the SCFM*, or any other kind of information on financial monitoring (including the fact of submission of such information).

- To retain documents relating to financial transactions subject to monitoring under the Law (including documentation relating to the identification of persons undertaking transactions) for five years from the transaction.

- To establish procedures for internal financial monitoring and appoint a compliance officer.

5.2   Identification procedures

The general requirements concerning identification rules are set out in the anti-money laundering law. A primary financial monitoring entity must identify the persons engaged in **financial transactions subject to financial monitoring** on the basis of a face-to-face interview using original documents or duly certified copies. This identification of persons may only be dispensed with if the persons involved in the transaction have already been subject to identification procedures or if they are both banks registered in Ukraine.

The Ukrainian Banking Law sets out additional requirements for identifying clients in the following cases:

- clients opening accounts in the bank;

- clients performing cash transactions of more than UAH 50 000 (approximately US$10 000) without opening an account;

- attorneys or representatives authorized to act on behalf of the above-mentioned clients.

Banks and institutions providing other financial services may not open or maintain anonymous (numbered) accounts.

Banks may not enter into contractual relations with clients – legal entities or individuals – if they suspect that the entity or individual is acting on behalf of somebody else. They must identify the beneficial owner or the person on whose behalf the transaction is executed.

A bank has the right to require potential clients to provide documents and information to establish their identity, the nature of their activities and their financial state. If the client fails to provide the necessary documents or information or intentionally provides false information, the bank may not do business with the client. If there are reasonable grounds to believe that the client has provided false information or has intentionally provided information in order to deceive the bank, the bank is required to report the facts to *the SCFM*.

If there is a decision of an authorized state body on canceling state registration of a legal entity or declaring a natural person as deceased or missing, the bank shall close accounts of such entity and immediately inform *the SCFM* about such accounts and shall not transfer funds or in any other manner dispose of money at these accounts until obtaining instructions from *the SCFM*.

A primary financial monitoring entity must keep all the information and the documents obtained with the purpose of identification of the client in the client's file.

5.2.1 Resident and non-resident individuals

The following information is required for identification of Ukrainian residents: surname, first name, patronymic, date of birth, series and number of passport (or other identification document), date of issue and issuing agency, place of residence (based on the registration of the permanent address indicated in the passport) and identification number from *the State Register of Natural Persons – Payers of Taxes and Other Compulsory Payments*. Banks may also request information about an individual's occupation.

For non-residents the following information is required for identification: surname, first name, patronymic (if any), date of birth, series and number of passport (or other identification document), date of issue and issuing agency, citizenship, place of residence or temporary stay.

Banks have the right to demand information required for client identification purposes from state bodies, banks and other legal entities, which are obliged to provide such information without charge within ten working days after receiving the inquiry.

5.2.2 Legal entities

For the purpose of identifying Ukrainian-resident legal entities the following information must be obtained: name, legal address, state registration documents (including Charter documents, information about managers and their functions, etc.), identification code from *the Unified State Register of Enterprises and Organizations of Ukraine*, references of the bank which opened the account and account number.

For non-resident legal entities banks must obtain: full name, location and details of the bank that opened the account and account number, a notarized and legalized copy of the Certificate of Incorporation (copy of legalized abstract from trade, banking or judicial register or proof of registration by local authorities of foreign state regarding registration of the legal entity, certified by a notary).

In addition, under *the Banking Law* the bank must identify (1) the individuals or legal entities that own the applicant, (2) the individuals or legal entities having direct or indirect control of the applicant and obtaining economic benefit from its activity; (3) individuals or legal entities with a significant shareholding (more than 10% according to recommendations of *the NBU*) in the applicant; (4) individuals or legal entities authorised to represent this legal entity. If the applicant fails to provide the information, the bank may not open an account and may not service any existing account with the applicant.

Banks have the right to demand information concerning the identity of any applicant and its managers from state bodies exercising control over it or supervising its activities, from banks or from other legal entities. Such information must be provided within ten working days free of charge.

5.3   Financial transactions subject to financial monitoring procedures

Preferably before undertaking a transaction, a primary financial monitoring entity is required to determine whether the transaction is subject to financial monitoring. If so, details of the person performing the transaction, the type of financial transaction, the reasons for it, its date and amount must be entered in the register kept for this purpose. Detailed procedures for banks are laid down by *the NBU*; for casinos and gambling institutions *by the Cabinet of Ministers of Ukraine*; and for traders in securities by *the SCSSE*.

A primary financial monitoring entity may refuse to execute any transaction if it considers that the financial transaction is subject to financial monitoring pursuant to the Law; details of the transaction and of the persons engaged in it must be submitted to *the SCFM*.

The anti-money laundering Law also provides for **internal financial monitoring and compulsory financial monitoring.** Internal financial monitoring includes the activity of primary financial monitoring entities on detection of financial transactions (relevant activity) that may be connected with legalization (laundering) of the proceeds, pursuant to the Law, as distinct from compulsory financial monitoring as described below. According to the anti-money laundering Law all operations subject to financial monitoring (internal or compulsory) must be detected and records must be retained for 5 years. These must be disclosed to *the SCFM* on its request; to the court based on a court order or decision; and to officials of the NBU during inspection under banking supervision and control procedures. The list of features describing financial transactions subject to internal financial monitoring is wide and based on such criteria as '*substantial* increase of the account balance', '**considerable** increase of the amount of cash', '**large** block of shares'. The NBU recommends that individual banks set their own parameters based on their judgment, furthermore, when a primary financial monitoring entity has grounds to believe that a financial transaction is aimed at laundering of proceeds **any** financial transaction, however small, should be subject to internal financial monitoring.

A financial transaction (relevant activity) which is subject to compulsory financial monitoring must be reported to *the SCFM* within 3 days. Compulsory financial monitoring includes measures taken by the SCFM in order to analyze the information on financial operations submitted by the primary financial monitoring entities, as well as the measures on checking such information pursuant to the laws of Ukraine.

5.3.1 Financial transactions subject to internal financial monitoring

A **financial transaction** (relevant activity) is subject to internal financial monitoring provided it has one or more of the following features:

1. Non-standard or excessively complicated financial transaction that has no evident economic sense or obvious legal aim, including:

   - Receipt by a primary financial monitoring entity of funds from a person that proposes or agrees to receive a significantly lower than normal rate of interest, or to pay a significantly higher than normal commission for similar deposits and transactions.

   - Transactions where the client insists on deviating from the entity's established terms, norms or procedures for conducting such transactions.

   - Significant last-minute changes into the previously agreed pattern of financial transaction, particularly changes pertaining to the movement of funds or other kinds of property, including repeated changes of bank references of beneficiary after the first order for transfer of funds was issued or payment documents endorsed, as well as issuing order for transfer of funds to beneficiary using two or more bank accounts of other persons.

   - Submission of unverifiable information.

   - Inability to satisfactorily identify counterparties, acceptance of funds (payment documents for payment of such funds) from a person that transfers the funds to another party of a civil law agreement, which results in return of funds without conducting of a financial transaction due to the failure to locate such other party or due to the refusal of such party to accept the funds.

   - Customers' refusal to provide the information specified by the laws and internal documents of a primary financial monitoring entity.

   - Regular conclusion of short-term agreements by a person or the use of other derivative financial instruments, particularly those that do not envisage the provision of basic assets, pertaining to financial transactions with one or several counteragents resulting in permanent profit or permanent losses of the customer.

   - Acceptance of funds (or payable financial instruments) by a primary financial monitoring entity from a person who repeatedly exchanges securities for other securities within the same year without receiving or providing cash indemnity related to such exchange.

   - Occurrence of an insured loss within a short time after conclusion of an insurance contract.

2. Non-compliance of a financial transaction with the activity of legal entity defined by statutory documents of such entity, including:

   - Sudden substantial increase of the account balance amount not directly connected with the person's activity with further transfer of such amount to another primary financial monitoring entity or if the balance amount is used for purchase of foreign currency (with transfer in favor of a non-resident) or bearer securities.

   - Absence of clear connection between the nature and kinds of a person's activities with the services for which the customer applies to a primary financial monitoring entity.

- Regular presentation of checks issued by a non-resident bank and endorsed by a non-resident, for collection or payment if this is inconsistent with the customer's normal pattern of activity.

- Credit to a person's account of a large number of payments from natural persons in relatively small amounts, including those through the cash department of an entity of primary monitoring, unless the person's activity involves rendering services to the general public or collecting compulsory and voluntary payments.

- Considerable increase of the amount of cash being transferred to account of a person that customarily effects cashless settlements.

- Credit to the account of a considerable amount of cash that is inconsistent with the account-holder's known income or activity.

- One-off dealings in large blocks of shares that do not freely circulate in the organized market unless the account holder is a professional operator in the securities market or the securities have been assigned in settlement of a liability.

3. Repeated financial transactions whose nature gives grounds to believe that their aim is to evade the financial monitoring procedures established by the Law, including:

- Regular credit of cash to a person's account (if the person is a legal entity and such placement is not connected with its main activity), with further transfer of the entire sum or its bigger part within one trading day or the next day to a customer's account opened at another primary financial monitoring entity, or in favor of third persons, including non-residents.

- Transactions conducted via an intermediary who fulfills the person's order without direct (personal) contact with a primary financial monitoring entity.

4. Any financial transactions, when a primary financial monitoring entity has grounds to believe that a financial transaction is aimed at laundering of proceeds.

5.3.2 Financial transactions subject to compulsory financial monitoring

A **financial transaction** is subject to compulsory financial monitoring if it exceeds UAH 80 000 (approximately US$15 800) or the equivalent in foreign currency and it has one or more of the following characteristics:

- Transfer of funds to or from an anonymous (numbered) account abroad or to an account with a financial institution in a country included in the list of offshore zones (which currently includes 37 tax haven jurisdictions) determined by *the Cabinet of Ministers*.

- Sale or purchase of checks, traveler's checks or other similar payment facilities for cash.

- Transactions in which at least one of the parties is a physical or legal entity that is registered, located or resident in a *NCCT* or has an account with a bank registered in an *NCCT*.

- Transfer of funds in cash abroad with a request to give the recipient the funds in cash.

- Placement of funds to an account in cash with their subsequent transfer to another person during the same or the next trading day.

- Placement of funds to an account or writing off the funds from an account of a legal entity within three months from the day of registration of such entity, or placement of funds to an account or writing off the funds from an account of the legal entity that has had no transactions on the account from the date it was opened.

- Opening an account and assigning the funds on it for the benefit of a third person.

- Transfer of funds abroad by a person in cases when no foreign economic contract was concluded.

- Exchange of banknotes, particularly of foreign currency, for banknotes of another nominal value.

- Carrying out financial transactions with bearer securities not placed in depositaries.

- Purchase of securities for cash.

- Payment of insurance compensation to a person or receipt of insurance premium.

- Payment of lottery, casino or other gambling winnings.

- Pledging of precious stones, metals and other valuables to a pawnbroker.

5.3.3 Financial transactions connected to financing of terrorism

A primary financial monitoring entity immediately report an intended transaction to *the SCFM* if any party or beneficiary is included in the Ukrainian government's *List of Persons Connected to Terrorism Activity*. The primary financial monitoring entity must suspend the transaction for 2 working days, during which *the SCFM* may order a further suspension of up to 5 days by informing the primary financial monitoring entity and appropriate law enforcement agency. The *List of Persons Connected to Terrorism Activity* is defined by *the Cabinet of Ministers of Ukraine* based on Ukrainian and foreign courts decisions and information filed by *the UN institutions*.

5.4 Reporting suspicious transactions or activities

For banks, the procedure for reporting financial transactions subject to compulsory financial monitoring to *the SCFM* is established by *the NBU*. For other primary financial monitoring entities it is determined by the Cabinet of Ministers of Ukraine.

If an employee of a primary financial monitoring entity engaged in financial business has reasonable grounds for believing that a financial transaction is aimed at laundering the proceeds of crime, the entity concerned must report the transaction to *the SCFM*. If there is any suspicion that the transaction is connected with terrorist activity, terrorist acts or terrorist organizations, the entity must immediately inform both *the SCFM* and the law-enforcement bodies.

Submission of information to *the SCFM* by primary financial monitoring entities is not considered to be a breach of banking or commercial confidence. The primary financial monitoring entities and their personnel are immune from liability for submission of such information as long as they acted pursuant to the Law.

The information submitted under the above mentioned procedure may be exchanged, disclosed and protected by *the SCFM*, primary financial monitoring entities, and the executive agencies and *the NBU* only in certain cases provided by Law.

The SCFM may send information related to money laundering on request of the relevant foreign authority based on the mutual international agreements.

6   Conclusion

As a developing European country still going through the process of transition, Ukraine is faced with many challenges including an extensive and resilient 'shadow' economy and a high degree of involvement of criminal groups in business and state power structures. Recognizing the vulnerability of the Ukrainian banking and financial system to exploitation for money laundering purposes, the Ukrainian government is making great efforts to prevent this activity. The anti-money laundering measures taken in Ukraine have been recognized by *FATF* as being sufficient to exclude Ukraine from *the list of the NCCT*.

Addresses

National Bank of Ukraine
Department on Prevention of Using
Banking System for Money Laundering and
Financing of Terrorism
9 Instytutska Street, 01601 Kiev
Ukraine
Tel +38044 226 2967
Fax +38044 230 2033
(38 044) 253-77-50
www.bank.gov.ua/Fin_mon/index.htm

State Committee for Financial Monitoring
24 Biloruska Street, 04050 Kiev
Ukraine
Tel +38044 594 1601
Fax +38044 594 1600
sdfm@sdfm.gov.ua
www.sdfm.gov.ua

Abbreviations

FATF	Financial Action Task Force of the OECD
NBU	National Bank of Ukraine
SCFM	State Committee for Financial Monitoring
SCRFSM	State Commission Regulating the Financial Services Markets
SCSSE	State Commission on Securities and Stock Exchange

Bibliography

National Bank of Ukraine: Guidance Note to banks for the prevention of Money Laundering, http://www.bank.gov.ua/Fin_mon/Methodol/index.htm.

MIDDLE EAST

Graham Lovett is the Managing Partner of Clifford Chance's Dubai office and also Head of Litigation and Dispute Resolution for the Middle East Region. Prior to his arrival in Dubai in March 2004, Graham was based in Clifford Chance's London office. Graham specializes in commercial litigation, arbitration and ADR. He has experience of multi-jurisdictional litigation and arbitration (LCIA, ICC and UNCITRAL) including in the United States, Russia, Italy, Germany, Hong Kong and Singapore. Graham is part of the firm's highly regarded International Arbitration Group, and also a Member of the Chartered Institute of Arbitrators (MCIArb).

Charles Barwick was admitted as a Solicitor of the Supreme Court of England and Wales in 2002. Charles' practice includes a broad mix of commercial litigation, arbitration and advisory work for international clients across the Gulf States and throughout the Middle East.

Firm's profile

Clifford Chance is a truly integrated global law firm which operates as one organization throughout the world. Our aim is to provide the highest quality professional advice by combining technical expertise with an appreciation of the commercial environment in which our clients operate. With 28 offices in 19 countries, the firm operates across all business cultures and offers full service advice to clients in key financial and regulatory centres in *Europe*, *the Middle East*, the *Americas* and *Asia*. Clifford Chance's lawyers advise internationally and domestically, under both common law and civil law systems.

United Arab Emirates

Graham Lovett/Charles Barwick

Gulf Managing Partner/Associate

Clifford Chance LLP
3rd Floor, The Exchange Building
Dubai International Financial Centre
P.O. Box 9380
Dubai
United Arab Emirates

Tel +9714 3620 444
Fax +9714 3620 445
graham.lovett@cliffordchance.com
charles.barwick@cliffordchance.com
www.cliffordchance.com

Anti-Money Laundering: International Law and Practice.
Edited by W.H. Muller, C.H. Kälin and J.G. Goldsworth
© 2007 John Wiley & Sons, Ltd

Contents – United Arab Emirates

Introduction

This chapter considers the *Federal laws of the UAE* in existence at the time of writing[1] and which are applicable throughout the *UAE*, as well as the laws of the *Dubai International Financial Centre* (*'DIFC'*), a financial free zone situated in the Emirate of Dubai that has its own laws and regulations.

1 Background to UAE Law

1.1 Source of legislation

The *UAE* is a Federation of seven Emirates (*Abu Dhabi, Ajman, Dubai, Fujairah, Ras Al Khaimah, Sharjah and Umm Al Quwain*) (*'the Federation'*). The basic foundation for all law in the UAE is the Islamic Shari'ah. The Federal Constitution expresses Islamic Shari'ah to be the main source of legislation. Upon this foundation, various Federal laws (applicable throughout the Federation) and local laws applicable solely in each Emirate have been enacted governing, among other things, civil and commercial transactions, contract and legal procedures for each Emirate. There may be some laws (in the form of decrees or instructions issued by each Emirate) that are not published but which nevertheless may be generally applicable.

1.2 No concept of judicial precedent

There is no concept of judicial precedent in the *UAE* (although an informal system of precedent does operate in the *Federal Supreme Court* and *Dubai Court of Cassation*) which means that the decisions of a court in one case will have no binding authority in respect of another case. There is also no formal system of court reporting. **Accordingly, it is not always possible to reach a conclusive interpretation on the laws of the UAE** or how the UAE courts would view particular transactions in applying the relevant anti-money laundering laws.

2 Legal framework

2.1 UAE law

Anti-money laundering provisions in the *UAE* are mainly found in the following laws (listed chronologically):

2.1.1 *Federal Law No. 6 of 1974* concerning Charitable Organizations.

2.1.2 *Federal Law No. 3 of 1987* concerning the Promulgation of the Penal Code (the 'Penal Code').

2.1.3 *Federal Law No. 4 of 2002* concerning the Criminalization of Money Laundering.

2.1.4 *Federal Law No. 8 of 2004* concerning the Financial Free Zones and Free Trade Zones.

2.1.5 *Federal Law No. 1 of 2004* on Combating Terrorism Offences.

2.1.6 *Federal Law No. 13 of 2004* concerning Supervision of Import/Export & Transit of Rough Diamonds.

---

[1] August 2006.

2.2 Central Bank regulations

In relation to banks, money exchanges, finance companies and financial institutions, the *Central Bank* regulations concerning *Procedures for Anti-Money Laundering* (No. 24 of 2000) also apply. **The Regulations (examined in further detail below) contain a significant number of examples of suspicious transactions for certain types of banking activity** (Cash Transactions, Investment-Related Transactions, International Banking and Financial Transactions, Secured and Unsecured Loans and Electronic Banking Services).

2.3 Terrorism financing

Federal Law No. 1 of 2004 on Combating Terrorism Offences makes the financing of terrorist activities a criminal offence. The offence is made out in relation to anyone who provides, collects, carries or transfers property directly or indirectly, with the intention that they are to be used to finance terrorist acts. Punishment for a breach of the law is life imprisonment.

2.4 UAE Penal Code

Chapter 4 of the *UAE Penal Code* relates to the 'concealment of things deriving from crimes'. Under *Article 407* any individual who knowingly conceals or takes possession of things deriving from a crime (even if he did not participate in the crime) shall be liable to the punishment prescribed for the underlying crime. The offence also extends to anyone who acquires the property in ignorance of the underlying crime, but in circumstances where it was possible to establish the illegality of the source of the property (i.e. wilful ignorance). In the latter case the maximum punishment is prescribed as a maximum period of imprisonment for 6 months, or a fine not exceeding AED5000, or both.

3 Scope of application of Federal Law No. 4

3.1 Overview

In this chapter we have concentrated on **Federal Law No. 4 of 2002 on the Criminalization of Money Laundering (*'Federal Law No. 4'* 2.1.3 above), as it is by far the most comprehensive of all UAE anti-money laundering legislation.** Any reference to an Article, unless stated otherwise, means an Article contained in *Federal Law No. 4*. Its provisions are applicable to individuals, as well as 'Financial Institutions' and 'Other Financial, Commercial and Economic establishments', if the money laundering is intentionally committed in their names or for their accounts.[2]

3.2 Definition of money laundering

Money Laundering is defined as 'Any act involving transfer, conversion or deposit of Property, or concealment or disguise of the true nature of that Property, which were derived from any of the offences stated in Clause (2) of Article (2) herein'.

---

[2] Federal Law No. 4 of 2002, Article 3.

3.3　Scope of financial institutions

The expression '**Financial Institutions**' covers 'any bank, finance company, money exchange house, financial or monetary intermediary or any other establishment licensed by the *Central Bank*, whether publicly or privately owned'.[3]

3.4　Licensed insurance companies and stock exchanges also included

The application of *Federal Law No. 4* extends to Financial Institutions (as defined) and also to 'establishments licensed and regulated by agencies other than the *Central Bank*, such as insurance companies, stock exchanges and others'.[4]

4　Primary offences

4.1　Definition of money laundering

Article 2(1) sets out the definition for the offence of money laundering:

> **Where any person intentionally commits or assists in the commission of any of the following acts in respect of Property, derived from any of the offences stated in clause 2 of this Article, such person shall be considered a perpetrator of the Money Laundering offence:**

(a) the conversion or transfer or deposit of Proceeds, with intent to conceal or disguise the illicit origin of such Proceeds;

(b) the concealment or disguise of the true nature, source, location, disposition, movement, rights with respect to, or ownership of proceeds.

(c) the acquisition, possession or use of such proceeds.[5]

'Property' is defined widely and means, 'assets of every kind, whether corporeal or incorporeal, moveable or immoveable, and legal documents or instruments evidencing title to those assets or any rights related thereto'.

4.2　Offences

The act will only fall under the money-laundering regime if the Property derives from the following offences (contained in Article 2(2)):[6]

(a) narcotics and psychotropic substances;

(b) kidnapping, piracy and terrorism;

(c) violations of the law of the environment;

---

[3] Federal Law No. 4 of 2002, Article 1.
[4] Federal Law No. 4 of 2002, Article 1.
[5] Proceeds are defined in The Law as '*any property resulting directly or indirectly from the commission of any of the offences stated in Article 2(2)*'.
[6] Federal Law No. 4, Article 2(2).

(d) illicit dealing in firearms and ammunition;

(e) bribery, embezzlement and damage to public property;

(f) fraud, breach of trust and related offences; and

(g) any other related offences referred to in international conventions to which the *UAE* is a party.

4.3   No reference to theft

At first sight, Article 2(2) seems to comprise a comprehensive list of serious criminal offences. However, no specific reference is made to the offence of theft. This is likely to be covered by the expression '*and related offences*' in (f) above.

5   The Anti-Money Laundering and Suspicious Cases Unit

5.1   Financial Information Unit

Article 7 of Federal Law No. 4 directed the *Central Bank* to set up a **Financial Information Unit (an 'FIU')** to deal with money laundering and suspicious cases, and to provide a centre for reporting. The FIU was also directed to make the information available to law enforcement agencies to facilitate their investigations. It was also empowered by Article 7 to facilitate the exchange of information with its counterparts in other countries, either pursuant to a convention, or simply on the basis of reciprocity.

5.2   AMLSCU

The UAE *Central Bank* had already pre-empted the legislation by setting up an FIU in July 1999 in the form of the Anti-Money Laundering and Suspicious Cases Unit ('AMLSCU'). The AMLSCU is the region's first dedicated anti-money laundering body staffed with over 100 specialists. As well as receiving and exchanging information, the AMLSCU can issue freezing orders to freeze funds anywhere in the UAE's financial system for up to 7 days whilst the activity is being investigated. The AMLSCU also acts as a focus and information exchange for other UAE government agencies that are involved in the investigation of money laundering and terrorist financing.

6   Regulatory supervision

6.1   Licensing and supervision agencies

Article 11 of Federal Law No. 4 provides that the agencies concerned with the licensing and supervision of Financial Institutions or Other Financial, Commercial and Economic Establishments are required to establish appropriate mechanisms to ensure compliance by those institutions they oversee with anti-money laundering rules and regulations, including the reporting of suspicious cases.

6.2   Central Bank

The UAE *Central Bank* is the predominant supervisory authority of the country's financial institutions in respect of compliance with anti-money laundering obligations, although other public institutions also play roles in the process.

6.3   Powers of government institutions

In order to assist with the investigation of suspected money laundering activities, Article 4 gives a number of powers to various UAE Government institutions charged with the responsibility for enforcing the Law. So, as well as giving the UAE *Central Bank* power to freeze accounts, Article 4 also permits the **Public Prosecutors Office** to seize property or the proceeds of crime, as well as giving the UAE Courts powers of attachment over assets derived from money laundering offences (although attachment of property with financial institutions can only be executed through the UAE *Central Bank*).

6.4   Maximum cash limits

Under Article 6, the UAE *Central Bank* also has the authority to set a maximum limit on the amount of cash that may be brought into the UAE without the need to declare it.

7   Central Bank Anti-Money Laundering Regulation 24/2000 ('The 2000 Regulation')

7.1   Central Bank Notice 163/98 re: Suspicious account movements

(a) **In February 1998, the UAE *Central Bank* issued a Notice to Banks (163/98) stating that *Central Bank* examiners had detected that movements in some accounts were not commensurate with the income of the concerned individual or corporate entity.** The Notice required banks to seek clarification from customers in the form of 'convincing explanations', although immediate notification was required to the UAE *Central Bank* where:

(b) Substantial remittances were received into an account without justification, especially when the account owner remitted or withdrew the amounts after a short period from deposit; and

(c) The account owner continuously deposited other individuals' cheques of medium/large cash amounts, which indicated that the account owner was carrying out funds management directly or indirectly.

7.2   No provisions on 'tipping off'

The 1998 Notice did not contain provisions relating to tipping-off, nor did it contain any guidance for the administration of anti-money laundering reporting.

7.3   The 2000 Regulation of suspicious transactions

On 14 November 2000, the UAE *Central Bank* issued the 2000 Regulation. The 2000 Regulation supplements previous *Central Bank* circulars that made reference to banking transactions of a suspicious nature, although it only imposes a duty of vigilance and lays down various procedures that have to be complied with. It does not impose any criminal liability, simply that the failure to report unusual and suspicious transactions will be penalized 'in accordance with prevailing laws and regulations'. The criminal liability followed with Federal Law No. 4.

---

[7] REF: 24/2000.

7.4   Scope of 2000 Regulations

The 2000 Regulation applies solely to operations of banks, money exchangers, financial companies and financial institutions operating in the UAE, and imposes a duty to monitor and report suspicious transactions. It also provides guidance on the administration of anti-money laundering controls and reporting, as well as directing banks to appoint a compliance officer to be responsible for anti-money laundering reporting and the training of bank staff.

7.5   Personal nature of obligations

Under the 2000 Regulation, all banks, moneychangers and other financial institutions as well as board members, managers and employees have a personal obligation to report any unusual transactions to the AMLSCU.

7.6   Know your customer obligations

7.6.1   Know your client obligations

Know your customer requirements have been in existence since 1993 following the publication by the UAE *Central Bank* of Regulation 14/93 regarding the opening of accounts.

7.6.2   Documentation

The 2000 Regulation reinforces Regulation 14/93 in terms of customer documentation required, record keeping and retention

7.6.3   Account Opening Procedures

When opening an account, a financial institution should obtain all information and necessary documents which include the full name of the account holder, the current address and place of work. It must also verify identity by physical inspection of the original passport and retention of a copy. When juridical persons open an account, a financial institution should obtain all information and documents with regard to that entity, particularly a copy of the trade licence, whose renewal date should be registered in order that the institution can ensure it keeps a copy of a valid trade licence at all times. The institution should also obtain the name and address of the main account holder, as well as the names and addresses of the partners.

7.6.4   Identity checks for non-account holders

When non-account holders wish to pay by cash for transfers/drafts, banks and money changers are required carefully and systematically to verify the identity of such customers in all transactions where the value of transaction is AED2000 for money changers and AED40 000 for banks. This required identification includes details such as name and address of the beneficiary and physical verification of identity. If money laundering is suspected, the identity of the customer must be verified regardless of whether the concerned amount is over AED40 000.

7.6.5   Money changers

Money changers operating within the UAE have to record details of persons transferring an amount of AED2000 or more and must ensure the correct identity by checking a passport, Labour Card or UAE Driving licence. They must also record the telephone number of the individual concerned.

7.6.6   Records must be retained for minimum 5 years

The Bank or financial institution must also set up a records system, which includes a copy of the passport/trade licence and information on the funds flowing through the accounts, including destination of such money. **These records must be kept and made available for a minimum of 5 years**. This includes all account-opening documents, which should be kept for a minimum of 5 years after the closing of the account.

8   Penalties in case of breach

8.1   UAE signatory to Vienna Convention

Federal Law No. 4 is intended to send a clear signal to the international community that the UAE is determined, as a signatory of the 1988 UN Convention (the 'Vienna Convention'), to uphold and comply with the Vienna Convention in addition to other more recent international initiatives to combat the funding of terrorism. The Law imposes criminal sanctions on both individuals and financial services providers.

8.2   Penalties for individuals and establishments

Individuals and establishments are subject to severe penalties for violation of the anti-money laundering legislation. **A person found guilty of the offence of money laundering under Article 2(1)[8] is liable to be sentenced to a term of imprisonment of not more than seven years and will be subject to fines of between AED30 000 and AED300 000.**[9]

8.3   Intention required

Under Article 3 'Financial Institutions' and 'Other Financial, Commercial and Economic establishments' shall be criminally liable of the offences of Money Laundering if intentionally committed in their respective names or for their accounts.

8.4   Applicable fines

Financial Institutions and Other Financial, Commercial and Economic establishments operating in the UAE who violate provisions under Article 3 will be subject to fines of between AED300 000 and AED1 000 000. Additionally, the proceeds of crime or unlawful property will either be confiscated or subject to other action if they have already been converted into, or mixed with, other property derived from lawful sources.

8.5   Personal responsibility

Chairman, directors, managers and employees of financial institutions or other financial, commercial and economic establishments who know of, yet fail to report to the AMLSCU, any act which occurred and was related to the money laundering offence, will be punished by imprisonment and/or by a fine of between 10 000 and AED100 000.[10]

---

[8] Federal Law No. 4 of 2002.
[9] Federal Law No. 4 of 2002, Article 13.
[10] Federal Law No.4 of 2002, Article 15.

9   Defence in respect of breaches of confidentiality

9.1   Immunity from liability for good faith disclosure

All financial institutions, financial, commercial and economic establishments and their respective directors, employees and authorised representatives are immune from civil, criminal and administrative liability if they are required to provide information in good faith for the purpose of reporting suspicious transactions.[11] The immunity extends to the disclosure of any information which might breach legislative, contractual and administrative provisions made to safeguard confidentiality unless it can be shown that such disclosure was made in bad faith.

10   Ancillary offences

10.1   Tipping off

10.1.1   Definition of 'tipping off'

Article 16 of Federal Law No.4 of 2002 broadly equates to the offence referred to in many other jurisdictions as 'tipping off'. Consequently, 'whoever informs any person that his transactions are being scrutinised for possible involvement in suspicious operations, or that security authorities or other competent authorities are investigating his possible involvement in suspicious operations', shall be guilty of an offence under the Law and be liable to criminal sanctions.

10.1.2   Imprisonment and fines

Any individual found guilty under this Article will be punished by imprisonment for a term not exceeding one year or by a fine of between AED5000 and AED50 000 or by both penalties

10.2   False notification

10.2.1   Definition

Article 17 makes it a criminal offence for any person to make in bad faith a false notification of money laundering to the relevant authorities in the UAE with the intent to cause damage to another person. This provision is designed to prevent the frustration of the Law's principal objectives by 'time-wasters' and other malicious individuals who cause unnecessary diversions of the authorities' time and resources in investigating such reports.

11   Dubai International Financial Centre ('DIFC')

11.1   DIFC is a financial free zone

In order to encourage foreign investment, the Government of the UAE has permitted the creation of a broad range of special economic zones, including free zones, for the development of a liberal, market-oriented legal and regulatory structure.

---

[11] Federal Law No. 4 of 2002, Article 20.

11.2   Established by Federal Decree

The DIFC was established as a financial free zone pursuant to Federal Decree No. 35 of 2004 and Dubai Law No. 9 of 2004 establishing the Dubai International Financial Centre 2004. Unlike some other free zones in the Middle East region, the DIFC has a physical geographical boundary within the Emirate of Dubai.

11.3   Legal and regulatory framework

The DIFC's legal and regulatory framework is effectively "best of breed", and has taken the most effective elements from a number of jurisdictions, primarily Europe, North America and the Far East (participants in the DIFC will, for example, recognise much from the *UK's Financial Services and Markets Act and Financial Services Authority* regulation). The legal and regulatory framework is therefore very familiar to those who operate on an international platform, and has been the culmination of extensive consultation and advice.

11.4   Civil and commercial laws do not apply in DIFC

Importantly, the UAE federal law allows for the dis-application of federal civil and commercial laws from financial free zones, although federal criminal law is still applied. Therefore, whilst a whole new raft of legislation has been introduced within the DIFC, the UAE criminal law is still applicable. As the anti-money laundering law falls under the ambit of criminal legislation, the UAE law on anti-money laundering is still applicable within the DIFC.

11.5   DFSA is the integrated regulator for activities in or from DIFC

The Dubai Financial Services Authority ('DFSA') is the integrated regulator for all financial and ancillary services undertaken in or from the DIFC. The DFSA administers certain DIFC laws,[12] and authorises, licences and registers individuals and institutions to operate within the DIFC.

11.6   The AML module

The anti-money laundering provisions applicable within the DIFC are found in the DFSA anti-money laundering module and apply to every Authorised Firm. The module makes clear that its provisions are in addition to any obligations required by UAE law, and should not be relied upon to interpret or determine the application of money laundering laws of the UAE. Although the detailed (and comprehensive) requirements of the DFSA anti-money laundering module are outside the scope of this chapter, the notable point is that the guidance dovetails into UAE law requirements for reporting suspicious transactions. Authorised Firms are therefore required to determine whether a suspicious transaction requires a 'corresponding' Suspicious Transaction Report to the AMLSCU, and if so, a copy of that external report must also be made available to the DFSA at the same time.

---

[12] Primarily those that are pertinent to regulatory activity such as the Regulatory Law, Trust Law, Data Protection Law, Markets Law, Collective Investment Law and the Law Regulating Islamic Financial Business.

12   Summary

12.1   International cooperation

The money laundering legislation in the UAE and DIFC are regarded as internationally credible and conform with *Financial Action Task Force* recommendations ('FATF 40'). The UAE has become one of the leading country's in the region to combat terrorist financing and money laundering. It is a member of the 14-member *Middle East North Africa Financial Action Taskforce*. In June 2002, the AMLSCU of the UAE *Central Bank* was the first Gulf country FIU to join the prestigious *Egmont Group*.

12.2   AMLSCU reported performance

By 2005 the AMLSCU had investigated over 2000 cases, of which 27 were referred to the public prosecutor. According to newspaper reports,[13] the UAE froze 17 suspicious bank accounts holding USD1.348 million.

12.3   Proposed changes to legislation

There is a notable increase in the publicly stated determination of the UAE *Central Bank* and Government to do even more to combat money laundering and terrorist financing. The Governor of the UAE *Central Bank* has recently confirmed his intention to update its legislation, increase education of money laundering countermeasures and forge closer ties with its neighbours and the international community. For example, in March 2006 the UAE signed a memorandum of understanding with the *United Kingdom* whose aim is to improve the exchange of financial information relating to money laundering and terror financing between the two countries. The rapid economic growth of the UAE, together with its close ties with the West, will ensure that it will retain its position as the foremost proponent of anti-money laundering practices in the region.

Addresses

Central Bank of the UAE
Anti-Money Laundering Suspicious Cases
Unit (AMLSCU)
P.O. Box 854
Abu Dhabi
UAE
Tel +971 2 666 8496
Fax +971 2 6674501
cbuaeamlscu@cbuae.gov.ae
www.centralbank.ae.

DFSA
Supervision Division
Level 13, The Gate
P.O. Box 75850
Dubai
UAE
Tel +971 4 362 1546
Fax +971 4 362 0810
info@dfsa.ae
www.dfsa.ae

---

[13] The Gulf News, 7 March 2005.

Abbreviations

AED	Arab Emirate Dirhams
AMLSCU	Anti-Money Laundering and Suspicious Cases Unit
DFSA	Dubai Financial Services Authority
DIFC	Dubai International Financial Centre
FATF 40	Financial Action Task Force recommendations
FIU	Financial Information Unit
UAE	United Arab Emirates

Bibliography

Central Bank of the UAE: Laws, Regulations and Procedures Implemented in the United Arab Emirates for Anti-Money Laundering and Combating Terrorism Financing, UAE, 2005.

DFSA Rule Book: Anti-Money Laundering Module (AML) [Ver 2/01-06].

www.centralbank.ae.

ASIA PACIFIC

Chee Fang Theng is a tax partner with the Singapore law firm of Khattar Wong. Her areas of work include trusts, estate and succession planning, corporate structuring, international tax planning, stamp duties, property tax and goods and services tax. She has advised multinational corporations, international shipping, aviation, major oil companies, public listed institutions, foreign banks, and high net-worth individuals, and has handled tax litigation cases before the Board of Review, High Court and Court of Appeal. She has contributed chapters and articles to international publications on tax and trusts, and participated in various Law Society committees set up to examine proposed tax and trust legislation.

Firm's profile

KhattarWong is one of Singapore's leading full-service law firms and has earned a strong reputation in the areas of banking, finance and property; corporate and securities laws; and litigation, and possesses an outstanding tax team. Clients repeatedly choose the firm for its experienced lawyers, dedication to client service and consistent delivery of client-centric solutions. It also provides advice across multiple jurisdictions through both its Shanghai and Beijing offices and its broad network with other regional practices covering Southeast Asia and India.

Singapore

Chee Fang Theng

Partner

Tax & Trusts Department

KhattarWong
80 Raffles Place #25-01
UOB Plaza 1
Singapore 048624
Singapore

Tel +65-6238 3019
Fax +65-6534 1090
cheefangtheng@khattarwong.com
www.khattarwong.com

Anti-Money Laundering: International Law and Practice.
Edited by W.H. Muller, C.H. Kälin and J.G. Goldsworth
© 2007 John Wiley & Sons, Ltd

Contents – Singapore

Introduction

In recent years, there has been a dynamic growth in financial activities, which has turned Singapore into a full-service global financial centre with a sophisticated and extensive network of banks, financial institutions, asset managers and advisors carrying out wealth management, capital market and treasury activities involving diverse investment products. The value of the assets under management is estimated to be approaching $1 trillion.[1] These activities are supported by good telecommunications, transport infrastructure and other support facilities.

The importance of the financial system to the economy and the need to avoid disruption to its operation by placing heavy emphasis on anti-money laundering and the countering of terrorist financing concerns is clearly recognized by the government. Therefore a robust framework of legislation, regulatory enforcement and international co-operation has been put in place.

1 The legal framework

1.1 Licensing and registration requirements

Certain business activities or business sectors are more susceptible to money laundering, such as banks, finance companies, money-remittance, insurance, trust and companies service providers, lawyers and accountants. They are therefore subject to specific laws (such as the Banking Act, Finance Companies Act, Securities & Futures Act, Insurance Act) as well as additional regulation and/or professional guidelines.

Banks, trust companies, insurance companies, moneylenders, money-changers and remitters are regulated by specific legislation and need to be licensed in order to operate in Singapore. Contravention is punishable by a fine or imprisonment or both.

1.2 Banking secrecy and trust company secrecy

The rationale for having confidentiality provisions in respect of trust and banking matters is to ensure that third parties who have no business to enquire into the private affairs of a person do not gain easy access to such financial information for their own unscrupulous purposes so that they are able to act to the detriment of such person. This may be necessary, for instance, to protect a business from commercial espionage, or to avoid being the target of criminals in kidnappings.

1.2.1 Banking secrecy

Customer information cannot be disclosed by a bank in Singapore or by its officers or any person, except where expressly provided by the Banking Act ('Banking Act') (s 47, Third Schedule, BA). The situations for which disclosure may be made are listed in the Third Schedule to the BA. A customer may also enter into an express agreement with the bank providing for a higher degree of confidentiality than that which is prescribed by statute. Disclosure is specifically permitted where it is necessary for a police or public officer duly authorized under specified written law to carry out investigation or prosecution or to receive the complaint or report, or to any court.

---

[1] 2006 Budget Speech by Finance Minister on 17 February 2006.

This provision will apply to approved merchant banks with modifications as prescribed by the MAS. The penalty for contravention in the case of an individual is a fine not exceeding S$125 000 or imprisonment for a term not exceeding 3 years or both. In other cases, the penalty is a fine of up to S$250 000.

1.2.2 Trust company secrecy

Trust companies are also not subject to similar secrecy provisions imposed by the Trust Companies Act ('TCA') (s 49, Third Schedule TCA). Information regarding a protected party (referred to as 'protected information') cannot be disclosed by a licensed trust company or any of its officers to any other person except as expressly provided in the TCA. A protected party may also enter into an express agreement with a licensed trust company for a higher degree of confidentiality than that prescribed in the TCA.

The obligation of any officer or other person who receives any protected information continues after the termination or cessation of his appointment, employment, or other capacity in which he had received such information. Where the MAS, in the course of inspection, investigation or regulating a licensed trust company, incidentally obtains any protected information which is not necessary for the supervision or regulation of the licensed trust company, then, such information shall be treated as secret by the MAS.

The penalties for contravention are similar to those applicable for the violation of the banking secrecy provisions.

1.3 Criminalization of money laundering and financing of terrorist acts

1.3.1 Introduction

Money laundering is a process to conceal the benefits derived from drug trafficking or criminal conduct by giving them the appearance of having originated from legitimate sources. This process usually involves three stages: (1) placement, which is the physical disposal of the funds; (2) layering, which is the creation of layers of financial transactions to distance and disguise the funds from their criminal sources; (3) integration, which is to place the funds back into the financial system appearing to be derived from legitimate sources.

This is in contrast to terrorist financing, where the sources may be either legitimate or illegitimate. For instance, the sources for terrorist funding may be criminal activities like drug trafficking, fraud, extortion or kidnapping. The sources may also be legitimate, such as donations from persons sympathetic to the cause, or income from legitimate businesses belonging to the terrorist organizations. Where the funds are from legitimate sources, the associated transactions may not necessarily be complicated. However, some of the techniques would be similar to those for money laundering, in order to conceal the connection between the funds and the terrorist organizations.

The legal framework for anti-money laundering and countering of financing of terrorism comprises of the following legislation:

(1) Corruption, Drug Trafficking and Other Serious Crimes (Confiscation of Benefits) Act.

(2) Monetary Authority of Singapore (Anti-Terrorism Measures) Regulations 2002.

(3) Terrorism (Suppression of Financing) Act.

1.3.2   Corruption, Drug Trafficking and Other Serious Crimes (Confiscation of Benefits) Act (Chapter 65A, 2000 Revised Edition) ('CA')

Offences

The following are offences under the CA:

(a) Assisting another to retain the benefits of drug trafficking and criminal conduct (s 43, 44 CA). A person may be liable to a fine of up to S$200 000 or to imprisonment for up to 7 years or both if convicted.
However, a person will not be guilty of this offence if he discloses the arrangement to an authorized officer:

  (i) prior to the commission of the act, and the act is committed with the consent of the officer;

  (ii) after the commission of the act, but is made on his own initiative and as soon as is reasonable.

The disclosure will not be regarded as a breach of any restriction against disclosure imposed by law, contract or rules of professional conduct. Further, the discloser will not be liable in damages for loss arising from the disclosure.
It is also a defence to prove that:

- he did not know and had no reasonable ground to believe that the arrangement related to proceeds derived from criminal conduct;

- he intended to disclose to an authorized officer;

- there is reasonable excuse for his failure to disclose; or

- where a person enters into the arrangement in the course of his employment, he disclosed to the appropriate person according to the procedure established by his employer.

The requisite mental element, which is in accordance with the FATF recommendations, is based on an objective test rather than a subjective test, namely, actual knowledge or reasonable grounds to believe, rather than purely based on actual knowledge alone.

(b) Concealing or transferring benefits of drug trafficking and criminal conduct (s 46, 47 CA). The penalty upon conviction is a fine of up to S$200 000 or imprisonment of up to 7 years or both.

(c) Tipping-off (s 48 CA). The punishment upon conviction is a fine of up to S$30 000 or imprisonment of up to 3 years or both. There is an exception which allows a lawyer or his employee to make disclosure to a representative of his client in the course of his legal professional work, or to any person for the purpose of legal proceedings, except where the disclosure is made with a view to furthering any illegal purpose.

(d) Any conduct engaged on behalf of a body corporate by a director, employee or agent, or by any other person with their agreement, will be deemed to have been engaged by the body corporate. The director, employee or agent is required to be acting within his actual or apparent authority (s 52 CA). Where a body corporate is guilty of an offence under the CA, and that offence is found to have been committed with the consent of, or attributable to the neglect of a director, manager, secretary or similar officer or any person purporting to act in that capacity, such person will also be guilty of the offence and punished accordingly (s 59, CA).

1.3.3   Confiscation of benefits

The CA also provides for the confiscation of benefits derived by a person from drug trafficking offences and serious offences upon his conviction (s 4 and 5, CA). The list of drug trafficking offences is set out in the First Schedule, and includes trafficking, manufacture, importation and exportation of controlled drugs, cultivation of cannabis, opium and coca plants, as well as money laundering. The list of serious offences is set out in the Second Schedule of the CA, and includes hijacking of aircraft, kidnapping, bribery, counterfeiting coin, murder and other Penal Code offences, as well as assisting another to retain, conceal and transfer benefits from criminal conduct. The High Court may issue restraint orders to prohibit any person from dealing with his realizable property, as well as charging orders to secure payment to the Government in respect of such benefits (s 15, 16, 17 CA). A restraint order may apply to all realizable property, whether or not described in the order, to prevent a person from dealing with it (which would include making payment to any creditor, or removing the property from Singapore) (s 16 CA). A charging order is limited to the amount payable under the confiscation order once it has been made, but may be made upon the value of the property charged prior to that (s 17 CA). The charging order may be made upon property held beneficially by the defendant, or by any person whom the defendant has made a gift under any trust or of specified assets which is caught by the CA. The specified assets refer to immovable property in Singapore, securities of the Government or any public authority, stock of any body incorporated in Singapore, stock of any body incorporated outside Singapore which is registered in a place within Singapore, and units of any unit trust where the register of unit holders is kept in Singapore. A gift is caught by the CA if it was made by the defendant during the period of 6 years before proceedings for drug trafficking or serious offences were instituted against him or where a confiscation order is made against him (s 12(7), (8) CA). A third party is protected if he makes an application to court before the confiscation order is made, and the court is satisfied that he was not involved in the drug trafficking or criminal conduct, and had acquired the interest for sufficient consideration and without knowing that the property was involved or derived from drug trafficking or criminal conduct under circumstances which do not arouse a reasonable suspicion (s 13 CA).

1.3.4   Scope of application

The CA applies to drug trafficking offences and serious offences committed in Singapore and outside Singapore (s 2 CA). Drug trafficking offences are listed in the First Schedule of the CA, whilst serious offences are listed in the Second Schedule. The list of serious offences includes offences under the Arms and Explosives Act, Arms Offences Act, Chemical Weapons (Prohibition) Act, Children and Young Persons Act, Computer Misuse Act, Corrosive and Explosive Substances and Offensive Weapons Act, Hijacking of Aircraft and Protection of Aircraft and International Airports Act, Kidnapping Act, MAS Act, Penal Code, Securities and Futures Act, Terrorism (Suppression of Financing) Act and United Nations Act. Tax evasion and fiscal offences are not included. It also applies to property situated in Singapore and elsewhere (s 3 CA). A person is taken to be convicted of drug trafficking or a serious offence, if he absconds (s 26 CA). A person is taken to have absconded if – (1) he dies after investigations have commenced, but before the institution of proceedings or conviction, or (2) if he cannot be found, apprehended or extradited after 6 months from the commencement of investigations. Proceedings under the CA can be instituted or continued against the personal representatives. If there are no personal representatives, then against the beneficiaries who are specified by the court upon the application of the public prosecutor (s 28 CA). A confiscation order may be made in relation to the estate of a deceased defendant. However, the personal representative or beneficiary will not be liable to imprisonment if the estate's property is inadequate to satisfy the confiscation order.

1.3.5 Duty to make disclosure

A person who knows or has reasonable grounds to suspect that any property represents the proceeds of, was intended or actually used in connection with drug trafficking or criminal conduct, due to any information or matter arising in the course of his trade, profession, business or employment, must disclose to an authorized officer as soon as reasonably practicable (s 39 CA). However, it is not an offence for a lawyer, his clerks, employees and interpreter to fail to disclose items subject to legal privilege, which is defined to mean the communications between a lawyer and his client or client's representative for the giving of legal advice, or communications made in connection with or in contemplation of legal proceedings (s 35 CA). The disclosure to an authorized officer is not a breach of any restriction against disclosure imposed by law, contract or rules of professional conduct, and the person making disclosure will not be liable for loss arising from the disclosure or any act or omission as a consequence of the disclosure.

A suspicious transaction reporting officer (STRO) may communicate anything disclosed to him or an authorized officer pursuant to s 39 of the CA to a corresponding authority of a foreign country if the following conditions are satisfied (s 41 CA):

(a) The corresponding authority of the foreign country has an arrangement to communicate similar information upon request by Singapore.

(b) The STRO is satisfied that the corresponding authority has given appropriate undertakings to protect the confidentiality and to control the usage of the communication, including an undertaking not to use it as evidence in any proceedings.

(c) Such other conditions prescribed by the Minister.

1.3.6 Powers of investigations and arrest

An authorized officer means (s 2 CA):

(a) an officer of the Bureau;

(b) an appointed special investigator of the Corrupt Practices Investigation Bureau;

(c) an appointed Commercial Affairs Officer;

(d) a police officer; and

(e) any other person authorized by the Minister.

The High Court may grant an order to produce material for the purposes of investigations in drug trafficking and serious offences (s 30, 31 CA). An authorized officer may make the application to court in relation to non-financial institutions, whilst the application must be made by the attorney-general or a person duly authorized by him in relation to financial institutions. Financial institutions for the purpose means licensed banks, approved merchant banks, licensed finance companies, holders of capital markets services licenses, licensed financial advisers, registered insurance companies, licensed intermediaries, and other persons prescribed by the Minister. However, licensed money-changers and remitters are not included (s 2 CA).

An authorized officer or officer of customs may arrest without warrant any person whom he reasonably believes has committed an offence under the CA (s 55 CA). An authorized officer who is not a police officer may exercise investigative powers for seizable offences conferred upon a police officer by the Criminal Procedure Code (Cap. 68) in a case relating to an offence under the CA.

An authorized officer can only disclose information obtained by him for the performance of his duties or functions, and not for any other purpose (s 56 CA). The penalty for contravention is a fine of up of S$2000 or imprisonment of up to 12 months or both.

Any person who obstructs or hinders an authorized officer in the discharge of his duty is liable upon conviction to a fine of up to S$2000 or imprisonment of up to 6 months or both.

1.3.7 Retention of financial records by financial institutions

Every financial institution is required to retain financial transaction documents for the minimum retention period of 5 years (s 37 CA). Where the document relates to the opening of an account or deposit box, the 5 years is computed from the date of closure of the account or deposit box. In any other case, the 5 years is computed from the day the transaction takes place.

1.3.8 Monetary Authority of Singapore (Anti-Terrorism Measures) Regulations 2002

Introduction

The MAS exercised its powers pursuant to s 27A(1)(b) of the MAS Act to make these Regulations, which have the objective of giving effect to Resolution 1267 (1999), Resolution 1373 (2001) and Resolution 1390 (2002) of the Security Council of the United Nations.

S 27A of the MAS Act allows the MAS to issue directions to a financial institution or class of financial institutions, and to make regulations concerning any financial institution or class of financial institutions or relating to the activities of any financial institution or class of financial institutions, as it considers necessary in order to discharge or facilitate the discharge of any obligation binding on Singapore by virtue of a decision of the Security Council of the United Nations.

A financial institution to which a direction is issued or which is bound by any regulations must comply with the direction or regulations notwithstanding any other duty imposed on the financial institution by any rule of law, written law or contract. A financial institution will not, in carrying out any act in compliance with any direction or regulations, be treated as being in breach of any such rule of law, written law or contract.

1.3.9 Scope of application

The Regulations apply to all branches and offices of financial institutions which are:

(a) incorporated in Singapore, whether located in Singapore or elsewhere; and

(b) incorporated outside Singapore, that are located in Singapore.

The Regulations also covers terrorist acts outside Singapore, in relation to the public of a country other than Singapore.

1.3.10 Prohibitions

Financial institutions are prohibited from doing the following:

(a) Provision or collection of funds for terrorists, where it knows or has reasonable grounds to believe that the funds will be used to commit any terrorist act (para 5 of the Regulations).

(b) Dealing with the property of terrorists, except with the written approval of the MAS (para 6 of the Regulations).

(c) Provision of resources and services for the benefit of terrorists, except with the written approval of the MAS (para 7 of the Regulations).

1.3.11 Terrorism (Suppression of Financing) Act (Chapter 325, 2003 Revised Edition) ('TA')

Introduction

The TA was enacted to give effect to the International Convention for the Suppression of Financing of Terrorism.

Offences

The following are offences under the TA:

(a) Providing or collecting property for terrorist acts (s 3, TA).

(b) Providing or inviting others to provide property and financial services for terrorist acts (s 4, TA).

(c) Use or possession of property for terrorist purposes (s 5, TA)

(d) Dealing with property of terrorists by any person in Singapore or a Singapore citizen outside Singapore (s 6, TA).

A person convicted of any of the above offences is liable to a fine of up to S$100 000 or imprisonment of up to 10 years or both.

Scope of application – extra-territoriality

A person who commits an act or omission outside Singapore, that would constitute the offence of providing or collecting property for terrorist acts (pursuant to s 3 TA), provision of property and services for terrorist purposes (pursuant to s 4 TA) or use or possession of property for terrorist purposes (pursuant to s 5 TA) if committed in Singapore, is deemed to commit the act or omission in Singapore and may be tried and punished accordingly (s 34(1) TA).

If a Singapore citizen commits the offence of dealing with property of terrorists (pursuant to s 6 TA) or failure to disclose (pursuant to s 8 TA) outside Singapore, he may be dealt with as if the offence had been committed in Singapore (s 34(2) TA).

Where there is no treaty or other agreement in force between Singapore and a country which is a party to the Convention for the Suppression of the Financing of Terrorism adopted by the General Assembly of the United Nations on 9th December 1999, an order may be made under s 17 of the Mutual Assistance in Criminal Matters Act (s 32 TA):

(a) declaring that country as a prescribed foreign country; and

(b) applying that Act as if there were a treaty or agreement under which that country has agreed to provide assistance in criminal matters to Singapore.

Terrorism financing offences are deemed to be included in the list of extradition crimes set out in the First Schedule to the Extradition Act (s 33 TA).

Duty of disclosure

Every person in Singapore and every Singapore citizen outside Singapore has the duty to inform the Commissioner of Police if he has control of any property belonging to terrorists, or has information in respect of any property belonging to terrorists (s 8, TA). Every person in Singapore who has information of material assistance in preventing the commission of a terrorism financing offence or in securing the apprehension or conviction involving terrorism financing must disclose the information to a police officer (s 10, TA). The failure to disclose may result in a fine of up to S$50 000 or imprisonment of up to 5 years or both.

Powers of confiscation, audit, forfeiture and investigations

The Minister may require any person or class of persons to determine on a continuing basis whether they are in possession or control of property owned or controlled by any terrorist (s 9, TA). Failure to comply is an offence resulting in a fine of up to S$50 000 or imprisonment of up to 5 years or both.

The attorney-general may make an application to a judge for an order of forfeiture in respect of property owned or controlled by a terrorist, or which will be used to facilitate a terrorist act (s 21, TA). The judge may set aside any transfer of property that occurred after the seizure of the property or service of a restraint order, unless the transfer was made for valuable consideration to a person acting in good faith (s 29, TA). The judge may also make an order for forfeiture where he is satisfied on the balance of probabilities that the property is owned or controlled by a terrorist, or which will be used to facilitate a terrorist act (s 24, TA). Where such property has been mixed with other property, the forfeiture order will only relate to the portion of the mixed property which represents the property owned or controlled by terrorists.

A judge may, upon an *ex parte* application by the attorney-general, issue a warrant to search and seize property situated in Singapore in respect of which an order of forfeiture could be made (s 11(1)(a), TA). The judge may also issue a restraint order in respect of property situated in or outside Singapore, prohibiting any person from disposing or dealing with any interest in that property (s 11(1)(b), TA). Property which has been seized or is subject to a restraint order may be detained for a period of up to 6 months from the seizure or issuance of the restraint order. The period may be extended if proceedings are instituted, or if a judge orders the continuation upon application by the attorney-general that the property is required for investigations or evidence (s 20, TA).

2 Regulatory framework

A fine balance has to be struck between not over-regulating so as to facilitate business and financial activities, as well as the need for regulation to catch and prevent money laundering and financing of terrorism activities.

2.1 Monetary Authority of Singapore (MAS)

The MAS is empowered to supervise and regulate the financial institutions in Singapore (s 21 MAS Act). The MAS is authorized to issue guidelines and operational regulations upon financial institutions, and to revoke the licence of any financial institution which fails to comply (section 28 MAS Act). Some of the specific legislation, for instance, the Banking Act, Financial Advisers Act, Insurance Act, and Securities and Futures Act, also confer powers upon the MAS to issue regulations and guidelines.

The MAS has issued notices on the prevention of money-laundering to the following financial institutions:

(1) Notice to merchant banks (MAS 1014) dated 22 February 2000.

(2) Notice to finance companies dated 22 February 2000.

(3) Notice to money-changing licensees and remittance licensees dated 24 April 2000.

(4) Notice to banks (MAS 626) dated 11 November 2002 issued pursuant to s 54A (now renumbered as s 55) of the Banking Act.

(5) Notice to life insurers (MAS 314) dated 11 November 2002 issued pursuant to s 64 of the Insurance Act.

(6) Notice to financial advisers (FAA N06) dated 11 November 2002 issued pursuant to s 58 of the Financial Advisers Act.

(7) Notice to holders of a capital markets services licence dated 11 November 2002 issued pursuant to s 101 of the Securities and Futures Act.

(8) Notice to persons approved to act as trustees for collective investment schemes (SFA 13-N01) dated 11 July 2003 issued pursuant to s 293 of the Securities and Futures Act.

These notices were issued with a view to preventing the financial system from being used in furtherance of money laundering activities, taking into account the provisions of the CA as well as the Financial Action Task Force 40 Recommendations.

Where Singapore-incorporated financial institutions have branches or subsidiaries overseas, they have to ensure that the group policy on money laundering is communicated to their overseas offices and that the standards for identity verification and record keeping under Singapore law are adhered to. Where the laws and regulations of the host country conflict with the notices, then the branch or subsidiary should comply with the laws and regulations of the host country and inform the head office of any departure from the group policy.

The basic principles and policies adopted to combat money laundering are as follows:

(a) Customer identification/know your customer.

(b) Compliance with laws.

(c) Co-operation with law enforcement agencies.

(d) Policies, procedures and training.

2.1.1 Customer identification

Financial institutions must obtain satisfactory evidence of the identity and legal existence of persons applying to do business with them. Such evidence should be substantiated by reliable documents and other means. During the business relationship, if the financial institution doubts the accuracy of the information relating to the customer's identity or there are signs of unreported changes, then it must take steps to verify the identity of the customer or beneficial owner.

Where the financial institution acquires the entire business or product portfolio of another financial institution, it is not necessary for the identity of all existing customers to be re-identified provided that all customer account records are acquired with the business, and due diligence enquiries do not raise doubts as to whether previously adopted anti-money laundering procedures satisfy Singapore requirements.

The customer identification procedures for non-face-to-face verification should be at least as stringent as those for face-to-face verification. Some of the measures suggested include obtaining an independently verified telephone contact, confirmation with the employer of the applicant's employment, confirmation of address through an exchange of correspondence, and obtaining a copy of the applicant's document of identity certified by lawyers or notary publics. Reasonable steps should be taken to avoid fraud, single or multiple fictitious applications.

Where the applicant is an unlisted company or unincorporated business, and none of the directors or partners are already known to the financial institution, then the principal directs, partners or shareholders must be identified according to customer identification procedures set out for personal applicants.

Financial institutions dealing with shell companies (entities which have no business substance) are cautioned to obtain satisfactory evidence of the identity of the beneficial owners. The use of trustees, nominees and fiduciaries (intermediary) may mask the origins of funds derived from drug trafficking or criminal conduct. Therefore financial institutions should obtain satisfactory evidence of the intermediary's identity and the nature of their duties. Where the intermediary is a financial institution authorized and supervised by the MAS in respect of its business in Singapore, or is a subsidiary of such a financial institution, then the intermediary may be relied upon to verify the beneficial owners' identity. Where the intermediary is a financial institution supervised by an overseas regulatory authority which has provisions equivalent to those set out in the notices, then it would be reasonable for the financial institution to accept a written assurance from the intermediary that the beneficial owners' identity has been obtained and the intermediary is satisfied with the source of funds. Where the intermediary does not fall within these categories, then the financial institution has to obtain satisfactory evidence of the beneficial owners' identity and source of funds. If satisfactory evidence of the beneficial owners cannot be obtained, then the financial institution has to consider whether to proceed, and to record any misgiving and special attention to monitoring the account.

2.1.2 Compliance with laws

Record keeping by financial institutions involving customers and transactions must meet the requirements of the law, and allow the relevant authorities, internal and external authorities to reliably determine the transactions and compliance with the notices. The records must also allow any transaction effected via the financial institution to be reconstructed, and to satisfy any enquiry or order from the relevant authorities in Singapore as to disclosure of information.

2.1.3 Co-operation with law enforcement agencies

Financial institutions must clarify the economic background of any transaction or business relationship, if its form or amount appears unusual in relation to the customer or the financial institution, or if the economic purpose or legality of the transaction is unclear. A non-exhaustive list of suspicious transactions is set out by way of example in the Appendix, and the identification of such transactions should prompt enquiries and further investigations Investigations on the source of funds. In this regard, financial institutions must implement adequate systems for detecting suspicious transactions, as well as institute a system for reporting suspicious transactions. This may include appointing senior person(s) or an appropriate unit to report to the STRO. As the obligation to report is on the individual who becomes suspicious of a money laundering transaction, officers and employees of the financial institution should be made aware of their statutory obligation to make such reports. Where it becomes necessary to make further enquiries of the customer, care should be taken to ensure that the customer does not become aware that his name has been brought to the attention of the STRO.

Financial institutions should not make a disclosure which is likely to prejudice an investigation under the CA, as tipping off is an offence. It is also an offence if the financial institution contravenes a production order issued by the court without reasonable excuse, or provides material known to be false or misleading in purported compliance with a production order without indicating how the material is false or misleading or providing the correct information which is in its possession or can be reasonably obtained. Hindering or obstructing an authorized office in the execution of a search warrant, or otherwise in the discharge of his duty under the CA, is also an offence.

2.1.4 Policies, procedures and training

Financial institutions should appoint a senior officer as compliance officer or set up a designated compliance unit headed by a senior officer to ensure expeditious action to any matter requiring special attention under the notices and the CA, and to advise management and staff on in-house instructions which are issued to promote adherence to the notices. The in-house audit must also regularly monitor the effectiveness of measures taken to counter money laundering. Training to raise awareness of the statutory obligations is recommended especially for new staff, 'front-line' staff, staff dealing with new customers, and supervisors and managers.

On 29 December 2006, MAS issued a Notice MAS 626 (pursuant to section 55 of the Banking Act (Cap. 19)) titled 'Prevention of Money Laundering and Countering the Financing of Terrorism', which takes effect on 1 March 2007 (except for Paragraph 9 of the Notice, which takes effect on 1 July 2007). This Notice deals with terrorist financing, enhanced customer due diligence for politically exposed persons, correspondent banking and wire transfers.

Apart from its powers to issue guidelines and regulations, the MAS also conducts regular inspections of the financial institutions to ensure compliance.

2.2   Law enforcement

The central authority for reporting and investigations of money laundering offences is the Commercial Affairs Department (CAD), which is part of the Singapore Police Force. The Suspicious Transactions Reporting Office (STRO), which comes under the CAD, is responsible for receiving suspicious transaction reports for further investigations. The STRO is authorized to share information with a foreign corresponding authority which has entered into an arrangement to make similar communications upon Singapore's request, and where the appropriate undertakings have been obtained for protecting the confidentiality and usage of the communications (s 41 CA).

2.3   Other guidelines

(a) The Association of Banks (ABS) has issued guidelines on the prevention of money laundering. Although these guidelines are not legally binding, the ABS Council has the power to impose penalties on members. Where a member resigns, or is suspended or expelled, MAS will be notified and the inter-bank markets facilities will not be available to such member.

(b) The Law Society and the Institute of Certified Public Accountants of Singapore have also issued guidelines on money-laundering. These professional guidelines however do not have force of law. There are however proposals to change the rules governing the legal profession to reduce the risk of money laundering.

3   International co-operation

3.1   Membership of international groupings

Singapore is a signatory to various conventions targeted at preventing drug-trafficking, money laundering and terrorism, such as the Convention against Illicit Traffic in Narcotics, Drugs and Psychotropic Substances 1988 and the International Convention for Suppression of the Financing of Terrorism 1999.

Singapore is also a member of the Financial Action Task Force (FATF), Egmont Group, and the Asia Pacific Group on Money Laundering.

3.2   Mutual assistance and exchange of information

3.2.1   Mutual Assistance in Criminal Matters Act (Chapter 190A, 2001 Revised Edition) ('MA')

Introduction

The MA was enacted to facilitate the provision and obtaining of international assistance in criminal matters.

Scope of application

The MA does not prevent the provision or obtaining of international assistance in criminal matters from the International Criminal Police (Interpol) or any other international organization (s 4, MA). Further, MA also does not authorize the extradition of any person (s 5, MA).

Requests by Singapore

A request for assistance from the foreign authority may only be made by the attorney-general (s 7, MA) for the following:

(a) Taking of evidence in the foreign country (s 8, MA).

(b) Arranging for the attendance of the person in Singapore to give evidence or assistance relevant to a criminal matter involving a Singapore offence (s 9, MA). However, such a person who is in Singapore pursuant to such a request has certain immunities and privileges (s 11, MA):

    (i) not to be detained, prosecuted or punished in Singapore for any offence which occurred before his departure from the foreign country pursuant to the request;

    (ii) not to be subjected to any civil suit in respect of any act or omission before his departure from the foreign country, being a civil suit which he could not be subjected if he was not in Singapore; and

    (iii) not to be required to give evidence or assistance in relation to any criminal matter in Singapore other than the criminal matter to which the request relates.
Further, a statement shall not be used in the prosecution of the person for an offence against Singapore law without the consent of the foreign authority, unless it relates to perjury, contempt of court, impeaching his credibility or as evidence (where he makes an inconsistent statement whilst giving evidence) (s 12, MA).

(c) Enforcement and satisfaction of a Singapore confiscation order (s 13, MA).

(d) Assistance in locating or identifying persons (s 14, MA).

(e) Assistance in service of process (s 15 MA).

Requests to Singapore

Requests for assistance by foreign countries must be made to the attorney-general (s 19 MA).

A request for assistance will be refused if the attorney-general is of the opinion that (s 20(1) MA):

(a) The foreign authority has not complied with the terms of any treaty or agreement between Singapore and that country.

(b) The request relates to investigation or punishment of a person for an offence of a political character.

(c) The request relates to the investigation or punishment of a person for an offence only under military law (and not ordinary criminal law) if it has occurred in Singapore.

(d) There are substantial grounds for believing that the request was for investigating or otherwise causing prejudice to a person on account of his race, religion, sex, ethnic origin, nationality or political organization.

(e) The request relates to the investigation or punishment of a person for which he has been convicted, acquitted or pardoned by a competent court or authority in the foreign country, or has undergone the punishment provided by law.

(f) The request relates to the investigation or punishment of a person for an act or omission which would not have constituted a Singapore offence had it occurred in Singapore.

(g) The request relates to an offence of insufficient gravity.

(h) The thing requested for is of insufficient importance to the investigations or could reasonably be obtained by other means.

(i) It is contrary to public interest to provide the assistance.

(j) The appropriate authority fails to undertake that the thing will not be used only for the criminal matter in respect of which the request was made, except with the consent of the attorney-general.

(k) In the case of a request for assistance in obtaining evidence or service of process, the appropriate authority fails to undertake to the attorney-general, upon request, anything obtained pursuant to the request upon completion of the criminal matter.

(l) The provision of the assistance could prejudice a criminal matter in Singapore.

The attorney-general may exercise his discretion to refuse a request for assistance by a foreign country (s 20(2) MA):

(a) Pursuant to the terms of any treaty or agreement between Singapore and that country.

(b) If the attorney-general is of the opinion that the provision of assistance would prejudice the safety of any person in Singapore or elsewhere.

(c) If the attorney-general is of the opinion that the provision of assistance would impose an excessive burden on the resources of Singapore.

(d) If that country is not a prescribed foreign country and the appropriate authority does not give an undertaking to the attorney-general that the foreign country will, subject to its laws, comply with a future request for assistance in a criminal matter from Singapore.

The foreign authority may make a request in relation to a criminal matter in that country to the attorney-general for the following:

(a) Assistance in obtaining evidence (s 21 MA).

(b) Producing a particular thing or thing of description of thing in Singapore (s 22 MA).

(c) Assistance for attendance of person in foreign country (s 26 MA).

(d) Enforcement of a foreign confiscation order or restraint, and the attorney-general may make an application to the High Court for the registration of the confiscation order (s 29, 30 MA).

(e) Assistance in search and seizure, and the attorney-general may make an application for a search warrant (s 33, 34 MA).

(f) Assistance in locating or identifying persons, which may be forwarded by the attorney-general to the appropriate agency in Singapore (s 37 MA).

(g) Assistance in service of process (s 38 MA).

3.2.2   s 32 of the Terrorism (Suppression of Financing) Act ('TA')

Where there is no treaty, memorandum of understanding or other agreement in force between Singapore and a country which is a party to the International Convention for the Suppression of the Financing of Terrorism, then an order may be made under s 17 of the MA to declare that country as a prescribed foreign country, and apply the MA as if there were a treaty, memorandum or other agreement under which that country agreed to provide assistance in criminal matters to Singapore (s 32 TA).

3.3   Extradition

3.3.1   Introduction

The Extradition Act ('EA') has a separate regime providing for the extradition of fugitives to and from:

(a) foreign States

(b) Commonwealth countries

(c) Malaysia.

A fugitive is a person who is accused of an extraditable crime within the foreign State or Commonwealth country.

An extraditable crime in relation to a foreign State means an offence committed in the foreign State which would constitute an equivalent offence in Singapore as described in the First Schedule of the EA. An extraditable crime in relation to a Commonwealth country is similarly defined, but with the additional condition that the maximum penalty is either death or not less than 12 months.

3.3.2   Jurisdiction as to offences committed at sea or in the air

The Minister or magistrate may exercise the powers conferred by the EA if the vessel where a fugitive who committed an offence on the high seas or outside Singapore airspace comes into any port or aerodrome in Singapore (s 40 EA).

3.3.3   Simultaneous requisitions

Where the requisition for the surrender of a fugitive is received from more than one foreign State or declared Commonwealth country, the Minister may surrender the fugitive to such State or country as he thinks fit. The Minister will consider all circumstances of the case, in particular (s 41 EA):

(a) the relative seriousness of the offences;

(b) the relative dates on which the requests were made; and

(c) the citizenship or other national status of the fugitive and his ordinary residence.

3.3.4   s 33 of the Terrorism (Suppression of Financing) Act ('TA')

Any terrorism financing offence will be deemed to be included in the list of extradition crimes listed in the First Schedule to the Extradition Act. Where there is no extradition treaty between Singapore and a country which is a party to the International Convention for the Suppression of the Financing of Terrorism, a notification in the Gazette under s 4 of the EA may be made to apply the EA as if there were an extradition treaty.

4   Conclusion

Singapore is categorized as Group I within the Financial Stability Forum (FSF) groupings in a 2000 report by the FSF. The FSF groupings range from Group I to III. Countries falling within Group I are regarded as having sound legal infrastructures and supervisory practices which adhere to internationally accepted standards, as well as having sufficient resources to ensure a high level of supervision and co-operation. Singapore has sound measures to prevent money laundering and terrorist financing, in the form of strong legislation and effective enforcement, and is also deeply involved in international co-operation in these areas.

Bibliography

2006 Budget Speech by Finance Minister, Singapore on 17 February 2006.

Banking Act (Chapter 19, 2003 Revised Edition).

Finance Companies Act (Chapter 108, 2000 Revised Edition).

Securities & Futures Act (Chapter 289, 2002 Revised Edition).

Insurance Act (Chapter 142, 2000 Revised Edition).

Trust Companies Act 2005 (Act 11 of 2005).

Money-Changing and Remittance Businesses Act (Chapter 187, 1996 Revised Edition).

Moneylenders Act (Chapter 188, 1985 Revised Edition).

Corruption, Drug Trafficking and Other Serious Crimes (Confiscation of Benefits) Act (Chapter 65A, 2000 Revised Edition).

Monetary Authority of Singapore (Anti-Terrorism Measures) Regulations 2002.

Terrorism (Suppression of Financing) Act (Chapter 325, 2003 Revised Edition).

Financial Action Task Force 40 Recommendations.

Notice to merchant banks (MAS 1014) dated 22 February 2000.

Notice to finance companies dated 22 February 2000.

Notice to money-changing licensees and remittance licensees dated 24 April 2000.

Notice to banks (MAS 626) dated 11 November 2002 issued pursuant to s 54A (now re-numbered as s 55) of the Banking Act.

Notice to life insurers (MAS 314) dated 11 November 2002 issued pursuant to s 64 of the Insurance Act.

Notice to financial advisers (FAA N06) dated 11 November 2002 issued pursuant to s 58 of the Financial Advisers Act.

Notice to holders of a capital markets services licence dated 11 November 2002 issued pursuant to s 101 of the Securities and Futures Act.

Notice to persons approved to act as trustees for collective investment schemes (SFA 13-N01) dated 11 July 2003 issued pursuant to s 293 of the Securities and Futures Act.

Convention against Illicit Traffic in Narcotics, Drugs and Psychotropic Substances 1988.

International Convention for Suppression of the Financing of Terrorism 1999.

Mutual Assistance in Criminal Matters Act (Chapter 190A, 2001 Revised Edition).

Extradition Act (Chapter 103, 2000 Revised Edition).

2000 Report by the Financial Stability Forum.

Takashi Nakazaki is an associate at Anderson Mori & Tomotsune, with broad experience in the areas of financial regulations, securities transactions, business dispute resolution, intellectual property (copyright law) and cyber law. More specifically, Mr Nakazaki has experience concerning disputes over various technologies including cross-border online transactions, real estate online auctions, electronic banking, and cyber money, computer software for medical devices, genetic engineering, open source software and file sharing software. He has also been involved with a wide range of matters dealing with the liquidation of real estate and bonds. Mr Nakazaki earned a Bachelor of Laws degree from Tokyo University, Faculty of Law in 1998 and is admitted to practice in Japan.

Firm's profile

Anderson Mori & Tomotsune, one of the largest law firms in Japan with approximately 200 bilingual lawyers, was formed from the merger of two of Japan's leading firms, Anderson Mori and Tomotsune & Kimura. Since the origin of its predecessors in 1952, the firm has historically represented multinational, overseas corporations. Supplementing its Tokyo main office, it also operates an office in Beijing, which is prepared to meet the needs of clients engaging in business in China.

Japan[1]

Takashi Nakazaki

Attorney-At-Law

Anderson Mori & Tomotsune
Izumi Garden Tower
6-1, Roppongi 1-chome,
Minato-ku, Tokyo 106-6036
Japan

Tel +81-3-6888-1101
Fax +81-3-6888-3101
takashi.nakazaki@amt-law.com
www.andersonmoritomotsune.com/en/lawyer/02/prof/0245.html

[1] I would like to thank Kunihiko Morishita, a partner of Anderson Mori & Tomotsune (AM&T), for providing helpful comments. I am also grateful to Duke Takashi Fujiyama, a foreign legal associate, and Kenneth Lam, a foreign legal clerk, of AM&T, for their assistance in preparing this chapter.

Anti-Money Laundering: International Law and Practice.
Edited by W.H. Muller, C.H. Kälin and J.G. Goldsworth
© 2007 John Wiley & Sons, Ltd

Contents – Japan

1 Legislative history

Until recently, Japanese legislation focused on drug-related money laundering. *The Law Concerning Special Exceptions to the Narcotic Drugs and Psychotropic Substance Control Law, Etc.* (*Kokusaitekina Kyouryokunomotni Kiseiyakubutsunikakaru Fuseikouiwo Jochousuru Kouitouno Boushiwohakarutameno Mayaku oyobi Kouseishinyakutorishimarihouno Tokureitouni kansuru Houritsu* Law No. 94 of 1991, as amended; more commonly known as the Anti-Drug Law (the '*ADL*')), which was enacted in 1991 and became effective in 1992, laid the legal foundation for preventing and prosecuting drug-related money laundering activities. The Ministry of Finance (*Ohkurashou*) then issued a 1992 administrative directive, *Kuragin* No. 1283, to implement the **ADL**. This administrative directive was subsequently incorporated into the guidelines *Re: Supervision of Financial Institutions, Etc. Book I for Deposit-Taking Financial Institutions (Jimu guideline Daiichi Bunsatsu Yokin Toriatsukai Kinyuukikankankei)* issued by the Financial Supervisory Agency (*Kin-yuukantokuchou*) in October 1998 (as amended; the '*FSA Guidelines*'). The 1998 amendment to *the Foreign Exchange and Foreign Trade Law* (*Gaikokukawase oyobi Gaikokubouekihou* Law No. 228 of 1949, as amended; the '*FEL*') required banks and money exchangers operating in Japan to seek identification from customers in certain cases in order to prevent money laundering; however, the **FEL** did not proscribe any penalty for any such banks and money exchangers that fail to obtain such identification.

In 1999, Japan expanded the scope of its anti-money laundering efforts through the enactment of *the Law Concerning Punishment of Organized Crimes and Regulation of Criminal Proceeds, Etc.* (*Soshikitekina Hanzaino Shobatsu oyobi Hanzaishuuekino Kiseitouni kansuru Houritsu*; Law No. 136 of 1999, as amended, more commonly known as the Anti-Organized Crime Law (the '*AOCL*')). The **AOCL** took effect on 1 February 2000 and proscribed not only money laundering occurring in connection with illegal drug transactions but also money laundering occurring in connection with several other specified types of criminal activities. The **FSA** Guidelines were amended in January and February 2000 to conform to the **AOCL**.

In 2002, the Japanese government ratified *the International Convention for the Suppression of the Financing of Terrorism* (the '*ICSFT*'). The **ICSFT** and the United Nations' Security Council's resolution No.1373 requires the Japanese government to establish measures that (i) criminalize the provision and collection of funds for terrorists; (ii) provide for the forfeiture of terrorist funds and asset freezing in preparation for forfeiture; (iii) require financial institutions to report suspicious transactions associated with terrorist funds; (iv) require financial institutions to identify their customers; and (v) require financial institutions to maintain records on transactions. Japan has satisfied those requirements. In that connection:

- For (i), (ii) and (iii) mentioned above, Japanese legislation focused on terrorism-related money laundering. In 2002, Japan expanded the scope of its anti-money laundering efforts through the enactment of the *Act on Punishment of Providing Funds for Criminal Acts with Threatening the Public (Koushuutou Kyouhakumokutekino Hanzaikouinotameno Shikinno Teikyoutouno Shobatsuni kansuru Houritsu*; Law No. 67 of 2002, as amended, more commonly known as the Punishment of Providing Funds for Terrorism Law). This new law, which took effect on 2 July 2002, established the crime of terrorist financing. The **AOCL** proscribes money laundering in connection with the crime of terrorist financing.

- For (iv) and (v) above, the *Act on Customer Identification and Retention of Records on Transactions by Financial Institutions, Etc. (Kin-yuukikantouniyoru Kokyakutouno Hon-ninkakunintouni kansuru Houritsu*; Law No.32 of 2002, as amended; more commonly known as the Customer Identification Law (the *'CIL'*)), which was enacted in 2002 and became effective on 6 January 2003, obligates financial institutions to confirm the identities of their customers and keep records on their transactions. The **CIL** was amended in order to prevent fraudulent parties from deceiving victims into transferring money to bank accounts under false names and its title was changed to the *Act on Customer Identification and Retention of Records on Transactions by Financial Institutions and Restriction on Misuse of Bank Accounts (Kin-yuukikantouniyoru Kokyakutouno Honninkakuninntou oyobi Yokinkouzatouno Fuseinariyounoboushini kansuru Houritsu)* in 2004. This amendment does not directly affect anti money-laundering policies.

- For (iv) and (v) above, also, by the 2002 amendment to the **FEL**, banks and money exchangers operating in Japan may be penalized if they fail to try to obtain identification from customers in certain cases. The 2002 amendment provided the ability to exchange information on international terrorists among Japan governmental ministries. The 2004 amendment allowed the Government to take measures in enforcement only by prior cabinet council approval and an ex post facto Diet permit.

Both the 1991 **ADL** and the 1999 **AOCL** penalize activities related to money laundering, such as the concealment and receipt of illicit proceeds from crimes or illegal transactions respectively covered by these laws. They also impose an obligation on financial institutions to ascertain the identity of their customers in connection with certain types of transactions, and to report suspicious transactions to competent authorities. (In order to avoid duplication, the reporting obligation under the **ADL** was abolished upon the **AOCL** becoming effective.) Both the 2002 **CIL** and the 1949 **FEL** impose an obligation on financial institutions to ascertain the identity of their customers in connection with certain types of transactions, and to book and maintain records on transactions.

2 The Japan Financial Intelligence Office ('JAFIO')

2.1 Function as an intelligence center

Under the **AOCL**, the reports from the various financial institutions, both government and private, are ultimately forwarded to the Commissioner of the Financial Services Agency (the *'FSA'*, *Kin-yuuchou*). Procedurally, the various financial institutions file all suspicious transaction reports to the government agency or ministry which has jurisdiction over them (**AOCL** Art. 54, Para. 1). The supervising government entity then forwards these reports to the **FSA** Commissioner (**AOCL** Art. 54, Paras. 3&4 and Art. 55). The functions of the **FSA** Commissioner in connection with money laundering are delegated to *the Japan Financial Intelligence Office ('JAFIO') (Tokutei Kin-yuu Jouhoushitsu)* within the **FSA**.

2.2   Cooperation with law enforcement agencies

When suspicious transactions are reported to **JAFIO**, the **AOCL** requires **JAFIO** to review and analyze the reported information and then to provide such information to the various law enforcement authorities, such as the National Police Agency, the Public Prosecutors Office and the Securities and Exchange Surveillance Commission, for further action in cases where such information will assist in the investigation of criminal cases or violations of laws (**AOCL** Art. 56, Para. 1). Furthermore, **JAFIO** is authorized to provide such information to the relevant foreign institution, subject to confirmation of the Ministry of Justice and the Ministry of Foreign Affairs in certain circumstances (**AOCL** Art. 57, Paras. 1&4).

3   The Anti-Organized Crime Law ('THE AOCL')

3.1   General

The **AOCL** has two main aims: (i) to toughen the punishment of organized crime; and (ii) to restrict money laundering. In order to regulate money laundering, the **AOCL** provides for criminalization of money laundering acts, impositions of penalties, forfeiture of profits from crime, freezing of forfeited assets, and a 'suspicious transaction' reporting system, amongst other stipulations.

3.2   Dealings with crime proceeds

3.2.1   Crime proceeds

In general, crime proceeds (as that term is defined in the **AOCL**) means property derived from certain criminal acts, and include returns on investment of crime proceeds, as well as any other assets which have been indistinguishably commingled with crime proceeds.

3.2.2   Concealment of crime proceeds (AOCL Art. 10)

The concealment or disguise of crime proceeds is prohibited and may lead to imprisonment with labor for up to five years or a fine of up to ¥3 000 000, or both.

3.2.3   Receipt of crime proceeds (AOCL Art. 11)

In general, any person who knowingly receives crime proceeds may be imprisoned with manual labor for up to three years or fined up to ¥1 000 000, or both. To commit this crime, a person must knowingly receive crime proceeds. However, if a person receives crime proceeds and reports the matter to the police at once; the person will not be taken to have committed this crime.

3.2.4   Forfeit of crime proceeds or imposition of penalties

In general, crime proceeds are subject to forfeiture, and in the event that direct proceeds from crime have been converted to another form, penalties may be imposed in order to recover an equivalent value. Note that intangible assets such as monetary claims obtained by crime (but which are not crime proceeds) are also subject to forfeiture or penalty under the **AOCL**.

3.3 Suspicious transaction reporting system

3.3.1 General

Under Art. 54 of the **AOCL**, if a financial institution suspects that certain assets or funds are crime proceeds, that institution must report the suspicious transactions to the agency that has jurisdiction over it (in the case where such agency is the **FSA**, then to **JAFIO**). Financial institutions are not allowed to disclose to the parties involved that such a report has been or will be made (**AOCL** Art. 54, Para. 2). The agency receiving the reports is required to forward the same to **JAFIO**.

3.3.2 Relevant reporting institutions

The **AOCL** imposes reporting obligations concerning suspicious transactions on a wide range of Relevant Reporting Institutions which receive money from customers such as banks, trust banks, insurance companies (including foreign insurance companies), securities companies (including foreign securities companies), Japan Post, money-lenders, futures trading companies and investment trust management companies (**AOCL** Art. 54, Para. 1; *Cabinet Order Concerning Reporting of Suspicious Transactions* (*Utagawashii Torihikino Todokedeni kansuru seirei*; Cabinet Order No. 389 of 1999, as amended; '**COCRST**'), Art. 1, Paras. 1&2) (collectively, the 'Relevant Reporting Institutions' in this chapter).

3.3.3 Suspicious cases to be reported

As mentioned below, the **FSA** Guidelines set out lists of examples of typical 'suspicious transactions' that Relevant Reporting Institutions must report to the **FSA**. These lists are prepared respectively for depository financial institutions (this list also applies to finance companies as well as securities finance companies as a reference), insurance companies, securities companies and foreign securities companies (this list also applies to securities investment trust management companies, investment corporations and securities investment advisers).

The **AOCL** requires a Relevant Reporting Institution to file the reports mentioned above if it should reasonably suspect that the monies received by such Relevant Reporting Institutions in the course of its business are Crime Proceeds or if it should reasonably suspect that the other party to a transaction for such business of such financial institution or the like is committing an act constituting an offence against **AOCL** Art.10 or **ADL** Art. 6 (**AOCL** Art. 2, Paras. 2 to 7 and Art. 54, Para. 1). As the list of such important crimes is wide, encompassing homicide to violations of securities legislation, the reporting Relevant Reporting Institutions need not be overly concerned about the specific crime with which the suspicious transaction is concerned. Practically speaking, as long as the case falls under any of the examples set out in the **FSA** Guidelines, the financial institution must file a report with **JAFIO** unless the relevant transaction is clearly not concerned with any crime.

Other than discussed above, since September 2001, the **FSA** has requested that Relevant Reporting Institutions report transactions it should reasonably suspect are connected with the Taliban and those associated with the Taliban as transactions suspected to have relations with criminal activities.

3.3.4 Elements of the criteria for assessing whether a transaction is 'suspicious'

Whether an event is 'suspicious' should be judged with respect to the average knowledge and experiences in the relevant financial business industry and in consideration of various factors such as the usual transaction status with the relevant customer; mode of remittance, especially whether the amount or frequency of a relevant transaction or a remittance is unreasonably high in view of the relevant customer's occupation and business.

3.3.5 Reporting matters/form

The **AOCL** requires Relevant Reporting Institutions to prepare reports on suspicious transactions in accordance with the form on the website of the **FSA** (**AOCL** Art. 54, Para. 1; *Ordinance Concerning Manner of Reporting in Suspicious Transactions, Etc.* (*Utagawashii Torihikino Todokedenohouhoutouni kansuru meirei*; Office of Prime Minister and Ministry of Justice Joint Ordinance No. 1 of 1999), Art. 1 and Annexed Forms 1 to 4). Such reports must contain the following information:

(1) Name and address of the reporting financial institution.

(2) Date and place at which the reported suspicious transaction took place.

(3) Nature of the business of the reporting financial institution with which the reported suspicious transaction is concerned.

(4) Description of the property relating to the reported suspicious transaction.

(5) Name, trade name and address or location of the party who performed the reported suspicious transaction.

(6) Reasons for making a report on the reported suspicious transaction.

(**AOCL** Art. 54, Para. 1; **COCRST**, Art. 3, Para. 2).

The **AOCL** permits Relevant Reporting Institutions to file reports on electronic media. In such case, they must file, on submission of a floppy/optical disc, the report using the form on the website of the **FSA** (Annexed Form 5).

3.3.6 Sanctions for non-reporting

As stated above, the **AOCL** obligates the Relevant Reporting Institutions to report suspicious transactions to competent authorities including the **JAFIO**; however, it imposes no sanctions or penalties against institutions failing to comply with this obligation. Many legal analysts think that the Japanese legislators may have assumed that a financial institution operating in Japan would comply voluntarily to preserve its reputation and public image.

4 The Customer Identification Law (CIL)

4.1 Customer identification obligation in general

The **CIL** was established and took effect on 6 January 2003. The Japanese Diet says that the goals of the **CIL** include (a) to help the Japanese government enforce the **ICFST** in Japan, (b) to make the reporting of suspicious transactions related to terrorist funds and money laundering by financial institutions more effective, and (c) to promote the customer management system of financial institutions,. The Japanese Diet says that another purpose of the **CIL** is to prevent the provision of funds to terrorists and money laundering through financial institutions and that the **CIL** accomplishes these aims in general by issuing warnings and preventing bank counter transactions with nefarious purposes and by enabling investigative organizations to trace those funds effectively. In 2004, the Japanese Diet changed the **CIL**'s title to '*the Act on Customer Identification and Retention of Records on Transactions by Financial Institutions and Restriction on Misuse of Bank Accounts*'. In this revision, provisions regarding the prohibition of the sale and purchase of bank accounts were added to the **CIL** (**CIL** Art. 16-2). The additional provisions have the aim of preventing fraud crimes in which victims are deceived into transferring money to bank accounts using a false name, which has been recognized as a serious social problem since 2004.

4.2   Financial institutions subject to the customer identification obligation

The **CIL** imposes identification obligations in relation to certain transactions on a wide range of financial institutions which receive money from customers, such as banks (including foreign banks and trust banks), insurance companies (including foreign insurance companies), securities companies (including foreign securities companies), trust companies, money-lenders, futures trading companies and investment trust management companies (**CIL** Art. 2) (collectively, the 'CIL-Related Institutions' in this chapter).

4.3   Transactions requiring customer identification

4.3.1   Transactions requiring customer identification

The transactions (as defined by the Order on Customer Identification and Retention of Records on Transactions by Financial Institutions and Restriction on Misuse of Bank Accounts (the 'CIO') (*Kin-yuukikantouniyoru Kokyakutouno Honnninkakuninntou oyobi Yokinkouzatouno Fuseinariyounoboushini kansuru Houritsu Sekourei;* Cabinet Order No. 261 of 2002, Art. 3)) for which a CIL-Related Institution would be required under the **CIL** to obtain Customer Identification may be classified amongst three categories, being (i) the commencement of ongoing transactions between CIL-Related Institutions and customers; (ii) any non-ongoing transaction of more than ¥2 000 000; and (iii) when suspicious details are given as customers' **personal specific items** (as hereafter defined in Section 4.4.1). Type (i) includes the conclusion of a deposit contract; conclusion of a trust agreement; conclusion of a money loan and credit contract; and conclusion of a sale and purchase contract of a foreign means of payment, claimable rights or others (hereinafter referred to as the 'Transactions' in this chapter). Moreover, a CIL-Related Institution has been required under the **CIL** to obtain Customer Identification in the case of remittance in person in cash of more than ¥100 000 since January 2007 (this does not apply to the case of electronic fund transfer).

4.3.2   Transactions that do not require customer identification

The **CIL** does not require CIL-Related Institutions to obtain Customer Identification for transactions such as derivative transactions and brokerage, agency or proxies of derivative transactions.

That is those transactions are deemed under Japanese law to be in no danger of being used as a method of concealment or receipt of crime proceeds (CIO Art. 3).

4.3.3 Whether or not a transaction requires customer identification – FAQ

(a) For assignments of accounts receivable, Customer Identification is not needed.

(b) When CIL-Related Institutions conduct the sale and purchase or borrowing and lending of securities with each other, generally, both CIL-Related Institutions need to perform customer identification. However, in practice, most CIL-Related Institutions may be regarded as customers which have already been identified, as stated in Section 4.6 (CIO Act. 3, Para. 1, Items 9&10).

4.4 Customers to be identified and personal specific items in customer identification

4.4.1 General

When CIL-Related Institutions perform transactions in areas of its respective main business, the CIL-Related Institutions shall confirm details (the '**personal specific items**') prescribed in each item following, by means of viewing the driver's license of the customer or by other means (e.g. money exchange business for money exchanger) in Art. 2 of CIO (hereinafter referred to as the 'Financial Business') with the customers (defined in Section 4.4.3) prescribed in each following item (**CIL** Art. 3):

(1) Natural person: Name and address or place of residence and date of birth.

(2) Juridical person: Name and location of main office.

(3) The Japanese government, a local public body, a corporation or foundation without personality, etc.: Name and address or place of residence and date of birth of a natural person who is in charge of the Transactions (as that term is defined in the **CIL**).

The above information is regarded as a focal point because the person in charge (whether in category (1), (2), or (3)) may be an important clue in the tracing of funds related to terrorism and crimes.

As general rule, in relation to identification of a natural person and a person in charge, the CIL-Related Institutions should institute procedures of identification only at the beginning of the transactions. However, in relation to a corporation or foundation without personality, the CIL-Related Institutions should institute identification procedures on each change of a natural person in charge.

4.4.2 The Japanese government, a local public body, a corporation or foundation without personality

Because the true identity of the Japanese government and local public bodies are clear, the **CIL** does not request their identification.

Because a corporation or foundation without personality has no certification measures, the **CIL** does not request their identification. Foreign governments, foreign governmental organs, foreign local public bodies, foreign central banks or international organs with which Japan associates are treated the same as the Japanese government.

4.4.3 Customers – indirect customers to be identified

The CIL-Related Institutions need to identify beneficiaries of a trust (with a customer, hereinafter referred to as the 'Customers' in this chapter) as well as the trustor with some exceptions.

4.4.4 Whether customers are to be identified or not – FAQ

(a) When CIL-Related Institutions make a contract with a guarantor or receive a payment from a guarantor, Customer Identification for the said guarantor is not needed.

(b) When CIL-Related Institutions enter into a transaction with a subsidiary or a related company of the same group as the Financial Institution, each such subsidiary and related company requires Customer Identification because they have different judicial personalities.

4.5 Customer identification methods and documents for customer identification

4.5.1 General

Customer Identification methods are different for face-to-face identification and non face-to-face identification. In face-to-face identification, there are two methods, being (i) presentation of public certificate documents which may be obtained by the customer or representative themselves, such as a driver license, a health insurance certificate or a alien registration certificate; and (ii) presentation of public certificate documents which may be obtained by a third party, such as a residence certificate, and followed by the sending of the bank book or other document relating to the transaction with the said customer or a person in charge to an address of the customer mentioned in the said personal identification document by registered mail, *kakitomeyuubin*, or by mail of which a record is made of acceptance and delivery as a special mail system.

In non face-to-face identification such as by way of mail and over the Internet, there are also two methods, being (i) the receipt of public certificate documents which may be obtained by the customer or representative themselves, or its copy from the said customer, accompanied with the sending of documents relating to the transaction to an address of the customer mentioned in the said personal identification document or its copy by registered mail, etc. as a special mail system, etc.; and (ii) use of an electronic signature.

Natural person	Presentation of public certificate documents which may be obtained by the customer or representative themselves, such as a driver license	
	Presentation of public certificate documents which may be obtained by a third party, such as a residence certificate	Sending documents relating to the transaction to an address of the natural person mentioned in the said personal identification document or its copy, by registered mail, etc.

		Receipt of public certificate documents or their copies sent by the customer or representative	
Judicial person	Natural person in charge	Same as for natural persons	
	Judicial person	Presentation of the certification documents of the judicial person	
		Receipt of certification documents of the judicial person sent by the natural person in charge	Sending documents relating to the transaction to an address of the judicial person mentioned in the said personal identification document or its copy, by registered mail, etc.
Non Japanese Natural Person/Non Japanese Judicial person		Same as for natural persons. As the case may be, similar documents are permitted.	
Japanese government, etc.		Natural person in charge, same as for natural persons	

4.5.2   Certificate documents' period of validity for identification

Certification documents	Validity period
Certified copy of family register, residence certificate, seal registration certificate, certified copy of corporate register	So long as the stamped date of receipt or date of issue of the document is within six months before the day of their presentation or sending to the CIL-Related Institutions
Alien registration certificate, a health insurance certificate	So long as the documents are valid on the day of their presentation or sending to the CIL-Related Institutions.

4.6   Interactions with customers for whom personal identification has already been confirmed

If CIL-Related Institutions have already confirmed the personal identification of customers (meaning personal identification following the **CIL** or the **FEL** identification procedures) and keep a **personal identification record** (meaning the **personal identification record** following the **CIL** or the **FEL** identification procedures), the said CIL-Related Institutions may thereafter satisfy their Customer Identification obligations if:

(i) The CIL-Related Institutions are personally acquainted with a customer or a person in charge.

(ii) The customer presents a bank book, a seal registered to the CIL-Related Institutions, or a cash card.

(iii) The customer correctly provides a secret item such as a pass code, bank account number together with a customer's birthday, or the transaction status between the customer and Financial Institution.

4.7   Duty of making a personal identification record

Whenever CIL-Related Institutions confirm personal identification, the CIL-Related Institutions shall immediately make a record (hereinafter referred to as the '**personal identification record**' in this chapter). The **personal identification record** must include the items such as (i) the name of the person whose personal identification was confirmed, including other items which are needed to identify the said person; (ii) the name of the person who made the personal identification document, including other items which are needed to identify the said person; (iii) the date on which the personal identification document or its copy was presented or sent, the date when it was presented or sent; (iv) the date on which the personal identification was confirmed; and (v) the contents of the transaction in which the personal identification was confirmed, etc.

CIL-Related Institutions shall keep **personal identification records** for seven (7) years after concluding the specified exchange transaction or the day designated by the Ordinance of the Ministry of Finance. **Personal identification records** may take the form of a hard copy, electric record or micro film.

4.8   Duty of making a transaction record

Whenever CIL-Related Institutions enter into a transaction related to financial business, except for micro transactions such as money exchange under the amount equivalent to ¥2 000 000, funds transfer under the amount equivalent to ¥10 000 and transactions without money transfer, etc., the CIL-Related Institutions shall immediately make a record of such transaction (hereinafter referred to as the '**transaction record**' in this chapter) (**CIL** Art. 5). The transaction record must include the items such as (i) the items sufficient to identify the relevant counterparty; (ii) the date of the transaction; and (iii) the kind and amount of the transactions. Inner control activities within each Financial Institution, such as paying wages to its employees, are not considered to be transactions related to financial business.

CIL-Related Institutions shall keep transaction records for seven (7) years after concluding the specified transaction or after the day designated by the Ordinance of the Ministry of Finance. **Personal identification records** may take the form of a hard copy, electric record or micro film.

4.9   Immunity of financial institutions

When the customers or a natural person in charge who intends to perform a specified exchange transaction refuses to comply with a request to confirm personal identification, the CIL-Related Institutions have the right to refuse to perform their duty related to the said specified exchange transaction until the said customer or natural person in charge complies (**CIL** Art. 6). To 'refuse to comply with a request' includes (but is not limited to) the aggressive indication of an intention to not comply with the personal identification procedure. This intention may be indicated by act or omission. However, for example, if the CIL-Related Institutions have no contact with a customer, this will mean that the CIL-Related Institutions cannot confirm the customer's intention and therefore this provision will probably not apply to the financial institution in that circumstance.

4.10 Supervision, inspection, and corrective measures for personal identification and the personal identification record

Any administrative government agency may request CIL-Related Institutions to report and file documents on their business (**CIL** Art. 7). Also, administrative government agencies may inspect CIL-Related Institutions.

When an administrative government agency finds that a Financial Institution breached its duty to create and maintain **personal identification records** with regard to transactions, that administrative government agency has the authority to issue a correction order to the said financial institution (**CIL** Art. 9).

4.11 Sanctions

4.11.1 Sanctions on financial institutions for breach of the customer identification obligation

Any person (such as an officer or an employee of the CIL-Related Institutions) who breaches a corrective order stated in Section 4.10 shall be liable to penal servitude for a term not exceeding two years, to a fine not exceeding ¥3 000 000, or both (**CIL** Art. 14). Any person who breaches a corrective order exhibiting uncooperative attitudes to reporting and inspection as specified by Art. 7 and Art. 8, Para. 1 of the **CIL** shall be liable to penal servitude for a term not exceeding one year, to a fine not exceeding ¥3 000 000, or both (**CIL** Art. 15). When a representative of a juridical person, an agent, an employee, or other worker of a juridical person commits any offense mentioned in Arts. 14 and 15 in regard to the business of the juridical person, the juridical person shall be liable for a fine not exceeding ¥300 000 000 (in the case of breach of Art. 14) or ¥2 000 000 (in the case of breach of Art. 15), in addition to the punishment of the offender himself/herself (**CIL** Art. 17, Items 1&2).

CIL-Related Institutions are regarded as performing their duties satisfactorily as long as they judge whether information provided by customers, including documents and statements, is true or false using the care required in normal financial transactions. Therefore, if a normal level of care is taken, even if the CIL-Related Institutions fail to detect the provision of false information by a customer, they will not necessarily be considered to have failed their duties regarding customer identification.

4.11.2 Sanction on customers

Any person providing false information on identification for the purpose of concealing **personal specific items** shall be liable for a fine not exceeding ¥500 000 (**CIL** Art. 16).

5 The Foreign Exchange and Foreign Trade Law ('THE FEL')

5.1 General

For the purpose of preventing money laundering, the **FEL** has two main contents, i.e. to oblige the banks (defined in Section 5.2 below) to obtain an approval from a competent minister before they make payments or perform capital transactions (defined in Section 5.2 below) related to terrorism, and to oblige the FEL-Related Institutions (defined in Section 5.5 below) to perform personal identification checks before they make contracts related to capital transactions, etc.

5.2 Payments and capital transactions requiring approval

Any resident or non-resident who wishes to make a payment from Japan to a foreign country, to a prohibited person specified by a competent minister (e.g. a terrorist), and any resident who wishes to make a payment to or receive a receipt from a non-resident who is a prohibited person specified by a competent minister is required to obtain permission from the competent minister (**FEL** Art. 16 and *the Foreign Exchange Order* (the 'FEO') (*Gaikokukawaserei;* Cabinet Order No. 260 of 1980, Art. 6)).

If the competent minister deems that a person, who has made a payment or received a receipt subject to the said requirement without obtaining the said permission will possibility make a payment or receive a receipt of the same kind again without obtaining the said permission, the Minister may, for a term of one year or shorter if the Minister determines, prohibit the said person, or impose, as prescribed by a cabinet order, on the person, a requirement to obtain a permission for, all or part of payments from Japan to a foreign country (excluding those made through foreign exchange transactions by banks (as defined in Art. 2, Para. 1 of *the Bank Law (Ginkouhou)* (Law 59. 1981)), Japan Post and certain other financial institutions (the 'Banks' in this chapter) or payments and receipts made between a resident and non-resident (excluding those made through foreign exchange transactions by banks).

Any resident or non-resident who wishes to enter into a capital transaction defined by Art. 20 of **FEL** (hereinafter the 'Capital Transactions') with a prohibited person specified by a competent minister (e.g. a terrorist) needs to obtain a permission from the competent minister.

5.3 Obligation of legality confirmation

A bank shall not enter into a foreign exchange transaction with a customer for payment or receipt unless it confirms either that the said payment or receipt is not any of the following items or (if the said payment or receipt is deemed to be any one of them) that the said customer obtains an approval for the said payment or receipt, (**FEL** Art. 17).

(a) Payment or receipt for which a requirement to obtain a permission is imposed by the Minister (**FEL** Art. 16).

(b) Payment or receipt resulting from one of the capital transactions for which requirement to obtain a permission is imposed by the Minister (**FEL** Art. 21).

(c) As follows (FEO Art. 7):

　　(1) Loan or guarantee transactions made as those being directly related to export or import of goods, or acts related to transfer of a right of mining, industrial property rights or the like

for which requirement to obtain a permission is imposed by the Minister (**FEL** Art. 24, Paras. 1&2).

(2) Service transactions performed by a resident for a non-resident and transactions concerning the sales and purchases of goods involving the movement of goods between foreign countries for which the Minister imposes a requirement to obtain a permission (**FEL** Art. 25, Para. 4).

(3) Any direct domestic investment, such as acquisition of any company's stock or share, transfer of stock or share of any company other than listed companies, etc. for which the Minister imposes a requirement to give notification (**FEL** Art. 26, Para. 2).

(4) Importation of goods with respect to which Art. 52 of the **FEL** imposes an obligation to obtain an approval.

5.4 Customer identification obligation in general (FEL Arts. 18 & 22-2)

As of 6 January 2003, the **FEL** was amended; the Japanese Diet says that the goals of such amendment are to create a more effective approval system for suspicious transactions related to terrorist funds and to take substantial measures to freeze assets in accordance with the **ICFST**. In this revision to the **FEL**, a sanction for breach of the customer identification obligations was introduced and the scope of the transactions under the customer identification obligations was enlarged, including capital transactions.

5.5 Financial institutions subject to the customer identification obligation

Under the **FEL**, whether a given person subject to the Customer Identification Obligations depends on the type of the transaction. Concerning the exchange transactions concerning a payment or receipt with a non-resident, or a payment to a foreign country from Japan, only the banks are required to satisfy the Customer Identification Obligation. However, concerning the conclusion of contracts related to capital transactions and the conclusion of a deposit contract; conclusion of a trust agreement; conclusion of a money loan and credit contract; and conclusion of a sale and purchase contract of a foreign means of payment, claimable rights, etc. (FEO Art. 11-5) in addition to the banks, a certain range of financial institutions which receive money from customers, i.e., insurance companies (including foreign insurance companies), securities companies (including foreign securities companies), trust companies (including foreign trust companies), futures trading companies (the 'FEL-Related Institutions' in this chapter) (**FEL** Art. 22-2) are required to satisfy the Customer Identification Obligation. Also, a person who conducts foreign money exchange business (which means to sell and purchase foreign currencies or travelers checks as a business) shall owe the same obligation of customer identification as the FEL-Related Institutions.

5.6 Transactions to be accompanied by customer identification

5.6.1 Transactions specified by FEL Art. 18 and FEO Art. 7

The transactions specified by **FEL** Art. 18 are exchange transactions (excluding the payment or receipt of small amounts (under the amount equivalent to ¥2 000 000 of payments or receipts)).

5.6.2   Transactions specified by FEL Art. 22-2 and FEO Art. 11-5

Transactions (as defined by FEO Art. 11-5) for which a bank or a FEL-Related Institution would be required under the **FEL** to obtain customer identification may be classified amongst three categories, being the same as those listed under the **CIL** and summarized in Section 4.3.1 above (for the purposes of the **FEL**, the matters set forth in Section 4.3.1 shall apply for this Section 5.6.2). Type (i) includes the conclusion of a deposit contract between a resident and a non-resident; conclusion of a trust agreement between a resident and a non-resident; conclusion of a money loan and credit contract between a resident and a non-resident; and conclusion of a sale and purchase contract of a foreign means of payment, claimable rights between a resident and a non-resident or others.

5.6.3   Transactions specified by FEL Art. 22-3

If a person, who conducts foreign money exchange business (meaning to sell and purchase foreign currencies or travelers checks as a business), performs money exchange (excluding exchanges under the amount equivalent to ¥2 000 000) with a customer, that person is subject to the Customer Identification Obligation (FEO Art. 11-6).

5.7   Customers to be identified and personal specific items in customer identification

5.7.1   General

The **FEL** requires FEL-Related Institutions to confirm details by means of viewing the driver's license of the customer or by other means, when the FEL-Related Institutions perform exchange transactions (excluding payments or receipts under the amount equivalent to ¥2 000 000) concerning a payment or receipt with a non-resident, or a payment to a foreign country from Japan with the customer prescribed in each of the items set out in section 4.4.1 above (**FEL** Art. 18, Paras. 1&2). The particular **personal specific items** which need to be confirmed for different types of customers in these circumstances are the same as those listed under Section 4.4.1 above. Also, general comments made in Section 4.4.1 are equally applicable to this section.

5.7.2   Japanese government, a local public body, a corporation or foundation without judicial personality

For identification of the Japanese government, local public bodies and corporations or foundations without judicial personality, the **FEL** and relevant related regulations are in substance equivalent to those described in Section 4.4.2 above.

5.7.3   Customers – indirect customers to be identified

The governing regulation on this point is FEO Art. 11-4. As its provisions are effectively equivalent to those summarized in Section 4.4.3 above, please refer in general to the comments in that section.

5.8 Interactions with a customer for whom personal identification has already been confirmed

This provision applies only to the transactions specified as type (i) stated Section 5.6.2.

If FEL-Related Institutions have already confirmed the personal identification of a customer (meaning personal identification following the **CIL** or the **FEL** identification procedures and keep a **personal identification record** (meaning the **personal identification record** following the **CIL** or the **FEL** identification procedures), the said FEL-Related Institutions are thereafter exempt from the customer identification obligation. Other exemption cases are defined by Art. 11-5, Para. 2 of the FEO.

5.9 Duty of making a personal identification record

All transactions specified in 5.3 are subject to the same regulation on this point. The governing regulation on this point is **FEL** Art. 18-3. As its provisions are effectively equivalent to those summarized in Section 4.8 above, please refer in general to the comments in that section.

5.10 Immunity of financial institutions

All transactions specified in 5.3 are subject to the same regulation on this point. The governing regulation on this point is **FEL** Art. 18-2. As its provisions are effectively equivalent to those summarized in Section 4.9 above, please refer in general to the comments in that section.

5.11 Corrective measures for personal identification and the personal identification record

All transactions specified in 5.3 are subject to the same regulation on this point. The governing regulation on this point is **FEL** Art. 18-4. As its provisions are effectively equivalent to those summarized in Section 4.9 above, please refer in general to the comments in that section.

5.12 Sanctions

5.12.1 Sanctions on financial institutions that breach the customer identification obligation

In general, banks and FEL-Related Institutions that breach their customer identification obligations are subject to sanctions under the **FEL** similar to those specified under Art. 14 of the **CIL**. Additionally, the sanctions relating to breach by persons related to a Financial Institution as specified by Art. 17 of the **CIL** are similarly stipulated by the **FEL**. Therefore, please see Section 4.11.1 for general comments and a discussion of the sanctions specified by these articles.

5.12.2 Sanction on financial institutions for payment, receipt, capital transactions without approval

Any person (such as an employee of a bank) who makes a payment, receive funds, or enter into a capital transaction without an approval breach their obligations under Art. 16, Paras. 1–3 and Art. 21, Paras. 1–2 of the **FEL** and shall be liable to penal servitude for a term not exceeding three years, or to a fine not exceeding ¥1 000 000 (when three times the amount of the subject matter of contravention exceeds ¥1 000 000, the fine shall not exceed the three-times amount), or both (**FEL** Art. 70, Items 3&7). When a representative of a juridical person, an agent, an employee, or other worker of a juridical person commits any offense mentioned in Art. 70 of the **FEL** in regard to the business of the juridical person, the juridical person shall be liable for a fine not exceeding ¥3 000 000, in addition to the punishment of the offender himself/herself (**FEL** Art. 72, Para. 1).

5.12.3   Sanction on customers

Any person providing false information on identification for the purpose of concealing **personal specific items** shall be liable for a fine not exceeding ¥500 000 (FEL Art. 71-2).

6   International cooperation

6.1   JAFIO's information sharing system with other countries' FIUs

JAFIO has recently signed bilateral information exchange agreements regarding suspicious transactions connected with money laundering or terrorist financing with the US, the UK, Belgium, Canada, Australia, Korea, Hong Kong, Thailand, Indonesia, and Singapore. These signed agreements will foster the exchange of financial intelligence and will enhance the information available to Japanese law enforcement and intelligence agencies. For example, in addition to the formal relationships set forth in those agreements, it is not unreasonable to expect that the Japanese governments informal working relationships and connections with the relevant authorities in those other countries would improve as a result of those agreements.

6.2   International assistance

The government may assist by acting on international legal assistance requests by foreign governments regarding the enforcement of forfeitures and penalty collections ordered by final adjudication of a foreign court and the freezing of assets for their enforcement under certain circumstances (**AOCL** Art. 59). In case of requested assistance relating to enforcement of forfeiture and penalty collection, prior examination by court, the Japanese prosecutor must claim that the requirements of the article 62 are satisfied (**AOCL** Art. 62)

7   The direction of anti-money laundering regulations reforms

7.1   The schedule of establishment of the ACPTPC

In light of the current domestic status of circulation of profits related to crimes including terrorism funds and the necessity of strengthening Japan's anti-money laundering measures based on the Forty Recommendations of FATF, the Japanese Government will establish *'the Act Concerning Prevention of Transferring Profits related to Crimes' (Hanzainiyoru Shuuekino Itenboushini kansuru Houritsu;* the '*ACPTPC*'). The **ACPTPC** will be established based on the contents of the **CIL** and Chapter V of the **AOCL**, i.e., the provisions concerning the customer identification and the suspicious transaction reporting system. The **ACPTPC** is scheduled to be discussed in the Japanese Diet from early spring of 2007. On behalf of the **FSA**, the National Police Agency will be in charge of the **JAFIO** under the **ACPTPC**.

7.2 Enlarging the scope of businesses subject to customer identification and reporting obligations

The **ACPTPC** will have the discretion to enlarge the scope of businesses subject to obligations of customer identification and reporting of suspicious transactions, with the power to add non-financial businesses such as dealers in precious stones, dealers in precious metals, real estate agents, credit card businesses, finance lease businesses, post-office box agencies, and telephone reception agencies, in addition to financial institutions under the **CIL** and Chapter 5 (Art. 54–58) of the **AOCL**. Among the abovementioned professions, lawyers oppose that enlargement. Although the initial bill of the **ACPTPC** contained five professions such as lawyers and public tax accountants, those professions were exempted from certain obligations in the **ACPTPC** which was finally submitted to the Diet.

Abbreviations

ACPTPC	The Act Concerning Prevention of Transferring Profits related to Crimes
ADL	The Anti-Drug Law
AOCL	The Anti-Organized Crime Law
CIL	The Customer Identification Law
CIO	The Order on Customer Identification and Retention of Records on Transactions by Financial Institutions and Restriction on Misuse of Bank Accounts
COCRST	Cabinet Order Concerning Reporting of Suspicious Transactions
FSA	The Financial Services Agency
FEL	The Foreign Exchange and Foreign Trade Law
FEO	The Foreign Exchange Order
ICFST	The International Convention for the Suppression of the Financing of Terrorism
JAFIO	The Japan Financial Intelligence Office

Bibliography

Bank of Japan: http://www.fsa.go.jp/fiu/fiue.html.

Financial Action Task Force ('FATF'): http://www.fatf-gafi.org/pages/0,2966,en_32250379_32235720_1_1_1_1_1,00.html.

Financial Services Agency ('FSA'): http://www.fsa.go.jp/en/index.html.

Headquarters' Decision for the Promotion of Measures Against Transnational Organized Crime and Other Relative Issues and International Terrorism: http://www.kantei.go.jp/foreign/policy/index/sosikihanzai/index_e.html.

Japan Financial Intelligence Office ('JAFIO'): http://www.fsa.go.jp/fiu/fiue.html.

Ministry of Economy, Trade and Industry ('METI'): http://www.meti.go.jp/english/index.html.

Ministry of Finance ('MOF'): http://www.mof.go.jp/english/index.htm.

National Police Agency: http://www.npa.go.jp/english/index.htm.

Wolfsberg Standards: http://www.wolfsberg-principles.com/translations-japanese.html.

Donna Li is a partner at AllBright Law Offices, which is the largest law firm in Shanghai, China. Ms Li received her J.D. degree from Albany Law School of Union University, her M.A. degree from University of Notre Dame, and her B.A. degree from Beijing International Studies University. Ms Li is admitted in the State of New York. Prior to joining AllBright Law Offices, she worked in the New York offices of Kaye Scholer LLP as a corporate associate and Pillsbury Winthrop LLP as a finance associate, both of which are large American law firms. Ms Li has broad experience in the areas of merger and acquisition, banking, corporate and finance laws, with a focus on international business transactions. She advises multinational corporations on their investments, operations, legal compliance and employment issues in China. She also advises Chinese companies and entrepreneurs on their business activities in the USA and Hong Kong. She has represented many US, European, Japanese and Chinese clients from various industries in a wide range of practice areas, including banking, finance, joint venture, wholly owned foreign enterprise, merger and acquisition, regulatory and compliance matter, trademark and copyright, licensing, leasing, trade, employment, tax, and real estate. Ms Li is listed in the special millennium edition of *Who's Who in American Law* published by Marquis, and in *The Asia Pacific Legal 500* consecutively since 2002 as one of the leading banking lawyers in China.

Gu Xiao Rong is the Director of Law Institute of Shanghai Academy of Social Sciences and Deputy Director of Shanghai Law Society. Currently Mr Gu is also serving as a member of Shanghai Municipal People's Congress and a councilor of China Law Society. Mr Gu has extensive legal research experience including Chinese finance law, securities law, company law and criminal law, and is the author of various publications. He supervises candidates of Ph.D. in law at China People's University, East China University of Politics and Law and Shanghai Academy of Social Sciences.

Organization's profile

Institute of Law, Shanghai Academy of Social Sciences was established in 1958, aimed at doing research on law and its branch sciences, seeking to solve major theoretical and practical issues concerning *China*'s legislation. The *Institute* has accomplished many projects, which have won good academic and social assessment. The current research projects of the *Institute* include *Internationalization of Punishment Regime on Financial*. Presently, the *Institute* has senior staff of 15 persons, 6 doctors, and 14 bachelors. The *Institute* is licensed to grant bachelor and doctor degrees. To the year of 2003, the *Institute* published 200 books and over 1750 papers and research reports.

China

Donna Li

Partner

AllBright Law Offices
Citigroup Tower, 14/F
33 Hua Yuan Shi Qiao Road,
Pudong New Area
Shanghai, P.R. China 200120

Tel +8621 61059000
Fax +8621 61059100
donnali@allbrightlaw.com;
www.allbrightlaw.com

Gu Xiao Rong

Director

Institute of Law
Shanghai Academy of Social
Sciences
gxr@sass.org.cn

Anti-Money Laundering: International Law and Practice.
Edited by W.H. Muller, C.H. Kälin and J.G. Goldsworth
© 2007 John Wiley & Sons, Ltd

Contents – China

1 Introduction

In recent years, money laundering in *China* has been rampant. 'Dirty money' from abroad has come into *China* for laundering under the cloak of investment, lawless gains have flowed out of the country via illegal private banks, and corrupt embezzlers have taken advantage of various channels for laundering and transferring illicit money. The *International Monetary Fund* has estimated that the annual amount of dirty money laundered in *China* is up to RMB200–300 billion. The money laundering situation is very severe.

As an important member of the *United Nations*, *China* is actively involved in controlling money laundering through international cooperation and has adopted effective measures on legal, systemic and organizational levels.

2 The primary anti-money laundering legal system

China is a member of the *United Nations Anti-Drug Treaties*, the *United Nations Convention against Transnational Organized Crime*, the *United Nations Convention against Corruption*, as well as other international conventions. Following international guidelines, *China* has established anti-money laundering legal systems that can be divided into three aspects: **laws, rules, and regulations**.

2.1 Laws

Article 191 of the current **Criminal Law of the PRC (***中华人民共和国刑法***)** adopted in 1997 provides for the crime of money laundering. In December 2001, the *Standing Committee of National People's Congress* (*SCNPC;* 全国人大常委会) amended the **predicate offences** for money laundering to include smuggling, drug crimes, **organized crimes by criminal syndicates**, and **terrorist activities**.

Article 191 of the *Criminal Law of the PRC* was amended to be: '*Whoever, while clearly knowing that the funds are proceeds or gains illegally obtained from **drug crimes, organized crimes by criminal syndicates, terrorist activities, or smuggling**, commits any of the following acts in order to cover up or conceal the source or nature of the funds shall, in addition to being confiscated of the said proceeds and gains, be subject to fixed-term imprisonment of no more than five years or criminal detention, and shall be fined with no less than 5% but no more than 20% of the amount of money laundered in addition to the above punishments or separately; if the circumstances are serious, he shall be subject to fixed-term imprisonment of no less than five years but no more than ten years, and shall also be fined with no less than 5% but no more than 20% of the amount of money laundered:*

(i) *providing fund accounts;*

(ii) *helping exchange property into cash or any financially negotiable instruments;*

(iii) *helping transfer capital through transferring accounts or any other form of settlement;*

(iv) *helping remit funds outside of the territory of China;*

(v) *covering up or concealing by any other means the source or nature of the illegally obtained proceeds and gains.*

Where an entity commits the crime as in the preceding paragraph, it shall be fined, and any person who is directly in charge and any other person who is directly responsible for the crime shall be subject to fixed-term imprisonment of no more than five years or criminal detention; if the circumstances are serious, any of them shall be subject to fixed-term imprisonment of no less than five years but no more than ten years.'

Section 10, Article 4 of the *Amendment to the Law of the PRC on the People's Bank of China (中国人民银行法修正案)* (December 2003) provides that the **People's Bank of China (PBOC; 中国人民银行)** will be responsible for '*directing and planning the anti-money laundering by financial institutions as well as capital monitoring*'.

In October 2006, *SCNPC* adopted the *Anti-Money Laundering Law of the PRC*. The *Law* provides for such issues as preventing and monitoring money laundering and preventing its predicate offences, obligations of anti-money laundering by financial institutions and specific non-financial institutions, investigation procedures for anti-money laundering, and international cooperation. In addition, *SCNPC* has adopted the *Sixth Amendment to the Criminal Law of the PRC (中华人民共和国刑法修正案(六))*, which expands the scope of predicate offences for money laundering to include **corruption and bribery, financial fraud, and crimes destroying financial administration order**.

2.2   Rules

Currently, there are administrative rules in *China* that are related to anti-money laundering, such as the *Provisions on the Real Name of Individual Deposit Account (个人存款帐户实名制规定)*, promulgated by the *State Council (国务院)* with Order No. 285 on 20 March 2000. Prior to issuance of such rules, any person could open a bank account under a false name and hide his/her identity.

2.3   Regulations

In January 2003, the **PBOC**, as the central bank of the *PRC*, promulgated three regulations on anti-money laundering: *Regulations for Anti-Money Laundering by Financial Institutions (金融机构反洗钱规定)*, *Administrative Measures for the Reporting of Large-Value and Suspicious RMB Payment Transactions (人民币大额和可疑支付交易报告管理办法)*, and *Administrative Measures for the Reporting by Financial Institutions of Large-Value and Suspicious Foreign Exchange Transactions (金融机构大额和可疑外汇资金交易报告管理办法)* (collectively referred to as the *One Regulation and Two Measures*). Prior to the promulgation of the *One Regulation and Two Measures*, the government authorities in charge had also adopted the following regulations related to money laundering:

- *Circular of Administration on Large-Value Cash Payment (关于大额现金支付管理的通知)* by the *PBOC* in August 1997.

- *Circular of Core Principles of Effective Bank Monitoring (有效银行监管的核心原则的通知)* by the *PBOC* in March 1998.

- *Implementing Rules for the Regulations of the PRC on Administration of Foreign-Funded Financial Institutions (中华人民共和国外资金融机构管理条例实施细则)*, originally by the *PBOC* in January 2002, then replaced by the China Banking Regulatory Commission in July 2004, respectively.

- *Guidelines on Internal Control of Commercial Banks (商业银行内部控制指引)* by the *PBOC* in September 2002.

- *Guidelines on Supervision of Commercial Banks' Offices Abroad (商业银行境外机构监管指引)* by the *PBOC* in August 2001.

- *Supplementary Circular of Relevant Issues on Investment by Domestic Residents in Domestic Listed Stock Held by Foreign Investors (关于境内居民投资境内上市外资股有关问题的补充通知)* by the **State Administration of Foreign Exchange (SAFE; 国家外汇管理局)** in February 2001.

- *Circular on Set-up of Case Transfer System and Strengthening of Work Cooperation (关于建立案件移送制度和加强工作协作配合的通知)* by the *State Auditing Administration (国家审计署)* and the *Ministry of Public Security (国家公安部)* in April 2000.

- *Circular of Interim Measures for Administration on Carrying Foreign Exchange Into and Out of the PRC Territory (携带外汇现钞出入境管理暂行办法)* by *SAFE* and the *General Administration of Customs (国家海关总署)* in August 2003.

In addition, the *PBOC* also consecutively promulgated the *Measures on Administration of RMB Bank Settlement Account (人民币银行结算帐户管理办法)*, the *Measures on Administration of Bank Cards Business (银行卡业务管理办法)*, the *Measures on Settlement by Domestic Letter of Credit (国内信用证结算办法)*, the *Interim Regulations on Cash Management(现金管理暂行条例)*, the *Provisions on Administration of RMB Deposit by Entities (人民币单位存款管理规定)*, etc.

The above regulations provide for measures preventing money laundering mainly from the following aspects: (i) control on large-value cash transactions; (ii) control on foreign exchange transactions, carrying or remitting money into or out of the *PRC*; (iii) report on large-value payment transactions; (iv) account management system; (v) administration on payment system; (vi) internal control system; etc. The operational practice of the above regulations is a good start for the *PBOC* to implement the *One Regulation and Two Measures* in 2003.

3   Operational framework for anti-money laundering

Presently in *China*, the *PBOC*, the *Ministry of Public Security*, the *SAFE* and financial institutions have formed an operational framework and mechanism for anti-money laundering.

3.1   Anti-Money Laundering Bureau

In September 2001, the *PBOC* set up the *Team for Anti-Money Laundering (反洗钱工作领导小组)*, which directs and plans the work for anti-money laundering within the financial industry in *China*. In July 2002, the *PBOC* established the *Anti-Money Laundering Office (反洗钱工作处)* and the *Payment Transaction Monitoring Office (支付交易监测处)*, which are responsible for detailing work for anti-money laundering, formulating anti-money laundering regulations in financial industry, and promulgating relevant regulations and measures.

In September 2003, the *PBOC* formally established an *Anti-Money Laundering Bureau (反洗钱局)* in *China* pursuant to the authorization of the *Circular of Opinions on Adjustment of Main Functional Internal Bodies and Personnel Administration of PBOC (关于中国人民银行主要职责内设机*

构和人员编制调整意见的通知), which was issued by the *Office of Committee of Central Government Bodies Administration (中央编制委员会办公室)*. In addition, the function of organizing and coordinating anti-money laundering work originally assumed by the *Ministry of Public Security* was transferred to the *PBOC*, and thus made it *China*'s primary authority in charge of anti-money laundering. The main responsibilities of the *Anti-Money Laundering Bureau* are as follows:

- *organizing and coordinating anti-money laundering measures by the state;*

- *studying and formulating anti-money laundering plans and policies of financial institutions;*

- *conducting **international cooperation** and exchange on anti-money laundering;*

- *collecting and tracing information on suspicious payment transactions in RMB and foreign exchange provided by various governmental departments; and*

- *transferring to judicial authorities any transaction involved in crime and assisting judicial authorities in investigation.*

3.2   China Anti-Money Laundering Monitoring and Analysis Center

In the first half of 2004, a specialized anti-money laundering intelligence department of *China*, namely the *China Anti-Money Laundering Monitoring and Analysis Center (**CAMLMAC**; 中国反洗钱监测分析中心)*, was established with the approval of the central government. The *Center* is affiliated with the *PBOC*, and its main responsibilities are collecting information on large-amount and suspicious transactions, clearing up and analyzing transaction information, providing analysis results to relevant judicial authorities, and engaging in intelligence exchange.

3.3   Focus of Anti-Money Laundering Bureau and the CAMLMAC

The relationship between the *CAMLMAC* and the *Anti-Money Laundering Bureau* of the *PBOC* is that the *Anti-Money Laundering Bureau* is an internal administrative body of the *PBOC*, while the *CAMLMAC* is an institution directly affiliated with the *PBOC*. Functionally, the *CAMLMAC* is an intelligence institution specializing in providing intelligence and information, while the *Anti-Money Laundering Bureau* is responsible for enforcing *China*'s anti-money laundering policies based on the intelligence provided by the *CAMLMAC*.

3.4   SAFE

The *SAFE* is responsible for formulating standards and rules for reporting large-amount and suspicious foreign exchange transactions, as well as for providing relevant supervision and administration. In March 2003, the *SAFE* set up an anti-money laundering office under its administration and inspection department for the purposes of supervising and controlling cross border money laundering activities. It is responsible for collecting, sifting, screening, and analyzing large-amount and suspicious money transfer data reported by banks, and reporting any suspicious foreign exchange transactions to the *SAFE* for inspection after primary examination.

3.5   Anti-money laundering obligation of commercial banks

Presently, Chinese commercial banks also set up their own anti-money laundering divisions that are responsible for reporting large-amount and suspicious foreign exchange transactions.

Commercial banks and relevant financial institutions are required to know their customers and report large-amount and suspicious payment transactions to the supervisory department of the *PBOC*, as well as assist the *PBOC*, the *Ministry of Public Security*, and the judicial authorities in investigating crimes involving money laundering.

3.6 Ministry of Public Security

In April 2002, the *Ministry of Public Security* set up its money laundering crime investigation department under its economic crime investigation bureau. This department is in charge of investigating money laundering activities reported by banks and the *SAFE*.

4 International cooperation on anti-money laundering

The Chinese government has actively participated in international cooperation against money laundering. In addition to being a member of the *United Nations Anti-Drug Treaties*, the *United Nations Convention against Transnational Organized Crime*, the *United Nations Convention against Corruption*, as well as other important international treaties, *China* has put forth its best efforts in participating in the *Financial Action Task Force on Money Laundering (FATF)*, the *Anti-Money Laundering Team of the Asia-Pacific Region*, and other relevant international organizations.

From 2001 to the end of 2002, relevant Chinese authorities assisted foreign police from 17 countries and regions in investigating more than 70 criminal cases involving money laundering.

After the 11 September 2001 terrorist attack on the *United States of America*, the *PBOC* sent lists of bank accounts of several suspicious terrorist organizations and their members to all banks in *China* pursuant to *Resolution No. 1373* of the *United Nations* and as per the request of the *US* government. The *PBOC* required banks to pay close attention to and carefully examine these accounts, and report the results to the *United Nations* and the *United States* immediately. *China*'s cooperation won praise from world anti-terrorist and anti-money laundering organizations.

China also entered into more than **70 police cooperation agreements** and memoranda of understanding against crime with dozens of countries, and signed **extradition agreements with over 20 countries**. From the establishment of the economic crime investigation bureau of *Ministry of Public Security* in 1998 through the first half of 2004, *China* successfully caught more than 230 persons, approximately 1/3 of whom were escaped criminals from over 30 countries and regions in *Europe*, *North America*, *South America*, *Australia*, *South-East Asia*, *Russia*, etc. Among those criminals were corrupt embezzlers, smugglers, and drug trade criminals who took part in money laundering.

China participated in the *First General Meeting of the Eurasian Group Against Money Laundering and Terrorism Financing (EAG)* held in *Moscow*, *Russia* on 8 December 2004. In the General Meeting, members discussed the internal institution establishment, listened to the report on anti-money laundering and terrorism financing by the *World Bank*, and adopted the work plan of 2005. This entails that the *EAG* would enter into the actual operational stage with respect to cooperation in anti-money laundering and anti-terrorism financing. It also approved the focus for 2005, which was as follows: (i) procuring members to promote relevant standards relating to anti-money laundering and anti-terrorism financing; (ii) formulating and implementing common actions and measures within the authority of financial intelligence organizations; (iii) evaluating effectiveness of measures relating to anti-money laundering and anti-terrorism financing; (iv) coordinating with relevant international organizations, teams, or countries in respect of the cooperation plan; (v) analyzing the development of money laundering and terrorism financing; and (vi) sharing their relevant experience in anti-money laundering and anti-terrorism financing.

Despite the achievement on international cooperation, there are still a lot of improvements to be made on anti-money laundering, Such improvement will be discussed in details in Section 5.4.1.

5 Further issues and measures

5.1 Improving the criminal legislation on predicate offences for money laundering

With respect to the seven categories of predicate offences for money laundering provided for in the *Criminal Law of PRC*, namely, drug trade, organized crimes by criminal syndicates, terrorist activities, smuggling, corruption and bribery, financial fraud, and crimes destroying financial administration order, currently in China, there is discussion as to whether these should be further expanded. There are mainly three opinions among the academia, legislators and practitioners, which are as follows:

(i) The predicate offences for money laundering should be expanded to apply to all crimes that may produce yields, as provided in Paragraph 1, Article 6 of the *United Nations Convention against Transnational Organized Crime (Convention)*, which states that the precondition for money laundering crime is '*knowing clearly that certain assets or property is obtained from crime, . . .*'.

(ii) The predicate offences for money laundering should include embezzlement, and tax and foreign exchange fraud in export in addition to the present offences.

(iii) The predicate offences for money laundering may not be expanded until it is necessary to add other crimes in accordance with actual situations. There is only one case of punishment for the crime of money laundering from 1997 to date in *China*, which indicates that the *Criminal Law* is capable of covering present activities relating to money laundering.

The second opinion above is well supported for the following reasons:

(i) *China* has signed the *Convention*, which provides that '*each contractual state shall seek to apply Paragraph 1, Article 6 to the widest range of predicate offences*'. As such, expanding the scope of predicate offences for money laundering to include the additional aforementioned offences complies with the requirement of the *Convention*.

(ii) The fact that only a handful of money laundering crimes are discovered each year in *China* should not be considered as evidence that there is no need to further improve the current legislation in connection with money laundering activity. Failure to make improvements may be due to the inability to recognize issues and lack of familiarity with the procedures by people in charge of anti-money laundering in *China*. Improvement of the criminal legislation on money laundering, therefore, would make the pertinent laws more practicable and effective in combating money laundering crime and its predicate offences.

In addition to enlarging the scope of predicate offences for money laundering, it also has been proposed to: (a) further clarify judicial interpretation on the degree of criminal offences; (b) impose a higher penalty amount on money laundering; (c) increase the term of imprisonment from the current maximum of 10 years to exceed 10 years or life detention; and (d) adopt extraterritorial jurisdiction over any predicate offence as long as the related money laundering activity occurs in *China*. Because money-laundering activities often involve corporate entities or professional institutions, it is also important to vest in judicial authorities the right to revoke business licenses and professional qualifications of those that are found guilty of money laundering.

5.2   Improving relevant legal system – the Anti-Money Laundering Law

The *Anti-Money Laundering Law of the PRC (反洗钱法)* (the ''*Law*'') has been adopted by the *National People's Congress (全国人大)*. The main purpose of this *Law* is to prevent money laundering and its predicate offences, maintain the financial order and secure the economic safety of the state.

This *Law* mainly regulates and prevents money laundering, while punishment for and combating against money laundering crime is governed by the *Criminal Law of PRC*. As such, the term 'anti-money laundering' in the *Law* shall be limited to preventing and supervising money laundering. The supervising parties include financial institutions, specific non-financial institutions and relevant departments of the *State Council*. The methods of anti-money laundering include the customer identity verification system, customer identity data and transaction records maintenance system, reporting large-value and suspicious transaction system established and performed by various financial and specific non-financial institutions, as well as the supervision, administration, investigation and international cooperation conducted by relevant departments of the *State Council*.

5.2.1   Supervision and administration of anti-money laundering

Since many government offices are involved in anti-money laundering, a supervision and administration system with clear responsibilities and good cooperation among administrative, judicial and industrial supervising departments needs to be established for the purpose of enhancing overall anti-money laundering capability. The *Law* provides that the *Anti-money Laundering Administrative Department of the State Council (国务院反洗钱行政主管部门)* shall be in charge of the administration of anti-money laundering work of the state, and relevant departments of the *State Council* shall administer the anti-money laundering within their respective scope of duties and shall cooperate with each other.

With respect to the clarification of detailed responsibilities for anti-money laundering, the *Law* provides that the *Anti-money Laundering Administrative Department of the State Council* shall: (a) organize and coordinate the anti-money laundering work of the State, (b) draw up anti-money laundering policy, (c) be responsible for money monitoring, investigation and international cooperation, (d) be in charge of supervision and administration of anti-money laundering conducted by financial institutions, including formulation of standards and requirements of prevention and supervision rules, as well as (e) perform the functions of supervision and inspection. Relevant departments of the *State Council* shall be responsible for supervising and administering the anti-money laundering conducted by the institutions of the industry under its charge, formulating standards and requirements of prevention and supervision rules for anti-money laundering by the institutions of the industry under its charge, as well as defining the functions of supervision and inspection. Meanwhile, they shall also have the obligation to report on suspicious transactions discovered during their work.

The ***Anti-Money Laundering Information Center (AMLIC;*** 反洗钱信息中心*)*, a bridge to preventing, supervising, and combating anti-money laundering, shall be responsible for receiving, analyzing, and transferring relevant information of anti-money laundering. It is an important institution for the anti-money laundering task. As such, the *Law* provides that the *Anti-money Laundering Administrative Department of the State Council* shall set up the *AMLIC*, and further provides its functions in detail.

Furthermore, to supervise carrying large-value cash and bearer instruments in and out of the territory of *China* for money laundering, the *Law* provides that the *Customs* shall report relevant information to the *Anti-money Laundering Administrative Department of the State Council*.

5.2.2 Anti-money laundering obligation of financial institutions and specific non-financial institutions

As the main channel of financing in modern society, financial institutions are the places that money laundering happens frequently. As such, the focus of preventing and supervising money laundering should be placed on financial institutions, through which the movement of abnormal funds may be monitored and reported, and proceeds of crime may be detected and controlled. However, financial institutions are not the only channel for money laundering, and with the improvement and perfection of supervisory rules for financial institutions, money laundering activities begin to penetrate into non-financial institutions. Thus, **the *Law* provides that not only financial institutions such as banks, securities companies, and insurance companies, but also specific non-financial institutions such as real estate sellers, precious metal and jewelry dealers, auction enterprises, mortgage firms, law firms, and accounting firms shall have the obligation to prevent, supervise, and combat money laundering**.

To cause all anti-money laundering regimes to become an integral part of the daily operation mechanism of the above institutions, and clarify the respective responsibilities of institutions and individuals, the *Law* provides that the financial institutions and specific non-financial institutions shall set up an internal control regime for anti-money laundering, establish a specialized anti-money laundering department or appoint a specialized person in charge, and carry on anti-money laundering training and publicizing.

To establish the corresponding relationship between customer identification and funds and transactions at the beginning when proceeds of crime enter into transactions, and to identify the true nature of funds and the real purpose of transactions and trace actual owner and beneficiary afterwards, the *Law* provides that financial institutions and specific non-financial institutions shall establish a customer identification system, which will be used to carefully identify, verify, and register the identity information of a customer and its agent and beneficiary. Furthermore, the institutions shall not provide service to those customers whose identifications are not clear. To facilitate verification of customer identity, the *Law* provides that financial institutions and specific non-financial institutions may verify relevant customer information with authorities of public securities and industry of commerce.

In addition, to fully utilize the anti-money laundering regime to combat corruption, the *Law* provides that financial institutions and specific non-financial institutions shall verify the identity of certain government officials in accordance with the conditions provided in the *Law*, and monitor their accounts and movement of funds.

To provide documents for analysis, investigation, and detection of anti-money laundering information, the *Law* provides that financial institutions and specific non-financial institutions shall keep customer identity and transaction information for a certain period of time. In accordance with the limitation of prosecution of the *PRC* and international general rules, the *Law* provides that customer identity information shall be kept for at least 5 years from the end of the business relationship, and transaction information shall also be kept for at least 5 years from completion of the transaction and the information relating to suspicious transactions shall be kept for at least 20 years.

The illicit fund movement often happens in abnormal large-value transactions. The *Draft* provides the reporting regime for large-value and suspicious transactions, which requires financial institutions and specific non-financial institutions to timely report to the *AMLIC* certain abnormal large-value transactions that lack obvious economic and lawful purpose. Such reports will be important hints for detecting and tracing illegal offences.

5.2.3 Anti-money laundering investigation regime

Money laundering activities are mainly in the form of fund movement and transfer. With the development of payment and settlement technology, the transfer and withdrawal of domestic or transnational funds become easier and more prompt. Especially, in cases of transnational fund transfer, once completed, the fund will be difficult to supervise and recall. To efficiently solve the problems of movement and transfer of crime proceeds under urgent circumstances, the *Law* provides that the anti-money laundering administrative department of the *State Council* has the right to conduct an investigation on anti-money laundering, and may take inquiring, reviewing, reproducing, sealing, and interim freezing measures.

Meanwhile, to avoid power abuse and protect legitimate property rights of entities and individuals, the *Law* expressly limits the conditions, subjects, and approving process and period to some investigating measures. The limits are as follows:

(i) Only those documents or materials that might be transferred, concealed, revised or destroyed can be sealed, and only those account funds that might be transferred abroad can be frozen.

(ii) Only the anti-money laundering administrative department of the *State Council* can adopt the measure of interim freezing subject to the approval of the person in charge of the *Anti-money Laundering Administrative Department of the State Council*.

(iii) The interim freezing shall not exceed forty-eight (48) hours. If the financial institutions did not receive the notice of sequential freezing order issued by the relevant public security bureau within 48 hours after taking such interim freezing measures in accordance with the requirement from the *Anti-money Laundering Administrative Department of the State Council*, the frozen assets shall be released immediately.

5.2.4 International anti-money laundering cooperation

To enhance the international anti-money laundering cooperation, fulfill *China*'s obligations of the international convention, and protect *China*'s good image in the world, Chapter 5 of the *Law* provides for basic principles of international anti-money laundering cooperation and general rules for information exchange and judicial cooperation methods.

5.2.5   Legal liability

To punish malfeasance, the *Law* provides that the officials of the anti-money laundering administrative department and other relevant departments of the *State Council* shall be held legally liable if they violate the rules in making inspections, taking interim freezing measures or implementing administrative punishment, or if they tip off anti-money laundering information, divulge trade secrets or personal privacy, or take any other action that is not in compliance with their duties. The legal liability should be a penalty or administrative punishment, etc.

To punish non-performance of anti-money laundering, the *Law* also provides for various legal liabilities of financial institutions and specific non-financial institutions and their senior managers and directly responsible officials for their non-performance of any anti-money laundering obligation. Considering that many of the above institutions are state-owned, to punish only the institution would, for all intents and purposes, be ineffectual. Thus, the *Law* provides a 'double punishment regime', which specifically entails punishment for both the institution as well as its senior managers and directly responsible officials.

Meanwhile, to guarantee a smooth process for anti-money laundering investigations, the *Law* provides for corresponding legal liabilities for financial institutions and specific non-financial institutions for their non-cooperation with anti-money laundering investigation.

5.3   Establish and improve institutional rules for anti-money laundering

At present, many commercial banks establish their own rules and self-discipline standards for anti-money laundering based on which institutional rules for money laundering may be considered. The mechanisms they take include '*know your customer*', report on large-value transactions, report on suspicious transactions, and records keeping.

5.4   Further improve the anti-money laundering system

Anti-money laundering is a new task for *China*. To accomplish this task, *China* has a long way to go and is making further improvements in several aspects.

5.4.1   Further improve international cooperation procedures

China has actively participated in international cooperation against money laundering, and has made great achievements in this respect. Presently, mainly bilateral cooperation between countries or regions, and cooperation through the *International Criminal Police Organization (Interpol)* are used to combat international crime, including economic and money-laundering crimes. In practice, *China*'s local public security bureaus should first report to the *Ministry of Public Security*, which then contacts the police authorities or Interpol of the state. Such procedure takes time and may translate into loss of opportunities for solving such cases. To enhance work efficiency, the relevant department of the State such as the *Ministry of Public Security* may, except for in some major and complex cases, authorize relevant authorities in big cities such as public security bureaus in *Shanghai* and *Guangzhou* to conduct international police cooperation directly with respect to ordinary money laundering cases before reporting to the *Ministry of Public Security*.

5.4.2 Establish and improve an anti-money laundering information system

SAFE has designed and developed an information system for large-value and suspicious foreign exchange transactions. The system is in use by banks, *SAFE*, public security bureaus, and other government offices. From March to October 2003, *SAFE* received 2 021 300 reports on large-value and suspicious foreign exchange transactions from all banks allowed to engage in foreign exchange business in *China*, which totaled US$490 035 billion. The public security bureaus, with the cooperation of *SAFE*, destroyed 'underground banks' and illegal foreign exchange transaction places, in which several billion RMB was involved. For large-value and suspicious RMB transactions, *China* has also set up reporting, collecting, and recording systems.

5.4.3 Form cooperative relationships among various departments

The *PBOC* has set up an anti-money laundering network according to '*One Rule and Two Measures*'. Financial institutions are the main entities through which dirty money is laundered, so the focus of anti-money laundering should be banks and stock and insurance companies. Divisions such as the *Customs*, foreign trade, industry and commerce, tax, public security, and judicial authorities are also involved. Anti-money laundering is a united task, which requires effort and cooperation from all divisions.

5.4.4 Expedite professional training

In order to accomplish the new task of anti-money laundering, anti-money laundering enforcers should be well-trained. As such, it is urgent to implement and expedite professional training. The *Anti-Money Laundering Bureau* of the *PBOC* is proposed to take lead in editing training materials and providing professional training to leaders and compliance officers of commercial banks and relevant financial institutions for this task.

6   Conclusion

In conclusion, the following aspects may be considered to further improve the anti-money laundering system in *China*:

(a) practice of laws and regulations;

(b) clarification of responsibilities and functions of various departments on all levels;

(c) clarification of responsibilities and functions of individuals within financial institutions;

(d) establishment of information collection and analysis systems; and

(e) cooperation among different organizations and departments.

Addresses

PBOC
32 Chengfang Street
Xicheng District
Beijing
PRC, 100800
Tel +8610 66194114
Fax +8610 66195370
www.pbc.gov.cn

SAFE
Huarong Building
18 Fucheng Road
Haidian District
Beijing
PRC, 100037
Tel +8610 68402265
www.safe.gov.cn

Ministry of Public Security
14 East Chang An Street
Beijing
PRC, 100741
www.mps.gov.cn

Abbreviations

AMLIC	Anti-Money Laundering Information Center
CAMLMAC	Chinese Anti-Money Laundering Monitoring and Analysis Center
Convention	*United Nations Convention against Transnational Organized Crime*
EAG	Eurasian Group against Money Laundering and Terrorism Financing
FATF	Financial Action Task Force on Money Laundering
Interpol	International Criminal Police Organization
PBOC	People's Bank of China
PRC	People's Republic of China
SAFE	State Administration of Foreign Exchange
SCNPC	Standing Committee of National People's Congress

Bibliography

Liang, Y.: Payment Transactions and Anti-Money Laundering, China Finance Publisher, Beijing, 2003.

Shen, L.: A Trans-Territory Contest, Liberation Daily, 11 May 2004.

Sun, M.: All-day-long Monitoring on 300 Billion Dirty Money, Anti-Money Laundering Intelligence Organization Sneak In, 21st Century Business Herald, 7 July 2004.

Wang, C.: Legislative Process of Anti-Money Laundering Law Is Officially Launched, China Youth Daily, 15 July 2004.

Steven Rudolf Sieker is a Partner in the International Tax Group of Baker & McKenzie in Hong Kong, China. His practice focuses on Hong Kong, Canadian and Asian regional tax advisory work, estate planning and tax litigation. In addition, he advises on money laundering law and regulation for multinational companies and financial institutions. Mr Sieker has written and contributed to a number of publications internationally. He is a past member of the Hong Kong Inland Revenue Department Board of Review. Mr Sieker was formerly a Vice-President with HSBC Guyerzeller Bank AG, and is a former Clerk to the Supreme Court of Canada. He holds a Bachelor of Arts (Honours) First Class degree from the University of Alberta and a Bachelor of Laws degree from Dalhousie University. He is admitted as a Solicitor in Hong Kong and England and Wales, and as a Barrister and Solicitor in Alberta, Canada.

Lee Travis Benjamin is an Associate in the International Tax Group of Baker & McKenzie in Hong Kong, China. His practice focuses on international tax advisory and tax controversy work for multinational companies, financial institutions and investment funds. In addition, he advises on money laundering law and regulation for financial institutions. Prior to commencing with Baker & McKenzie, Mr Benjamin practiced in corporate and indirect tax in the Hong Kong and Melbourne offices of an international firm. Mr Benjamin holds Bachelor of Arts and Bachelor of Laws degrees from the University of Queensland, as well as a Master of Laws degree from the University of Melbourne. He is admitted as a Solicitor and Barrister in New South Wales, Australia, and is a Registered Foreign Lawyer in Hong Kong.

Firm's profile

Founded in 1949, **Baker & McKenzie** is a global law firm of more than 3300 locally qualified, internationally experienced lawyers and 5500 other professionals and staff in 70 offices in 38 countries. The firm provides dedicated legal and associated business services across the broad spectrum of commercial law.

Hong Kong*

Steven R. Sieker

Partner, International Tax Group

L.T. Benjamin

Associate, International Tax Group

Baker & McKenzie
14th Floor Hutchison House
10 Harcourt Road
Hong Kong

Tel +852 2846 1888
Fax +852 2845 0476
steven.sieker@bakernet.com
www.bakernet.com

* This chapter is current as of the date of submission (16 September 2006)

Anti-Money Laundering: International Law and Practice.
Edited by W.H. Muller, C.H. Kälin and J.G. Goldsworth
© 2007 John Wiley & Sons, Ltd

Contents – Hong Kong

1 Introduction

The *Hong Kong Special Administrative Region of the People's Republic of China* (*Hong Kong*) has a legal and regulatory framework to deal with **money laundering** and countering **terrorist financing** (CTF). Recent case law suggests that *Hong Kong*'s anti-money laundering (AML) laws are vigorously applied by the police, prosecutors and the Courts alike.

Hong Kong does not have a consolidated AML/CTF statute. However, AML/CTF legislation has been developed through the criminal law to address the problems associated with the laundering of proceeds from **drug trafficking** and serious crimes, as well as to give effect to anti-terrorism measures. Essentially, *Hong Kong*'s statutory AML/CTF regime is contained in three ordinances:

- The *Drug Trafficking (Recovery of Proceeds) Ordinance* (*DT(RP)O*).

- The Organized *and Serious Crimes Ordinance* (*OSCO*).

- The United *Nations (Anti-Terrorism Measures) Ordinance* (*UN(ATM)O*).

The *DT(RP)O* came into force in September 1989. It provides for the tracing, freezing and confiscation of the proceeds of **drug trafficking** and creates a criminal offence of **money laundering** in relation to such proceeds.

The *OSCO* was modeled on the *DT(RP)O* and contains substantially the same operative provisions. The *OSCO* was brought into operation in December 1994. It extends **money laundering** offences to cover the proceeds of all **indictable offences**, which effectively covers the proceeds of almost all 'crime' in *Hong Kong*.[1]

The *UN(ATM)O* was enacted in July 2002 and a substantive part of it came into operation in August the same year. The *UN(ATM)O* fully implements the mandatory elements of *United Nations Security Council Resolution (UNSCR) 1373* and selected aspects of the *Financial Action Task Force's (FATF) Special Recommendations*. The *UN(ATM)O* prohibits any person within *Hong Kong* from providing or collecting funds for terrorists, and requires disclosure of suspected **terrorist property**.

In a regulatory context, the *Hong Kong Monetary Authority* (*HKMA*), which has supervisory powers over *Authorized Financial Institutions* (*AFIs*), has issued a *Guideline on Prevention of Money Laundering* (*HKMA Guidelines*), as well as the *Supplement to the HKMA Guidelines*, which cover AML/CTF for these organizations.[2]

Additionally, the *Hong Kong Securities and Futures Commission* (*SFC*) and the *Hong Kong Insurance Authority* (*OCI*) have issued various guidance notes, which provide an AML/CTF regulatory regime for non-*AFI* corporations (and licensed representatives) in the securities and insurance sectors respectively.

---

[1] This chapter focuses on the *OSCO*, as the AML/CTF legislation of broadest application in *Hong Kong*.

[2] This chapter focuses on the *HKMA Guidelines* and *Supplement to the HKMA Guidelines* because AFIs are the private sector organizations most likely to be required to make a AML/CTF disclosure.

2 Legal framework

2.1 Money laundering

The offence commonly known as **money laundering** is contained in *section 25(1)* of the *OSCO*. It creates a criminal offence of dealing with property knowing, or having reasonable grounds to believe, that the property is the proceeds of an **indictable offence**.[3] All liability under the *OSCO* falls on natural persons, not corporations. In this connection, Hong Kong's AML legislation is quite different from that of other jurisdictions in which the actions or knowledge of natural persons (i.e., employees) are taken to be the actions or knowledge of the corporation when an employee is acting in the course of their employment.

The criminal provisions in relation to **money laundering** extend to failing to report knowledge or suspicion that any property represents proceeds of, was used in connection with, or is intended to be used in connection with an **indictable offence** to an authorized person.[4]

Please see Section 3 for an analysis of the application of the *OSCO*.

2.2 Terrorist financing

Terrorist financing is a criminal offence under the *UN(ATM)O*. Specifically, *section 7* prohibits any person from providing or collecting by any means, directly or indirectly, funds with the intention that the funds be used; or knowing the funds will be used, in whole or in part to commit one or more terrorist acts (whether or not the funds are actually used).

Section 8 of the *UN(ATM)O* provides that, except under the authority of a licence granted by the *Hong Kong Secretary for Security,* no person may make any funds or financial (or related) services available, directly or indirectly, to or for the benefit of, a person who the first-mentioned person knows or has reasonable grounds to believe is a terrorist or a terrorist associate (at the time of writing, *section 8* is not yet in operation).

Liability under *sections 7 and 8* of the *UN(ATM)O* rests with natural persons within and outside *Hong Kong* who are *Hong Kong* permanent residents, as well as a body incorporated or constituted under *Hong Kong* law.

2.3 Criminal liability of legal entities

Legal entities (such as corporations) do not have a 'criminal liability' under the *OSCO* for **money laundering** offences. A *Hong Kong* incorporated corporation (or like entity) can face a 'criminal liability' under *sections 7 and 8* of *UN(ATM)O* for **terrorist financing**.

2.4 Confiscation of assets

Section 8 of the *OSCO* empowers the *Court of First Instance* or the *District Court* to make confiscation, charging and enforcement orders. Charging orders may be made in respect of:

---

[3] Defined in *section 23A* of the *Crimes Ordinance* to mean any offence other than an offence which is triable only summarily. This effectively means almost all crimes in *Hong Kong*.
[4] Defined in *section 2(1)* of the *OSCO* to be any police officer; any member of the *Customs and Excise Service*; and any other person authorized in writing by the *Secretary for Justice* for the purposes of this Ordinance. In practice, the authorized person is an officer of the *Joint Financial Intelligence Unit (JFIU)*.

- land in *Hong Kong*;

- shares of any company incorporated in *Hong Kong*;

- shares of any company incorporated outside *Hong Kong*, that are registered in a register kept in any place in *Hong Kong*; and

- units of any unit trust that is registered in a register of unit holders that is kept at any place within *Hong Kong*.

Additionally, enforcement orders may be made over any property:

- held by the defendant;

- gifted by the defendant to any person; or

- which is subject to the effective control of the defendant.

Sections 13 and *14* of the *UN(ATM)O* contain forfeiture provisions in respect of **terrorist property**.[5]

2.5 Implementation of specific international sanctions

2.5.1 United Nations Sanctions

Hong Kong enacted legislation to give effect to the *UNSCR*s concerning terrorism and **terrorist financing** under the *United Nations Sanctions Ordinance*.

2.5.2 Support to sanctions of other jurisdictions

Hong Kong has not implemented laws or regulations to provide support to sanctions of other jurisdictions.

2.5.3 Adherence to FATF Recommendations

According to the 2002-3 FATF Annual Report (which contains the most recent reference to Hong Kong's compliance with FATF recommendations), Hong Kong is in full compliance with 28 of the 40 FATF recommendations. Hong Kong is also in compliance with four of the FATF's special recommendation and in partial compliance with three.

3 The scope and application of the OSCO

3.1 Dealing with the proceeds of an indictable offence

Money laundering is made an offence in *Hong Kong* by *section 25(1)* of the *OSCO*:[6]

> '*A person commits an offence if, knowing or having reasonable grounds to believe that any property in whole or in part represents any person's proceeds of an* **indictable offence**, *he deals with that property.*'

---

[5] Defined in *section 2(1)* of the *UN(ATM)O* to include the property of a terrorist or terrorist associate; or any other property consisting of funds that – are intended to be used to finance or otherwise assist the commission of a terrorist act; or were used to finance or otherwise assist the commission of a terrorist act.

[6] Please note that all section references in *section 3* are to the *OSCO* unless specifically noted.

3.1.1 A person

Any natural person, and not a corporation, is liable under *section 25(1)*. The scope of the offence is not limited to persons who supply advice or financial services in regulated sectors.

3.1.2 The elements of the offence

The *Court of Appeal* in *HKSAR v Li Ching*[7] found that there was no obligation under *section 25(1)* to establish that the **indictable offence** had been committed or that the property dealt with by the defendant was in fact the proceeds of an **indictable offence**. This view was approved by the *Court of Appeal* in *HKSAR v Wong Ping Shui*,[8] which considered that:

> *The scheme or system by which money is laundered is intrinsically a criminal scheme. It is not necessary to launder money which is legitimately and honestly acquired. Criminality is implicit in such an enterprise: proscribing it is what the legislature intended and what the draftsman set out to achieve.*

In the *Court of Final Appeal* in *HKSAR v Wong Ping Shui*,[9] the Court stated that there is a difference between a **money laundering** offence in *section 25(1)* and handling stolen goods (an offence in *section 24* of the *Theft Ordinance*). Under the *Theft Ordinance*, the quality of the goods in question forms part of the *actus reus* (a guilty act) of the offence, which places the onus of proof on the prosecution to demonstrate that the defendant did handle stolen goods. The provision defines the *mens rea* as the dishonest belief or knowledge that the goods are stolen. This can be distinguished in relation to *section 25(1)*:

> *The mental element to be proved, whether in terms or knowledge or belief on reasonable grounds, is directed merely at the property being dealt with.*

On this basis, the case law suggests that the quality of the property dealt with by the defendant is characterized by the defendant's knowledge or belief. In order to prove the *mens rea* under *section 25(1)*, it is sufficient for the prosecution to demonstrate that the defendant either knew or had reasonable grounds to believe that the property represented the proceeds of an **indictable offence**. In the *Court of Final Appeal* in *HKSAR v Wong Ping Shui*, Mr Justice Ribeiro noted:

> *. . . it is wholly implausible that the legislature could have intended proof of **money laundering** offences to require proof of the underlying criminal offences that generated the money being sanitized. There is the obvious likelihood that such activities would be cloaked in secrecy and that they may well have taken place in one or more foreign jurisdictions.*

3.1.3 Knowledge

Dealing with property that represents the proceeds of crime is an offence under *section 25(1)*. The intention of *section 25* is to catch a person who knowingly and willingly launders (or assist other persons in this respect). According to *Atwal v Massey*, knowledge is a subjective test unrelated to the objective determination of what a reasonable man would have known in the circumstances.[10]

---

[7] [1997] 4 HKC 108.
[8] CACC 251/2000.
[9] [2001] HKLRD 346, [2001] HKCFAR 29.
[10] [1971] 3 All ER 881.

Notwithstanding this, 'knowledge' for the purposes of *section 25(1)* is almost certainly wider than 'actual knowledge', and includes constructive knowledge. For example, in the English case of *James & Son Ltd v Smee*, Justice Parker held that:

> knowledge ... includes the state of mind of a man who shuts his eyes to the obvious or allows his servant to do something in the circumstances where a contravention is likely not caring whether a contravention takes place or not. [11]

3.1.4   Reasonable grounds to believe

The other aspect of *mens rea* in *section 25(1)* is wider in scope. It requires a person to have reasonable grounds to believe that property represents the proceeds of an **indictable offence**. The *Court of Appeal* in *HKSAR v Shing Siu Ming* considered the issue in the context of a similar provision in the *DT(RP)O*:[12]

> ... The prosecution has to prove knowledge of trafficking or that a defendant had reasonable grounds to believe that there was trafficking. The prosecution is not called upon to prove actual belief. It would be sufficient to prove reasonable grounds for such a belief and that the defendant knew of those grounds.

Moreover, the *Court of Appeal* outlined the objective and subjective matters that must be proved to show that a defendant had 'reasonable grounds to believe' that property represented the proceeds of crime:

> This phrase we are satisfied, contains subjective and objective elements. In our view it requires proof that there were grounds that a common sense, right-thinking member of the community would consider were sufficient to lead a person to believe that the person being assisted was a drug trafficker or had benefited therefrom. That is the objective element. It must also be proved that those grounds were known to the defendant. That is the subjective element.

HKSAR v Shing Siu Ming was approved by the Appeal Committee of the *Court of Final Appeal* in *Seng Yuet Fong v HKSAR*.[13]

On the issue of reasonable grounds in relation to the source of a person's property, Justice Line in *HKSAR v Yam Ho-Keung*,[14] held that:

> It seems clear to me that when an event can reasonably be explained on the basis of a few grounds, the man contemplating the issue holds reasonable ground for belief in them all. By using the term 'having reasonable grounds to believe' the draftsman and the legislature clearly made a conscious departure from the old phrase 'knowing or believing'. The effect is to make the offence a wide one. It means that people who deal in cash in circumstances which produce the limited list of inferred explanations as arises here are caught by the section. Another way of putting it is that the words of the section are aimed at condemning the man who reasonably foresees that he may be dealing in the proceeds of an **indictable offence** yet nonetheless goes on to do it. I do not consider that such a man was not within the sights of those who promoted the Organized and Serious Crimes Ordinance.

---

[11] [1954] 3 All ER 273.
[12] [1997] 2 HKC 818.
[13] FAMC 26 of 1998.
[14] DCCC 621 of 2001.

Section 25(1) provides that a person may commit the offence of **money laundering** without having any criminal intent or purpose. Notwithstanding that a person has dismissed the prospect that property is the proceeds of crime, *section 25(1)* may still apply if reasonable grounds exist to suggest that the property is proceeds of crime. *Section 25* cannot be circumvented by failing to make rational enquiries or seeking information if the situation is such that a common sense person would have grounds to believe that the property represented the proceeds of crime. As a consequence, there is a very real practical risk that *section 25(1)* will apply to unwary people.

3.1.5 Indictable offences

A money laundering offence is limited to dealing with property that a person knows or has reasonable grounds to believe represents the proceeds of an **indictable offence**.[15] This *de minimis* threshold is of little significance, as most criminal offences in *Hong Kong* are **indictable offences**. Under the *Crimes Ordinance*, an **indictable offence** means 'any offence other than an offence which is triable only summarily'. As a result, *section 25(1)* covers almost all offences, including tax evasion, gambling, fraud, corruption, piracy and drug trafficking.

3.1.6 Property

'Property' is widely defined in *section 2(1)* by *section 3* of the *Interpretation and General Clauses Ordinance* to include 'money, goods, choses in action and land; and (b) obligations, easements and every description of estate, interest and profit, present or future, vested or contingent, arising out of or incident to property as defined in paragraph (a) of this definition'.

3.1.7 Dealing with property

Practically all property and business transactions represent 'dealing' with property for the *section 25* purposes. *Section 2(1)* provides a non-exhaustive definition of 'dealing' to include:

- receiving or acquiring the property;

- concealing or disguising the property (whether by concealing or disguising its nature, source, location, disposition, movement or ownership or any rights with respect to it or otherwise);

- disposing of or converting the property;

- bringing into or removing the property from *Hong Kong*; or

- using the property to borrow money, or as security (whether by way of charge, mortgage or pledge or otherwise).

Section 25(1) is based on the property dealing taking place in *Hong Kong*. The case of *HKSAR v Yeung Ah Lung*[16] involved a person charged with dealing with property, knowing or having reasonable grounds to believe that the property represented the proceeds of a crime committed in *Hong Kong*. The *Court of Appeal* held that there was no provision which could bring the action

---

[15] In *Lam Hei Kit v HKSAR* (FAMC No. 27 of 2004) the Appeal Committee of the *Court of Final Appeal* held that it was not reasonably arguable that a charge of dealing with property known or believed to represent the proceeds of an indictable offence contrary to *section 25(1)* of the *OSCO* was a nullity if the underlying offence was not specified by the arresting officer.

[16] CACC 506/2003.

within *section 25(1)*, as the act of dealing with the property took place outside *Hong Kong*. It was immaterial for these purposes that the primary predicate offence occurred in *Hong Kong*.

3.2   Failure to disclose knowledge or suspicion (reporting obligations)

The section of the *OSCO* most likely to give rise to practical issues for professionals is *section 25A(1)* which provides that:

Where a person knows or suspects that any property:

(a) in whole or in part directly or indirectly represents any person's proceeds of;
(b) was used in connection with; or
(c) is intended to be used in connection with,

*an **indictable offence**, he shall as soon as it is reasonable for him to do so disclose that knowledge or suspicion, together with any matter on which that knowledge or suspicion is based, to an authorised officer.*

A person who fails to disclose his knowledge or suspicion to the authorities in accordance with *section 25A(1)* commits an offence under *section 25A(7)*. As a consequence, a person who knows or has reason to believe that property constitutes the proceeds of crime cannot extricate himself from criminal liability by declining to deal with the said property. *Section 25A(1)* imposes an obligation on that person to disclose his knowledge or suspicion to the authorities.

In the English case of *Squirrell Ltd v National Westminster Bank plc,*[17] it was observed that while the purpose is not to turn innocent parties into criminals, it is intended to put them under pressure to provide information to the authorities to enable the latter to obtain information about possible criminal activities and to increase their prospects of being able to freeze the proceeds of crime.

The terms '**indictable offence**' and 'property' appear in *section 25(1)* and apply equally to *section 25A(1)*. However, *section 25A(1)* has application to a person who knows or suspects that property represents the proceeds of, was used in connection with, or is intended to be used in connection with, an **indictable offence**. The situations which may lead to a potential criminal liability under *section 25A(1)* are thus much wider, and the *mens rea* threshold considerably lower, than that of *section 25(1)*.

3.2.1   Suspicion

The suspicion test is a subjective test and may be distinguished from *section 25(1)* in which there is no reference to reasonableness and, as a consequence, no objective benchmark of when a person should or should not suspect that property represents the proceeds of crime. As a result, a person who does not suspect that property represents the proceeds of crime or who will not be guilty of an offence under *section 25A(1)*. Notwithstanding this, a defendant may encounter difficultly in convincing a Court that his lack of suspicion was honestly held where a ordinary man would have been suspicious about the property in question. It is possible that the personal knowledge and experience of the defendant will be a significant consideration in determining his state of mind. Finally, as discussed in Section 3.1.3., knowledge may include constructive knowledge, and therefore willful blindness may not be a defence.

---

[17] [2005] EWHC 664, [2005] 2 All ER 784.

The case law implies that *section 25A(1)* is a considerably lower *mens rea* threshold than the test of having 'reasonable grounds to believe' in *section 25(1)*. In the case of *Hussien v Chong Fook Kam*,[18] the Privy Council considered the test of 'reasonable suspicion' which appeared in the *Malaysian Criminal Procedure Code*, which authorized a police officer to arrest a person whom he reasonably suspected of being guilty of an offence. Lord Devlin said:

> *Suspicion in its ordinary meaning is a state of conjecture or surmise where proof is lacking: 'I suspect but I cannot prove.' Suspicion arises at or near the starting-point of an investigation of which the obtaining of prima facie proof is the end.*

The view in *Hussien v Chong Fook Kam* is supported by the case of *Pang Yiu Hung Robert v Commissioner of Police*. In this case, Justice Hartman cited Lord Devlin and Scott LJ with endorsement, stating that: 'suspicion is not to be equated with prima facie proof'.

3.2.2 Disclosure to an authorized officer

A person who knows or suspects that property is connected with an **indictable offence** is required to disclose that knowledge or suspicion, together with any matter on which that knowledge or suspicion is based, to an authorized officer 'as soon as it is reasonable' for him to do so. *Section 25A(4)* provides that it is a defence for a person who is employed by another at the time he knows or suspect that property is connected with an **indictable offence** to report his knowledge or suspicion to an 'appropriate person' in accordance with the internal reporting procedures established by his employer.

Any police officer, member of the *Hong Kong Customs & Excise Department* (*C&E*) or other person authorized by the *Secretary for Justice* is an authorized officer for the purposes of *section 25A(1)*. Information obtained under *section 25A(1)* may be disclosed by any authorized officer to the *Department of Justice*, the *Police Force*, *C&E*, the *Immigration Department* and the *Independent Commission Against Corruption* (*ICAC*) for the purpose of combating crime.[19] In practice, disclosures under *section 25A(1) OSCO* are made to the *Joint Financial Intelligence Unit* (*JFIU*), a body jointly run by staff of the *Hong Kong* Police Force and the *C&E*.

For further information, please see: http://www.info.gov.hk/police/jfiu/english/index.htm. *JFIU* – GPO Box 6555, Hong Kong. Telephone: +852 2866 3366.

3.3 Tipping-off

Section 25A(5) is a *tipping-off* offence and is intended to preserve the integrity of an investigation by the authorities into money laundering. The scope of *section 25A(5)* has yet to be tested in the courts. *Section 25A(5)* creates the offence of disclosing information. . .

3.3.1. Defences

It is a defence in proceedings against a person for the offence of tipping-off to prove that: (a) he did not know or suspect that the disclosure concerned was likely to be prejudicial to the investigation; or (b) he had **lawful authority or a reasonable excuse** for making that disclosure.[20] 'Lawful

---

[18] [1970] AC 942.
[19] *OSCO, section 25A(9).*
[20] *OSCO, section 25A(6).*

authority' in this context is thought to require more than a contractual or professional obligation which are overridden by *section 25A(5)*.

3.4 Extraterritorial application

The legislature clearly intended that the *OSCO* should have extraterritorial application. *OSCO* extends not only to property which is known or believed to represent the proceeds of **indictable offences** committed in *Hong Kong*, but also to property which represents the proceeds of **conduct** which takes place overseas which **would** constitute an **indictable offence** if it had occurred in *Hong Kong* (under *section 25(4)*).

The implications of this rule were illustrated in the football match-fixing case of *Lok Kar Win v HKSAR*.[21] The *Court of First Instance* held that *section 25(4)* was specific and unambiguous and catered specifically for the situation where there has been **conduct** abroad. The provision did not require the commission of a foreign offence. Justice Burrell considered that what constituted 'ill-gotten gains and dirty money' for the purposes of *section 25(1)* had to be judged by the standards of *Hong Kong* and not the standards of the foreign jurisdiction where the profit was made. The *Court of Final Appeal* agreed, holding that the determining factor for the purposes of *section 25(4)* is the conduct complained of as judged by *Hong Kong* law, and not whether that conduct constituted an offence in the foreign country where it occurred.

It was clearly contemplated by the Courts in *Lok Kar Win* that a person may commit an offence under *section 25(1)* by dealing with property which represents the proceeds of conduct which would constitute an **indictable offence** in *Hong Kong* but which was not illegal in the jurisdiction in which it occurred. Presumably, this applies to the reporting obligations under *section 25A(1)*.

Section 82 of the *Inland Revenue Ordinance*, provides that tax evasion can constitute an **indictable offence**. To a similar effect, in the *Court of Appeal* in *HKSAR v Li Ching*[22] involving the conviction of a *Hong Kong* resident under *section 25(1)* for dealing with the proceeds of foreign tax evasion in the *People's Republic of China*, Justice Mayo said:

> ... *section 82(1)(g) is of assistance. This subsection is so widely framed that it is not possible to conceive of tax evasion in China which would not fall foul of the section. Mr. Wong who is representing the Applicant attempted to draw an analogy with handling stolen goods. This attempt was not convincing as it is clear that section 25 of the Organized and Serious Crimes Ordinance, Cap. 455 is framed in different terms to section 24 of the Theft Ordinance, Cap. 210. In particular under section 24 the prosecution must establish that goods in question have been stolen. There is no similar requirement concerning the proceeds of an **indictable offence**.*
>
> *There can be no doubt that if section 82 of the Inland Revenue Ordinance and section 25 of the Organized and Serious Crimes Ordinance are read together and the Judge accepted that the Applicant believed that the moneys in question were the proceeds of tax evasion in China he was guilty as charged.*

Hence, it is irrelevant, strictly speaking, whether the conduct abroad was a crime in that jurisdiction. The rationale for such a law is that it allows *Hong Kong* to prosecute someone for reprehensible conduct abroad even if the laws in that jurisdiction do not cover the offence.

---

[21] [1999] 4 HKC 783 and 796.
[22] [1997] 4 HKC 108.

3.5   Remittance agents and money changers

The *OSCO* also requires remittance agents and money changers to keep records of customers' identity and particulars of remittance and exchange transactions of HK$20 000 or more or of an equivalent amount in any other currency. *Authorized Institutions* are technically exempted from this requirement (please see Section 4.1 in relation to *HKMA Guidelines* in this area).

4   Regulatory guidelines

As indicated under Section 3.2, the *OSCO* imposes considerable reporting requirements in relation to knowledge or suspicion in respect of (and together with) information of tainted property. These obligations apply to all natural persons, not to corporations. Hence, employees of, for example, banking institutions, have an obligation to disclose knowledge or suspicion in accordance with *section 25A(1)* of the *OSCO*. The *HKMA*, *OCI* and *SFC* have also issued guidelines on AML/CTF (including disclosure of knowledge).

4.1   HKMA Guidelines

The *HKMA* is empowered to issue guidelines pursuant to its industry supervisory function under *section 7(3)* of the *Banking Ordinance*. The *HKMA* first issued the *HKMA Guidelines* in 1993. Following the enactment of the *OSCO* in 2000, the *HKMA Guidelines* were amended to provide for detailed customer verification and record-keeping requirements. In June 2004, a *Supplement to the HKMA Guidelines* (and accompanying *Interpretative Notes*) was published to take account of global developments. Combined, the *HKMA Guidelines* and the *Supplement to the HKMA Guidelines* are the most comprehensive AML/CTF regulatory guidelines in *Hong Kong*.

4.1.1   Application

The *HKMA Guidelines* apply to all banking and deposit taking activities in *Hong Kong* carried out by *Authorized Institutions*, as well as their subsidiaries in *Hong Kong* (*AIs*). *AIs* that fail to comply with the *HKMA Guidelines* may have their respective regulatory licence revoked or varied.

4.1.2   Verification of identity of applicants for business

The *HKMA Guidelines* and the *Supplement to the HKMA Guidelines* require *AIs* to verify their customer's (and potential customer's) identity on the basis of appropriate documentation. Additionally, AIs must record the identity and other relevant information about their customers. This extends to any customer claiming to act on behalf of another person.[23]

For the purposes of the *HKMA Guidelines*, evidence of identity may be regarded as satisfactory if:

- it is reasonably capable of establishing that the applicant for business is whom he claims to be; and

- the *AI* that obtains the evidence is satisfied, in accordance with its internal procedure, that it does establish that fact.

---

[23] *Guidelines on Prevention of Money Laundering*, para. 5.1.

Specific rules apply to accounts for individuals; corporations; clubs, societies and charities; unincorporated businesses; shell companies; trust, nominee and fiduciary accounts. It is intended that AIs implement on-going monitoring of, and maintain up-to-date information on, all customer accounts.[24]

*AI*s must also identify the beneficial ownership and control of the customer, especially where the customer is a non-listed company[25] or is a trust/nominee,[26] and special rules apply to correspondent banking relationships.[27]

4.1.3   Customer acceptance policy

*AI*s should determine the risk profile for their customers, and for customer groups. The *Supplement to the HKMA Guidelines* suggests that the following factors should be taken into consideration in this regard:

- The customer's origin (e.g., place of birth, residency), the customer's business location (including incorporation), whether the customer is otherwise connected with *Non-Cooperative Countries and Territories*[28] designated by the *FATF*, or those known to the *AI* to lack proper AML standards.

- The customer's background or profile, being linked to, a politically exposed person or otherwise being an individual with high net worth whose source of funds to be credited to an account (both initially and thereafter) is unclear.

- The customer's industry, which may be susceptible to **money laundering** risk, such as money changers or casinos.

- For corporate customers, seemingly unnecessary or complex ownership structures.

- Any other information that may suggest that the customer is high risk (e.g., knowledge that the customer has been refused a banking relationship by another *AI*).[29]

In addition, an *AI* that is considering establishing a relationship with a person suspected or suspected to be a *Politically Exposed Person* (*PEP*) should undertake extra customer due-diligence, including for the companies that are clearly related to him.[30] Importantly, an *AI* should also ascertain the source of funds before accepting a *PEP* as a customer. The decision to open an account for a *PEP* should be taken at a senior management level.[31]

4.1.4   Remittance

In relation to remittances, the *Supplement to the HKMA Guidelines* provide that:

- An ordering *AI* in a remittance transaction must disclose the originating customer's name and account location and account number. The remittance message should also contain the

---

[24] *Supplement to the HKMA Guidelines*, sections 12 and 13.
[25] *Supplement to the HKMA Guidelines*, section 4.
[26] *Supplement to the HKMA Guidelines*, section 5.
[27] *Supplement to the HKMA Guidelines*, section 11.
[28] *Supplement to the HKMA Guidelines*, section 14.
[29] *Supplement to the HKMA Guidelines*, para. 2.3.
[30] *Supplement to the HKMA Guidelines*, para. 10.5.
[31] *Supplement to the HKMA Guidelines*, para. 10.5.

customer's address or other unique reference (e.g., date of birth, identity document number or other customer identification number).[32]

- Similarly, an *AI* handling incoming remittances for a beneficiary should conduct enhanced scrutiny of, and monitor for, remittance messages that do not contain complete originator information.[33]

4.1.5   Record keeping

The *OSCO* entitles a Court to examine past transactions to assess whether a defendant has benefited from an **indictable offence**. In this connection, the *HKMA Guidelines* effectively recommend that the following information be maintained:

- the beneficial owner of the account (including for accounts opened on behalf of a third party);

- the volume of funds flowing through the account; and

- for selected transactions – the funds' origin (if known), the form in which the funds were offered or withdrawn, i.e. cash, cheque etc., the identity of the person undertaking the transaction, the funds' destination, the form of instruction and authority.[34]

The *HKMA Guidelines* also recommend that *AI*s consider the statutory requirements and the needs of the investigating authorities against normal commercial considerations. However, wherever practicable the following document retention periods should be followed:

- account opening records – copies of identification documents should be kept in file for six years[35] following the closing of an account;

- account ledger records – six years from entering the transaction into the ledger;

- records in support of entries in the accounts in whatever form they are used, e.g. credit/debit slips and checks and other forms of vouchers – six years from when the records were created; and

- remittance and money changing transactions records for non-account holders – six years from when the records were created.

It is suggested that retention may be by way of original documents, stored on microfilm, or in computerized form, provided that such forms are accepted as evidence under *sections 20 to 22* of the *Evidence Ordinance*.[36]

4.1.6   Reporting of suspicious transactions

The *JFIU* is the reception point for disclosures under the *OSCO*.

As indicated in Section 3.2, under *section 25A* of the *OSCO*, the obligation to report is on the individual who has knowledge or suspicion of a **money laundering** transaction. This applies

---

[32] *Supplement to the HKMA Guidelines*, para. 9.2.
[33] *Supplement to the HKMA Guidelines*, para 9.7.
[34] *HKMA Guidelines*, para. 7.2.
[35] Six years is the statutory limitation period for certain classes of claims under the *Limitation Ordinance*.
[36] *HKMA Guidelines*, para. 7.4.

equally to reporting knowledge or suspicion about **terrorist property**, as per *section 12* of *UN(ATM)O*.[37] The *HKMA* recommends that each *AI* appoint a designated officer or officers (Compliance Officer) who should be responsible for reporting to the *JFIU* in accordance with *section 25A* of the *OSCO*. The Compliance Officer should also be the person to whom all internal reports are made.[38] From a legal perspective, the liability of an employee making a report to the Compliance Officer is effectively extinguished once the report is made, after which liability shifts to the Compliance Officer in accordance with *section 25A* of the *OSCO*.

The *HKMA* recommends that Compliance Officers keep a register of, and acknowledge, all reports made to the *JFIU* and all reports made to them by employees in accordance with internal procedures.[39]

4.1.7   Staff education and training

The *HKMA Guidelines* request that *AI*s make their employees aware of their personal legal obligations under the *OSCO*. Specifically, *AI*s should inform their employees that they are personally liable for failure to report information to the Compliance Officer/authorities.

Employees should be advised to promptly report suspicious transactions to their *AI*'s Compliance Officer, even if they do not know precisely what the underlying criminal activity is or whether illegal activities have occurred. AIs should therefore provide anti-money laundering training to their local as well as overseas staff.

For further information, please see: http://www.hkma.gov.hk. *HKMA* – 55th Floor, Two International Finance Centre, 8 Finance Street, Central, Hong Kong. Telephone: +852 2878 8196.

4.2   SFC Guidelines

The *SFC* regulates the activities of corporations licensed under the *Securities and Futures Ordinance* and associated entities that are not *AFI*s, as well as licensed representatives. The *SFC* has issued a *Guidance Note on Prevention of Money Laundering and Terrorist Financing* that came into operation in April 2006. It is largely principles-based and implements a risk-based framework providing licensed corporations and their associated entities with the ability to determine their customers' risk profile utilizing specified criteria. The *Guidance Note on Prevention of Money Laundering and Terrorist Financing* suggests that higher-risk customers should be subject to rigorous customer due-diligence measures while lower-risk customers are entitled to a more basic screening.

For further information, please see: http://www.sfc.hk. *SFC* – 8th Floor, Chater House, 8 Connaught Road Central, Hong Kong. Telephone: +852 2840 9222.

4.3   OCI Guidelines

The *OCI* regulates issued a *Guidance Note on Prevention of Money Laundering* to insurance companies and brokers in July 2005.

---

[37] *Supplement to the HKMA Guidelines*, section 15.
[38] *Guideline on Prevention of Money Laundering*, para. 9.3.
[39] *Guideline on Prevention of Money Laundering*, para. 9.4.

The *Guidance Note on Prevention of Money Laundering* provides detailed direction on customer acceptance, customer due diligence, record keeping, suspicious transaction reporting and staff training and screening for insurance companies, in line with the global insurance AML/CTF trends. Moreover, the *Guidance Note on Prevention of Money Laundering* provides common examples of money-laundering techniques involving insurance products and outlines a number of suspicious transaction types, to help insurance companies to recognize such transactions.

For further information, please see: http://www.oci.gov.hk. *OCI* – 21st Floor, Queensway Government Offices, 66 Queensway, Hong Kong. Telephone: +852 2520 2728.

5 AML/CTF supervision

The *Hong Kong Police Force* and the *C&E* have responsibility to supervise AML/CTF compliance in *Hong Kong*. These two bodies are assisted by organizations such at the *ICAC*.

The role of the *JFIU* is to receive and store suspicious transactions reports and to pass them to the appropriate investigative unit.

As indicated in section 4, the *HKMA* has supervisory powers over the regulation of *AI*s. The *SFC* regulates the activities of corporations licensed under the *Securities and Futures Ordinance* and associated entities that are not *AFI*s, as well as licensed representatives. Likewise, the *OIC* plays the same role for insurance companies and insurance brokers. Failure to comply with the AML/CTF guidelines determined by these bodies may affect corporate licensing.

6 Law enforcement

The AML/CTF laws are enforced by the *Hong Kong Police Force* and *C&E*. Both agencies work closely with financial regulators and the *Department of Justice* in investigation and prosecution.

6.1 Penalties

The penalties for breach of the key operative provisions of the *OSCO* are as follows:

- Dealing with the proceeds of an indictable offence (*section 25(1)*): where convicted on indictment the person is liable for a fine of HK$5 000 000 and to imprisonment for 14 years; or on summary conviction to a fine of HK$500 000 and to imprisonment for three years.

- Failure to disclose knowledge or suspicion (*section 25A(1)*): a maximum penalty of three months' imprisonment and a fine of HK$50 000.

- 'Tipping off' *section 25A(5)*: the person will be guilty of a criminal offence carrying a maximum penalty of HK$500 000 and imprisonment of three years.

The penalties for breach of the key operative provisions of the *UN(ATM)O* are as follows:

- Providing or collecting funds with the intention that they be used commit a terrorist act (or knowledge thereof) (*sections 7 and 8*): a penalty of a fine (of an unlimited amount) and imprisonment for 14 years.

- Failure to disclose knowledge or suspicion (*section 12*): a maximum penalty of three months' imprisonment and a fine of HK$50 000.

7 International cooperation

Hong Kong has been a member of the *FATF* since 1990 and is a founding member of the *Mutual Legal Assistance Agreements*.

Addresses

Joint Financial Intelligence Unit (JFIU)
GPO Box 6555
Hong Kong
Tel +852 2866 3366
http://www.info.gov.hk/police/jfiu/english/
index.htm

Hong Kong Monetary Authority (HKMA)
55th Floor, Two International Finance Centre
8 Finance Street, Central
Hong Kong
Tel +852 2878 8196
http://www.hkma.gov.hk

Securities and Futures Commission (SFC)
8th Floor, Chater House
8 Connaught Road Central
Hong Kong
Tel +852 2840 9222
http://www.sfc.hk

Hong Kong Insurance Authority (OCI)
21st Floor, Queensway Government Offices
66 Queensway
Hong Kong
Tel +852 2520 2728
http://www.oci.gov.hk

Abbreviations

AFIs	Authorized Financial Institutions
AML	Anti-Money Laundering
C&E	Hong Kong Customs & Excise Department
CTF	Countering Terrorist Financing
DT(RP)O	Drug Trafficking (Recovery of Proceeds) Ordinance
FATF	Financial Action Task Force's
HKMA	Hong Kong Monetary Authority
HKMA Guidelines	Guideline on Prevention of Money Laundering
Hong Kong	Hong Kong Special Administrative Region of the People's Republic of China
ICAC	Independent Commission Against Corruption
JFIU	Joint Financial Intelligence Unit
OCI	Hong Kong Office of the Commissioner of Insurance
OSCO	Organized and Serious Crimes Ordinance
PEP	Politically Exposed Person
SFC	Hong Kong Securities and Futures Commission
UN(ATM)O	United Nations (Anti-Terrorism Measures) Ordinance
UNSAR	United Nations Sanctions (Afghanistan) Regulation
UNSCR	United Nations Security Council Resolution

Bibliography

Broome, J.: Anti-money laundering: international practice and policies, Sweet & Maxwell Asia, Hong Kong, 2005.

Hopton, D.: Money laundering: a concise guide for all business, Gower, England, 2005.

Savla, S.: Money laundering and financial intermediaries, Kluwer Law International, The Hague, 2001.

Stessens, G.: Money laundering: a new international law enforcement model, Cambridge University Press, UK, 2000.

Andrew White holds an appointment as a Senior Fellow in the Faculty of Law, University of Melbourne, where he lectures in both the LLB and JD Programs; holds an academic staff appointment in the Centre for Corporate Law and Securities Regulation; and conducts research in Islamic law in the Asian Law Centre. During the past 25 years, Mr White has been a practicing attorney representing individual, corporate and government clients in matters relating to Islamic commercial law, international trade and commercial transactions. His professional tenure includes time engaged as a partner in a major international law firm based in the USA, as a senior attorney in a law firm in Europe, and as principal in his own law firm. He lectures and publishes extensively in the USA, Europe and Australasia on a wide range of legal topics of academic interest as well as topics of interest to legal and business professionals.

Organization's Profile

Australia's first university law course began at the **University of Melbourne** in 1857. The nation's oldest law school, the Melbourne Law School has approximately 3500 students enrolled in course work and research-based degrees, and approximately 90 academic staff engaged in teaching and diverse research. Located within the Law School are the renowned Centre for Corporate Law & Securities Regulation, the Asian Law Centre, and eight additional research centres of international standing.

Australia

Andrew White

Faculty of Law

University of Melbourne
Victoria 3010
Australia

Tel +61 3 8344 6847
Fax +61 3 8344 4546
andrew.white@unimelb.edu.au
www. http://www.law.unimelb.edu.au

Anti-Money Laundering: International Law and Practice.
Edited by W.H. Muller, C.H. Kälin and J.G. Goldsworth
© 2007 John Wiley & Sons, Ltd

Contents – Australia

1 Introduction

Motivated at least in part by heightened concerns regarding terrorist activity, especially in the wake of the London bombings in July 2005, Australia has committed to major reforms of its **anti-money laundering** and **counter-terrorism financing (AML/CTF)** laws. Although terrorists and their sponsors may use both legally and illegally obtained monies to carry out their activities, strengthened AML/CTF laws yield the double-dividend of preventing significant funds being diverted to facilitate terrorist activity, and at the same time discouraging financial fraud and other forms of criminal activity (especially drug-related and large-scale organized crime) by making them less profitable. The Australian Government currently is dedicated to undertaking 'a fundamental overhaul of Australian legislation' and implementation of global anti-money laundering standards, aimed at ensuring that Australia does not become 'a soft touch for money launderers and terrorist financiers'.[1] This chapter will summarize the existing legislative and regulatory framework in Australia for combating money laundering and terrorist financing, including especially the *Financial Transaction Reports Act 1988 (Cth)*, the *Proceeds of Crime Act 2002 (Cth)*, and the activities of the *Australian Transaction Reports and Analysis Centre (AUSTRAC)*. The chapter will also summarize proposed AML/CTF legislation which has been released by the Australian Government in draft form (the '**revised exposure draft AML/CTF Bill 2006**'), currently being finalized by the Attorney-General's Department for anticipated introduction to the Australian Parliament at some time in 2006. The revised exposure draft AML/CTF Bill 2006 is based upon Australia's commitment to implementation of a range of global anti-money laundering standards issued by the *Financial Action Task Force* (the *FATF Forty Recommendations*[2] regarding money laundering plus the *FATF Nine Special Recommendations*[3] regarding terrorist financing), as well as Government committee investigations and extensive consultation and public comment during two rounds of revision and release of exposure drafts for comment. Notwithstanding the considerable groundwork undertaken by the Government in arriving at a final draft for submission to Parliament, however, it is important to note that this chapter is only able to review and comment upon the proposed legislation released in revised exposure draft AML/CTF Bill 2006, draft AML/CTF Rules, and commentary as of 15 September 2006. The form or substance of any final AML/CTF legislation promulgated by Parliament in this respect cannot be predicted.

2 Overview of existing AML/CTF regulation and legislation in Australia

The Australian Government has estimated that between AUD\$2–3 billion is laundered in Australia each year.[4] This occurs through a wide variety of means and methods. Money laundering is

---

[1] Minister for Justice and Customs, 'Australia endorses global anti-money laundering standards' (media release: 08 December 2003). www.ag.gov.au/agd/www/Justiceministerhome.nsf/Page/
RWP448419DCA3156F1BCA256DF5007A C772?OpenDocument as of 15 September 2006.

[2] Text, Interpretive Notes, Glossary, and other materials regarding the *Forty Recommendations* may be accessed at www.fatf-gafi.org/document/28/0,2340,en_32250379_32236930_33658140_1_1_1_1,00.html#40recs as of 15 September 2006.

[3] Text, Interpretive Notes, Guidance Notes, and other materials regarding the *Nine Special Recommendations on Terrorist Financing* may be accessed at www.fatf-gafi.org/pages/0,2966,en_32250379_32236947_1_1_1_1_1,00.html as of 15 September 2006.

[4] Financial Action Task Force/Group d'action financière, 'Summary of the Third Mutual Evaluation Report: Anti-Money Laundering and Combating the Financing of Terrorism – Australia' (FATF/OECD: Paris 14 October 2005).

accomplished primarily through the legitimate channels of securities dealers and financial services providers, of retail banks and credit unions, and even through gambling houses or casinos. By using such legitimate and often unwitting participants, combined with false identities and forged documents, illegal money laundering may 'slip below the radar' of regulatory and criminal law enforcement bodies. Of course, money laundering in Australia also occurs through various illegal vehicles. These include the time-honored smuggling of cash in and out of the country, ranging to more up-to-date and sophisticated schemes involving the mixing of criminal proceeds with legitimate business profits, often by professionals whose primary or even sole business activity is laundering money. In Australia, a comprehensive regulatory and legislative scheme ensures relatively effective oversight and investigation with respect to significant financial transactions. This is accomplished primarily through the *Financial Transaction Reports Act 1988* and its enforcement mandate by the *Australian Transaction Reports and Analysis Centre (AUSTRAC)*. Moreover, various Federal and State/Territory[5] criminal laws, such as the **Criminal Code Act 1995** *(Cth)* and the *Proceeds of Crime Act 2002*, address the receiving or possessing of money or other property derived from criminal activities or which may be used in committing a crime – including terrorist acts. This regime of various laws, although generally regarded as quite comprehensive, however, has been determined by the Government to be currently in need of updating to meet 'the challenges posed by increasingly sophisticated money laundering and terrorist financing techniques'.[6] A report issued by the Financial Action Task Force (**FATF**) evaluated Australia's AML/CTF laws against the international standards set forth in the *FATF Forty Recommendations* regarding money laundering plus the *FATF Nine Special Recommendations* regarding terrorist financing.[7] Based on an on-site visit and review, as of April 2005, the *FATF* determined that Australia's AML/CTF laws were fully compliant with respect to only twelve of the *FATF Forty Recommendations* on money laundering. The *FATF* report also found that Australia is non-compliant ('major shortcomings with a large majority of the essential criteria not being met') with respect to nine of the *FATF Forty Recommendations*, and only partially or largely compliant with respect to the remainder of the money laundering recommendations. Moreover, with respect to the *FATF Nine Special Recommendations* regarding terrorist financing, the *FATF* evaluation did not find Australia to be fully compliant with respect to any of those recommendations, although it was found non-compliant with only one of the *FATF Nine Special Recommendations*. The Australian Government's proposed updates to the current laws, while only tentative and not in effect as of the writing of this chapter, are discussed below with respect to revised exposure draft AML/CTF Bill 2006.

2.1   Financial Transaction Reports Act 1988

The *Financial Transaction Reports Act 1988*[8] *(FTR Act)*, together with the *Proceeds of Crime Act 2002* discussed later in this chapter, forms the primary framework of anti-money laundering and counter-terrorism financing efforts in Australia. The *FTR Act*, as its name indicates, is primarily a reporting law, with secondary investigation, enforcement, and record-keeping requirements.

---

[5] While AML/CTF efforts occur at both the Federal and State/Territory level in Australia, only Federal legislation is discussed in this chapter.

[6] Minister for Justice and Customs, 'Australia fighting money laundering and terrorist financing' (media release: 17 October 2005). www.ag.gov.au/agd/WWW/justiceministerHome.nsf/AllDocs/ 2DCD3F1AC23A43A8CA25709E0027F92E? OpenDocument as of 15 September 2006.

[7] Financial Action Task Force/Group d'action financière, 'Summary of the Third Mutual Evaluation Report: Anti-Money Laundering and Combating the Financing of Terrorism – Australia' (FATF/OECD: Paris 14 October 2005).

[8] Act No. 64 of 1988 as amended, taking into account amendments up to Act No. 86 of 2006.

The *FTR Act* states that its primary object is to facilitate the administration and enforcement of taxation laws, and it does provide significant assistance to investigations of evasion and attempted evasion of tax laws. Its express further objectives, however, are to facilitate the administration and enforcement of other Commonwealth and Territories laws, as well as making information available to the States for the administration and enforcement of States' laws, as well. As such, the reporting and record-keeping requirements set forth in the *FTR Act* also provide an important tool in combating specifically-defined 'suspect transactions', including money-laundering offenses under the *Proceeds of Crime Act 2002* and financing of terrorism offenses under the *Criminal Code Act 1995* or the **Charter of the United Nations Act 1945 (Cth)**.

The *FTR Act* accomplishes its stated objectives primarily by imposing significant financial transaction reporting and record-keeping requirements with respect to 'cash dealers', solicitors, and certain persons who transfer or receive currency into or out of Australia. The *FTR Act* also permits inspection of certain financial information and the premises of cash dealers and even solicitors, and specifies certain documents retention requirements. Finally, as discussed below in this chapter, the objectives of the *FTR Act* are enforced by the *Australian Transaction Reports and Analysis Centre (AUSTRAC)*. In that regard, *AUSTRAC* is specifically established and authorized by the *FTR Act* to oversee compliance with the reporting requirements of the *FTR Act* and, further, to act as Australia's specialist **Financial Intelligence Unit *(FIU)***, providing financial transaction reports information to State, Territory and Australian law enforcement and revenue agencies.

2.1.1 Cash dealers – definition

Cash dealers are the primary focus of the requirements of the *FTR Act*. Under the *FTR Act*, the definition of a 'cash dealer' includes

- financial institutions, including authorized deposit-taking institutions and co-operative housing societies;
- financial corporations (as defined in the *Constitution*);
- insurers or insurance intermediaries;
- financial services licensees (as defined in the *Corporations Act 2001*) whose license covers either or both dealing in securities or dealing in derivatives;
- trustees or managers of unit trusts;
- persons who are bullion sellers;
- certain persons involved in the business of collecting, holding, exchanging, or delivering currency;
- certain persons involved in the business of making funds available or arranging for funds to be made available in or outside of Australia;
- persons in the business of operating gambling houses or institutions;
- bookmakers and other persons operating totalisator betting services.

2.1.2 Cash dealers – reporting requirements

Cash dealers specifically are required to comply under the *FTR Act* with reporting requirements in the event of certain **significant cash transactions**, **suspect transactions**, and **international**

funds transfers. In particular, where a cash dealer is a party to a 'significant cash transaction' (defined by the *FTR Act* as one which involves the transfer of currency of not less than AUD 10 000 in value),[9] Section 7 of the *FTR Act* requires the cash dealer to prepare and communicate to the Director of *AUSTRAC* certain 'reportable details' of that transaction. These reportable details, which are set forth in Schedule 1 of the *FTR Act*, include

- the parties' names and addresses;
- the nature and date of the transaction;
- the method used by the cash dealer to identify the identity of the persons conducting the transaction with the cash dealer; and
- the total amount of currency, total monetary amount, and any foreign currency involved in the transaction.

Similarly, under Section 16 of the *FTR Act*, a cash dealer must prepare and communicate to *AUSTRAC* a report of all suspect transactions to which the cash dealer is party.[10] 'Suspect transactions' are defined by Sections 16(1) and 16(1A) as those transactions which the cash dealer has 'reasonable grounds to suspect':

- may be relevant to an investigation of actual or attempted tax evasion;
- may be relevant to investigation or prosecution of an offense against a Commonwealth or Territory law;
- may be of assistance to enforcement of the *Proceeds of Crime Acts (1987 and 2002)* or regulations made under those Acts; or
- is preparatory to the commission of a financing of terrorism offense or relevant to the investigation or prosecution of a person for a financing of terrorism offense.

Finally, in accordance with Section 17B of the *FTR Act*, a cash dealer who sends out of Australia or receives into Australia an international funds transfer instruction must prepare a report of the instruction, if either the cash dealer or the person on whose behalf the cash dealer is acting is not an authorized deposit-taking institution. The report must be sent to AUSTRAC or, in the case of certain reports or classes of reports so nominated by AUSTRAC, the report is not sent to AUSTRAC and instead retained by the cash dealer for a period of seven years.

2.1.3   Cash dealers – identity information requirements

In addition to the above outlined transaction reporting requirements with which cash dealers must comply under the *FTR Act*, cash dealers also must collect and hold identifying information regarding persons who open certain specified accounts or become signatories to certain specified accounts. In particular, the identity information requirements of the *FTR Act* apply to all accounts with cash dealers which are safe deposit facilities or arrangements.[11] In addition, the identity information requirements of the *FTR Act* also apply to accounts with cash dealers (other than safe deposit facilities or arrangements) in which either (i) the credit balance exceeds AUD 1000

---

[9] Excluding defined 'exempt cash transactions' under Section 9 of the *FTR Act*.

[10] Under Section 17 of the *FTR Act*, the cash dealer receives protection where information is disclosed under Section 16 of the FTR Act, such that the cash dealer "shall be taken, for purposes of Section 400 of the Criminal Code, not to have been in possession of that information at any time."

[11] Section 18(1)(b) of the *FTR Act*.

or (ii) at any time after 30 days from the day the account is opened or the person becomes a signatory on the account, the aggregate of the amounts credited to the account within the last 30 days exceeds AUD 2000.[12] The defined '**account information**'[13] which must be collected and held by the cash dealer includes:

- an account number or other information identifying the account;

- the name and address (not a Post Office Box) of the account holder;

- whether the account is held in a business name, and a copy of the certificate of registration or application for registration if not registered;

- whether the account is held in a corporate name, and a copy of any certificate of incorporation.

Similarly, the defined '**signatory information**'[14] which must be collected, verified, and held by the cash dealer includes:

- the name of the signatory in relation to the account and, if an unincorporated association, a copy of the instrument authorising the signatory to sign;

- any other name by which the signatory is commonly known;

- an identification record for the signatory.

The defined '**identification record**'[15] must include either (i) an '**identification reference**'[16] for the signatory (a written and signed reference by an 'acceptable referee' providing certain information about both the signatory and the referee, and stating that the referee has examined a specified identification document,[17]), or (ii) if the cash dealer is an 'identifying cash dealer',[18] a record of a prescribed verification procedure.[19]

If the cash dealer does not have the required account information or signatory information, the account is blocked until the cash dealer has the information.[20] Moreover, it is an offense for the signatory knowingly to make a withdrawal from a blocked account, and it is an offense under certain specified circumstances for the cash dealer to allow such withdrawal.[21]

Finally, it is important to note that all records (or copies of the records) of any information made or obtained by a cash dealer while obtaining account information or signatory information must

---

[12] Section 18(1)(a) of the *FTR Act*.

[13] Section 3 of the *FTR Act*.

[14] Section 3 of the *FTR Act*.

[15] Section 20A of the *FTR Act*.

[16] Section 21 of the *FTR Act*. For convenience, *AUSTRAC* Form s.21 'Reference from an Acceptable Referee' is a simple fill-in form available through the *AUSTRAC* website at www.austrac.gov.au/guidelines/forms/21.pdf as of 15 September 2006.

[17] A 'primary identification document', such as a birth certificate or other document defined by Section 3 of the *FTR Act* or a defined 'secondary identification document'. [Section 21 of the *FTR Act*.] If no primary identification document is examined by the referee, then the cash dealer must give notice of that fact to *AUSTRAC*. [Section 22 of the *FTR Act*.]

[18] As defined in Section 8A of the *FTR Act*.

[19] Either the so-called '100-point verification procedure' based upon inspection of certain documents, each of which is weighted with a certain value of points, or another verification procedure approved by *AUSTRAC* for the cash dealer. [Section 20A(1)(b) of the *FTR Act*.] For convenience, *AUSTRAC* Forms 201 and 202 provide a simple fill-in guide to the 100-point verification, available through the *AUSTRAC* website at www.austrac.gov.au/guidelines/forms/201.pdf and www.austrac.gov.au/guidelines/forms/202.pdf, respectively, as of 15 September 2006.

[20] Section 18(2) and (2A) of the *FTR Act*.

[21] Sections 18(4)-(4B) of the *FTR Act*. An offense against these sections may be punishable upon conviction by a maximum imprisonment of two years. [Sections 18(6) of the *FTR Act*.]

be retained by the cash dealer for a period of seven years after the relevant account is closed. In addition, the cash dealer must maintain a complete copy and a register of all documents released prior to the end of the seven-year period. The penalty for failure to comply with these requirements carries a penalty of one year imprisonment.[22]

2.1.4   Solicitors – reporting requirements

Solicitors are also subject to the reporting requirements of the *FTR Act*. Much like cash dealers, if a solicitor (or a solicitor corporation or partnership of solicitors) is a party to a 'significant cash transaction' (not less than AUD 10 000 in value) in the course of practicing as a solicitor or solicitors, Section 15A of the *FTR Act* requires the solicitor (or corporation or partnership) to prepare and communicate to the Director of *AUSTRAC* certain 'reportable details' of that transaction. These reportable details, which are set forth in Schedule 3A of the *FTR Act*, include:

- the nature and date of the transaction;
- the total amount of currency, the total monetary amount of the transaction, and the foreign currency involved in the transaction, if any;
- the names and addresses of the parties to the transaction;
- the address at which the transaction was conducted;
- certain details regarding any principal on whose behalf a party to the transaction conducted the transaction; and
- certain details regarding any cheque or banker's draft involved in the transaction.

2.1.5   All persons – international transfers not less than AUD 10 000

In addition to the reporting requirements imposed on cash dealers and solicitors with respect to certain significant cash transactions and international wire transfers in and out of Australia, Section 15 of the *FTR Act* also imposes reporting requirements on persons who:

- transfer Australian or foreign currency into or out of Australia;
- or who receive Australian or foreign currency from outside Australia;
- in an amount not less than AUD 10 000 in value.

Certain persons, including commercial passenger carriers and commercial goods carriers, may be exempted from the reporting requirements where the currency is carried by a passenger or unwittingly on behalf of another person.[23] Significantly, contravention of Section 15 of the *FTR Act* is a strict liability offense[24] and also is punishable upon conviction by imprisonment for a maximum term of two years.

2.2   Australian Transaction Reports and Analysis Centre (AUSTRAC)

The *Australian Transaction Reports and Analysis Centre (AUSTRAC)* is the primary agency responsible for collecting financial intelligence and regulating a wide range of cash dealers

---

[22] Section 23 of the *FTR Act*.
[23] Section 15(2) – (4).
[24] See Section 6.1 of the *Criminal Code Act 1995*.

and others involved in financial transactions in Australia. *AUSTRAC* was established under the *FTR Act* as an authority within the Australian Attorney-General's portfolio, reporting to the Minister for Justice and Customs. As noted in the sections of this Chapter above, *AUSTRAC* is the responsible agency charged with collecting various financial transactions information under the *FTR Act*, as well as ensuring compliance by cash dealers and others with the reporting and identity verification requirements of the *FTR Act*. In addition, *AUSTRAC* analyzes the financial transactions information it collects, and provides intelligence and other assistance regarding that information to various Commonwealth, State and Territory law enforcement agencies, security and revenue agencies. These include, most notably, the

- *Australian Tax Office (ATO)*
- *Australian Security Intelligence Organisation (ASIO)*
- *Australian Federal Police (AFP)*
- *Australian Securities and Investments Commission (ASIC)*
- *Australian Crime Commission*
- *State and Territory Police Services and Revenue Authorities.*

By sharing information both on-line and through exchange of data extracts, *AUSTRAC* and these various partner agencies are able to effectively combat money laundering, major crimes and tax evasion in Australia. Moreover, *AUSTRAC* actively participates in bilateral and multilateral relationships with a number of significant foreign Financial Intelligence Units *(FIUs)*, including the Egmont Group of Financial Intelligence Units (over a hundred *FIUs* worldwide), the Asia Pacific Group on Money Laundering (thirty-two member countries, including the United States and Canada), and the Financial Action Task Force *(FATF)* on money laundering.

2.3 Proceeds of Crime Act 2002

The *Proceeds of Crime Act 2002*[25] (the *'PoC Act 2002'*) is the primary legislation by which a court may deprive criminals of the proceeds and benefits of their criminal conduct. It is intended to attack the profit-motive of organized criminal activities, including money-laundering, trafficking in drugs and people, and major financial fraud. In addition, the *PoC Act 2002* implements Australia's obligations under the **UN Suppression of Financing of Terrorism Convention** and relevant **UN Security Council Resolutions** regarding the seizure of terrorism-related property. In accomplishing its intended objectives of deterrence, punishment, and deprivation of the fruits of a crime, the *PoC Act 2002* uses an effective regime of civil forfeiture. Unlike the **Proceeds of Crime Act 1987 (Cth)** which, operating in addition to and parallel with the *PoC Act 2002*, only allows court ordered confiscation of property from persons actually convicted of a crime, the *PoC Act 2002* provides a simpler procedure which *does not require conviction* as a condition to confiscation. Under the *PoC Act 2002*, instead, the court may order restraint and forfeiture of a person's assets where the court decides it is *more probable than not* that the person committed a serious offense and that the assets in question are the proceeds of that conduct. Given the harshness of the civil forfeiture provisions of the *PoC Act 2002*, it should be noted that there are provisions for relief from the effects of restraining orders or forfeiture orders authorized by the

---

[25] Act No. 85 of 2002 as amended, taking into account amendments up to Act No. 86 of 2006.

PoC Act 2002, such as where a party is able to prove to the Court that his or her assets were lawfully derived or where a forfeiture order would cause a hardship to the party's dependent(s).

In addition to the confiscation scheme summarized above, the *PoC Act 2002* also contains information gathering and monitoring provisions. For example, the *PoC Act 2002* provides for the issuance by the court of **examination orders**,[26] requiring persons to appear and give evidence in certain specified situations relating to restraint or forfeiture of property. The *PoC Act 2002* authorizes the court to issue **production orders**,[27] requiring persons to produce or make available for inspection to authorized officers certain **property-tracking documents**.[28] These include documents relevant to identifying, locating or quantifying property of any person:

- who has been convicted of, charged with, or whom it is proposed to charge with, an indictable offense; or

- whom there are reasonable grounds to suspect of having engaged in conduct constituting a terrorism offense; or

- whom there are reasonable grounds to suspect of having, within the last 6 years, engaged in conduct constituting any other serious offense.

These also include documents relevant to identifying, locating or quantifying:

- proceeds of an indictable offense, or an instrument of an indictable offense, of which a person has been convicted or with which a person has been charged or is proposed to be charged; or

- proceeds of a terrorism offense, or an instrument of a terrorism offense, that a person is reasonably suspected of having committed; or

- proceeds of any other serious offense, or an instrument of any other serious offense, that a person is reasonably suspected of having committed within the last 6 years.

Further, the *PoC Act 2002* authorizes certain officers of the *Australian Federal Police* or the *Australian Crime Commission* to give written notice[29] to a financial institution requiring the institution to provide to an authorized officer any information or documents relevant to any one or more of the following:

- determining whether a specified person is an account holder with the financial institution;

- determining whether a particular person is a signatory to an account with the financial institution;

- the current balance of the account held by the particular person;

- transactions details on such an account over a specified period of up to 6 months;

- details of any related accounts;

- any transaction(s) conducted by the financial institution on behalf of a specified person.

Finally, the *PoC Act 2002* authorizes a court to issue a **monitoring order**[30] to a financial institution, requiring it to provide certain authorized officers with information about transactions

---

[26] Sections 180–182 of the *PoC Act 2002*.
[27] Sections 202–212 of the *PoC Act 2002*.
[28] Sections 202 of the *PoC Act 2002*.
[29] Sections 213–218 of the *PoC Act 2002*.
[30] Sections 219–224 of the *PoC Act 2002*.

during a particular period, through an account held with the institution by a particular person who is, has been, or is about to be involved in or benefiting from the commission of a serious offense, or where the account is being used in the commission of a money-laundering offense.

2.4   Criminal Code Act 1995

Facilitated in part by the reporting and investigative provisions set forth in the *Financial Transaction Reports Act 1988* and the *Proceeds of Crime Acts (1987 and 2002)*, the *Criminal Code Act 1995*[31] sets forth a series of statutes which expressly address money laundering offenses.[32] In particular, a person is guilty of an offense of money laundering if the person deals with money or property which:

- is the proceeds of a crime *and believed by the person to be such*, or is intended by the person to become an instrument of crime; *or*

- is the proceeds of a crime, or there is a risk that it will become an instrument of crime, and the person is *reckless* as to the fact that it is proceeds of crime or the fact that there is a risk that it will become an instrument of crime (as the case requires); *or*

- is the proceeds of a crime, or there is a risk that it will become an instrument of crime, and the person is *negligent* as to the fact that it is proceeds of crime or the fact that there is a risk that it will become an instrument of crime (as the case requires).

'Dealing with money or other property'[33] is defined by the Act to include receiving, possessing, concealing or disposing of money or other property; importing money or other property into, or exports money or other property from, Australia; or engaging in a banking transaction relating to money or other property. The actual offense under which the person may be convicted, and the penalty imposed, depends upon whether the person's dealing is with actual knowledge, recklessness or negligence, as well as the value of the money or property involved at the time of the dealing.

The *Criminal Code Act 1995* also expressly addresses the offenses of terrorism financing and the financing of terrorists.[34] It is an offense under the Act if a person provides or collects funds and the person is reckless regarding whether they will be used to facilitate or engage in a terrorist act. Further, it is an offense if a person intentionally makes funds available to another person or collects funds on his behalf, and is reckless regarding whether the other person will use the funds to facilitate or engage in a terrorist act. The penalty for conviction of the offenses of financing terrorism or financing a terrorist is imprisonment for life. Significantly, a person commits an offense of financing terrorism or financing a terrorist even if a terrorist act does not occur or the funds will not be used to facilitate or engage in a specific terrorist act.

Finally, it should be noted that the Criminal Code Act 1995 also makes it an offense for a person to dishonestly supply information relating to the person, which may be used (either alone or in conjunction with other information) to access funds, credit or other financial benefits.[35]

---

[31] Act No. 12 of 1995 as amended, taking into account amendments up to Act No. 86 of 2006.
[32] Division 400 of the *Criminal Code Act 1995*.
[33] Section 400.2 of the *Criminal Code Act 1995*.
[34] Division 103 of the *Criminal Code Act 1995*.
[35] Part 10.8 of the *Criminal Code Act 1995*.

'Dishonesty' is measured against the standards of ordinary people. Conviction carries a penalty of imprisonment for five years.

2.5   Charter of the United Nations Act 1945

The *Charter of the United Nations Act 1945*[36] makes it an offense for a person to hold a '**freezable asset**' and use or deal with the asset, allow the asset to be used or dealt with, or facilitate the use of the asset or dealing with the asset.[37] A freezable asset is one owned or controlled by a **proscribed person or entity**, or derived from such an asset. 'Proscribed persons or entities' are those persons listed as such by the Australian Minister of Foreign Affairs, in accordance with regulations of the Governor-General of Australia and decisions of the United Nations Security Council Committee '**UN 1267 Committee**' established pursuant to UN Security Council Resolution 1267.[38] The **Consolidated List**, containing several hundred names, is maintained by the Minister in accordance with the *Charter of the United Nations (Terrorism and Dealings with Assets) Regulations 2002*[39] and is available from the Australian Department of Foreign Affairs and Trade (DFAT).[40] While the *Charter of the United Nations Act 1945* does not expressly refer to assets of those involved in terrorism financing, it and the *Charter of the United Nations (Terrorism and Dealings with Assets) Regulations 2002* were promulgated in order to give effect to UN Security Council Resolutions 1267 and 1373, among others, calling upon member states to suppress terrorism financing and to freeze, without delay, financial assets or economic resources of persons who commit, or attempt to commit, terrorist acts.

3   The proposed reforms to AML/CTF laws in Australia

As discussed above in this chapter, the *FATF* report issued in October 2005 noted that Australia's AML/CTF laws (as of April of that year) were fully compliant with respect to *only twelve* of the *FATF Forty Recommendations* on money laundering, and were fully compliant with *none* of the *Nine Special Recommendations* regarding terrorist financing. Following release of the *FATF* report, the Australian Government released its '**exposure draft AML/CTF Bill 2005**' in December 2005. This first draft revised AML/CTF legislation had been a work in progress since at least December 2003, when the Government had announced it would proceed with an overhaul of Australia's AML/CTF system as part of its commitment to implementing the *FATF Forty Recommendations* and the *FATF Nine Special Recommendations*. As part of the process of preparing the first draft AML/CTF Bill, the Government established a Ministerial Advisory Group, undertook consultations with industry groups, and conducted a series of roundtable meetings involving the financial sector, gambling sector, bullion dealers, and the legal and accounting professions.

Reflecting in-principle agreements reached through these Government-industry consultations, the Government announced that it would implement the reform process in two tranches. The first

---

[36] Act No. 32 of 1945 as amended, taking into account amendments up to Act No. 124 of 2002.
[37] Unless solely for the purpose of preserving the value of the asset. *Charter of the United Nations Act 1945*, Section 20(3).
[38] Adopted by the UN Security Council on 15 October 1999. A copy of the resolution is available at http://daccessdds.un.org/doc/UNDOC/GEN/N99/300/44/PDF/N9930044.pdf?OpenElement as of 15 September 2006.
[39] Statutory Rules 2002 No. 314 as amended, made under the *Charter of the United Nations Act 1945*, taking into account amendments up to SR 2003 No. 168.
[40] The Consolidated List is available through DFAT's website at www.dfat.gov.au, as of 15 September 2006.

tranche covers the financial and gambling sectors, bullion dealers, and lawyers and accountants (but only to the extent that they provide services in direct competition to the financial sector). The second tranche will be to address AML/CTF obligations of real estate agents, jewellers, and lawyers and accountants not providing specified financial services. Significantly, the Council of Australian Governments has also resolved formally to work with the Commonwealth in undertaking a number of key actions toward strengthening Australia's counter-terrorism laws, including consultation by the Commonwealth with the States and Territories regarding the possible enactment of laws to prevent the financing of terrorism by non-profit or charitable institutions, as well.

The exposure draft AML/CTF Bill 2005, together with draft AML/CTF Rules, draft guidelines, and explanatory materials, was released by the Australian Government for public comment between 16 December 2005 and 13 April 2006. During that time, the Senate Legal and Constitutional Legislation Committee also conducted an inquiry into the exposure Bill and published a report of its inquiry at the close of the public submissions period. Based upon the public submissions and the findings of the Senate committee, the Government then released revised exposure draft AML/CTF Bill 2006, together with an incomplete set of revised draft AML/CTF Rules,[41] for public comment between 13 July 2006 and 04 August 2006. In releasing the revised exposure draft AML/CTF Bill 2006 and Rules, the Government indicated its intent to make the second draft Bill more 'risk-based' than the first draft, clarifying various sections to permit reporting entities to be able to apply risk-based systems and controls as part of their mandatory AML/CTF programs of customer identification and other obligations under the legislation. This could help reduce compliance costs for at least some reporting entities, although certain reporting obligations, record-keeping requirements and other obligations also have been expanded in the most recent draft.[42]

As a cautionary reminder, it is important to note that this chapter is only a summary of the proposed legislation released in revised exposure draft AML/CTF Bill 2006, the revised draft AML/CTF Rules, and commentary as of 15 September 2006. It is anticipated that the revised exposure draft AML/CTF Bill 2006 and revised draft AML/CTF Rules will undergo further revision to reflect the comments submitted during the three-week exposure period concluded in August 2006. It also is likely that the revised exposure draft AML/CTF Bill 2006 will be reviewed by the Senate Legal and Constitutional Legislation Committee. The form and substance of any final AML/CTF legislation promulgated by Parliament in this respect, therefore, cannot be predicted. Moreover, as of 15 September 2006, no transition period has been decided.

3.1   The revised exposure draft AML/CTF Bill 2006

The revised exposure draft AML/CTF Bill 2006, the second draft of the *Anti-Money Laundering and Counter-Terrorism Financing Act 2006* (the *'AML/CTF Act'*), promotes Australia's international commitments to combat money laundering and financing of terrorism. It is intended that the objects of the *AML/CTF Act* will be achieved by, among other things, requiring that certain information be provided by specified **reporting entities** to Australian government authorities. In

---

[41] Certain specified Rules will be completed only after additional consultation with industry sectors and other interest groups. Moreover, it is anticipated that additional Rules will continue to be made on an as-needed basis, to address or clarify administrative issues or any unintended consequences of the legislation. AUSTRAC is responsible for making the AML/CTF Rules, pursuant to the revised exposure draft AML/CTF Bill 2006.

[42] A copy of revised exposure draft AML/CTF Bill 2006, the revised draft Rules, and a useful summary of the differences between the two exposure drafts can be found at www.austrac.gov.au/aml/index.htm, as of 15 September 2006.

complying with the *AML/CTF Act*, for example, reporting entities generally will be required to carry out a procedure for verifying a customer's identity before providing a designated service to the customer. Reporting entities will also be required to report to *AUSTRAC* (and, in some cases, to customs or other law enforcement officers) all suspicious matters, certain transactions above a specified threshold, designated services that relate to international funds transfer instructions, and cross-border movements of physical currency and bearer negotiable instruments. In addition, the *AML/CTF Act* will require reporting entities to have and comply with anti-money laundering and counter- terrorism financing programs.

3.1.1 Reporting entities/designated service providers

The reporting entities to whom the *AML/CTF Act* will apply are financial institutions and other persons who provide a '**designated service**', defined in the revised exposure draft AML/CTF Bill 2006 as including:

(a) The following services undertaken by authorized deposit-taking institutions,[43] banks, credit unions, or other persons specified in the AML/CTF Rules:

- as an account provider, opening an account, allowing a person to become a signatory on a new or existing account, or allowing a transaction to be conducted in relation to the account;

- as a deposit-taker, accepting money on deposit or allowing a transaction to be conducted in relation to a deposit;

- as an issuer or seller of traveler's checks, cashing or redeeming a traveler's check;

- as an originating or destination institution, accepting or making money available under certain specified funds transfer instructions;

- issuing a bill of exchange, a promissory note, or a letter of credit.

(b) The following services undertaken in the course of carrying on a business:

- making a loan or, in the capacity of a lender, allowing the borrower to conduct a transaction in relation to the loan;

- factoring a receivable;

- forfeiting a bill of exchange or a promissory note;

- supplying goods (not acquired by a consumer) under a finance lease;

- as a lessor under a finance lease (involving goods not acquired by a consumer), allowing the lessee to conduct a transaction in relation to the lease;

- supplying goods (not acquired by a consumer) to a person by way of hire-purchase;

- as a supplier of goods (not acquired by a consumer) to a person by way of hire-purchase, allowing the person to conduct a transaction in relation to the hire-purchase agreement;

---

[43] Bodies corporate under the *Banking Act 1959*, the Reserve Bank of Australia, and persons who carry on State banking within the meaning of the Constitution.

- as agent of a person, acquiring or disposing of a security, a derivative, or a foreign exchange contract, where the service is not specified in the AMC/CTF Rules;

- as agent of a person, acquiring or disposing of a bill of exchange, a promissory note, or a letter of credit, where the service is not specified in the AML/CTF Rules;

- certain specified issues or sales of securities or derivatives;

- as provider of a pension or annuity, accepting payment of the purchase price for a new pension or annuity;

- providing a custodial or depository service, or a safe deposit box or similar facility, where the service is not an exempt legal practitioner service;

- guaranteeing a loan or, as guarantor of a loan, making a payment to the lender;

- exchanging currency (regardless of whether Australian or not);

- collecting or holding physical currency, not collected as consideration for the supply of goods or services (other than the service of collecting or holding physical currency) or as a donation to a charity;

- preparing a pay-roll on behalf of a person from physical currency collected, or delivering physical currency (including pay-rolls) to a person.

(c) The following services:

- as an account provider for an account, as a building society or credit union, or as a trustee or manager of a trust, providing a checkbook or a similar facility, or a debit card, that allows the holder of the account or beneficial interest in the trust to draw a check on or debit an account held by such account provider, building society or credit union, or trustee or manager;

- issuing a stored value card, where the monetary value on the card is not less than AUD 1000 or such other amount specified in the regulations;

- increasing the monetary value stored on a stored value card, where the increased monetary value is not less than AUD 1000 or such other amount specified in the regulations;

- issuing or selling a money order, postal order or similar order with a face value not less than AUD 1000 or such other amount specified in the regulations;

- cashing or redeeming a money order, postal order or similar order with a face value not less than AUD 1000 or such other amount specified in the regulations, as an issuer or seller of the order;

- accepting money or property from a transferor to be transferred under a designated remittance arrangement;

- making money or property available to an ultimate transferee under a designated remittance agreement;

- as issuer, redeeming a bearer bond;

- issuing, accepting a premium, or making a payment in relation to a life policy or a sinking fund policy;

- certain specified activities as a trustee under a superannuation fund (other than a self-managed superannuation fund);

- certain specified activities as a 'retirement savings account'[44] provider;

- buying or selling bullion;

- providing certain specified gambling services; and

- providing such other services as are specified in the regulations.

Finally, the geographical scope of the *AML/CTF Act* will extend only to Australian residents and others with a clear legal nexus to Australia. That is, the reporting requirements will be imposed only where:

- the designated service is provided at or through a permanent establishment of the provider in Australia;

- the service provider is a resident of Australia and the designated service is provided at or through a permanent establishment of the provider in a foreign country; or

- the service provider is a subsidiary of a company that is a resident of Australia and the designated service is provided at or through a permanent establishment of the provider in a foreign country.

3.1.2   Procedure for verifying a customer's identity

Based upon the text of the revised exposure draft AML/CTF Bill 2006, the *AML/CTF Act* generally will require reporting entities to verify the identity of all new customers before providing designated services to them.[45] There are, however, some exceptions:

- Designated services provided by a reporting entity through its foreign office will not be covered by the identity verification requirements of the *AML/CTF Act*.

- Trustees of superannuation funds or authorized deposit funds and providers of retirement savings accounts (accepting a contribution, roll-over, or transfer of funds where the member has not yet reached preservation age), are exempted from the *AML/CTF Act*'s identity verification requirements.

- With respect to existing customers at the time of the *AML/CTF Act*'s commencement, the reporting entity can continue to provide the designated service to that customer without first undertaking the identity verification procedures of the *AML/CTF Act*, unless a '**suspicious matter reporting obligation**' (discussed below in this chapter) arises.

- With regard to certain low-risk designated services,[46] the reporting entity also can provide the designated service to that customer without first undertaking the identity verification procedures of the *AML/CTF Act*, unless a suspicious matter reporting obligation arises.

---

[44] As defined in the *Retirement Savings Accounts Act 1997*.

[45] The *AML/CTF Act* will permit identity verification to be carried out after provision of the designated service, in special cases to be specified in the AML/CTF Rules. No such Rules have been released yet. It is anticipated that they will be released following further consultation with industry and other interest groups.

[46] Low-risk designated services will be defined by the AML/CTF Rules. No such Rules have been released yet, and it is anticipated that they will be released only on an as-needed basis to identify any low-risk designated services.

Other exemptions and 'special circumstances' that justify carrying out the identity verification procedures after the commencement of a designated service may be provided by the AML/CTF Rules. In all cases, however, reporting entities will be required to carry out ongoing customer due diligence and, as discussed below in this chapter, to undertake **identity reverification** procedures in certain circumstances set forth by the *AML/CTF Act* and AML/CTF Rules. '**Ongoing due diligence**' involves the reporting entity monitoring its provision of the designated service in Australia, with a view to identifying, mitigating and managing the risk of money laundering and financing of terrorism. Significantly, breach of the *AML/CTF Act*'s ongoing due diligence requirement will be an offense punishable by fine and/or imprisonment of up to two years, as well as by civil penalty.

Generally, a reporting entity will be required to have in place a customer identification program that includes appropriate risk-based systems and controls designed to enable the reporting entity to be 'reasonably satisfied', as to certain minimal 'know your customer' (the '**KYC information**'). The KYC information to be collected and verified at the relevant times will depend upon whether the customer is an individual, a company, a trustee, a partner in a partnership, an association, a registered co-operative, or a government entity. The KYC information to be collected and verified will also depend upon whether the reporting entity has determined (based upon the appropriate risk-based systems and controls it is required to put in place, as well as money laundering and terrorist financing risks relevant to the designated service provided) that additional KYC information must be collected.

In the case of an individual, for example, a reporting entity will be required by the AML/CTF Rules to collect, at a minimum, information regarding the customer's full name, date of birth and residential address, and the reporting entity will be required to verify, at a minimum, the customer's full name and either the date of birth or the residential address. Moreover, if the reporting entity has determined (based upon the appropriate risk-based systems and controls and/or money laundering/terrorist financing risks) that additional KYC information must be collected, the further KYC information to be collected may include:

- the customer's name and any aliases, residential address, place and date of birth, country(ies) of citizenship, and country(ies) of residence;

- the customer's occupation or business activities;

- the nature of the customer's business with the reporting entity – including the purpose of specific transactions or the expected nature and level of transaction behavior;

- the income or assets available to the customer, and the customer's financial position;

- the customer's source of funds, including the origin of funds, and the beneficial ownership of the funds used by the customer with respect to the designated services; and

- the beneficiaries of the transactions being facilitated by the reporting entity on behalf of the customer including the destination of funds.

As noted above, similar KYC information rules will apply to companies, trustees, partners, associations, registered cooperatives, and government entities. In the case of individuals, however, the verification procedures in the AML/CTF Rules will also contain 'safe harbor' provisions. Where the relationship with the customer is of medium or lower money laundering or terrorist financing risk, the reporting entity can verify the customer's name, date of birth, and residential address from certain specified identification documents or through certain specified reliable and independent electronic data.[47]

In addition to the initial verification requirements set forth in the draft AML/CTF Rules, if a reporting entity at any time has reasonable grounds to doubt that a customer or agent for the customer is the person he or she claims to be, then the reporting entity will be required to re-verify the person's identity. Re-verification must be undertaken as soon as practicable and, in any event, within 14 business days. In meeting its re-verification obligations, a reporting entity will be required to take appropriate and reasonable steps, or other appropriate action in light of the money laundering or terrorist financing risk, to satisfy itself whether or not the customer or agent for the customer is the person he or she claims to be.

Finally, it should be noted that based upon the text of the revised exposure draft AML/CTF Bill 2006, the *AML/CTF Act* and the AML/CTF Rules will permit applicable customer identification procedures or applicable agent identification procedures to be carried out on behalf of a reporting entity by another person who is:

- an agent of the reporting entity;

- another reporting entity; or

- accredited under the AML/CTF Rules.[48]

Under the revised exposure draft AML/CTF Bill 2006, an agent for these purposes includes certain internal agents of the reporting company, certain external agents of the reporting company, and certain internal agents of external agents of the reporting company.

3.1.3   Reporting to *AUSTRAC*

Based upon the text of the revised exposure draft AML/CTF Bill 2006, the *AML/CTF Act* will impose four types of reporting obligations[49] on reporting entities:

- A reporting entity will be required to give AUSTRAC a report about any **suspicious matter**.

- A reporting entity that provides a designated service involving a **threshold transaction** will be required to give AUSTRAC a report about the transaction.

- A reporting entity that provides a designated service relating to an **international funds transfer instruction** will be required to give AUSTRAC a report about the provision of the service.

- A reporting entity may be required to give an **AML/CTF compliance report** to AUSTRAC during relevant reporting periods.

A suspicious matter reporting obligation arises under the revised exposure draft AML/CTF Bill 2006 where the reporting entity or its authorized agent (for purposes of the applicable customer identification procedures described above) has reasonable grounds to believe that:

---

[47] In order to use electronic verification, the reporting entity must also verify that the customer has a credit or transaction history for at least the past three years.

[48] There is presently no need identified by the Government for such accreditation Rules, but they will be drafted as necessary where accreditation of identification service providers is requested by the industry.

[49] The first three listed here will not apply to a designated service that is of a kind specified in the AML/CTF Rules; a designated service that is provided in circumstances specified in the AML/CTF Rules; or a designated service that is provided by a reporting entity at or through a permanent establishment of the entity in a foreign country.

- The customer or customer's agent is not who that person claims to be.
- The provision or prospective provision of a designated service either:
  - may be connected with a breach, or an attempted breach, of a taxation law;
  - may be connected with a breach, or an attempted breach, of a law of a State or Territory that deals with taxation;
  - may be connected with an offense against a law of the Commonwealth or of a State or Territory;
  - may be of assistance in the enforcement of the *Proceeds of Crime Act 2002* or regulations under that Act; or
  - may be of assistance in the enforcement of a law of a State or Territory that corresponds to the *Proceeds of Crime Act 2002* or regulations under that *Act*;
- The provision, or prospective provision, of a designated service is preparatory to the commission of an offense of terrorism financing or an offense of money laundering, as defined in the *AML/CTF Act.*
- Information that the reporting entity has concerning the provision or prospective provision of a designated service may be relevant to the investigation or prosecution of a person for an offense of terrorism financing or an offense of money laundering, as defined in the *AML/CTF Act.*

In the case of the first two above-listed types of suspicious matters, the reporting entity will be required under the *AML/CTF Act* to give AUSTRAC a report about the suspicious matter within 3 business days after the day on which the reporting entity or its authorized agent forms the relevant suspicion. In the case of the last two above-listed suspicious matters involving terrorism financing and money laundering offenses, the reporting entity will be required to give AUSTRAC a report about the suspicious matter within 24 hours after the time at which the reporting entity or its authorized agent forms the relevant suspicion. The required contents of the report is specified by the draft AML/CTF Rules, and includes the name, address, date of birth and other information regarding the identity of the customer, and a detailed statement of the matter that triggered the suspicion.

A threshold transaction with respect to which a reporting entity is required under the revised exposure draft AML/CTF Bill 2006 to give AUSTRAC a report is a transaction involving the transfer of not less than AUD 10,000 in physical currency or e-currency, or in an amount or form (including other forms of property) otherwise specified by regulation as a threshold amount for a specified transaction. In the event of a threshold transaction, the reporting entity will be required to give AUSTRAC a report of the transaction within 10 business days after the day on which the transaction takes place. In addition, under the draft AML/CTF Rules, the reporting entity will be required to provide specific details in respect of the transaction, including the name, address and other identifying information regarding the customer, and the date, amount, and description of the threshold transaction.

Only certain designated services relating to international funds transfer instructions must be reported by a reporting entity under the revised exposure draft AML/CTF Bill 2006. These include authorized deposit-taking institutions, banks, credit unions, or other persons specified in the AML/CTF Rules accepting or making available money under an international funds transfer instruction, or the acceptance or making available of money or property as a result of a transfer under a designated remittance agreement relating to an international funds transfer instruction. The provision of such a service must be reported to AUSTRAC within 10 business days after the day on which the service is commenced. However, any transactions as to which regulations provide an exemption from these requirements of the *AML/CTF Act*, or which fall below a threshold amount or value specified by regulation, are excluded from this reporting requirement.

Finally, AML/CTF compliance reports may be required under the *AML/CTF Act*, but only as required by the AML/CTF Rules. In particular, the revised exposure draft AML/CTF Bill 2006 requires that *if* the AML/CTF Rules define a specified reporting period and a specified lodgement period beginning at the end of the reporting period, which may be recurring periods, *then* a reporting entity must, within the lodgement period for a reporting period, give AUSTRAC a report about the reporting entity's compliance with the *AML/CTF Act*, the regulations and the AML/CTF Rules during the reporting period. The draft AML/CTF Rules do not contain any such requirements, however, although the Government has stated that such Rules will be completed following further consultation with industry sectors and other interest groups.

3.1.4 AML/CTF programs by reporting entities

An important part of the legislation to be included in the *AML/CTF Act*, set forth in the revised exposure draft AML/CTF Bill 2006, is that every reporting entity, before it commences to provide a designated service, will be required to adopt and maintain an anti-money laundering and counter-terrorism financing program that applies to the reporting entity. Significantly, failure to implement such a program, as well as failure to comply with a program so adopted, will each be offenses which carry a significant monetary penalty (120 penalty units) and/or imprisonment for two years. The program adopted may be either a standard AML/CTF program that applies only to the reporting entity or a joint program that applies to a group of reporting entities in a particular designated business group. Its primary purpose must be to identify, mitigate, and manage risk the reporting entity may reasonably face that the provision of a designated service at or through the reporting entity's permanent establishment in Australia might involve or facilitate money laundering or terrorism financing, as well as to comply with all requirements specified in the AML/CTF Rules. In addition, with respect to a reporting entity that provides a designated service at or through a permanent establishment in a foreign country, the program adopted must also ensure that the reporting entity takes such action as is specified in the AML/CTF Rules in relation to the provision by the reporting entity of designated services at or through a permanent establishment of the reporting entity in a foreign country.

In addition to the primary purpose of identifying, mitigating, and managing risk, the draft AML/CTF Rules also require that the adopted AML/CTF program must be designed *to identify significant changes* in the ML/TF risk (particularly with respect to the requirements of the AML/CTF program) and assess the ML/TF risk posed by *new designated services, new methods of designated service delivery*, and *new or developing technologies used for the provision of services*, prior to introducing the services or adopting the methods or technologies. Furthermore, the AML/CTF program must extend to all areas of the reporting entity's business that are involved in the provision of a designated service, including functions by third parties.

Finally, the draft AML/CTF Rules require that the AML/CTF program include:

- an AML/CTF risk awareness training program, with specified appropriate training for employees;

- an employee due diligence program;

- appropriate records to demonstrate to AUSTRAC that the program meets requirements in the AML/CTF Rules;

- approval and oversight of the program by the reporting entity's governing board (and if none, then by the CEO or equivalent) and senior management;

- a designated 'AML/CTF Compliance Officer' at the management level;

- regular independent program review by either an internal or external party, with the results of the review provided to senior management; and

- regard to any feedback by AUSTRAC with respect to the reporting entity's performance on the management of ML/TF risk.

The above-listed requirements of an AML/CTF risk awareness training program, an employee due diligence program, and appropriate documentation do not apply to a reporting entity with a permanent establishment in a foreign country. However, such a reporting entity must still comply with the other requirements and put in place appropriate risk-based systems and controls to the extent reasonable and practicable under the circumstances and with regard to local laws of the foreign country. In addition, the reporting entity must report to AUSTRAC if it is unable to put in place such appropriate risk-based systems and controls due to a prohibition of local laws in the foreign country. Significantly, if the reporting entity is regulated by an AML/CTF regime in the foreign country which is comparable to that in Australia, then it is necessary to consider only minimal additional risk-based systems and controls.

3.1.5 Cross-border movements of physical currency and bearer negotiable instruments

The revised exposure draft AML/CTF Bill 2006 provides that cross-border (into or out of Australia) movements of physical currency with a total value of not less than AUD 10 000 must be reported to AUSTRAC or to a customs officer or a police officer.[50] A person who is about to leave Australia or who arrives in Australia must, if required to do so by a police officer or a customs officer (and subject to examination and search):

- declare whether or not the person has with him or her any Australian currency or foreign currency;

- declare the total amount of any Australian currency or foreign currency that the person has with him or her; and

- declare whether or not, to the best of the person's knowledge and belief, the required report has been given in respect of any Australian currency or foreign currency that the person has with him or her; and

---

[50] Customs officers and police officers must forward the report to AUSTRAC within 5 days.

- produce to the officer any Australian currency or foreign currency that the person has with him or her.

The reporting requirement for physical currency does not apply to commercial passenger carriers, if the person carrying the currency is a passenger, nor does it apply to commercial goods carriers where the physical currency is carried on behalf of another person who has not disclosed to the carrier that the goods carried on behalf of that other person include physical currency.

Similarly, persons who are about to leave Australia must, if required to do so by a police officer or a customs officer (and subject to examination and search):

- declare whether or not the person has with him or her any bearer negotiable instruments;

- declare the amount payable under each bearer negotiable instrument that the person has with him or her; and

- produce to the officer each bearer negotiable instrument that the person has with him or her.

If a bearer negotiable instrument is produced to a police officer or a customs officer by a person leaving or arriving in Australia, the officer may require the person to give a report about the instrument to AUSTRAC, or to a customs officer or a police officer.[51]

3.1.6 Defenses to civil and criminal proceedings; other provisions of the revised exposure draft AML/CTF Bill 2006

The discussion in this chapter of the revised exposure draft AML/CTF Bill 2006 and draft AML/CTF Rules is not intended to be exhaustive or all-inclusive, especially as it is uncertain at the time of this writing as to what further changes will be made to the draft Bill and the draft Rules. A number of provisions are not mentioned in this chapter. One important provision which is likely to remain in the new *AML/CTF Act*, however, should be kept in mind with respect to all the requirements of the *AML/CTF Act* and AML/CTF Rules: the revised exposure draft AML/CTF Bill 2006 includes a 'good faith' protection from civil liability for actions or omissions to act in compliance with the *AML/CTF Act* and AML/CTF Rules, as well as a general defense to criminal and civil penalty proceedings where reasonable precautions have been taken and due diligence has been exercised.[52]

Addresses

Attorney-General's Department, Commonwealth of Australia
Central Offices
Robert Garran Offices
National Circuit

Barton ACT 2600
Australia
Tel +61 2 6250 6666
Fax +61 2 6250 5900
www.ag.gov.au

---

[51] Customs officers and police officers must forward the report to AUSTRAC within 5 days.
[52] Sections 195A and 195B, respectively, of the revised exposure draft AML/CTF Bill 2006.

Australian Crime Commission
Postal address:
GPO Box 1936
Canberra City 2601
Street address:
68 Northbourne Avenue
Canberra ACT 2601
Australia
Tel +61 2 6243 6666
Fax +61 2 6243 6687
www.crimecommission.gov.au

Australian Federal Police
Postal address:
PO Box 401
Canberra City 2601
Street address:
Cnr Unwil Place & Streeton Drive
Weston ACT
Australia
Tel +61 2 6223 3000
www.afp.gov.au

**Australian Transaction Reports &
Analysis Centre (AUSTRAC)**
Postal address:
PO Box 5516
West Chatswood NSW 1515
Australia
Tel +61 2 9950 0827 (Australia: 1300 021
037)
Fax +61 2 9950 0054
www.austrac.gov.au

**Department of Foreign Affairs and
Trade, Commonwealth of Australia
(DFAT)**
R.G. Casey Building
John McEwen Crescent
Barton ACT 0221
Australia
Tel +61 2 6261 1111
Fax +61 2 6261 3111
www.dfat.gov.au

Abbreviations

AML/CTF	Anti-Money Laundering and Counter-Terrorism Financing
AML/CTF Act	Anti-Money Laundering and Counter-Terrorism Financing Act 2006
AUSTRAC	Australian Transaction Reports and Analysis Centre
DFAT	Australian Department of Foreign Affairs and Trade
FATF	Financial Action Task Force
FIU	Financial Intelligence Unit
FTR Act	Financial Transaction Reports Act 1988 (Cth)
KYC	'know your customer'
ML/TF	money laundering and terrorism financing
PoC Act 2002	Proceeds of Crime Act 2002 (Cth)

David Craig is a partner specialising in banking and finance law. David worked for two years with New York law firm, Cravath, Swaine & Moore before returning to Bell Gully and becoming a partner in 1999. David has experience in domestic and international banking and capital markets transactions. He is particularly experienced in the use and regulation of derivative instruments and acts as the New Zealand counsel to ISDA and ISMA. David is a regular contributor to a number of international finance law journals and regularly speaks on banking and finance issues at international conferences. He is a committee member of the Australasian Banking and Financial Services Law Association. David is named as a Leading Individual in banking and finance by the *Asia Pacific Legal 500* 2005/2006. *Chambers Global* 2006 also lists David as a Leading Individual in banking and finance and describes him as 'a very commercial capital markets specialist'.

Simon David is a solicitor in Bell Gully's Wellington office. Simon has worked in the banking and finance team since joining the firm in 2004. Simon has experience in acting for lenders and borrowers in a broad range of international and domestic financing and property transactions. In particular, Simon has been involved in documenting a number of secured and unsecured lending transactions, including syndicated lending and group borrowing. Simon regularly advises New Zealand and overseas corporates on New Zealand regulatory requirements, including company law and personal property securities matters.

Firm's profile

Bell Gully is New Zealand's leading commercial law firm and the firm of choice for international businesses investing or operating in New Zealand. Bell Gully is also one of New Zealand's oldest law firms. The firm is the result of a merger between Bell Gully & Co of Wellington, founded in 1860, and Buddle Weir & Co of Auckland, founded in 1840. Our expertise and experience is consistently recognised by influential independent commentators. Bell Gully was named New Zealand Law Firm of the Year by the International Financial Law Review for the third consecutive year in March 2006.

New Zealand

David Craig

Partner

Simon David

Solicitor

Bell Gully
HP Tower
171 Featherston Street
(PO Box 1291)
Wellington
New Zealand

Tel +64 4 915 6839
Fax +64 4 473 3845
david.craig@bellgully.com
www.bellgully.com

Anti-Money Laundering: International Law and Practice.
Edited by W.H. Muller, C.H. Kälin and J.G. Goldsworth
© 2007 John Wiley & Sons, Ltd

Contents – New Zealand

1   Introduction

1.1   The role of FATF in New Zealand

New Zealand has been a member of the *Financial Action Task Force on Money Laundering* ('FATF') since 3 April 1991. As a member, *New Zealand* has a commitment to have legislation in force that implements the *FATF* 40 Recommendations (the 'Recommendations') on money laundering and terrorist financing. The *Financial Transactions Reporting Act 1996* (the 'FTRA'), which came into force on 1 August 1996, is *New Zealand's* primary legislation prohibiting money laundering.

All members of *FATF* are required to have their compliance with the Recommendations assessed by *FATF* on a regular basis. *FATF* most recently assessed *New Zealand's* compliance in October 2003, with a report of *FATF's* findings (the 'FATF Report') being released in August 2005.[1] **Although *FATF* found *New Zealand's* compliance with the Recommendations to be 'generally sound', it stated that 'some minor legislative changes, combined with additional resources and organisational changes, could further enhance the system'.**[2]

In response to the FATF Report, *New Zealand* is currently reviewing the *FTRA* and the role of *New Zealand's* central bank, the *Reserve Bank of New Zealand* (the 'RBNZ'), in preventing money laundering activities in *New Zealand*. Changes are expected to be implemented by 2008.

1.2   Introduction to New Zealand's anti-money laundering legislation

By comparison to other jurisdictions, ***New Zealand* has a largely deregulated financial sector**. The *New Zealand Government* relies on market forces and self-regulation within the financial sector, rather than providing a strict supervisory role. Legislation and regulator activity tends to focus on disclosure and monitoring the behaviour of financial institutions, rather than extensive prescriptive and proscriptive rules.

As stated above, the *FTRA* is *New Zealand's* principal money laundering legislation. Other legislation includes: the *Crimes Act 1961*, the *Misuse of Drugs Act 1975*, the *Terrorism Suppression Act 2002*, the *Proceeds of Crime Act 1992* and the *Mutual Assistance and Criminal Matters Act 1992*. The *FTRA* is outlined below in Section 2. The other legislation is outlined in Section 3.

2   The Financial Transactions Reporting Act

2.1   Defined terms

The following defined terms are the key to understanding the scope of the *FTRA's* obligations.

(a) *Financial institutions*: The obligations under Parts II to IV are obligations of financial institutions. The definition of 'financial institution' includes most organisations that provide

---

[1] Financial Action Task Force on Money Laundering, New Zealand: Report on the Observance of Standards and Codes – FATF Recommendations for Anti-Money Laundering and Combating the Financing of Terrorism, International Monetary Fund, Washington, DC, August 2005.
[2] Money Laundering and New Zealand's Compliance with FATF Recommendations – A Discussion Document, Ministry of Justice, Wellington, August 2005, p. 5.

financial services (such as banks, life insurance companies, share brokers and investment managers). Others, such as lawyers and accountants, are included to the extent that they receive funds from clients for deposit or investment. The definition also includes casinos and real-estate agents, because these types of businesses are particularly vulnerable to use in money laundering operations. In addition, persons whose business or a principal part of whose business involves borrowing, lending or investing money or managing funds on behalf of others are included within the definition.

(b) *Facility*: An account or arrangement that is provided by the financial institution and through which a *'facility holder'* may conduct two or more *'transactions'*.

(c) *Facility holder*: The person in whose name the facility is established. This includes any person who is authorised to conduct transactions through a facility.

(d) *Occasional transaction*: Any transaction that involves the transfer of cash and that is either not conducted through a facility or is conducted through a facility but the person conducting the transaction is not a facility holder.

(e) *Transactions*: Broadly, a transfer of funds by any means.

2.2   Outline of obligations on financial institutions

The *FTRA* requires financial institutions to comply with certain verification and reporting requirements in relation to facility holders either resident, or transacting, in *New Zealand*.

In general terms, financial institutions have the following obligations under the *FTRA*:

- to verify the identity of facility holders (Part II);
- to report suspicious transactions (Part III);
- to retain verification and transaction records (Part IV); and
- to report imports and exports of cash (Part V).

2.3   Obligations on financial institutions to verify identity (Part II)

Sections 6 to 12 of the *FTRA* require financial institutions to verify the identity of customers in certain circumstances. **Identity must be verified**:

(a) Where a person applies to become a facility holder (whether in relation to an existing facility or the establishment of a new facility).

(b) Where a person is conducting an occasional transaction and either:

(i) the amount of cash involved in the transaction is at least NZ$10 000 (approximately US$6200); or

(ii) the person conducting the transaction, or someone else, is conducting other occasional transactions, the total cash involved is at least NZ$10 000 and the financial institution believes on reasonable grounds that the transactions have been structured to avoid the specified threshold.

(c) Where:

    (i) a person is conducting occasional transactions through a financial institution; or

    (ii) a facility holder is conducting a transaction through its facility;
and, in either case:

    (iii) the financial institution has reasonable grounds to believe that the person is conducting the transaction on behalf of others; and

    (iv) either:

- the amount of cash involved is at least NZ$10 000; or

- the person conducting the transactions, or someone else, is conducting other transactions, the total cash involved is at least NZ$10 000 and the financial institution believes on reasonable grounds that the transactions have been structured so as to avoid the specified threshold.

(In this case, the financial institution must verify the identity of the persons on whose behalf it is believed the transactions are being conducted.)

(d) Where a person conducts a transaction (whether or not involving cash) and the financial institution has reasonable grounds to suspect a money laundering offence.

2.3.1   Procedures for verifying identity

Where a financial institution is required to verify the identity of a person, section 12(1) of the *FTRA* provides that verification must be '***by means of such documentary or other evidence as is reasonably capable of establishing the identity of that person***'.

The Best Practice Guidelines for Financial Institutions (the 'Best Practice Guidelines') issued by the *Financial Intelligence Unit* (the 'FIU') states that:[3]

> The Act is deliberately silent on exactly what evidence is 'reasonably capable' of proving a person's identity... As a general rule, institutions are required to verify identity from a document or documents obtained from a reputable and identifiable source, such as the New Zealand Government issued identification, or by way of reference from a reputable and identifiable party.

Whether a person's identity has been sufficiently identified by a financial institution will largely depend on the **type and source** of the documentation relied on. The Best Practice Guidelines list the following documents as examples of possible forms of identification:[4]

- an ATM or credit card (provided that the signature has been verified); or

- a driver's licence; or

- a passport.

---

[3] Best Practice Guidelines for Financial Institutions, New Zealand Police Financial Intelligence Unit, Wellington, September 2005, p. 20.
[4] Best Practice Guidelines for Financial Institutions, New Zealand Police Financial Intelligence Unit, Wellington, September 2005, p. 20.

The Best Practice Guidelines also recommend that financial institutions check a second form of identification to verify the address of a person (such as an original utility bill).[5]

2.3.2   Timing of identity verification

Generally, a financial institution will be required to verify the identity of the relevant person **before a transaction** is carried out or an account is opened.

2.3.3   Previous identification

Section 12(2) of the *FTRA* provides that a financial institution can rely on a **previous identification** '*if the financial institution has reasonable grounds to believe that the evidence is still reasonably capable of establishing the identity of that person*'. However, the Best Practice Guidelines state that:[6]

> In a situation where there has been a significant time lapse between dealings with a particular customer, it may be sensible to renew the verification to ensure that the financial institution is dealing with the same person.

2.4   Obligations to report suspicious transactions (Part III)

Where any person conducts or seeks to conduct any transaction through a financial institution and the financial institution has **reasonable grounds to suspect**:

(a) that the transaction is or may be relevant to the investigation of any person for a money laundering offence; or

(b) that the transaction is or may be relevant to the enforcement of the *Proceeds of Crimes Act,*

the financial institution must, **as soon as reasonably practicable after forming the suspicion**, report that transaction to the *Commissioner of Police*.

The number of suspicious transactions being reported to the *New Zealand Police* has increased dramatically, with over 12 600 suspicious bank transactions being reported in the last two years.[7] This increase has been attributed to heightened awareness by the *New Zealand* public towards money laundering.

2.5   Retention of records (Part IV)

The *FTRA* requires financial institutions to keep and maintain records relating to transactions and verification of customers. These records must be kept in writing and in English, or at least be readily convertible to written English.

---

[5] Best Practice Guidelines for Financial Institutions, New Zealand Police Financial Intelligence Unit, Wellington, September 2005, p. 21.
[6] Best Practice Guidelines for Financial Institutions, New Zealand Police Financial Intelligence Unit, Wellington, September 2005, p. 21.
[7] *Scanlon Sean*: Bank Scams Double Since 2003, The Christchurch Press, Christchurch, 6 January 2006, p. 5.

2.5.1   Obligation to keep transaction records

Section 29 of the *FTRA* requires a financial institution to keep such records as are reasonably necessary to enable a transaction through that financial institution to be readily reconstructed at any time by the *Commissioner of Police*. The amount of information required to be retained will vary for each transaction. However, at a minimum, transaction records should contain the following information:

   (i) the nature of the transaction;

  (ii) the amount of the transaction;

 (iii) the date on which the transaction was conducted;

  (iv) the parties to the transaction;

   (v) where applicable, the facility through which the transaction was conducted; and

  (vi) the name of the officer, employee or agent of the financial institution who handled the transaction, if that person has face-to-face dealings with any of the parties to the transaction and has formed a suspicion about that transaction.

Records must be retained for **at least five years** after the completion of the transaction.

2.5.2   Obligation to keep verification records

Section 30 of the *FTRA* provides that, where a financial institution is required to verify the identity of a person, the financial institution must keep such records as are reasonably necessary to enable the nature of the evidence used for the purposes of that verification to be **readily identified** at any time by the *Commissioner of Police*.

Where records relate to the verification of the identity of a person in relation to a facility, the records must be retained for not less than five years from the date the person ceases to be a facility holder. In all other cases, records must be retained for not less than five years from the date that the verification is carried out.

2.6   Obligation to report imports and exports of cash (Part V)

Part V of the *FTRA* requires every person who enters or departs *New Zealand* with cash on hand of NZ$10 000 or more to report that cash to a customs officer in the prescribed form. If a customs officer suspects a person of carrying unreported cash, he or she may detain and search that person.

2.7   Offences

Where any financial institution fails to comply with its obligations under Part II, III or IV of the *FTRA*, that financial institution commits an offence and is liable to a fine of NZ$100 000 in the case of a body corporate and NZ$20 000 in the case of an individual.

Where any person fails to report cash imports or exports in breach of Part V of the *FTRA*, that person is liable to a fine not exceeding NZ$2000.

Recently, the courts have started to take a hard line towards compliance with the *FTRA*. In *Police v E-Trans International Finance Limited* (District Court, Auckland, 6 July 2004), at paragraph 27, Justice FWM Elrea held that:

> compliance with the legislation is, in the Court's view, important not only in terms of apprehension of those who seek to use the financial institutions of this country for laundering money illegally gained, and the detection of crime so that persons conducting such transactions can be traced; it is also relevant to the prevention of such crime by making clear that this country will not be a 'soft touch' for international drug dealers and international criminals of other types.

2.8 Defence

If a financial institution fails to verify or report a transaction in breach of the *FTRA*, there is a defence available in each case. The financial institution must prove that it took all '*reasonable steps*' to ensure that it complied with the *FTRA* or that, in the circumstances, it could not reasonably have been expected to ensure that it complied with the provision.

In determining whether a financial institution took all reasonable steps to comply, a *New Zealand* court will have regard to:

- the nature of the financial institution and the activities in which it engages; and

- the existence and adequacy of any procedures established by the financial institution to ensure compliance with the relevant provision, including (without limitation) staff training and audits to test the effectiveness of any such procedures.

2.9 Vicarious liability

Under section 53 of the *FTRA*, employers and principals are liable for any acts done or omitted by employees, whether or not the acts or omissions are done with the knowledge or approval of the employer or principal. Where any person is acting as the agent of another, then that other person is liable for any acts or omissions of the agent unless the acts or omissions were done by the agent without the principal's express or implied authority.

Under section 54 of the *FTRA*, where any body corporate is convicted of an offence, each of its directors and officers concerned in the management of that body corporate is also guilty of the offence if it is proved that the act or omission that constituted the offence took place with the knowledge, authority, permission or consent of that director or officer.

3 Other legislation

3.1 Crimes Act and Misuse of Drugs Act

Section 243 of the *Crimes Act* and section 12B of the *Misuse of Drugs Act* both create offences of money laundering. These offences involve dealing in property that is the proceeds of serious crime or a specified drug offence for the purpose of concealing that property (punishable by seven years' imprisonment) or having possession of such property with intent to engage in a money laundering transaction (punishable by five years' imprisonment).

Knowledge of money laundering offences may be inferred from objective factual circumstances, including wilful blindness and recklessness.

3.2   Proceeds of Crime Act

The *Proceeds of Crime Act* provides for the restraint of property where a person is convicted or charged with a serious criminal offence. It also provides for the property to be forfeited to the *Crown*. In addition, if a person has derived benefits as a result of committing an offence, the court may assess the value of the benefits and order the offender to pay the *Crown* a pecuniary penalty.

3.3   Mutual Assistance and Criminal Matters Act

The *Mutual Assistance and Criminal Matters Act* facilitates the provision and obtaining by *New Zealand* of international assistance in criminal matters including assistance in money laundering investigations and property forfeiture actions.

3.4   Terrorism Suppression Act

The *Terrorism Suppression Act* (the 'TSA') implements *New Zealand's* international obligations[8] by prohibiting the funding of terrorist acts and terrorist entities. In particular, the *TSA* makes it an offence, without lawful justification or reasonable excuse:

(a) wilfully to provide or collect funds intending that they be used, or knowing that they are to be used, in order to carry out terrorist acts; or

(b) to '*deal with*'[9] any '*property*'[10] knowing that the property is owned or controlled by an entity designated as a terrorist entity or an associated entity (or derived or generated from such property); or

(c) to make available any property, or any financial or related services, either to or for the benefit of an entity, knowing that the entity is designated as a terrorist entity or as an associated entity.

Under the *TSA*, the *Prime Minister* has the power, following consultation with the *Attorney-General*, to designate an entity as a terrorist entity or associated entity and to direct that the making of a designation order be publicly notified in any manner or form that the *Prime Minister* thinks fit.

The *TSA* provides that any person in possession or immediate control of property, suspecting on reasonable grounds that the property is owned or controlled by an entity designated as a terrorist or associated entity (or derived or generated from such property) must, as soon as practicable after forming that suspicion, report to the *Commissioner of Police*.

---

[8] These obligations arise under Resolution 1373 (2001) of the Security Council of the United Nations adopted under Chapter VII of the United Nations Chapter on 28 September 2001, the International Convention for the Suppression of Terrorist Bombings adopted by the General Assembly of the United Nations on 15 December 1997, the International Convention for the Suppression of the Financing of Terrorism adopted by the General Assembly of the United Nations at New York on 9 December 1999, the Convention on the Physical Protection of Nuclear Material done at New York and Vienna on 3 March 1980 and the Convention on the Marking of Plastic Explosives for the Purpose of Detection done at Montreal on 1 March 1991.

[9] '*Deal with*' is broadly defined and means to use or deal with the property, in any way and by any means, and includes allowing the property to be used or dealt with, or facilitating the use of it or dealing with it.

[10] '*Property*' includes real or personal property of any description, whether situated in New Zealand or elsewhere, whether tangible or intangible.

Proceedings may be brought in *New Zealand* for financing of terrorism if the acts alleged to constitute the offence took place outside *New Zealand* but were directed towards terrorist acts being done within *New Zealand*.

To date, no terrorist financing has been reported in *New Zealand*.[11]

4   Proposed amendments to the FTRA

4.1   First discussion document

In response to the FATF Report, the *Ministry of Justice* released a discussion document[12] in August 2005 suggesting a number of possible amendments to the *FTRA,* which would place further obligations on financial institutions. These amendments include:[13]

- extending due diligence measures to properly verify the identity of third parties for whom a customer is acting;

- retaining files relating to business relations (in addition to verification and transaction records) for no less than five years;

- providing the *New Zealand Police* with financial records upon request;

- reporting funds or property suspected to be related to terrorist financing or owned or controlled by terrorist organisations;

- paying special attention when dealing with persons from countries whose money laundering regulations do not comply with the Recommendations;

- higher recruitment standards and more staff training for financial institutions;

- the mandatory appointment of compliance officers;

- ensuring foreign branches and subsidiaries comply with New Zealand standards; and

- preventing criminals from controlling financial institutions.

4.2   Second discussion document

At the time of publication, the *Ministry of Justice* has released a second discussion document.[14] Generally, this document supports the legislative framework outlined in this chapter. However, while the first discussion document contemplates reforms being in the form of amendments to the *FTRA*, the second discussion document contemplates replacement legislation. Other than the legislative reforms already referred to in this chapter, proposed changes include:

---

[11] Financial Action Task Force on Money Laundering, New Zealand: Report on the Observance of Standards and Codes – FATF Recommendations for Anti-Money Laundering and Combating the Financing of Terrorism, International Monetary Fund, Washington, DC, August 2005.

[12] Money Laundering and New Zealand's Compliance with FATF Recommendations – A Discussion Document, Ministry of Justice, Wellington, August 2005.

[13] Money Laundering and New Zealand's Compliance with FATF Recommendations – A Discussion Document, Ministry of Justice, Wellington, August 2005, p. 15.

[14] Anti-Money Laundering and Countering the Financing of Terrorism: New Zealand's Compliance with FATF Recommendations – Second Discussion Document, Ministry of Justice, Wellington, June 2006.

- increased and expanded customer due diligence requirements; and

- the establishment of a new supervisory body to work along side the *FIU*. The role of this body would be to identify money laundering risks, oversee implementation and compliance with anti-money laundering requirements and educate affected industries and the public generally.

It is expected that this replacement legislation would be in force by 2008.

5   The principal anti-money laundering regulators in New Zealand

5.1   New Zealand Police

Two sections of the *New Zealand Police* deal specifically with financial crime.

5.1.1   Financial Intelligence Unit

The *FIU* is based in *Wellington*. It receives and investigates suspicious financial transaction reports under the *FTRA*. The *FIU* also monitors large amounts of cash crossing New Zealand borders. Since 1997, the *FIU* has been a member of the *Egmont Group*, an informal forum that provides international support and information sharing opportunities in respect of preventing domestic money laundering.

The *FIU* is responsible for publishing guidance notes under the *FTRA* to be used by all financial institution. The Best Practice Guidelines were issued in September 2005.

Generally, the *FIU* will receive and review a suspicious transaction report and refer it to the Proceeds of Crime Unit (the 'PCU') for further investigation.

5.1.2   Proceeds of Crime Unit

The *PCU* is based in *Auckland*, *Hamilton*, *Wellington* and *Christchurch*. It is responsible for investigating offender's assets and making applications to the court for the restraint or forfeiture to the *Crown* of proceeds of serious crime or drug offences.

Two other *Crown* agencies that have responsibility for controlling money laundering are the *New Zealand Customs Department* and the *Serious Fraud Office*.

5.2   Reserve Bank of New Zealand

In accordance with the *Reserve Bank of New Zealand Act 1989*, the *RBNZ* is responsible for the **registration and prudential supervision** of all registered banks. The *RBNZ* requires all registered banks to have procedures in place that implement and comply with the standards outlined in the *Basel Committee's 'Statement of Principles on Prevention of Criminal Use of the Banking System for the Purpose of Money Laundering'*[15] and paper on *'Customer Due Diligence for Banks'*.[16]

---

[15] Statement of Principles on Prevention of Criminal Use of the Banking System for the Purpose of Money Laundering, Basel Committee on Banking Supervision, December 1998 at www.bis.org/bcbs/publ.htm.

[16] Customer Due Diligence for Banks, Basel Committee on Banking Supervision, October 2001 at www.bis.org/bcbs/publ.htm.

Nine of *New Zealand's* registered banks are also members of the *New Zealand Bankers' Association* (the 'NZBA'). The NZBA was established in 1891 and acts as a forum for registered banks. The NZBA issues Money Laundering Procedures and Guidelines, which are available to all its members.

It has been proposed in a Cabinet Paper[17] released on 7 December 2005 that the *RBNZ* should be the single universal prudential regulator or a 'mega-regulator' for the whole of the domestic financial sector (including banks, insurance companies, building societies and credit unions). A consequence of this initiative may well be that these non-bank financial institutions are required to comply with the anti-money laundering standards expected of registered banks.

Addresses

New Zealand Police
Office of the Commissioner
180 Molesworth Street
P.O. Box 3017
Wellington
New Zealand
Tel +64 4 474 9499
Fax +64 4 498 7405

Ministry of Justice
FATF Interagency Working Group
P.O. Box 180
Wellington
New Zealand
Tel +64 4 918 8800
Fax +64 4 918 8820

Abbreviations

FATF	Financial Action Task Force on Money Laundering
FIU	Financial Intelligence Unit
FTRA	Financial Transactions Reporting Act 1996
NZBA	New Zealand Bankers' Association
PCU	Proceeds of Crime Unit
RBNZ	Reserve Bank of New Zealand
TSA	Terrorism Suppression Act 2002

Bibliography

Anti-Money Laundering and Countering the Financing of Terrorism: New Zealand's Compliance with FATF Recommendations – Second Discussion Document, Ministry of Justice, Wellington, June 2006.

Best Practice Guidelines for Financial Institutions, New Zealand Police Financial Intelligence Unit, Wellington, September 2005.

---

[17] Cabinet Paper CBC (05) 276: Domestic Institutional Arrangements for Financial Sector Regulation, The Treasury, Wellington, 7 December 2005.

Cabinet Paper CBC (05) 276: Domestic Institutional Arrangements for Financial Sector Regulation, The Treasury, Wellington, 7 December 2005.

Claridge, A.: Huge Leap in Dodgy Dealing Linked to Crime, The Christchurch Press, Christchurch, 29 December 2004.

Financial Action Task Force on Money Laundering, New Zealand: Report on the Observance of Standards and Codes – FATF Recommendations for Anti-Money Laundering and Combating the Financing of Terrorism, International Monetary Fund, Washington, DC, August 2005.

Money Laundering and New Zealand's Compliance with FATF Recommendations – A Discussion Document, Ministry of Justice, Wellington, August 2005.

Money Laundering & Terrorist Financing Typologies 2004–2005, Financial Action Task Force on Money Laundering, Paris, 10 June 2005.

Money Laundering, Financial Stability Department, Reserve Bank of New Zealand, Wellington, August 2003.

Scanlon, S.: Bank Scams Double Since 2003, The Christchurch Press, Christchurch, 6 January 2006.

AFRICA

Pieter Smit is a Senior Manager at the Financial Intelligence Centre in South Africa where he is responsible for the development of anti-money laundering policy and legislation and the Centre's role in South Africa's response to money laundering and terrorist financing. He holds a Bachelors degree in law from the University of Pretoria and an LLM, with major subjects in banking and exchange law, from the University of Johannesburg. He started his career as a public prosecutor. Then, as a State Law Advisor of the South African Law Reform Commission, he was responsible for projects which resulted, among others, in legislation on money laundering, asset forfeiture, mutual legal assistance and extradition. Before joining the Financial Intelligence Centre he was attached to the Asset Forfeiture Unit in the office of the National Director of Public Prosecutions as an advocate.

Organisation's profile

The **Financial Intelligence Centre** is the financial intelligence unit in South Africa. It is primarily responsible for the identification of proceeds of crime and the combating of money laundering activities and the financing of terrorism. The Centre also has a responsibility to monitor compliance with, and give guidance on the implementation of, money laundering laws. In addition the Centre provides advice of a policy nature and formulates proposals on the development of legislation to address issues concerning money laundering and terrorist financing.

South Africa

Pieter Smit

Senior Manager

Financial Intelligence Centre
240 Vermeulen Street
Pretoria 0002
South Africa

Tel +27 12 309 9200
Fax +27 12 309 9480
pieter.smit@fic.gov.za
www.fic.gov.za

Anti-Money Laundering: International Law and Practice.
Edited by W.H. Muller, C.H. Kälin and J.G. Goldsworth
© 2007 John Wiley & Sons, Ltd

Contents – South Africa

1   Chapter overview

This chapter deals with the legislative response in South Africa to the phenomenon of money laundering.

An analysis is made of the **current money laundering offences** in South Africa. These are money laundering, assisting another to benefit from proceeds of unlawful activities, acquisition, possession or use of proceeds of unlawful activities and failure to report suspicion regarding proceeds of unlawful activities. In each case the elements of the offence are discussed and a few examples of what may happen in practice are given. The development of these provisions is also explored by taking a brief look at the predecessors of the current money laundering offences.

South Africa also has a structure for **recovery of the proceeds of criminal activity** that is close to the height of the evolutionary scale of proceeds of crime models. The South African model comprises of a conviction-based confiscation procedure as well as a so-called civil forfeiture procedure without requiring a conviction. This chapter takes a brief look at these procedures. The steps that make up these procedures are explained and the procedures are distinguished from each other.

In addition the chapter describes South Africa's **regulatory framework of preventative control measures**. These are measures concerning client identification, record-keeping, reporting of information and internal compliance structures which apply to a broad range of financial and non-financial institutions.

The chapter takes a brief look at one of the structures created specifically to address money laundering in South Africa, namely the South African **financial intelligence unit** known as the *Financial Intelligence Centre*.

Lastly the chapter provides a short overview of measures concerning **extradition and mutual legal assistance**.

2   Introduction

South Africa is a regional financial centre with a modern financial system and banking infra-structure. There are more than 50 registered banks in South Africa offering a range of services and products. In addition a full range of sophisticated financial services are offered by non-bank financial institutions including long and short-term insurance companies, financial advisors and intermediaries, investment managers, securities brokers, and collective investment schemes.

South Africa has an exchange control regime in place. Currency exchange is only permitted by Authorised Dealers in Foreign Exchange, which are appointed by the Minister of Finance and regulated by the Exchange Control Department of the SARB. The majority are banks that are also appointed as Authorised Dealers.

South Africa has developed a comprehensive legal structure to combat money laundering. The main statutes are the *Prevention of Organised Crime Act*, 121 of 1998 and the *Financial Intelligence Centre Act*, 38 of 2001. The Minister of Finance is the responsible Minister on policy measures and issues concerning money laundering.

South Africa became a member of the Financial Action Task Force in June 2003. In August 2002 South Africa became a member of the Eastern and Southern African Anti-Money Laundering Group.

Early typologies research indicates that criminals use various means to launder their proceeds in South Africa. These indicate that the means used include the purchase of properties and goods, the establishment of companies and trusts for laundering the proceeds of crime, the misuse of businesses, the use of casinos, and using the informal, cash-based sector. The money laundering investigations that have occurred involved predicate offences of fraud, theft, corruption, racketeering, and gambling.

3 Criminalisation of money laundering

The current provisions dealing with the manipulation of the proceeds from unlawful activities are contained in the *Prevention of Organised Crime Act*. This Act contains three offences which combine to criminalise a wide range of money laundering activities. These are the offences of money laundering, assisting another to benefit from the proceeds of crime and of acquisition, possession or use of such proceeds.

3.1 Money laundering

The **money laundering offence** is contained in section 4 of the Prevention of Organised Crime Act. This provision criminalises entering into any agreement, arrangement or transaction in connection with the proceeds of crime which has, or is likely to have, the effect of concealing or disguising the nature, source, location, disposition or movement of those proceeds or of enabling any person who has committed an offence to avoid prosecution to remove or diminish those proceeds.

3.1.1 Guilty action

One of the common elements of an offence under South African law is a guilty action or omission (the '*actus reus*'). In the case of the money laundering offence the action is either to enter into an **agreement or arrangement in connection with certain property**, or to perform another action in connection with that property. In short this could be anything done in respect of the property in question.

The agreement or arrangement need not be legally enforceable. Even where a criminal looks to launder proceeds from a criminal activity through illegal or unenforceable transactions would the action be committed. Such cases would not amount to an attempt to commit money laundering but to the completed offence.

The qualification of the action is that it **must have a certain consequence**, or it must be at least likely to have a certain consequence. The consequence can be one of three alternatives. It can be

- to conceal or disguise the nature, source, location, disposition or movement of the property or the ownership thereof or any interest that anyone may have therein; or
- to enable or assist an offender to avoid prosecution; or
- to enable or assist an offender to remove or diminish the proceeds of some criminal activity.

The relevant consequences need not have been realised, as long as it is likely that the agreement or arrangement could have resulted in one of those consequences. The court will have to determine what is likely to result from a specific agreement or arrangement. It is suggested that the court will do this by reference to what can generally and according to reasonable experiences be expected to result from an agreement or arrangement. The use of the word 'likely' indicates that it is not any result, however remote, that is intended here.

The fact that the agreement or arrangement need not be legally enforceable and the fact that the relevant consequence need not be realised means that in almost any circumstance will the completed offence be committed. It is only where the agreement or arrangement was initiated but not concluded where there would be room for a charge of attempt to commit money laundering.

3.1.2 Proceeds as an objective fact

The property in connection with which the action is to be performed must be the 'proceeds of unlawful activities'. The phrase 'proceeds of unlawful activities' is defined in the *Prevention of Organised Crime Act*. The factors referred to in this definition are facts which can be determined objectively:[1]

> **'proceeds of unlawful activities'** means any property or any service advantage, benefit or reward which was derived, received or retained, directly or indirectly, in the Republic or elsewhere, at any time before or after the commencement of this Act, in connection with or as a result of any unlawful activity carried on by any person, and includes any property representing property so derived;

The property in question **must have been derived from unlawful activities**. This unlawful activity could have taken place **anywhere and at any time**. South Africa followed an '**all crimes**' **approach to defining the scope of the money laundering offence**. It is not limited by reference to the type of underlying criminal activity from which the laundered proceeds are obtained. This means that any profit-generating activity which constitutes and offence under South African law qualifies as a so-called predicate offence.

The money laundering offence in the *Prevention of Organised Crime Act* does **not require a conviction** for the underlying criminal activity which gave rise to the proceeds in question. It is also not necessary to prove that the criminal proceeds originated from a specific instance of criminal activity.

3.1.3 Intent and negligence

The required form of guilt (mens rea) for the money laundering offence is expressed in the phrase '**knows or ought reasonably to have known**'. The knowledge element of the offence in the *Prevention of Organised Crime Act* relates to **intent** as a form of guilt and includes **actual knowledge as well as constructive knowledge** of the fact that the property in question is the proceeds of crime.

Constructive knowledge exists if a person believes that there is a reasonable possibility that a fact is true but fails to obtain information to confirm or reject that belief.

In practical terms, in relation to the money laundering offence, this means that a person who believes that there is a possibility that the property with which he or she is dealing is the proceeds of criminal activities, but turns a **blind eye** to that possibility, will be held to have known the property to be criminal proceeds and therefore to have intended to launder those proceeds.

The description of the phrase 'ought reasonably to have known' in the *Prevention of Organised Crime Act* relates to **negligence** as a form of guilt. The phrase 'ought reasonably to have known'

---

[1] Section 1(1) of the Prevention of Organised Crime Act.

refers to a fact of which a diligent and vigilant person would be aware. To this person is attributed the general knowledge, skill, training and experience that may be reasonably expected of a person in the position in question and the actual knowledge, skill, training and experience of the person whose actions are under consideration.

To put this in practical terms again, a person ought to be aware of the fact that he or she is dealing with the proceeds of criminal activities if a reasonably diligent and vigilant person in his or her position, with the knowledge, skill, training and experience that may be expected of such a person, would have been aware thereof.

The formulation of the money laundering offence in the *Prevention of Organised Crime Act* clearly includes both intent and negligence as required forms of guilt. These may appear to be technical or legalistic issues but it can have serious consequences for a person or organisation that does not take cognisance thereof.

The fact that the *Prevention of Organised Crime Act* clearly defines the knowledge element to include facts that a person believes to possibly exist, without having actual knowledge thereof, means that there is more room to conclude from the objective surrounding circumstances of a particular case that a person was aware that the property in question is the proceeds of crime. The effect of this is that whenever something appears to be out of the ordinary a person will not be allowed to ignore that fact and in so doing to avoid liability.

Furthermore by expressly describing the negligence element the *Prevention of Organised Crime Act* places a duty of diligence on every person and organisation that is at risk of coming into contact with the proceeds of criminal activities. This duty entails that persons should acquire the knowledge, skill and experience and undergo the training that will be necessary to identify situations where they are dealing with the proceeds of criminal activities. The duty also requires that persons should in fact constantly apply their knowledge, skill, training and experience so that they will be alerted when they come across something out of the ordinary.

In short the formulation of the money laundering offence makes it clear that a person will not be allowed to simply raise his or her shoulders and say, 'I did not know'.

It may be helpful to give an example of what may happen in practice to illustrate some of the points made above:

A member of an organised criminal group 'Mr X' approaches a financial intermediary for assistance in disposing of an exceptionally large amount of cash. The cash was obtained by members of the organised criminal group through the sale of contraband. The intermediary suggests that Mr X divides the cash and makes a number of investments such as purchasing a single premium endowment policy, a collective investment scheme and securities on a securities exchange. The intermediary then proceeds to place the various investments on Mr X's behalf and hands the relevant policy documents, certificates and other documents to Mr X.

The knowledge element which must be applied to Mr X and the intermediary in a money laundering prosecution is that each of them must have known, or ought reasonably to have known, that the cash is the proceeds of unlawful activities.

In Mr X's case this does not present a problem. Being a member of the organised criminal group he will have actual knowledge of this fact. As a result he will be held to have had the necessary intent to launder the criminal proceeds.

The intermediary may have constructive knowledge of this fact. If circumstances described above raised the intermediary's suspicion as to the legal source of the money and he chose to ignore this and continue entering into the contracts, he will be regarded as having knowledge of its illegal source. As a result he will be held to have had the necessary intent to launder the criminal proceeds.

If these circumstances did not raise any suspicions in the intermediary but a reasonable person in the same circumstances would have become suspicious and refused to proceed with the investments on Mr X's behalf, the intermediary will be regarded as being negligent.

3.2   Assisting another to benefit from proceeds of unlawful activities

Assisting another to benefit from the proceeds of unlawful activities refers to the offence of a person who knows or ought reasonably to have known that **another person** has obtained the proceeds of unlawful crime and who enters into an agreement, arrangement or transaction which facilitates the retention or the control by that other person of those proceeds is facilitated, or by means of which the proceeds are used to make funds available to that other person or to acquire property on his or her behalf or to benefit him or her in any other way.

3.2.1   Guilty action

The action described in this offence is to enter into an agreement or arrangement with another person in connection with certain property. The agreement or arrangement entered into is qualified by one of two consequences. The first consequence is that the retention or the control of the proceeds of criminal activities by the other person be facilitated. The other is that the proceeds of the criminal activities be used in one of three ways:

- to make funds available to the other person;

- to acquire property on his or her behalf; or

- to benefit him or her in any other way.

In the first case the consequence, namely the facilitating of the retention or the control of the proceeds of criminal activities, must have realised for the completed offence to be committed. If this consequence did not realise the accused may be convicted of an attempt to commit this offence.

In the second case it is important to note that the consequence is not for the funds to be made available to the person in question or the property to be acquired on his or her behalf or that he or she have benefited in some way. The required consequence of the agreement or arrangement entered into is just that the proceeds of the criminal activity be put to use to achieve one of these purposes. The offence will have been completed once the proceeds are used with one of these purposes in mind, regardless of whether the purpose is in fact achieved.

The person performing the action **must be somebody other than the person who initially obtained the proceeds**. It can be any person who launders the proceeds by transacting with either the criminal who had derived the proceeds or another person who has control over those proceeds or stands to benefit from them.

The property in connection with which the action is to be performed must be the 'proceeds of unlawful activities'. The definition of 'proceeds of unlawful activities' in the *Prevention of Organised Crime Act* will apply in this respect.[2] This means that the court will have to refer to objectively determinable facts presented in evidence when considering the nature of the property involved. These facts would have to show that the nature of the property falls within the definition.

Concerning the property it is important to note that the description of the offence does not require the terms of the agreement or arrangement to involve the property in question directly. This means that the agreement or arrangement does not have to refer in any way to the property that forms the proceeds of unlawful activities.

> It may be helpful again to refer to the earlier example of what may happen in practice to illustrate the points made above concerning the relation between the agreement or arrangement entered into and the proceeds of unlawful activities:
> One of the investments made on Mr X's behalf is the purchase of a single premium insurance policy. Once the policy is purchased and the premium paid the policy becomes an instrument representing the original proceeds of the unlawful activity. This instrument now facilitates Mr X's control over the proceeds.
> The policy can also be used to make funds available to Mr X, for example by surrendering the policy or using it as security for a credit agreement.

3.3 Acquisition, possession or use of proceeds of unlawful activities

Acquiring, possessing or using the proceeds of unlawful activities refers to the offence of a person who acquires, uses or has possession of property and who knows or ought to have known that it is the proceeds of crime of another person.

3.3.1 Guilty action

The action in this offence consists merely of doing one of three things with the proceeds of unlawful activities. These are:

- to acquire the proceeds of unlawful activities;

- to use the proceeds of unlawful activities; or

- to possess the proceeds of unlawful activities.

Somebody other than the person acquiring, using or possessing those proceeds must have committed the unlawful activities from which the property has been derived.

3.4 Penalties

The *Prevention of Organised Crime Act* prescribes serious maximum penalties for these offences, namely a fine of R100 000 000 (±US$16 867 000), or imprisonment for a period not exceeding 30 years.

---

[2] Section 1(1) of the Prevention of Organised Crime Act, discussed above.

4   Confiscation and forfeiture

The recovery of the proceeds of criminal activity can have a significant impact on the ability of organised criminal groups to perpetuate their criminal activities. For this reason the combating of money laundering on the one hand and the recovery of the proceeds of criminal activity on the other, should form two components of a strategy to combat organised crime.

The *Prevention of Organised Crime Act* contains two separate procedures for depriving criminals of their proceeds of criminal activities. The first is a **confiscation** procedure[3] and the second is a **civil forfeiture** procedure.[4]

The confiscation procedure may only be instituted **once a person is convicted of an offence**.[5] The procedure consists of an enquiry instituted by the trial court at the request of the public prosecutor. The purpose of the enquiry is to **determine the benefit** the offender has derived from the offence of which the offender is convicted and other related unlawful activities. This enables the court to order the confiscation of the value of that benefit.[6] This is referred to as a confiscation order. The confiscation order is similar to a judgment for the payment of a sum of money and is made in addition to any sentence that the court may impose.

Although the confiscation enquiry may only be instituted after conviction the procedure to be followed at the enquiry **is a civil procedure**.[7] This means that the rules of evidence applicable in civil proceedings apply at such an enquiry and that the burden of proof is one of a balance of probabilities.

For a confiscation order to function effectively it must be supported by a pro-active measure to obtain control over the offender's realisable property before the making of a confiscation order. This is necessary in order to prevent a person who may be subjected to a confiscation order from disposing of property that may be used to satisfy the order or diminishing its value, before the confiscation order is made. Such an order is referred to as **a restraint order**.[8] The aim of the restraint order is to **freeze** the financial position of the offender or suspected offender and it may be granted even while the investigation is still pending.

The civil forfeiture procedure allows for the forfeiture of property **without first obtaining a conviction** against any person. It is a procedure based on the nature of the affected property itself. The property in question **must be tainted**, either through being the proceeds of unlawful activities or through being used in connection with the commission of an offence.[9]

The procedure is initiated by the making of a preservation of property order.[10] The preservation of property order serves a similar function as a restraint order in the confiscation procedure namely to gain control over property that may be forfeited to the State.

A hearing to determine whether the property is indeed tainted follows the preservation of property order.[11] This must be proven at the hearing on a balance of probabilities. A person with an interest

---

[3] Chapter 5 of the Prevention of Organised Crime Act.
[4] Chapter 6 of the Prevention of Organised Crime Act.
[5] Section 18 of the Prevention of Organised Crime Act.
[6] *Ibid.*
[7] Section 13 of the Prevention of Organised Crime Act.
[8] Section 26 of the Prevention of Organised Crime Act.
[9] In the Prevention of Organised Crime Act this is referred to as an instrumentality–see section 1(1) of the Act.
[10] Section 38 of the Prevention of Organised Crime Act.
[11] Section 50 of the Prevention of Organised Crime Act.

in the property concerned may participate in the forfeiture hearing in one of two ways. The person may oppose the application on the basis that the property is not tainted. Alternatively the person may apply for the exclusion of his or her interest in the property on the basis that he or she was unaware that the property is tainted.[12] If the court finds that the property is tainted it makes an order declaring the property forfeit to the State.[13]

5   Preventative control measures

The two key items on the shopping list of a money launderer are an effective financial system, and weak controls over access to a financial system. The regulatory control measures in the South African anti-money laundering framework are contained in the *Financial Intelligence Centre Act*. These measures cover four broad areas namely the identification of clients, record-keeping, reporting of information and internal policies to facilitate compliance.

5.1   Scope of regulatory control measures

The control measures of the *Financial Intelligence Centre Act* apply to a wide variety of financial and non-financial institutions referred to in the Act as 'accountable institutions'.[14]

5.1.1   Banking sector

All institutions carrying on the **business of a bank** as defined in the *Banks Act,* 94 of 1990, are included in the Schedule of accountable institutions. In other words, any institution carrying on a type of business for which a banking licence is required is an accountable institution. This covers a broad range of banking services including commercial banking, corporate banking and private banking.

In addition the scope of the *Financial Intelligence Centre Act* also includes other forms of banking institutions such as mutual banks, as defined in the *Mutual Banks Act*, 124 of 1993, and the Post Bank, constituted under the *Postal Services Act*, 124 of 1998.

5.1.2   Non-bank financial institutions

The *Financial Intelligence Centre Act* applies to a large number of **non-bank financial institutions**. Many of these institutions offer financial services which are also offered by banks, but which can be offered without the requirement of having a banking licence. These include bureaux de change and money remitters.

The *Financial Intelligence Centre Act* also applies to a variety of **financial service providers and intermediaries**. These include:

- life insurers,
- managers of collective investment schemes,
- financial instrument traders,
- securities brokers,

---

[12] Section 52 of the Prevention of Organised Crime Act.
[13] Sections 48 and 50 of the Prevention of Organised Crime Act.
[14] Schedule 1 to the Financial Intelligence Centre Act.

- investment advisors and intermediaries, and

- investment managers.

5.1.3   Non-financial institutions

The *Financial Intelligence Centre Act* also includes as accountable institutions a number of institutions that are not regarded as part of the mainstream financial sector, but can nevertheless facilitate access for criminal proceeds to the financial sector. These include:

- attorneys,

- providers of services to trusts,

- estate agents, and

- gambling institutions.

5.2   Obligations of accountable institutions

5.2.1   Client identification

The first set of obligations imposed by the *Financial Intelligence Centre Act* require accountable institutions to **establish and verify the identities of their clients**. The underlying principle of this obligation is that institutions must know who they are doing business with and must avoid engaging in business with anonymous or undisclosed clients, or clients using false identities.

The obligation to identify clients is expressed in the form of a prohibition against doing business with unidentified clients. The *Financial Intelligence Centre Act* expressly prohibits accountable institutions from entering into business relationships or carrying out single transactions with clients unless the clients' identities have been established and verified.[15]

The steps to establish and verify clients' identities are provided for in regulations made under the *Financial Intelligence Centre Act*. These include, for example for natural persons, that the person's name, date of birth, identity number or passport number and, in most cases, residential address be obtained and confirmed.

In the case of corporate entities the information to be obtained and confirmed include the details of incorporation such as the registered name and address and the registration number, as well as information concerning the identities of the majority shareholders, directors and those entitled to transact on behalf of the corporation.

The regulations also refer to the information to be obtained in respect of other business forms such as partnerships and trusts. In respect of partnerships information must be obtained concerning the trading name of the partnership and the identities of all partners and persons entitled to transact on behalf of the partnership. In respect of trusts information must be obtained concerning the name and number of the trust and the geographic area where the trust is registered as well as information concerning the identities of the founder, trustees, named beneficiaries and persons entitled to transact on behalf of the trust.

The obligations to establish and verify the identities of clients also apply to those that deal indirectly with accountable institutions such as agents and principals of clients.

---

[15] Section 21 of the Financial Intelligence Centre Act.

5.2.2 Record-keeping

The second set of obligations under the *Financial Intelligence Centre Act* requires institutions to **keep records of their clients' identities and their transaction activities**. The purpose of the record-keeping requirement is to ensure that a transaction or series of transactions can be reconstructed in the course of an investigation, indicating not only what had happened but also who had been involved.

The *Financial Intelligence Centre Act* requires accountable institutions to keep record of the information obtained during the identification process concerning the identities of clients entering into business relationships, or conducting single transactions. Apart from the information pertaining to clients' identities, this section also requires accountable institutions to keep record of:

- the nature of the business relationship or transaction entered into;

- the amounts involved in a transaction;

- the parties to a transaction; and

- the particulars of all accounts involved in a transaction.[16]

The records pertaining to the establishment of a business relationship (in other words records of clients' identities) must be kept for a minimum of **five years** after the business relation is terminated. Records pertaining to a particular transaction must be kept for a period of five years after the transaction is concluded.

The *Financial Intelligence Centre Act* allows for the storing of records in electronic format and by third parties.

5.2.3 Reporting of information

The third set of obligations under the *Financial Intelligence Centre Act* requires institutions to report information to the *Financial Intelligence Centre* (the financial intelligence unit for South Africa).

The *Financial Intelligence Centre Act* contains four reporting duties. The current reporting obligation relates to the reporting of **suspicious or unusual transactions**.[17] This obligation applies not only to the financial and other institutions that are referred to in the *Financial Intelligence Centre Act* as accountable institutions, but to all businesses and also to all persons in charge of or employed by a business. This obligation requires the relevant institutions to report any suspicion that:

- The business has received or is about to receive the proceeds of crime or property which is connected to terrorist financing.

- A transaction or series of transactions to which the business is a party:

    - facilitated or is likely to facilitate the transfer of the proceeds of crime or property which is connected to terrorist financing;

    - has no apparent business or lawful purpose;

---

[16] Section 22 of the Financial Intelligence Centre Act.
[17] Section 29 of the Financial Intelligence Centre Act.

- is conducted to avoid giving rise to another reporting duty under the *Financial Intelligence Centre Act* ;

- may be relevant to the investigation of tax evasion or attempted tax evasion;

- relates to terrorist financing.

- The business has been used or is about to be used in any way for money laundering or to facilitate terrorist financing.

The obligation to report suspicious or unusual transactions **also applies to aborted transactions**, in other words transactions which have been initiated, or about which enquiries have been made, but which are not concluded.

'**Tipping-off**', in other words the unauthorised disclosure that a report of this nature has been made is an offence.

The other reporting duties under the *Financial Intelligence Centre Act* are all threshold-based reporting duties. The first of these is a duty to report **large cash transactions**. These are transactions involving cash amounts exceeding a prescribed limit. [18] The second is a duty to report the movement of amounts of cash exceeding a prescribed limit across South Africa's borders.[19] '**Cash**' for the purposes of these provisions refers to physical currency (notes and coins) of South Africa or any other country. The third threshold-based reporting duty requires the reporting of **electronic transfers of funds** exceeding a prescribed limit across South Africa's borders.[20]

The obligations to report large cash transactions and cross-border electronic transfers apply to accountable institutions. The obligation to report large cash transactions also applies to dealers in motor vehicles and dealers in Kruger Rands.

The limits for these reporting obligations are set by the Minister of Finance by regulation. The provisions in which the threshold-based reporting obligations are obtained are not yet in operation which means that the relevant thresholds have not yet been fixed. The Minister may make different sets of regulations in respect of different classes of accountable institutions which implies that the limits for the reporting of large cash transactions and cross-border electronic transfers may differ in respect of different classes of accountable institutions.

The obligations to make reports under the *Financial Intelligence Centre Act* **overrides all obligations of confidentiality** or secrecy.[21] The only exception is the common law right to legal professional privilege as between an attorney and the attorney's client. This means that an attorney does not have to report information which was communicated to him or her in confidence by a client for the purposes of legal advice or litigation which is pending or contemplated or which has commenced, or by a third party for the purposes of litigation which is pending or contemplated or has commenced. All other information at the disposal of an attorney must be reported in terms of the reporting obligations referred to earlier, even if the information is of a confidential nature.

Persons making reports under the *Financial Intelligence Centre Act* enjoy a considerable amount of **protection** under the Act.[22] A person who initiated or contributed to a report is protected from criminal or civil liability which may otherwise result from the disclosure of information

---

[18] Section 28 of the Financial Intelligence Centre Act.
[19] Section 31 of the Financial Intelligence Centre Act.
[20] Section 31 of the Financial Intelligence Centre Act.
[21] Section 37 of the Financial Intelligence Centre Act.
[22] Section 38 of the Financial Intelligence Centre Act.

in accordance with a reporting obligation. Such a person can also not be compelled to testify in any criminal proceedings that may arise from a report which he or she had initiated or to which he or she had contributed. The person may nevertheless choose to testify voluntarily. In addition, evidence concerning the identity of a person who initiated or contributed to a report is not admissible in criminal proceedings, unless the person chooses to testify in those proceedings.

5.2.4   Internal compliance measures

The *Financial Intelligence Centre Act* requires accountable institutions to underpin the client-identification, record-keeping and reporting obligations with their own **internal rules** to give effect to these obligations.[23] An accountable institution's internal rules must cover all the obligations in terms of the *Financial Intelligence Centre Act* that apply to that institution.

Accountable institutions must also **provide training** to all staff members who are associated with the carrying out of the institution's obligations under the *Financial Intelligence Centre Act*.[24]

Accountable institutions must also appoint persons such as **compliance officers** who are responsible for ensuring compliance by the employees of accountable institutions, and the accountable institutions themselves, with the *Financial Intelligence Centre Act*.[25]

5.3   Supervision of compliance

The various supervisory bodies, such as the *South African Reserve Bank* for banks and the *Financial Services Board* for non-bank financial institutions, are **responsible for supervising compliance** with the *Financial Intelligence Centre Act* by the institutions supervised by them.[26]

The *Financial Intelligence Centre* may refer possible failures of compliance with the *Financial Intelligence Centre Act* to the various supervisory bodies. When the Centre refers a matter to a supervisory body, the supervisory body must investigate the matter and take steps to remedy it.[27]

5.4   Penalties

The *Financial Intelligence Centre Act* contains a number of offences relating to contraventions of, or the failure to comply with these preventative control measures. The maximum penalties for these offences range from a fine of R10 000 000 (±US$1 687 000) or imprisonment for a period of 15 years for offences such as failures to identify clients or report information to a fine of R1 000 000 (±US$810 000) or imprisonment for a period of 5 years for offences such as failures to implement internal rules and provide training.

6   The Financial Intelligence Centre

The *Financial Intelligence Centre* is established by the *Financial Intelligence Centre Act*.[28] The Centre is the **financial intelligence unit** in South Africa and its **main objectives** are to assist in the identification of the proceeds of unlawful activities and the combating of money laundering and terrorist financing activities. The *Financial Intelligence Centre* exists in order to

---

[23] Section 42 of the Financial Intelligence Centre Act.
[24] Section 43 of the Financial Intelligence Centre Act.
[25] Section 43 of the Financial Intelligence Centre Act.
[26] Section 45 of the Financial Intelligence Centre Act.
[27] Section 44 and 45 of the Financial Intelligence Centre Act read together.
[28] Section 2 of the Financial Intelligence Centre Act.

make information collected by it available to investigating authorities, the intelligence services and the South African Revenue Service and to exchange information with similar bodies in other countries.[29]

The **functions** of the *Financial Intelligence Centre* include the **processing, analysing and interpreting** information obtained by it (mainly information concerning suspicious financial activities which are reported to the Centre), with a view to **inform, advise and co-operate with investigating authorities**, supervisory bodies, the South African Revenue Service and the intelligence services.[30] In other words, the *Financial Intelligence Centre* supplies investigating authorities with possible leads of a financial nature concerning money laundering and other criminal activities and supports them in their investigations on the basis of its analysis and interpretation of the information at its disposal.

The *Financial Intelligence Centre* provides information to investigating authorities on its own initiative as well as upon request.

The *Financial Intelligence Centre* also **monitors compliance** with the provisions of the *Financial Intelligence Centre Act* and **gives guidance** to accountable institutions, supervisory bodies and other persons regarding the performance by them of their duties under the Act.

The *Financial Intelligence Centre Act* provides the *Financial Intelligence Centre* with a number of **powers** to enable it to perform its functions. One such power is the power to **intervene in on-going transactions**.[31] The *Financial Intelligence Centre* may instruct an institution not to proceed with the carrying out of a transaction which has been reported to it, if it believes that the transaction involves the proceeds of crime or may constitute money laundering or terrorist financing. If such a transaction is already completed the *Financial Intelligence Centre* may instruct an institution not to proceed with any subsequent transaction in respect of the funds in question. The *Financial Intelligence Centre's* intervention in a transaction is valid for a period of five days.

The *Financial Intelligence Centre Act* also enables the *Financial Intelligence Centre* to **request confirmation from an institution that a specific person is a client of that institution**.[32] This enables the *Financial Intelligence Centre* to assist investigating authorities in focusing investigations on the institutions where a person engages in financial activities, and reduces wasted effort in locating a person's financial records.

The *Financial Intelligence Centre* may also **monitor the transaction activity of a person** with a specific institution.[33] The *Financial Intelligence Centre Act* enables the *Financial Intelligence Centre* to obtain an order from a judge, obliging an institution to report all transactions of a specific client for a three-month period. This period may be extended if required. The power to monitor a person's transaction activity with a particular institution provides a powerful tool to establish a financial profile of that person.

The *Financial Intelligence Centre Act* allows the *Financial Intelligence Centre* to share information with financial intelligence units as well as investigating authorities outside South Africa. Towards this end the *Financial Intelligence Centre* became a member of the Egmont Group in 2002.

---

[29] Section 3 of the Financial Intelligence Centre Act.
[30] Section 4 of the Financial Intelligence Centre Act.
[31] Section 34 of the Financial Intelligence Centre Act.
[32] Section 27 of the Financial Intelligence Centre Act.
[33] Section 35 of the Financial Intelligence Centre Act.

7   International co-operation

International co-operation in respect of the administration of criminal justice is regulated in South Africa by the *Extradition Act*, 67 of 1962, and the *International Co-operation in Criminal Matters Act*, 75 of 1996.

The *Extradition Act* provides for **extradition** of fugitives who are accused or convicted of an offence which is punishable by a term of imprisonment of more than six months in terms of the laws of South Africa and a requesting state. The *Extradition Act* allows extradition to countries with which South Africa has extradition agreements as well as on an *ad hoc* basis. The *Extradition Act* allows for the extradition of South African foreign nationals alike.

Coercive measures for **mutual legal assistance** are provided in terms of the *International Co-operation in Criminal Matters Act*. These measures include obtaining of witness testimony in respect of investigations and prosecutions, the enforcement of fines and other pecuniary penalties and the enforcement of freezing and forfeiture orders. The provision of mutual legal assistance under the *International Co-operation in Criminal Matters Act* is not predicated on formalities such as dual criminality, reciprocity or the existence of an agreement or treaty

South Africa has acceded to the UN Convention against Illicit Traffic in Narcotic Drugs and Psychotropic Substances (Vienna Convention) and is a signatory of the UN Convention against Transnational Organised Crime (Palermo Convention). Both these conventions have been ratified by the South African Parliament. In addition South Africa has become a party to a large number of the so-called anti-terrorism conventions of the United Nations including the International Convention on the Suppression of the Financing of Terrorism.

Address

Financial Intelligence Centre
240 Vermeulen Street
Pretoria
South Africa
0002

Private Bag X115
Pretoria
South Africa
0001
Tel +27 12 309 9200
Fax +27 12 309 9480
www.fic.gov.za
Contact person: Pieter Smit
pieter.smit@fic.gov.za

INDEX